W9-CLB-394

KIDNAP

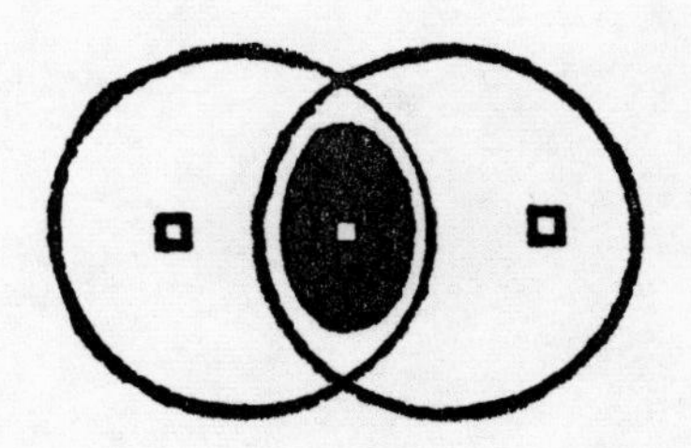

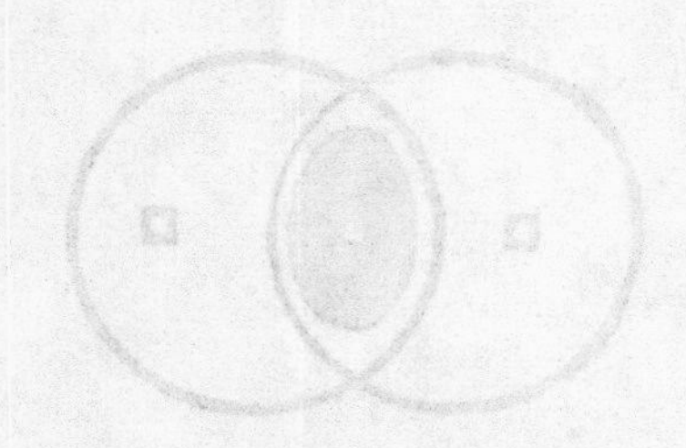

KIDNAP

THE STORY OF THE LINDBERGH CASE

by George Waller

THE DIAL PRESS 1961 NEW YORK

Library of Congress Catalog Card Number: 61-7368

For Joan

W

DESIGNED BY WILLIAM R. MEINHARDT
MANUFACTURED IN THE UNITED STATES OF AMERICA

CONTENTS

LIST OF ILLUSTRATIONS

Lindbergh

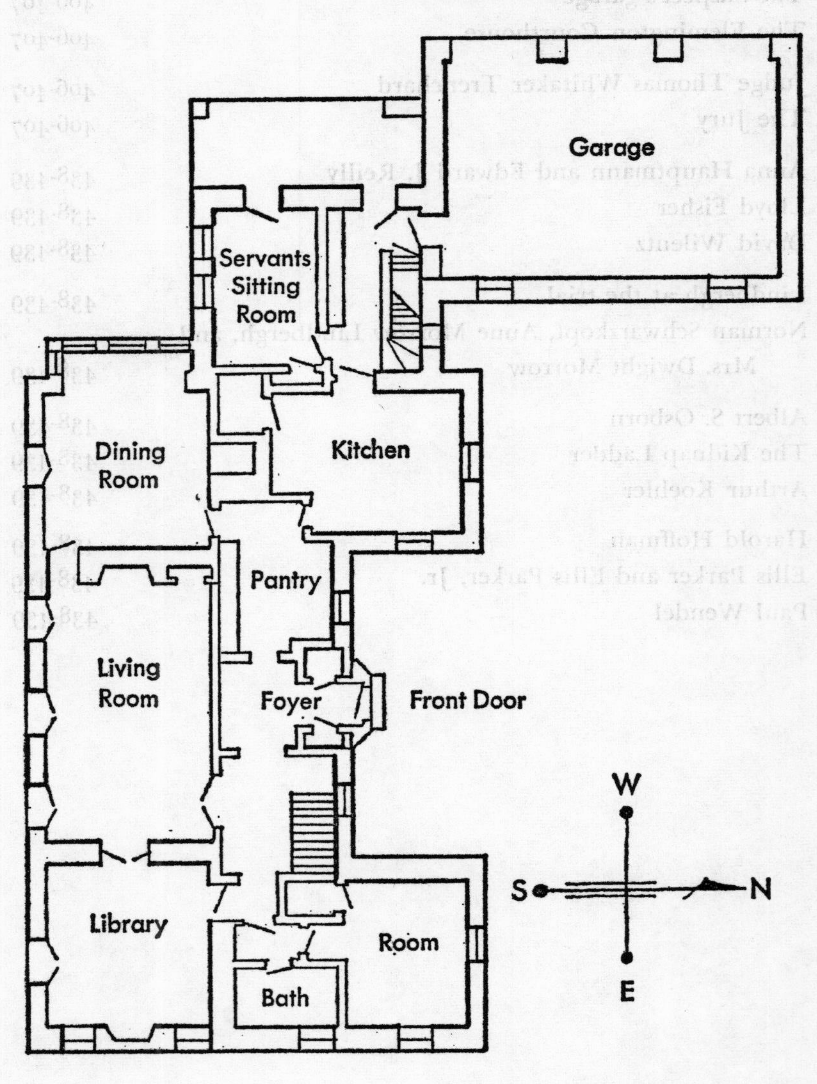

FIRST FLOOR

House

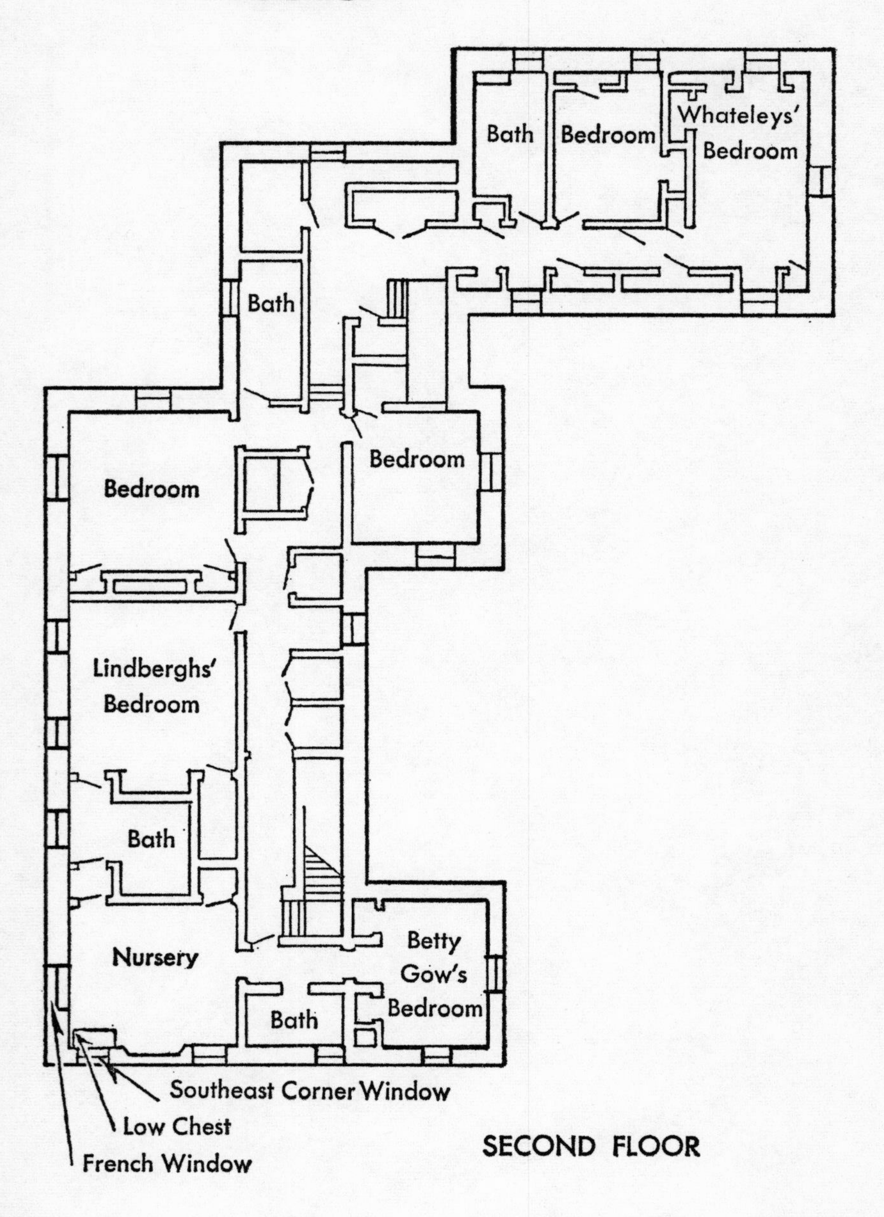
Bath
Bedroom
Whateleys' Bedroom
Bath
Bedroom
Bedroom
Lindberghs' Bedroom
Bath
Nursery
Betty Gow's Bedroom
Bath
Southeast Corner Window
Low Chest
French Window
SECOND FLOOR

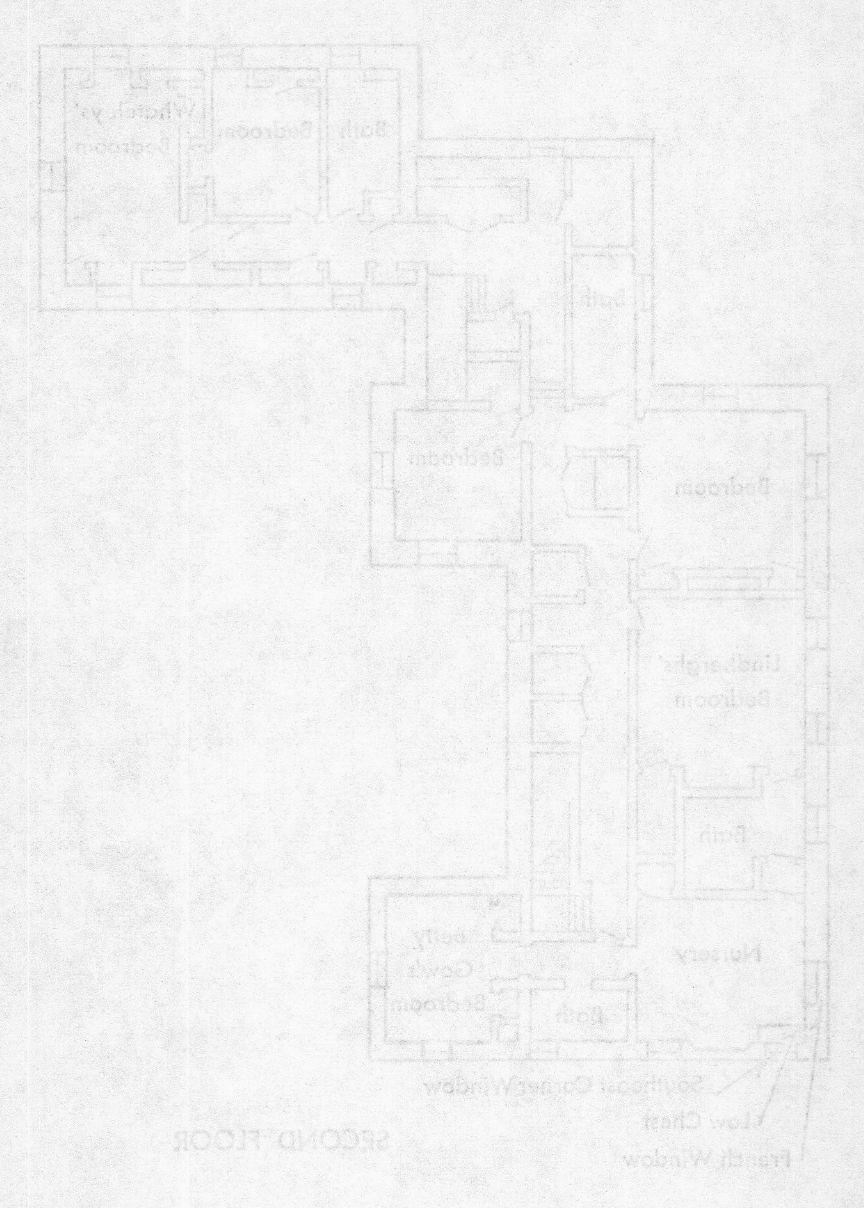

Part One

THE CRIME

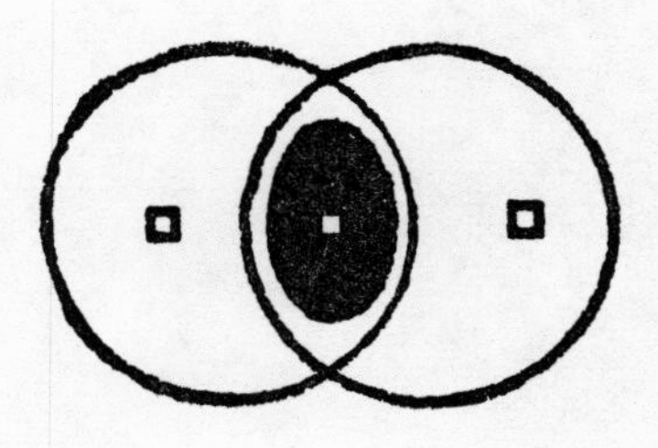

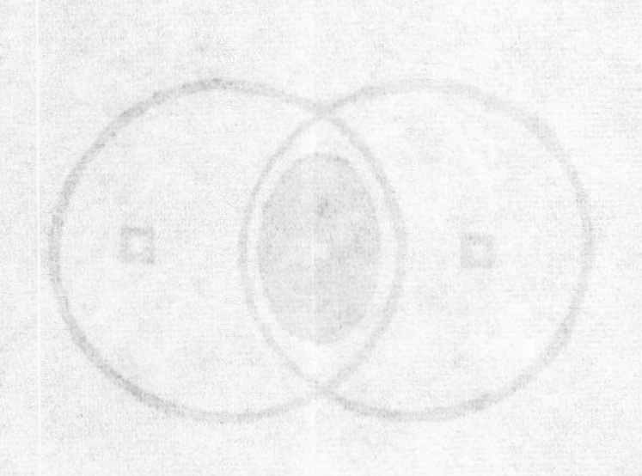

1

Tuesday, March 1, 1932, was cold and windy, with a clinging dampness. Despite the unpleasant weather, in midafternoon Anne Morrow Lindbergh went out for a breath of fresh air. She hadn't felt free to leave the house before because the baby wasn't well, but a while ago his nurse had arrived to help take care of him.

Returning from her stroll, Anne Lindbergh paused at the southeast corner of the house and looked up at the second-story nursery windows, then picked up a few pebbles from the moist, clayey ground and tossed them against the corner windowpane. Presently Betty Gow, the nurse, appeared. Smiling, she turned away and came back with the little boy in her arms. She pointed down to his mother and he smiled in recognition. Anne Lindbergh waved. Betty raised the baby's hand and waved it back.

Two hours later, a few minutes before five o'clock, Betty sat down to tea in the servants' quarters with Oliver Whateley, the butler, and his wife Elsie, the housekeeper-cook. Oliver had served tea to Mrs. Lindbergh in the living room and Betty had brought the baby from the nursery to play with his mother. Outside, in the pale dwindling light, the wind sighed through the trees and rattled the house shutters.

The cold and dampness were why Anne Lindbergh and the baby were still here today in the new house Charles Augustus Lindbergh had built in New Jersey near the village of Hopewell. It was the Lindberghs' custom during the winter months to spend the weekdays with Anne's widowed mother, Mrs. Dwight Morrow, at Next Day Hill, her fifty-two-acre estate in Englewood, New Jersey, and the week ends in their own home. Mrs. Morrow had still not recovered from the shock of her husband's death the previous summer and she welcomed the young family's company. Also, the new house wasn't quite ready; most of the windows lacked curtains, and other finishing touches were needed.

Over the week end, however, the little boy had developed a cold —nothing serious, but his mother didn't like the idea of taking him back to Next Day Hill in the raw weather. She decided, and her husband agreed, that it would be better to stay on at Hopewell for an extra day or so.

Betty and the Whateleys discussed this and other matters over their tea. All three had come from Scotland to domestic service in America, and Oliver in particular still spoke with a burr. Middle-aged and agreeably efficient, the Whateleys had been a superior sort of wedding present to Charles and Anne Lindbergh from the Morrows.

Betty Gow had come well recommended to take charge of Charles, Jr., a few months after he was born. Like the Whateleys, she enjoyed and was proud of her position; Mrs. Lindbergh was friendly and considerate and of course Colonel Lindbergh was world-famous. The nursemaid's job had still another advantage: Anne Lindbergh liked to take care of the baby herself on the week ends, which in effect gave Betty two days off each week instead of the customary one. And Next Day Hill, where she usually stayed, was much closer to New York than the Hopewell place—and Betty, who at twenty-seven had a slender, attractive figure, dark bobbed hair and blue eyes, was as interested in dates as the next young woman.

Anne Lindbergh had telephoned Betty twice about the baby's condition, yesterday morning and again this Tuesday morning, when she had said that, since the weather showed no signs of improving, the nurse might as well come and help look after him. The Morrow household was staffed by twenty-nine servants, so Betty had had no difficulty arranging for Ellison, the second chauffeur, to drive her to Hopewell.

But she'd had to rule out a date she had made for that evening with a friend, Henry Johnson. She had gone out with him the evening before and, when he had learned that Mrs. Lindbergh was still uncertain when she would return with the baby, he had asked to see Betty again the next night. Before leaving, she had telephoned him at his boarding house to explain, but he was not in his room and she had left a message for him to call her later at the Lindbergh place.

At a quarter to six, the sudden, lively appearance of Charles Augustus Lindbergh, Jr., interrupted the servants' tea. Fair-haired and blue-eyed, with a dimple in his chin that resembled his father's, he came galloping into their sitting room, shouting a baby jumble of words that almost but not quite made sense; twenty months old, he was just beginning to talk. As he ran around and around the table, shouting now at Betty and now at Elsie, there was nothing to indicate the small imperfection with which he had been born: two toes of his right foot overlapped slightly.

His cold seemed much improved. Leaving his mother to finish her tea, he had charged off to visit the other members of the household and see what the wire-haired fox terrier was up to.

The terrier was a present from the child's paternal grandmother, Mrs. Evangeline Lindbergh. Some hopes had been entertained for him as a watchdog, but in the year and a half he had spent with the Lindberghs and the Morrows he had proved anything but reliable—at times indifferent to outdoor noises that real watchdogs would have thought worth investigating, at others hysterically agitated by domestic sounds no more sinister than the closing of the oven door.

Looking around apprehensively as the little boy ran into the room, the terrier had squeezed lower in his basket and pretended that he was not at home; ever since Charles, Jr., had learned how to use his legs, life for the dog had become much too busy.

Betty spared him an evening romp. She took the baby's hand, announced that it was time for his supper and led him upstairs to the nursery.

Planned with care by the young parents (Charles Lindbergh was twenty-eight when his son was born, Anne twenty-three), the nursery was light and airy and gave a corner view from three windows—the largest, a French window, faced south; the others faced southeast. Beneath the French window a substantial box with double doors contained small Charles' personal fortune—his toys; a low chest stood beneath the southeast corner window. On the fireplace mantelpiece was a porcelain rooster flanked by two smaller birds, and a kiddie car rested near the hearth. A folding pink-and-green screen, decorated with farmyard animals and a little red schoolhouse, stood close to the maple crib.

The child had his meals at a small maple table in the center of the room. Securing him in his chair, Betty went downstairs again to the kitchen for his cereal. He ate it docilely, and she was about to get him ready for bed when his mother came into the nursery to help.

Although her father was a multimillionaire and the American ambassador to Mexico, Anne Morrow had been virtually unknown when Charles Lindbergh proposed to her three years before. Newspaper reporters had discovered her to be a slim girl with brown hair and blue eyes, sensitive and rather shy, who liked to write poetry. She looked tiny beside her tall husband, too fragile for adventurous trips; but two years after they were married she accompanied him on an aerial tour of the Orient and, he proudly reported, helped in everything except the actual piloting of their plane.

Still docile, Charles, Jr., offered no objections as the two women undressed him and slipped on his night clothes. Betty gave him a spoonful of the mild laxative prescribed when his sniffles had set in. He didn't like its taste and dashed most of it down the front of his woolen sleeping suit. And so he was undressed again.

Betty had a thought. "Mrs. Lindbergh," she said, "let me run up a proper little flannel shirt to put on next to his skin. It won't take more than a few minutes."

Anne Lindbergh agreed and Betty went down to the kitchen, where Elsie gave her a pair of scissors and said she would bring a needle and thread. Betty returned to the nursery. While the boy and his mother played together, she cut the material for the night-shirt from a flannel petticoat Charles, Jr., had worn when he was an infant, trimming it so that part of the petticoat's embroidered, scalloped hem became the shirttail.

A moment later Elsie appeared with needles and thread; a practiced seamstress, Betty had the shirt finished in a jiffy. She rubbed the child's chest with Vicks ointment; then again, his mother helping, dressed him for the night. At last ready for bed, he wore the new flannel shirt, stitched with English-spun blue silk; over it a sleeveless wool shirt cut low in front and back; diapers and rubber pants; and, over all, a fresh woolen sleeping suit. Since he had a tendency to suck his thumbs, Betty attached a thumbguard to each hand.

She put him into his crib and drew the covers snugly to his chin, making sure that the sheets and blanket would not slip by fastening them to the mattress with two large safety pins. Then, with Anne Lindbergh's help, she attended to the windows and shutters. Leaving the French window ajar to admit a bit of air, they closed the other windows after locking the shutters—all except a balky pair at the southeast corner window. These had warped and wouldn't quite shut, so that the metal bar would not slide across into its socket.

At seven-thirty Anne Lindbergh left the nursery. Betty sat beside the crib to wait until Charles, Jr., fell asleep.

Wailing over the damp woods and muddy fields, the wind restlessly stirred the shutters. Betty sat quietly, now and then glancing at the boy's face. Soon she heard his breathing fall into the steady pattern of sleep. She looked at her watch in the soft light; it was just eight o'clock.

Putting out the light, she went downstairs to the living room and told Anne Lindbergh that her son was sleeping peacefully.

2

Charles Lindbergh, Sr., arrived at his new home shortly before eight-thirty. He had had a busy day in New York, visiting the offices of Pan American Airways, Transcontinental Air Transport, Inc., and spending several hours in the Rockefeller Institute for Medical Research, rounding it off with a trip to his dentist. In the pressure of these appointments, his usually excellent memory had faltered; he had forgotten that this evening he was to have addressed some two thousand New York University alumni, who were expectantly assembled at dinner.

Colonel Lindbergh had chosen the location for his house after much thought. He wanted a home that would be shut off from the world, yet fairly handy to New York. This estate of five hundred acres seemed to offer the ideal combination. The formidable wilderness of the Sourland mountains guarded it from the north; swamps and barren fields lay to the south; and New Jersey's capital city, Trenton, was only fourteen miles away.

Two and a half stories high, the house was built in a vaguely French manorial style of fieldstone covered with whitewashed cement. A white picket fence surrounded it, and behind it a windmill added a colorful touch. Encircled by thick woods, the house sat in a clearing on the brow of a small hill which sloped down to a level stretch where work on Lindbergh's private airfield had begun.

Entering by the main door, one came into a large foyer and faced a flight of wide stairs to the second floor. Off the foyer was a spacious living room with a fireplace; flanking the living room on one side was the dining room, on the other the library. Elsewhere on the first floor were the kitchen and, adjoining it, the pantry and the servants' sitting room. Beyond these was a three-car garage, the terminus of a wide court at the end of the driveway.

On the second floor, over the living room, were Charles and Anne Lindbergh's bedroom and a bathroom, through which they could enter the nursery, situated over the library. Betty Gow's bedroom was directly across the hall from the nursery. There were three guest rooms on the second floor and, over the garage, Oliver and Elsie Whateley's bedroom.

Hopewell, the nearest village, was three miles away over a dirt lane and hard-surfaced road.

Lindbergh had hoped his new home would afford him the privacy an average citizen enjoyed, but even while the house was being built countless pictures of it—some captioned "A Nest for the Lone Eagle"—had appeared in the press, and when it was completed the public's interest had seemed to increase. Nearly five years had passed since his solo flight across the Atlantic in the flimsy *Spirit of St. Louis;* he was a husband and father and an airlines consultant; but, though loath to acknowledge it, Charles Augustus Lindbergh remained in the eyes of millions the audacious, modest, gangling kid of 1927—and the object of their passionate curiosity.

Sounding the horn of his tan Franklin sedan as he came up the driveway, he wheeled the car into the garage and entered the house through the servants' quarters, pausing in their sitting room, where Betty and Elsie were having dinner, to ask about Charles, Jr. Betty told him that the youngster was in bed asleep and feeling much better.

In the living room, having heard the car's horn, Anne Lindbergh was expecting her husband. She accompanied him upstairs for the few minutes it took him to wash and then came down with him again to the dining room, where Oliver Whateley was waiting to serve the evening meal.

He had just started when Henry Johnson phoned. Betty Gow explained how she happened to be there and said she was sorry she couldn't keep their date. After a few minutes she said good-by and hung up. She returned to the servants' sitting room and had her coffee, then switched on the radio and made herself comfortable with a magazine.

When they had finished their meal, the Lindberghs went into the living room. Oliver removed the remaining dishes to the kitchen and helped his wife with them. Then Elsie asked Betty if she'd like to go upstairs and see her new dress. They went off together and Oliver settled down in the sitting room to read the *Saturday Evening Post.*

In the living room, Charles and Anne Lindbergh sat on a sofa before the fire, chatting against the cozy background of burning logs and the rise and fall of the wind in the chimney. It was a few minutes past nine.

Suddenly Lindbergh turned his head. "What was that?" he said. Anne asked what he meant.

He had heard a sound, he said, a sound like breaking wood, yet it hadn't seemed like a tree bough snapping off in the wind. Anne said she'd heard nothing. They waited a moment, then resumed their talk. On a night such as this, all kinds of sounds could be picked up by the wind's fingers—and no one else in the house seemed to have been alarmed by it, certainly not the fox terrier, dozing in his basket; if the curious noise had reached his ears, he had comfortably ignored it.

A little while later they went upstairs to their bedroom and talked for some twenty minutes more; then Lindbergh bathed, dressed again, and went down to his desk in the library to dispose of some work. The desk faced the library's southeast corner window, and through the curtainless glass and open shutters he could look out into the black, noisy night.

Anne began to get ready for bed. She wasn't feeling very well and thought she might have caught the baby's cold.

In the Whateleys' bedroom, Elsie and Betty were exchanging domestic gossip, the new dress having been thoroughly discussed. Betty looked at her watch; it was ten o'clock. "I must go to the baby," she said. Every night at this time she took Charles, Jr., on a final trip to his bathroom; pausing briefly for a parting word, she started along the hall toward the nursery.

A moment later, Anne Lindbergh rang for Elsie. When the housekeeper appeared, Anne asked if she might have a hot lemonade; she then went to turn on the water for a bath.

In the hall, as she was leaving, Elsie saw Betty approaching. Betty asked if Mrs. Lindbergh was in her room and she said yes.

"I wonder if she wants to see the baby," Betty said. "I am just going in."

"Well, if she wants to, she is going through the other way," Elsie replied, gesturing toward the bathroom and its connecting door to the nursery.

She went downstairs and told her husband of Mrs. Lindbergh's request. Oliver put aside his magazine and joined her in the kitchen, putting on the kettle while she got out a lemon.

Betty went back along the hall and entered the nursery. She left the lights off, as she always did when she came into the baby's room at night, because she was afraid the sudden brightness might startle him—but she left the door open so that the hall lights would enable her to see. She crossed to the French window and closed it. Then she plugged in an electric heater and stood waiting until the room began to lose its chill. Warming her hands so that they wouldn't be cold on the child's skin, she crossed to his crib and let her eyes become accustomed to the patch of darkness.

Suddenly, oddly, she realized that she did not hear the soft sound of his breathing. She bent swiftly and felt all over the crib. It was empty.

His mother had taken him, of course. Betty walked down the hall to the Lindberghs' bedroom door, knocked and entered. Anne Lindbergh came from the bathroom.

"Mrs. Lindbergh, do you have the baby?" Betty asked.

Anne looked surprised. "Why, no," she said, "I don't have him."

"Where is the Colonel?" Betty said quickly. "He may have him. Where is he?"

"Downstairs in the library," Anne said.

Betty ran down. Lindbergh was at his desk, reading. "Colonel," she asked breathlessly, "do you have the baby?"

He stared at her.

"No. Isn't he in his crib?"

"No!"

Lindbergh ran past her and up the stairs, and Betty followed.

Anne Lindbergh had gone into the nursery, hastily searched the crib, and returned to her bedroom. Now her husband ran into the baby's room, saw too that the crib was empty, and inspected it closely.

The bedclothes seemed untouched, still forming the contours of the child's body. The two large safety pins with which Betty had fastened the blanket and sheets to the mattress were undisturbed, and Lindbergh could see the impression left by his son's head on the pillow. It was obvious that the little boy had not clambered out of the crib by himself.

The young father hurried through the bathroom to his bedroom and took a Springfield rifle from his closet. He swiftly returned to the nursery and Anne followed, nervously clutching her robe.

He turned and faced her. "Anne, they have stolen our baby."

In a hushed voice, Anne said, "Oh, my God. . . ."

3

Something on the radiator grating beneath the southeast corner window caught Lindbergh's eye. Going closer, he saw an envelope. He left it there, untouched, and warned Anne and Betty not to touch it, or anything else, until the nursery had been examined for fingerprints.

The window, they noted, was the one with the balky shutters that couldn't be locked and wouldn't quite shut. The sash was closed, but the shutters were partly open; on the sill and on a suitcase that lay on the low chest directly beneath the window were smudges of reddish yellow clay—footprints, perhaps. Still another clay smudge, even less distinct, was on the floor. All were too blurred to show the clear outline of a foot, but Lindbergh saw that the clay was the same as that of the soil directly outside.

He hesitated for an instant, then asked Betty to send Oliver Whateley.

The kettle having come to a boil, Elsie was cutting the lemon for Anne Lindbergh's lemonade when Betty ran into the kitchen. She told Oliver the Colonel wanted him at once and added, as though she couldn't believe it, "The baby's gone." The butler hurried off as Elsie stared.

"What do you mean?" she asked.

"Why, Elsie, the baby is gone," Betty said again.

Elsie dropped her knife and started after her husband. She came upon him at the top of the stairs, with Colonel Lindbergh.

"Where is Mrs. Lindbergh?" she asked.

Lindbergh pointed to the nursery. "In there."

Elsie went in and saw Anne looking into the empty crib. She stood beside her, comfortingly, then persuaded her to return to her bedroom and gently helped her dress, hearing again and again Anne's whispered monotone, "Oh, God . . oh, God."

The nearest police headquarters was in Hopewell. The young father told Oliver to call the police chief, Harry Wolfe. The butler had regained his professional poise; he said calmly into the phone, "Colonel Lindbergh's son has been stolen. Will you please come at once?"

Lindbergh had half expected to learn that the telephone wires had been cut. Now, as he heard Oliver's voice, he went downstairs to make two calls of his own: the first to the New Jersey State Police, the second to his friend and attorney, Colonel Henry C. Breckinridge, in New York. He asked them to come.

At half past ten, Anne Lindbergh, Elsie, and Betty began to search the house. They searched every room, every closet. They opened the doors of the kitchen cabinets, peered into the laundry and storage bins, looked everywhere the baby might have been hidden or, though it seemed improbable, might have hidden himself.

Carrying his rifle, Lindbergh had gone outside and started along the road north of the house. Oliver had followed him and now drove slowly behind the young man in a car he had taken from the garage, weaving from side to side so that the headlights played on the shadowy fields.

In the black distance, other lights appeared. They grew rapidly from pinpoints to the bright beams of a police car. A moment later it stopped and two officers got out: Harry Wolfe, the Hopewell police chief, and his constable Charles E. Williamson.

Lindbergh led them to the nursery. He pointed out the clues he had found and told them not to touch anything. After a few minutes, they went downstairs and outside again to continue the search.

Anne Lindbergh, Elsie, and Betty sat in the living room. They had done everything possible; now they could only wait. Anne sat stiffly without speaking, and the servants shared her silence. As much as they wished to comfort and reassure her, they didn't know what to say. They could think only of the little boy, not quite over his cold, somewhere in the raw night, and hope that whoever had lifted him so quickly and silently from his crib had brought a blanket to wrap him in.

Outside, despite the darkness, Wolfe and Williamson were discovering new evidence. Two holes had been pressed into the reddish yellow clay directly beneath the southeast corner nursery window, and nearby was a shallow impression that could have been a footprint. Some sixty feet farther away, Wolfe's flashlight found a ladder.

Rather, the parts of a ladder. It had been built, crudely but ingeniously, in three sections—the side rails of the bottom section far enough apart to permit the middle and top sections to nest between them, so that it could be compactly carried. The top section of the ladder was lying by itself ten feet farther on. The middle and bottom sections were connected by a dowel pin—a round wooden rod thrust through matching holes in the side rails where the sections joined to lock them together when the ladder was extended and raised. At this juncture, the top rung of the bottom section and one of its rails were badly split.

Studying the splintered wood, the young father thought of the sound he had heard while he and Anne sat in the living room, the sound he had wondered about and then dismissed. At that instant, the kidnaper must have been carrying the child from the nursery; must have climbed down the ladder, stepped on the rung where the two sections met—and where the ladder was weakest—and broken it.

Wolfe and Williamson carried the still-attached sections to the two holes they had found and carefully inserted the ladder's legs. They fitted snugly.

Exploring further, they came upon a three-quarter-inch chisel. They were speculating as to its purpose (had it been brought to pry open the shutters and window?—needlessly, since neither had been locked) when several members of the New Jersey State Police arrived: Colonel H. Norman Schwarzkopf, the commanding officer; his deputy, Major Charles Schoeffel; Detectives Lewis J. Bornmann and Nuncio De Gaetano; and Trooper Joseph Wolfe.

Colonel Henry Breckinridge came soon afterward.

Once again, Lindbergh led the way to the nursery and pointed out the clues, particularly the envelope lying on the radiator grating. He called downstairs to Betty Gow and asked her for a knife. She brought a penknife, gave it to him, and returned to the living room.

Trooper Wolfe used the blade to carry the envelope to the fireplace mantelpiece, where it would not interfere with their examination of the window and shutters and the smudged-clay footprints. It rested there, undisturbed, until a few minutes past midnight, when Corporal Frank A. Kelly, a fingerprint specialist, arrived.

Kelly drew on a pair of gloves, picked up the envelope, and placed it beside his kit on the maple table in the center of the room. As the others watched, he carefully went over it for fingerprints. He found none.

In a sudden silence, interrupted only by the wind on the shutters, Major Schoeffel took the envelope and slit it neatly with the knife. He drew out a note scrawled in pencil and studied it briefly. Then, with a look at Harry Wolfe, the Hopewell police chief, he said to Lindbergh, pointedly, "Now, who do you want to see this note, Colonel?"

Wolfe interpreted the words as a hint that his services were no longer required and, with Constable Williamson, he left.

Schoeffel gave the note to Lindbergh. It read:

> Dear Sir
>
> Have 50000$ ready 25000$ in 20$ bills 15000$ in 10$ bills and 10000$ in 5$ bills After 2–4 days we will inform you were to deliver the mony We warn you for making anyding public or for notify the police The child is in gut care
>
> Indication for all letters are singnature and three holes

Lindbergh glanced at the signature. It was curious and unmistakable. Two circles interlocked; within the ellipse formed where they overlapped was an egg-shaped oval. The circles were outlined in blue, the oval was solid red, and three square holes pierced all three parts of the design in a horizontal line.

Charles Lindbergh was a well-to-do young man. He was the technical adviser for two major airlines, Pan American Airways and Transcontinental Air Transport, Inc. When he joined Transcontinental, in 1928, he was given $250,000 in cash and an option to purchase stock in the company, with the understanding that he would use the full payment to do so. Pan American had also given him an option to buy company stock, and he had made other well-chosen stock investments. From each airline he also received a salary. All in all, it was estimated, his assets amounted to a good deal more than half a million dollars.

Anne Lindbergh was a member of one of the wealthiest families in America. Recently, New Jersey tax experts had said that the payment in 1932 of $1,019,000 in inheritance taxes by the estate of Anne's father, Senator Dwight W. Morrow, would save the state from going into the red by some $400,000.

The $50,000 ransom, therefore, would seem to pose no problem.

The problem, the young father thought as he studied the note again, was how to get the money to the kidnapers—and it was a dilemma of his own making. The note warned him not to call the police; he had taken that step before reading it.

He turned to the others in the nursery and told them there must be no interference—no police activity, newspaper publicity, or friendly efforts to help that would prevent him from paying the ransom and reclaiming his son.

Colonel Breckinridge, his close friend, backed him. Schwarzkopf, the State police commandant, said that he understood and sympathized but wondered just how far a policy of noninterference could be put into effect.

In the early morning hours, while Anne roamed restlessly through the house and Corporal Kelly looked for fingerprints on the ransom note, the nursery's southeast corner shutters, windowpane and sill, the baby's crib and the wall alongside it, Lindbergh and the others made a further search of the grounds.

4

Thirty minutes after Oliver Whateley's call to Hopewell, three states had received the alarm by police teletype and the city editors of their metropolitan morning newspapers had started to remake the front pages. The activity and publicity Lindbergh had hoped to forestall were taking form.

Scores of reporters headed for the Lindberghs' house. Hundreds, soon thousands, of others—bystanders, onlookers, souvenir hunters, the merely curious—joined the rush as the news spread.

They were only to be expected, in the light of Lindbergh's undiminished fame. The history of that fame had its real beginning in 1919 when a New York hotel owner, Raymond Orteig, announced that he would award $25,000 for the first nonstop flight between New York and Paris. For eight years, all attempts to win the prize came to grief. In May 1927, three planes, tuned up and ready to go, waited on Roosevelt Field in New York: the *America,* with a crew headed by Commander Richard Evelyn Byrd; the *Columbia,* manned by Clarence Chamberlin and Lloyd Bertaud; and the *Spirit of St. Louis,* in which a twenty-five-year-old airmail pilot proposed to make the trip alone. Stormy Atlantic skies held them back, and as the days passed it became a matter of feverish interest to see which plane would beat the others in getting off.

For good reasons, the *Spirit of St. Louis* was the popular favorite. It was the smallest, a single-engine, rather myopic craft (it had been necessary to put a periscope in the cockpit to give the pilot a field of vision); it didn't carry a sextant or even a radio (every inch of space was needed for extra gasoline) and would be navigated over the perilous sea by dead reckoning. But above all, its pilot—the papers called him the Flying Kid—was young and alone. He came of a wholesome Swedish-American background (his father had been a congressman, his widowed mother was a schoolteacher)—and had an irresistible grin and a fine head of hair.

A few minutes before eight o'clock on the morning of May 20, Charles Lindbergh lifted the overloaded *Spirit of St. Louis* through a curtain of mist and headed for Paris. The country seemed to hold its breath as the small silver-coated plane droned into the Atlantic silence. That night, forty thousand people, at Yankee Stadium for the Sharkey-Maloney heavyweight fight, rose to their feet, bowed their heads and prayed for "Lindy." Millions joined them and, the next morning, agreed that their favorite wit and homespun philosopher, Will Rogers, again had hit the nail on the head when he wrote in his nationally syndicated comments on the news: "No attempt at jokes today. A slim, tall, bashful, smiling American boy is somewhere over the middle of the Atlantic Ocean, where no lone human being has ever ventured before." Will was by way of being a flyer himself.

On the evening of the twenty-first, after thirty-three and a half hours in the air, having flown 3610 miles without a stop, the *Spirit of St. Louis* landed at Le Bourget airport near Paris.

As the news raced across the front pages, the New York *Evening World* sold 114,000 additional copies; others did as well or better. President Calvin Coolidge assigned a warship, the USS *Memphis,* to bring the hero and his famous plane home; if anyone thought the thrifty chief executive was going to extremes the criticism was not heard.

When Lindbergh arrived, Mr. Coolidge welcomed him with the longest public flow of words that had passed the President's pinched-in lips since his annual message to Congress. Fifty-five thousand congratulatory telegrams were delivered to the young man during his short stay in Washington; thousands more followed him to New York. Eighteen hundred tons of torn-up paper snowed from office windows as he rode in a motorcade up Broadway; 155 tons had greeted the premature Armistice news in 1918.

Captain Lindbergh was commissioned colonel. He was awarded the Distinguished Flying Cross and the Congressional Medal of Honor. He could not remember all his foreign decorations. A promoter guaranteed him two and a half million dollars for an aerial tour of the world; Hollywood offered him seven hundred thousand for a movie appearance. Lindbergh, Texas, announced its new name.

The hero seemed annoyed with the hullabaloo, but his behavior merely made him appear more heroic. To a people inured to heavy-handed crime and light-fingered graft, cheap theatrics, blatant sex and idols who had proved to be weak in the joints, Charles Lindbergh came as a knight in shining armor.

He rejected the gaudy big-money offers and shied from the public eye. His demeanor was so earnest, simple and warmly appealing that the newspapers quickly cast him in a new role: Prince Charming. Only one thing was lacking, they felt—a romance. It was not lacking for long.

In December, Lindbergh flew the *Spirit of St. Louis* to Mexico on a good-will tour. In Mexico City he fell in love with Anne Morrow, daughter of the U.S. ambassador; and after she returned to the family's New Jersey estate he pursued his courtship by flying low over the Morrow mansion and dipping his plane's wingtips. Their romance and marriage were looked upon as an enchanted idyl, uniting a young man of modest background and a girl of great wealth and high social position.

"No living American commanded such unswerving fealty," a popular historian wrote. "You might criticize Coolidge or Hoover or Ford or Edison, but if you decried anything that Lindbergh did, you knew that you had wounded your auditors. For Lindbergh was a god."

The first headlines appeared—LINDBERGH BABY KIDNAPED. The clamor and alarm soared sky-high. There was "an intense feeling of individual and personal affront," said a young New York psychiatrist, "at this crime against the adored citizen of the world." Along with a great many others in his profession, he inquired into the psychological aspects of the theft.

President Herbert Hoover deplored the kidnaping. The governor of New Jersey called emergency police conferences. Bishop Manning of New York issued a special prayer "for immediate use"—he and his clergy could not wait until Sunday, he declared, to pray for the baby's safe return. The president of the American Federation of Labor asked every member to join in tracking down the kidnapers. Commander Evangeline Booth of the Salvation Army requested her officers to give their aid and mentioned "the miraculous accomplishments with which God has honored our movement along these very lines through our Lost and Found Department."

A few people remained calm.

One was Mrs. Evangeline Lindbergh, Charles' mother. She seldom missed a day at Cass Technical High School in Grosse Point, Michigan, where she taught chemistry; she had not been absent even when her son was flying the Atlantic. She was at her desk the day after the kidnaping. Anne Lindbergh had called her the night before. The older woman had said that they must try not to worry too much.

In his column, Will Rogers wrote:

> What a shock to everybody; but how much more of a one it is when you have seen the baby and seen the affection of the mother and father and the whole Morrow family for the cute little fellow.
>
> Two weeks ago Sunday, Mrs. Rogers and I spent the day with them. The whole family interest centered around him. He had his father's blond curly hair, even more so than his dad's. It's almost golden and all in little curls. His face is more of his mother's. He has her eyes exactly.
>
> His mother sat on the floor in the sun parlor among all of us and played blocks with him for an hour. His dad was pitching a soft sofa pillow at him as he was toddling around. The weight of it would knock him over. I asked Lindy if he was rehearsing him for forced landings.
>
> After about the fourth time of being knocked over, he did the cutest thing. He dropped of his own accord when he saw it coming. He was just stumbling and jabbering around like any kid twenty months old.
>
> He crawled up in the back of the Morrow automobile that

was going to take us home and he howled like an Indian when they dragged him out.

I wish we had taken him home with us and kept him.

In Chicago, in a Cook County jail cell where he was waiting for transfer to the federal penitentiary in Atlanta to serve an eleven-year income-tax evasion sentence, Al Capone, the chief American gangster, responded to the news with two moves, one public, the other private. Publicly, he offered ten thousand dollars for the return of the child and the apprehension of the kidnapers, and said: "It's the most outrageous thing I ever heard of. I know how Mrs. Capone and I would feel if our son were kidnaped, and I sympathize with the Lindberghs. If I were out of jail I could be of real assistance. I have friends all over the country who could aid in running this thing down."

Privately, Capone got in touch with Arthur Brisbane, a featured Hearst newspaper columnist, with another kind of offer: if the U.S. would restore his freedom, he would restore the Lindbergh child to its parents. Brisbane reported the offer in his front-page column.

Mrs. Maude Ballington Booth, a leading official of the charitable organization called Volunteers of America, sent a telegram to every large paper and news agency:

> Mrs. Maude Ballington Booth, little mother of the prison world, wishes to send through your columns to her boys of the underworld on behalf of the Lindbergh baby: "Having been in touch with those who are outside the law for nearly forty years, I know how many of you are good at heart and you will sympathize with these agonized parents. As your little mother, I plead with all the tens of thousands of you I have known or helped to aid in finding the baby. You have means of learning the truth which no officer of the law could have. Let every manly criminal join this search and prove that he will not condone this brutal crime."

In Washington, reported *The New York Times,* "Immediate pressure for early passage of the measure making kidnaping a Federal offense is held certain as the result of the kidnaping of Colonel Lindbergh's son." But Professor Albert Einstein, asked for his opinion by shipboard reporters, held that "kidnaping is a sign of lack of sanity in social development and not a lack of laws."

Franklin Delano Roosevelt, governor of New York, declared that the state police system lay at the Lindbergh family's disposal. Foreign prime ministers sent their nations' regrets and sympathy. Mrs. Carl Hanna, wife of the owner of the Cleveland *News,* recommended flinging German police dogs into the hunt. Ellis H. Parker, often described as a rustic Hawkshaw as a result of his talent for arresting unsuspected wrongdoers in Burlington County, New Jersey, announced that he was available to take charge of the case, then sulkily disclaimed any interest in it when his offer was refused.

In Washington, D.C., Gaston Bullock Means, ex-private detective, ex-secret operative for the Department of Justice during the Harding administration, requested and received an interview with Colonel M. Robert Guggenheim, of the wealthy and public-spirited Guggenheim family. If given the proper assistance, Means told Colonel Guggenheim, he was confident that, with his knowledge of the ways of the underworld, he could quickly clear up the Lindbergh kidnaping and restore the baby to its parents. Guggenheim said he would like to hear more.

Many others wished to help. Among them was a man named Arthur Koehler.

Koehler lived in Madison, Wisconsin, where he was chief wood technologist in the Forest Service of the United States Department of Agriculture. In his office in the Service's laboratory, Koehler pursued infinitely delicate investigations into the weaknesses, strengths and commercial possibilities of thousands of samples of wood. His impressive lore traced back to his earliest years in Manitowoc, Wisconsin, when he discovered that his father's favorite retreat was one that, for a small boy, probably could not be equaled by any other in the world—a carpentry shop, filled with delightful wood shavings and curious wooden shapes and shining instruments. From then on, Arthur Koehler was dedicated to wood.

On the morning of March 2, sitting down to breakfast, hearing the cheerful racket made by his infant son, who was thumping a spoon on the tray of his high chair, Koehler looked at his newspaper and saw the astounding headline: the Lindbergh child had been stolen. The kidnaper or kidnapers had left several clues behind—footprints, a chisel, a ladder.

In his office, Koehler wrote to Colonel Lindbergh. Through the facilities of the Forest Service Laboratory, he said, if given a sample of wood from the ladder he might be able to determine where the wood had come from: what section of the country, what mill and lumberyard. The information might be valuable.

Koehler addressed, sealed and stamped an envelope and put the letter in the mail, where it joined thousands of others sent to the Lindberghs.

5

Charles Lindbergh sat down to his breakfast on the morning of March 2 and found that he could not eat it. He had had no sleep, had not bothered to shave. He wore an old pair of gray pants, a leather jacket and an open-neck shirt.

The long night of searching had yielded several clues: the ladder, the chisel, the smudged clayey marks in the nursery, and the footprints outside. Of the footprints, the larger had been found in the mud beneath the southeast corner nursery window, close to the deep indentations left by the ladder's legs.

This larger footprint was 12⅛ inches long and 4¼ inches wide. There were ridges in the print; Detective Nuncio De Gaetano had speculated that some sort of wool covering must have been worn over the shoe.

Another, smaller footprint had been discovered nearby. It seemed to indicate that the kidnaper had a confederate, perhaps a woman, who had waited close to the ladder to take the baby from his arms.

But was the kidnaper a man, after all? The true size of the foot was obscured by the thick covering.

The young father rose from his untouched food and returned to the search.

He had said that he wanted no police interference, but the presence of the police was essential: to run the twenty-line telephone switchboard that had been set up in the garage, where Colonel Schwarzkopf had established his headquarters, and to keep back the army that was in effect besieging the house—reporters and cameramen, souvenir hunters, gawkers and gapers, gossips and cranks and excited amateur detectives.

Among them was a Mrs. Antonia Cholowski, who made her living as a pig-slaughterer in the Hopewell countryside. She had heard some talk in the back country, the Sourlands, she said, about "kidnaping the Lindbergh baby" before the kidnaping had taken place. An odd tribe of people lived in tar-paper shacks among those trackless hills; many were descendants of the Hessian mercenaries who had come to America under British command during the Revolution and stayed in the new country, marrying squatters' daughters and Indians and runaway Negro slaves. Led by Mrs. Cholowski, State troopers searched countless shacks, cross-examined the natives, and found nothing.

A tall, handsome, dignified man was admitted through the police cordon because of his apparent sincerity and intelligence. He had a message that could be given to no one but Anne Lindbergh. She was lying down when he was brought to her bedroom door. Holding out his arms, he began Hamlet's soliloquy.

And Lindbergh's wishes could not stop the Jersey State police from investigating and speculating.

Captain John J. Lamb, head of the State police detective branch, considered two possibilities. Was the kidnaping an inside or an outside job?

There was much to support the first possibility. Nursemaid Betty Gow knew the day before the kidnaping that the baby had a cold and that the Lindberghs would not be returning to Englewood as they normally did. Betty had come to the Hopewell place on Tuesday well aware that the baby would be in his nursery that night. Of course Oliver and Elsie Whateley also knew.

According to the Lindberghs' best recollection, no one aside from relatives and friends—and Betty Gow and the Whateleys—had been in the nursery since the house had reached its present stage of near-completion. No one except relatives and friends—and Betty and the Whateleys—had ever handled the baby. If a stranger had found his way to the crib in the dark nursery that night, had picked up the child, carried him to the window and down the ladder, wouldn't the baby have cried out?

Who had discovered that the baby wasn't in his crib? Betty. How had she looked when she announced the shocking news? Her voice, Lindbergh remembered, was "quite excited" but certainly not hysterical. Neither then nor later did she break down and weep. Could that have been because she had known that the baby was in safe hands?

But if it had been an inside job, Captain Lamb asked himself, why the complicated, risky business of the ladder?

Say that the ladder was only camouflage—the chisel and footprints too. Say that Betty and the Whateleys, operating a long-rehearsed plan, had kept an eye on the Lindberghs, taken the baby from the crib, brought him down by the servants' stairs, and given him to a confederate waiting outside the back door. It was perfectly possible.

As for the confederate—did Betty have any close friends?

She did, Captain Lamb learned. She had a friend who seemed to be very much interested in her, a young man named Henry Johnson, nicknamed Red, the color of his hair.

In 1931, Red Johnson had had a summer job as a deck hand on Thomas W. Lamont's yacht, the *Reynard*. In August, while the yacht was anchored off North Haven, Maine, where the Morrows vacationed (Dwight Morrow and Thomas Lamont knew each other well through their joint partnership in J. P. Morgan & Company, the banking house), the good-looking, husky young sailor had been introduced by one of the Morrow chauffeurs to Betty Gow, then staying with Anne Lindbergh and the baby at the Morrow summer place. Betty and Red took to each other at once; when the Lamont yacht, as if in the interest of their developing romance, conveniently moored herself in the Hudson near the New Jersey palisades, it was easy enough for Red to drive over to Englewood in his car and pick up Betty for a date—a visit to Palisades Amusement Park, boating, movies, dancing. Red had a brother, John, who lived in a small house outside Hartford, Connecticut, where Betty once had visited.

So, there was Betty's sweetheart, a young sailor who had seen a good deal of the pleasures enjoyed by the rich, who knew very well how wealthy the Morrows were, and who—it turned out—had scant regard for the immigration laws of the United States: a native of Norway, he had jumped ship and entered the country illegally.

Red Johnson had been picked up for questioning by the police. In his car they had found an empty milk bottle. Asked what it was doing there, he had replied that he liked to drink milk while driving.

Captain Lamb knew that Charles and Anne Lindbergh and Anne's mother were convinced that none of the servants in either household had had anything to do with the crime; Lindbergh believed that the kidnaping had been planned and carried out by an underworld gang. The police were determined nevertheless to investigate every aspect of the inside-job possibility. All twenty-nine of the Morrow servants, and the three Lindbergh servants, were being questioned, a process that would require several weeks, since so many of them were of European origin; to do a thorough job it would be necessary to inquire into each one's family background and circumstances.

6

Lindbergh was one of the millions of people who read the Arthur Brisbane column reporting that Al Capone had offered to restore the kidnaped child if the United States would give him back his freedom. The Internal Revenue Service of the Treasury Department was responsible for the gangster's imprisonment for income-tax evasion; Lindbergh called the Secretary of the Treasury,

Ogden Mills, and told him about the Capone offer. Could anything be done about it? The Secretary said he would look into the matter.

He sent for Elmer Irey, who headed all of the Treasury's law-enforcement agencies, including the Intelligence Unit of the Internal Revenue Service, the unit that had actually jailed Capone, told Irey of Lindbergh's call and suggested that he go to Hopewell, talk to him and help in every way he could. But, Mills added, he must warn Lindbergh that the Treasury would not cooperate in any arrangements he might wish to make with Capone.

Irey went to Hopewell the next day. Pleased by this prompt response, Lindbergh nevertheless felt that he should make one thing clear. He had called the Treasury about Capone's offer, he said, because he was determined to explore every possible chance of getting his child back; but he wouldn't ask for the gangster's freedom in exchange for his son even if it meant saving the baby's life.

It was very unlikely, Irey replied, that Capone knew who had stolen the child or where he was. Word had leaked to him that Capone had confided that one of his own gang, Bob Conroy, was the kidnaper—but Irey knew for a fact that on the night of the crime Conroy was some two hundred miles from Hopewell.

The information relieved Lindbergh. He told Irey he would be grateful if he, or a few of his associates, would stay on. Irey assured him that the Treasury was ready to do everything it could; at this point, however, it was necessary to await developments, and he asked Lindbergh to call him in Washington as soon as any came up in which he could be of help.

The young father resumed his long vigil. He and Anne had scarcely slept since the night the baby had been stolen, and the light cold she had caught from the child had steadily worsened, arousing not only her family but also the servants to concern for her health. Dressed in a plain navy-blue sports frock with a white collar, a blue plaid scarf tied around her dark hair, ready to leave at a moment's notice, to go anywhere if she and Charles should be called, her face betraying the strain, Anne nevertheless wandered around the house and the grounds, ignoring all pleas to rest.

She was in the third month of her second pregnancy. Of course it was the missing and not the expected child that dominated her mind. Anne called the lost baby "Charles," as she called her husband, with no pet diminutive name for either. But the father had a pet name for his son. He referred to Charles Augustus Lindbergh, Jr., as "It." Lindbergh had regarded the *Spirit of St. Louis* almost as a living thing, speaking of the two of them as "We," revealing the profound affection he felt for that frail, marvelous craft; after his son was born, the feeling of closeness and love was transferred to the baby.

And the little boy had begun to copy him. Anne and Betty Gow had heard the baby ask where "It" was and when "It" was coming home; unmistakably, he had meant his father. Charles, Jr., called his nurse "Gow," and it was a family joke that he had pronounced her name before making his first attempt to say "Mother" or "Mommy."

In her restless tour of the house and grounds in search of something, anything, to do to hasten her child's return, it occurred to Anne Lindbergh that there was one thing that could and should be done.

On the morning of March 3, the front page of every major newspaper carried her appeal:

> Mrs. Anne Morrow Lindbergh asks that the baby's diet be adhered to, as follows:
> A half cup of orange juice on waking.
> One quart of milk during the day.
> Three tablespoons of cooked cereal morning and night.
> Two tablespoons of cooked vegetables once a day.
> The yolk of one egg daily.
> One baked potato or rice once a day.
> Two tablespoons of stewed fruit daily.
> A half cup of prune juice after the afternoon nap.
> Fourteen drops of viosterol, a vitamin preparation, during the day.

This means of communicating with the kidnapers suggested to the Lindberghs that another kind of appeal was possible. And so, later on March 3, with Colonel Breckinridge's approval, they wrote a second message:

> Mrs. Lindbergh and I desire to make a personal contact with the kidnapers of our child.
>
> Our only interest is in his immediate and safe return and we feel certain that the kidnapers will realize that this interest is strong enough to justify them in having complete confidence and trust in any promises that we may make in connection with his return.
>
> We urge those who have the child to select any representatives of ours who will be suitable to them at any time and at any place that they may designate.
>
> If this is accepted, we promise that we will keep whatever arrangements that may be made by their representative and

ours strictly confidential and we further pledge ourselves that we will not try to injure in any way those connected with the return of the child.

CHARLES A. LINDBERGH
ANNE LINDBERGH

Going over these words once more before releasing them to reporters, Colonel Breckinridge thought that some explanation should be made. "We are counting," he said, as he handed out the typewritten slip, "upon the personal statement to create a feeling of confidence in the minds of the persons who now have the baby, so they will feel free to establish a contact with us. Colonel Lindbergh is not afraid. Certainly the kidnapers cannot believe he would trifle with them in a matter of such extreme importance to him. He will meet them anywhere, under any conditions they may wish to lay down, even to going into the underworld itself, to meet the men who have his baby and arrange for his return."

Learning of the assurances the Lindberghs were about to give, Attorney General William A. Stevens of New Jersey issued a statement of his own. He understood the parents' concern, he said, but he must make it clear that they, as private citizens, did not have the authority to promise immunity to the criminals; that the police officers of New Jersey had no such authority; that a crime had been committed and must be answered for. Although the Lindberghs in effect had said they would not prosecute, ". . . We [the State of New Jersey] will," Stevens concluded.

On March 4, when their message and Colonel Breckinridge's explanation appeared, the Lindberghs had other matters to think about.

A letter had arrived. Thousands of letters had arrived since the morning of March 2; this one was different in that it showed an unmistakable relationship to the original kidnap note: it bore the same identifying symbol, the two interlocking circles traced in blue, with the solid red oval in the center and the three square holes.

The letter had been mailed in Brooklyn the evening before at nine o'clock. It read:

Dear Sir. We have warned you note to make anything public also notify the police now you have to take consequences—means we will have to hold the baby until everything is quite. We can note make any appointments just now. We know very well what it means to us. It is realy necessary to make a world affair out of this, or to get your baby back as soon as possible to settle those affair in a quick way will be better for both—don't by afraid about the baby—keeping care of us day and night. We also will feed him according to the diet.

We are interested to send him back in gut health. And ransom was made aus for 50000 $ but now we have to take another person to it and probably have to keep the baby for a longer time as we expected. So the amount will be 70000 20000 in 50$ bills 25000 $ in 20$ bill 15000 $ in 10$ bills and 10000 in 5$ bills Don't mark any bills or take them from one serial nomer. We will form you latter were to deliver the mony. But we will note do so until the Police is out of the cace and the pappers are quite. The kidnaping we prepared in years so we are prepared for everyding.

The avalanche of mail flowing each day to the Lindbergh home came through the detectives' hands. As they studied the letter, Captain Lamb and his associates noted the German words *gut* and *aus*. They did not conclude from these words, and the clumsy spelling and construction, that the writer necessarily was a German. Perhaps the letter had been dictated to the writer; perhaps the words and sentence structure had been contrived to lead the police astray. One thing they did believe: the letter did not say "I" but "we," which bore out their conviction—and the conviction of Lindbergh, Breckinridge and Schwarzkopf—that they were dealing with an underworld gang.

It seemed to the Lindberghs and Breckinridge that, in order to deal swiftly and successfully with a gang, it would be advisable to have a representative or representatives who possessed firsthand knowledge of the underworld.

Another letter arrived, brought from New York by James Phelan, one of Breckinridge's staff. It had been mailed to the attorney at his office at 25 Broadway and was accompanied by a note requesting him to hand it to Colonel Lindbergh. The note was unsigned but the spelling and punctuation were familiar, and so was the identifying symbol.

The latest letter said:

Dear Sir: Did you receive ouer letter from March 4. we sent the mail in one off the letter—near Boro Hall, Brooklyn. We know Police interfer with your privatmail. How can we come to any arrangements this way. in the future we will send ouer letters to Mr. Breckenbridge at 25 Broadway. We believe polise captured two letter and let not forwarded to you. We will not accept any go-between from your sent. We

> will arrang theas latter. There is no worry about the boy. He is very well and will be feed according to the diet. Best dank for information about it. We are interested to send your boy back in gut health.
>
> It is neccisery to make a world-affair out of it, or to get your boy back as soon as possible. Why did you ignore ouer letter which we left in the room the baby would be back long ago. You would not get any result from the Polise becauce our dinaping was pland for a year allredy. But we were afraid the boy would not be strong enough.
>
> Ouer ransam was made out for 50000 but now we have to put another to it as propperly have to hold the baby longer as we expected so it will be 70000$ 20000 in 50$ bills 25000 in 20$ bills 15000$ in 10$ bills and 10000 in 5$ bills. We warn you again not to mark any bills or take them from one ser. No. We will inform you latter how to deliver the mony but not before the polise is out of this cace and the pappers are quite.

"We will not accept any go-between from your sent"—which might mean "from your side" or "sent by you." But Breckinridge did not waver in his conviction that a go-between familiar with the underworld was essential. The name of Morris Rosner had been given to him as that of a man fully equipped to deal with underworld gangs. In an interview, Rosner was found to be acceptable. At the Lindbergh home, where he was installed, he announced that he would need two people to assist him. He would stay in Hopewell and direct the operations of his assistants, who would be stationed in New York. He knew just the two men he wanted: Salvatore Spitale and Irving Bitz.

On March 6, another Lindbergh announcement appeared on the front pages:

> If the kidnapers of our child are unwilling to deal direct we fully authorize "Salvy" Spitale and Irving Bitz to act as our go-between. We will also follow any other method suggested by the kidnapers that we can be sure will bring the return of our child.
>
> CHARLES A. LINDBERGH
> ANNE LINDBERGH

Colonel Schwarzkopf did not approve of these appointments, but bowed to the parents' wishes. As soon as the backgrounds of Rosner, Spitale and Bitz had been investigated and established by the newspapers, a good deal of criticism was heard. The Reverend Charles E. Coughlin, pastor of the Shrine of the Little Flower in Royal Oak, Michigan, a popular clergyman whose radio audience ran into the millions, said that he was ". . . shocked to learn that Colonel Lindbergh has been driven to deal with underworld characters in an effort to regain his child. . . . Surely, this is the most outrageous committal ever seen by the American public. Do you know who these men are? They are unlawful. They are racketeers. They are the new almighty that we have in the United States. In all the history of civilization there was never such an admission made by any country. And that is what Prohibition has done for us—Prohibition, that has not made the country safe for democracy but instead has made it safe for the bootleggers, the gangsters, and thugs. Such are the people Colonel Lindbergh felt it necessary to appoint."

Other clergymen felt the same way.

Salvatore Spitale and Irving Bitz established headquarters in a speakeasy on Forty-first Street, New York. Here, shortly after their appointment, they were apprehended by the police, brought into federal court, and charged with conspiracy to violate federal law, the Prohibition amendment, by landing a cargo of liquor at Gerrittsen Beach in Brooklyn. But the charge couldn't be made to stick, and Spitale and Bitz returned to the speakeasy.

Salvatore Spitale's word was respected in the underworld. Thirty-five, a quiet, well-dressed man, he had begun his professional life as a bouncer in a Williamsburg dance hall and gradually worked up to become the owner or part-owner of Harlem cabarets, midtown speakeasies and restaurants.

Irving Bitz, according to newspaper investigation, was "a much less important figure." He had done time in Atlanta for peddling dope and had served as strong-arm man for gangster Jacob "Little Augie" Organ.

Their chief, Morris Rosner, referred to himself as a former government agent. He did not mention that he was under indictment for grand larceny in a stock-selling promotion in which the public was said to have lost more than two million dollars. This disclosure by the inquisitive press did not shake his position in the Lindbergh household.

Rosner asked for and received the original ransom note that had been left in the nursery; tracings were made of it for his, Spitale's and Bitz's use, and the note returned to Colonel Lindbergh. The three special representatives then announced that they were ready to open negotiations with the underworld. There followed a flurry of reports of mysterious comings and goings at all hours from and to the speakeasy headquarters. Rosner, Spitale and Bitz were said to have been seen at various points along the Eastern seaboard and as far inland as Chicago and Detroit. To newspaper readers, Detroit suggested the Purple Gang, almost as well known as Capone's organization. A report appeared that a certain Harry Fleischer, previously an important member of the Purple Gang, had been seen thirty miles off Scotland Light on a rum-running boat with two other men and "a crying baby." A conflicting report had it that, at about the same time, Fleischer was seen walking around with a woman and a baby in the neighborhood of the White House.

Rosner granted an interview, printed on March 12. He had definite knowledge, he said, that the Lindbergh baby was alive and would be returned to its parents. "My statement," he concluded, "does not represent my opinion but is based on what I actually know."

The case, it seemed, was about to break.

The young father and mother, the police, the reporters, the world waited.

7

Dr. John Francis Condon, an elderly educator, had grown impatient with waiting and leaving arrangements to the underworld.

Dr. Condon was seventy-two but had the body of a much younger man, thanks to his lifelong devotion to athletics. More than six feet tall, he was proud of his firm muscles and solid two hundred pounds. He lived with his wife Myra in a comfortable two-story house at 2974 Decatur Avenue, near 201st Street, in what he called "the most beautiful borough in the world—the Bronx." Their daughter, also named Myra, had followed in her father's footsteps as a teacher until her recent marriage to Ralph Hacker, a young architect. The Condons' two sons, John and Lawrence, were lawyers.

John F. Condon could look back on a good, full life. After taking his Bachelor of Arts degree at the College of the City of New York in 1884 and his M.A. at Fordham University, he had taught in city schools for the next forty-six years without missing a single scheduled class. Now retired, his life was scarcely less active than before: he lectured at Fordham on pedagogy, gave swimming lessons to those of his students who were interested and spoke on a multitude of subjects at schools and organizations throughout the city.

Ruddy, with gray hair and gray mustache, Dr. Condon was patriotic, religious, sentimental. His clothes, somewhat old-fashioned, always looked neat, and he favored a black derby hat. He was fond of conversation, and talked well, and frequently.

On the night of March 1 Dr. Condon kept a lecture engagement at Morris Evening High School and afterward joined a group of friends at Bickford's in Fordham Square. Dr. Condon's record of attendance at Bickford's for the last twelve years was almost as good as his record of conducting classes; he sat with the same friends at the same table, drinking coffee, analyzing world affairs and local events. Because of Dr. Condon's group and their erudite discussions, Bickford's was popularly known as the "Cafeteria College of the Bronx."

Tonight, the round-table talk roamed from the merits of various police systems, foreign and domestic, to intricate mathematical problems. Shortly before twelve o'clock, a newsboy started shouting outside. He came into the cafeteria. Dr. Condon and his friends stared at the huge black letters he displayed: LINDBERGH BABY KIDNAPED.

There was little more than the bare, staggering announcement, but it was enough to hold the group beyond their usual parting time. At last Dr. Condon got up to walk home, a distance of half a mile. More extras had appeared; he bought them and, erect and brisk, strode toward Decatur Avenue.

For the next three days Dr. Condon thought of little else but the kidnaping. From the bottom of his heart he believed in America as the first nation of the world, its people the finest, its chief citizens the most distinguished, its heroes the boldest and noblest. Of those heroes, Charles A. Lindbergh was his favorite. It seemed to Dr. Condon that in stealing the Lindbergh child the kidnapers had shamed America's name.

On March 5 there was a family dinner at the Condon home. Mrs. Condon, Myra, John and Lawrence saw that the head of the family was upset. The day's news had crowned his indignation with outrage: Charles and Anne Lindbergh had appointed Salvatore Spitale and Irving Bitz as agents to conduct negotiations with the kidnapers. An editorial accompanied the press announcement, proclaiming the editors' sense of shock that the Lindberghs had found it necessary to employ the underworld in an effort to reclaim their child. It seemed to be a confession that the United States itself could not do so.

Dr. Condon said emphatically to his wife, daughter, and sons that, by golly, Uncle Sam *would* restore the baby—and he would help!

Soon afterward, he went to his study. The family glanced at one another; they knew what Dad was doing—writing a letter.

He was. In purple ink (ink he manufactured himself, preferring it to the commercial brands) and his elegant Spencerian hand, Dr. Condon wrote to the editor of his favorite newspaper, the Bronx *Home News*.

"I offer," he wrote, "all I can scrape together so a loving mother may again have her child and Colonel Lindbergh may know that the American people are grateful for the honor bestowed upon them by his pluck and daring.

"Let the kidnapers know that no testimony of mine, or information coming from me, will be used against them. I offer $1000.00, which I've saved from my salary (all my life's savings), in addition to the suggested $50,000. I am ready, at my own expense, to go anywhere, also to give the kidnapers the extra money and never utter their names to anyone.

"If this is not agreeable, then I ask the kidnapers to get any Catholic priest, with the knowledge that every priest must hold inviolate any statement which may be made by the kidnapers."

The Bronx *Home News* was Dr. Condon's favorite newspaper for several reasons. Though often scoffed at by worldly critics (some professed to have seen on its front page the headline BRONX MAN HURT, followed by the information that a Bronx tourist in Japan had suffered quite painful lacerations of the left leg during a typhoon that wiped out ten thousand Japanese), the paper was indifferent to jokes and gibes, convinced that to its readers the Bronx and the affairs of Bronx citizens were matters of supreme interest. Dr. Condon agreed. Then too, the *Home News'* owner and publisher, James O'Flaherty, had been a friend of his ever since, as youths, they had played ball together. Over the years, the paper had published a great number of Dr. Condon's contributions, including poetry, several of which voiced his indignation at a turn of events and were signed L. O. Nestar (Lone Star), J. U. Stice (Justice), or another pseudonym that had captured his fancy.

His letter was not received in time for the March 7 issue of the *Home News,* but the next day it occupied a prominent place. The paper commented editorially: "In offering to act as go-between in negotiations for the return of the Lindbergh baby, Dr. Condon said that he was doing so on his own initiative and would be responsible to no person for information which he might obtain from the abductors."

If little or no attention was paid to the March 8 edition of the *Home News* in Manhattan, Brooklyn, Queens and Staten Island, in the Bronx it received more than enough to make up for the other boroughs' neglect. Dr. Condon's telephone rang constantly; his family and most of his friends—and many people he had never heard of—were skeptical if not frankly critical. Didn't he realize that everyone would be laughing at him for assuming that the Lindbergh kidnapers read the Bronx *Home News*? Why had he made such a fool of himself?

Dr. Condon replied patiently: "I want to see that baby's arms around his mother's neck once more."

His faith was strengthened by the support of an old friend, Al Reich—Alfred Jacob Reich, an ex-heavyweight boxer with whom Dr. Condon attended various sports events.

March 9 was a busy day. Dr. Condon gave four lectures at widely separated points; but, buoyed up by his extraordinary constitution, he wasn't tired when he reached home a little after ten. It was Mrs. Condon's custom to place his mail just beneath a bronze Tiffany clock, the chief ornament of the dining-room mantel. Tonight, there was more correspondence than usual. That was only to be expected in the continuing backwash of his Bronx *Home News* letter.

One envelope caught Dr. Condon's eye because of the large block letters and the form of the address:

MR DOCTOR JOHN F. CONDON
2974 DECATUR AVENUE
NEW YORK

He opened it first. The effect was stunning. Dr. Condon found a chair, sat down, and read the crudely penciled letter again.

> Dear Sir: If you are willing to act as go-between in Lindbergh cace pleace follow stricly instruction. Handel incloced letter *personaly* to Mr. Lindbergh. It will explain everything. Don't tell anyone about it. As soon we found out the Press or Police is notifyed everything are cansell and it will be a further delay.
>
> Affter you gett the mony from Mr Lindbergh put these 3 words in the *New York American*
>
> MONY IS REDY
>
> Affter notise we will give you further instruction. Don't be affrait we are not out fore your 1000$ keep it. Only act strickly. Be at home every night between 6–12 by this time you will hear from us.

The long white envelope also contained a smaller white envelope. On it were two lines of writing in the same hand:

Dear Sir: Please handel incloced letter to Colonel Lindbergh. It is in Mr. Lindberg interest not to notify the Police.

Don't tell anyone about it, the unknown author had written; but Dr. Condon felt in need of friendly counsel. His first impulse was to turn to his wife, but she and the rest of his family were uneasy about his determination to help Uncle Sam solve the Lindbergh case. He decided he would consult Al Reich.

At this time of night, Al was usually to be found at Max Rosenhain's restaurant having a late snack. Dr. Condon put the small envelope back into the large one, hurried outside and boarded a streetcar.

But when he reached the restaurant, at 188th Street and Grand Concourse, Al was not there. Rosenhain, an old acquaintance, hadn't seen Al all night; possibly he was away on some real-estate deal, a business in which Dr. Condon shared some of his interests.

Dr. Condon could not repress his news. He told Rosenhain that he had heard from the Lindbergh kidnapers. Rosenhain seemed doubtful; Dr. Condon gave him the letter. Then he explained that he had to move fast; had to get to the Lindberghs as soon as possible. That was why he wished to find Al. He himself couldn't drive; Al had a car and was an excellent driver.

Max Rosenhain looked around the restaurant, pointed to a table. There sat their friend Milton Gaglio, a clothing salesman, who owned a car.

After hearing the news, Gaglio volunteered to drive Dr. Condon to Hopewell. But he suggested—and Rosenhain agreed—shouldn't Dr. Condon first telephone Colonel Lindbergh?

Dr. Condon went to the telephone booth. After explaining to the voice that answered the Lindberghs' telephone that he had a message for Colonel Lindbergh and that he had been instructed to give it to no one else, he was told by a second voice that he was now speaking to the person in charge of all telephone messages for the Colonel. Dr. Condon identified himself by reciting his list of degrees and other honors, including the title of professor. They seemed to produce a favorable impression, for when he again demanded to speak to Lindbergh, a third voice said that this was Colonel Lindbergh speaking.

Dr. Condon explained about the letter. He was asked to read it. When he had finished, he said that it contained another envelope, which he had not opened. "Please open the letter and read it to me," the voice said.

Dr. Condon opened the small envelope, took out a piece of paper and read:

Mr Colonel Lindbergh Hopewell

Dear Sir: Mr Condon may act as go-between. You may give him the 70,000$ make one packet the size will be about—

Here, Dr. Condon explained, there was the drawing of a box, the dimensions printed alongside, seven by six by fourteen inches. He resumed:

We have notifyed you already in what kind of bills. We warn you not to set any trapp in any way. If you or someone els will notify the Police ther will be a further delay. Affter we have the mony in hand we will tell you where to find your boy. You may have a airplane redy it is about 150 mile awy. But before telling you the adr. a delay of 8 houers will be between.

Dr. Condon stopped. The voice asked if that was all. It seemed tired, almost disinterested.

No, Dr. Condon discovered, that was not quite all. At the bottom of the letter was a strange device. "Colonel," he said, "I do not know whether this is important or not, but there are what I might call a secantal circle, that is, one circle cutting in the other, the same as a secant cuts through a circle. Is it important?"

The voice at the other end of the wire was suddenly alive with excitement. "I'll get an auto and come to you," it said. "Where are you?"

"I am in the Bronx," Dr. Condon said. "But you don't have to. You have enough to do. I will come down to you—to Hopewell."

He hung up.

There was no question but that it was his mention of the odd pattern at the bottom of the letter that had produced the dramatic change. Dr. Condon studied the pattern again. He had never seen anything like it. Two overlapping blue circles, which might have been made by daubing the bottom rim of a bottle with ink and pressing it against the paper, formed an inner oval which was colored a solid red, much as if the misshapen cork of a red-wine bottle had been used as a stamp; cutting across the curious design were three rough holes.

It was close to midnight. Max Rosenhain asked if he could come too; Dr. Condon welcomed his company. Milton Gaglio led them to his car and they started for Hopewell.

8

Two hours later they finally found the Hopewell crossroads; they had lost their way three times. A policeman standing nearby listened to their story and said that he would guide them to a gate on Featherbed Lane, which ran toward the Lindbergh house. Someone was waiting by the gate—a tall, slender gray-haired man, with a little mustache. He opened the gate and came up to them.

He impressed Dr. Condon at once; he was obviously a gentleman, courteous, well-spoken, well-dressed. He rode with them to the big house at the end of the driveway. They entered it through the kitchen, and their companion—who had asked for their names but not given his—introduced himself as Henry C. Breckinridge, Colonel Lindbergh's friend, adviser and spokesman.

Max Rosenhain said facetiously that they, the three visitors, represented a sort of international committee, "a Wop, a Jew, and a Harp." He was nervous.

Lindbergh, Breckinridge said, was waiting upstairs to see Dr. Condon, and led him to a second-story bedroom. Presently a tall young man entered the bedroom; recognizing him, Dr. Condon got up from his chair and shook Charles Lindbergh's hand.

The old man produced the two letters. The second letter was the more important: it carried the distinctive interlocking symbol. There could be no doubt about it, Lindbergh said, it was the same signature. It couldn't be a forgery, because the symbol had never been printed in the newspapers.

Breckinridge agreed. In his opinion, he said, Dr. Condon should be their intermediary: his frankness, good will and sincerity were evident. He suggested that they turn the ransom money over to him.

But Dr. Condon objected. First, he thought, they should look into his record, verify his standing. That would not be necessary, Lindbergh said. Since it was so late, he went on, he hoped Dr. Condon would spend the night in his home.

Dr. Condon was glad to accept, but he wondered if arrangements could be made to ensure his return to Fordham by four o'clock the next afternoon for a lecture. Lindbergh replied that he could count on it.

Unfortunately, there wasn't a spare room for Max Rosenhain and

Milton Gaglio. They shook hands with Lindbergh and left, promising to say nothing about the events of the evening.

Dr. Condon had a favor to ask: he wondered if he might have the pleasure of meeting Mrs. Lindbergh.

Lindbergh took him to the room where she was resting and introduced him. Dr. Condon observed that there were tears in her eyes.

"What are you crying for?" he asked in a gentle voice. "I am going to bring your baby back."

Then he added, smiling:

"Look at the Colonel here. I think he's jealous of an old fellow like me!"

Anne smiled, gave a little laugh. After they left the room, Lindbergh said that it was the first time she had laughed since the night their child had been taken.

To Dr. Condon the mother's smile and laughter were ample reward for his arduous night. He was struck by the word Lindbergh had used. *Taken*—not *kidnaped.*

There was just one empty room in the house, Lindbergh explained, the nursery; he apologized that he could not provide a bed, not even a cot. Could Dr. Condon make out camp-style on the floor? Dr. Condon said that of course he could. The young man went to get sheets, a blanket, a pillow. In his absence, Dr. Condon studied the nursery, noting the empty maple crib, the kiddie car, the porcelain birds on the fireplace mantel, the farmyard animals and little red schoolhouse decorating the folded screen.

Lindbergh returned and quickly made up a bed on the floor close to the crib. He apologized again for these makeshift accommodations, hoped his guest would be able to sleep well, and said good night.

Dr. Condon undressed, meditated for a few minutes, and then knelt beside the crib. He prayed for help and guidance and vowed that he would not rest until the little boy was back in his mother's arms.

At eight o'clock the old man rose, stretched his stiff limbs, dressed and made another survey of the room. Apparently the crib had not been disturbed since Charles Lindbergh, Jr., had last slept in it. The bedclothes were fastened to the mattress with two large safety pins. An idea occurred to Dr. Condon. Removing the safety pins, he slipped them into a small canvas pouch he always kept in his pocket for various odds and ends.

Next, opening the doors of the box beneath the French window, he found many of the baby's toys, among them the tiny wooden figures of a lion, a camel and an elephant. He was studying these when the bedroom door opened and his host entered, wishing him good morning.

Indicating the three wooden animals, Dr. Condon asked permission to take them with him: when he saw the baby, he would ask him to identify the toys and pronounce their names. Perhaps Colonel Lindbergh could remember how his son had said the words? It seemed to him, the young man said, that the baby had had no trouble with *lion* and *camel* but that he pronounced elephant *el-e-punt.*

Good, Dr. Condon commented. If the little boy recognized the toys and called the elephant an el-e-punt, he could feel sure that the baby was Charles Augustus Lindbergh, Jr., and not another child substituted by the kidnapers in order to make further ransom demands for the real baby.

Dr. Condon then confessed that he had taken the safety pins from the crib. Above all, he had to be certain of the identity of the persons he would be dealing with. He would show them the pins, ask them where they had seen the pins last, and also ask where they had been fastened to the mattress. The correct answers would establish them as the kidnapers.

Lindbergh approved. They went down to breakfast.

Alone for a few minutes in the breakfast room, Dr. Condon was served a preliminary cup of coffee by Betty Gow. Soon he was joined, for a breakfast of orange juice, bacon and eggs, toast and coffee, by Charles and Anne Lindbergh, Mrs. Dwight Morrow, Breckinridge, and a police lieutenant whose voice Dr. Condon recognized as that of the first man to whom he had spoken over the telephone the night before.

After breakfast, Lindbergh, Breckinridge and Dr. Condon had another talk. He was convinced, the young father said, that Dr. Condon was in touch with the persons who had taken his son. Shortly, he would get together the $50,000 in the specified bills, and later he would raise the additional $20,000 the kidnapers had demanded.

He held out a piece of paper to Dr. Condon. The old man read:

March 10, 1932

We hereby authorize Dr. John F. Condon to act as go-between for us.

Charles A. Lindbergh
Anne Lindbergh

Breckinridge would take care of the "Money is ready" message that same afternoon, but they must think up some special name for the signature; the newspapers must not learn that Dr. Condon was in touch with the kidnapers. An idea occurred to Dr. Condon. If you put his initials, J.F.C., together and pronounced them quickly, the result was a new, individual name, known to them, and recognizable to the kidnapers, but meaningless to anyone else.

Jafsie.

Lindbergh thought the new name an excellent idea.

And so the message to be inserted in the New York *American* would read:

I accept. Money is ready. Jafsie.

For an hour Dr. Condon studied the most recent photographs of Charles, Jr., and took several of them with him when, a little later, he left for the Bronx. He also took the two safety pins, the lion, the camel, the elephant—and the Lindberghs' thanks and the memory of the tears in Anne's eyes.

Breckinridge drove; the trip required far less time than Dr. Condon's midnight journey to Hopewell. Pulling up in front of the neat two-story house on Decatur Avenue, Breckinridge proposed that, since Dr. Condon's home would be the keystone of the case while negotiations with the kidnapers were under way, perhaps the doctor could put him up during that time. He would do everything in his power, he said, to keep his presence a secret from the newspapers, but he felt that he should be on hand.

Dr. Condon did not hesitate. For as long as he wished, Colonel Breckinridge must consider the Condons' home to be his own.

9

In Washington, Colonel M. Robert Guggenheim, who on March 2 had received a call from the ex-secret operative Gaston B. Means, waited in vain for further word from him.

Gaston Means had in fact abandoned Colonel Guggenheim's offered help for even more promising assistance.

Fifty-three years old, half bald, with a substantial stomach and the easy tongue and affability of a successful former salesman, Means had lived a life of many changes. He was well-born: the Means family had owned the rich plantation acres of Blackwelder's Spring near Concord, North Carolina, for more than a century. His great-grandfather had been governor of the state, his father mayor of Concord, his uncle chief of police.

After graduating from the University of North Carolina, Gaston Means had decided against following the family tradition of working the land and standing for public office; he became a salesman for Cannon Mills, and prospered. He liked the life, the constant change of scene, the entertaining. His tall figure took on weight; his face another chin; by the time he was in his early thirties Means weighed more than two hundred pounds.

Perhaps a thinner man would not have had the disturbing and painful experience that marred one of Means' trips. Occupying an upper Pullman berth, in the middle of the night he was violently precipitated to the aisle of the car and badly bruised. He and the porter discovered that a supporting chain had snapped. Means sued, and won. Evidence produced by the Pullman Company that the faulty chain had been sawed halfway through by unknown hands was not considered conclusive enough to tip the balance.

In 1914, with the outbreak of war, Means joined the William J. Burns detective agency and secured the private account of Count von Bernstorff, German ambassador to the United States, at a fee of a thousand dollars a week. Means lived in style in a Park Avenue apartment, entertained often and well and pursued several romances.

Mrs. Maude King, a young, attractive, wealthy widow, was one of his romantic interests. Her late husband's relatives were so impressed by Means' knowledge of the world, high finance and politics that when he offered to manage the King estate they gave him the job. His investments, chiefly in cotton, didn't seem to be profitable, but the family's confidence held firm.

Means often spoke nostalgically of the South; Mrs. King, a Chicago girl, said she would like to visit the old plantation. During the visit they went on a picnic with tragic consequences. Arrested, Means explained to the police that he and his guest had taken a revolver with them, for target practice. He had gone for a drink of spring water, leaving the gun in the crotch of a tree—a safe place, he had thought. Not safe enough; in his absence, by some deadly mischance Mrs. King had fired the revolver; the bullet had entered her head behind the left ear. At his trial, Means did not agree with the prosecuting attorney's statement that, according to her family, Mrs. King hated guns and was the last person in the world to wish to handle one. The jury sustained Means; he was acquitted.

That ended the King estate job. He got another through William Burns, the new chief of the Department of Justice's Division of Investigation, who remembered Gaston Means as a successful private operative and approved his application to become a Department of Justice secret agent.

In 1930, looking back on those hectic days, Means declared that hundreds of thousands of dollars had passed through his hands, payoffs to various members of the Harding administration and "the Ohio gang." He recollected that among other secret missions he had been employed by Mrs. Harding to investigate the President's rumored backstairs romance with pretty Nan Britton. Because of the evidence he had uncovered, Means said he would always believe that a mortal jealousy lay behind Warren Harding's death in San Francisco in 1923. The public was told it was due to an apoplectic stroke.

Means had had ample opportunity to ponder the past during a two-year term in the federal penitentiary in Atlanta after he was found guilty of having conspired to violate the Eighteenth Amendment. Released, he soon returned on a fresh two-year rap, this time for swindling via the mails. He was a superb convict, praised by the warden as an example for others, less decorous, to emulate.

The Communist conspiracy then engaged Means' attention. He attacked it at the expense of the National Civic Federation, which financed his investigations to the tune of two hundred thousand dollars. The two hundred thousand ran out; the conspiracy remained undefeated. Means was, comparatively speaking, idle.

On the morning of March 2, he read the headlines and called Colonel Guggenheim. And on March 4, while Guggenheim waited to hear more, Gaston Means telephoned Mrs. Evalyn Walsh McLean.

He knew a good deal about her. The daughter of Thomas Walsh, a Colorado mine millionaire, and the estranged wife of Edward Beale McLean, publisher of the Washington *Post,* Mrs. McLean prided herself on her position in Washington society and spent lavishly to maintain it; she owned and often wore, despite its evil three-century reputation, the 44½ carat midnight-blue Hope diamond. She was a friend of the Lindberghs and, moreover, a friend of Captain Emory S. Land, USN, Mrs. Evangeline Lindbergh's cousin.

Means knew, too, that there had been a tragedy in Mrs. McLean's life after she became the owner of the huge ill-starred two-million-dollar diamond. She had been haunted by the premonition that her son, Vinson—called in the newspapers the "Hundred Million Dollar Baby"—would be kidnaped and held for ransom. From his birth in 1909, the little boy was strictly guarded. He was eight years old when, one day, he managed to get away from his guards. A delivery truck drove up to the estate; the gates were unlocked and opened; Vinson, playing nearby, scampered through. His guards ran after him; he ran harder, dodging traffic. Struck by a car, he died in the street.

Means sat in the living room of the great McLean house, Friendship, in the Georgetown section of Washington. "Mrs. McLean," he said, "I've come to realize that honesty is the best policy. I've made mistakes, bad mistakes. I've served jail sentences for them. But I want to do more. I want to do something to wipe out my past record so that I can hold up my head again and look my fellow citizens squarely in the eye."

Mrs. McLean had agreed to the meeting when Means had given her a hint, over the phone, of its purpose. He had suggested that she ask Captain Land to be present.

"I know the head of the Lindbergh kidnap gang," Means continued. "With your help, I can have the baby back to his mother inside two weeks."

His past errors, he said, had brought him into touch, in the Atlanta Penitentiary, with criminals of all stripes. The head of the Lindbergh gang was one of them and they had come to know each other well. The man trusted him, knew him for a straight-shooter. He had given his terms to Means for the safe return of the Lindbergh child.

"He wants a hundred thousand dollars," Means said.

Mrs. McLean did not seem taken aback.

Means thought a code might be helpful in further discussions or communications. For example, the leader of the kidnap gang—a man known to the underworld as The Fox—would be number 19. Mrs. McLean would be number 11. Another point: the kidnapers had insisted that the child must be delivered to a Catholic priest, and the priest must swear that under no circumstances would he describe the man or men who had given him the baby.

Both Mrs. McLean and Captain Land said that this seemed reasonable. Mrs. McLean thought she knew exactly the man for the job: the Reverend J. Francis Hurney, pastor of the Church of the Immaculate Conception. She would have a talk with him. If Father Hurney said yes, she would ask him to meet Means the next day.

After their meeting, Father Hurney told Mrs. McLean he had thought Means forthright, sincere, and it was obvious that he knew what he was talking about—his references to the underworld were unmistakably genuine. Father Hurney said he would be glad to serve. But perhaps, first, Mrs. McLean should obtain the Lindberghs' approval of the plan.

Captain Land volunteered to go to Hopewell and put it up to Lindbergh.

The following day, March 6, Captain Land came back from his Hopewell trip; both Lindbergh and Breckinridge, he reported, were convinced that the underworld was responsible for the kidnaping, a conviction borne out by what Means had said. Lindbergh, therefore, gave his approval; but in the event of success, he wanted it understood that he would repay the ransom to Mrs. McLean. And of course he approved her insistence on secrecy.

On March 7, Mrs. McLean went to her bank and, in the president's office, was given the sum of one hundred thousand dollars in old, worn bills—so stipulated by the kidnapers through Gaston Means. She took an additional four thousand in crisp new currency. This four thousand dollars, Means had explained, was for his personal expenses.

Gravely, Means accepted the money; it was a serious business they were engaged in, and none knew where it might lead—to a happy ending, he hoped; but if not, if Father Hurney didn't receive the stolen child, it was agreed that the hundred thousand was to be returned to Mrs. McLean.

No one outside their group must know what was going on. Mrs. McLean must not say anything to friends, business advisers, attorneys.

She gave her word.

10

In Norfolk, Virginia, another man of the cloth, the Very Reverend Harold Dobson-Peacock, dean of Christ Episcopal Church, was waiting for an urgent caller.

He had identified himself over the phone as John Hughes Curtis, president of the Curtis Boat Building Corporation. Last night, Curtis had said—the night of March 9—he had an extraordinary experience. He wanted to tell the dean about it face to face, as soon as possible.

Dobson-Peacock knew John Hughes Curtis not as a friend but by reputation: a popular man who led an active social life, husband of a charming wife, Constance Curtis; father of two children, John Hughes, Jr., twelve, and Constance, eleven.

A little after noon, Curtis pulled up in his green sedan. A big man, tanned, muscular, his face was solemn. Dean Dobson-Peacock took him to a room where they could be sure of no interruption and closed the door.

The night before, Curtis began, there had been a meeting at the Norfolk Country Club, attended by all yachtsman members, since the matter was pressing: winter storms had raised havoc with the piers and moorings.

Curtis had been one of the last to leave the meeting, almost the very last, except for the driver of an old Hudson that, as he prepared to swing out of the drive, had come alongside. Curtis realized that the car's driver had not been at the meeting at all, as he had first assumed; he recognized him as a person who was hardly on good terms with decent society, a man of many aliases, formerly a rum-runner. Curtis had once repaired a boat for him. In spite of his dubious background, Sam—the handiest of his several names—had always seemed to be a pretty square-dealer; Curtis had never caught him in a lie or an attempted fraud; indeed, thought fairly highly of him, had even put in a good word for Sam once in a while with the Coast Guard.

"What are you doing here?" Curtis had demanded. "What's the matter?"

Sam had left his old car and got in beside Curtis. "Mr. Curtis," he said, "please don't get sore, but I want you to swear you won't tell anyone what I'm going to tell you now."

Curtis had never seen the ordinarily cocksure Sam so shaken. He agreed to tell no one.

In the next moment he understood the reason for Sam's concern. Sam had been selected as an intermediary by the Lindbergh kidnapers.

It was not a part he had chosen for himself, Sam had continued; they had come to him. They wanted him to ask Curtis to form a committee of a few prominent Norfolk citizens to deal on the one hand with Colonel Lindbergh and on the other with the gang.

Curtis had been puzzled. Why should they choose him? Why come to Norfolk, Virginia—why not negotiate with Lindbergh through people closer to his home, in New Jersey or New York?

The reason, Sam had explained, was that the gang feared the New Jersey and New York gangs; also, they would demand a split.

Then how about the two men, Spitale and Bitz, whom Lindbergh had appointed to deal with the underworld?

The gang wrote them off as a joke, Sam declared.

Curtis had thought it over. He foresaw all kinds of complications, he told Dean Dobson-Peacock, and had said as much to Sam. "I can't get in touch with Colonel Lindbergh," he had said angrily. "It's impossible. He must have a million people bothering him. Damn it, I could wring your neck!"

Sam had repeated his plea: "Don't get sore." At the very least, wouldn't Mr. Curtis think about it? If they had a chance to get the Lindbergh baby back, could they refuse?

Curtis had regained his better senses; there was much in what Sam said. All right, he had said, he would think about it, and arranged to call Sam the next morning.

Sam had climbed back into his old Hudson and driven off.

At home, Curtis had sat up late. The thing was not so fantastic after all. He had repaired boats for rum-runners; what dockyard man along the coast hadn't? In a manner of speaking, the gang would feel they had a connection with him. And he remembered Sam's reputation as a square-dealer.

Finally, Curtis had thought of his two young children and decided that he would do all he could to help the Lindberghs.

The following morning, he had announced his decision to Sam. He had gone further; he had hit on the one man of all men in Norfolk who, he thought, should be able to reach Colonel Lindbergh—Harold Dobson-Peacock.

Sam had been pleased with the news. The Lindbergh baby, he had assured Curtis, was in good health; with this he had hung up, and Curtis had made his call to the dean.

Pipe in mouth, Dobson-Peacock considered John Hughes Curtis' indeed quite extraordinary experience. How odd, he thought, that while the Lindberghs were trying to make contact with the kidnapers through the underworld, the kidnapers were trying to make contact with the Lindberghs through respectable citizens!

It was true that he should be able to reach the family. He knew Anne Morrow Lindbergh and her mother.

At fifty-two, the dean had had a distinguished career in his church. An Englishman, he had served in the war, from which he carried two wound-scars, and in 1927 had been called abroad to become rector of the Episcopal cathedral in Mexico City, where he had met Dwight Morrow, United States ambassador to Mexico, and his charming family. The Morrows were acquainted with Dobson-Peacock's wife and his daughter, Marjorie, who had made her debut into Norfolk society last year. Certainly he could identify himself satisfactorily to Charles Lindbergh!

It seemed to him, he said at last, that the story Mr. Curtis had told fitted logically into the setting as he understood it. Such shocking crimes as the Lindbergh kidnaping were only a natural outgrowth of the prohibition law, which the dean had denounced as the most asinine ever imposed on a liberty-loving people. It had spawned a new class of criminals; contemptuous of all authority, there was nothing they dared not touch. Well, the crime had been committed; it remained to save the baby. Since the gang had seen fit to approach Curtis and Curtis, with some reason, had approached him, he would be glad to help.

First, Curtis and the dean agreed, they must telephone Colonel Lindbergh, describe the situation, and volunteer to act as negotiators.

Dobson-Peacock felt that this important call required special facilities, which could be provided by the central office of the telephone company in Norfolk. By the time they arrived there, it was early afternoon. In guarded terms, the dean explained his requirements to an official of the company; a special booth was made available and a special operator began the business of getting in touch with Lindbergh in Hopewell.

Dean Dobson-Peacock was not the most patient of men, and reaching the Lindbergh home seemed an unduly complicated operation. Finally a voice answered. Was this Colonel Lindbergh? No, it was not. Then let him speak to the Colonel, the dean said, and gave his name. Colonel Lindbergh was not available. Was Mrs. Morrow available? No.

The dean's patience wore thinner. Just who *was* available?

It appeared that a man described as Colonel Lindbergh's secretary, a Mr. Rosner, would be willing to speak to him.

A flat voice asked what the dean wanted. Again Dobson-Peacock identified himself and spoke of his friendship with the Morrows. Then he introduced Curtis.

Once more Curtis described his meeting with Sam. Rosner seemed curiously indifferent. He had no suggestions to make and the telephone call, so important in prospect, petered out in long, dispiriting silences.

There was nothing to do but hang up.

Back in his rectory, the dean's annoyance grew. He was not accustomed to such treatment. He, who might be called one of the leading churchmen in the East, had in effect been shrugged off by an individual whose speech betrayed anything but breeding and education. If this person Rosner was Lindbergh's secretary, the Colonel's affairs would appear to be in deplorable shape.

Yet what could he do? The dean telephoned Curtis to see if any new ideas had occurred to him. So far none had, but Curtis promised to call at once if he thought of a fresh approach to the problem.

It was not Curtis who thought of a new approach; it was his wife Constance.

The daughter of a well-to-do Brooklyn dentist, Constance Robeteau had brought a comfortable dowry to her marriage to Curtis fifteen years before. From their apartment house at Redgate Avenue and Manteo Street she conducted a busy social life, and affectionately and efficiently looked after her husband, son, and daughter. She had been of great help and comfort to Curtis when, in 1931, the Curtis Gas Engine and Boat Company, after a prosperous career that included a major contract with the German government, had run into difficulties and gone bankrupt with liabilities of $365,000.

Without her, as Curtis often said, he did not know what he would have done.

Now, as before, she came to his aid. He told her about Sam and Dobson-Peacock and the exasperating call to Hopewell. Constance pointed out that there was a man in Norfolk with a personal, exceptional link to Colonel Lindbergh himself. He was, of course, Admiral Guy Burrage. John should tell *him* the story. Certainly Admiral Burrage would be able to get Lindbergh on the phone, if anyone could.

Curtis agreed; but out of common courtesy he thought he should first propose the idea to Dean Dobson-Peacock. Yes, Constance said, that was only right.

Curtis waited until the next day, March 11, before returning to the dean's home. The dean listened to Constance Curtis' suggestion without the enthusiasm that might have been expected; however, its merit was unassailable.

Gray-haired, lean and upright despite his sixty-seven years, Vice Admiral Guy Hamilton Burrage, USN (Ret.), lived in comfortable, unpretentious circumstances in his gabled house at 731 Yarmouth Street. As Constance Curtis had recalled, his connection with Lindbergh was an unusual one. In 1927, Admiral Burrage had been in command of all American naval forces in European waters, flying his flag from the new 7500-ton cruiser *Memphis*. It was brought to the admiral's attention in May that a young man had set out alone to fly the Atlantic; if he came down somewhere short of his goal, Paris, in the ocean, it would be up to Burrage's command to try to rescue him.

Admiral Burrage was destined to meet Charles Augustus Lindbergh in a happier setting than a rescue at sea. After the President of the United States had decided that the national hero should be brought home in the style he deserved, Lindbergh boarded the *Memphis*; Admiral Burrage had the welfare of the famous young man in his keeping during the few days it took the cruiser to steam across the Atlantic, and it had been he who, getting in touch with Mrs. Evangeline Lindbergh by radio, had arranged to bring her to her son's side when the warship docked.

Again Curtis told his story. When he had finished, Admiral Burrage sat in silence for several moments, then said emphatically: "I'd go to the ends of the earth, if necessary, to help Colonel Lindbergh get his baby back!"

For some hours they discussed the kidnaping, and Burrage recalled various incidents and anecdotes from the days he had spent with Lindbergh. It was well he did, for, when at length he picked up the telephone and called Lindbergh's home, his statement that he was Admiral Guy Burrage was not accepted at its face value.

After several voices had spoken to him, still another came over the wire. This, it said, was Colonel Lindbergh. "This is Guy Burrage, Colonel," the admiral said cordially. But the other hesitated. Would the admiral mind very much relating some of the things that had occurred while the two of them were on the *Memphis?* Admiral Burrage retold the anecdotes he had told Dobson-Peacock and Curtis and followed with Curtis' account of the conversation with Sam.

The call had lasted almost a half hour when Admiral Burrage said good-by. It had not been satisfactory. There had been no positive response to his question: should he and the dean and Curtis meet with Sam and begin negotiating with the kidnapers? The best thing to do, Burrage told the others, would be for him to write a letter to Lindbergh asking if they might come to Hopewell.

Because, the admiral said slowly, he had the curious conviction that it wasn't Charles Lindbergh he had spoken to.

11

In the classified columns of the March 11 editions of the New York *American,* a small advertisement read:

MONEY IS READY. JAFSIE.

Shortly after noon, Mrs. Condon heard the telephone in her house in the Bronx.

She was alone. Dr. Condon had told her that he expected to be away all day, and their guest, Colonel Breckinridge—the gentleman her husband had brought home the previous day—was at his office.

The telephone was in the hall. Mrs. Condon picked up the receiver and said "Hello?"

A man's voice inquired if Dr. Condon was at home. No, she replied, her husband was lecturing; he had said he would return in the early evening, soon after six. If the caller wished, she would be glad to write down his name.

The caller ignored the invitation; he curtly instructed her to tell Dr. Condon not to go out that night. He would call again, he said, around seven. He hung up.

The quality of his voice made an impression on Mrs. Condon. It was a thick, deep voice, strongly accented.

As he had promised, Dr. Condon arrived home a few minutes after the Tiffany clock had struck six. Breckinridge came soon afterward. Dr. Condon was still examining his mail when his wife remembered the noontime call. The caller had said he would telephone again at seven. The possible significance of the hour struck Dr. Condon: in their instructions, the kidnapers had written that they would get in touch with him between six and twelve o'clock at night. This man had called just after the appearance of the message in the *American*. It seemed quite possible that he was one of the kidnap gang.

Al Reich arrived; he had agreed to drop in every evening in case he could be of help. Joined by the Condons' daughter Myra, the small group waited, watching the clock's hands slowly turn toward seven.

The hour struck. Nothing happened. Breckinridge began to pace nervously. Something must have gone wrong, he declared. Perhaps——

The telephone bell cut him off.

Dr. Condon ran into the hall, lifted the receiver, and said, "Hello?" A deep voice asked if he was Dr. John F. Condon. Yes, he said; who was calling? The voice asked if he had received the letter with the distinctive signature, the overlapping circles. *Signature,* the old man noted, was pronounced *sing*nature.

He said that he had. How else would he have known what message to put in the *American?*

The caller said that he had seen the message.

Dr. Condon asked where he was calling from and was told Westchester.

The caller inquired if Dr. Condon wrote pieces for the newspaper once in a while.

Dr. Condon said yes, he did. Now his excitement rose: he heard the caller tell someone else that Dr. Condon wrote articles for the papers.

Instructions followed. Dr. Condon was told that he must stay at home every night—the same hours, six to twelve. Soon he would receive another note; he must be sure to do exactly what the note said, otherwise everything would be finished.

Dr. Condon promised to obey.

Another voice spoke. Dr. Condon could not mistake the words; they were in Italian, of which he had some knowledge—*statti citto,* a colloquial expression. In English, it would be *Shut up!*

The first voice then said that very soon Dr. Condon would hear from the gang again.

That was all. To the little group awaiting him, the old man told all he had heard: that he was to stay at home, that another note would arrive for him, that the caller's voice was heavily accented, an accent that seemed to be consistent with the phrasing and spelling in the ransom notes; that he was not alone; and that it would seem that the person with him was Italian, just as it would seem that he himself was German.

Breckinridge said he was sure that they were in direct touch with the kidnapers. Two things must be done: first, the money must be assembled in the specified denominations; second, to deliver the money, they must find a box of the size described in the note.

An idea occurred to Dr. Condon. Upstairs, he had a ballot box dating from the year 1820, a gift from one of his friends on City Island, where real-estate affairs often took him and Al Reich. With its brass bindings and lock, the box was unmistakable. Dr. Condon did not propose to use it but rather to have a copy of it made, with the same brass fittings. The new box would have a veneer composed of five different kinds of wood. After the money had been transferred in it, the box—if found again—would provide valuable evidence, perhaps even point to the kidnapers.

Breckinridge approved, and it was agreed that the next day Dr. Condon would find a cabinetmaker to work on the box.

Al Reich said good night and left; he would be on hand again, of course, the next evening. Dr. Condon saw that all the doors were locked; then he and Breckinridge slowly mounted the stairs to their bedrooms.

Breckinridge was much moved by the events of the evening, most particularly by Dr. Condon's role. He put his hand on the old man's arm. He knew very well, he said, how strongly opposed the Condon family was to the doctor's participation in the case, and he sympathized with them. If, as he and Dr. Condon hoped, the latter should be called on to negotiate face to face with the kidnapers, he might be in danger. He wished, Breckinridge went on, that there were other means of dealing with the kidnapers, but the task had fallen to Dr. Condon as the kidnapers' choice. He only hoped that Dr. Condon would be given a reward in keeping with the trial he and his family were going through.

The old man smiled. Yes, he had a reward in mind, he said, but it might turn out to be too great!

Breckinridge was puzzled. A reward too great for the Lindberghs to pay?

The reward he had set his heart on, Dr. Condon said, still

smiling, was the privilege of putting the baby back in his mother's arms.

Breckinridge looked at him. He felt sure, he said, that the reward could be arranged.

The hands of the Tiffany clock pointed to six. It was the evening of March 12; once more the little group was gathered downstairs in the Condons' home.

Dr. Condon gave a report on his activities of the day. He had gone to see a first-rate Bronx cabinetmaker, with whom he had left the ballot box. The duplicate box was to be constructed as he had described; the cabinetmaker promised to have it within four days; the cost would be three dollars, materials and workmanship included.

Seven o'clock; half-past seven. There was the sound of footsteps on the veranda. The doorbell rang.

Dr. Condon hurried to the door. Two men greeted him, his companions of that blundering night ride to Hopewell—Max Rosenhain and Milton Gaglio. They had stopped by, Rosenhain explained, to see what was happening and if they could be of help.

The old man invited them in. Breckinridge remembered them and was grateful for their earlier services; it concerned him, though, to think that if the kidnapers were hiding nearby watching the house, waiting for the proper moment to make their approach, the unexpected appearance of Rosenhain and Gaglio might alarm them. But it couldn't be helped.

Eight-thirty. The doorbell again.

At Mosholu Parkway and Jerome Avenue in the Bronx, John Joseph Perrone had had a slow evening on the hack stand. A fare finally showed up, a young man who told Perrone to take him to 3440 Knox Place. After collecting the fare and a modest tip, Perrone turned his cab around and drove slowly east.

At Knox Place and Gun Hill Road he was hailed by a man who came running toward him with hand upheld. Perrone stopped; the man came up to the cab, tried to open the right front door. Perrone lowered the window. Something seemed to be bothering the other; several times he glanced around as he spoke.

"Do you know where Decatur Avenue is?"

"Yes, sure," Perrone said.

"Do you know where 2974 is?"

"Sure!"

The man put one hand into his overcoat pocket, drew out an

envelope; put his hand back into the same pocket and, looking intently at Perrone, brought out a dollar bill. He gave envelope and bill to the driver; on the envelope was written the address and a name: *Dr. Condon.*

Then he walked to the rear of the cab and began to write on a piece of paper, glancing at the car's license plate. Perrone debated getting out and asking him what it was all about, then decided against it. He put the cab in gear and started toward 2974 Decatur Avenue.

Dr. Condon opened the front door. A stranger stood there; parked at the curb in front of the house was a cab. "Are you Dr. Condon?" the driver asked.

Dr. Condon nodded. The other held out a long white envelope; Dr. Condon saw the familiar large, awkward handwriting spelling out his name and address.

He went back inside, opened the envelope and read:

> Mr Condon
>
> We trust you but we will note come in your Haus it is to danger. even you can note know if Police or secret servise is watching you
>
> follow this instruction. Take a car and drive to the last supway station from Jerome Ave. here 100 feet from the last station on the left seide is a empty frankfurther stand with a big open porch around. you will find a notise in senter of the porch underneath a stone. this notise will tell you were to find uss.
>
> Act accordingly
>
> After ¾ of a houer be on the place. bring mony with you.

As before, the intricate symbol-signature appeared at the bottom.

bring mony with you. But that was impossible, Breckinridge said; he didn't have it—it would take some time to assemble the specified bills; besides that, the new box wouldn't be ready for a few days.

Dr. Condon was not disturbed. Here was his chance to meet the kidnapers, the personal contact he had been waiting for. He could explain about the money; but now, above all, he must do exactly what they said, so far as he could. They gave him three-quarters of an hour to get to the frankfurter stand. How could he make it in that time?

Al Reich said he would drive him.

Breckinridge came down the steps with them to Al's Ford coupé. He shook their hands and gave them his blessings.

It was a dismal night; the cold wind had kept most of the Bronx at home; old leaves, bits of rubbish, paper scraps stirred and scuttled along the gray streets. Dr. Condon pulled his overcoat tighter, patted one pocket to make sure again that the little canvas pouch was there. Al spoke uneasily; he was worried about his friend and counseled him to be careful. But Dr. Condon was not concerned. He had always kept himself in excellent shape, he reminded Al, and he knew how to use his fists if it should prove to be necessary.

Here was Jerome Avenue. Traffic was even scantier. The gloomy blocks rushed by under the street lights. Al slowed the car as they neared the last subway station, and both men peered ahead. On the west side of the street stood a frail, melancholy booth, the deserted frankfurter stand, girdled by a dilapidated porch.

Al made a U turn and came to a halt in front of the stand. Dr. Condon left the car, climbed a sagging board step to the porch. Precisely in the center lay a large flat rock. He picked it up and found another long white envelope, the same kind he had seen earlier.

He carried the envelope toward the car and stopped beneath a street lamp. Al leaned curiously from the coupé as Dr. Condon slit the envelope and took out a small piece of paper. He read aloud, for the other's benefit:

> Cross the street and follow the fence from the cemetery direction to 233rd Street.
>
> I will meet you there.

233rd Street, Al reckoned as Dr. Condon got back into the car, would be about a mile ahead.

Now they came to a scene even more dismal than the deserted streets. On one side lay the bare acres of Van Cortlandt Park, dispiriting enough but a good deal more cheerful than the opposite side, the great stony sprawl of Woodlawn Cemetery, securely locked in for the night behind its nine-foot iron fence.

Al responded to the forbidding sight with a quip. When Dr. Condon was plugged by the kidnapers, at least he wouldn't have too long a journey to his final resting place.

Al slowed the car and stopped some fifty feet short of 233rd Street. Here was one of the cemetery's main entrances, a three-sided space spanned by heavy locked gates.

It seemed to Dr. Condon that this must be the spot the note-writer had had in mind. He started to get out. Al said he would go with him; with luck, he'd be able to grab the fellow. But Dr. Condon would have none of it. The writer expected one man, not two, he pointed out, and any attempt to catch him might interrupt the negotiations, even end them. Dr. Condon's job was to get the baby; then it would be the police's job to capture the kidnapers. He had no intention of trying to ambush or deceive them; the important thing was to establish an atmosphere of confidence.

Reluctantly Al agreed.

Dr. Condon walked along the empty street to the cemetery gates. He stood before them, glanced around, saw nothing; but he sensed that he was being watched. It might be only his imagination, of course. Or it might be that he, or they—the note-writer and his Italian confederate—were surveying him: was this Dr. Condon or a chance loiterer? How could he settle that question? Ostentatiously, Dr. Condon took the note from his pocket, slowly read it again, put it back.

Still nothing happened.

Puzzled, Dr. Condon went back to the car. Al looked at him questioningly: what was what? Dr. Condon said he did not know.

It was quarter past nine. They had arrived at the rendezvous in plenty of time; that couldn't be the trouble.

The old man returned to the Woodlawn gates and waited again. It was cold; fortunately he had worn the warmer of his two overcoats.

Nine-thirty came; he stirred restlessly.

Something white waved in the chill night air.

Dr. Condon stared. It was a cloth, perhaps a handkerchief, held in a man's hand. The hand moved up and down between two vertical iron bars of the gates; the man who held it was inside the cemetery.

Dr. Condon strode toward the gates. As he advanced, the hand was withdrawn. Against the background of naked trees and tombstones, a dim figure faced him, masked by a handkerchief held over the face, so that only the eyes were visible under the low-pulled hat brim.

Dr. Condon heard the voice he had heard the night before—thick, deep, heavily accented. It asked if he had received the note. Dr. Condon replied that he had.

The voice continued:

"Did you got it, the money?"

"No," Dr. Condon said. "I couldn't bring the money until I saw the package." By *package* he meant the kidnaped child.

A sound came to their ears: the dull crunch of a footfall inside the cemetery. The voice cried, "There is a cop!" Thrusting the handkerchief he had held to his face into a pocket of his overcoat, the figure took hold of one of the gate bars, hauled himself up hand over hand, vaulted over the top and landed lightly beside Dr. Condon. He put his right hand in his coat pocket, where, the old man thought, he might have a gun.

"Did you send the cops?" he demanded accusingly.

"No!" Dr. Condon said. "I gave you my word I wouldn't do that, and I've kept my word!"

"It is too dangerous," said the other; and, turning, he ran north along the street.

Dr. Condon ran after him, shouting, "Come back! Come back! Come back here! Don't be cowardly!" In vain.

The cemetery gates, the cemetery guard whose footfall they had heard, the cemetery itself, fell behind. His quarry, Dr. Condon knew from his brief inspection, was far younger than he, but the old man kept within hailing distance. He was not too far behind when the other ran into Van Cortlandt Park and bolted into a clump of trees and bushes.

Dr. Condon bolted in too, and almost crashed into him. Grabbing the other's arm, he spoke severely:

"You mustn't do anything like that! You are my guest!"

The other was sullenly silent. Dr. Condon looked about him and saw a park bench. He pulled his quarry toward it, sat him down. Again he spoke sternly. He shouldn't have run off and left him, a poor schoolteacher who had come all the way to the cemetery to see him!

"Don't ever do it again!" Dr. Condon admonished. "I am square with you!" Therefore, he concluded, the other should be square with him.

For a few minutes they sat in silence, looking across the barren park to 233rd Street. Some three hundred feet away, Al Reich's car hadn't moved.

With his left hand, the younger man held his overcoat collar tightly around his chin; his right hand remained in his coat pocket. At last he spoke.

"It is too dangerous," he said. "It might be twenty years." He paused. "Or burn. Would I burn if the baby is dead?"

Appalled, Dr. Condon faced him directly. *Dead?* What did he mean? What were they doing there if the baby was dead?

But he was reassured. The baby was not only alive but in good health, the other said. It was getting more to eat than its mother had asked for. The mother shouldn't worry, the father shouldn't worry, Dr. Condon shouldn't worry.

His tone, even more than his words, relieved Dr. Condon; it showed no evasiveness, no telltale shiftiness of a guilty conscience. The old man sat back.

"How do I know I am talking to the right man?" he asked.

Dr. Condon had received the letters with the circle signatures, the other said, and the old man noted again that the word was given the same odd pronunciation, *sing*nature. From his pocket he took the small canvas pouch, opened it, and removed the safety pins. He held them up and asked if his companion had seen them before.

"The baby was held in the crib by safety pins," the other said.

Satisfied, Dr. Condon went on to other matters. "You know my name," he said. "Please tell me yours."

"John," the other replied.

Here was a coincidence! John, Dr. Condon pointed out, was *his* first name, too.

"Are you a German?" he inquired.

"No. Scandinavian."

"What would your mother say, John, if she knew you were engaged in a thing like this?"

"She wouldn't like it. She would cry."

"Then leave it!" Dr. Condon said. "Come with me. I have a thousand dollars of my own available, and you can have it."

"We don't want your money," John said.

We—not *I*. Dr. Condon seized on this. Who, he asked, were "we"?

He was only a go-between, John replied; the head of the gang was Number 1, a very big man who had once worked for the government. Number 2 was a smart man also. He knew Dr. Condon; he had told the gang that Dr. Condon was a fine man.

Well then, Dr. Condon said, perhaps he and Number 2 could meet. Things might move a little faster if this were arranged.

No, John said, it couldn't be done. Since Dr. Condon would recognize him, Number 2 felt that such a meeting would lead to his capture.

The old man returned to his earlier appeal. "Leave them, John! I will give you my money and I will go over to Jersey and collect the rest for you, if it is within my power. There are a number of lawyers in my family and if it is within the law, I will get Colonel Lindbergh to go along with you to the last degree. But if you fail me, I'll follow you all the way to Australia. Leave them!"

"No," John said.

"Why?"

"The leader would smack me up. They would drill me."

"You mustn't be afraid of anything like that," Dr. Condon said.

"Do what you think is right, while you have the time, for your mother's sake." He waited hopefully, but the other was silent. "You will be caught, John."

"No," his companion said. "We prepared a year for this."

The bitter wind nipped the skin; John drew his overcoat lapels closer. "John," Dr. Condon said earnestly, "you have nothing to be afraid of. I have been square all my life and I am square now. You have nothing to fear from me. Take down that coat—the fabric is too thin. I have two coats, and I will give you one if you are in want."

John shivered, coughed. Dr. Condon nodded gravely. "The inroads of pulmonary disease seem to start. Let me go over and get you some medicine. I will do anything I can to straighten this matter out—anything!"

John did not respond. Dr. Condon tried another approach, asking where the baby was now.

The baby was on a boat, John told him, some six hours away by ordinary travel. Two women were aboard, in charge of the child.

Dr. Condon asked how would he recognize the boat.

The masts were marked with white cloths; besides, John added, when it was time for Colonel Lindbergh to come for the baby, he, John, would stand on the shore and signal to the crew.

John's share of the ransom, Dr. Condon inquired, after a pause —what was it to be?

Twenty thousand was to go to Number 1, John replied; the other five members of the gang—there were six altogether—would each receive ten thousand.

That made seventy thousand, Dr. Condon pointed out. Not fair! The original sum was fifty thousand.

Yes, John said, but Lindbergh had not followed instructions; he had called in the police, he had complicated everything, made it more difficult and dangerous. They had to think of themselves. Maybe they would need lawyers. They had to put aside some of the money for lawyers.

Dr. Condon observed that the most ticklish job had been assigned to John, yet he was to receive only half the leader's payoff. He knew that only too well, John said. He was sorry he had gotten mixed up in it.

Quickly, Dr. Condon pursued this admission. "John," he begged, "take me to the baby! I will go as a hostage!"

John did not understand. "Hostage?"

"I mean, I will go and stay there until you get the money. Let me be with the baby! I have three toys belonging to the baby and there are three words I know that the baby knows."

John looked off into the distance and then shook his head.

Noting the direction of his glance, Dr. Condon asked: "Your friend is with you?" John said nothing. "Why not call him?" the old man pressed. "I will go with both of you. Two against one is fair. The only thing I want is the baby."

"No," John said. "I must not call my friend. He would kill me. And I must not take you back with me."

The night seemed colder. John shifted on the bench. Hastily, Dr. Condon said that he had set his heart on placing the child in its mother's arms, but he would not insist on this; if John preferred, the child could be given to a priest.

John ignored the suggestion; he must be going, he said; Dr. Condon should have brought the money.

There seemed little point in trying to continue, but Dr. Condon asked again about the stolen child. So long as he could be satisfied that the baby was well, he said, it would be possible to arrange for its return and the payment of the ransom. His voice rose and he admonished John with an uplifted finger:

"I promised Colonel Lindbergh and Mrs. Lindbergh to help get their baby back. That is what I am out for—nothing else."

Again John reassured him. Before long he would be given the little boy—"You can put the baby's arms around Mrs. Lindbergh's neck," he added. Also, the baby was in better health than it had ever been; that was the message Number 1 had instructed him to give Dr. Condon when they met. And now he needed proof for Number 1 that he had talked with Dr. Condon—proof Dr. Condon must supply by writing and inserting an advertisement in the next Sunday's Bronx *Home News*. It would read: *Baby is alive and well. Money is ready.*

The old man agreed, then put his hand on the other's arm as he seemed about to rise. There was something troubling him, he said. The newspapers had been making much of police suspicions of Henry Johnson, the sailor friend of the baby's nursemaid, Betty Gow. Dr. Condon didn't know Johnson but he had friends who did, Norwegians who worked in the boatyards on City Island, and all insisted that the young man was innocent.

Of course he was innocent, John replied a bit heatedly—and so was Betty Gow! Neither of them had had anything to do with the kidnaping! Why did Dr. Condon pay attention to such talk?

"Maybe you think we are not the right parties," he went on. "We *are* the right parties!"

He would prove it. On Monday morning, not later than ten o'clock, he would send Dr. Condon a token.

What kind of a token?

John said: "I will send you the sleeping suit of the baby."

"You will send me the baby's sleeping suit?"

"I will." John got up from the bench. "I must go," he said. "I waited too long already."

Dr. Condon rose too. They faced each other, shook hands, and said good night. John walked off, almost casually, toward the north and vanished in the darkness.

The old man looked at his watch. It was quarter to eleven. They had been on the park bench for more than an hour.

At home, Dr. Condon gave Colonel Breckinridge a description of the evening from beginning to end. He added a few details. John's accent, he said, changed such words as "boat" into *boad,* "right" into *ride,* "would" into *vould.* Although he had kept his coat collar raised, Dr. Condon had glimpsed his mouth, which was small. The eyes, of course, he had clearly seen; deep-set eyes. His cheekbones were high, his complexion light. Dr. Condon would put his height at about five feet nine and his weight at about that of a middleweight, around 165 pounds. The middleweight comparison was apt, Dr. Condon continued; he had trained many athletes and he knew a wiry, muscular body when he saw one; and then too, how lightly John had vaulted over the cemetery gate!

One phrase struck Breckinridge; John had said, had he, that the gang had prepared for the kidnaping for a year?

Yes, Dr. Condon assured him. It testified to the gang's thoroughness.

There was a larger significance, Breckinridge explained. In one of the ransom letters, a letter Dr. Condon hadn't seen, the writer had spoken of the year they had spent preparing to steal the child. John's remark was fresh proof that they were in personal contact with the same people.

One more task remained for Dr. Condon. Taking pen and paper, he wrote:

BABY ALIVE AND WELL. MONEY IS READY. CALL AND SEE US. JAFSIE.

The advertisement appeared in the Sunday edition of the Bronx *Home News.* That evening, Lindbergh telephoned Elmer Irey of the Treasury Department in Washington. The time for exchanging ransom and child was almost at hand, he said, and Irey's experience and advice would be immensely helpful. Would he come back on the case?

Irey promised to come as quickly as possible.

12

John Hughes Curtis was growing discouraged. Here it was March 15 and still no word from Colonel Lindbergh. Three days ago, on March 12, Admiral Guy Burrage had written to him at Hopewell and suggested meeting there so Curtis, Dobson-Peacock, and Burrage could discuss with Lindbergh the overtures Sam, the former rum-runner, had made. Why hadn't he replied? Too busy? It could hardly be that he was indifferent!

Curtis was inclined to drop the whole business. He had tried to help the Lindberghs in their hour of need, he said, but from all appearances it was a waste of time.

Dean Dobson-Peacock strongly disagreed, as did Admiral Burrage. It was true that Burrage had felt doubtful about his phone conversation with Lindbergh; perhaps he *had* talked with an imposter—but his letter to Lindbergh must have got through. Surely there would be an answer! There was no sense in quitting when they had barely begun.

Curtis agreed to wait a few more days.

March 17. Now Burrage himself was puzzled. Why was there no reply?

For the moment, the question was brushed aside; Curtis had news. He had heard from Sam, he told the admiral and Dobson-Peacock, and Sam had said that the gang was getting restless. They were anxious to have the arrangements settled; they knew as well as anyone else that the Lindbergh baby was dynamite.

But the Lindberghs could be assured, Sam had said, that the baby was receiving the best treatment money could buy. The gang had engaged a special nurse for him and she was following the diet Anne Lindbergh had given the newspapers, right down to the viosterol. Too, the nurse had bought a new outfit for the little boy in one of the Norfolk shops. But with every passing day the danger increased and they didn't like it a bit.

Here was the most interesting point, though, Curtis went on. He was sure it had been a slip of the tongue because the next instant Sam had tried clumsily to cover up: he had said something about the baby's being *on a boat.*

Now when it came to boats, Curtis was an expert. If you wanted to hide out on a boat, where would you be most likely to take it? To one of the thousands of tiny coves and inlets of Chesapeake Bay, or right out to sea, beyond the international limit.

Searching for the gang through all those remote, secluded inlets would be a weary, time-consuming task with no assurance of success. If, on the other hand, the negotiating committee had to put out to sea, it would need a seagoing craft. And Curtis had been promised the use of one, the magnificent yacht *Marcon* owned by hotel magnate Colonel Charles H. Consolvo and skippered by Captain Frank H. Lackmann. Curtis knew them both. No sooner had Colonel Consolvo heard that he might be of help than he had offered the unlimited use of his yacht, which was ready to sail at a moment's notice.

March 18. Sam had been in touch with him again, Curtis reported to the dean and the admiral. The gang had instructions to transmit to Lindbergh; they wanted some solid sign of his good faith. They would be satisfied, they said, if he would deposit in a Norfolk bank the sum of $25,000 in the names of the three negotiators.

Curtis had replied, he told the others, that they would put the proposal up to Lindbergh—if they ever heard from him!—but that Sam must understand and make clear to the gang that they would not collect a single penny until the baby had been handed to its father and Lindbergh had identified him.

At last Lindbergh wrote to Admiral Burrage. He would be glad to receive Burrage, Dobson-Peacock and Curtis at his house on Tuesday, March 22. A happy thought struck the dean. It would be wonderful if the baby could be returned to its mother's arms on the coming Sunday, March 27—Easter Sunday!

13

Arriving home from early church on Sunday, March 13, Dr. Condon looked at his copy of the Bronx *Home News* and found the advertisement inserted at John's request:

BABY ALIVE AND WELL. MONEY IS READY. CALL AND SEE US. JAFSIE.

He stayed in the house the rest of the day, but the promised token did not come. It might be well to prod John and his associates with another *Home News* ad. Dr. Condon composed one, to appear the next day:

MONEY IS READY. NO COPS. NO SECRET SERVICE. NO PRESS. I COME ALONE, LIKE LAST TIME. JAFSIE.

He was going through the following morning's mail when his wife called him to the telephone. Dr. Condon heard John's familiar voice; there had been a delay in sending the baby's sleeping suit but it would come, as he had said.

Tuesday, March 15, dragged by; no letter, no call, no sleeping suit. But the morning mail delivery on March 16 was substantial; it included a package wrapped in brown paper, securely bound, addressed to Dr. Condon. The handwriting was unmistakable. He didn't open it; he wanted Breckinridge to do that.

Breckinridge rushed from his office; Dr. Condon, his wife and daughter watched as he undid the knots, opened the paper. It contained a soft, folded garment of gray wool. Breckinridge could not positively identify it; for that they would have to wait for Lindbergh. Breckinridge had already telephoned him, and Lindbergh would get there as soon as he could, but he was in a state of siege at Hopewell; there was a twenty-four-hour watch on the house and, unless he wished to bring a cavalcade of reporters hot on his heels, he had to slip out unnoticed.

He wasn't able to come until long after nightfall. At half past one in the morning, Thursday March 17, Dr. Condon's doorbell rang. A tall, slim figure stood on the veranda—an odd figure, wearing large amber glasses, a cap pulled low and no overcoat though the night was bitter. Lindbergh's voice identified him.

He examined the gray woolen garment. It was a child's sleeping suit, twenty-four inches long, buttoned up the back with four buttons above and two buttons on the flap below. There was a small breast pocket; a red label on the neckband gave the manufacturer's name.

It was spotlessly clean.

The sleeping suit, Lindbergh said, was exactly like his son's; in all probability it was the one he had been wearing on the night of the kidnaping. But, the young father wondered, why had it been cleaned? Obviously that had been done or it would be soiled, after all this time.

A note was attached to the suit:

> Dear Sir. Ouer man faill to collect the mony. There are no more confidential conference after we meeting from March 12. those arrangements to hazardous for us.
>
> We will note allow ouer man to confer in a way like befor. circumstance will note allow us to make a transfer like you wish. It is impossibly for us. Wy shuld we move the baby and face danger. to take another person to the plase is entirely out of question. It seem you are afraid we are the right party

and if the baby is all right. well you have ouer singnature. it is always the same as the first one, specialy them 3 holes [The same design had been drawn in here.]

Now we will send you the sleepingsuit from the baby. besides it means 3$ extra exspenses becauce we have to pay another one. Pleace tell Mrs. Lindbergh note to worry the baby is well. we only have to give him more food as the diet says.

You are willing to pay the 70000 note 50000$ without seeing the baby first or note. let us know about that in the New York American. we can't do it other ways becauce we don't like to give up ouer safty plase or to move the baby. If you are willing to accept this deal put these in paper

I accept Mony is redy

Ouer program is:

After 8 houers we have the mony received we will notify you where to find the baby. If there is any trapp you will be responsible what will follows.

One sentence puzzled Lindbergh and Breckinridge: *circumstance will note allow us to make a transfer like you wish.* Dr. Condon knew the explanation: he had told John that if he did not wish to give the baby to him, he could give the boy to a Catholic priest—or, if he preferred, remove him to a different hiding place, where Dr. Condon might visit him to satisfy himself that he was the Lindberghs' son.

It seemed to Lindbergh that so far John and his accomplices had been faithful to their promises, and therefore it was reasonable to conclude that they would deliver the baby as soon as they had been given the money. He thought that should be done as soon as possible, and that no traps should be set for the kidnapers. Dr. Condon agreed; but before paying the money, shouldn't they first positively identify the boy? In fact, he had already indicated as much, in the latest advertisement he had prepared, one that was to appear later today, the seventeenth. It read:

I ACCEPT. MONEY IS READY. YOU KNOW THEY WON'T LET ME DELIVER WITHOUT GETTING THE PACKAGE. LET'S MAKE IT SOME SORT OF C.O.D. TRANSACTION. COME. YOU KNOW YOU CAN TRUST JAFSIE.

All very well, Lindbergh thought, but they'd be taking a terrible chance if, by insisting on safeguards, they prolonged negotiations to the point where the kidnapers lost patience. The gang had been told before that the money was ready; according to their letter, it seemed that they wished to be assured of it again—so by all means put the ad they asked for in the *American.*

The three men drafted the new advertisement:

I ACCEPT. MONEY IS READY. JOHN, YOUR PACKAGE IS DELIVERED AND IS O.K. DIRECT ME. JAFSIE.

Then they had sandwiches and coffee, and the young father resumed his disguise for the return trip to Hopewell. He took the sleeping suit with him.

The money *was* ready. That afternoon, Thursday, March 17, armed guards from J. P. Morgan & Company brought fifty thousand dollars to the Fordham branch of the Corn Exchange Bank, where Dr. Condon and Henry Schneider, the bank manager, had arranged for its deposit. Fifty thousand, not seventy thousand. Lindbergh said he would raise the additional twenty thousand later, but getting together even the amount of cash originally demanded by the kidnapers had been difficult; he had been obliged to sell blocks of stocks at a heavy sacrifice in order to make up the full sum and would have to sell more at the same low prices to get the extra twenty thousand.

Of course it was true, as Dr. Condon understood, that the young man could turn to a number of sources and raise as much cash as he might require; the Morrows and business and private friends had offered to help immediately after the kidnaping; but in this intensely personal matter, Lindbergh wished to handle everything on his own, to be under no obligations, or as few as possible.

Dr. Condon was incensed, therefore—and Breckinridge too—when a front-page newspaper story reported a rumor that the Morgan firm had made $250,000 available to Lindbergh for the ransom. It was outrageous, Breckinridge declared. The kidnapers would read the story, accept it as gospel, and think: what pikers we've been! And their demands would be jacked sky-high.

That was bad enough. Another rumor printed in the papers seemed even worse. A syndicate of gangsters, it was said, was prepared to deliver the stolen child to his parents immediately upon receipt of satisfactory ransom. Dr. Condon did not doubt the existence of the gangster syndicate; gangsters infested his beloved country and the thought infuriated him, but if they had made any such offer—and to whom?—it was a fake. He sat down and wrote to the Bronx *Home News*:

It is my sincere hope that our sworn officials may have their acumen and insight directed in proper channels to

> drive from the face of the earth this great canker-sore of our nation, the stratum known as the organized gangster-kidnapers, whose lawlessness makes a mockery of the laws of the greatest country on God's earth and who are a menace to public decency and public safety.

Dr. Condon did not wish to have his name in the columns of the *Home News* or indeed of any metropolitan paper at this time; the made-up signature *Jafsie* had appeared so often that there was much speculation about it. And so, after some thought, he signed his letter of protest *P. A. Triot.*

Many letters had come to the *Home News* asking about the Jafsie advertisements. The publisher, the editor and the assistant editor knew who Jafsie was and the importance of keeping his identity secret if Dr. Condon's house was not to be besieged as was Lindbergh's. In an effort to convince their curious readers that Jafsie was as much a figure of mystery to the *Home News* as to anyone else, and to direct suspicion away from the truth, the paper said:

> . . . another advertisement for insertion under the heading of "Special Notices" was received at the *Home News* office in the mail this morning. While the advertisement itself contained the familiar "Jafsie" signature, the note requesting its publication was unsigned and the origin of the ad, like that of those previously received, is unknown. There has been nothing to indicate definitely that the ads have any bearing on the Lindbergh kidnaping and their significance is a matter of conjecture.

Dr. Condon had followed the kidnapers' instructions, and yet—by the end of Saturday, March 19—he had not heard from them again. Or had he? In the evening, he told Breckinridge a puzzling and perhaps significant experience he had had during the day.

Weeks before, he had promised to preside at the opening ceremonies of a charity bazaar in the Bronx, the proceeds to go toward building a chapel for the jail on Hart's Island. The bazaar had been well attended; all kinds of things were on sale, and Dr. Condon had mixed with the crowd, offering help and advice wherever needed. His eye had fallen on a small, dark-skinned woman—an Italian, he guessed. She had looked back at him, and it had seemed to Dr. Condon that she was appealing for help. He volunteered his. What could he do for her? She was interested in buying a violin, she had replied. There were several violins on display; Dr. Condon had explained that their prices depended on several factors: the wood, the age, the maker of the instrument. He had picked up a couple to illustrate his points.

Suddenly the woman had craned up to him and whispered: "Nothing can be done until the excitement is over. There is too much publicity. Meet me at the depot at Tuckahoe on Wednesday at five in the afternoon. I will have a message for you."

Dr. Condon had been left holding a violin, watching her small figure dart through the crowd. He remembered that in his first conversation with John over the telephone he had heard a man at the other end of the wire speak two words in Italian.

Certainly, Breckinridge said, Dr. Condon should be at the Tuckahoe railroad station on Wednesday at five.

They wrote still another advertisement:

INFORM ME HOW I CAN GET IMPORTANT LETTER TO YOU. URGENT. JAFSIE.

All through Sunday the twentieth, there was no news. But Monday morning's mail was fruitful—a letter, postmarked March 19, 7:30 P.M., Station N, New York. The familiar symbol-signature identified its source. Dr. Condon read:

> Dear Sir: You and Mr. Lindbergh know ouer Program If you don't accept den we will wait untill you agree with ouer deal. We know you have to come to us anyway But why should Mrs. and Mr. Lindbergh suffer longer as necessary We will note communicate with you or Mr. Lindbergh until you write so in the paper.
>
> We will tell you again; this kidnaping cace whas prepared for a year already so the Police won't have any look to find us or the child you only puch everyding further out did you send that little package to Mr. Lindbergh? it contains the sleepingsuit from the Baby. the baby is well.

On the reverse side of the page there was a final sentence:

> Mr. Lindbergh only wasting time with his search.

They had advertised that Jafsie accepted, that the money was ready, that Jafsie was waiting for further instructions, yet the kidnapers offered no instructions and seemed to feel that Jafsie had not accepted their terms! Why?

All they could do, Breckinridge said, was to continue with their messages. They prepared another ad.

THANKS. THAT LITTLE PACKAGE YOU SENT ME WAS IMMEDIATELY DELIVERED AND ACCEPTED AS REAL ARTICLE. SEE MY POSITION. OVER FIFTY YEARS IN BUSINESS AND CAN I PAY WITHOUT SEEING THE GOODS? COMMON SENSE MAKES ME TRUST YOU. PLEASE UNDERSTAND MY POSITION. JAFSIE.

They decided that the ad should run for three consecutive days, Wednesday the twenty-third, Thursday the twenty-fourth, Friday the twenty-fifth.

Keeping the mysterious rendezvous at the Tuckahoe station, Dr. Condon was on the platform before five. He waited well past the hour but there was no sign of the small dark woman.

The latest in the series of ads appeared for the three days and brought no answer. But on its last day, the twenty-fifth, Dr. Condon was concerned by an infinitely graver matter. Were the kidnapers through with him? Was his usefulness to the Lindberghs at an end? So the headlines seemed to imply.

The newspaper story came from Norfolk, Virginia. There, on the afternoon of March 24, it was learned that three well-known Norfolk citizens—John Hughes Curtis, Dean Harold Dobson-Peacock, Admiral Guy H. Burrage—were in communication with the Lindbergh kidnapers.

14

Late Tuesday afternoon, March 22, Curtis, Dobson-Peacock and Burrage drove up the driveway to the Lindbergh house.

Charles Lindbergh was waiting for them, with Colonel Schwarzkopf of the State Police. In the young man's greeting to Admiral Burrage there was no trace of the diffidence the voice that had professed to be his had conveyed over the telephone, and the admiral did not refer to it.

He led his visitors to the library, and once more Curtis related his experiences with Sam, coming last to the token of good faith the kidnapers demanded: twenty-five thousand dollars to be deposited by Lindbergh in a Norfolk bank in the names of the three intermediaries.

Lindbergh had listened in silence, and when Curtis finished he still didn't speak. Curtis asked him to name the sum he would pay for his child's return. The young man replied that he must have absolute proof that Sam and the men behind him really were the kidnapers before he would commit himself to any arrangements.

Curtis had told Sam that no ransom would be handed over until Lindbergh actually held his son in his arms, Dobson-Peacock pointed out.

Lindbergh said he was sure of their good intentions—how could he help but be, since his old and respected friend Admiral Burrage was a member of the group?—but he had to tell them that he thought they were being deceived. He had excellent reasons for thinking so, which he wasn't free to reveal.

But he could not rule out any possibility, however dubious it might seem. There was an easy way for Sam to convince him that he represented the kidnapers. Let Sam give Curtis, or Dobson-Peacock, or Burrage, a photograph of the baby taken since the night he had disappeared, or a few words in writing from the gang signed with a certain symbol.

Curtis agreed to the proposal, and Lindbergh thanked them for all their trouble. Would they stay for dinner?

They would.

Back in Norfolk, on the afternoon of the twenty-fourth, Dean Dobson-Peacock was called by a reporter. Word had leaked out that he, Curtis and Burrage were involved in the search for the Lindbergh child; was it true?

It seemed to the dean that it would be worse to have the press speculate on the matter than to release some information, and so he granted an interview.

It was true, he said, that they had seen Colonel Lindbergh; true, also, that they were in touch with the kidnap gang. Furthermore, they had reason to be hopeful that the case would soon be happily concluded with the return of the baby.

"We believe," Dean Dobson-Peacock continued, "that the kidnapers are acting in good faith. They want to deliver the baby and are willing to wait for their compensation until after it has been delivered. We have a good idea where the child is—to say any more now would prejudice the case."

Why was the dean so sure they were in contact with the right gang? Did he have any proof?

"Proof?" he cried. "What more proof is needed than that the kidnapers have agreed to turn the baby over to us and demand no payment until Colonel Lindbergh has taken the child in his arms and said, 'This is my baby'?"

Dobson-Peacock's interview was held early enough to be published in the Norfolk evening papers; the next morning there were repercussions. Colonel Schwarzkopf, with Lindbergh's approval, issued a statement. "The three citizens of Norfolk who visited Colonel Lindbergh," he said, "gave him information which, on being investigated, was found to have no special significance."

A good deal of guessing followed. Did Lindbergh really feel that the information "had no special significance"? Or did he simply want the police to *think* he regarded it as insignificant? Did Schwarzkopf himself believe it? For in spite of what he had said, he had asked for the help of the Virginia and Maryland police in combing through the myriad harbors, coves and inlets of the Chesapeake.

John Hughes Curtis was aroused by the controversy. He regretted the publicity, he told reporters, but since Schwarzkopf seemed so skeptical, he would like the Jersey police chief to know that, just three hours after the intermediaries returned home, Sam called from Philadelphia. Curtis had told him they had visited Lindbergh and that he insisted on proof that Sam's gang was holding the baby as hostage. All right, Sam had said, he'd get proof.

"I am awfully, awfully sorry the report of our visit was made public," Curtis concluded. "It may be the cause of the child's not being recovered as we had planned. I am hopeful, however, that we will be able to bring about the desired results. It would be an awful thing if the publication of our visit to Colonel Lindbergh and his agreement to permit us to carry on the negotiations should result in the child's not being returned to his anxious and heartbroken parents. I'll say this—until it is proved to me that I am the victim of a hoax, or until, on the other hand, our negotiations prove unsuccessful, I'm going to see to it that all this unwise publicity is stopped."

15

Dr. Condon's fears were allayed: it was obvious from Colonel Schwarzkopf's statement that Lindbergh put little faith in the new development. Breckinridge, too, didn't believe there was much if anything in it. Then why hadn't there been an answer to the ads that had appeared during the last three days?

What else was there to do but draft still another?

MONEY IS READY. FURNISH SIMPLE CODE FOR US TO USE IN PAPER. JAFSIE.

It was published on Saturday, March 26. Sunday was a long, drawn-out day of waiting; so was Monday.

But Tuesday morning brought a letter:

> Dear Sir: It is note necessary to furnish any code. You and Mr. Lindbergh know ouer Program very well. We will keep the child in ouer save plase until we have the money in hand, but if the deal is note closed until the 8 of April we will ask for 30000 more. also note 70000—100000
>
> How can Mr. Lindbergh follow so many false clues he knows we are right party ouer singnature is still the same as in the ransom note. But if Mr. Lindbergh likes to fool around for another month, we can help it.
>
> once he has to come to us anyway but if he keeps on waiting we will double ouer amount. there is absolute no fear aboud the child. It is well.

The interlocking circles followed.

Now, Breckinridge said, they must act. What had their carefully worded messages achieved?—a threat to raise the ransom! He called Lindbergh, who agreed, and at midnight drove to Dr. Condon's house for a conference.

Dr. Condon persisted in his argument that the kidnapers would eventually accept a cash-on-delivery arrangement, or at least would let him have a glimpse of the boy before he handed over the money—which, he said, should be fifty thousand, not seventy. But the others were firm; there must be no more shilly-shallying. Lindbergh had raised the additional twenty thousand (altogether, to raise $70,000 in cash he had had to sell $350,000 worth of stocks). Their message must be a simple, complete capitulation. It must read:

I ACCEPT. MONEY IS READY. JAFSIE.

The advertisement appeared on Thursday, March 31. The next morning Dr. Condon received an answer, a letter with a Fordham Station postmark:

> Dear Sir. Please handel inclosed letter to Col. Lindbergh.
> It is in Mr. Lindbergh interest not to notify police.

The enclosure read:

> Dear Sir, have the money ready by Saturday evening. We will infor you where and how to deliver it. have the money in

one bundel we want you to put it in a sertain place. ther is no fear that somebody els will take it, we watch everything closely. Pleace let us know if you are agree and read for action by saturday evening. if yes put in the paper

Yes everything O.K.

It is a very simble delivery but we find out very son if there is any trapp. After 8 houers you gett the adr. from the boy. on the plase you find two ladies. they are innocence.

If it is to late we put it in the New York American for Saturday morning. Put it in New York Journal.

To Dr. Condon, the most important point was: *After 8 houers you gett the adr. from the boy*—meaning, of course, *of* the boy. Breckinridge suggested that, to be absolutely sure the exchange would take place, the ad should appear on Saturday, April 2, in both the morning *American* and the evening *Journal.*

Lindbergh gave Dr. Condon written authority to pay seventy thousand dollars to "whomsoever in his judgment" were the kidnapers and said he would take Dr. Condon by car to the rendezvous the kidnapers named. He had been urged by friends, by Schwarzkopf and other police officials to hide men in the neighborhood of the rendezvous, but he would not; that would be setting a trap, which the kidnapers had so often warned him against. He could not wait any longer, things must be finished now, this week end, the baby returned to his father and mother. It had been an almost unbearable ordeal for Anne Lindbergh to examine the sleeping suit, and every hour of waiting intensified the strain.

Lindbergh left for Hopewell, saying he would be back the next day, Saturday, April 2.

His great worry now was that something might happen to frighten off the kidnapers before the next day. *After 8 houers you gett the adr. from the boy.*

In answer to Lindbergh's call Elmer Irey, the Treasury's chief law-enforcement officer, had returned to Hopewell, accompanied by two agents of the Internal Revenue Service's intelligence unit, Frank J. Wilson and Pat O'Rourke; a third, Arthur P. Madden, had come from Chicago. They had stayed on at Hopewell to try to be of help.

Lindbergh's offer of immunity to the kidnapers, his rejection of any plan that might arouse their suspicion and fear of a trap, his insistence that his son's safety came first, had originally been viewed by Irey with sympathy and respect. But the Treasury man felt that the time had come to speak frankly; otherwise, he saw a very real chance that the kidnap gang would get away scot-free.

Irey told the young man that he disapproved of the way the ransome bills had been assembled. There wasn't a single gold note in the package, he pointed out, to make the money easier to trace. Also, he was opposed to turning over the cash without first recording the serial number of every single bill.

But Lindbergh objected. He was convinced that the kidnapers would keep their promises to him, and he meant to keep his promises to them. Irey stood his ground. The package of ransom bills would have to be reassembled so as to include gold notes and the serial numbers of all the bills listed, he said, or the Treasury would play no part in the case. The federal government could not be put in the position of aiding the kidnapers and compounding a felony.

Lindbergh hesitated. Well, he said, he would think about it.

It was a hard decision to make, but Irey's arguments won. The ransom package was returned from the Fordham bank to J. P. Morgan & Company, where Treasury agents Wilson and Madden were already at work with fourteen Morgan clerks, making up two new packages according to Irey's specifications. Any purely domestic bank would have found it difficult, if not impossible, to meet his demands, Irey knew, for the nation's economic woes had drained off their gold reserves; but J. P. Morgan & Company, with its broad international business relations, would certainly have a large supply of gold notes on hand.

After some eight hours' work, the job was finished. The first package contained fifty thousand dollars, of which thirty-five thousand was in gold certificates. The second, much smaller package consisted of four hundred fifty-dollar gold notes which Wilson and Madden were confident would be fairly easy to spot once the kidnapers started to pass them.

Altogether, there were 5150 bills. No two serial numbers were in sequence, a fact the agents confirmed as the number of each bill was recorded.

The bills were wrapped and tied with a particular kind of paper and string, easy to identify by matching them with samples that were put in a Morgan vault.

16

On the Lindbergh place, Betty Gow and Elsie Whateley were taking an early afternoon stroll; in the last few weeks, it had become a daily habit. Today, Friday, April 1, marked the end of a month since the kidnaping. Neither Betty nor Elsie had left the estate in that time, but it hadn't seemed like an isolated life; there were the State troopers, the visitors, the constant attempts by press and radio reporters and photographers to break through the police cordon, and the sudden, mysterious comings and goings of Colonel Lindbergh and Colonel Breckinridge.

In the last few days both women had been conscious of a sharpening tension; they felt something was about to happen. "Something," of course, could only be the return of the baby. Various signs seemed to point to it. Colonel Lindbergh had brought back his son's sleeping suit—at least, both Anne Lindbergh and Betty were almost positive that it was the baby's. And then, Anne Lindbergh's aunt, Mrs. Agnes Morrow Scandrett, had returned from a European trip, her ship cabin loaded with toys for the little boy. Wasn't that a hopeful omen?

After talking for a while with the troopers on guard at the gate house, Betty and Elsie started back up the gravel driveway, the way they had come. They had covered the same ground dozens of times in the past weeks, but now they made a discovery that somehow or other had skipped their notice before. They saw it at the same time. Quickly Betty picked it up. They knew at once what it was—one of the baby's thumbguards, tied exactly as Betty had tied it in the nursery on the night of March 1.

They ran to the house to show it to the young parents. Another good omen! Wasn't it? Wasn't it?

17

Saturday April 2.

In Washington, Mrs. Evalyn Walsh McLean waited for more news from Gaston Means. March had been an exasperating month for both of them: several times Means had seemed to be on the verge of the happy ending he and Mrs. McLean hoped for, only to see their hopes shattered at the last moment.

No one was really to blame, Mrs. McLean realized; they were dealing with a gang, and the chief of the gang was a suspicious and cautious man—he had to be, in his dangerous way of life. He had explained to Mrs. McLean, through Gaston Means, that other gangs were always on his trail, trying to get the Lindbergh baby away from him.

Means telephoned to say he had the feeling they would be out of the woods within the next few days, maybe within the next few hours.

In New York, a US Navy Vought Corsair piloted by Lieutenant George Richard landed and discharged its solitary passenger, John Hughes Curtis. All the facilities of the Navy's Hampton Roads base had been made available to the Norfolk group by order of Rear Admiral W. D. MacDougall, commandant of the Norfolk Navy District.

Crossing to Trenton, New Jersey, Curtis telephoned Lindbergh. The Colonel was not at home, he was told. But, Curtis protested, he had with him a messenger from the kidnapers with a letter that he would place only in Lindbergh's hands.

Curtis left a number for Lindbergh to call back, and waited impatiently. At length the phone rang. He would be busy for at least several hours, Lindbergh said; the gang's messenger would have to wait. Curtis replied that he didn't think he could persuade him to, because of the constant danger. It couldn't be helped, Lindbergh told him; he had urgent business elsewhere.

That morning the message demanded by the kidnapers had appeared in the New York *American:*

YES. EVERYTHING O.K. JAFSIE.

In the late afternoon, Dr. Condon and Charles Lindbergh began their final preparations. Dr. Condon brought out the duplicate ballot box. He had underestimated the sheer bulk of the ransom bills in the denominations the kidnapers had listed, twenty-five thousand dollars in twenty-dollar bills, fifteen thousand in ten-dollar bills, ten thousand in five-dollar bills; there were 4750 bills in the fifty-thousand-dollar package alone. He managed to wedge the bigger package into the box, although in the process it split on one side. That wasn't necessarily a disadvantage—it might even serve as extra evidence in the future, and the box was still sturdy. The smaller package of money went in fairly easily. Dr. Condon closed the box but didn't lock it; the key, too, might serve as evidence.

The kidnapers' note had said that they should be *read for action* on Saturday evening. *They* were ready; now it was up to the kidnapers to tell them what to do.

The Condons, Lindbergh, Breckinridge and Al Reich sat down to wait.

Dr. Condon was composed; his family was on edge. The old man was the only person who, having seen John, could identify him. Surely it must have occurred to John—as it had occurred to Lindbergh and Breckinridge—that, after receiving the ransom, it would be a simple matter to remove the one witness who could expose him. If Dr. Condon wished to withdraw even now, Lindbergh had said, he would understand.

Dr. Condon had firmly declined.

An hour passed; another. It was almost eight. The doorbell rang.

Myra opened the door; her father was just behind her. Dr. Condon saw a short thin dark man, quite young, nondescriptly dressed. A cab waited at the curb, but this wasn't the same driver who had delivered an earlier message. He handed an envelope to Myra, returned to the cab and drove off.

Lindbergh opened the envelope and read:

> Dear Sir: Take a car and follow Tremont ave. to the east until you reach the number 3225 East Tremont ave.
> It is a nursery
> Bergen
> Greenhauses florist
> There is a table standing outside right on the door. You find a letter undernead the table covert with a stone, read and follow instruction.

The symbol-signature appeared beneath the last word. But there was more:

> Don't speak to anyone on the way. If there is a radio alarm for policecar, we warn you we have same equipment. have the money in one bundel
> we give you ¾ houer to reach the place.

Dr. Condon picked up the tightly stuffed box and started with Lindbergh for the Colonel's car, but Al had a suggestion: why not take his Ford coupé instead? John had seen it before, and a new car might make him suspicious.

Lindbergh nodded. Al gave him the key.

Sitting close to Lindbergh in the car's narrow seat, Dr. Condon saw that his young companion was armed. A shoulder holster bulged beneath his jacket.

The first rendezvous had been a graveyard; so, it turned out, was the second: St. Raymond's Cemetery. The J. A. Bergen greenhouses and flower shop were close by. The shop was closed and dark, the display table outside the door bare of flowers.

Dr. Condon got out of the Ford, looked under the table and saw a stone. He lifted it, picked up the envelope beneath and returned to the car.

They read the note under the dash light:

cross the street and walk to the next corner and follow
Whittemore Ave to the soud
take the money with you. come alone and walk
I will meet you

Lindbergh started to get out, but Dr. Condon stopped him; the note said that Jafsie must come alone. He glanced at the ransom box on the seat between them, decided to leave it there. First, he said, he wanted to talk to John.

He started off.

Whittemore Avenue was a dirt road; the corner street lamp seemed only to intensify the surrounding shadows. Row upon row of gravestones flanked the shabby path and faded into the darkness. Any number of men might be hidden there, Dr. Condon reflected, perhaps the whole kidnap gang. He determined not to follow the instructions but instead to walk east on Tremont so that he could peer behind the tombstones closest to him.

After some three hundred feet he passed the cemetery gates, turned and slowly went back. He stood indecisively, looking around, then called to Lindbergh in the coupé:

"I guess there's no one here. We'd better go back."

Almost immediately, he heard a voice.

"Hey, Doctor!"

A figure rose behind a gravestone some distance within the cemetery and gestured to him.

"Hey, Doctor, over here!" the voice called again—so loudly, it seemed to Dr. Condon, that Lindbergh too must have heard it.

"All right," the old man said. He started toward the tombstone, but the figure moved off, zigzagging among the graves. Dr. Condon followed. To the left he saw a lane leading into the cemetery, flanked by a wall perhaps five feet high. The figure crossed the wall and the lane and stooped behind a hedge about as high as the wall.

"Here, Doctor."

"All right," Dr. Condon said again. He went up to the hedge and peered through the thinly matted branches at the stooping figure. Annoyed, he said: "Stand up!" The other obeyed.

Dr. Condon recognized John.

Tonight, in the dim light, he didn't bother to conceal his face. He wore a dark suit and a fedora hat with a snapdown brim.

"Did you got it, the money?"

"No," Dr. Condon said. "I didn't bring the money. It is up in the car."

"Who is up there?"

"Colonel Lindbergh."

"Is he armed?"

"I don't know," Dr. Condon said. Then he added: "No, he is not."

John demanded the money, but Dr. Condon refused. "Not until you give me a receipt showing me where the baby is."

He didn't have any such paper, the other said, but he would go and get it—it would take just a few minutes—if at the same time Dr. Condon would go to Colonel Lindbergh and come back with the seventy thousand dollars.

"John, listen," the old man said. "You want that money. Colonel Lindbergh is not so rich. These are times of depression. Why don't you be decent to him?"

The gang's first demand, he pointed out, had been for fifty thousand dollars. Lindbergh had that amount with him, but he hadn't been able to raise the extra twenty thousand. Fifty thousand was a lot of money, a fortune. It was there in the car; if John would give him a note of directions, in a few minutes the gang would be rich.

John considered this. "Well, all right," he said at last. "I suppose if we can't get seventy, we get fifty."

He turned and strode away. Dr. Condon hastily took a watch from his vest pocket; later on, he thought, he might be able to find the place where John wrote, or obtained, the note by establishing the length of time it took him to go there and return, and the place might supply a clue to the gang's identity.

The watch was one of the old teacher's most prized possessions. Originally designed for a Chinese emperor, it sounded the time in a musical sequence of hours, quarter-hours and minutes. Dr. Condon touched the control and a tiny chime rang nine times. A pause. Three chimes signifying the first quarter-hour. Another pause. One chime. It was sixteen minutes past nine o'clock.

As he started back toward the car, another thought occurred to him. In their first meeting, John had said that he was afraid of the gang's leader; now it seemed that John *himself* was the kidnap boss —and afraid of no one! How else could he decide so calmly to settle for fifty thousand when the gang had demanded seventy?

Lindbergh peered from the coupé and Dr. Condon quickly described his talk with John and the outcome of his bargaining. For that, the young man said, he was grateful. Removing the smaller of the two packages, he handed the box with its fifty-thousand-dollar bundle to the other.

Dr. Condon returned to the rendezvous. Soon he saw the dark figure threading toward him between the tombstones. He pressed the ingenious clock. The tiny chime again sounded nine times, then three, then fourteen: twenty-nine minutes past nine. It had taken

John thirteen minutes to go to wherever he had kept the note or had written it and come back.

Dr. Condon rested the ransom box on his forearm, to show John that he had lived up to his part of the agreement, and said, "Give me the note."

John's hands were buried in his coat pockets. "I got the note," he said, "but don't open it yet." It wasn't to be opened, he added, for six hours.

"I have never betrayed a confidence," Dr. Condon assured him. "I have carried out every order of both parties the best I could. I won't open it. I will take it up to Colonel Lindbergh."

John took an envelope from his left coat pocket and handed it across the hedge to Dr. Condon, who at the same instant passed the box to John's right hand.

The old man stored the envelope safely in his own coat pocket and turned to leave.

"Wait a minute," John said. Kneeling behind the hedge, he placed the box on the ground, opened it, took out the package and removed a sheaf of bills. "I want to see if it is all right, if these bills are marked."

"If these bills are marked, I know nothing about it, John," Dr. Condon said. "I had nothing to do with it and didn't see them."

John seemed to be satisfied; he restored the bills and stood up. "The crowd thinks you're fine," he told Dr. Condon. "All of them said your work was perfect."

"I know of no other way," Dr. Condon replied. "John," he added, "if you give me a chance to get that baby, everything will be all right. But if you don't, I will follow you to Australia!"

John held out his hand. "Your work was perfect," he repeated. "Good night."

They shook hands over the hedge.

"Good night, John," said Dr. Condon. "Remember—don't try to double-cross me!"

For a moment he stood watching John's retreating figure, then returned to the car. He gave Lindbergh the envelope and told him John's stipulation that it was not to be opened for six hours. Lindbergh stared at the envelope, turning it in his hands. Well, he said, if that was the agreement, they would live up to it.

Studying the expression on his young friend's face, Dr. Condon was troubled. He asked him to drive not to Decatur Avenue but to a small empty house on the southeast side of Westchester Square, a mile or so from the cemetery. As they stopped in front of the empty house, Dr. Condon explained that it was one of his real-estate holdings; here they could be sure they wouldn't be disturbed.

They walked to the stoop and sat down, and Dr. Condon started to speak, warming to his subject the more he saw the justice of it. It was he, he pointed out, who had given his word to John—Lindbergh had made no promise of any kind. And having paid a fifty-thousand-dollar ransom, at least they were entitled to assurance that the note was not a fake, did in fact tell where they would find the stolen child. If John had played them false, each minute might lessen their chances of recovering the baby.

Lindbergh thought for a moment. Yes, he said, Dr. Condon was right; and he opened the envelope. The familiar handwriting met their eyes:

> the boy is on Boad Nelly. it is a small Boad 28 feet long. two person are on the Boad. the are innosent. you will find the Boad between Horseneck Beach and Gay Head near Elizabeth Island.

At last!

The young father and the old man were in high spirits as they drove back to Decatur Avenue.

Some miles away, Captain Richard Oliver of the New York City police also returned home. From various scraps of information and from an order issued by Police Commissioner Edward P. Mulrooney [on the night of April 2, the order read, the territory above 125th Street and the Harlem River was forbidden ground to all New York detectives], Captain Oliver had deduced that tonight Lindbergh or his representatives would meet the kidnapers and arrange for the return of his son.

Oliver had his own theory about the kidnap gang. He was convinced that they were second-raters who had blundered into the big time. No topnotch organization would appoint the clumsy John its negotiator. In Oliver's opinion, John was either the intermediary for a "cheap" gang or belonged to a gang that somehow or other had got hold of the distinctive ransom signature and was trying to chisel in.

Oliver had decided to act by himself. If he could find the rendezvous, and if John came to it alone, he meant to take him prisoner —or play the part of a mobster and force John to lead him to the gang's hideout.

And so he had ignored the Commissioner's order. Wearing plain clothes, he had waited in the vicinity of the Condons' house and, in his own car, had trailed Lindbergh and Dr. Condon.

At the cemetery, well hidden, he had watched Dr. Condon for a few minutes as the old man set out. And then Oliver had hesitated. What if the baby was about to be returned? What if, by his risky and unauthorized scheme, he permanently destroyed the arrangements? What if he should cause the final loss of the child?

The thought had been too much for his earlier resolution. Captain Oliver had left the cemetery and headed home.

18

While Dr. Condon told the good news to his wife and daughter and Al Reich, Lindbergh and Breckinridge were busy at the telephone. Presently, Lindbergh announced that the two were ready to leave. Would Dr. Condon and Al like to go with them? It would soon be midnight, and Dr. Condon had had an active day and night, but he declared that not for anything would he stay behind when they were so close to the moment he had thought and spoken of so many times, when he would put the baby in its mother's arms.

They drove downtown. Lindbergh parked in front of a private home at 2 East 72nd Street, just off Central Park—Mrs. Morrow's town house—and they went inside.

Several men were waiting in the library. Breckinridge introduced Dr. Condon to two of them, Treasury agent Frank Wilson and his superior, Elmer Irey, and Dr. Condon began to speak about his experiences of the evening. He felt a little proud, he confessed, of having saved twenty thousand dollars of Colonel Lindbergh's money.

The Treasury men stared at him. Just how, Irey asked, had he managed to do that?

Dr. Condon explained. Irey's expression puzzled him. He asked if anything was the matter.

Controlling himself with difficulty, Irey said that yes, something was. The twenty-thousand ransom package, which Dr. Condon had not given to John, contained four hundred fifty-dollar gold certificates—notes that would have been the easiest to spot when the kidnapers passed them. The Treasury men had made up the package with this in mind, and now Dr. Condon had ruined the plan. Thanks to him, the biggest gold certificates the kidnapers would pass were the twenty-dollar denomination. Fifty-dollar gold notes were comparatively rare; twenty-dollar gold notes weren't.

Dr. Condon was crestfallen. No one had told him the special significance of the smaller package. If only he had known!

That was true, Irey admitted; it was really not his fault. Putting a better face on it, he said that perhaps Dr. Condon could help in another way, by telling him about John.

Dr. Condon described how John had appeared to his observant schoolmaster's eye during their two meetings. He noticed that as he talked one of Irey's companions was sketching on a piece of paper—a sketch that resulted in a fairly good likeness of John.

Irey asked if Dr. Condon could identify the spot where John had jumped over the cemetery wall; perhaps he had left his footprints there. Dr. Condon was sure he could.

Lindbergh and Breckinridge joined them. All arrangements had been made, Lindbergh said, and they were ready to go and get his son. Breckinridge, Dr. Condon, Al and Elmer Irey got into Lindbergh's car and the Colonel took the wheel.

Irey wondered if Dr. Condon had any idea where John had gone for the note of instructions they were about to follow. Somewhere within thirteen minutes' brisk walking time from the spot where he and John had met, Dr. Condon replied; he was certain, because he had noted the time with his watch. He took out the watch now and saw that it was past two o'clock, the early morning of Sunday, April 3.

Where were they bound? Irey told him: the airport in Bridgeport, Connecticut. Colonel Lindbergh had made the necessary calls and everything was prepared.

But when they came to the airport, three hours later, it seemed that everything was not prepared. They waited for an hour. The rising sun glinted on the waters of Long Island Sound, and with it came the bellow of powerful airplane engines. Entranced, Dr. Condon watched a formidable shape wheel in the sky. A flying boat! It was a Sikorsky amphibian, Irey explained, ideally suited to the job of spotting the *Nelly* from the air and putting down beside her.

The pilot climbed out and he and Lindbergh inspected the ship. Then Lindbergh gestured to the cabin. But when Al Reich, following the others, started to enter, the young father stopped him. After picking up his son, he said, he intended to land at the Aviation Country Club in Hicksville, Long Island. Someone would have to take his car there and wait for them. Would Al do this? Al nodded.

Lindbergh gunned the engines and the Sikorsky grumbled into the brightening sky.

Looking around, Dr. Condon saw, tucked in one corner of the cabin, a baby's clothes and a bottle of milk.

Vineyard Sound, in Massachusetts waters, is bounded on the northwest by the Elizabeth Islands, on the southeast by the island of Martha's Vineyard; it varies in width from two to four miles and is some seventeen miles long.

During the morning of April 3—a fine, clear morning—islanders, fishing-boat crews and pleasure-seekers were puzzled by the strange antics of a two-engine amphibian. The plane scoured the whole Sound, but concentrated on a roughly triangular section at the southern end. Expertly if (it seemed at times) hazardously piloted, it often flew so close to the water that it appeared about to settle alongside some fishing boat or pleasure craft; then the engines would gather volume and the plane would rise, swing wide, turn and again swoop low.

Coast Guard cutters from nearby Cuttyhunk Island turned up in the area, and the gray blur of a small Navy warship swam over the horizon. As the sun mounted toward noon, word of these activities went to Boston, Providence and Bridgeport newspapers; someone suggested that the searching plane must be connected with the Lindbergh kidnaping. The reporters gathered.

John's note had said that the boat *Nelly* was "between Horseneck Beach and Gay Head near Elizabeth Island." Dr. Condon remembered that John had told him the boat could be identified by white cloths on the masts.

But for all their low-level crisscrossing over the water, the bright, clear morning passed without their seeing a small boat with white cloths on the masts.

It was noon. A day, a night, part of another day had passed without more than a cat nap for Dr. Condon. Still he watched as keenly as ever, his senses as alert as when he had waited in the cemetery for John to bring him the instructions. But he was hungry.

He saw that they were turning away from the search area. For some minutes the plane roared ahead in level flight. Now they were swooping low. Had the young father, at the controls, spotted a boat that might be the *Nelly*? Eagerly Dr. Condon looked out. He saw that they were at water level, settling down in a flurry of spray. The engines turned over a last time; the silence, after hours of close thunder, came as a shock.

They had landed beside Cuttyhunk Island. A group of excited men waited on the dock. Lindbergh shook his head, said nothing in answer to the reporters' questions; Breckinridge said only that there was no news—no news—no news.

A fine lunch was served them at the Cuttyhunk Hotel, and Dr. Condon put it to good use. Lindbergh ate little.

Through the afternoon hours, the Sikorsky amphibian continued to stitch back and forth over the waters of Vineyard Sound, but with no luck. Something had gone wrong, something must have interfered with the kidnapers' arrangements. Perhaps the Coast Guard activity had alarmed them, caused them to disguise the *Nelly,* or put in at some secluded cove. In any event there seemed little point in going on with the search for the time being. The Sikorsky made one last futile swing through the Sound at low level, then gained altitude, leveled out, and pointed its stubby nose for Long Island and the Aviation Country Club at Hicksville.

Al Reich had had a tedious day of waiting with the car. They were too tired to tell him much; anyway, the answer was plain: they had not found the baby.

Dr. Condon's family was waiting for the old man when he arrived home. They had bought the morning papers, full of the amphibian's search; the reporters at Cuttyhunk had mistaken him for the Norfolk boatbuilder, John Hughes Curtis, whose contact with the kidnap gang had said that the Lindbergh baby was being kept on a boat.

Finally, Dr. Condon was able to get to bed. He was very tired, so tired he couldn't sleep, his mind bemused with crowded pictures: John in the cemetery; the rush to Manhattan; the drive to the airfield; the great plane, the long, anxious, useless search.

According to schedule, an advertisement appeared on April 4 and 5 in the columns of the New York *American,* the New York *Evening Journal* and the Bronx *Home News*:

YES. EVERYTHING O.K. JAFSIE.

19

Charles Lindbergh drove home alone. Anne would be up, waiting for him and their child. Even before he reached the house he saw that everything was ready to welcome the baby. No lights had burned in the nursery since the night of the kidnaping, but now its windows glowed.

They had heard the car; Anne was at the door. Charles told her the story. It was just a delay, he was sure. In spite of the thoroughness of their search, he could have missed the *Nelly*—or the kidnapers could have become frightened and hidden the boat's name, or left Vineyard Sound. To show how confident he was, he called Newark airport and gave instructions to make ready for flight the next day a Lockheed-Vega monoplane. The ship had been held for his use; the airport staff arranged to fly it to the nearer Teterboro airport in Hasbrouck Heights, New Jersey.

Early the next morning, carrying a small blanket and a suitcase, Charles clambered into the monoplane. Less than an hour's flight brought into view the familiar Elizabeth Islands, Martha's Vineyard and the dark blue Sound. The Coast Guard cutters were still there. Again, people on land and sea craned their heads as the plane criss-crossed the Sound.

Halfway through the afternoon, Lindbergh landed at a country airport and asked about a boat named *Nelly*. No one knew of such a boat. He took off again.

It was half past six when he brought the plane back to Teterboro airport. He climbed out, blanket and suitcase under one arm.

In the nursery the welcoming lights shone against the gathering darkness.

For his part, Dr. Condon was not idle. He remembered Elmer Irey's question: could he identify the spot in St. Raymond's Cemetery where John had crossed over the wall? Driven by his son-in-law Ralph Hacker and accompanied by a Department of Justice agent, he set out to find the spot. Hacker took with him materials with which to preserve any evidence they might discover.

Dr. Condon led the way to the wall, to the place where, as he remembered, John had jumped over. At the base of the barrier a man's footprint was deeply pressed into the ground. Hacker poured fluid plaster into it and some minutes later extracted the print in a plaster mold.

Next, the three tried to find a clue to John's line of retreat after he had taken the ransom box from Dr. Condon, but this search was fruitless.

So passed April 4. Dr. Condon's depression was not improved to see the YES. EVERYTHING O.K. JAFSIE ad in the papers. It would be there the next day, too. No doubt John also saw it. He was certain, the old man told Breckinridge, who had returned to the Condon home, that this was only a temporary postponement, that John would soon be in touch with them again.

Breckinridge agreed; they must be patient and not worry. But it might be wise, Dr. Condon thought, to urge John on a little, show him they were concerned. He proposed another ad, and wrote it out for Breckinridge's inspection:

> WHAT IS WRONG? HAVE YOU CROSSED ME? PLEASE, BETTER DIRECTIONS. JAFSIE.

Breckinridge approved, and Dr. Condon gave the ad to the newspapers with instructions to run it until further notice.

April 5. No word from John.

Lindbergh had talked with Curtis, now on his way back to Norfolk; in the absence of proof, the young man still felt that the Norfolk group had been deceived, but he was determined to keep every door open.

April 6. Lindbergh decided to ask for help from the government.

None of the ransom money had been marked, but the Morgan clerks had listed the serial numbers, in the event the kidnapers came to trial. The twenty-dollar bills were either United States of America gold certificates or Federal Reserve notes; the tens were gold certificates, the fives United States notes.

The Treasurer of the United States, W. O. Wood, immediately agreed to send a circular with the serial numbers to banks throughout the world, and a message asking every teller to keep his eye open for the listed bills and, upon seeing one, to call or wire the United States Treasury.

Many somewhat similar circulars went to banks in the ordinary course of Treasury business, but in two respects this stood out. Though it said nothing about the Lindbergh case, the amount listed—fifty thousand dollars—was the same the papers had mentioned as the sum demanded by the kidnapers and the circular was unusually long and detailed: fifty-seven pages of fine print.

In a Newark bank, a teller was struck by these facts. He asked a friend, a reporter on the Newark *News,* whether he was imagining things or did his friend also see a connection between the circular and the Lindbergh case? The newspaperman did. Lindbergh must have handed over fifty thousand to the kidnapers and failed to receive the child in return. Now, with the government's help, he was trying to track down the gang.

The Newark *News'* city editor thought so too. The story went into print and the wire services distributed it. Too late Lindbergh explained the fatal damage it might cause: the kidnapers might conclude that he did not trust them.

He felt that he must give the gang an explanation. On April 9, he handed Schwarzkopf a statement, to be broadcast that night over every radio network:

> Colonel Lindbergh has authorized the statement that a ransom of $50,000 was paid to the kidnapers—properly identified as such—upon their agreement to notify him as to the exact whereabouts of the baby. The baby was not found at the point designated.
>
> Several days were permitted to elapse to give the kidnapers every opportunity to keep their agreement.

It was not intended to use the numbers on the specie in which the ransom was paid, but inasmuch as the kidnapers have failed to keep their agreement and have not communicated since the ransom was paid, it is felt that every remaining possible means must be utilized to accomplish the return of the baby, and to this end the cooperation of the Federal Government was requested in tracing the bills used.

"The transaction had no relation to our negotiations," Curtis and Dobson-Peacock told reporters. "We still have faith in the parties with whom we have been dealing." But they added that the payment of the fifty thousand dollars "will add to the difficulty of bringing the negotiations to a successful consummation."

Monday, April 11. Dr. Condon's name dominated the front page of the Bronx *Home News.* Since the payment of the ransom had been made known, the paper, with Dr. Condon's consent, had decided to reveal the part it and he had played. The *Home News* had barely appeared when reporters and photographers descended on Dr. Condon's immaculate lawn, ran riot through the flower beds, and, in the house, drowned the ticking of the Tiffany clock.

Yes, the old man told them, he was confident the kidnapers would keep faith with him. The reason for this initial failure was the gang's fear of a trap. "Colonel Lindbergh will hear from them in a day or so and his child will come back to him," he declared. "The kidnapers just haven't had time to make proper arrangements."

A reporter asked, "Don't you think the fact that over a week has elapsed since you paid the money is proof that Colonel Lindbergh was duped?"

"No! There were too many airplanes and Coast Guard cutters cruising around in the vicinity where the child was to be turned over."

New Jersey State and New York City police officers arrived with a request for a description of John; Dr. Condon gave it, then took them to the places where he and John had met.

Some officers felt that the kidnapers, including John, might have deliberately committed a petty crime and let themselves be captured, in order to lie low in jail until the hue and cry died down. Each day Dr. Condon traveled downtown to New York City police headquarters, inspected rogues-gallery photographs and studied the daily line-up. He also recorded John's accent, as he remembered it.

In Greenwich, Connecticut, Mrs. Ella Decornille was about to close her smart pastry shop on West Putnam Road when she saw a green Packard town car stop outside.

Mrs. Decornille watched the liveried chauffeur leave the wheel and open the back door. She knew fine clothes when she saw them, and the clothes worn by the lady who stepped gracefully out of the car were very fine: a gray felt hat, a gray tweed coat, with a string of green-silvery beads to set off the ensemble.

The woman came into the shop. Her complexion was rather dark and her age, Mrs. Decornille thought, must be somewhere in the forties. She asked for a loaf of home-baked bread and one of the fresh strawberry pies. Mrs. Decornille wrapped them and received in return a twenty-dollar bill. She rang up the sale on the cash register, sorted the change, then glanced at a newspaper list, pasted beside the machine, of the serial numbers of the Lindbergh ransom bills.

Mrs. Decornille realized that she held one of the bills in her hand.

She announced her discovery in a startled voice to the customer. The lady grabbed the bill and darted from the shop. The car left in a hurry.

Mrs. Decornille called the police.

20

Appraised by the McLean butler, Gaston Means explained that Mrs. McLean was expecting him. She was—impatiently. She was greatly disturbed, she said, after Means had been shown into the living room, by the amazing revelations of the past few days. A person in the Bronx, a schoolteacher called Jafsie, had been dealing with what he said was the Lindbergh kidnap gang; and Colonel Lindbergh had given fifty thousand dollars to him, which Jafsie said he had turned over to one of the gang.

To make things even more upsetting, there were these three men in Norfolk who said *they* were dealing with the kidnap gang.

One could not doubt the word of a man like Admiral Burrage, Mrs. McLean pointed out. And Colonel Lindbergh was convinced of Jafsie's reliability.

Which gang was Mr. Means dealing with? The Fox's gang, or this Jafsie individual's gang, or the Burrage–Curtis–Dobson-Peacock gang? And which gang had the baby?

The explanation was simple, Means assured her: There weren't three kidnap gangs; there was only one. Dr. Condon's gang, the Burrage–Curtis–Dobson-Peacock gang and his—Gaston Means'—gang were the same. Why had the Jafsie negotiations fallen through? Why hadn't the child been delivered? Because the gang suspected that the serial numbers of the ransom bills had been kept—and their suspicion had proved justified. The Norfolk group would be no more successful in getting the baby. Mrs. McLean had read in the papers about the Coast Guard's activity around Chesapeake Bay; it had scared off the gang. They had decided that only through Means could matters be brought to a satisfactory conclusion.

Now, Means continued, to let Mrs. McLean in on developments: The Fox had called him to Aiken, South Carolina. There he had seen the child. *He had seen Charles Augustus Lindbergh, Jr.* The kidnapers had sworn that it was the Lindbergh child, and he was convinced they had told the truth. He had held the baby in his arms. The baby had blue eyes, blond hair, was dressed in a knitted cap, a buff coat, brown shoes and white stockings. Not only had the baby's age and appearance convinced him; even more convincing was the gang's willingness to send motion pictures of the child to the parents.

Mrs. McLean asked if the baby were still in Aiken. Yes, Means replied; that was why he had called on her. The kidnapers had taken the baby to Aiken because they knew Mrs. McLean owned a summer home there. They were afraid to come to Washington and give the baby to Father Hurney because of the police and federal authorities; but if Mrs. McLean would go to Aiken, everything could be wound up. He was confident of this, Means said, so confident that it wouldn't be necessary for Father Hurney to come with them to receive the child, as originally planned. But they must hurry; the kidnapers were suspicious, could easily change their minds.

Mrs. McLean hurried. She arrived in Aiken the next day. Means left her at her house, promising to return shortly with The Fox. He was as good as his word. Here was the gang leader Mrs. McLean had heard so much about, a middle-sized brown-haired man with a mustache and horn-rimmed glasses. His behavior was quite in character for an underworld boss. His eyes shifted continuously, surveying the room. Then he insisted on examining the entire house. It was a big house and the inspection took some time. The Fox, Means whispered to Mrs. McLean, was searching for hidden microphones.

He found none. Still he seemed uneasy. He would have to confer with the other members of the gang, he told Mrs. McLean. After that he would visit her again. If in the meantime she said so much as a word about him to anyone except Means, she would regret it. Mrs. McLean vowed she would be silent.

She was excited, not only by having seen The Fox in person but also by the prospect of the baby's return—today, perhaps; if not, certainly within the next few days. She told Means she felt much encouraged, and he admitted that he was satisfied with their progress.

His satisfaction proved to be premature. When The Fox came back, he said he had been unable to convince the others that everything was on the level; they thought they had been ill-advised to come to Aiken and stay so long, when safety lay in moving from place to place. They were afraid a trap had been set for them, and so they had left Aiken. In fact, they had left the United States. They were in Juarez, Mexico, just across the border from El Paso, Texas. Mrs. McLean must follow. They would bring the baby across the border to her in El Paso. But, as before, she would have to hurry.

One thing more, The Fox added: it would be wise if Mrs. McLean brought a trained nurse with her; the baby was ill—not seriously, but anything might develop unless he had competent care.

Mrs. McLean promptly obtained the services of Elizabeth Nelson, a professional nurse. Informed of the circumstances and the importance of saying nothing to anyone, Miss Nelson assured her employer that not for the world would she betray her confidence. Means assigned the nurse the code number 29.

They left for El Paso, where Means crossed the border to Juarez. He returned downcast. Things had taken an unexpected twist. The gang was so afraid of the ransom bills they had received from Dr. Condon, with serial numbers that had been plastered all over the country, that they had spent only five hundred of the fifty thousand dollars and didn't dare touch a dollar of the balance. They refused to surrender the baby unless Mrs. McLean gave them an additional thirty-five thousand dollars in brand-new, unmarked, unlisted bank notes. In return, she could have Lindbergh's forty-nine thousand five hundred, which was useless to them.

Mrs. McLean had handed out a hundred thousand dollars plus Means' personal expenses; she was a wealthy woman, but thirty-five thousand more in cash would be a little hard to come by. She would need time to raise it. Means understood, he assured her; nevertheless, for the sake of the baby, she must hurry.

Mrs. McLean left for Washington; Miss Nelson stayed in El Paso, as did Means, to be on hand for the exchange.

To get the money in a hurry, Mrs. McLean turned over several jeweled bracelets and a two-foot rope of diamonds to Elizabeth Poe, a friend on the Washington *Post,* and asked her to pawn or sell them. Miss Poe thought it was strange that anyone so rich should need money so urgently. The more she thought about it, the more suspicious she became. She kept the jewels and phoned Mrs. McLean's attorneys, who called their client.

Mrs. McLean reluctantly told them why she had to have the cash, and they advised her in strong terms to break off all connections with Gaston Means. On April 17 she phoned him in El Paso. She was sorry, she said, but she no longer believed that he could restore the baby. Their association must end and he must return the one hundred thousand to her.

Means said that he too was sorry, especially since they were on the brink of success. But he would not attempt to dissuade her, and of course he would return the hundred thousand dollars, which he had concealed for safekeeping in his brother's home in Concord, North Carolina. He would go to Concord at once, get the money, bring it to Washington, and hand it to Mrs. McLean.

21

His and Anne's hopes cruelly dashed, Charles Lindbergh turned to the Norfolk group. And here there was promising news. On Monday, April 18, John Hughes Curtis came to Hopewell to report it to him.

Curtis had set up New York headquarters at the Prince George Hotel on East 28th Street and enlisted the help of an old friend, Edwin Bruce, who drove him to the Lindbergh place. The kidnapers had taken him partly into their confidence, Curtis said; he'd been given the address of a house in Newark and there had met Sam and a fellow called Dynamite, a Scandinavian type, about forty-two, the captain of the schooner on which they were holding the baby. And there was a third man. The others called him John. He was fairly young and spoke with a heavy accent and had a trim, muscular body, all tallying with Dr. Condon's description of *his* John. Moreover, he had spread out some bills on a table, and their serial numbers were among those in the published list of bank notes Dr. Condon had given John.

Curtis had wanted to take a few to show Lindbergh but was told nothing doing—the gang had confidence in him or they wouldn't be dealing with him, so why shouldn't Lindbergh trust him too? Curtis had lost his temper. They had a hell of a nerve, asking Lindbergh to pay a second ransom! They laughed at him. Did he think they'd ever intended to settle for the original sum? From the beginning they'd counted on two payments.

They deserved to hang for such cold-blooded trickery, Curtis had shouted. Forget it, they'd advised him good-naturedly. Then they had set a new rendezvous, near Cape May, New Jersey.

So the baby was on a boat, after all; John hadn't lied in his note of instructions, at least not to that extent. Encouraged, Lindbergh said he'd like to be somewhere in the neighborhood when the meeting took place. Curtis saw no reason he shouldn't. There was a little hotel in the village of Cape May Court House; Lindbergh could take a room and call him at the Prince George, so that when Curtis heard from the gang he'd be sure of reaching him.

The next evening, Lindbergh, Edwin Bruce and Lieutenant Richard, the Navy pilot assigned to the Norfolk group, drove to the hotel and called the Prince George. Curtis was waiting. He'd had word from the gang and would come at once. He got to Cape May Court House at midnight. The gang would take him on board their schooner, he reported, if Lindbergh would agree to two conditions: that there would be no special Coast Guard activity in the area and that he wouldn't publish the serial numbers of the bills after the second payment had been made and the child returned.

Tell them he agreed, the young man said.

All right, Curtis said, now for it! He had no idea what would happen next but he'd return as soon as the gang put him ashore after the meeting.

He came back soon after daybreak, tired but cheerful. A lot had happened; things were moving at last. He'd been picked up by two women in an old Ford sedan equipped with a two-way radio for keeping in touch with the constantly moving schooner. One of the two women, a blonde called Hilda, was Dynamite's wife—his real name was Olaf Larsen, Curtis had learned—and the other, Inez, was her sister, also married to a schooner captain. Hilda, who spoke with a German accent, had been quite talkative; she and Olaf had three boys, ranging from seven to twelve, and she was a nurse.

A boat was waiting and soon Curtis was on board the schooner, a two-masted Gloucester fisherman with a temporary deck cabin aft painted white and a dark-green hull. Dynamite was there, and John, and Sam—his real name turned out to be Morrie Truesdale—and two more men, Eric and Nils. But the baby wasn't on the schooner; or at least so Dynamite and John said—for all Curtis knew, of course, the little boy could have been hidden somewhere below. The important thing was that Dynamite had promised to have the schooner, and the baby, in the vicinity of Block Island early the following morning, Thursday the twenty-first. Curtis was to get a chart of Block Island waters and one of the gang would telephone him the exact rendezvous.

That wasn't quite all. The gang had opened up even more and revealed how the baby had been kidnaped.

Curtis glanced a little apologetically at Lindbergh and said this wasn't necessarily what he believed, simply what he'd been told: the child had been stolen with the help of one of his three servants.

The servants were above suspicion, Lindbergh protested.

It was just what he'd been told, Curtis pointed out again, not necessarily the truth; but true or not, the plan had been worked out in detail. They'd shown him a chart of Lindbergh's house, furnished by this servant. John had struck up an acquaintance with the servant in a roadhouse outside Newark, and they'd agreed that the baby represented a lot of easy money, if they worked together. As a first step, they had ascertained from a doctor how much chloroform could be safely given to a child of that age to keep him quiet. Then, on the night of March 1, John, Eric and Hilda had waited in a green Hudson sedan on the driveway a few hundred feet from the Lindbergh home; Sam and Nils were posted as lookouts in another car farther on. The servant had signaled from the house, John and Eric propped the ladder up to the nursery window, climbed in, chloroformed the baby and—given the all-clear by the servant—walked boldly down the stairs, out the front door, and down the drive to the Hudson. The two cars sped to Cape May, where Inez was waiting with a boat to take them to the schooner.

It was Hilda, Curtis finished his account, who'd written the original ransom demand and the succeeding notes sent by the kidnapers.

Daybreak of the twenty-first found the four men, in a small fast craft Lindbergh had rented, at the rendezvous point near East Quarter Light just off the high clay bluffs of Block Island. They were right on time, obeying the directions Curtis had received by phone after their return to the Prince George; but there was no sign of a two-masted Gloucester schooner with white cabin and dark-green hull.

They waited in vain.

Curtis said it seemed clear something had frightened off the gang, perhaps the fishing boats at work in these waters. There was nothing to do but go back to New York and wait for further instructions.

Lindbergh thought of Anne, at home. He had had the release of this activity, but she must wait in the house with the empty nursery. Waiting, always waiting.

22

The beautiful yacht *Marcon,* fuel tanks full, ready for sea, lay at a Norfolk pier in the late afternoon light Friday, April 22, while Captain Frank Lackmann watched for his expected passengers, John Hughes Curtis, Alex Swanson and party. They arrived just before six. Swanson was a tall, slim young man who shook hands with the yacht's skipper rather shyly and seemed unaccustomed to the sound of his own name. That was natural; he was very new to it. It had been adopted to put newspapers off the scent, but Captain Lackmann reflected that it would take a pretty nearsighted reporter not to recognize Charles Lindbergh a couple of hundred yards away.

The others were Edwin Bruce, Lieutenant Richard, and Captain Kenneth Whiting, commandant of the Norfolk Air Station. Richard and Whiting carried a Browning machine gun, rifles, and pistols, and Lindbergh had a pistol in a shoulder holster under his jacket. Bruce merely brought two cameras, motion-picture and still. He had thought it discreet to pack them in his suitcase; if he saw them, Lindbergh might object.

Of the original Norfolk group, Admiral Burrage and Dean Dobson-Peacock remained behind, as before, since it was Curtis who was actively in touch with the gang—although the dean also had been active the preceding few days. He was still puzzling over his adventure, wondering if he actually had been the victim of an attempted high-handed fraud.

A strange, rough voice had informed Dobson-Peacock over the telephone that if he wanted the Lindbergh negotiations to end successfully he must hurry to New York and register at the Park Lane Hotel under the name James Hill. The dean had done so and had been escorted by a stranger to another hotel, where a well-dressed middle-aged man had said flatly that for fifty thousand dollars he and the other stranger were prepared to put the stolen child in the dean's hands.

Dobson-Peacock had managed to get away—they had become increasingly demanding, even threatening, advising him to handle the deal alone if he knew what was good for him—only after promising to return the next day. He had reported to Curtis at the Prince George, and Curtis had said he could forget the whole thing as a fake, because the real kidnapers had communicated with him again, confirming his suspicion that the Block Island waters had been too crowded for comfort, setting up a new rendezvous twenty miles at sea. If that too should fail, they would sail the schooner south and exchange the baby for the second ransom payment somewhere off the Virginia coast, at a point to be arranged. In those waters, Curtis could use to good advantage Colonel Consolvo's earlier offer of his yacht *Marcon.*

The new rendezvous did fail. The next one was set by the gang for some twenty miles east of the Chesapeake lightship. The vessel the *Marcon* was to meet, Curtis told Lackmann and Whiting, was a Gloucester fishing schooner, dark green hull, white cabin aft, flying white towels from her forward mast for positive identification. The gang had given him her name: the *Mary B. Moss.*

Whiting offered to scout ahead in a seaplane. Lindbergh and Curtis gratefully approved the idea.

The *Marcon* sailed at 6:40 P.M. and reached the rendezvous in the small hours of the next morning, April 23. Lindbergh was on the bridge; he and the others scanned the choppy seas. They were empty. But at 6:35 A.M. a vessel was sighted; it seemed to be a fishing schooner. The machine gun was put in position and the *Marcon* slapped on speed. Swiftly her quarry's outline grew in Lindbergh's binoculars. It was a fishing boat, all right, and this was the place——

But where were the identifying white towels?

Curtis shook his head. It wasn't a Gloucester schooner, only a fishing smack.

The *Marcon* swung around, idled back and forth through the rendezvous area. Curtis went below for a pill. He always had been an indifferent sailor; the weather was brisk and he expected the worst.

Whiting returned from a scouting tour with no news. The meeting had been arranged for early morning; at a little past one in the afternoon the yacht put back for Norfolk. Lindbergh helped with the mooring lines.

Well, Curtis said, he thought he'd better go ashore and try to contact the gang to see if there was an explanation.

There was—from Dynamite, read to Curtis over the phone by Hilda: *Has yacht double exhaust? Heard your exhaust. Had company. Be patient. Will break through.*

The weather steadily worsened during the next day and they sighted no other craft at sea; after the *Marcon* made port Captain Lackmann considered it best to stay there until Tuesday morning, when the skies were clearer. The yacht cast off. Today, perhaps, would be the day. At nine, a report came from Whiting in the seaplane. He had spotted a vessel flying something white from her mast. The *Mary B. Moss?* No; when the *Marcon* overhauled the new suspect, the "something white" turned out to be her crew's washing, flapping in the wind.

Wednesday's weather was dirty again; the yacht did not sail. Curtis took advantage of their enforced idleness to fly to New York.

He had invested a lot of time and more money than he could afford in the search since the night Sam had approached him, and he was worried not only about expenses but, much more, about his wife Constance. She was ill; his long absences and the knowledge that he was mixed up with gangsters weren't helping her to get well. Richard Lee of the New York *Daily News* had put in a bid for the exclusive story of Curtis' dealings with the kidnapers, providing he could make the baby available solely to *Daily News* photographers, and it had occurred to him that another big paper might top the *News*. So he had arranged for William E. Haskell, Jr., assistant to the president of the New York *Herald Tribune,* to discuss things with him at the Prince George.

Curtis told Haskell the kind of story he could write and suggested an advance payment of twenty-five thousand dollars. Haskell telephoned the *Tribune*'s managing editor, Grafton Wilcox, and then said the idea was acceptable and the paper wasn't opposed to a twenty-five thousand advance—but not until the baby was found and Colonel Lindbergh approved the story and consented to its publication.

Since the child's return was expected any day now, Curtis said, he'd start writing his story as soon as he could squeeze in the time.

Admiral Burrage came down to the *Marcon* for a visit and Lindbergh described the weary, frustrating search. "These are the hardest days for me," he said. Thursday the twenty-eighth was another tedious day of waiting. Edwin Bruce went ashore and brought back the Norfolk newspapers and a variety of candies for Lindbergh.

As usual, the papers carried a story on the case. This one concerned Salvatore Spitale and Irving Bitz, who were withdrawing, they had announced, because Lindbergh no longer respected their advice. They had strongly opposed paying fifty thousand dollars for Dr. John F. Condon to hand over to the alleged kidnapers, but Lindbergh had ignored their protest.

That evening Navy technicians installed a new, improved two-way radio on the yacht; Naval Radioman Pratt joined the crew.

On Friday the twenty-ninth Curtis returned, and in midafternoon the *Marcon* set out for Cape Henry, the easternmost point on the route from Norfolk to the Atlantic. She was overhauled by a Coast

Guard cutter on a routine check, and Curtis made a joke of it. They'd better watch their step!—he had in his wallet a letter from a high-ranking Coast Guard officer notifying all cutters to stay clear of any craft on which John Hughes Curtis was a passenger.

At Cape Henry, Lindbergh took a swim and with Curtis, Bruce and Richard practiced firing a few of the guns aboard, using a fishnet stake as the target. In the morning, from three to six, he kept watch, then made breakfast for himself in the galley. At half-past three that afternoon, Saturday April 30, the *Marcon* was some twelve miles east of the Chesapeake lightship, but neither yacht nor seaplane sighted the *Mary B. Moss*. Curtis, seasick, admitted that it was discouraging; still, Dynamite had told them to be patient.

A gale kept the *Marcon* in port through May 2, but the next day she was at sea again.

A discussion of tactics took place, to which Curtis, with his restless stomach, listened uneasily. It was obvious, the others pointed out, that the gang was intensely suspicious, afraid of any sign of possible trouble. On the other hand, Curtis had mentioned that letter of his from the Coast Guard. If he could get on board the *Mary B. Moss,* the letter would be bound to give the gang confidence. But how to get on board? Well, there was Whiting's seaplane; Curtis could join him in it and they could land alongside the schooner. All very well, but wouldn't the plane's Navy insignia alarm the gang and drive them away? Someone came up with the answer: Curtis could parachute down from the seaplane near the *Mary B. Moss;* the gang would *have* to rescue him from the sea.

It seemed a sound idea. As for the jump itself, Lindbergh told the pensive Curtis, there was really nothing to it, and he explained the technique of parachuting into rough seas. Then he paused thoughtfully. It had to be admitted that some risk was involved, and Curtis was the only one who could identify the kidnapers. All in all, perhaps they'd better forget it. Curtis agreed.

During the day, the United States battleship *Utah* steamed across the horizon but the *Mary B. Moss* was nowhere to be seen.

The next day at sea, Radioman Pratt advised Captain Lackmann that a Navy plane was taking off with a message for Curtis. The yacht stood by, engines idling. Presently the plane appeared, swung low and released a lifebelt. The message was bound to it.

It was from Curtis' good friend A. L. Foster of Atlantic City, New Jersey, who owned a rugged eighty-five-foot ketch, the *Cachalot*. She was at their service, Foster wrote, whenever they needed her.

Curtis and Lindbergh had discussed this before. The young man had become increasingly disturbed by their failure to sight the schooner; he had been away from home a long time and Anne was worried, just as was Constance Curtis. The news had leaked out that he was on the *Marcon;* reporters and photographers had poured into Norfolk; and the weather had been almost consistently against them. Couldn't they establish a new rendezvous farther north?

Curtis had said he'd ask Hilda to see how the gang felt. Their answer was favorable: if the *Marcon* and the *Mary B. Moss* continued to miss each other, they'd shift the rendezvous north. Then Curtis had wired Foster, asking if he could use the *Cachalot,* better suited to stormy waters than the luxurious *Marcon.*

Wednesday, May 4—no contact. On Thursday the *Marcon* waited in the vicinity of Cape Charles while Whiting flew into the teeth of a stiff wind, looking for the *Mary B. Moss.* In spite of the rising seas and his internal unhappiness, Curtis said: "If Whiting reports anything out there, we'll go out even if we wash the deckhouse off."

Whiting saw nothing. The *Marcon* returned to Norfolk.

This same Thursday, Gaston Means was in trouble.

Mrs. McLean had waited patiently for him to pick up the one hundred thousand dollars and return it to her as promised; finally she had spoken to her attorneys. The U.S. Department of Justice, qualified to act because Means had received the money in the District of Columbia, was informed of her experiences and a warrant issued for the arrest of Gaston Bullock Means and one "The Fox" on the charge of having defrauded Evalyn Walsh McLean of one hundred thousand plus four thousand dollars—Means' expenses.

All through the last part of April and the first days of May, Justice Department agents had kept an eye on Means, waiting for him to leave his home in Chevy Chase, Maryland, and step into federal territory, where the warrant was valid. Eventually he did; the agents' car forced his to the curb and he was arrested. He learned the reason in the office of J. Edgar Hoover, chief of the department's Division of Investigation: Means had convinced Mrs. McLean that he could restore the Lindbergh baby in return for a hundred-thousand-dollar ransom. He had restored neither the child nor the money. The charge was "larceny after trust"—embezzlement.

Not true, Means replied. Admittedly, he hadn't restored the baby—his operations had been cut short at their most promising point—but as for the hundred thousand dollars (his expense fee was nonreturnable), it was news to him that Mrs. McLean didn't have it. He had picked up the cash at his brother's home in Concord, North Carolina, and was driving to Washington to give it to Mrs. McLean when, in Alexandria, Virginia—just a few miles from his destination—a car had drawn alongside his and forced him to stop.

The driver, a stranger, had leaned out and whispered one word: *eleven.* Its significance was plain. Eleven was the code number Means had assigned Mrs. McLean, to identify her in their dealings with the kidnap gang. What else could it mean but that the stranger was an agent appointed by her to intercept Means and collect the money?

"I was certain of it," he said, "so I gave him the hundred thousand dollars."

He had taken it for granted, Means continued, that her agent had passed on the money to Mrs. McLean. It came as a shock to learn that he had not. The agent's perfidy was obvious.

Now that the matter had been cleared up, Means assumed that he was free to return to his private affairs.

It seemed that he was not. United States Attorney Leo A. Rover frankly doubted the veracity of his account, and Means was arraigned. Rover asked for bail of one hundred thousand dollars. "In view of Means' record," he said, "and what we know of him and the things he is capable of, it is the government's view that a bond in the full amount of the alleged defalcation be required for his appearance, because we feel that otherwise he would not be present when his case is called for trial."

On Friday, May 6, high wind and waves hammered the Virginia coastline; the *Marcon* could not sail. But the morning of May 7 brought a pleasant change; Captain Lackmann awoke to find that the seas had calmed. It was a perfect day. He looked for Curtis, Lindbergh, Bruce and Lieutenant Richard, but they had gone. Curtis had left a note: *Frank—you will hear from me. Please stay here at least two days before you move. Then stand by. Thanks. J. C.*

Captain Lackmann had not been told, but the day before Curtis had returned from a trip ashore with further word from Dynamite. The captain of the *Mary B. Moss* was in favor of moving their operations to New Jersey waters at once.

Before boarding the *Cachalot,* Curtis kept an appointment in New York with Haskell of the *Herald Tribune.* They discussed the story Curtis was to write while Ruth Gay, a young secretary he had hired, took notes. After Haskell left, Curtis started to dictate his experiences, but soon broke off because, as he explained to Bruce, who had driven him to the city and was listening, he had to find out from the gang where the new rendezvous was to be.

On Sunday May 8 A. L. Foster, at his home at 6001 Ventnor Avenue, Atlantic City, received the telephone call he had been expecting: the Lindbergh party would be there tomorrow, Curtis said. He had called Hilda in Freeport, Long Island, where she was staying, and she had passed along word from Dynamite that the new rendezvous would be the waters off Cape May, near Five Fathoms Banks. The *Mary B. Moss* would no longer fly white towels from her forward mast; instead, both schooner and ketch would identify themselves by flashing their foremast lights.

The small group—Lindbergh, Curtis, Bruce, Richard—arrived at Foster's home the next afternoon. The young father was in cheerful spirits; after all the exasperating delays, he was certain that his son would soon be in his arms—late tonight perhaps, or the next morning. He was so confident that he arranged a radio code to flash word to friends on shore when the little boy was safely aboard the *Cachalot;* they in turn could keep him advised of shoreside developments.

The *Cachalot* sailed at seven in the evening. Five hours later she arrived in the rendezvous waters. Lindbergh took turns at the helm with Foster and, when the other was at the wheel, busied himself flashing signals from the foremast into a night of rising wind and mounting seas. Almost always, it seemed, they were dogged by wretched weather, adding to the difficulties of making contact between two small craft.

The signals continued, but no answering flash gleamed in the darkness. For four and a half hours of the early morning of Tuesday May 10, the ketch crisscrossed the area.

A gray dawn broke. By five o'clock it was plain that the new rendezvous had failed.

The *Cachalot* returned to Cape May Harbor and Curtis went ashore to try to learn what was wrong. Lindbergh stayed aboard, attending to odd jobs and helping the steward with the meals.

Curtis came back looking gloomy. He had talked with Inez in a cottage on the Cape May shore. Previously, she had talked by radio to Dynamite on the *Mary B. Moss,* still at sea. The schooner was making very heavy weather of it, she had been told; the men were surly and resolved to turn the baby over to Lindbergh as soon as they possibly could. Curtis said that even Inez appeared to be feeling the strain; her voice had trembled and she looked pale and drawn.

If only the storm would pass! But Wednesday, May 11, showed no signs of clearing and the *Cachalot,* sturdy but less seaworthy than a Gloucester schooner, could not safely leave port. Curtis went to nearby Atlantic City to dictate more of his story to Ruth Gay, and

Bruce and Lieutenant Richard left for a visit to New York. Lindbergh remained aboard—and, later on, listened to news from Washington that Gaston Means, after six days in jail, had succeeded in having his bail reduced to fifty thousand dollars, posted that not inconsiderable sum and been released.

By the next morning, Thursday, the storm had died to low winds and a cold drizzle. Curtis came back from Atlantic City but Bruce and Richard, in the belief that the ketch would still be stormbound, stayed in New York.

The *Cachalot* put to sea. She threaded back and forth across the waters off Five Fathoms Banks, searching for the schooner. Again Lindbergh flashed identifying signals from the foremast light. If there were answering signals from the *Mary B. Moss,* he and his companions failed to see them.

23

The dreary weather of Thursday May 12 reached in from the sea to the Sourlands country. The windshield wiper on William Allen's truck swabbed steadily as he drove with a load of timber along the back road linking Princeton and Hopewell. A thin, forty-six-year-old Negro employed by a firm of house-movers, he remarked to his companion, Orville Wilson, that he'd be glad when the afternoon's work was finished and he could go home to his wife and kids in Trenton.

They drove through Mount Rose, hardly a village, just a few houses and a general store. Hopewell, rather more than a mile ahead, had been little if any better known to the world until the Lindberghs had built their home across the valley—about a mile away as the crow flies, five miles or so by the winding roads. One could get a pretty good view from here of the white house with the windmill in back, but it was a familiar sight to Allen and he didn't bother to turn his head.

Beyond Mount Rose the road was deserted in the rain. Allen pulled over to one side, explaining his purpose to Wilson, who replied that it seemed to him Allen might have had the foresight to stop at a service-station rest room and avoid having to wade into the damp woods.

Allen scrambled through the thicket of second-growth maple and locust trees, some fifty feet into the woods. Bending his head to duck a low-hanging branch, he stopped short. Then, slowly, he advanced to investigate the thing he had chanced upon.

It lay in a small hollow, half-buried by a drift of rotting leaves and dirt. The skeleton of an animal, Allen thought. He looked closer. A human foot protruded from that small mound of death.

In the truck, Orville Wilson saw his friend running from the woods.

"My God," Allen yelled, "there's a child—a dead child over there!"

Wilson got out; Allen led him to his find. They bent over it. It lay face down in the shallow pit. Wind and rain and time and scavengers had worked upon it, but it was still recognizable as a child's body.

The little that was left of the hair seemed to be blond; some fragments of clothing clung to the figure. Wilson touched it tentatively but Allen stopped him before he could clear off the partial covering of sodden leaves. Everything, he said, must be left exactly as he had found it.

"What you going to do?" Wilson asked.

Allen took a moment to steady his nerves. "Report it to Charlie Williamson!"

The truck roared down the sloping road to Hopewell. Constable Charles E. Williamson, who on the night of March 1 had answered the telephone call from the Lindbergh house, was in the barbershop. "Could you talk to me a couple of minutes?" Allen asked.

"Sure," Williamson said. "Talk to you for five, if you want me to." The smile left his face as Allen described the small body lying in the woods.

Williamson got out of the barber chair in a hurry and beckoned Allen to follow him. In the township police station Allen repeated the story to Chief Harry Wolfe. Wolfe telephoned Colonel Schwarzkopf at New Jersey State Police headquarters. Listening, William Allen began to grasp the significance of what he had found.

Trooper Andrew Zapolsky was the first of the State police to reach the place in the woods where Allen and the Hopewell officers were waiting. Kneeling beside the shallow grave, he carefully lifted the body and turned it over. The face was quite well preserved. Zapolsky took a child's portrait from his jacket and held it beside the small head. He did not need long to compare the two and come to a conclusion.

At sea, the drizzling rain continued and a few whitecaps began to kick up under the freshening wind. Visibility was poor. In this weather another craft might loom up in the murk with no more than a moment's warning. But the *Cachalot* was plainly visible; her foremast light unceasingly blinked on and off in response to the tireless fingers of the young man in the pilot house.

There was no answer.

In her son-in-law's continued absence, Mrs. Dwight Morrow had joined Anne at the Hopewell house. Through Thursday afternoon they waited for the call they had expected every day since Charles had left to meet the kidnapers. The gray light waned; it seemed that once more they were to be disappointed.

At the grave, William Allen and the others were joined by a group of officers, detectives and troopers, headed by Inspector Harry Walsh of the Jersey City police. Trooper Zapolsky's conclusion, they agreed, was correct, but Inspector Walsh thought it would be wise to obtain additional proof before informing the family. He studied the shreds of cloth clinging to the body. Perhaps the nursemaid, Betty Gow, would have samples of the clothing the baby wore on the night of March 1. He set off for the Lindbergh house.

The others fanned out to search for clues. The hunt for Charles Augustus Lindbergh, Jr., had spread fairly well throughout the world, to ships and trains, airplanes and automobiles, but it had not touched this spot so close to home—although some seventy-five feet away from the small mound emergency telephone wires had been strung through the woods.

Inspector Walsh was calm, seemingly engaged in routine police business, as he asked Betty Gow if he might have a sample of the baby's night clothing. Betty replied that she had exactly what he wanted: she had kept the remnant of the flannel petticoat from which she had improvised a nightshirt after the little boy had spilled his medicine. And from Elsie Whateley she could get the spool of blue silk thread she had used for the stitches. Betty went upstairs, returned and gave them to Walsh, who calmly thanked her.

He drove back to the grave. The flannel petticoat and fragments of clothing matched. So did the blue thread, when held against the few stitches that were visible.

The garments must be preserved as evidence, Walsh said; with a stick, he delicately raised the body. But he wasn't careful enough; the stick slipped and penetrated the head, leaving a small, pencil-size hole. He tried again. There were no more accidents as he removed the remains of the rotted nightshirt and the sleeveless wool shirt that had been worn over it.

Taking the dripping clothing, Walsh returned to the Lindbergh house and informed Colonel Schwarzkopf that there was no longer any doubt.

On its seventy-second day, May 12, 1932, the search for Charles Augustus Lindbergh, Jr., was ended.

Schwarzkopf sent for Betty Gow. The nursemaid looked at the shreds of flannel and wool and seemed to sense their meaning. Her fingers were shaky as she placed the petticoat's embroidered, scalloped hem over the scalloped flannel shirttail. The design was identical. She plucked at a wisp of the familiar blue thread until she could bring herself to speak. Yes, she said at last, they were part of the baby's clothes. Where had the police found them?

Schwarzkopf told her.

Even with the evidence before her eyes, it was not easy for Betty to believe the truth. The truth, so she and Anne Lindbergh thought, was that the baby was hidden on a schooner somewhere in the Atlantic; at any moment they would hear from the Colonel that he had met the kidnapers and rescued his son. It simply could not be that the small body lying in the woods was their little boy.

But it *was* true, Schwarzkopf said.

The moment had come to tell Anne Lindbergh.

Betty wondered: Shouldn't her husband be told first?

The news was being radioed to him on the *Cachalot,* Schwarzkopf said. They could no longer delay telling the mother.

Anne was with Mrs. Morrow as Schwarzkopf came into the room.

He had very bad news to give them, he said. The baby was dead. The body had been found a few miles from the house, in the woods. He had been dead, it seemed, since the night of March 1. There was no possibility whatever of a mistake. And it would serve no purpose, Schwarzkopf ventured, for either of them to see the body.

Mrs. Morrow put her arms around her daughter. As quietly as he could, Schwarzkopf left the room.

No answer came from the *Cachalot* in response to the message repeatedly flashed to her in the prearranged code. Was the ketch in trouble, or had her radio broken down? To Colonel Breckinridge, reached in his New York office with the news, it seemed a last unbearable irony that the whole world should know—as very soon now it must know—that the Lindbergh baby was dead while the father still searched for his son. Coast Guard officials agreed and cutters put out to find the *Cachalot.*

The State police had set up quarters in the garage of the Lindbergh house; from there, at a little after five, a trooper telephoned

Paul Gebhart's general store in Hopewell, which had become a gathering place for newspaper and radio reporters. "There will be an important announcement at Colonel Lindbergh's garage," he said, and added that it would be a good idea for the reporters to get there as fast as they could. He phoned the same message to the press room of the State House in Trenton.

The Hopewell men made it first, but those from Trenton weren't far behind. In the garage, grouped around a long wooden mess table, they waited for Schwarzkopf to speak. At 6:45 P.M. the hum of talk fell away. In silence they listened to the rain, then Schwarzkopf began:

"We have to announce that apparently the body of the Lindbergh baby was found ——"

He hesitated, the sentence incomplete; even to him, though he had known the news for hours, it sounded as incredible as it did to the two dozen men facing him.

Beginning again, he told about William Allen's discovery in the woods. Before he could finish, there was a break for the door to send the four shattering words *Lindbergh baby found dead* over the wires. Schwarzkopf's sharp voice held his audience until he had read the last of his statement. Then he let them go.

Coroner Walter Swayze's funeral parlors at 415 Greenwood Avenue in Trenton served as the county morgue; that evening, two detectives arrived with a visitor. There might, there just might have been a mistake. Was there anyone who would know as certainly as the mother? Yes; the nurse.

Betty Gow was led to the autopsy table. She looked down, then put her hand to her eyes and turned her face away. No, she said when she was able to speak, there had not been any mistake.

After performing an autopsy Dr. Charles H. Mitchell, official physician of Mercer County, where the body was found, wrote his report. In the space under the heading *Diagnosis of the Cause of Death,* he noted:

The child died of a fractured skull caused by external violence.

He did not add, since it wasn't necessary, that it was a severe, extensive fracture. On the inner wall of the skull, at the point of fracture, there were the remains of a blood clot. The child, therefore, was alive when the fracture occurred; the blood clot simply would not be present had he not been when he was struck or when he fell.

At the very minimum, Dr. Mitchell estimated, the Lindbergh baby had been dead for two months, probably for days longer.

The weather-stained *Cachalot* slipped into Cape May Harbor and tied up at her familiar mooring in the thickening darkness.

No message had reached her during the day. No Coast Guard vessels had crossed her path. There had been no glimpse of a light flashing through the murk in answer to hers. But with better weather, for which there seemed to be some prospect, perhaps tomorrow the long-delayed rendezvous with the *Mary B. Moss* would take place.

So Lindbergh hoped, and Curtis said the same as he went ashore —he was spending the night in Atlantic City.

Lindbergh again remained on board, occupying himself with the usual small jobs.

Later, Edwin Bruce and Lieutenant Richard returned from their stay in New York. They knew of the discovery in the Jersey woods; boarding the ketch, they saw, to their dismay, that Lindbergh did not. In greeting them he merely reported another day of failure; maybe tomorrow their luck would change.

Bruce and Richard glanced at each other. Lindbergh sensed their uneasiness. He began to ask if anything was wrong, but fell silent and turned away.

Bruce made himself speak. "Colonel, I have a message for you. They have found the baby——" He broke off nervously as Lindbergh wheeled and stared at him.

"Found——?"

Bruce finished quickly. "He is dead."

24

Lindbergh baby found dead.

A hush of stunned disbelief seemed to fall throughout the world.

Almost the first public figure to express his shock and sympathy to the Lindberghs was President Ortíz Rubio of Mexico, who felt particularly close to the young couple; Charles Lindbergh and Anne Morrow had fallen in love in Mexico City. Through a correspondent of *The New York Times,* Señora Rubio sent a message of her own: "The death of the Lindbergh baby goes to the hearts of all the mothers of the world. I am full of grief for Mrs. Lindbergh, who weeps inconsolable for the loss of her little one."

The Vatican appealed for justice. In Santa Monica, California, Will Rogers wrote:

"There's nothing one can say that means anything in a time like this. I knew the little fellow, held him in my arms a few weeks before he was killed. I hope the responsible ones are caught, and caught quickly, and that there's a full measure of justice ready for them when they bring them in."

In Royal Oak, Michigan, the Reverend Charles E. Coughlin said: "The baby's death is a challenge to eradicate the gangster and the hoodlum from our society. My deepest sympathy goes out to Colonel and Mrs. Lindbergh. May their sorrow be an incentive to every American to make this a better country for the children of the growing generation."

Commander-in-Chief Evangeline Booth of the Salvation Army wired the Lindberghs:

"My heart bleeds for you in your indescribable grief. Every sorrow has its Olivet. There will be comfort in knowing that your darling has been and is now with the children bright in glory and will never know sorrow."

In New York, the *Daily News* said:

> GET THE LINDBERGH KILLERS!
>
> The kidnaped Lindbergh baby has been found—slain.
>
> The damnable fiends, the inhuman monsters, who kidnaped the baby and presumably were responsible for the bilking of Colonel Lindbergh out of $50,000 are still at large.
>
> Until the killers are tracked down and brought to justice, the children of America will not be safe. And the rest of the world will be able to point to this country and say: "That is the country where criminals can persecute decent citizens in absolute defiance of the law."
>
> Does the Federal Government wish to preserve its integrity and its dignity, and so preserve the power of all other governmental agencies in this country?
>
> If it does, it will put its best men on the trail of these fiends, and keep them on the trail until the fiends are captured and convicted of first degree murder.
>
> The American people, shocked and grieved, will, we believe, demand such action by the Government in a voice that cannot be ignored.

In Grosse Point, Michigan, Mrs. Evangeline Lindbergh prepared to join her son and daughter-in-law. A telephone call had come to her from the Lindbergh home late in the afternoon, just after she had returned from her classroom. Mrs. Lindbergh had not missed a day at school since the kidnaping; she had told her pupils that she would be grateful if they would not say anything about the baby's disappearance, and they had complied.

In Washington, Mrs. Evalyn Walsh McLean shut herself off from the press; in Norfolk, Admiral Guy Burrage told reporters that he had nothing to say. But Dean Dobson-Peacock confessed that he was baffled by the tragic discovery. "I cannot understand why the group we were dealing with should have continued the negotiations when they learned there would be no advance payment," he said. "There would be no point in it with the baby already dead."

Captain Frank Lackmann, still standing by on the *Marcon,* had a theory that, he believed, completely cleared up this point. The long cat-and-mouse game with the *Mary B. Moss* had been deliberately contrived by the kidnapers in an attempt to maneuver the *Marcon* far enough out to sea so that they could safely abduct Lindbergh himself.

In New Jersey, John Hughes Curtis was in a State police car, bound for Hopewell. He was certain, he told reporters, that he had been in contact with the gang who had not only stolen but—as they now knew—killed the Lindbergh baby. "They knew too much," he said. "They had too many definite bits of evidence to be any other than the murderers themselves."

In the Bronx, Dr. John F. Condon swore that from this day forward, if need be to the end of his life, he would spare no effort to track down John and his accomplices; that it *was* John and his gang who had kidnaped and killed the child, the old man was convinced. To reporters, he recalled the question John had asked him in the cemetery: "*Would I burn if the baby is dead?*" It had given him pause, but then John had persuaded him that the baby was alive and in good health. It was John's guilty conscience that had asked that question, Dr. Condon said.

In the woods between Mount Rose and Hopewell, State troopers stood guard over the shallow hole that had held the small body, and close by, on the rainswept road where William Allen had stopped his truck, cars drove bumper to bumper. Still more of the curious came on foot. At the spot Allen had entered the woods, now barricaded and guarded by troopers, the mounting traffic had converged into a tangle in which almost no movement was possible. Peddlers hurried up with peanuts and popcorn; others hawked postcards of the Lindbergh house. An enterprising merchant from Trenton arrived with the materials to set up a refreshment stand, and soon the smell of hot dogs was in the air.

Charles Lindbergh drove through the night toward his home.

25

In the pale early light of Friday May 13 the rain still fell.

Two new visitors, Henry Breckinridge and a New York physician, Philip Van Ingen, arrived at Walter Swayze's funeral parlors in Trenton. Dr. Van Ingen had delivered Charles Lindbergh, Jr.; he had last seen and examined the child only ten days before he was stolen. In the examination he performed now the doctor measured the size of the skull, studied the number and shape of the teeth—there were sixteen; eight upper and eight lower—and finally inspected the two overlapping toes of the right foot. His finding, and that of chemists who had analyzed the hair and compared it with the souvenirs of baby hair kept by Mrs. Morrow, confirmed Betty Gow: there had been no mistake. In view of this proof, it was announced, it would not be necessary to put Charles and Anne Lindbergh through the ordeal of identifying their son.

Coroner Swayze signed a certificate of death, which he filed at the New Jersey Department of Health, and was given a permit for cremation.

In midafternoon Colonel Schwarzkopf and other officials came to the mortuary, making their way through the sightseers waiting in the rain. Another car drove up. The crowd's patience was rewarded; the murmur of voices rose to an excited babble. The papers had said he wouldn't come, but here he was: Colonel Lindbergh.

He was bareheaded. His face looked tired, older than his years. Breckinridge, who had returned to Hopewell, followed him from the car. The young man walked swiftly into the mortuary; the older man paused, looking at a familiar figure in the crowd, the tall, upright figure of Dr. John F. Condon. Breckinridge gestured as if to ask him if he wished to go inside; Dr. Condon shook his head.

In the room where the body lay, Schwarzkopf and the others watched as Lindbergh walked to the sheet-covered table. He indicated the sheet. "Take that off," he said. A member of the coroner's staff removed the covering and stepped back, leaving the young man alone at the table.

He stared at his son. A flush came into his face. He bent over, examined the mouth, counted the teeth. He inspected the two small overlapping toes. Then he left the table.

In an adjoining room, Erwin E. Marshall, Mercer County prosecutor, approached him. "Colonel Lindbergh," he asked, "are you satisfied that it is the body of your baby?"

"I am perfectly satisfied that it is my child," Lindbergh replied.

The body was wrapped in a shroud and placed in a small oak coffin. At half past four a gray hearse left the funeral parlor. One car followed. Schwarzkopf drove; in the back sat Lindbergh and Breckinridge.

The two cars slowly climbed the Jersey hills; an hour later they reached their destination, Rose Hill Cemetery in Linden, south of Elizabeth. M. L. Howard, supervisor of the cemetery, directed the removal of the tiny coffin to the crematory chapel. Lindbergh walked close behind his son. Breckinridge and Schwarzkopf let him go alone.

No religious service had been asked for. The coffin was carried by elevator to the floor below. The young man followed down a short flight of stairs.

Alone, he watched as the glass doors of the cremation chamber opened and the coffin was rolled in. The doors were sealed. Flames burst from the fireclay of the chamber. Lindbergh pressed closer to the doors. The white heat mounted. He stared into the heart of the flames. Then there was nothing more to see.

The supervisor told him that the ashes would be kept at the crematory until an urn was provided. "Thank you," Lindbergh said.

Schwarzkopf was again at the wheel for the journey to Hopewell through the failing light.

26

Dr. Condon had not made the trip from his home in the Bronx merely to stand with the staring crowd outside the Swayze funeral parlors. He was there because on Thursday evening, several hours after the appalling discovery, he had been summoned by the New Jersey State Police to the Lindbergh home, and on Friday, still in Hopewell, had gone to Trenton to see this next-to-the-last stage in the brief history of the child whose living body he had hoped to place in its mother's arms.

Colonel Schwarzkopf had summoned not only Dr. Condon but also John Hughes Curtis and Morris Rosner. He was anxious to act rapidly in advance of the criticism he felt sure would soon be directed at the fruitless State police efforts to arrest the kidnapers.

Following his announcement that the child had been found, he had recalled the reporters to hear another statment. "As long as there was a possibility of the baby's being alive," he had told them, "the police have been acting with a certain amount of suppressed activity in order not to interfere with any negotiations that might result in the baby's safe return. Now that the body of the baby has been found, every possible effort will be used to accomplish the arrest of the kidnapers and murderers."

To Colonel Schwarzkopf, every possible effort meant, to begin with, getting every bit of information from Condon, Curtis and Rosner regarding their dealings with the gang. It seemed obvious to the State police head and his detectives that the three men had been the victims of a gigantic hoax. For when Morris Rosner had told reporters on March 12 that he had definite knowledge that the Lindbergh baby was alive and would be returned to its parents, the child's body had been lying in its grave for days. Similar assurances had deceived Curtis and Dr. Condon.

Or *had* Dr. Condon been deceived? After all, it was he who, in a sense, had invited the extortion of the ransom money and then given the fifty thousand dollars to the gang. Why had he chosen the Bronx *Home News* to publish his letter offering his services as intermediary, why not one of the great metropolitan New York dailies? How was it that his letter, after appearing in a paper of such modest circulation, had been answered so promptly? Was it because he knew that the Bronx was the base of the gang's operations and that they read the *Home News?*

Why had he been so eager to risk not only his life savings but, in dealing with dangerous men, his life itself? Couldn't the answer be that he was tied in with the gang?

On the other hand, he had held out against paying the ransom money until he had seen and identified the baby. Also, he had saved Lindbergh twenty thousand dollars. But mightn't he have done that to remove suspicion from himself? Twenty thousand dollars wasn't too much to sacrifice to go scot-free. Perhaps the ransom money was buried in a spot known only to Dr. Condon, in St. Raymond's Cemetery or even in the garden of his home.

Curtis arrived first, just after midnight on the morning of Friday May 13. Lindbergh drove up soon afterward, and Curtis went forward to speak to him. He couldn't feel more shocked, he said; Lindbergh had his heartfelt sympathy. Everything the gang had told him had convinced him that the child was alive. Callously deceived, as Lindbergh and he and Dobson-Peacock and Burrage had been, it was only left for him to lend all the help he could in the pursuit, capture and conviction of the men who had perpetrated the murder and the hoax.

Lindbergh thanked him.

Captain John Lamb of the State police and Special Agent Frank Wilson of the Internal Revenue Service were waiting to interview Curtis; but first, in answer to his questions, Lamb described how the baby's body had been found and added that William Allen had been cleared of any suspicion of complicity.

Then Lamb questioned Curtis. The officer was mainly interested in the *Mary B. Moss;* what did she look like? Choosing his words carefully, since Lamb wasn't so familiar as he with marine terms, Curtis described the Gloucester fisherman from hull to mastheads. Lamb thanked him for his thoroughness; now, he said, the police could set out after the gang even though they were still somewhere at sea.

Wilson went to telephone the schooner's description to the Treasury Department. When he came back, he told Lamb and Curtis that the information would be passed on to the Coast Guard, whose cutters and amphibian planes would search the coastal waters from Yarmouth, Nova Scotia, to the Florida keys, with particular attention to the rendezvous area near Cape May.

Lamb returned to his questions. He would like Curtis to begin at the very beginning, the first dealings he had had with the Lindbergh kidnapers. Curtis nodded. He cast his thoughts back to the night he had described so often, when Sam had waylaid him.

By two o'clock in the morning, Curtis' throat was dry; he asked for a glass of orange juice. Continuing, he described his telephone calls to Hilda on Long Island. Wilson asked if he remembered the number. Yes, Curtis replied: Freeport 5630.

Morris Rosner and Dr. Condon arrived at the Lindbergh home within a few minutes of each other. They were shown to separate rooms and told how important it was for the police to have every possible scrap of information.

Rosner said he would describe from first to last his and Spitale's and Bitz' activities.

After the Lindberghs had appointed them to act as their intermediaries with the underworld, they had been shown the original ransom note and been given tracings of the symbol signature. The tracings had been extremely useful in the hundreds of contacts they had made. If asked to, he'd try to describe every one of those contacts, but he thought it would be a waste of time, since most of them had turned out to be cheap grifters, tinhorns, petty crooks, trying to chisel in. However, one had seemed to be on the level.

"From this contact, which we made shortly before March twelfth," Rosner went on, "we had every reason to believe that we were dealing with the kidnapers and that the baby was alive and safe." That was why he had given his March twelfth statement to the press. And he was still convinced that they had been dealing with the real gang; to prove they had stolen the child, the gang had submitted a symbol signature that was identical to the tracings the intermediaries had been given.

Rosner concluded his account. Would he be willing to repeat it to the Bronx grand jury, if Bronx District Attorney Charles B. McLoughlin thought it necessary? Certainly; he wished to do everything he could to bring the guilty to justice.

Dr. Condon began his story by saying that he had been wantonly abused and deceived, and, through him, so had the parents of the dead baby; his one desire was to help.

As the old man proceeded, he was repeatedly interrupted by questions; he welcomed them, though many seemed to suggest that he wasn't telling all he knew. Calmly he responded to the insinuations with the reminder that every step he had taken had been approved by Lindbergh and Breckinridge.

He did not tell his questioners—they did not ask—his own theory of how the baby had died.

Bitterly reflecting after the shock of the baby's death, Dr. Condon had recalled how the crib looked during his overnight stay in the nursery. The two large safety pins were thrust through the blankets and mattress on either side of the child's neck, directly above the shoulders, snugly securing the bedcovers under his chin. He couldn't have been pulled from the head of the crib without removing the pins, and both Anne Lindbergh and Betty Gow were positive that the pins had not been disturbed. Obviously, then, Dr. Condon reasoned, the baby had been pulled from the foot of the crib.

Why hadn't he cried? It would have been difficult if not impossible to keep a hand clasped firmly over his mouth while he was pulled from under the covers. There had to be a safer way, and Dr. Condon was sure he knew what it was. The child had been strangled *first,* or smothered, or struck so hard that his skull was fractured, *then* taken from the crib. It was a dead body that the kidnaper had carried through the window and down the ladder and across the muddy fields to its grave in a drift of rotting leaves.

Dr. Condon came to the end of his story. There were no more questions, but he was informed that he would have to repeat it the next day to District Attorney McLoughlin. Dr. Condon said he would be happy to.

For their part, the police did not tell Dr. Condon their tentative theory. Perhaps chloroform had been used to stifle the child's cries, and its heavy odor had escaped through the partly open French window in the fifty minutes or so that elapsed between the theft and its discovery—but in any event, the police thought it likely that the baby was alive when carried from the room.

He might very well have died shortly after, in which case the ladder probably had been the cause of his death. Using the same four kinds of wood, cut to the same dimensions and placed in the same positions, police carpenters had built exact duplicates of the forty-pound ladder the kidnapers had abandoned in their flight and had conducted some experiments beneath the southeast corner nursery window. During one of these a duplicate ladder had split—in exactly the same places the kidnapers' ladder had split—under the weight of an officer who was climbing down with a bundle to simulate the stolen child. He had been flung not outward but inward—into the whitewashed wall of the house. The thirty-three-inch, thirty-pound bundle (the baby's height and weight) had fallen heavily against the wall; its "skull" had collided sharply with a window sill.

Assuming it to be the actual child, possibly the impact killed him. Possibly not. Perhaps he survived the fall and the kidnaper, clutching the little boy, ran down to Featherbed Lane, where the gang's car was waiting. Then the car sped over the hill road along which William Allen was to drive his truck seventy-two days later. From the spot where Allen had parked, the Lindbergh house was visible across the small valley. That night, a half-hour or so after the kidnaper had fled from the partially darkened house, the gang saw that every room was streaming with light. It could only mean that the theft had been discovered, which in turn might well mean that every road in the area was blocked and every passing car searched by police. Which meant that their small prisoner must be hidden in their car so cleverly he would never be discovered—or he must be disposed of.

The second course had seemed safer.

Perhaps Charles Augustus Lindbergh, Jr., was already dead. If not, he died then. The shallow grave was dug in the woods and the body hastily buried. The kidnapers' car drove safely back to wherever it had come from.

So ran the State police theory.

John Hughes Curtis retired to the sofa reserved for him in the Lindberghs' library and, worn out, quickly fell asleep. He slept late into the morning. Rising, he ate an excellent breakfast. Then two State detectives came to him with a request: first, would he accompany them to Cape May and show them the spot on the coastal road where he had first met Hilda and Inez in the two-way-radio-equipped Ford sedan, then guide them to the cottage where, on May 10, he had talked with Inez?

Certainly, Curtis said.

They drove to the Cape May road. But more than three weeks had gone by since Curtis had first met Hilda and Inez, and it had been quite dark at the time. In addition, he had been preoccupied with thoughts of strategy. He did his best to point out the place, but he confessed it was difficult.

In the circumstances, one of the detectives assured him, it would require both an extraordinary memory and unusual eyesight to recognize the spot. But finding the cottage should be relatively easy, since Curtis had visited it only a few days ago.

When he tried, another difficulty arose. It hadn't occurred to Curtis before but, as they now saw, the cottages along the Cape May shore were all pretty much alike. The three men waded through the damp knee-deep grass, inspecting one bungalow after another. At last Curtis was forced to throw up his hands. For the life of him, he declared, he couldn't single out the cottage.

The next day, the fourteenth, he was asked to retell his whole story, since some police officers—a group headed by Inspector Harry W. Walsh of the Jersey City police—had heard it only at second hand. Curtis obliged. A police stenographer recorded his words.

When he had finished, Curtis asked if the police could do without his assistance for the short time it would take him to visit his family and dispose of some business papers in his office. Inspector Walsh talked it over with his associates. He told Curtis that, reasonable though his request was, and much as they—family men themselves—would like to grant it, the fact was that the whole case against the *Mary B. Moss* gang rested on him, and the police couldn't take any chances with his safety. Who knew better than the gang that only Curtis could identify them? No; he must bear with the authorities for a while longer and stay where he was. But Walsh would send an officer to get the business papers, so at least Curtis would have that off his mind.

The dismal weather of the long search vanished in brilliant sunshine on Sunday May 15. At sea, Coast Guard cutters, Navy destroyers and aircraft widened their quest for the *Mary B. Moss.*

At Hopewell, Colonel Breckinridge had some unpleasant information he felt it his duty to give Lindbergh.

It seemed that for some time Dr. Condon had been subjected to a steady stream of hate mail. One letter had informed him that he would find enclosed in the envelope an authentic likeness of the kidnaper known as John. A small mirror fell out. And he and Mrs. Condon had received so many crackpot and threatening phone calls, often with the charges reversed, that in mid-April he had arranged for his number to be changed from Sedgwick 3–7154 to a private listing, Sedgwick 3–1177.

Breckinridge said that Dr. Condon warranted better treatment. Lindbergh agreed; the same Sunday, he wrote to the old man:

> My dear Dr. Condon:
>
> Mrs. Lindbergh and I want to thank you for the great assistance you have been to us. We fully realize that you have devoted the major portion of your time and energy to bring about the return of our son. We wish to express to you our sincere appreciation for your courage and cooperation.
>
> Sincerely,
>
> Charles A. Lindbergh

He gave copies of the letter to reporters for publication.

Sunday had been a peaceful day for John Hughes Curtis. He had wandered around the grounds (a police officer, of course, was always within sight, evidence of Inspector Walsh's concern for his safety), listened to radio reports of the continuing search for the *Mary B. Moss,* read the newspapers, played a game of checkers.

But on Monday, the sixteenth, he was again asked to help out. Curtis had described each member of the kidnap gang in such detail that it was evident he had used his eyes well. Perhaps he would be able to pick out from a rogues' gallery the photos of two or three or maybe even all of the gang.

At police headquarters in Newark, Curtis carefully inspected picture after picture in the rogues' gallery file. But though it seemed likely that at least some of the gang had criminal records, apparently they'd managed to stay clear of police photographers.

Then Curtis paused and pointed to a picture he had turned up. It looked like one of the kidnapers.

The detectives studied the man's history; he was a bad sort, allright, but for many months he had been an inmate of the New Jersey State Hospital for the Insane in Morris Plains, where he was to this day.

There remained the hope of locating the house in Newark where, early in April, Curtis had said, he had talked with Morrie Truesdale (alias Sam), Olaf Larsen (alias Dynamite) and John and had been incensed by the calm admission that they had planned from the beginning to collect two ransom payments. Some six weeks had passed and he couldn't remember the address, but Curtis thought he recalled the route he had been told to take to the house, and certainly he'd recognize the place if he saw it.

The detectives and Curtis drove through the busy Newark streets. The car stopped, turned, retraced its course, turned again as Curtis peered from the window. Time and again they twisted and circled, following his directions. The afternoon wore on. At last he shook his head. Too much time had passed, he said disconsolately, and now he was thoroughly confused. He didn't know how to reach the house.

They drove back to Hopewell.

During the evening, Curtis listened to a radio news broadcast which reported among other things that the Coast Guard was still searching for the *Mary B. Moss,* then he walked restlessly around the house. Everyone seemed to avoid him this evening; no one was willing to join him in a quiet game of checkers. He went to his sofa in the library but found he didn't feel like going to sleep, returned to the living room, took another turn around the house.

Just before midnight, a familiar and friendly face appeared. Inspector Harry Walsh had been busy on a police errand in the neighborhood and had thought he would drop by. Curtis greeted him gratefully and proposed a game of checkers. Walsh said all right, fine. In better spirits, Curtis brought out the checkerboard and the two men sat down.

As they played, the inspector inquired about Mrs. Curtis and the two children—how were they? Curtis had telephoned his wife that afternoon to ask how she was feeling. She was still not at all herself, he told Walsh, and it worried him. The children had asked him when he was coming home. They were all very close, and he missed them sorely.

Troubled by his thoughts, his mind strayed from the checker game. Walsh suggested that they step outside for a breath of air.

In the courtyard, in the cool spring night, Curtis spoke again about his wife. Surely the two of them had had more than their share of hard times! Only last spring his Gas Engine and Boat Company, of which he had been very proud, had gone bankrupt with liabilities of three hundred sixty-five thousand dollars, and he had had a breakdown. If it hadn't been for his wife's help and understanding, he didn't know what might have happened.

Walsh nodded sympathetically. He could understand, he said, what a great weight Curtis must have on his mind at this time.

There was a pause.

Wouldn't it be a relief, Walsh went on, if Curtis got rid of some of it?

How could he do that? Curtis asked.

Well, Walsh replied, he'd feel a lot better if he told the *real* story of his activities in the Lindbergh case. "If you haven't told the truth," he said, "why don't you go in and tell it now?"

But, Curtis protested, he *had* told the truth!

Walsh looked off, as if he hadn't listened, then said that so many puzzling things had turned up that it was hard for anyone to believe he had told the real story.

"The smartest thing you can do," Walsh advised in his friendly manner, "is to tell Colonel Lindbergh the truth."

Curtis said nothing. They stood for a moment in silence.

The inspector remarked how pleasant and peaceful the night was. But it was getting late. An hour had passed since he had come by and he would have to be getting along. No doubt Curtis was tired. After all, he had had a long day.

Walsh moved as if to leave.

Then Curtis spoke.

"The only thing I told him that isn't true," he said, "is that I saw the ransom money."

Walsh considered this. "Why not go in and tell Colonel Lindbergh?" he suggested. "That's the thing that convinced him you really were in contact with the kidnapers."

Curtis hesitated, then nodded. They returned to the house and Walsh sent word to Lindbergh that he would like to see him. In a few minutes the young man joined them, and the three went into the dining room.

In a strained voice, Curtis told Lindbergh that he had lied when, on two occasions, he said he had seen and checked the serial numbers of some of the ransom bills. He had felt compelled to deceive Lindbergh in order to convince him of the desperate need for speed in dealing with the gang.

Lindbergh looked at Curtis wordlessly; then, with a gesture of disgust, he stood up and walked quickly from the room.

Walsh sent for another officer, Lieutenant Arthur Keaton of the State police, and a police stenographer. Curtis repeated his statement: It was not true that he had seen and handled some of the Lindbergh ransom money; however, in every other respect he had told the truth.

The stenographer asked if that was all. Curtis nodded.

"Why don't you be open and honest about the whole affair?" Walsh said.

He had been, Curtis insisted, he had been! He had lied only in that one little detail!

The stenographer left the room. Walsh said that perhaps they had better go over the whole story still another time.

Once more Curtis described his encounter with Sam, once more told how he had sought the help of Dean Dobson-Peacock and Admiral Burrage. After two hours Walsh decided that the session had lasted long enough; Curtis hadn't said a single thing that was new. He stood up, interrupting the long recital. "Why not have it off your mind?" he said in a tired voice. "I'm going to bed."

As he started to leave with Keaton, Curtis bounded from his chair so abruptly that it banged against the wall. "All right, I'll make a statement!" he cried. "Get me a typewriter! I'll make a statement and sign it!"

Keaton brought a typewriter and some paper. Curtis inserted a sheet and sat thinking, and Walsh told him that since he was making a voluntary statement, he must say so.

Curtis began to type. There were few pauses. The paper read:

> Statement of John Hughes Curtis, 702 Redgate Avenue, Norfolk, Va. Made by my own hand and own free will. Referring to the two statements made previously by me in regards to the Linbergh Case.
>
> At the present time I am sane, but I honestly believe that for the last seven or eight months I have not been myself, due to financial troubles.
>
> I was apparently brought back to my senses by my telephone conversation with my wife this afternoon when she told me of the troubles she was having and how the children missed me, also by my conversation with Inspector Harry W. Walsh.
>
> I desire to state that my remarks about the newspapers are true and can be verified, this is in reference to my story about Mr. Haskell and Mr. Willcox of the Herald Tribune, Mr. Lee of the News and Mr. Turin and Fox, offering me money of my knowledge of the Linbergh Case or pictures of the baby.
>
> The matter was brought to my attention during a conversation and due to what I now believe was a distorted mind by brooding over it, I became insane on the subject for the time being, which caused me to create the story in its entirety., which were untrue in every respect
>
> I never knew such people that I named to Colonel Linbergh and they were creatures of a distorted mind, with the exception of Morrie Truesdale, who had no connection with the crime.
>
> I exceedingly regret that I caused Colonel Linbergh and others any inconvenience and wish it were in my power to correct my wrong.
>
> In justice to my wife and two children I trust that it is in the

> power of Colonel Linbergh to forgive the inconvenience, worry and injustice I did him in his time of grief.
>
> This statement has been brought about by the realization of the wrong I have done.

Curtis signed his full name to the paper; underneath the word *Witness* in the lower left-hand corner the two officers signed theirs, prefaced by their ranks. Walsh added the time: 4:35 A.M., May 17, 1932. Then he took Curtis to the library sofa that was his bed. He felt sorry for him, Walsh said, and even sorrier for his wife and children; but in his opinion, no matter how severely Curtis was punished it would be small payment for the cruelties he had inflicted on Charles and Anne Lindbergh.

Curtis' shoulders slumped; tears came to his eyes and rolled down his ruddy cheeks. Walsh left him.

Late in the afternoon of May 17, Colonel Schwarzkopf called a press conference. Curtis sat with lowered head as Schwarzkopf read the confession. The reporters found it hard to believe. The *Mary B. Moss,* that sturdy schooner—Dynamite and John and the others—Hilda and Inez and the old Ford equipped with the powerful radio—all a fake? They tried to question Curtis, but Schwarzkopf intervened. Curtis, he said, had made another statement, which he would now read.

The second typescript said flatly that the Very Reverend Dean H. Dobson-Peacock had so relished the prestige and publicity he had received as one of the negotiating committee in the Lindbergh case that he had not only encouraged Curtis but had stood in the way of his attempt to end the fraud three days after Admiral Burrage had written to Lindbergh on March 15. Up to that time, nothing had been heard from Lindbergh and Curtis had said that he wished to drop the whole affair. But Dobson-Peacock had strongly disagreed, and his opinion had prevailed.

Schwarzkopf continued with Curtis' statement:

> Many of the stories that appeared in the newspapers were manufactured by Dobson-Peacock and were untrue, and he had knowledge of their untruthfulness at the time he released them for publication. I know from my own experience with the Dean that the only interest he had throughout this matter was one of satisfying his desires for publicity, and the more he got, the better he liked it. . . . I became annoyed and went to Admiral Burrage about it, and it was agreed that in the future the Admiral would handle the publicity and nothing but

the real facts as delivered by me would be released for publication.

Putting the two typescripts away, Schwarzkopf told the reporters that he would like to say a few words of his own. In a telephone call to Norfolk several hours earlier, he had asked Dobson-Peacock to come to Hopewell today. The dean had declined; moreover, he had said that he doubted it would be possible for him to leave Norfolk and come to Hopewell at any future date. Two telegrams sent to him had been ignored. It all demonstrated, Schwarzkopf said, that although he was deeply involved in the case, Dobson-Peacock was unwilling to help the police set the facts straight; and, unfortunately, so long as he stayed clear of New Jersey, nothing could be done about it.

In Norfolk, during the evening of May 17, reporters told Constance Curtis of her husband's confession. Shocked and frightened, she was put to bed under a doctor's care. Admiral Burrage, when informed, said sharply: "I will not make any statement now and I do not expect to make any in the future."

Dean Dobson-Peacock was far more responsive; he couldn't believe, he said, that John Hughes Curtis had simply invented the gang and his dealings with them. He went on: "I knew he had a nervous breakdown some time ago and has been under a terrible strain during the past few weeks. I did not know, however, that he had been laboring under a hallucination regarding his negotiations for the recovery of the baby. I can't believe he made a statement declaring it all a fake." As for Curtis' charge that he might have cut short the hoax, the dean said indignantly:

"I don't know what he is talking about. He told Admiral Burrage and myself he would not go into the case at all unless he could get our cooperation. We freely gave our assistance, hoping to have the pleasure of returning the stolen baby to its parents. We were in accord at all times. I cannot understand how he could have done such a thing. It just seems impossible."

But wasn't it true, a reporter persisted, that the dean was flattered by the attention he was getting and would have been satisfied just with the publicity? Dobson-Peacock's tone grew sharper. No publicity of any kind, he pointed out, had come to the negotiators until March 24, after they had returned to Norfolk from the visit to Lindbergh's home. That was when the reporters had first interviewed him. And that was nine days after the time Curtis had said he was inclined to give up the whole thing. In view of those facts, how could anyone charge that he was a publicity-seeker?

Finally, although he refused to go to Hopewell, he would be glad to talk to anyone the New Jersey police cared to send to him.

In New York, Richard Lee of the New York *Daily News* and Grafton Wilcox of the *Herald Tribune* denied the implication in Curtis' statement that by offering to buy his account of the case they had induced him to prolong the fraud. They had signed no contract, and their verbal understanding was that no payment would be made until Curtis had handed over the Lindbergh child to its parents—a condition Curtis had known he could not carry out.

William Haskell of the *Herald Tribune* added that Curtis' imagination had been prodigal. He had said that while they were aboard the *Marcon* the searchers had sighted the *Mary B. Moss* but were unable to approach her because of the high sea; and, staring across the waves at the craft on which his son was held, Lindbergh had tried to leap overboard and swim to it. Curtis said they had been forced to hold him back.

Charged with having knowingly and wilfully given false and untrue reports of the person or persons guilty of the crimes of kidnaping and murder, for the purpose of hindering the apprehension of those persons, John Hughes Curtis was placed under arrest. Bail was fixed at ten thousand dollars. Since it wasn't forthcoming, he was taken to the Hunterdon County jail in Flemington, New Jersey.

There, on Friday, May 20, he sat in his cell, waiting for trial.

In the grand jury room of the Bronx Supreme Court building, Dr. Condon described to the Bronx County grand jury his experiences since the night he had volunteered to serve as intermediary in the Lindbergh case. His manner was that of a teacher addressing his pupils, and he drove home his points by chalking on a blackboard helpful diagrams and words John had mispronounced.

Later that afternoon, a young American woman with close-cropped blonde hair and a confident grin climbed into a monoplane at Harbor Grace, Newfoundland. She took off at ten to six.

Fourteen hours and fifty-six minutes later the monoplane landed in a pasture near Londonderry, in Northern Ireland, and the pilot stepped out. Yes, Amelia Earhart Putnam told the press, she was happy to be the first woman to have flown the Atlantic alone, and especially pleased that she had done it in the fastest time yet—but she wished her fuel had held out long enough to carry her to Paris.

Exactly five years before, she reminded her interviewers, Charles Augustus Lindbergh had landed the *Spirit of St. Louis* in Paris, and she felt that on this twenty-first day of May, the anniversary of his historic arrival, it would have been a small tribute to the Lone Eagle if she too had made it to Le Bourget.

Part Two

THE CAPTURE

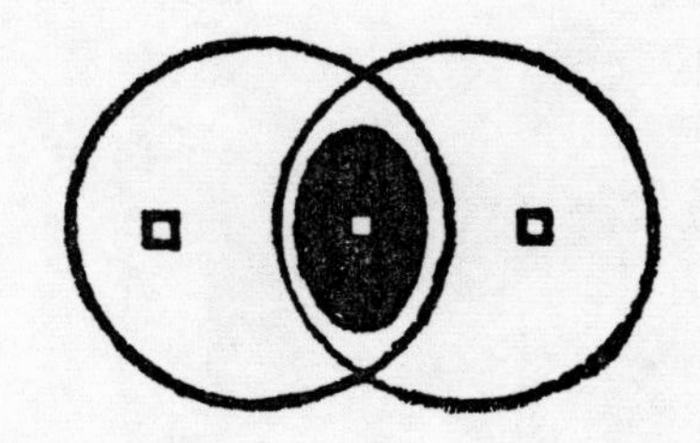

1

Colonel H. Norman Schwarzkopf was not a police officer in the usual sense; he had never patroled a beat, served as a detective, or specialized in the strategy of running down criminals. But as his exemplary military history proved, he was a man well equipped to command.

A 1917 graduate of the United States Military Academy, Lieutenant Schwarzkopf had won his captain's bars after three months of active service as an artillery officer in the World War. In 1921, when he was twenty-six, he had been selected over older and more experienced men to take charge of the newly formed New Jersey State Police. Under his guidance the unit had grown into a semi-military elite corps, clad in campaign hats and smart horizon-blue uniforms with flaring yellow-striped riding breeches.

At thirty-seven, well liked and securely established in his third five-year term of office, Colonel Schwarzkopf had seemed to be above reproach. The kidnaping and haphazard discovery of the body of Charles Augustus Lindbergh, Jr., swept away this apparent immunity; harsh critics attacked his handling of the case. Admittedly he had been inhibited by Charles Lindbergh's fear for his son's life, and his officers had had to proceed with the utmost caution, but in the face of all that had occurred was there any reason to believe that they could solve the crime even if given their head?

Schwarzkopf's critics thought not. They suggested that the State police, though admirably suited to preserve everyday law and order, were incapable of coping with such a major case; that they were insufficiently trained in modern detection techniques; that more money had gone into uniforms than laboratory equipment; and that the temperament of the corps, thanks to Schwarzkopf's zealous tutelage, was hostile to the spirit of cooperation that must obtain if the kidnapers and murderers were to be brought to justice.

The critics enlarged upon the charge of noncooperation. They recalled that within four days after the kidnaping representatives of the federal government had gone to the Lindbergh home and offered every assistance it was in their power to give. Since kidnaping was not a national offense, federal investigators were not completely free to act; but no law stood in the way of their providing advice and technical help. Apparently neither had been wanted. Their suggestions had been received politely; no use had been made of their scientific equipment. Although federal agents had stayed close to the scene of the crime, they had been little more than unofficial observers, barely informed by the State police of developments in the case.

Detective Sergeant James J. Finn of the New York City police had met similar indifference. True, Lindbergh had telephoned Police Commissioner Edward P. Mulrooney in the early morning hours after the kidnaping and asked to borrow Finn for the case (in the tumultuous reception New York had given the Lone Eagle after his return from Paris, Finn had been one of his guards and Lindbergh had admired his efficiency) and, welcoming him to Hopewell, had told Finn to do everything he could, go as far as he liked. But neither these instructions nor the New York City postmarks on the ransom-note envelopes, indicating that the kidnaping was at least partly a New York police affair, had made the New Jersey detectives more communicative, and Finn had left with the observation that he could learn as much about the case by reading the newspapers.

Early in the morning of Friday May 13, the day after the child's body had been discovered in the Jersey woods, President Herbert Hoover had announced:

"I have directed the law-enforcement agencies and the several Secret Services of the Federal Government to make the kidnaping and murder of the Lindbergh baby a live and never-to-be-forgotten case, never to be relaxed until the criminals are implacably brought to justice. The Federal Government does not have police authority in such cases, but its agencies will be unceasingly alert to assist the New Jersey police in every possible way until this end has been accomplished."

The agencies named by the Chief Executive included the Division of Investigation of the Department of Justice, the Secret Service of the United States Treasury, the espionage and police arms of the Coast Guard, the Bureau of Narcotics, the intelligence unit of the

Bureau of Internal Revenue, the Bureau of Prohibition, the Postal Inspection Service, and the Bureau of Customs.

The President had instructed the Attorney General of the United States to inform Governor A. Harry Moore of New Jersey that this great array lay at his disposal. Realizing that a confusion of talents might result when so many were offered, the attorney general had added a suggestion in his letter to the governor: a coordinator of tested ability was available in the person of J. Edgar Hoover, director of the Justice Department's Division of Investigation.

The response had been disappointing. Though there was now no reason to restrict the search for fear of jeopardizing the Lindbergh baby's safety and an army of government agents stood ready to help, the New Jersey police still seemed reluctant to share their secrets: the clues, evidence and statements by "witnesses" gathered so far.

But the great federal machine could not stand idle. One witness, at least, was not controlled by the New Jersey police, and federal agents and New York City detectives had begun to act on his information: Dr. Condon's description of John. And there were the clues supplied by the ransom bills. *John* undoubtedly was a false name; Dr. Condon, despite his trained mind and schoolteacher's eye, might have erred in his description—but the ransom bills were real.

Dr. Condon had paid the ransom on Saturday April 2. A week later an alert teller had discovered one of the bills, a twenty-dollar note, in the 96th Street and Amsterdam branch of the East River Savings Bank in Manhattan. The bill had been deposited on Monday April 4 to the account of David Marcus. Unable to trace the bill's history, Mr. Marcus had quickly proved himself to be above suspicion.

David Marcus' twenty-dollar bill had been the first of a cautious trickle, seeping one at a time into shops, stores and banks, invariably in the smaller denominations: ten- and five-dollar notes. As each was discovered and reported, the lead was promptly pursued.

Frank Wilson, head of the intelligence unit of the Internal Revenue Bureau, continued to represent the Treasury's interest in the case, assisted by special agents Arthur Madden and Pat O'Rourke. Led by Thomas H. Sisk, special agents of the Justice Department's Division of Investigation also engaged in the hunt (still other Justice agents were probing the whereabouts of the elusive figure known to the underworld, according to Gaston Means, as "The Fox"). And at New York City police headquarters, James Finn, promoted from sergeant to acting lieutenant, directed twenty-three of the department's ablest detectives in a daily search for suspects.

Charles Augustus Lindbergh, Jr., was dead and the early bungling of the case could never be repaired; but now other, more experienced hands would bring it to a speedy and successful close.

So, at least, special agents Wilson and Sisk and Lieutenant Finn were resolved.

2

Colonel Schwarzkopf answered his critics sharply: their charges of bungling and mishandling simply were not true.

Thirty New Jersey detectives and troopers, supervised by Captain John Lamb and Inspector Harry Walsh, had devoted thousands of hours to a round-up of clues and questioning of possible suspects and witnesses. They had examined the thirty-two Lindbergh and Morrow household servants and their relatives, friends and acquaintances. Each one had had to furnish a record of his activities during the year before the kidnaping. The architects, bricklayers, carpenters, plumbers—the whole construction crew that had built the Lindberghs' new home had been questioned. Major Charles Schoeffel, deputy commander of the State police, had gone to England to enlist Scotland Yard's help in an investigation of the background and past associations of Betty Gow and the Whateleys. The stories told by eyewitnesses—or people whose experiences shortly before the kidnaping seemed to bear out the known facts—had been recorded and dovetailed and checked.

Still, the criticism stung. And so, at his headquarters in Trenton, with Lamb and Walsh, Schwarzkopf once again reviewed the history of their investigation; once again went over the stories told by various people who had been near the scene of the crime just before March 1.

A few of these accounts seemed particularly promising.

It was early one evening in mid-February that Millard Whited first saw the stranger. Whited was driving to his farmhouse over the dirt road that bordered the Lindbergh estate, about a mile away from the new house itself, after a day of logging. His supper was waiting and he was hungry; still, he slowed the old truck as the stranger came into view—strangers were a rarity in the Sourlands.

The stranger was standing at the side of the rode. He glanced incuriously at Whited; Whited stared back. The stranger didn't call out or gesture to ask for a lift; he just stood there while Whited's dilapidated truck creaked past.

A week later, he was driving from Hopewell along another back road when he came to the crossroad leading to the hamlet of Zion, a mile and a half from the gate to the Lindbergh place. A man walked out from the patchy undergrowth, started across the road and stopped and peered at Whited. It was the same stranger. This time, Millard Whited made a point of noting his clothes. The stranger wore a gray felt hat tipped forward a little and a gray suit. He was carrying an overcoat. Whited seemed to catch a flicker of surprise on his face—perhaps he recognized the old truck and its driver—then the face became impassive again.

Whited drove on. There was something on that man's mind, he told himself.

Shortly before noon on March 1, old Amandus Hochmuth was taking the air and waiting for entertainment in front of his house. The source of the entertainment he hoped for was the nearby intersection of the Mercer County highway and the lane leading to Charles and Anne Lindbergh's new home. The turn from the highway into the lane seemed easy; many drivers attempted it without sufficiently slackening their speed and landed in the roadside ditch.

The small disasters—nobody was ever seriously hurt—delighted Amandus Hochmuth. For a good number of his eighty-four years he had watched the intersection. He could remember one week when no fewer than seven cars had plunged into the ditch! Of course you could hardly expect a fine week like that to come along more than once or twice in a lifetime.

Mr. Hochmuth's hopes rose with the hum of an approaching car. A rather dirty green sedan, it was coming from Hopewell, traveling at a pretty good clip, forty-five miles an hour or so. Sure enough, the driver seemed to be aiming for the sharp, deceptive turn. Mr. Hochmuth adjusted his glasses. Almost certainly this was one for the ditch! But no; at the last second the driver slammed on his brakes and the dirty green sedan screeched to a halt at the very edge of the ditch. The driver glared at Amandus Hochmuth, who had to smile at the man's sudden loss of dignity.

The car had stalled. As the driver tried to start it, Mr. Hochmuth began to walk toward him. He noticed that there was a ladder in the car, jostled into an awkward position by the abrupt stop. The driver adjusted the ladder. Then the engine caught and the green sedan hurried away.

Amandus Hochmuth remembered the car, the angry driver, the ladder. The next day the State troopers came around asking questions, and he told them the story.

Young Ben Lupica lived with his parents in Hopewell and attended Princeton Preparatory School. Driving home after his classes on the afternoon of March 1, he paused as usual at the family's

Rural Free Delivery mailbox, which was quite near the Lindbergh gatehouse. After he picked up the letters, Ben drove a little way along the narrow road and parked at the side to read his mail.

As he read, he heard a car coming toward him. Traffic was sparse here; Ben glanced up. It was a dark blue or black sedan, a Dodge, a '28 or maybe '29 model, with Jersey plates. Its course was eccentric. Approaching at a fast pace, it swerved in front of Ben, then pulled up with a jerk and stopped on the wrong side of the road at the top of a short track that led to a cornfield.

The driver seemed to be in his middle thirties. His face was thin, sharp-featured, and he wore a dark felt hat and a dark overcoat. Ben started his car and drove past the other. Glancing at it to make sure he had enough clearance, he noticed that there were two sections of a ladder resting on the top of the front seat beside the driver and reaching from the windshield to the rear window of the sedan.

A few days later, when State troopers showed him the ladder sections that had been found near the Lindbergh house, Ben said he couldn't be sure but they might be the sections he had seen.

But if this man and Amandus Hochmuth's angry driver and Millard Whited's stranger were members of the kidnap gang, the prime question remained: how could they have known that Anne Lindbergh and the baby would be in the new Hopewell place on the night of March 1, a Tuesday, contrary to the family's habit of spending weekdays in the Morrow mansion in Englewood? And known the location of the baby's nursery and that the shutters of the southeast corner nursery window were so badly warped they couldn't be latched? Finally, how could they have known precisely when to time the job—between eight o'clock, when the baby fell asleep and Betty Gow left him, and about half past nine, when the Lindberghs went to their bedroom suite that connected with the nursery, and Anne, not feeling too well, decided to go to bed?

Schwarzkopf, Lamb and Walsh felt sure that the answer was obvious: the gang had had inside help.

It would seem that the theft had been planned well in advance, in which case the kidnapers probably had conspired with one or more of the servants to steal the child on a week end. But Betty Gow had learned before noon of Tuesday, March 1 (and undoubtedly Oliver and Elsie Whateley had learned even earlier) that Anne Lindbergh and her son would be in the Hopewell house that night—plenty of time to inform the kidnapers of the extended stay and for the gang to take advantage of it.

Of course it was possible that the information hadn't gone

straight to the gang; that the three servants, one or all of them, had acted unwittingly—they might have mentioned the news to someone who had passed it on to the kidnapers.

Considering this, Schwarzkopf and Lamb and Walsh thought they had better have another look at Henry Johnson's story. For Red Johnson was Betty Gow's boy friend, and at around half past eight on the night of March 1 Betty had told him that the little boy had come down with a cold and she was at the Hopewell place to help take care of him. Red was familiar with the layout of the Lindberghs' house; he had been inside it three times while visiting Betty, the third time just two weeks before the kidnaping.

On the whole, questioning Henry Johnson had been rather pleasant, Lamb and Walsh recalled; he was a likable fellow. A twenty-six-year-old Norwegian with thick reddish hair, he had spent the previous spring and summer and early fall as a deck hand on the Thomas Lamont yacht *Reynard*. He had been told to rejoin the yacht on March 1, but before that Tuesday came along the date had been changed to March 15.

When he wasn't on the water, Red had shared a room in a boarding house in Englewood, not too far from Betty Gow and their friends of the Morrow domestic staff.

What had he said about his activities on the night of March 1? Schwarzkopf and his two aides turned to Henry Johnson's statement.

Early Tuesday evening, Red drove toward the Morrow estate in his green Chrysler coupé. He had a date with Betty Gow. He had had a date with her the previous night and the night before that, but this would be a bit different—a double-date with Johansen Junge and his wife Marguerite, a seamstress on the Morrow staff.

On the way, Red picked up Johansen and they tried to decide the best way to spend the evening, finally agreeing to leave the decision to the women. But when they arrived at the Morrow mansion, only Marguerite was there. She explained that Betty had telephoned Red's boarding house that morning but had missed him. Their date would have to be postponed; the Lindbergh baby had a cold and Mrs. Lindbergh had asked Betty to come to Hopewell to help look after him.

Red thought he had better call Betty. He waited until the night telephone rates went into effect and called from a drugstore in Englewood. The baby was better, Betty said, but even so they were staying over—at least for the night, perhaps longer. Well, Red said, maybe in the morning he'd drive up to Hartford, Connecticut, to visit his brother John; maybe by the time he returned Betty would be back in Englewood.

He rejoined the Junges and suggested a spin around the town in his car. Two hours or so later, he said good night to them and drove back to the boarding house on James Street. Heimo Hatsu, his roommate, was already in bed. They exchanged a few words and Red turned in.

The next morning, Wednesday March 2, Johnson rose early and set out again in his coupé. He stopped for breakfast at the Grand Restaurant on Palisades Avenue in Englewood. The waitress told him the news: the little Lindbergh boy had been kidnaped! Red couldn't believe it. "Why," he said, "I was talking with the baby's nurse last night and she said the baby was all right!"

After breakfast, he drove to a grocery store opposite Englewood's police headquarters. As usual, he took an empty milk bottle with him. Red was fond of milk; he liked to say that he was on a milk diet. He had made a habit of buying it here and, at the same time, turning in the empty bottle, which saved the small but in the long run considerable extra expense of the two-cent deposit on every new quart. Then he set off for his brother's house.

On the highway leading out of the Fordham district of the Bronx, a hitchhiker hailed the coupé. Red stopped and invited him to hop in. They introduced themselves: the other was John Fernnino, a day laborer, bound for his home in Southport, Connecticut.

Red spoke of the Lindbergh kidnaping, at such length that Fernnino remarked he seemed to know a great deal about the baby. Red explained that the little boy's nursemaid was a particular friend. With an ease born of habit, he uncapped his milk bottle and drank from it as he drove; he was on a milk diet, he told Fernnino. Finishing the quart, he tossed the bottle behind the seat, to be returned when he bought a fresh one.

In Bridgeport, Fernnino thanked Red for the lift and said good-by. Red drove on. At about half past one he arrived at his brother's house in West Hartford. He was still there when on Friday, March 4, Hartford police officers took him into custody. They had been notified by phone where to find him by New Jersey detectives who had questioned Betty Gow and learned about Red.

They peered into his car and fished out the empty milk bottle. All right, they asked, where had he hidden the baby? Red smilingly explained that he knew nothing about the stolen child; *he* drank milk—he was on a milk diet!

At Hartford police headquarters, Captain Henry Gauthier of the Jersey City detective squad had questioned him closely; Gauthier had been sent to get the truth from Red and he meant to do it.

Red told him the same story he had earlier told the Hartford police. Ordered to tell it again, he did, without a single discrepancy. He told it still again without change after Gauthier escorted him back to New Jersey and turned him over to the State police.

The story stood up—as Schwarzkopf, Lamb and Walsh had to admit. If Red had been an agent or an informant in the kidnap plot, it would seem that he had been unaware of his role. He was still in custody, handy for questioning in the light of future developments; this wasn't due to any connection with the Lindbergh case but to his admitted guilt in illegally entering the United States. Immigration officials, not the State police, now held Red.

If he had been anything but evasive, that couldn't be said of Violet Sharpe, a young serving maid on the Morrow domestic staff. Back in their own headquarters, the State police barracks in Alpine, Lamb and Walsh reviewed their experiences with Miss Sharpe.

Violet was English, twenty-eight years old, pretty, slightly plump, not at all the retiring kind, a bit temperamental on occasion but never uppish. In the two years she had been with the Morrows, Mrs. Morrow had had no reason to find fault with her. She had been hired directly after her arrival in New York from Toronto, where she had worked for six months. Her sister Emily was a maid in the Englewood home of Constance Chilton, co-owner with Elisabeth Morrow—Anne Lindbergh's sister—of a children's school.

Everyone on the staff at Next Day Hill liked Violet; in the case of the butler Septimus Banks, it had grown into a warmer interest. The other Morrow servants thought that Banks would soon overcome the hesitations of a middle-aged bachelor and pop the question.

Dignified, reserved, a model butler, Septimus Banks had served the Morrows for years; he had no visible flaws, although he could, if pressed, lead the way to a New York speakeasy or two that had known his custom.

On March 10, it had been Violet's turn to be questioned. Pursuing the usual routine, a State police car drove her from Englewood to the Lindbergh house for questioning by one group of detectives while another group, in her absence and without her knowledge, examined her room in the Morrow servant quarters.

The searchers had turned up various odds and ends: the names and addresses of several friends; a half-dozen business cards of a cab service called the Post Road Taxi Company in White Plains, New York; letters from her father and mother in the village of Beenham, England; a few books, including *The World's 100 Best Detective Stories* and *Murder on Broadway;* and a New York savings-account bankbook. Violet's salary as a member of the Morrow household was a hundred dollars a month, yet in the comparatively short time she had worked there her nest egg had grown to sixteen hundred; somehow or other she had managed, also, to send money regularly to her parents. Of course, she lived in and her expenses were low.

Violet had written a note to herself: *Banks promises to try and be straight for twelve months.*

Did *try and be straight* refer to that very slight spot on the butler's otherwise irreproachable person, his occasional visits to speakeasies?

At the Lindbergh house, Violet's questioners had been a good deal less successful. Her personal affairs, she had informed the detectives, were her own business. Patiently, they had explained that they merely wanted to know where she was and what she did on the day of the kidnaping, March 1. Finally, with occasional tart comments on people who poked their long noses where they weren't wanted, Violet had told them.

Anne Lindbergh had telephoned from Hopewell at about half past eleven in the morning and Violet had answered the Morrow phone. Mrs. Lindbergh had asked for Betty Gow and Violet had called her; later, Betty had told her that the baby had a slight cold and that she was going to Hopewell to help look after him.

At around a quarter to eight in the evening, a friend of Violet's—well, not really a friend; it would be more exact to call him an acquaintance—had telephoned and asked her to go to a movie with him. Violet had accepted, adding that she wasn't quite finished serving the Morrows' dinner but she was sure she could be ready by eight-thirty.

At eight-thirty on the dot, Violet said, her acquaintance had come up the back driveway to the pantry door. They had walked to his car, some distance off. A young man and a young woman were in the back seat; her acquaintance had introduced them. They had gone to the Englewood Theater and, after the movie, had driven directly back to Next Day Hill. That had been at a little before eleven. Her acquaintance had seen her to the servants' entrance and they had said good night.

Violet hadn't seen him since. She hadn't seen the young couple, either.

Here Violet's memory, balky at best, had failed completely.

Her acquaintance's name?

She couldn't remember.

The names of the couple?

That too escaped her.

The name of the movie they had seen?

She was unable to say.

Well, what had it been *about?*

She couldn't recall any of it.

The detectives had kept on: Where had she first met the acquaintance who had invited her to the movie?

Violet's memory had improved a bit. She had met him while out for a walk the previous Sunday.

The "previous Sunday" was two days before the kidnaping. That fact and the fact that Violet had learned on the morning of the kidnap day that the Lindberghs were staying over in Hopewell plus her evasiveness about the kidnap night—though little more than a week had gone by—had established her as a suspect in the case, and she had been put down for further questioning.

The many other matters demanding investigation had delayed it for more than a month.

Inspector Walsh had taken charge of the second questioning. It had occurred on April 13 in the Morrow home, where, Walsh thought, Violet might feel at ease—and more cooperative.

As if to justify this theory, her memory had taken a turn for the better. She hadn't been able to remember the movie, she said, because they hadn't gone to a movie at all. They had gone to a roadhouse, the Peanut Grill, "in one of the Oranges," maybe a half-hour's drive from Englewood.

A roadhouse, Walsh had pointed out, was a dubious place for such a respectable girl to visit, on such short notice, with three people who were little better than strangers.

Violet had flared up, defending her behavior; in doing so she had given the whole background of her outing on the kidnap night.

In the afternoon of the previous Sunday, she said, she and her sister Emily were strolling along Lydecker Street when a man waved from a passing green sedan. Violet thought he was one of her friends on the Morrow staff and so she returned his wave. The sedan had pulled over to the curb. As they came closer, Violet realized that she had made a mistake; she didn't know him.

He was young, twenty-three or so. Smiling, he had leaned out of the car. "I'm sorry," Violet said, "I thought I knew you."

"That's all right," he replied. "Where are you going?"

Down to the village, Violet answered—Englewood.

It so happened that the young man was going the same way and he offered the sisters a lift.

In the car, Violet and the young man had struck up an easy conversation, and pretty soon he had asked if she'd care to go to the movies the next evening. "No," Violet said, "I wouldn't care to." But she said it with a smile, and it was evident that the young man hadn't felt rebuffed. He had said he would phone and ask her out again and Violet had said O.K. Where could he call her? Violet gave him the Morrow number and told him to "ask for Violet."

On the following Tuesday evening around quarter to eight, as she had already explained, he had phoned and invited her to a movie. Accepting, she had instructed him to wait in his car at the same spot on Lydecker Street where they had met. But the young man didn't follow instructions: when Violet had glanced out of the pantry window at half past eight, there he was, walking toward the house from his car, which he had boldly parked in the driveway. His forwardness had annoyed Violet. Putting on her hat and coat, she had hurried out to meet him.

After she had been introduced to the young couple, they had driven to the Peanut Grill in Orangeburg, a small village in New York just across the state line. They had stayed there until about ten-thirty. Violet drank coffee; the others drank beer. They had danced and talked and had a nice time.

Back home, a few minutes before eleven, George Marshall, the Morrow night watchman, had admitted Violet to the estate; just after she entered the house Marguerite Junge had come in. Violet had teased her for being out so late. Not very long after that, the telephone had rung and Violet had answered it and heard the awful news that the baby was missing.

Having learned so much, Walsh had wished to learn more.

Who were the three people? Couldn't she remember their names?

She had been introduced to the young couple only by their first names, Violet had explained, and she simply couldn't remember them. But the name of the young man, she felt sure, was Ernie—not because she remembered it from the night of their date, for she honestly didn't, but because, a few days later, someone had called her to the phone and she had heard his voice—"This is Ernie speaking." He had asked her to meet him again the next Sunday, March 6. Violet had said all right. But there was a heavy rain on March 6 and she had decided to stay in. Ernie had called once more and again asked for a date but Violet had told him no, she was too busy.

And that, she told the inspector, had been the last of Ernie.

What did these three people look like?

Ernie, Violet said, was tall and thin, with fair hair and a fair complexion. The night she had seen him he was wearing a light gray hat, a dark gray overcoat and a navy-blue suit. The second young man was around Ernie's age; fair-haired too, but short. He wore a soft felt hat and a dark gray overcoat. The girl also was in the early twenties, a dark, pretty girl, medium height and build.

She wore a tiny black tam-o'-shanter hat and a navy-blue suit and black patent leather pumps.

How did they sound? How did they talk?

All three of them had sounded to Violet like native Americans.

Had anything struck her about the car, aside from its being a green sedan?

No, nothing, she replied. She couldn't give its make, couldn't be sure whether it had New York or New Jersey license plates.

"During the time you were in their company," Walsh concluded his questions, "was there any conversation concerning the Lindberghs or their baby?"

"Yes. The girl asked me, 'How is Lindy's baby?' "

"And what did you say?"

All she had told the girl, Violet said, was that Lindy's baby was a very cute little fellow.

There Walsh had rested. But only for the time being. He was not satisfied that Violet had given a faithful description of her activities on the night of March 1—and Captain Lamb agreed. Several points stood out:

After having worked at Next Day Hill for two years without once dating an outsider (so the other servants had testified) and having excellent reason to believe that Septimus Banks would soon ask her to marry him, why had Violet let herself be picked up on the street two days before the kidnaping?

Why had her sister Emily—who had been with Violet during the pick-up—applied on March 1, the day of the kidnaping, for a visa to return to England?

And why had Emily sailed for England on April 6, just four days after Dr. Condon had given fifty thousand dollars to a man who claimed to be a member of the kidnap gang?

Why, finally, had Emily taken care not to inform the police of her intention to sail?

Mrs. Dwight Morrow might steadfastly defend Violet's good name and insist that if the maid had supplied any information that had helped the kidnapers she had done so unwittingly, but Walsh and Lamb could not agree with this picture of naïve innocence. They had decided to put greater pressure on Violet, until she yielded the true story.

But then, on May 11, Violet had entered Englewood Hospital for surgery. It could not fairly be said that she had done so only to escape Walsh; for some time the Morrow family physician had been saying that her diseased adenoids and tonsils needed attention; still, the two officers wondered, why had she elected to act on his advice at this crucial point?

She was still in her hospital bed when the baby's body was discovered. Up to then Violet had maintained a show of good spirits —a smile, a wink, a pert remark; suddenly she became moody and withdrawn.

At last she had left the hospital and returned to the Morrow home; to speed her recovery Inspector Walsh had curbed his impatience for several days more. Now he felt that he could wait no longer. He notified Violet that he expected her to be available for another session of questioning on the evening of May 23.

3

Perhaps the keenest criticism of the New Jersey State police was directed at their handling of the clues; Colonel Schwarzkopf had to admit that it was somewhat justified. There had been errors of judgment, inexcusable carelessness, instances of simple oversight. But was there a police organization anywhere that would not have to confess on occasion to similar flaws? Considering the shock and confusion of the night of March 1, weren't some blunders to be expected?

The State police fingerprint expert, Corporal Frank Kelly, had reached the Lindbergh home soon after midnight. He had powder-dusted and processed the ransom note and envelope; thanks to Lindbergh's vigilance, no one in the nursery had handled them. Next he had processed the crib, the window sill, the faulty shutters, and other nearby surfaces. He had found no fingerprints, only blurred smudges that probably had been left by the Lindberghs, the servants, and the little boy himself.

Kelly had then examined the chisel and the ladder found outside the house on the soft damp ground. There were no fingerprints. At least so he had declared in his report; others were not so sure. One was Dr. Erastus Mead Hudson, a New York physician.

Dr. Hudson had asked permission to inspect the ladder surfaces for prints, explaining that his method was more searching than the process Kelly had used. The Hudson method, originally developed in France twenty years earlier, depended on silver nitrate, which, combining with the sodium chloride, or salt, secreted in all fingerprints, changed the silver nitrate into silver chloride. Since silver chloride was sensitive to light, Dr. Hudson had pointed out, exposure to sunlight would darken the areas touched by hand and bring out the fingerprints.

But Captain Russell A. Snook, supervisor of the State police Bureau of Identification, had observed that the Hudson method would be unlikely to produce anything of value, since the ladder had been handled by so many people after Kelly had finished with it. Nevertheless, on March 13 the doctor had been permitted to demonstrate his silver nitrate system—but only on a small part of the ladder. Kelly and Sergeant Louis Kubler, also of the Bureau of Identification, had watched. Then, taking over from Dr. Hudson, they had sprayed the whole ladder with silver nitrate, which, after exposure to light, had revealed no less than 125 finger marks and a veritable gallery of palm prints.

Hudson had advised the police to photograph the great variety of marks, and the Bureau had followed his advice. Their high hopes had come to nothing. Of all the marks, not one was a genuine fingerprint; and of the eight that could be identified, all had been made by the police.

The salt deposits left by fingers, Hudson had informed the press, could be counted on to remain intact for six months, if they were imprinted on wood that was kept inside a house at normal temperatures. If the State police had promptly accepted his offer—if every Tom, Dick and Harry in the organization had not passed the ladder from hand to hand, as they must have—perhaps its surfaces would have pointed to the man or men who had built it.

So the newspapers had charged. And even now, weeks later, as Schwarzkopf was well aware, the affair of the ladder was still referred to as an excellent example of State police bungling.

Their handling of the footprints was attacked with almost equal bitterness.

A trail of smudged prints daubed in reddish-yellow clay led across the floor from the nursery's southeast corner window to the baby's crib. Outside, a single large footprint faced the house near the southeast wall, and several smaller footprints had been found not far away. The texture of the daubs in the nursery matched the texture of the soil on which the house stood, as the investigating detectives and troopers had determined almost at once; their further investigations had scarcely risen above that elementary level.

Detective Lewis Bornmann had not measured the large footprint beneath the nursery window, although the butler, Oliver Whateley, had said that he had not gone outside the house in the hours immediately before the kidnaping and that neither he nor Lindbergh had been near the southeast wall in their first frantic search for the kidnapers. True, Detective Nuncio De Gaetano *had* measured the footprint, after noticing a series of ridges along one side which seemed to indicate that the shoe or boot had been covered with a thick-ribbed woolen sock; but it had not occurred to him to use a tape-measure—he had measured the print against the 14½-inch handle of his Eveready flashlight, making it out to be approximately 12⅛ inches long. De Gaetano had then matched the width of the print against the palm of his hand, which led him to estimate that it was 4¼ inches wide.

Trooper Joseph Wolfe had used another method of measuring. As he peered at the footprint in the beam of his flash, the thought had occurred to him that the print was slightly larger than his own shoe—size nine. He hadn't tried to determine whether the print had been made by a right or a left shoe.

Corporal Kelly, on the other hand, had photographed the footprint but, like Detective Bornmann, had not measured it.

Nobody had measured the smaller footprints in any way, by shoe, palm or flashlight handle. Of course, as Schwarzkopf knew, later developments made that oversight unimportant. Though at first Anne Lindbergh had said that she had not gone outside the house in the hours preceding the kidnaping—and Betty Gow and Elsie Whateley were sure that they too had remained inside during the blustery afternoon and evening—by and by she had remembered that after returning from her afternoon stroll she had stood on the damp soil beneath the nursery's southeast windows and thrown some pebbles against the corner windowpane to attract Betty's attention; and presently Betty had brought the baby to the window.

And so the smaller footprints had been accounted for. But the cursory treatment given the large print still rankled. Why had no one made a plaster-of-Paris cast? Even Dr. Condon, no police officer, had not been guilty of this neglect. With the assistance of his son-in-law Ralph Hacker, he had made a cast of the man's footprint in the soil at the base of the wall in St. Raymond's Cemetery. So far, the old man's zeal had led nowhere; still, as Schwarzkopf was in no mood to deny, it underscored the carelessness of the State police.

But these aspects of the investigation, regrettable though they were, didn't tell the whole story; there were other aspects in which the State police, and the Newark and Jersey City detectives Governor Moore had placed under Colonel Schwarzkopf's command for the duration of the case, had been alert and painstaking. Schwarzkopf thought so, anyway, and his two aides, Captain Lamb and Inspector Walsh, agreed.

To begin with: in the dusk of March 2, Lieutenant John J.

Sweeney of the Newark police, standing in the still-damp soil beneath the nursery's southeast corner window, had noticed two vertical gray scars, each about two inches long, on the white wall of the house, a couple of feet below and slightly to the right of the window shutters. It had occurred to him that the space between the scars approximated the width of a ladder and that they might have been caused by a ladder's slipping in the mud and scraping through the whitewash to the gray stone underneath. The next day, with the help of Corporal Kelly and others, Sweeney had tested his theory. Reassembling the three sections of the kidnap ladder —although one rung and the adjoining side rail had split, the ladder could still be made to stand—they had inserted the legs in the two holes in the muddy ground beneath the window. Legs and holes exactly matched; but when the ladder was propped against the house, its three sections—each approximately seven feet long —carried the top ends of the rails to a place on the wall well above the scars.

The puzzle was solved simply. When the top section of the ladder was removed, the tips of the rails came to rest directly over the scars.

Kelly had photographed the ladder in this position. Then Sweeney, with the aid of an extension ladder borrowed from the Lindbergh garage, had studied the scars through a magnifying glass and discovered wood splinters lodged in the masonry. Placing the top rung of his extension ladder on a level with the top rung of the kidnap ladder, he had been able to reach up, grasp the window casing, and hoist himself into the nursery; then he had reversed the process: he had swung out of the window and climbed down the ladder.

Later, the kidnap ladder—through one of the duplicates constructed by the police—had revealed additional information: the person who had used it to enter and leave the nursery weighed from 150 to possibly 179 pounds and was long-legged and agile.

The first deduction was based on the fact that, time after time, detectives and troopers of middle weights had climbed up and down the duplicate ladder without mishap—but an officer weighing 180 pounds had split the same rung and side rail in exactly the same places shown broken in the kidnap ladder. Since the baby had weighed 30 pounds, his abductor must have weighed at least 150—most likely more; for the ladder had supported the kidnaper on the way up, but had broken under the extra weight of the baby.

The second deduction came from the fact that the rungs were

roughly nineteen inches apart, six inches more than the distance between the rungs of an average ladder.

On March 8, in the Trenton laboratory of State police photographer George G. Wilton, the kidnap ladder had been photographed from every angle in the condition in which it had been found. Next, Captain Henry Gauthier, starting from the Lindbergh house and circling in ever-widening arcs, had shown the ladder to every builder, every carpenter and virtually every family within a radius of twenty miles. None had recognized it; all had disclaimed knowledge of who might have built it.

Schwarzkopf had then sent the ladder to the New Jersey Police Training School in Wilburtha, near Trenton, for analysis. Their tests had been inconclusive.

It had remained to enlist the aid of the federal government. In this connection, Schwarzkopf hadn't hesitated. Splinters of wood removed from the wall of the Lindbergh house and a few detached pieces and slivers taken from the ladder had been sent for analysis to the Forest Service Laboratory in Madison, Wisconsin; and, finally, arrangements had been made for the busy Corporal Kelly to take the ladder itself to Washington for study by the Bureau of Standards.

The chisel left behind after the kidnaping had been exhibited to every hardware-store clerk within twenty miles of the Lindbergh place. All had studied its Stanley trademark, its white beechwood handle flecked with brownish spots, its brass ferrule and three-quarter-inch blade, but none could recall having sold it. They said the chisel was such a common type that it might have come from any hardware store in the United States.

Although of course the ladder had revealed nothing about the character of the man who had climbed it, the information it had given about his height, weight and agility seemed to agree with Dr. Condon's description of John; in the night light of their two meetings, he had appeared to be about five feet nine and a half inches tall, around 165 pounds, and so wiry and nimble that he had vaulted easily over the nine-foot cemetery gate. And there was reason to believe that the same man had been in the nursery on the night of March 1; he had recognized the safety pins as those used to fasten the baby's bedclothes to the crib mattress.

But it seemed to Lamb and Walsh that the kidnaper had betrayed a good deal more about himself by the way his mind worked. Both in the clumsily composed ransom notes and in his behavior with Dr. Condon, they felt, John had told them quite a lot. True, there was no conclusive proof that he had written the notes, although Dr. Condon had heard him pronounce the word "signature" precisely as it was spelled in them: *sing*nature. And in the light of what had been pieced together, it seemed improbable that the notes had been dictated to him or represented anything but his own ideas as the actual leader of the gang. Any theory that John was guilty of no more than extortion was ruled out by the fact that he had produced the sleeping suit the baby had worn on the night of the kidnaping and, moreover, had attached to it a note in the same unmistakable handwriting.

Although even to a layman's eye certain conclusions seemed indisputable, in April Schwarzkopf had sent all fourteen kidnap notes to a handwriting expert, Dr. William T. Souder, for analysis; more recently, in search of an even more highly qualified opinion, he had told Captain Snook, the notes' custodian, to submit them to Albert S. Osborn, perhaps the best-known graphologist in the nation.

4

On May 23 the New Jersey authorities made two new moves against the kidnapers.

To prison wardens and police officials throughout the country, the State police sent circulars which reproduced the handwriting in two of the notes Dr. Condon had received and requested them to compare it with the handwriting of criminals in custody. And late that day, the State legislature authorized Governor Moore to offer a reward of twenty-five thousand dollars for information leading to the arrest and conviction of the kidnapers of any child under sixteen.

Colonel Schwarzkopf had an engagement at the Morrow mansion for the evening of the twenty-third; so had Charles Lindbergh. Inspector Walsh had asked them to be present during the third questioning of Violet Sharpe. Lieutenant Arthur Keaton joined them in the Morrow study as the inquiry began.

Violet repeated her account of her activities on the night of March 1. When she paused, as before, with her return to the Morrow estate, Walsh sharply took her up.

Why had she told the police one story on March 10 and quite a different story on April 13? Which was the truth?

Violet answered that the true story was the one she had told on April 13.

Why had she lied the first time?

She couldn't explain, Violet said. She must have been nervous; but then her mind had cleared and she told the truth.

Perhaps, Walsh suggested, her mind was even clearer now?

Violet nodded. She was flustered under the gaze of the four men, one of them the father of the dead child.

Then maybe with her clearer mind she could positively identify the three people with whom she said she had gone to the roadhouse?

Violet said sullenly that she couldn't tell him any more about them than she had already.

Was it her habit, Walsh asked, to let herself be picked up by strange men and taken to roadhouses?

Violet answered indignantly: Of course not! After all, her sister had been with her when the man in the green sedan had stopped. And she hadn't agreed to go to a roadhouse with him; she had accepted his invitation to go to a movie. Not until they had stopped at the Peanut Grill had she known he had other plans.

About that movie they never got to, Walsh went on; just when was it Ernie had suggested going to one?

When he called, Violet replied. How often did she have to tell him! Ernie had called at about a quarter to eight, before she'd finished serving the dinner, and had asked her to a movie!

Walsh stared at Violet as if he hadn't heard her correctly. Ernie telephoned her at around a quarter to eight on the evening of Tuesday, March 1?

Yes!

Walsh continued to stare at her. When he spoke, he took his time.

Wasn't it a fact, he said, that Ernie had telephoned her at one o'clock that afternoon; that she had talked with him just an hour and a half after she had learned, at eleven-thirty in the morning, that the Lindbergh baby had a cold and would be kept in the Hopewell house that night?

Violet flushed; she looked at her hands, folded in her lap, then nodded.

5

Albert Sherman Osborn had wondered about the handwriting in the Lindbergh kidnap notes and the information it might yield to the trained eye, as had many lesser-known graphologists, amateur and professional. He was gratified to have the notes submitted to him for analysis. The State police in so doing might be said to cap his long career. He could point to many appearances in court as an expert in cases involving disputed documents, and to a score of books on graphology, which in his view was an exact science. Osborn was seventy-one, and he looked the part of a scientist. He was tall, with a snowy head of hair and abundant mustache, and he wore glasses; his only infirmity was a slight deafness.

Several conclusions about the kidnap notes seemed to him so obvious as to be elementary. All fourteen notes had been written by the same hand. The same spelling appeared throughout: *anyding* for anything, *mony* for money, *boad* for boat, *ingnore* for ignore and, of course, *singnature* for signature. *G*s and *h*s were transposed, making light into *lihgt* and right into *rihgt*. The *x*s and *y*s were equally characteristic, the former resembling two *e*s laid back to back, the latter an undotted *j*. And of the 391 *t*s that Osborn numbered in the notes only three were crossed; of 304 small *i*s only seven were dotted.

New York invariably appeared as *New-York,* a European form.

The notes displayed other relationships. The writer referred in later messages to earlier statements: the amount of the ransom, the warning not to notify the police, the assurance that the child was in good hands. But the most dramatic similarity was the symbol at the bottom of every note—excluding the three sent to Colonel Breckinridge and Dr. Condon.

Strictly speaking, the signature-symbol did not come within the province of a handwriting expert; but in this and a few other respects Osborn felt justified in extending the range of his study. He examined the symbol as keenly as the handwriting itself.

In every instance, it appeared in the lower right-hand corner of the paper: two interlocking circles outlined in blue, the inner oval formed where they overlapped colored solid red. They were punched with three rough-edged square holes.

It seemed to Osborn that the circle imprints had been made with ordinary writing ink, Occasionally the outlines were blurred, indicating that a rubber stamp or any instrument designed for ink had not been used.

He recalled a phrase stressed in the first note and again later: *Specially them three holes,* the author had written. Osborn concentrated on the holes. In each symbol-signature, they had been punched by the same crude instrument: they bore the same relation to one another (the first and second holes were farther apart than the second and third) and also to the bottom and side edges of the paper. Osborn satisfied himself on this score by placing all eleven signed notes on top of one another, squaring the edges, and holding the sheets to the light. The three holes were lined up precisely: he could look through them.

He reached two more conclusions:

The writer's hand was disguised. Occasionally, the disguise was extravagantly complicated; in other places it faltered so as to be hardly any disguise at all, as if the writer had grown careless or forgetful.

The writer was of German origin. The notes pointed to a hard struggle to express in English thoughts formed in his or her native language. These errors almost certainly were not part of a disguise; they were too unconsciously revealing. The writer must have composed the notes painstakingly by referring to a German-English dictionary. Difficult polysyllabic words were correctly spelled; simple words—of which the writer apparently had felt confident—were misspelled. Entire sentences seemed hopelessly jumbled; translated literally into German, as they must have been framed in the writer's mind, they made sense.

The words and phrases that indicated the writer's origin were sprinkled throughout the notes. Typical examples were *gut, aus, uns.* "Sleeping suit" appeared as one word: in German it would have been *schlafanzug* or *schlafrock.* Dr. Condon was addressed as *Mr Doctor John F. Condon,* a proper German salutation. And then there was the hyphenated New-York and the writer's custom of placing the dollar sign after the figures.

Given such a unique combination of spelling and phraseology, Osborn thought, it should be possible to compose a handwriting test that would expose the writer of the kidnap notes. The test could be dictated to any person suspected of having played a part in the Lindbergh kidnaping, and the suspect's transcription then matched against the original writing in the notes. The style of the suspect's handwriting would not necessarily be significant, since the original writing had been disguised.

Osborn composed a test paragraph which minimized style. Spelling played a more important part in his calculations, and he avoided any words that might betray the purpose of the test by revealing to the suspect that the police were on the trail of the kidnapers-extortionists. On the other hand, he made full use of ordinary words that were misspelled in the notes: our, *ouer;* where, *were;* later, *latter;* not, *note;* anything, *anyding;* something, *someding.*

Sending the handwriting test with his report to Colonel Schwarzkopf, Osborn stressed that it must be dictated to the suspect, *not* shown. If, in the suspect's version, "our" turned up as *ouer* and "not" as *note,* and so on, any previously established link to the kidnaping would be drawn that much tighter.

6

While Albert Osborn worked over his analysis, several pieces of wood sent by the New Jersey State police arrived at the desk of Carlile P. Winslow, director of the Department of Agriculture's Forest Service Laboratory in Madison, Wisconsin. He referred the fragments to the chief wood-identification expert, Arthur Koehler; they came, Winslow said, from the Lindbergh kidnap ladder.

Koehler nodded. It had taken the samples some time to reach him, but here they were. In March he had volunteered his help in a letter addressed to Colonel Lindbergh. Later, reading that thousands of letters were piled up at the Hopewell house, he had concluded that it would be foolish to expect an answer; and none had come.

Now, perhaps, he could make good his unacknowledged offer.

Forty-seven, rather stooped, nearly bald, Arthur Koehler pursued the everyday routine of his work with wholehearted devotion. He lived not far from his office with his wife, two daughters, and a baby son. The Forest Service Laboratory was staffed with specialists; Koehler thought his specialty by long odds the most fascinating. Any problem that raised questions dealing with the growth and cellular structure of wood was his concern.

Raised on a farm, young Koehler had shown little liking for the life and had resolved to get away from it as quickly as possible; but the nearby woods had given him deep pleasure. Whenever he could, he had wandered, absorbed and observant, through them. He had grown acquainted with every aspect of the changing forest, and there were moments he cherished in memory: a perfectly still winter afternoon when he and a friend had sawed a birch tree so precisely that the completely severed trunk had remained upright. The faintest stir of air would surely have toppled it, but there had not been even a whisper of wind among the frozen trees. They had left it standing, a sort of miracle. The next morning Koehler had returned; the birch trunk lay on the snowy ground.

Koehler entered the University of Michigan, but though he had left the farm he had not left his beloved woods: his chosen study at the university was forestry. By his senior year he had progressed so rapidly that he was appointed assistant instructor in tree identification; after graduating in 1911 he had continued his studies in the laboratory, scrutinizing the patterns of wood pores, the structure of the different species' cells. And in 1928, he had begun to divide his time between the Forest Service Laboratory and the University of Wisconsin, where he lectured on wood.

Koehler's reputation had grown over the years; some people in the Midwest said his work was infallible. Litigants called him to court to testify in cases involving wood identification. And his list of publications steadily lengthened; by the time his superior, Carlile Winslow, put the pieces from the kidnap ladder in front of him, Arthur Koehler had written fifty-two booklets, bulletins and pamphlets out of his truly massive erudition.

Koehler dissected a sliver from the fragments of wood and placed it beneath his microscope. Pine; the kind of pine found in North Carolina and her sister states—second-growth pine. Another sliver was Douglas fir from west of the Rockies. Another was birch; still others were ponderosa pine, brought east from their native western forests.

But here was something else, something very interesting; several foreign fibers, plump as rope under the vast magnification. Some dull green, some black, some white, they were threads of wool, speared on the jagged wood edges. Apparently they had escaped detection by all the police experts who had examined the fragments.

Perhaps the threads had been snagged from the clothes of the kidnaper who climbed the ladder to the Lindbergh nursery.

Koehler untangled the wool fibers. He would mention them in his report to his superior, which would be sent on to Colonel Schwarzkopf.

At State police headquarters in Trenton, Schwarzkopf, Lamb and Walsh studied the reports Albert Osborn and Arthur Koehler submitted.

Having received facsimiles of two of the kidnap notes, police officials in other states had urged Schwarzkopf to distribute copies of the rest, but he had refused and insisted that there were good reasons for his refusal. He had always suspected that the notes had been written in a disguised hand; now Osborn had confirmed him. And the graphologist had provided a valuable test to be dictated to suspects. It had been risky enough before, when just two facsimiles had been distributed, for there was a chance that some might fall into the hands of reporters. Sending out copies of *all* the kidnap notes would simply be begging for trouble. Given the opportunity, every newspaper in the country would publish them; millions of readers would study them; among those millions were the kidnapers, who, if ever subjected to Osborn's test, would be warned against duplicating the handwriting in the notes.

Lamb and Walsh, too, found the Osborn and Koehler reports helpful. While they did not confirm, they did not refute an idea the officers had entertained earlier. The kidnap ladder, though roughly fashioned, was by no means an amateur job; whoever had made it possessed considerable mechanical ability. And one of the ransom notes testified to similar ability on the part of the writer: the drawing of the box in which the money was to be delivered was in proper perspective and showed a knowledge of cubic content.

Wasn't it possible, therefore, that the builder of the kidnap ladder and the writer of the kidnap notes were one and the same? If so, hadn't the fibers discovered by Arthur Koehler come from that person's clothing?

For a time, Lamb and Walsh thought so. But a stubborn memory nagged at Lamb. The ladder had been displayed to a great many people; to protect its surfaces, it had been wrapped in olive-drab and black-and-white woolen blankets.

Fibers from these blankets matched the fibers found by Koehler.

The most reliable lead, it seemed to Lamb and Walsh, remained the one they had pieced together before: the similarity between what the ransom notes said and what the man called John had said to Dr. Condon during their first meeting. Substantially the information was the same. And it fell into a pattern of opposites, pointing even more strongly to the conclusion that John and the note-writer were one. Time and again, in a transparent attempt to avoid capture, he had stated the exact opposite of the truth.

He had said that he was a Scandinavian, when everything known about him proved he was German.

He had said that the baby was in good health, when in fact the baby was dead.

He had said that the child was on a boat, when all the time the body lay in its shallow grave in the Jersey woods.

He had said that he was only a go-between for the kidnap gang—but did not everything about his behavior indicate that he was the gang's leader?

7

On Monday June 6, Charles Lindbergh resumed his normal pattern of life. For the first time since March 1, he went to his office at Transcontinental and Western Airways, "The Lindbergh Line" which had evolved from Transcontinental Air Transport, Inc.

His business interests had been largely ignored during the past months; other interests, too. Prominent among the latter was the experimental work he had been pursuing at the Rockefeller Institute for Medical Research with Dr. Alexis Carrel.

Lindbergh had met Dr. Carrel in 1930. The surgeon and experimental biologist, famous in scientific circles since 1912, when he had been awarded the Nobel Prize in physiology and medicine, had taken to the younger man, and Lindbergh had responded. Carrel had talked about his work; the transplantation of organs; transfusion; suturing blood vessels; and Lindbergh, with the other's encouragement, had begun to experiment with perfusion pumps, sterile glass chambers designed to supplement, assist, or even possibly, in an emergency, take the place of a human heart.

He had had to drop his experiments during the long search for his son; but now the search was over, the case was out of his hands; the professional manhunters were in charge. He would give them whatever help he could but his and Anne's personal welfare and peace of mind depended on their returning to a normal life as quickly as possible.

They had moved from the new house at Hopewell, at least for the time being. Anne's mother had urged them to come and live with her at Next Day Hill, which overlooked the splendid fifty-two-acre Morrow estate; it was from there on this June morning that Lindbergh had driven to his office in New York.

Later in the day, reporters learned that he was back at work. Secretaries were asked how he looked, how he had behaved. He had behaved the same as always, they agreed; but he looked older and, though naturally spare, he had lost a lot of weight, maybe as much as thirty pounds.

During the same morning, Governor A. Harry Moore of New Jersey was reminded anew of the case that, so far, his police had been unable to solve. William Allen, the Negro truck driver who had chanced upon the baby's body, was appearing in a Coney Island sideshow, gaudily decked out with a troupe of wax figures that re-created the discovery and the Lindberghs' shock and grief.

Allen didn't have a steady job and he had a wife and four children to support. Well, Governor Moore decided, some other way would have to be found to support them. Telephoning the head of the New York City police, he acknowledged that Coney Island was outside the area of his authority, but he could not remain silent in the face of such brazen exploitation of the tragedy of two New Jersey residents, Charles and Anne Lindbergh.

He was assured that the New York police felt the same way. So did the Coney Island Chamber of Commerce. Already, Inspector James Fitzpatrick of the Coney Island precinct had been instructed by the Brooklyn Commissioner of Licenses to revoke William Allen's exhibition permit.

With new weapons, Inspector Walsh returned to his attack on Violet Sharpe's story. During the last session, the evening of May 23, Violet had had to admit that Ernie had telephoned her at one o'clock in the afternoon of the kidnap day, an hour and a half after she had learned that the Lindbergh baby would remain at Hopewell that night. The implication was plain: Violet could have informed Ernie of this with plenty of time for him to tell others.

Just who was Ernie?

By Thursday June 9, Walsh was in a position to aid Violet's uncertain memory.

He walked into the study of the Morrow mansion at eleven that morning; with him was Laura Hughes, who helped Mrs. Morrow with secretarial and other chores. Walsh sent for Violet and told her he wanted to hear her story again, from beginning to end.

Violet was nervous; the secretary's busy pencil, taking down each word, upset her. She went on with the familiar tale, less and less sure of herself, and Walsh pounced on every hesitation until it seemed to be a clumsy effort to hide guilty knowledge. At last, she had no more to tell.

Walsh took a photograph from his pocket. He instructed Violet to study it and then tell him if the man in the picture was Ernie.

Violet stared at the unsmiling face. Rogues'-gallery portraits are not noted for the subjects' vivacity of expression, and this was a police portrait.

"Yes," she said. "Yes, that's the man."

Walsh studied her. The picture she held was of Ernest Brinkert, petty thief and sometime operator of the Post Road Taxi Company of White Plains, New York. In March detectives had turned up a half dozen of the cab company's business cards in Violet's room; upon investigating they had learned that the service had gone out of business a year and a half before. But its records remained and they had supplied the name of Ernest Brinkert.

It had seemed to Walsh that Ernie Brinkert and the Ernie of Violet's story could be the same man.

He tapped the photo Violet held. Why hadn't she told him before who Ernie was?

She didn't know before, Violet replied.

"Yes, you did," Walsh said. "You had his cards among your personal effects."

"I did not!" Violet cried.

"I'm not going to argue with you. All I want to know is: is this or is it not the man you were with that night?"

Violet's voice rose still higher. "Yes, it is! Yes, it is!" Her body shook, and she burst into sobs.

Laura Hughes, alarmed, put down her pad and pencil and telephoned the Morrows' doctor. He came in a hurry.

Walsh would have to stop for the present, the doctor told him; Miss Sharpe's pulse was very fast, her condition semihysterical. Walsh assented and put the photo back into his pocket. He intended to resume the questioning the next day, this time in his office in the State police barracks in Alpine.

After a while, Violet was able to leave the study. As she passed by the desk, Laura Hughes glanced up sympathetically. To her surprise, Violet smiled and winked.

That evening, after reflecting on Inspector Walsh's ability to pluck unpleasant surprises out of his hat, Violet came to a decision. Walsh had said that he was going to question her the next day in Alpine. "They'll never take me from this house again!" Violet cried to her friends in the servants' hall. "They'll never question me again!"

At ten the next morning, Walsh picked up the phone in his office and called the Morrow mansion. He asked for Arthur Springer, who had been Dwight Morrow's secretary until the Senator's death and who was now Mrs. Morrow's personal secretary.

Mrs. Morrow was not at home, and Charles and Anne Lindbergh had left the house shortly before the call. Mrs. Morrow had gone to be with her brother-in-law, to receive the guests who presently would be arriving at his residence for the marriage the next day of a niece. A dinner in honor of the bride-to-be was to be held this evening.

Arthur Springer came to the phone, and Walsh said that he wished to question Violet Sharpe in his office; he had arranged for a physician to be present, so that no one need fear for her health. He was sending Lieutenant Keaton to drive Violet to Alpine; would Springer please have her get ready for the trip?

Springer called the servants' hall on the house phone and gave Violet the inspector's instructions. Violet didn't reply. She slammed down the receiver and ran to Septimus Banks.

"Walsh wants to question me again," she cried, "but I won't go! I won't! I won't!"

The butler tried to calm her, but Violet hardly seemed to hear. Shaking off his hand, she slipped past him into the pantry and reached for a large measuring glass on one of the shelves. She hurried upstairs to her room. On an upper shelf of her wardrobe closet, securely tucked away, was a six-inch-tall tin can. A strip of yellow paper glued around it bore a warning legend, heavily penciled: *Poison. Do not unpack.*

Violet took down the can and ripped off the paper strip. A thin trickle of fine powder glittered on her clothes and on the closet floor. She ran to the bathroom and poured a stream of shiny crystals from the can into the measuring glass. Some spilled over onto the smooth white washbasin surface. Violet turned one of the taps and poured enough water into the glass to dissolve the crystals. She went back to her room and put the can on a table. Then she raised the glass to her lips and drained it.

A dainty necklace of crystals, somehow still undissolved, clung to the bottom.

Violet put the glass beside the can on the table. She walked slowly down the stairs. Emily Kempairien, a chambermaid, was in the pantry. Violet started to speak to her. The words ended in a garble as she swayed, staggered and fell.

Emily Kempairien shrieked for help. Banks was the first person to reach the pantry. While he did his best to revive Violet, someone else brought Dwight Morrow, Jr. He knelt over Violet, then ran to the house phone and told Arthur Springer to get a doctor and notify the police.

The others helped Septimus Banks carry Violet to her room. Gently, he put her on the bed. By and by the doctor arrived; but Violet had died long before.

When Walsh heard the news, he and Lieutenant Keaton and Detective Corporal William Horn drove to Next Day Hill and were led to Violet's room. The chief of the Englewood police, Charles A. Peterson, was there. He showed them the can and the measuring glass on the table. A printed label on the can read: *Cyanide Chloride, 73–76 percent. Not to be used as an insecticide or fungicide.* The thin strand of potassium cyanide crystals still lay in the wet glass. Walsh was examining it when the coroner arrived to make his official pronouncement—Violet Sharpe was dead, a suicide—and to arrange for her body to be removed to the Greenleaf morgue in Englewood for a post-mortem.

Where had the can of poison come from? There was no record in the Morrow household or in any Englewood drug store of its purchase. The manufacturing chemists, Eimer & Amend, whose name was on the label, said that the deadly crystals were often used to clean silver and jewelry. In her frugal and tidy fashion, Violet apparently had brought the can with her to the Morrow house when she came to work there a little more than two years before.

The gala dinner for the bride-to-be was called off; it would be unthinkable, Mrs. Morrow declared, in the wake of the suicide of her pretty, vivacious English maid, whose innocence she would never cease to believe in. The elderly lady told reporters that Violet had "simply been frightened to death."

Walsh disagreed; he said Violet's death was an admission of guilt. Schwarzkopf thought so too. "The suicide of Violet Sharpe," he informed the press, "strongly tends to confirm the suspicions of the investigating authorities concerning her guilty knowledge of the crime against Charles Lindbergh, Jr."

If by killing herself she had confessed her complicity, was not Ernest Brinkert guilty too? A police alarm went out, calling for his arrest on sight.

Scotland Yard was cabled the same day and told that Violet Sharpe had taken poison rather than face further investigation; they were asked to find and arrest, if necessary, the dead girl's sister Emily, who had sailed for England on April 6.

On this same Friday, June 10, the White Plains police took two steps to hasten the arrest of Ernest Brinkert, who had operated the Post Road Taxi Company there. They called Dr. Condon, and that night he came to White Plains headquarters to study a rogues'-gallery photo of Ernie. "It looks something like the man who got the money," he said at last, "but this picture's too light to tell. I can't be sure."

Later, Detective Roy Turner of the White Plains force called on Mr. and Mrs. Thomas Fay at 50 East Post Road; the police had learned that the Fays had handled Brinkert's service calls while his company was in business. They talked freely about Ernie; not that he was a pleasant subject to discuss! Most people heartily disliked him; he was continually in debt and never paid up. As Mrs. Fay enlarged upon Ernie's failings, the telephone rang. Her husband answered, then turned with a look of surprise. Who should be calling but Ernie! Turner went to the phone and told Ernie who he was and why he was at the Fays'. Ernie said he had telephoned because he'd heard the police wanted him. "I'm coming in," he said. Turner asked where he was calling from, but Ernie refused to say. "I'm coming in myself," he declared, and hung up.

Detective Turner traced the call to a store at 126 Sickles Avenue in New Rochelle, a few miles south. He telephoned New Rochelle police headquarters and a posse of detectives set out to arrest Ernie.

They found him sitting quietly in his car outside the store. Another car was angled directly in front of his, and two men were jumping up and down and waving their arms to attract the attention of the police. They had recognized Ernie's green Nash sedan, after hearing about it and its owner on a radio broadcast, and had blocked it with their car while Ernie was still in the store.

Ernie smiled at the detectives as they warily approached with drawn guns. He didn't want any trouble, he told them; there was no need for it. He amplified this at New Rochelle police headquarters: he knew nothing about the Lindbergh kidnaping beyond what he'd read in the newspapers and heard over the radio; he and his wife Mary had spent the night of March 1 playing cards at the home of a friend, Frank Page, in Bridgeport; he had never met Violet Sharpe or her sister.

His story seemed preposterous, a patched-up job, invented with the help of his wife and his friend. How could he hope to get around the fact that Violet had identified him as her escort on the night of the crime? What about his business cards, found in her room?

Dr. Condon was summoned. The detectives watched with high hopes. Here was Jafsie and here too, perhaps, was the mysterious John.

Dr. Condon carefully inspected Ernest Brinkert, then shook his head. This man wasn't John; he had never seen him before.

By four o'clock in the morning neither the police nor the suspect had made any headway; Ernie insisted that he was telling the truth, the police that he was lying. He would be extradited to New Jersey, they said, as soon as the necessary official steps were taken. The sooner the better, Ernie observed; forget about the official steps! He signed a waiver and was started off in a police car for the New Jersey State Police barracks in Alpine, where Inspector Walsh was waiting for him.

Acting at once, Scotland Yard sent Detective Inspector John Horwell to Stourbridge, Worcester, where Emily Sharpe was spending the week end on the estate of Viscount Cobham as the guest of her brother, who was in service there. Horwell cabled Schwarzkopf:

I am satisfied that Emily Sharpe knows nothing about the Lindbergh business. She appears to be a girl of excellent character and has been in the best of situations.

Though he saw no reason why Schwarzkopf should be interested, Horwell had picked up a new bit of information from Emily, hitherto unsuspected even by her parents: Violet wasn't single, as Septimus Banks and everyone else in the Morrow house had thought. Two and a half years ago in London, just before sailing for Canada, she had married a George Payne. Emily had never met him and didn't know where he was.

She blamed Violet's suicide on the New Jersey police. "Ever since the baby disappeared," Emily had told British reporters bitterly, "Violet was badgered and questioned until she did not know what she was saying or doing. She was driven nearly mad. And it was all so cruel. Violet would never have done anything to the child or to anyone who wanted to find it."

Colonel Schwarzkopf expressed his sympathy for Emily Sharpe and the girls' parents, but he maintained it wasn't true that Violet had been unduly pressed or intimidated by his men. And their suspicion of her had been and was well founded. As proof, he gave reporters copies of the "contradictory and evasive" statements she had made during the questioning on March 10, April 13 and May 23.

Emily's remarks seemed to Inspector Walsh to be aimed squarely at him. "There is no basis for such criticism," he retorted. "She was always treated gently, never roughly. We pleaded with her to help us." Consider the facts: (1) Violet had told the police conflicting stories concerning her movements on the night of March 1; (2) she had persistently refused to reveal the identity of her escort on the night of March 1. And no one could deny that, after the discovery of the Lindbergh baby's body, Violet had changed from a cheerful, confident young woman to a morose shadow of herself. Why? It seemed obvious to the inspector: her conscience was torturing her. Until the child's body was found, she had taken it for granted that the kidnapers would return him to his parents, that she would be given her share of the ransom money and that no one would ever be the wiser.

The baby's death had shaken her; then she saw that the case against her was gradually pushing her into a corner from which there would be no escape. And so, Walsh concluded, she had taken the only way out—taken it just before she was to be questioned again, when her guilt would have been exposed.

The newspapers thought this a reasonable theory; and with Ernest Brinkert in custody—the Ernie of the green sedan—surely confirmation could not be long delayed.

It had been a long Saturday for Walsh; at six in the evening he was finally preparing to leave his office when a visitor was brought in. His name was Ernest Miller, he explained; he lived in Closter, New Jersey, he was twenty-two years old, and it was *he* who had dated Violet Sharpe on the night of March 1. He had heard about the police's interest in the other Ernie and wanted to put things straight.

Walsh felt confident that Ernest Brinkert was telling a cock-and-bull story about his innocent diversions on the night of the kidnaping, and he listened to Ernest Miller with open disbelief. He was telling the truth, the young man insisted. He had met Violet and Emily while they were taking a walk, and he had called Violet and made the date just as she said.

Then why, Walsh demanded, had Violet identified Ernest Brinkert as the man she had been out with?

It made no sense to Ernest Miller. Violet had known his name from the beginning. And he could back up his story. The young couple Violet had described were Elmer Johnson, also of Closter, and Katherine Minners, of Palisades Park, New Jersey.

Detectives brought in Katherine Minners; she corroborated Miller.

Sorely puzzled, Walsh informed Colonel Schwarzkopf. The newspapers would learn about it sooner or later, Schwarzkopf advised him, so he'd better get it over with at once.

With some diffidence, Walsh did so. "This is a peculiar turn of events," he admitted to newspapermen. "It is no fault of ours. I can't understand why Violet Sharpe, if she had nothing to do with the kidnaping, preferred death to revealing Miller's name. I cannot understand it at all."

The press quickly changed its line; it understood only too well! The New Jersey police, baffled by their failure to solve the Lindbergh crime, smarting under the criticism, had so persecuted Violet that she had swallowed poison.

English newspapers increased the angry chorus. Violet Sharpe's suicide was a disgrace to American justice; the New Jersey police had "added to the baby murder the death of a tortured girl," said the London *Daily Telegraph*. "They stand, or should stand, condemned in the eyes of all decent persons in the United States," said the Manchester *Guardian*.

From the cell in Hunterdon County Jail where he was awaiting trial, John Hughes Curtis told reporters that Violet Sharpe's family had his deepest sympathy. The accusations of police persecution were quite justified, he said. "Beatings evidently are a common practice with the New Jersey State police in gaining their ends, but they're not always necessary. Lying promises often work just as well."

Republican leaders in Congress charged that the State Police were simply inept tools in the bungling grasp of New Jersey's Democratic administration. Labor members of Parliament inquired what His Majesty's Government were doing to protect British citizens in foreign lands from police brutality. The Government was not idle, they were assured; His Majesty's acting consul-general in New York had been instructed to look into Violet Sharpe's suicide.

Reporters reminded Schwarzkopf that on June 10 he had said Violet Sharpe's suicide bore out his belief that she had advance knowledge of the kidnaping. Did he still hold that view? Schwarzkopf replied testily: "The fact remains that conflicting statements were made, that a false identification was made, that the identity of Miller was concealed, and that truths were denied." He promised to continue the investigation until the facts behind the suicide were established beyond question.

A point of possible interest occurred to Ernest Brinkert; he recalled that six days before the suicide, while he was working as a butler-chauffeur in New Rochelle, he had been approached by a man who had identified himself as a Justice Department agent. The agent had shown him one of the cab-company cards that had been found in Violet Sharpe's room and Brinkert had admitted that the cards were his. He couldn't explain how they had come into Violet's possession, but one thing was certain: he hadn't given them to her. He had never heard of Violet Sharpe. He had volunteered to go with the agent and clear it up with Violet, Ernie said, but the other evidently had thought such a step was unnecessary —he'd left, taking Ernie's chauffeur's license. The next thing he knew, Ernie said, Violet was dead and the police were broadcasting alarms for him.

Late Tuesday afternoon, June 14, a middle-aged man in black entered the Greenleaf morgue in Englewood. The attendants had come to expect him; it was his fourth visit in the past four days. They left him alone to his grief, standing with bowed head beside Violet's coffin.

She was buried at Brookside Cemetery, not far from the tomb of Dwight Morrow. There were red roses from His Majesty's acting consul-general, wreaths from the Morrows and their servants and Betty Gow and a last, special gift of flowers from the middle-aged man in black, Septimus Banks.

All right, Walsh asked, if she was innocent, why had Violet lied? In the foolish hope that somehow it would keep Banks from learning that she'd gone to a roadhouse with a virtual stranger?

Why had she taken poison? Yes, she'd become upset during the last questioning—but could anyone fairly say it had been harsh enough to drive her to suicide?

Innocent? Why should an innocent girl kill herself?

8

The trial of Gaston Means in the District of Columbia Supreme Court had begun on June 8; on June 15, the day of Violet Sharpe's burial, Means stood up to hear the result of Justice James M. Proctor's deliberations.

Means seemed confident. His aplomb had survived Mrs. McLean's testimony, and he had not been perturbed by the contempt with which United States Attorney Leo A. Rover had ticked off each incident in the case. The Fox was still at large but, the prosecutor charged, it was Gaston Means who had been the chief perpetrator of the fraud. With that, on June 10, Rover had finished his case and turned it over to the defense attorneys.

Counsel for the defense had rested without calling a single witness, not even Means.

On Monday June 13, Justice Proctor had referred the government's charge to the jury of eleven men and one woman, and they had weighed it for two hours. They had found Gaston Bullock Means guilty of larceny on two counts: one hundred thousand dollars for the so-called ransom and four thousand for what he had claimed were his unavoidable personal expenses.

Now, on the fifteenth, he waited to hear his sentence. The maximum penalty on each larceny count was ten years' imprisonment or a thousand-dollar fine, or both.

Justice Proctor addressed the court: "The Lindbergh case brought out all the best in the hearts of men, but also gave the opportunity to some to display the weakness and wickedness of human nature. The verdict of the jury in this case reveals that the defendant capitalized not only on the sweetest and tenderest emotions of the human heart but also the basest."

Means smiled at the judge. The smile brought out a dimple in his prosperous face.

He was sentencing Gaston Means, Justice Proctor concluded, to fifteen years' imprisonment, ten years for the larceny of one hundred thousand dollars and five years for the larceny of four thousand dollars.

The verdict seemed to gratify Means; his smile broadened. It was the third time he had been sentenced to a term in a federal penitentiary.

Dr. Condon said he'd be glad to look over a new collection of rogues'-gallery portraits in Inspector Walsh's office; when he walked in he held out his hand to the inspector—they had met before—but Walsh ignored it.

It was about time, he said, for Dr. Condon to confess the real part he had played in the kidnaping. What had he done with *his* share of the fifty thousand dollars? Did he expect anyone with any brains to believe he hadn't entered the case for the money?

If God in Heaven told him that story, Walsh scathingly declared, he wouldn't believe it.

Momentarily taken aback, Dr. Condon reflected that none of this should have come as a surprise. The New Jersey police hadn't come right out and said so but they'd hinted that he knew more than he chose to tell—might even be a full-fledged member of the kidnap gang. There were no rogues'-gallery pictures for him to inspect; just a trick to get him here. He resigned himself to another long session of questioning.

It lasted for four hours. Over and over, he repeated the story of his experiences with the man called John.

Walsh seemed to ponder. He asked if Dr. Condon played croquet. Yes, Dr. Condon replied, he did; in fact, he was a master of the game; but in sports his real preference was boxing.

Nothing more was said about croquet. Dr. Condon recalled having heard that the inspector had played checkers with John Hughes Curtis on the night Curtis had confessed. Why hadn't Walsh proposed checkers to him—why croquet. Puzzling?

Walsh suggested going out for a little fresh air. There was nothing Dr. Condon would enjoy more. Walsh had proposed a breath of air to Curtis, too, hadn't he? Did he think this was the infallible recipe for a confession?

They followed a winding path along the Jersey Palisades. Dr. Condon remarked on the various beauties of nature so abundantly displayed. At the end of the bracing stroll he was still chatting companionably.

Walsh had had enough; Dr. Condon was driven home to the Bronx.

On June 19, a Sunday, pupils of the Little Falls, Minnesota, grade schools filed into Memorial Park to dedicate a seedling to the memory of Charles Augustus Lindbergh, Jr. The seedling had been cut from a giant pine in Lindbergh State Park, on the site of the old Lindbergh homestead, where the Colonel's father had grown up. Two of the pupils had made a bird bath, which was installed at the foot of the slip of pine.

On Wednesday June 22, kidnaping became a federal offense as Congress approved the Lindbergh law, in effect another memorial to the child who three months and twenty-one days before had been lifted from his crib by unknown hands.

The following Monday, June 27, the trial of John Hughes Curtis began in the Flemington, New Jersey, courthouse.

Some in the courtroom wondered: trial for what? Curtis had confessed that he had made up the whole story of Sam and the gang and the fishing schooner—but what law had he broken?

The State's attorneys had found it an exasperating point. Nothing in the New Jersey statute books seemed to fit Curtis' case. Anthony M. Hauck, Jr., the chief prosecutor, had not been able to come closer than a charge of obstructing justice, wilfully misleading the police, a misdemeanor punishable by three years' imprisonment or a thousand-dollar fine, or both.

The old courthouse was crowded and the air was close. Charles Lindbergh sat with Hauck and his associate prosecutor, Harry Stout. Lindbergh seemed unaware of all the staring eyes. He did not glance at the man with whom he had spent so many days and nights at sea. But Curtis kept peering at Lindbergh; he seemed to be waiting for a friendly nod.

The Very Reverend H. Dobson-Peacock and Admiral Guy Burrage had declined all invitations to testify at the trial; defense counsel explained that they had no desire to expose themselves to New Jersey police hospitality; but Curtis was not altogether alone. His daughter Constance, a thin, pale eleven-year-old, was close beside him and often put her hand in his. She too watched the young man at the other table, barely ten feet away.

Hauck rose. "We will prove," he informed Judge Adam O. Robbins and the jury, "that John Hughes Curtis was actually in contact with the kidnapers, that he knew who they were and knew their whereabouts, and that he did not disclose their whereabouts to either Colonel Lindbergh or to the authorities because there was no satisfactory arrangement with Colonel Lindbergh as to the amount of the ransom."

Here was another question for the keener observers in the courtroom: if Curtis had confessed that his story was a hoax and that the kidnap gang did not exist, how could he have been "in contact" with them?

The prosecutor's staff had wrestled with that question for weeks. If Curtis was to be convicted of anything, they had decided, it would have to be shown that he had spun his yarns solely to prevent the New Jersey police from finding and arresting the kidnapers. But he could not have kept the police from finding the kidnapers if there *were* no kidnapers. It followed, they concluded, that Curtis had lied in saying that he had invented the kidnapers; he *had* known them, *had* known where they were and so had kept the police from apprehending them.

Lindbergh was called to the witness stand. The warm air had turned his cheeks pink, and his forehead was stippled with sweat. He spoke calmly in answer to Hauck's questions. He told how he had first met Curtis, had doubted that Curtis was really in touch with the kidnapers and finally—after Dr. Condon's efforts had failed—had come to believe him and therefore had taken part in the search for the *Mary B. Moss*.

C. Lloyd Fisher, a local man who was Curtis' defense counsel, rose to question Lindbergh. His manner was respectful. There was only a single time, Lindbergh readily admitted, when the money question had come up with Curtis—when the gang had suggested that the sum of twenty-five thousand dollars deposited in a Norfolk bank would prove Lindbergh's good faith—and he knew for a fact that Curtis hadn't made a cent out of the whole business.

"Now, Colonel," Fisher asked, "do you believe Curtis was ever in touch with the actual kidnapers?"

Lindbergh shook his head. "I do not at this time believe that Mr. Curtis was in contact with the kidnapers. I do not believe that he ever knew who took the child or in whose possession he was."

"Thank you, Colonel," Fisher said, and the young man left the witness chair.

He was followed by troopers, detectives and State police officials. Each one swore that in his opinion Curtis' story was a hodgepodge of lies.

Harry Stout summed up for the prosecution. After reading Curtis' confession to the jury, he turned and pointed to the prisoner. "There sits the most monumental liar God has ever permitted to tread this earth!" he shouted.

His meaning was obvious. The State still contended that Curtis had *not* lied in his original story; he had lied later, in his confession, in *saying* that he had lied.

Constance Curtis flushed, looked at Lindbergh, then down at the floor. She was not in the court the next day, when Judge Robbins endeavored to explain "this legal dilemma" to the jury of seven men and five women. They had heard the charge, the judge began—that Curtis had knowingly and wilfully obstructed justice by misleading and hindering the police. But unless the State had proved to the jury's satisfaction that Curtis had been in touch with the kidnapers and had known their whereabouts, they could not find him guilty as charged—and he was bound to point out to them that they had heard one witness after another swear that in their opinion Curtis had never known the kidnapers.

To find Curtis guilty, he concluded, the jury must be convinced that his original story to Dean Dobson-Peacock and Admiral Burrage and Colonel Lindbergh was true.

The jury retired. Four hours and five minutes later they returned and announced their verdict:

John Hughes Curtis was guilty as charged, but they recommended mercy.

Acting on their opinion, Judge Robbins sentenced Curtis to one year in jail, rather than the maximum three years the law provided, and fined him one thousand dollars. Lloyd Fisher announced that he would appeal the decision.

For the time being, the case against Curtis was closed. In the judgment of his peers, he had known who the Lindbergh kidnapers were, had known where they could be found, and had obstructed justice by refusing to give the information to the police. But in an interview the next day Colonel Schwarzkopf and other police officials insisted to reporters that Curtis had never had any information to give.

Who was right? the newspapers asked. And if Curtis had told the truth when he confessed that his story was a lie—if he *had* invented the kidnap gang—what was his motive? Even admitting that his tale had sprung from "a distorted mind," as he had said, he must have had a reason for entering the Lindbergh case.

Columnists and editorialists fished for an explanation: Curtis was deeply in debt; creditors were dunning him hard. By announcing that he was in touch with the kidnapers and winning Lindbergh's confidence, had he hoped that the actual abductors would reveal themselves to him, appoint him their intermediary—which would enable him to sell the story of the child's return to the highest bidder?

Or had he thought that his activities would put off his creditors? Surely not even the stoniest-hearted would risk public censure by dunning a man who was doing his best to reclaim Charles and Anne Lindbergh's baby son!

Or was a current Norfolk rumor true: that Curtis was in trouble with a group of rum-runners he had testified against some weeks before the kidnaping; that they had threatened him and his family with death and that in desperation he had created a fake gang to fend off a real gang?

Or had he simply been hungry for publicity?

Or *was* his story the truth? Was his admitted hoax a lie? Was his confession the real hoax? And if so, what was the motive behind it? Had he written it because the baby had been found dead and he was afraid that he might be accused of being an accomplice of the kidnapers and charged with murder?

Curtis sat in his cell as the questions piled up. A week later, free on ten thousand dollars bail raised chiefly through the efforts of his attorney, he went home to his family in Norfolk.

Charles and Anne Lindbergh's second child was expected in August. According to rumor, they had no intention of risking a second tragedy: they would sail for Europe for the birth. Nonsense, friends said; the Lindberghs were too level-headed for that: they meant to take up their life again, with their new baby, in the house at Hopewell.

But Mrs. Morrow, Anne's mother, was in Europe and Betty Gow was in Scotland—simply to spend a short holiday with her family, she had told reporters. It looked instead as if they were abroad to prepare the way for Anne.

Charles Augustus Lindbergh, Jr., had been born in the nursery at Next Day Hill—a gala night, the great house blazing with lights, friends pouring in. Tonight, Monday August 15, the house was mostly dark. A State trooper stood on guard at the gateway; three private detectives patrolled the grounds.

At three o'clock in the morning of the sixteenth, a car came to the door, people got in. It drove to 4 East 66th Street, New York. Anne Lindbergh was helped out and into her mother's town apartment. Very soon afterward, Anne's second son was born.

Dr. Everett Hawks, the obstetrician at the first birth, and his colleague, Dr. Edward H. Dennen, gave a few details to the press: the new baby weighed six pounds eleven ounces; he had not yet been named; mother and child were doing nicely.

The father had a few more words for the press, in a statement read by Colonel Breckinridge. Charles had written:

"Mrs. Lindbergh and I have made our home in New Jersey. It is naturally our wish to continue to live there near our friends and interests. Obviously, however, it is impossible for us to subject the life of our second son to the publicity which we feel was in large measure responsible for the death of our first.

"We feel that our children have a right to grow up normally with other children. Continued publicity will make this impossible. I am appealing to the press to permit our children to lead the lives of normal Americans."

9

The search continued.

For Frank Wilson of the Treasury Department and Thomas Sisk of the Department of Justice, the federal investigators in charge of the case, and for Lieutenant James Finn of the New York City police, it was chiefly a matter of waiting. Colonel Schwarzkopf still declined to reveal to these outsiders, as he regarded them, the evidence, clues and statements from suspects and witnesses the New Jersey police had gathered, even though the investigative arms of the two federal agencies and the criminal identification bureau of the New York police possessed clearly superior laboratory tools and technicians.

And so the "outsiders" were forced to concentrate on the ransom bills and to wait for the kidnapers' caution to give way to confidence, when the bills might be passed more freely.

Lieutenant Finn, a slight, sharp-faced man of fifty, began each day at headquarters by studying a large map of New York City and its environs. Colored pins dotted the map, each locating the spot where a ransom bill had been exchanged. They were all too few for Finn's taste; but, he thought, what could he expect? It was hard for bank tellers, storekeepers, clerks and collection agents to stay on the lookout for the bills. By now, autumn 1932, some two hundred fifty thousand copies of the Treasury's ransom circular had been distributed, but its fifty-seven pages were awkward to handle and the type listing the serial numbers of the bills was tiny and hard to read, with the result that most people had become bored with the task. Colonel Lindbergh had offered a two-dollar reward to every person who reported the receipt of a ransom bill; Finn himself had devised the least troublesome method of checking the numbers; federal agents and New York detectives had regularly made the rounds of the city banks to keep the tellers on the alert —and all these measures had helped, but not nearly so much as was hoped for.

To make the problem more difficult, only the smaller bills, the ten- and five-dollar notes, were being passed—less likely to attract attention. Not since a twenty-dollar bill had caught a teller's eye early in April had the kidnapers risked using another. Or, if they had, it had never turned up.

Impatient with their slow progress, Special Agent Wilson had taken the problem to United States Treasurer W. O. Wood and suggested that he secretly recall and retire specified issues of currency which would embrace the Lindbergh ransom money. Wood had broached the idea to other Treasury officials, who had pointed out that the nation's economy was not in the best of health and that if word of such a move leaked out it might touch off a panic. He had regretfully turned down Wilson's plan.

So, week by week, the colored pins on Lieutenant Finn's map increased with exasperating slowness—and each lead wound up nowhere.

Was there nothing else that could be done?

Finn remembered a talk he had had in April with Leigh Matteson of the International News Service. Ever since the kidnaping, Matteson had been convinced that only a lunatic would attempt such an act; seeking professional corroboration, he had asked the opinion of Dr. Lindsay R. Williams of the New York Academy of Medicine. Dr. Williams had referred him to Dr. Israel Strauss, chairman of the Committee on Medical Jurisprudence, who in turn had sent him to the committee's secretary, a young New York psychiatrist named Dudley D. Shoenfeld.

Matteson had broached his idea to Dr. Shoenfeld, and the psychiatrist had responded with a theory of his own. Shoenfeld's theory, Matteson had told Finn in April, was that the Lindbergh baby had been kidnaped by a lone man, an amateur rather than a professional criminal, impelled by acute psychic drives.

Well, that was nothing new. A number of people, police officers, federal agents—and armchair detectives—had always argued that the official theory that an organized gang was responsible was dead wrong; that it was the work of a single daring criminal.

Why would a professional gang pick on the national hero, they said, when there were so many less conspicuous and wealthier candidates for a quick trimming?

Would a gang be content with fifty thousand dollars? How much would that come to for each member? Chickenfeed.

Were the ransom letters, with their absence of threats to the child's safety, typical of professional kidnaping practice? They were not.

Would a gang have abandoned the ladder at the scene of the crime? Hardly, but an individual in hasty flight, the child in his arms, would have found it too cumbersome to lug along.

The official theory had remained unshaken. After all, who could deny the admitted fact that gangsters ruled all American crime?

Shut off by the New Jersey police, Finn and his detectives had had no opportunity to examine all the suspects; they had only the slow appearance of the ransom bills and Dr. Condon's description of John to work with.

In June Finn had issued a description of John to the press:

> Age, 30 to 35; height, 5 feet 9 inches; athletic build; speaks with Scandinavian or German accent; 150 to 160 pounds; rather light complexion; medium light hair; sharp almond eyes; high forehead, pointed chin; when last seen, wore soft brown hat, long black overcoat of light fabric, and black leather shoes.

Remembering Matteson's description of Dr. Dudley Shoenfeld's lone-operator theory, Finn wondered if the psychiatrist might not be able to help. He said as much to a colleague, who reminded him of a fact he very well knew: the higher authorities in the police department regarded with skepticism any theory advanced by any psychiatrist, psychoanalyst or whatever they wished to call themselves. Look at the racket these brain wizards had raised in the Loeb-Leopold case!

Still, Finn thought, a talk with Dr. Shoenfeld could do no harm and needn't be brought to the attention of the higher-ups. The psychiatrist might have more to contribute than the bare bones of the theory he had outlined to Leigh Matteson months before.

Dr. Shoenfeld did have a good deal more to contribute. His was a busy professional life, but he had spent a lot of time thinking about the Lindbergh case.

Thirty-nine, Dudley David Shoenfeld was a New Yorker, a graduate of New York University and Bellevue Medical College, Clinic Assistant and Adjunct Psychiatrist at Mt. Sinai Hospital, Chief of the Out-Patient Department of the Mental Health Clinic and Consultant Psychiatrist of the Hebrew Orphan Asylum. Despite these duties he also managed to teach mental hygiene at the Mt. Sinai Nurses Training School, child guidance at the New School for Social Research and to maintain his private practice.

Dr. Shoenfeld regarded the professional-gangster kidnaping theory as nonsense. Psychoanalytic studies had shown the typical American criminal to be contemptuous of the very rich, and especially the newly rich, convinced as he was that quick and easy fortunes could be made only by operating barely within the law, and often outside it. But these rich hypocrites pretended to be respectable, pious, patriotic—window-dressing to cover up their sins! They all deserved a good rooking.

Would any professional criminal have thought of Charles Lindbergh as a member of this phony-respectable, dirty-rich, stinking-hypocrite group? The national hero a fraud?

To ask the question, Dr. Shoenfeld thought, was to answer it.

It followed that no professional criminal or criminals would have seriously considered kidnaping Charles Lindbergh's baby boy.

Then who had stolen the child?

In the days following the crime, Dudley Shoenfeld had cast around for a motive. He remembered from his physics classes that if you knew the stimulus, you could predict the reaction. One might say, then, that if one knew, *really* knew, the victim of a crime (the *stimulus*) one could predict the nature of the man or men who had committed it (the *reaction*).

Perhaps the key lay in Charles Lindbergh himself.

In psychoanalytic terms, Lindbergh was as familiar to Shoenfeld as one of the case histories he had assembled in his Mental Health Clinic. He had been particularly struck by the fact that although Lindbergh had made a daring bid for fame—and won—he resented the world's interest in him and remained aloof from its gestures of admiration and affection. Shoenfeld thought Lindbergh could be compared to the new baby in the average American family, who soon senses that he is the most important member of the household and that he need do nothing in return for the attention he receives, even if he were able to respond intelligently. He may be indifferent or querulous or cantankerous; never mind, the adults in the family continue to shower attention on him, even though some of the younger members may bitterly resent the state of affairs, may even aggressively express their resentment. The baby knows that, in effect, he is all-powerful.

Was this a far-fetched analogy? To Shoenfeld, it seemed sound. Again and again magazine and newspaper writers and gossip columnists and radio commentators had pictured Lindbergh as a boy who had accomplished the feats of a man. He was boyish-looking, certainly, and he had a boy's coltish charm. And even in the midst of the crowds that had swarmed around him right after the famous flight, somehow he had seemed to be alone. His father was dead and his mother kept herself in the background. And so he had been adopted by the nation. As the nation's foster child and favorite son, he could do no wrong. Like the new baby, he was all-powerful.

In Lindbergh, then, the psychiatrist could see the *stimulus.* Surely the *reaction* was perfectly predictable.

The two could be linked as simply as this: (1) in the eyes of the American people Lindbergh was all-powerful; (2) someone whose position was inferior, even by normal standards, but who had delusions of omnipotence, regarded the young idol as a rival, an enemy. If he attacked and defeated his rival, he would prove that he was greater than Lindbergh.

Then a lone amateur must have committed the crime, acting boldly at the risk of great personal danger—in this man's fantasies just as Lindbergh would have acted! The kidnaper had demanded fifty thousand dollars, enough to take care of his material needs; but far more important to him was the significance of the abduction. The daring theft of the baby gratified his unconscious drive: it was a psychological truth that a child, especially a son, satisfied man's unconscious quest for immortality, and that the most devastating blow that could be dealt to the father's virility was an assault on his child.

Soon after the kidnaping, Dudley Shoenfeld came to another conclusion. Either by design or by purposeful accident, Charles Augustus Lindbergh, Jr., would be killed. Only in the baby's death could the kidnaper's unconscious find complete gratification.

By the end of March, the psychiatrist had seen no reason to change his views. Then in April had come the news of Dr. John F. Condon's negotiations with the man who called himself John. Shoenfeld saw his theories working out. Everything he read about John's behavior with Dr. Condon during their first meeting—the ease with which he overcame fear that he had been lured into a trap; his confident, chatty conversation, lasting more than an hour; the present tense of that vital question, "Would I burn *if the baby is dead?*"—indicated to the psychiatrist that John was the lone amateur of his speculations, that John thought of himself as all-powerful and that the Lindbergh baby had been killed.

On May 12, with the discovery of the child's body in the Jersey woods, the final point had been confirmed.

Despite this proof, Shoenfeld had to admit that his theories were based solely on newspaper reports. If only he could get to the fountainhead, the actual evidence itself! Keenly anxious to help, hopeful of proving that psychiatry could be valuable in tracking down a criminal, he wrote to the New York police asking for permission to examine the ransom notes.

Their reply astounded him: it seemed they were as much in the dark as he. They too were anxious to see the notes, but their requests had been refused by the New Jersey authorities.

To the scientist, the psychiatrist, this attitude was incomprehensible; but in the face of it, he could only watch the newspapers for further developments.

Summer had turned into fall. Now it was October. Unexpectedly, a call came from the police; the caller introduced himself as Lieutenant Finn and invited Dr. Shoenfeld to headquarters for a talk.

Shoenfeld was delighted. He found Finn an intelligent and conscientious officer who listened attentively as he presented his theories. In parting, after assuring him that much that he had said seemed sound and quite possibly would prove to be of help, Finn promised to make a new appeal to the New Jersey police for permission to inspect the ransom notes. This time, he would lend urgency to his request by pointing out that the notes were essential if Dr. Shoenfeld's analysis of the crime and the criminal was to be complete.

For a change, the new plea brought results. The New York police were still not to be permitted to see the jealousy guarded notes but at least Dr. Shoenfeld was to be given that rare privilege. Captain

Russell A. Snook, chief of the State police identification bureau, came to the doctor's office, bringing with him enlarged photostat copies of all fourteen ransom notes. Shoenfeld could keep the photostats, Captain Snook informed him, until he had completed his study. Colonel Lindbergh had expressed the hope that at that time the psychiatrist would come to the Morrow home in Englewood and explain his ideas to him and the New Jersey investigators.

Shoenfeld asked if he might bring Lieutenant Finn.

No, Captain Snook replied. The invitation was meant for the doctor alone.

This further evidence of the New Jersey police's determination to keep the center of the stage embarrassed Shoenfeld; nevertheless he accepted the invitation.

After Captain Snook left, Shoenfeld telephoned Finn and explained the request and its terms. Damned annoying, Finn said, but not surprising. He advised the psychiatrist to give his audience only a general outline of his ideas, and predicted that although the Jersey police apparently had not opposed Lindbergh's desire to hear Shoenfeld's views, they would resent his presence and would act on none of his suggestions.

Early in November, Dr. Shoenfeld went to Next Day Hill. Lindbergh, Captain Lamb, Inspector Walsh and other police officers were waiting for him in the library. He explained that his study of the ransom notes wasn't finished, but even so they had given him a few new ideas.

The photostats were spread on the library floor and Shoenfeld pointed out certain things that had struck him, linking them with his general theory of the crime and the criminal. He was speaking not as a handwriting expert, he emphasized, but as a psychiatrist.

Lindbergh nodded. He had nothing to say, however, when Shoenfeld completed his talk, and the police were no more forthcoming. The psychiatrist almost expected to be told that he must now return the photostats; instead, he was assured again that he could keep them until they had fully served their purpose.

Carrying with him a mental picture of the tall, silent, famous young man peering at the huge handwriting on the library floor, Dr. Shoenfeld went home.

Faithfully, he called Finn, who repeated his belief that the other's deductions offered definite possibilities. If he wasn't committed all the way to Shoenfeld's ideas, at least he was willing to go along. But, he stressed, this did not hold for his superiors. Some of them were definitely hostile and had suggested that Finn was a bit touched on the subject. In view of this, it would be a good idea if Shoenfeld would submit a written report, officially presenting his theory and conclusions.

Shoenfeld demurred. A full, official report, he said, would be studded with the kind of technical language that to the suspicious layman smacked of witchcraft. It would be safer to write a fairly simple report. He would save for Finn's more enlightened ears the delicate shadings of psychoanalytic interpretation of the ransom notes and the kidnaper and murderer who had written them.

Lieutenant Finn agreed. Much safer.

10

On Sunday evening, November 6, John Hughes Curtis drove north toward Flemington. Entering the courthouse the next day, he spoke warmly to his chief counsel, Lloyd Fisher, and genially waved to the others present: Assistant Attorney General Joseph Lanigan, Anthony M. Hauck, Jr., the prosecuting attorney, and Judge Robbins.

The business at hand had been carefully worked out in advance. Fisher asked the court to resentence John Hughes Curtis, and Lanigan and Hauck declared that they had no objections.

"This court," the judge said, "has imposed a term of one year in jail and a fine of one thousand dollars upon this defendant. It is now within the province of this court to suspend operation of the jail sentence, which I hereby do."

If the jail sentence was suspended, the fine was not. Curtis had come prepared to attend to that detail; smiling, he paid the fine with a thousand-dollar bill. To show that he nurtured no hard feelings, he shook hands with the judge and the State attorneys and returned to Norfolk, a free man. Later, he described this final act of a personal drama as "a vindication." Implying that he could have saved the thousand dollars if he'd wanted to take the trouble, Curtis told reporters he had paid rather than subject himself further to "the uncertainties of Jersey justice."

The November 8 headlines announced the defeat of President Herbert Hoover's bid for a second term in office. The victor, in a Democratic landslide swollen by the great depression, was the governor of New York, Franklin Delano Roosevelt.

11

On November 10, Dudley Shoenfeld submitted a memorandum to the New York City police. It explained in simple language the whys and wherefores of his theory and concluded with the statement that he had arrived at his beliefs soon after the crime; his study of the ransom-note photostats had simply supported his original conclusion.

Lieutenant Finn thought well of the report. Through Shoenfeld's reasoning, the figure of the man called John seemed to be drawing closer.

Now, the psychiatrist proposed, how about a blueprint for action, a step-by-step plan that he felt sure would finally expose John? Finn liked the idea. First they must have a synthetic portrait of their quarry. Shoenfeld set about sketching John from five points of view: his nationality, residence, occupation, mental and physical characteristics.

John was German. Shoenfeld was as sure of it as he was that John was the kidnaper, the killer, the writer of the ransom notes which unmistakably identified his nationality. He was an immigrant, still confused by the complexities of English, who continued to think in German. The errors in the notes were genuine errors, not a clumsy attempt to deceive the reader.

Newly arrived Germans almost invariably sought out their fellow countrymen (as did most immigrants) and settled among them, at least in the beginning of their life in America. There were several German communities in and around New York; the largest was Yorkville in Manhattan, but Shoenfeld was positive that John did not live in those crowded streets. It seemed clear that he lived in a German section of the Bronx. He read the Bronx *Home News,* that intensely parochial newspaper in which Dr. Condon had first stated his willingness to serve as go-between in the Lindbergh case; both his meetings with Dr. Condon had taken place in the Bronx; and his detailed directions to the old teacher showed that John was thoroughly familiar with the area.

To establish John as an inhabitant of the Bronx was an advance, but it hardly pinpointed him: the borough stretched over forty-one square miles and more than a million and a half people lived there.

John's occupation, third of the five points of view, was not so clear, but it was safe to say that he possessed some mechanical skill. The kidnap ladder was a home-made job, and he had sketched in proper perspective the box in which the kidnap money was to be delivered. Certainly he was accustomed to work with wood.

The most revealing evidence—the evidence, Shoenfeld maintained, that eventually would betray him—was the unconscious, telltale workings of John's mind shown in his conduct and in the ransom notes. John thought of himself as all-powerful. Since he was all-powerful, he could safely continue with the ransom negotiations although he knew he could not return the kidnaped child; even after his first alarm he could dismiss the threat of danger and calmly chat with Dr. Condon for more than an hour.

His blind faith in himself was apparent not only in the character of the notes but in the extraordinary number—fourteen—he had written. Their tone was cocksure, argumentative: "*Why did you ignore ouer letter?*" and "*How can Mr. Lindbergh follow so many false clues. . . .*" In effect, he was saying: *How can Lindbergh think for a moment that anyone but I could be brave enough and skillful enough and powerful enough to kidnap his son?*

And he was calmly confident that sooner or later, despite Lindbergh's foolish lack of perception and cooperation, he would bring the hero to heel. Twice he had written: "*You have to come to us anyway. . . .*"

But perhaps the most glaring example, an unconscious slip that in Shoenfeld's opinion fully betrayed John's complacent sense of omnipotence, was this sentence, also written twice: "*It is realy necessary to make a world affair out of this.*" He had meant to write "*It is* not *really necessary*" or "*Is it* really necessary?" But, elated by the international attention his feat had aroused, his unconscious had revealed his exultant pride.

Although he spoke occasionally about a "*trapp,*" John truly believed himself to be beyond capture and punishment. Again and again, in effect, he assured Lindbergh that consulting the police was a waste of time: "*. . . this kidnaping cace whas prepared for a year already. . . .*"

Through another slip, John revealed that unconsciously he identified himself with and possessed the powers of Charles Lindbergh. On the back flap of the envelope addressed to Colonel Breckinridge, John had written Lindbergh's name and address. This, of course, was the space customarily used by a letter-writer for his name and address. No matter what John's conscious reason might have been, in his unconscious he was saying *I am Lindbergh.*

And the striking symbol John had designed, the two interlocking circles forming an inner oval, colored red, where they overlapped, gave additional proof of his compulsive desire to identify. On every note addressed to Lindbergh the symbol served as the writer's signature. A signature says *I am;* the symbol used in place of a signature also said *I am*. Conscious, intelligent reasons may have caused John to use a symbol, but Shoenfeld was sure that his choice of this particular one was controlled by his unconscious, and that—together with other indications scattered throughout the ransom notes—it pointed to homosexual tendencies.

The symbol might also be construed as an airplane, with the vertical elliptical shape as the fuselage and the outer circles as the wings. With such a thought dictating his choice, John had pictured Lindbergh as the world pictured him: the American eagle, ruler of the airways. And here was another interesting point: during the World War, John's homeland had boasted a great aviator-hero whose skill and daring had aroused the admiration even of his enemies. He was Baron Manfred Albrecht von Richthofen, credited with a kill of eighty Allied warplanes, an ace of aces; the coveted if unofficial title of ace came with a fighting pilot's fifth kill. Lindbergh and von Richthofen may very well have been linked in John's imagination.

Von Richthofen, whose fighter plane was painted scarlet, had been called the *Red Knight*. If you regarded the signature-symbol as a plane, then the fuselage was red. All in all, Shoenfeld thought, there was ample evidence linking John with Lindbergh and von Richthofen: John was Lindbergh and again was von Richthofen; the three were bound together in a relationship affected by the homosexual tendencies John unconsciously revealed.

Therefore, couldn't an excellent case be made out that in John's mind the theft of Charles Lindbergh, Jr., was a victorious attack on the hero himself, a daring deed that proved that John was as brave and as skillful as Lindbergh? Hadn't *his* feat, the kidnap-murder, won as much world attention as Lindbergh's transatlantic flight?

Shoenfeld had observed several distinctive characteristics in the notes' writing: a marked tremor, a blurring of letters, a persistent omission of letters from some words and transposition in others: *rihgt, ingnore, singnature,* and so on. This seeming inability to spell and make sense frequently was followed by a stretch of comparative fluency. Numerous letters had been formed with a flourish, elaborately overdecorated. The style changed abruptly; at times it appeared that several writers had had a hand in composing the notes, which undoubtedly would lead a graphologist to say that the writing was disguised.

Perhaps so; but from a psychiatrist's point of view the tremor, the peculiar habit of spelling certain words in the writer's own way, the overdecoration, the sudden departures in style all suggested that John was in a state of *dementia praecox,* for which the newer, most commonly accepted term was *schizophrenia*—"a functional psychosis," in an encyclopedia's compact definition, "characterized by unrealistic behavior dominated by private fantasy."

An early symptom, often evident to the psychiatrist well before the full flowering of the illness, was the same feeling of omnipotence that marked John's actions and writing, and associated with it was the surly conviction that mysterious enemies were resolved to keep the schizophrenic from achieving his desires. Shoenfeld summed up this fourth view of John: if it was correct, then he must have spent at least a brief period in an institution. Shoenfeld further believed that if John suffered an acute mental breakdown before he was captured, it would take the form of mutism: he would not respond to questioning.

Shoenfeld came to the fifth point. On the basis of his analysis of John's mind, he felt that he could describe the kidnaper in physical terms. John was associated with Lindbergh in his private fantasies; he was jealous of Lindbergh, he resented his prestige, his importance—it might be said that John was the older child in the family dominated by a new baby. Resentful, envious, the older child longs to oust the new young rival. John, Shoenfeld believed, would turn out to be older, if not much older, than Lindbergh. Physically he would resemble Lindbergh.

There he was: the kidnaper, the killer, sketched from the inside out.

He was a German alien, with a German common-school education, who had settled in the United States not long ago. Possibly he made his living by working with wood; he might be a carpenter. He was a few years older than Charles Lindbergh, say thirty-three to thirty-six. He resembled Lindbergh. Very likely he had once been a patient in an institution. He was poor, perhaps unemployed, among the millions thrown out of work by the depression. If married, he was tyrannical; possibly childless. Although he could attract and be attracted to women, he spent many of his leisure hours with men. He was methodical, extremely cautious, with abnormal confidence in himself and little faith in those close to him.

Very well. But the major problem remained. In the well-nigh illimitable Bronx there might be hundreds of German immigrants who superficially could serve as a model for the portrait Shoenfeld had drawn. And a borough-wide manhunt, Lieutenant Finn knew, would alert John to the danger in which he stood and send him fleeing to safety.

Somehow, they would have to limit the area of their search.

The psychiatrist thought he had hit on a clue as to how that might be done.

In his final kidnap note—the note for which Charles Lindbergh had paid fifty thousand dollars and which, he had believed, would bring the happy ending to his and Anne's long wait for their stolen child—the kidnaper had written:

you will find the Boad between Horseneck Beach and Gay Head near Elizabeth Island.

Under the magnifying glass, it seemed to Shoenfeld, the words *Gay Head* betrayed signs of having been written originally as *Gun Hill,* and then changed.

Gun Hill Road was a principal thoroughfare in the Bronx. At the point where it was intercepted by Knox Place, a man—certainly it must have been John—had hired Joseph Perrone, the cab driver, to deliver a message to Dr. Condon. That point was a block away from Woodlawn Cemetery, where John and Dr. Condon had first met.

Perhaps the slip, the inadvertent original writing of *Gun Hill,* indicated the neighborhood in which John lived: a residential section either threaded, intersected or bordered by Gun Hill Road.

They studied a police map of the district and traced the places John had named in his directions to Dr. Condon. The cemeteries, Woodlawn and St. Raymond's, were miles apart. They concentrated on the maze of streets between the two points. The most promising section in which to look for their man appeared to be roughly a rectangle in the Williamsbridge section.

The west side of the rectangle, dominated by Woodlawn, was bounded by Jerome Avenue. The east boundary was the Boston Post Road. The northern side of the rectangle was formed by 233rd Street, the southern by Gun Hill Road. The shape of the rectangle, as the two men drew it on the map, ran east and west.

Approximately one square mile of the chosen area was inhabited. But they could further narrow the ground, draw the net tighter, if Shoenfeld's analysis was correct. If it was, John lived in a German community in this hypothetical hunting ground. Once they found such a community, Finn and Shoenfeld agreed, they had every reason to believe that patient, methodical police work would pluck from his fancied safety the kidnaper and murderer of Charles Augustus Lindbergh, Jr.

12

Anne Lindbergh and her new son continued to do nicely. He was christened Jon Morrow.

Not long after the baby's birth, his father bought a watchdog. A far cry from the fox terrier that had drowsed through the kidnaping, it was a Belgian police dog named Thor. Thor patroled the Morrow estate in Englewood; when a strange woman foolishly wandered onto the grounds, he tore her clothes.

Jon Morrow Lindbergh was four months old in December. During the month his father received a letter mailed from Roanoke, Virginia. The writer said that unless he was paid fifty thousand dollars, Charles Lindbergh's second son would be kidnaped.

A more detailed letter arrived, written in the same clumsy hand. It said:

> colonel lindbergh:
> sir i am sorry that i cant write english good but i hope that you have read my other leter. i told you that i wanted money to go away from the usa my home is across the ocean and i must have (50,000) fifty thousand or i will get your baby. dont that we can get it for we can and will if it takes years. i am sorry that you paid your money to the rong man when i now that he did not get your baby and if you not published it your baby would have ben with you today but you broadcast and it was in all the papers. he died of new monia. we have no warm place to stay now i do not want this little baby we want he money and it will cheaper to pay us the $50,000 your child is worth that you. we will leave this country and you can have your child allways and no more worry about. i am in a little town to day call roanoke, va. i live in a big city but i come to roanoke sometimes. you can 2 thousand in 500 bills in 10.00 5 in 20.00. 10 thousand in 50.00 bills 30 in 100.00 and i must put in a box so it will be safe. i no not yet what time i will get to the place where i want you yourself to put the money. it is that you go down to roanoke va and then go to rosewood ave. then go up this ave till you come to a clean looking log close to the side of the road left side then cross the road is a big white pine tree about 30 feet hi close to it is a rotten stump. you put the money in this stump and cover with trash and leave. this is close at the back of the white house and garage. be not later than january 5th. i hope you know enough not to publish this. whin you come do make up so no one will know you. i hope you understand i mean to do what i say.

Another letter followed:

> notice roanoke va.
> i hope you will now enough not to publish or to try to put the cops if so i will sure do my job and you will forever be

sorry. We hate this country and is enough of us to do you and yours and we will unless you put fifty thousand dollars at the place we have told you. rosewood ave or road grant ct. in a stump close to white pine tree on the right side of the road and not later than january 3, 1933 and put it thar yourself and fix yourself so no one will no you and no cops. if you do this as i ask you to i will promest you that you will never be bothered again and can live in pice the rest of your life and we will leve this place and never come back. the way we want the money.

two thousand in 5.00 bills
three do $10.00
five do do $20.00
ten do do $50.00
thirty do 100.00

fifty thousand in all. you do not take the numbers for not one will used in this country.

we want to say farewell to usa sorry my paper is not good but the best i got.

As each letter came, Lindbergh sent it to Colonel Schwarzkopf, who gave it to Captain Lamb. Lamb quickly determined that, aside from the sum of fifty thousand dollars, there were no similarities between the new letters and the original ransom notes.

After notifying the federal authorities, he sent photostats of the letters to the chief of police of Roanoke, Virginia, who summoned the head of his identification bureau, Detective Robert Johnson.

In a wooded section of the Roanoke suburb called Weaver Heights, Johnson found the "clean looking" log, the big white pine tree, and the rotten stump. Registering at a Roanoke hotel under the name John J. Jones, he wrote a letter identifying himself as Colonel Lindbergh's secretary and declaring that fifty thousand was far too much for Lindbergh to pay.

Johnson deposited his letter in the hollow rotten stump near the big white pine tree, then ostentatiously withdrew from the scene. He quietly returned to a hidden spot from which he could watch the stump.

Several hours later, he was forced to leave. When he went back to the stump, the letter was gone.

A new message arrived for John J. Jones at the Roanoke hotel. The tone was more threatening. The fifty thousand dollars must be paid or Colonel Lindbergh's baby would disappear.

Johnson explained in reply that Lindbergh had suffered financial reverses and simply could not manage that amount. He left the letter in the hollow stump; again an answer came to the hotel. Twenty-five thousand dollars had been trimmed from the asking price. Still too much, Johnson replied via the stump; Colonel Lindbergh would not go beyond seventeen thousand.

Here the negotiations rested for several days. On the first day of the new year, 1933, Johnson enlisted Detective Howard Ferguson's aid. One relieving the other, the two men constantly watched the stump from different vantage points. So far as they could see, no one ventured near it.

After six consecutive days and nights of this, Johnson called off their vigil, reporting to his chief that either the other party had detected them and thought it wiser to lie low for a spell or had given up the whole business. But his hopes were revived; a new letter informed him that the proposed seventeen thousand dollars would be acceptable. Johnson replied that the money would be deposited in a Roanoke bank and a check placed in the hollow stump. Next, in the president's office of the Roanoke State and City Bank, he described the plot and explained his strategy. Every teller was instructed to be on the lookout for a check for seventeen thousand dollars made out to Cash, signed by John J. Jones, bearing on its back the notation: *No transfer. To be delivered to bearer as per transfer agreement provided that it is presented to this bank.*

Johnson sealed the check in an envelope with a short note of instructions: the check must be endorsed by a code sign, *No. 2–XXX.* On the face of the envelope he wrote a warning that the enclosures were to be disregarded by all persons except those for whom they were intended. Then he put the envelope in the stump.

He was confident that the man or men who so mysteriously retrieved his letters from the stump without being seen were practically in his grasp. The check would be presented to a teller at the bank, the teller would signal the waiting police, and the police would swoop down.

But nothing happened.

A week passed, a second, a third.

Detective Johnson had never dealt with a more exasperating foe. It almost seemed that the others, whoever they were, took a mischievous delight in tantalizing him. And after three full weeks, the bank tellers could hardly be blamed for relaxing their watchfulness.

But one teller, W. M. Skelton, had not forgotten. At noon on Thursday February 9, he saw a thin young man in cap and windbreaker walk up to his cage and proffer a check made out to *Cash* in the amount of seventeen thousand dollars, signed by John J. Jones, bearing on its back the *No transfer* notation and the endorsement *No. 2–XXX.*

"I want to get this cashed," the young man said.

"All right," Skelton replied. "Just a minute." Turning, he gave the check to the bank's assistant cashier, Leigh Stevens, who recognized it and nodded.

"How do you want it?" Skelton asked the young man.

"Make it in big bills."

Leigh Stevens picked up a money sack and left the cage. Once out of sight, he telephoned Johnson at police headquarters. Surprised and pleased, Johnson summoned Ferguson, and both detectives hurried toward the bank.

Stevens neatly stacked several pads of blank receipts, almost the size of bank notes, wrapped them in brown paper, and tied the bundle with string. He dropped the bundle into the sack and walked slowly back to the cage. The detectives, he saw, were discreetly posted beyond the young man.

Skelton slid the check toward him and told him to sign it. He endorsed it *Roy Brown,* and the teller handed him the brown-paper parcel.

"Thank you," the young man said politely, and left the bank.

Johnson and Ferguson followed. A block away he was joined by a somewhat older man, who glanced behind and seemed to recognize the two detectives. He immediately made off in one direction, his companion in another. The officers ran after their original quarry and saw him slip into a parked car, where a young woman with a baby was waiting.

Johnson arrested them and took them to headquarters. Ferguson remained inconspicuously behind and soon arrested the second man as he warily approached the car.

The one who had offered the check proved to be Joseph Bryant, nineteen; the other, Norman Harvey, twenty-six; the young woman, Harvey's wife Elsie; the infant, their child. Both Bryant and Harvey lived within a half-mile of the rotten stump. Neither had a police record. Both swore they had had nothing to do with a plot to extort money from Charles Lindbergh.

Bryant said he had found the check by accident. Moonshiners kept liquor in hollow stumps throughout the woods, and he had hopefully looked for a drink in this particular stump. Instead, he seemed to have found a fortune. Feeling incapable of dealing with the tremendous windfall by himself, he had hastened to the Harveys' place, and they had agreed to share it with him after the check was cashed.

But Norman Harvey denounced this version. "No, sir!" he shouted. "It's a lie!" Bryant had offered to give him ten thousand dollars *if* he would endorse and cash the check. And he had refused.

It had been simply out of kindness, a favor to a friend, that he had driven Bryant to the bank.

Bryant and the Harveys were kept in custody. Washington was notified and federal agents arrived. Prolonged questioning failed to budge the suspects: they had had no hand in the Lindbergh plot. Handwriting tests were inconclusive; but the Bureau of Standards in Washington, with superior equipment, might be able to make more of them. In the meantime, Bryant and Harvey were formally charged under federal statutes with conspiracy and mailing threatening letters, and were held in default of twenty-five thousand dollars bail. A hearing was scheduled for Monday February 13.

On Monday, counsel for the government explained to United States Commissioner Charles D. Fox, presiding, that more time was needed to permit scientific tests of the handwriting samples, and a new hearing was scheduled for February 18. At the same time, Commissioner Fox drastically reduced the suspects' bail.

The February 18 hearing was also postponed; on February 24, government counsel pleaded for still more time. Commissioner Fox proposed a bargain: he would postpone the hearing until July if the government would consent to a new rock-bottom bond of a thousand dollars, which the suspects could raise and which would enable them to go free.

Government counsel agreed. Back to their woods went Joseph Bryant and Norman Harvey, to tell the adventure of the rotten stump and point out the stump itself to their friends.

13

In New York, detectives investigated the rectangular area in the Bronx where, Dudley Shoenfeld reasoned, the kidnaper-killer lived, most likely in a German community.

They returned with depressing news. There was no German community within the rectangle, they told Lieutenant Finn—or, for that matter, anywhere near it.

Finn notified Shoenfeld, adding that it might still be true that John's home was inside the rectangle, but so were thousands of other homes; its population was that of a fair-sized town. The problem remained formidable.

Leigh Matteson, the newspaperman whose interest in the case had brought Finn and Shoenfeld together, offered a suggestion. Some time ago, he said, it had occurred to Arthur Madden, the Treasury agent, that since an automobile must have been used by the kidnaper his license application must be on file. Why not tie this idea to the rectangle theory—ask the New York State Motor Vehicle Bureau to cull out the license applications which bore German names and street addresses inside the rectangle and then compare the handwriting on the forms with the handwriting in the ransom notes?

A good idea, the others agreed. Right now, in the files of the Motor Vehicle Bureau, John's true name and address might be waiting for them—written in John's own hand, so that for all his shrewdness he would deliver himself to the police. And John's hand was unmistakable: the *x*s that resembled *e*s laid back to back, the *y*s like undotted *j*s, the uncrossed *t*s and undotted *i*s, the habit of inverting *ght* to *hgt*.

Given a number of applications carrying German names and addresses within the Bronx rectangle, surely the handwriting experts would be able to point to the one that was John's!

But when Finn consulted the experts, he was told that the script that appeared on a typical license application form was so scanty that it would be useless to attempt a comparison. Trying to find the kidnaper-killer by this method would be a waste of time and effort.

The search—or, more accurately, the waiting for a break—must go on in the same old weary way. So it seemed.

14

Almost a year had passed since the kidnaping, and the crime was still unsolved. Once again Colonel Schwarzkopf asked himself: What more could his State police do?

His thoughts turned again to the clues, lingered over the kidnap ladder.

It had been examined for fingerprints and photographed from every angle; it had been exhibited to builders, carpenters, and dozens of families in and beyond the neighborhood of the Lindbergh house; slivers had been sent to the Forest Service Laboratory for analysis, and the ladder itself had been scrutinized by technicians of the Bureau of Standards. Nothing significant had come from any of this.

Then had the ladder revealed all it could tell about the man who had used it, the man who had built it?

Perhaps not. So far, the government's wood experts, the Forest Service people, had seen only fragments of the ladder. Perhaps if the whole thing were turned over to them they could pry loose a few secrets.

Major Robert Y. Stuart, chief of the Forest Service of the United States Department of Agriculture, enthusiastically agreed with Schwarzkopf. He had a man, Major Stuart said, who could literally make the ladder talk—Arthur Koehler.

Schwarzkopf remembered that it was Koehler who had found those threads tangled in slivers from the ladder; they'd turned out to have come from the blankets in which the police had wrapped it.

What was so remarkable about Koehler? Well, Stuart replied, he was more than just a wood-identification expert, he was by way of being a detective, and a great detective, too. In fact, in Wisconsin, where Koehler worked, he was called "a Sherlock Holmes of wood." Just the mention of his name had persuaded one particularly ingenious arsonist to confess.

Schwarzkopf's opinion of supersleuths who with trifling ease solved crimes that mystified the police was not high; still, he would take Stuart's word for it. Would he be willing to assign Koehler to the Lindbergh case and send him to New Jersey?

Major Stuart was willing.

Arthur Koehler said good-by to his wife and children and left for Trenton, where, at State police headquarters, Schwarzkopf introduced him to Captain Lamb. Lamb drove him to the Police Training School in nearby Wilburtha.

For the first time, Koehler saw the kidnap ladder itself. His impression was sharp and immediate. The man who had made it did not take pride in his work. Koehler had a craftsman's respect for fine carpentry; where another would notice only that the ladder had been roughly fashioned (but with a good deal of ingenuity, so as to fit two of its sections inside the third), he saw glaring evidence of a slapdash job. For the steps, the builder had used cleats: boards turned on edge and flimsily set into shallow recesses, rather than rungs or flat crosspieces snugly anchored in the side rails; his chisel had gouged unevenly and too deeply into the wood, and he had applied a dull handplane carelessly and inconsistently.

Koehler dissected the ladder. He carefully numbered each part; the bottom cleat became 1, the top cleat 11, the left-hand bottom side rail was 12, progressing in stagger sequence to 17, the right-hand top side rail.

Then he began to inquire through his microscope into the wood's secrets. The ladder-builder had used four kinds. The side rails of the bottom section were second-growth Southern pine; of the middle section, Douglas fir. Both had been used in the top section. The cleats, in the main, were ponderosa pine. The dowels that held the sections together when the ladder was raised were birch.

For four days Koehler scrutinized the numbered pieces, which as a matter of preliminary routine he had measured for length, width and thickness. His stock of information grew. Some of it seemed to him to be of great significance. Whereas it was interesting but not, perhaps, of much value to learn that two of the side rails made of Douglas fir were perforated with a few slanting, round nailholes, showing that the wood had served some earlier construction purpose, it struck Koehler with dramatic force to see that Rail 16, the left-hand Southern-pine side rail in the top section, contained four nailholes, all in the same end of the rail, and that the edges of the holes were clean—not marked by rust. Since rust marks meant moisture, the clean edges showed that wherever that particular board had been used before being built into the ladder, it had been inside, protected from the weather.

And these four nailholes were square, not round, as were the holes in the Douglas fir rails. It followed that the nailholes in Rail 16 had been made by the old-fashioned type of square cut nails.

The distances between the holes varied and the pattern was irregular. Two of them were at an angle and one slanted sharply.

Koehler established the size of the holes at the surface. Then, by a tedious, delicate process of measuring with a square cut nail of the same proportions, he proved to his own satisfaction that one could drive four such nails into the board at—not fifty or a hundred or a thousand but *ten thousand* other spots and not duplicate the unmistakable profile of the four original nailholes.

Koehler asked himself: What would your chances be of finding another board with four old-fashioned square cut nailholes that would precisely match the pattern of the nailholes in Rail 16 of the Lindbergh kidnap ladder?

He put the question in another way. If you found such a board, couldn't you say with almost absolute certainty that at some time in the past it had been nailed to the board that, later on, had been wrenched from it and made into Rail 16 of the ladder?

Considering the spacing of the nailholes, the depth and width, the angle of penetration, and the fact that they had been made by the old-fashioned square nails, the chance that such a board had *not* been nailed to the kidnap ladder board was, Koehler reckoned, mathematically almost nonexistent, say something like one in ten billion.

He employed conservative terms to mention his conclusion to Schwarzkopf and Lamb. When and if they arrested a suspect in the

Wide World

CHARLES AUGUSTUS LINDBERGH, JR.

Fair-haired and blue-eyed, with a dimple in his chin that resembled his famous father's, he was twenty months old and just beginning to talk.

UPI

CHARLES AUGUSTUS LINDBERGH

Nearly five years had passed since his flight across the Atlantic in the flimsy *Spirit of St. Louis,* but he remained in the eyes of millions the audacious, modest, ingenuously appealing kid of 1927.

Wide World

ANNE MORROW LINDBERGH

She looked tiny beside her tall husband, too fragile for adventurous trips, but two years after their marriage she accompanied him on an aerial tour of the Orient and, he proudly reported, helped in everything except the actual piloting of the plane.

THE CRIB
Warming her hands at the electric heater so they wouldn't feel cold on the little boy's skin, Betty Gow crossed to the crib and let her eyes become accustomed to the patch of darkness. Suddenly, oddly, she realized that she did not hear the soft sound of his breathing.

UPI

UPI

THE LINDBERGHS' NEW HOME
The brand-new house—shut off from the world, yet fairly handy to New York—wasn't quite ready; most of the windows lacked curtains, and other finishing touches were needed.

case, Koehler said, it would be a good idea to search his house and garage to see if they contained a strip of wood with nailholes—or possibly with the nails still in it—exactly matching those in Rail 16.

The ladder bore many other identifying marks, each testifying to the character of the workmanship. Koehler determined that a few curved rows of faint scratches had been inscribed by a handsaw, hastily or carelessly used, so that its teeth had snared in the wood. The recesses for the cleats in the side rails had been made by this saw. Its course could be measured by marks of from thirty-five to thirty-seven thousandths of an inch in thickness, the thickness of the saw blade. The chisel, too, had been used on these recesses, and both saw and chisel had cut in more deeply than was necessary.

And then there were the ridges left by the uneven blade of the handplane. Looming up under the magnifying glass like the spines of mountain ranges, they fell into patterns as unmistakable as a man's signature.

Where were those tools now, the plane and the saw (Koehler had the chisel); and where was the board with the pattern of nailholes matching the pattern in Rail 16? To know the answers would be to know who had committed the crime. Koehler didn't know. But just to be able to pose the questions was progress.

He did know that all the wood that had gone into the ladder had come into its builder's hands by devious routes from forest grove to sawmill to market—bought in the lumber market, or stolen, perhaps, just as the ladder was to be used to steal a child. And here was food for thought, as there was in the fact that, with the exception of Rail 16, all the ladder's side rails were one-by-four common—a lumber-trade term. The Southern pine was particularly plentiful, growing in a great many states. It sold so cheaply that Koehler was reasonably certain the pine in the ladder had not been shipped far to market.

Then there were the ponderosa-pine cleats. They had been cut from a single board five and five-eighths inches wide and at least four feet eleven-and-a-half inches long. It was also clear that the two side rails of Southern pine in the bottom section had been cut from one piece, at least fourteen feet long; this was proved by their grain, which matched end to end. But the Douglas fir rails didn't match, which meant that the builder had bought them in short lengths.

On March 8, Arthur Koehler wrote a report of his findings. Submitting it, he said that he would like to search the area around the Lindbergh estate on the chance that he might come across some of the same kind of wood that had been used in the ladder. Schwarzkopf approved, and Detectives Bornmann and De Gaetano were assigned to accompany Koehler.

His inquiry took a more athletic turn. He visited all the settlements in the neighborhood; he scoured through back yards and chicken runs and sheds and garages and outhouses and the homes of people whose names had been turned in to the police. More than once the two detectives had occasion to hoist him through the window of a temporarily vacant house. He ranged into the next county; but nowhere did he find a piece of wood to fit the definitions fixed in his mind.

What about the two birch dowels, used to hold the three sections of the ladder together? They hadn't been made by the builder; they were of a type—three-quarters of an inch in diameter—available in most hardware stores. The same kind of round wooden rod was often used to form mop handles.

The dowel pins in the ladder had been worn shiny. Koehler's inquiries revealed that similar birch dowels were turned out in some Massachusetts factories. He traveled to Massachusetts with the pins. It would be impossible, the factory people told him, to say that the pins had been made by a certain factory and delivered to certain outlets.

Had the ladder told him everything that it could tell? Koehler thought not. He said he would like to have the dissected parts in his laboratory in Madison for further study. Schwarzkopf agreed and the arrangements were made.

Koehler returned to his home and his family, and to a pleasant surprise. In his absence, a new workroom with the very best equipment had been set up for him in the Forest Service Laboratory. Again he settled down to study the ladder that, more than a year ago, had been raised to a window of the Lindbergh nursery, and that, when its scars and nailholes were properly interpreted—and Arthur Koehler knew this with absolute certainty—would point to the man who had stolen and killed Charles and Anne Lindbergh's baby son.

15

Lieutenant Finn, Special Agent Wilson of the Treasury Department, and Special Agent Sisk of the Department of Justice agreed that the break they had been hoping for had arrived.

The Hoover administration had departed, leaving the great depression. Industrial production stood at an appalling all-time low. Increased runs on the banks and the more and more popular habit of hoarding gold were shaking the country's financial structure. President Roosevelt had moved to halt these dangers by summoning a special session of Congress and asking it to approve the Emergency Banking Relief Act, which it hastily did. Next, he had explained the purpose of the act and other measures in a fireside chat to his fellow citizens. His talk was designed to persuade hoarders to return the gold to the banks. Many responded; within a few days some $633 million in gold coins and certificates were redeposited; but the Federal Reserve Board estimated that a billion dollars was still in private hands, $600 million in gold certificates, $400 million in gold bullion and coins.

The new Secretary of the Treasury, William H. Woodin, pointed out that hoarded gold served no useful purpose, whereas added to the deposits in the Federal Reserve banks it would supply a sound basis for currency and credit; but his mild words achieved little.

And so, on April 5, President Roosevelt exercised the powers granted to him by the Banking Relief Act. He directed all persons possessing gold (bullion, coins, or certificates) valued at more than a hundred dollars to deposit it in Federal Reserve banks, or banks that were members of the Federal Reserve System, on or before May 1, 1933, when the gold would be exchanged for other forms of currency. The penalty for noncompliance was a ten thousand dollar fine or ten years' imprisonment, or both.

As governor of New York, Roosevelt had offered the state's aid in the Lindbergh case; now, of course without realizing it, he had supplied the break. Finn and the others were convinced of it. Gold certificates made up almost two-thirds of the fifty thousand dollar ransom paid to John—and in just a little over three weeks his gold notes would be outlawed. If John held on to them and then tried to pass them, their very appearance should awaken suspicion and sooner or later sound an alarm. It was easy for a bank teller or a store clerk to become forgetful about checking the serial numbers of the Lindbergh ransom bills, but each gold certificate would carry with it a cry for attention that could hardly be ignored.

But this new development might well trap John by May 1 if he decided to play safe right away and turn in his gold notes. Finn, Wilson and Sisk hurriedly informed officials and cashiers of the Federal Reserve Bank of New York and affiliated banks in the city. Every teller must be on the lookout.

John's arrest seemed imminent. It seemed so imminent to Finn that he began to ponder the question of *how* he should be arrested and examined; both arrest and examination could be badly botched.

Finn asked Dudley Shoenfeld's advice, which was immediate and positive. John, he said, must be arrested away from his house. Then he would be bound to have at least one ransom bill with him: his psychological makeup compelled him to carry one or more bills wherever he went, since, in his unconscious, the ransom money was the symbol of his omnipotence.

Finn's matter-of-fact mind added that John certainly would take some of the ransom money whenever he went out because he would have to be continually alert for opportunities to exchange it.

In any event, a ransom bill on his person would enable the police to hold him. At home, John would have no special reason to keep money in his pocket. He might even regard his home as an unsafe place for the bills. Perhaps he had hidden them somewhere else.

The arrest, Shoenfeld continued, must be made discreetly if they were to get a confession. They must not clamp down on John as on an ordinary criminal and hustle him off for the routine, intimidating processes of examination. John lived in a special world. He thought of himself as surrounded by enemies. He should be taken into custody through a technical arrest and quietly removed to a secluded place—an apartment, say—where the surroundings would be relaxing and he might freely respond to questions of the sort a psychiatrist would address to the mentally diseased. The familiar, rough-and-ready police methods and the inevitable publicity would only confirm John's conviction that he lived in a hostile world; he would show his contempt for it, and demonstrate his superiority to it, by refusing to speak.

One week before May 1, fifty ten-dollar ransom bills turned up at the Chemical National Bank in New York; a few days later, fifty more were discovered at the Manufacturers Trust Company. None had caught the eye of a teller at the time of transaction.

May 1 arrived. In Manhattan, thousands of members and sympathizers of the Communist Party paraded to Union Square, where crowds cheered the May Day celebration. Other crowds hurried to the banks and lined up in queues, often as thick as three abreast, to exchange their gold for legal currency.

In the rush, would the sweating tellers remember to watch for those supremely important gold certificates that, in effect, would say, "Here I am—John"?

Finn, Wilson and Sisk waited through the day with as much composure as they could manage. No calls came in from the banks.

But the next day examination showed that $2980 in gold certificates, received by the Federal Reserve Bank of New York in a single transaction, bore serial numbers that fell within the ransom list. On the exchange slip was written *J. J. Faulkner, 537 West 149th Street, New York City.*

The teller who had taken the gold notes and the slip could remember nothing about J. J. Faulkner. The three investigators set out in pursuit.

There were no Faulkners at 537 West 149th Street.

They dug deeper. A dozen years ago a Faulkner *had* lived there, a J. Faulkner at that. And an automobile that had been stolen in Lakehurst, New Jersey, a few days before the Lindbergh kidnaping had been recovered not long afterward across the street from the house.

J. Faulkner proved to be Jane Faulkner; city marriage records showed that on May 21, 1921, she had married Carl O. Giessler, a naturalized German. Intensive police work tracked the Giesslers to their home in Larchmont, New York; but here the trail ran into a wall. Giessler was part owner of a Madison Avenue flower shop, unimpeachably respectable; he was able to prove that neither he nor Mrs. Giessler, née Faulkner, had any connection with the $2980 exchange slip or the kidnap-murder of the Lindbergh baby.

It seemed that the man who had filled in the slip had picked the name and address out of the air.

The high hopes the investigators had shared sank from their peak of April 5 until, soon after May 1, they reached the familiar level of watching and waiting. Federal Reserve Bank officials discovered that $700 million in bullion, coins and certificates remained in private hands. This meant that, though John had kept most of his gold notes, a great many other people also had kept theirs. In other words, John might have plenty of company while passing gold notes; they might even become so common as to arouse no interest at all when they appeared.

16

Gaston Means was on trial again. On Monday May 8, in the District of Columbia Supreme Court, he was charged with conspiracy to defraud Mrs. McLean of thirty-five thousand dollars, which he had told her the gang demanded because the serial numbers of the ransom bills they had collected from Dr. Condon had been so widely advertised.

Mrs. McLean told the jury the story of her dealings with Means and The Fox. She could see The Fox, if she cared to, as she spoke. Forty-two, medium height, well dressed, a bit plump, he seemed far less sinister in the courtroom than he had to Mrs. McLean in her Aiken place. He had been run to earth by agents of the Justice Department and arrested by New York detectives at his father-in-law's Brooklyn home. Records of the department's Division of Investigation divulged The Fox's real name, Norman T. Whitaker, a man with a family background as respectable as Means'—but he too had run into trouble with the law. They had met in the federal penitentiary at Leavenworth, Kansas.

According to Whitaker, he'd had nothing to do with the plot to defraud Mrs. McLean, but then she had been asked to come to New York for a police line-up. "That's Number 19," she had said, pointing to the diffident Whitaker. "That's The Fox."

Mrs. McLean finished her story. Neither Means nor Whitaker seemed disturbed by it.

The next day the courtroom was packed; Charles Lindbergh had offered to testify. He had arrived with Anne the evening before in the famous low-wing monoplane of their tour to the Orient in 1931. On the witness stand, he quietly described the kidnaping and the discovery of the baby's body. Together with the respectful questions put by the prosecuting attorney, the account required barely fifteen minutes.

Lindbergh was followed on the stand by Gaston Means.

He had avoided the witness chair in his previous trial, but now he seemed pleased to be in it, adjusting his bulk as comfortably as possible to its bony structure and smilingly awaiting the questions of his attorney, J. William Tomlinson.

The first question brought a hush to the room.

"Do you know who kidnaped the Lindbergh baby?"

"Yes."

"Do you know who got the fifty thousand dollars Colonel Lindbergh paid the kidnapers through Dr. Condon?"

"Yes."

"Do you know where the one hundred thousand dollars paid by Mrs. McLean is?"

"Yes."

Tomlinson paused. Then he asked Means to tell the true story of the Lindbergh kidnaping.

He had decided to testify, Means assured his attorney, solely to serve the truth. Then he stated that the leader of the kidnap gang was Wellington Henderson, head of the Communist Third International in the United States. Henderson's right-hand man was Irving Fenton, whom Means had met while serving an earlier sentence in the Atlanta penitentiary.

The original plan, he continued, was not to kidnap the baby but his *father*. Circumstances had forced the gang to steal the child instead. "But," Means added, "if Colonel Lindbergh had tried to enter the negotiations, as they had expected, he would have been captured and they would have asked a million dollars' ransom for him."

Irving Fenton had urged him to join the gang, but Means had refused. Nevertheless, Fenton told him about every move. The "actual engineers" of the abduction were Max Hassel and Max Greenberg, two of gangster Waxey Gordon's bootleg beer-runners, and it was Violet Sharpe who kept Henderson informed of Charles and Anne Lindbergh's activities. But in Means' honest opinion she didn't realize the significance of what she was doing.

Snatched by the gang on the night of March 1, the baby was taken to a "liquor dugout," a bootleg storage place, in New Jersey. Some days later, Henderson and Fenton came to see Means at his home. The two men were in a highly excited state. They told him that they had tried to deliver the child to Mrs. McLean at Fairview, her Maryland country home, but, contrary to their understanding of arrangements, she wasn't there. Recalling that Colonel M. Robert Guggenheim was a friend of the Lindberghs, they had driven to his home in Washington. He had refused to accept the baby.

So just where *were* they to deliver the child, Henderson had hotly inquired of Means, and were they or were they not to get the one hundred thousand dollar ransom?

Means did his best to reassure them. "I realized I was up against a hard proposition," he remarked parenthetically to the jury, "with Mrs. McLean falling down on me like that." The next day he told her about the opportunity she had missed and advised her to leave immediately for Fairview. She did so. But there was another hitch. While reconnoitering the grounds at Fairview, Henderson and Fenton observed that Mrs. McLean was accompanied by a maid, a nurse, two chauffeurs, and an unidentified man. He might very well be a plain-clothes man, they thought. And so, suspicious and afraid, they quickly drove away with the child.

Again they complained to Means. He realized that he would have to speak bluntly to Mrs. McLean. "I went to her and told her that she was violating our agreement by having so many people out there. I told her that if she kept putting obstacles in the way, there was no telling what would happen to the baby."

Mrs. McLean had a place in Aiken, South Carolina. Taking the baby with them, Henderson and Fenton and a few other members of the gang went there. Then Henderson summoned Means and led him to a parked car; and on the back seat of the car there was a child.

The child had blue eyes and blond hair. Means took him into his arms. The little boy, Henderson told him, was Charles Augustus Lindbergh, Jr.

But just when it seemed that the exchange of the child for the ransom money would surely take place, The Fox became suspicious of a trap and the gang hastily left for Juarez, Mexico.

Then his negotiations had had to be dropped, Means said—"temporarily dropped," or so he had thought.

He and The Fox had been instructed by Henderson to confer with Fenton in Chicago. Fenton showed them the forty-nine thousand five hundred dollars that remained of the sum Dr. Condon had paid, money they dared not use and wanted to hand over to Mrs. McLean in exchange for thirty-five thousand in unlisted bills. Fenton kept it in a locked box; he retained a key for himself and gave Means a duplicate to take to Henderson.

Means' next task was to deliver Mrs. McLean's hundred thousand to her in Washington. But on a bridge near Alexandria, Virginia, three men waved him to a stop with a red lantern. They were strangers, Means said, but identified themselves as Mrs. McLean's agents by uttering the secret code number, eleven.

They said that Mrs. McLean had ordered them to collect her money from him. His orders, he told them, were to deliver it to the lady herself.

"Those orders have been changed," the men replied.

In view of the change, and convinced that he was dealing with Mrs. McLean's authorized representatives, Means obeyed.

On May 17, five days after the baby had been found dead, Henderson came to see him. Means confronted him with the shocking news. Henderson laughed. It wasn't the Lindbergh child, he said; the body in the Jersey woods was a plant the gang had arranged.

If that was true, Means asked, how could Charles Lindbergh have identified the body?

Henderson shrugged it off. Lindbergh was mistaken. The baby was alive and well in Juarez at that very moment. The Communist Party of the United States had in its possession documents substantiating everything he had said.

Both Wellington Henderson and Irving Fenton, Means declared, could be found at either 2419 or 3419 Grand River Avenue in Detroit. And the hundred thousand dollars ransom was in a safety-deposit box in the name of Max Hassel in the Elizabethport Banking Company in Elizabeth, New Jersey.

Means was finished. The date was May 12, a year after the day William Allen had chanced upon the small body half-hidden beneath the dirt and sodden leaves of its quick grave.

United States Attorney Leo A. Rover, chief prosecutor, got up and said that the government would not cross-examine. He had no desire to lend importance to Gaston Means' fantasies by appearing to take them seriously. He sat down.

His colleagues whispered to him, however, and presently he rose again. He merely wanted to establish two facts: that the chief actors in Means' staggering tale were either dead or did not exist and never had existed, making it impossible for the prosecution to call them to affirm or deny Means' statements. Violet Sharpe was dead, and recently Max Hassel and Max Greenberg had been riddled with gunfire by persons unknown in the Elizabeth-Carteret Hotel in Elizabeth. A high-ranking Communist Party official had said "There is no such person as Wellington Henderson in the Communist Party. Gaston Means' testimony is a silly attempt to shift blame that not even enemies of the Communist Party can believe." Furthermore, Rover continued, of the two Detroit addresses given by Means, there was no 3419 Grand River Avenue and 2419 was the headquarters of the Workers, not the Communist, Party.

As for Max Hassel's safety-deposit box, which Means said contained Mrs. McLean's hundred thousand dollars (presumably turned over to Hassel by the three men who had collected it from Means), Justice Department agents discovered $214,000 in it and a note for fifty thousand dollars signed by an Elizabeth lawyer—but the denominations ranged from fifty- to five-thousand-dollar bills, whereas Mrs. McLean had given Means nothing larger than a hundred-dollar bill.

In Means, the prosecutor told the jury, American society found itself unwillingly possessed of a modern Baron Münchausen, "such a dyed-in-the-wool liar that if he ever told the truth, he'd lie to get out of it."

It took the jury two hours and twenty minutes to find Gaston Means and Norman Whitaker—who had declined to take the stand—guilty as charged. Each was sentenced to two years in prison.

With an affable smile for all, Gaston Means was led from the courtroom to resume his stay in the Atlanta penitentiary, a longer stay than he had foreseen. The Fox went with him.

17

Among the many scars on the kidnap ladder were some that claimed Arthur Koehler's particular attention. He had detected them during his original study of the ladder and noted them down as warranting further investigation. They appeared along the edges and both faces of each of the bottom side rails, Numbers 12 and 13—a series of tiny, shallow, almost imperceptible grooves. Koehler had recognized them at once for what they were: the marks made by the knives of a lumber-mill planer.

In his workroom, he carefully studied the grooves. A unique fact emerged through the microscope lens. Along one edge of each bottom rail—both of which originally had been part of the same strip of one-by-four-inch Southern pine—an imperfection in the blade of one of the planer's knives had carved a faint but unmistakable path. He measured the space between the barely distinguishable blemishes. They were the same distance apart. Precisely eighty-six hundredths of an inch separated one from the next.

Koehler felt a spark of excitement. He had all of the knife cuts photographed and the photos greatly enlarged. Then he studied the imperfect grooves again, as a fingerprint expert would examine enlargements of the fingers' identifying whorls. To Koehler's appraising glance, the blemishes made by the defective knife in effect were the fingerprints of the planer.

How could he find that planer?

First, he would have to determine its characteristics—speed, number of knives, and so on—since mill planers often varied. Koehler knew the usual type as intimately as he knew all woodworking equipment. Two revolving steel cylinders gripped the untrimmed board and thrust it between four cutter-heads: sets of protruding knives fixed at regular intervals around steel drums. Spinning at high velocity, the cutter-heads flicked minute semicircular fragments from the board as it passed between them—two face cutters first shaving the broad surfaces, two edge cutters then paring the narrow surfaces. When all four surfaces of the board had been dressed, two more revolving cylinders thrust it out of the planer. The speed of the feed rolls fixed the speed of its passage.

Studying the tiny blemishes on the matching edges of the two ladder rails, Koehler counted, from one to the next, six knife cuts. Since the blemishes could be called revolution marks (the defective blade had left its mark every time its cutter-head completely revolved), this meant that the edges of the original pine board had been trimmed by cutter-heads with six knives. And now the photo enlargements supplied another clue. Every eighth knife cut on the matching faces of the rails was faintly dissimilar, betraying the fact that one of the cutters' blades had not protruded as far as it should have and had not cut as fully into the wood as the others. This minute irregularity also formed a revolution mark, testifying that there were eight knives in the cutter-heads that had dressed the broad surfaces of the board.

Koehler measured the space between each casual discrepancy. They were exactly ninety-three hundredths of an inch apart.

He now knew the essential characteristics of the planer he sought. There were eight knives in its face cutters, six knives in its edge cutters, and they revolved at different speeds. A board traveled through the planer ninety-three hundredths of an inch for each revolution of the face cutters, eighty-six hundredths of an inch for every spin of the edge cutters.

Koehler jotted down a few calculations. He concluded that the original strip of Southern pine, of which the ladder's bottom rails had been part, had been dressed at the rate of about 230 feet a minute, more than twice the speed of the typical eastern mill planer. Even so, he was confident that his quest could be limited to the eastern states. Although Southern pine grew all over the country, it was so cheaply purchased that it would have been unprofitable to ship it far—from forest grove to mill, from mill to lumberyard or another source. And since the two portions of the pine strip lying before him had eventually turned up in New Jersey, Koehler felt reasonably sure they had been milled somewhere in the Atlantic states.

In the thousands of miles of the Atlantic area, however, there were hundreds of mills; and even should he find the mill, there would remain the considerable task of tracing the wood from the mill to the lumberyard that had purchased it, and from the lumberyard to the man who had bought, or stolen, the pieces he had used in making the kidnap ladder.

The first step, at least, was simple. Koehler took out his copy of the Southern Lumberman's Directory and turned to the list of planing mills from New York to Alabama. There were 1598 of them. He would have to approach each one.

He began to write a letter that could be mailed, simultaneously, to every mill listed. He said that he was anxious to locate a planer that fed lumber, particularly one-by-four-inch Southern pine, at a speed of 230 feet a minute and that had six knives in its edge cutters and eight knives in its face cutters, the first revolving faster than the second. He asked the mill-owner if he possessed such a machine. He also asked for a prompt reply.

18

Charles and Anne Lindbergh had made their home near Hopewell, and they had hoped to return to it. The white house on the hill overlooking the Sourlands had been kept in readiness for the homecoming by Oliver and Elsie Whateley.

In the middle of May, Oliver experienced an alarming increase in the mild internal pains that occasionally troubled him. He wouldn't have worried too much if Elsie had been there, but she was in England, visiting relatives, and he felt more than ever alone in the big house. He went to a doctor. The result was an emergency operation for a perforated ulcer.

Lindbergh visited Oliver twice in the Princeton hospital and telephoned several times. Elsie arrived at his bedside a few minutes before he died.

His death seemed to put the finishing touch to the idea of returning to the Hopewell place, an idea already shaken by the threatening letters from Roanoke and similar letters Charles and Anne Lindbergh had received and turned over to the police. The young parents came to a decision: since it seemed that it would be impossible for them to live a normal family life there, they would abandon the white house.

There had been offers for the hundred-thousand-dollar estate. Several were shocking: some people wished to turn the house into a kind of museum, open to the public for a fee. Souvenirs would be on sale, soft drinks, hot dogs. It could be a gold mine.

The Lindberghs decided to donate the estate as a welfare center for children.

They would form a board of trustees to manage it as a nonprofit corporation. They themselves would serve on the board; also Colonel Breckinridge, Owen Lovejoy, executive secretary of the Children's Aid Society in New York, and Dr. Abraham Flexner, director of the Institute for Advanced Study at Princeton University.

In June, Breckinridge filed the incorporation papers, setting forth the purpose of the organization: "To provide for the welfare of children, including their education, training, hospitalization, and other allied purposes, without discrimination in regard to race or creed."

Charles and Anne named it High Fields.

A few weeks later in the federal court building in Roanoke, Virginia, United States Commissioner Charles D. Fox reviewed the government's case against Joseph Bryant and Norman Harvey, accused of having attempted to extort fifty thousand dollars from Charles Lindbergh—and dismissed it.

The government's inability to make the charge stick was a great relief to Bryant; to Harvey, it was a matter of indifference. A week before, he had been sentenced to twelve years in the Virginia state penitentiary for killing a certain Curtis Edwards, who, Harvey said, had maliciously thrown rocks at his cottage one moonlit night.

19

In July, *The New York Times* added a new information service. It resembled the weather reports in that it was published regularly, in concise form, and was regarded as sufficiently interesting to grace *The Times'* front page. The new service was called *The Kidnaping Situation* and it gave readers up-to-the-minute facts on the latest abductions: who had been kidnaped, who had been released, how much ransom had been paid, what kidnapers had been caught.

The Times also published a summary, not unlike the baseball standings in the sports pages, listing the victims of the rapidly growing kidnaping business, now commonly known as the snatch racket. *The Times* made three significant points: prior to the abduction of Charles Lindbergh, Jr., only one kidnaping had been thought worthy of mention in the nation's press; of all the hostages taken for ransom, only the Lindbergh baby had been recovered dead; finally, the success of his abductors in extorting fifty thousand dollars from the parents had encouraged later kidnapers to demand larger and larger payments.

Attorney General Homer S. Cummings announced that the federal government was well aware of this growing threat to the public welfare and that new legislation to deal with it was being drafted for the next session of Congress. Meanwhile, he said, there were a few basic rules every family should obey if kidnapers struck:

1. Notify the nearest office of the Division of Investigation of the Department of Justice.
2. Dissuade outsiders, no matter how well-meaning, from injecting themselves into the case.
3. Leave the scene of the abduction unchanged until the authorities have examined it for evidence and clues.
4. Avoid publicity at all costs, for news of the crime would give notice to the kidnapers that the authorities had been appealed to, with the result that the hostage might be killed.

The attorney general urged all families threatened by kidnapers to take the Department of Justice into their confidence and assured them that any information they gave would be acted upon with the utmost skill and discretion.

Like *The Times,* Lloyds of London introduced a new service. Many wealthy Americans had requested the famous English underwriters to provide a hedge against possible abductions by issuing kidnap-insurance policies. The names of the insured could not be disclosed, of course, since the information might be regarded by kidnapers as an invitation to move in; but it was understood that the maximum protection Lloyds offered an adult was a hundred thousand dollars. For a child, Lloyds stipulated as maximum the sum paid for Charles Lindbergh, Jr.'s, dead body: fifty thousand dollars.

Lloyds also offered compensation for injuries sustained by a hostage while held by kidnapers.

20

Some lumber mills had replied to his request as speedily as Arthur Koehler had hoped; others had been exasperatingly slow. Day after day, from New York and New Jersey, from Pennsylvania and Maryland, from the Virginias and the Carolinas and Georgia and Alabama—from the entire span of the suspect territory—their letters had arrived at Koehler's workshop in the Forest Service Laboratory; day after day he had scanned them expectantly. Now he totted up the results.

Twenty-five mill owners thought they had a planer that fit Koehler's description. He could rule out two of these, however, because they had never handled one-by-four-inch Southern pine, the kind of boards from which the kidnap ladder's bottom rails had come.

Koehler wrote a second request to the twenty-three mills that remained: would they please send him samples of one-by-four boards their planers had dressed?

Again the response was erratic; a few samples came promptly, the rest at tedious intervals. Impatiently Koehler examined each piece as it arrived, scrutinized the planer's subtle scars, determined the revolution marks made by its cutter-heads and measured the distance between them, counted the number of knife cuts from one revolution mark to the next.

The marks and measurements he had memorized during his analysis of the ladder's bottom rails were thrown like a shadow from the pattern in his mind onto every sample of wood under his microscope. Time after time they failed to match.

Then one day in the quiet room they matched exactly. There it was, the piece he had hoped to get, a one-by-four-inch strip that had passed through a planer operating at precisely the same speed and with the same number of knives. Eight blades in the face cutters had dressed the strip every ninety-three hundredths of an inch; six blades in the edge cutters had trimmed it every eighty-six hundredths of an inch.

True, the planer had not left its fingerprints on the strip as it had on the ladder's bottom rails—the faint blemishes along one edge and the slightly irregular scars along one face. But Koehler hadn't expected to see them again. Long ago the defective knife that had caused the blemishes almost certainly had been sharpened or replaced and the maverick blade that had made the irregular nicks put back in line.

Still, he thought, further tests might be useful. He telegraphed the M. G. and J. J Dorn Company of McCormick, South Carolina (which had sent him the wood), and asked for additional samples—*but* samples taken from stock going on two years old. There was just a bare possibility, Koehler thought, that wood planed that far back and still on hand might reveal the "fingerprints." Eighteen months had passed since the kidnap ladder had been found, and it seemed likely that at least some of the wood used to put it together had been purchased a few weeks to a few months before the crime.

The new samples came. None bore the "fingerprints," and some showed a wider spacing between the revolution marks than others, which revealed the same intervals as the Dorn mill's previous sample. Koehler was puzzled. Different spacing meant different speeds. Why had some boards traveled through the planer faster than others?

The question was irritating; until he had the answer, he couldn't proceed.

Koehler again packed his bags, said good-by to his family and left for South Carolina.

At the Dorn mill in McCormick, he showed his Forest Service badge, introduced himself, and in turn was introduced to Joseph J. Dorn, one of the owners and a South Carolina state senator as well.

It was Koehler's habit to reveal as little of the nature of his missions as possible, but he felt that he could and should confide freely in Senator Dorn. The latter listened, assured him that the information would go no further, and with gratifying zeal ordered his mill hands to hunt from one end of the yard to the other and bring every old scrap of one-by-four Southern pine they could find. Maybe there was something around, he told Koehler, that would show the same so-called fingerprints as those engraved on the kidnap ladder's bottom rails.

No matching piece was found; but while the hunt was on, Koehler obtained the answer to the puzzle of the planer's performance. When it had been installed, Dorn explained, the planer had been equipped with a large pulley that produced too fast a feed. A smaller pulley sent by the factory hadn't helped; it was too slow. The mill had licked the problem by purchasing an in-between-size pulley from an Augusta, Georgia, hardware store. While it hadn't been designed for the planer, it worked fine. Even so, the standard pulleys were also used from time to time, which accounted for the different speeds.

Koehler had listened with growing interest. Could he see the middle-size pulley operate?

It was quickly installed and a board was fed between the planer's whirling cutters. When it emerged, its markings, except for the missing fingerprints, matched those on the ladder rails.

Koehler felt encouraged. It was only a tiny step forward, but with luck it might lead to giant strides.

When had the pulley been bought?

Dorn led Koehler to his office, thumbed through the ledgers and ran his finger to a date: September 1929.

The Lindbergh baby had been kidnaped on March 1, 1932. Koehler counted back. To trace the ladder rails to their ultimate owner, he would have to track down all the one-by-four-inch Southern pine the Dorn mill had sold during roughly twenty-nine months —quite a bit longer than the period he had hoped for.

But there was a way to simplify the task. Since the ladder was linked by the crime to New Jersey, it seemed sensible to limit the search to an area north of the Potomac. If not successful, he could broaden it later.

Koehler began to copy from the ledgers the date and destination of each shipment to that area. When he studied the finished list, it seemed to point unhesitatingly to his next move. Forty-six carloads, made up wholly or partly of the pine, had been sent north to twenty-five firms. Many of these firms no doubt had sold the wood to others, and these to still others, some of the lumber changing hands so often that he might never be able to trace it. But at least he knew where to start. Eighteen of the carloads had gone to two places within a twenty-five-mile radius of the Lindbergh home. These places were the Johns Manville plant at Manville, New Jersey, and a Trenton box factory.

Koehler thanked Senator Dorn and took the next train north.

The Trenton factory had received four carloads of the pine, the Manville plant fourteen. With Detective Lewis Bornmann, whom the State police had selected to accompany him on such calls, Koehler first visited Johns Manville.

He learned that the Dorn shipment had been disposed of soon after it arrived, sliced into short lengths and used to make crates for the company's products. Where had the wood been stored before it was cut up? Behind high wire fences—extremely difficult, Koehler saw at a glance, for a thief to climb. What lengths had the boards been cut to—how short? Too short, he found, to have been used for the kidnap ladder's bottom rails.

At the box factory in Trenton, Koehler was told a similar story and left similarly satisfied. The single board he had set out to trace had not been shipped there, either. He crossed the eighteen carloads off his list. Although he seemed to be moving sideways instead of forward, it was progress of a sort.

In pursuit of the twenty-eight carloads still to be accounted for, Koehler and Bornmann journeyed to New York City; upstate to Germantown; to Stamford and New Haven, Connecticut; to Boston and Springfield, Massachusetts. None of the lumberyards they visited had even a scrap of the Dorn pine left over; every piece had been sold. But some of the dealers recalled the stock, remembered people who had bought bits of it, and, consulting account books, supplied their names and addresses.

The new list, even longer than the first one, plunged Koehler into a house-to-house search that at times reminded him uncomfortably of the celebrated hunt for the needle in the haystack, a needle which, so far as he knew, had never been found. Not explaining his visits, but with the authority of his badge and Bornmann's police credentials, he embarked on a lengthy tour of the suspect points, stopping at each place to make a tiny dissection: a sliver of garage, a few ounces of attic, a morsel of hen coop, a chip of kennel, a fragment of baby's playpen, an inch or two of fence. Ringed by curious stares, he whittled piece after piece of pine, inspected them through his magnifying glass, thanked the sometimes hospitable, sometimes hostile owner and went on. Nowhere did he find a specimen that matched the wood pattern he had memorized.

Returning to New York, Koehler again began to check out the shipments from the Dorn mill.

The search narrowed; eliminating one entry after another, he arrived with Bornmann at a lumberyard in Ozone Park on Long Island, heard the same explanation he had been given so often: all of the Dorn pine had been sold. Every bit of it? The dealer nodded, then reflected. Now that he thought about it, he said, he remembered having used some of the one-by-fours to build storage bins.

He led them to the bins and, noting an awkwardly protruding board, sawed it off and handed it to Koehler. The light was dim and speckled with wood dust. Koehler carried the strip of pine into clear sunlight and studied it through his glass.

Faintly visible along one edge of the board and spaced equally apart were the familiar blemishes a defective cutter knife had engraved on the kidnap ladder's bottom rails. He turned to Bornmann with a smile. At last the pattern matched.

But not precisely. Although the tiny scars were the same, they were a trifle farther apart and closer to the center of the board edge than they appeared on the ladder rails.

Driving on with Bornmann, Koehler turned over the discrepancy in his mind. Wider spacing meant that the board had traveled through the planer at a swifter speed, but why? The Dorn pulleys, of course, he thought. This wood had been dressed when the original, fast-feed pulley was on the planer and the edge cutters were either in a higher or lower position than they occupied when the ladder-board had gone through.

His thoughts quickened. Ordinarily, except when the knives were sharpened, a planer's cutters were reset only after they had been replaced by other cutters temporarily employed to dress patterned stock. It would seem, therefore, that directly prior to the planing of the Ozone Park shipment, some patterned stock had been trimmed. If this were true, there was only one possible conclusion: both before and after the special order, the defective knife was at work—and before, and possibly after, the Ozone Park purchase, the middle-size pulley that had produced the marks on the ladder rails was on the planer.

Almost certainly the board he wanted had been part of a carload of Southern pine the Dorn mill had shipped directly before or immediately after the shipment to Ozone Park.

Koehler took the list from his pocket. The subsequent delivery had gone—twenty days later—to Youngstown, Pennsylvania. But these one-by-fours, he had noted parenthetically, had been dressed an eighth of an inch narrower than the ladder-board.

He looked at the entry two lines above. In November 1931, nine days earlier than the Ozone Park shipment, a portion of Southern pine of the precise width and thickness of the ladder rails had been included in a carload of lumber sent to Halligan & McClelland in New York City.

At Halligan & McClelland, Koehler asked his usual questions. As usual, the Dorn shipment had been sold—but to a single purchaser. The entire carload had been bought by the National Lumber & Millwork Company on White Plains Road in the Williamsbridge district of the Bronx.

Koehler and Bornmann were in good spirits as they left. It had been a long and arduous search, but if their luck held it seemed that they might soon find the needle in the haystack.

21

At police headquarters in New York, Lieutenant Finn's map of the city had taken on a brisk new look. The few scattered pins with which, more than a year before, he had started to record the appearances of the Lindbergh ransom money had multiplied into a miniature forest, a solitary green pin symbolizing the single twenty-dollar bill that had been reported, clusters of of red representing ten-dollar notes, thickets of black indicating the fives. The date on which each bill had been detected—and a corresponding pin stuck in the map—was meticulously marked.

Studying the map day after day, Finn had seen a pattern gradually emerge. Originally, the ransom-bills passer had set out in a different direction each time he disposed of the money, and when he eventually went back over the same routes he apparently never pressed his luck by turning up twice in the same place. But though he was cautious, he also was careless—or, to use Dr. Dudley Shoenfeld's diagnosis, he was a bit carried away by his sense of omnipotence. For one thing, he operated continuously in the same limited area; for another, he was most active in neighborhoods which appeared to be fairly convenient to where he lived. The pins were thickest along the subway and streetcar routes running north and south in the northeast sector of the city: along Lexington and Third avenues in upper Manhattan and the German-speaking district of Yorkville; across the Harlem River in the great bosom of the Bronx.

The Bronx was where he lived. It had to be. Fine lines had been drawn between each and every pin, so that the map now resembled a vast spider's web; but in the center, where the lines mainly intersected, a large, loose knot had formed. Somewhere inside that knot or close to it, Finn was convinced, was the man he wanted.

A series of threads spun from it toward the Fordham section of the borough, looped back toward Morris Park, and swept downward in a long curve dotted with red and black pins through the eastern length of Manhattan to Wall Street and City Hall and across the East River to Brooklyn—the pins becoming fewer and fewer the farther they appeared from the Bronx. A few ransom bills had turned up in Albany, Utica and Troy in upstate New

York, one as far away as Chicago, but Finn was confident that originally these too had been passed within the city limits.

Shoenfeld's analysis and most of the clues and now the map pointed to the Bronx as the place where John could be found. But the tangled web in the center sprawled over such a sizable area that it was no more helpful in establishing his exact whereabouts in the borough than the psychiatrist's conjectured rectangle.

Still, the various pins—or, more accurately, the ransom bills they represented—had gradually given flesh to John's features. For all the bank tellers, storekeepers, clerks and cashiers who did not notice the Lindbergh money, there were some, a praiseworthy minority, who did. When a bill was reported, a few of Finn's detectives hurried to the scene. Usually these sorties achieved nothing; the callers had not recognized the money until some time after they had received it and had only a hazy recollection, or none at all, of the person who had submitted it. But a few had observed and remembered him well, and their descriptions repeatedly agreed: he was a man with sharp blue eyes, high cheekbones, curiously flat cheeks (no bulge, no indentation) and a pointed chin; he spoke with a German accent and wore a soft felt hat pulled down over his forehead.

This singular portrait, which closely resembled Dr. Condon's earlier sketch, could mean only one thing, Finn thought: John was operating alone, trusting no one but himself to dispose of the ransom hoard. The way the money was tendered supported this view, for it was as unique as a signature.

Every bill was folded in half along its full length, then doubled over twice along its length, so that when it was unfolded and laid flat it displayed a pattern of creases dividing it into eight parts. John, his observers had noted, would take such a tightly compressed bill from the watch pocket of his trousers or the lower right pocket of his vest and toss it casually onto the counter to the clerk or cashier, who would have to smooth it open to make sure of its denomination.

Studying the money under his microscope, Dr. Alexander Gettler, the city's chief toxicologist, had drawn a few more details into the portrait. Many of the bills bore tiny glycerine esters on their surfaces, with now and then a touch of emery, suggesting that John was a carpenter who ground his own tools. And most of the bills had a musty odor, as though they had long been buried. One bill was marked with red and blue crayon.

Dr. Gettler had found no fingerprints on the bills, nor had he expected to; for though they unquestionably were present, on paper currency they were virtually impossible to detect. In any event, he had pointed out to Finn, John's prints would be hopelessly lost among an incalculable number of others.

As clue after clue pointed to New York's borough of the Bronx, Colonel Schwarzkopf had found it increasingly hard to justify New Jersey's proprietary role in the case. Who could argue, his critics said, against the weight of evidence? If the State police were to play *any* sort of role in apprehending the kidnaper, they would have to enlist the cooperation of the New York police; and what chance did they have of getting it unless they offered to cooperate in return?

Schwarzkopf had run out of answers to the rising clamor. He asked to join the hunt on the opposite side of the Hudson and threw open his files on the case to both the New York and federal operatives.

At this point, the federal men were all special agents of the Justice Department's Division of Investigation. On October 19, following a presidential directive, the Treasury Department had withdrawn from the search and Attorney General Cummings had turned over the government's interest in the kidnaping to J. Edgar Hoover. The change in policy was bound to expedite matters, the attorney general explained, because all information and activity would be in charge of the federal agency that had demonstrated it was best equipped to deal with abductors—since the enactment of the Lindbergh law, which made kidnaping a federal offense, Justice Department agents had solved every such case they had entered but two, and in both of these the victim's family had resisted their efforts to help. Furthermore, the Division of Investigation had built up the world's largest fingerprint file (the identities of some four million criminals were on record) and it possessed more information on kidnapers and their working methods than any other law-enforcement agency.

It all made excellent sense. The country waited with renewed expectation.

Special Agent Thomas Sisk was given command of fifteen of the division's investigators; each was armed with photos of a sketch of John by James T. Berryman, the well-known cartoonist of the Washington *Star,* who had drawn it from descriptions given by Dr. Condon and Joseph Perrone, the cab driver who had carried a message from the kidnaper. Five large maps of New York City's five boroughs were put up in the division's Manhattan office at 370 Lexington Avenue and were used to record the appearances of the ransom money.

With the way clear for concerted action, Captain Lamb had dispatched a dozen State detectives to New York, headed by Lieutenant

Arthur Keaton, and now all three units—New York police, New Jersey police and Justice Department agents—worked together in reasonable harmony. Each had its own ideas, its own techniques, its own sources of information and accumulation of clues, and each continued to operate independently; but there was a free exchange of evidence and advice. And they agreed that if one unit came upon a break in the case, it would promptly notify the others.

Sunday night, November 26, was clear and cold. Sitting inside her ticket booth, Mrs. Cecile M. Barr, the attractive young cashier of Loew's Sheridan Square Theater at Seventh Avenue and 12th Street in Greenwich Village, had carefully noted the biting weather in her daily record, since it was bound to affect receipts.

Business had indeed been slow, although the film was a lively one—*Broadway Through a Keyhole,* written by Walter Winchell and featuring Paul Kelly and Constance Cummings.

At half-past nine, Mrs. Barr began to count the receipts and check out the cash for the night. Suddenly, a tiny, tightly folded wad fell on the counter in front of her. Mrs. Barr looked up, a bit nettled; there had been something almost contemptuous in the way the man standing at the window had tossed it toward her.

She picked up the wafer-thin wad, a Federal Reserve note, and started to unfold it with a show of effort as she stared at her customer. He appeared to be in his middle thirties, wiry, of medium height and weight, and despite the sting in the air he wore no topcoat over his dark suit. A dark slouch hat was pulled down over his forehead and his blue eyes unwaveringly returned her look from a triangular face formed by high cheekbones, flat cheeks and a pointed chin.

Deliberately smoothing the note, a five-dollar bill deeply creased by the eight rigid squares into which it had been pressed, Mrs. Barr said crossly, "Well, what do you want?"

He seemed puzzled. There were three different prices, she explained. He stepped back and inspected the admission sign. "One forty," he said.

Mrs. Barr gave him a forty-cent ticket, made change, and pushed it toward him. He went inside the theater and she put the odd-looking note with the other receipts.

The next morning, the theater's assistant manager deposited them with William Cody, a teller in the Corn Exchange Bank, two blocks north on 14th Street. Leafing through the bills, Cody thought he saw a familiar serial number. He checked it against his list of the Lindbergh ransom bills; it matched.

At five o'clock, when she went on duty again, Mrs. Barr once more was confronted by the tightly folded five-dollar bill. This time it was in the hands of a police lieutenant—Lieutenant Finn, he had introduced himself. Could Mrs. Barr describe the person who had given the bill to her the night before? Mrs. Barr could, and did; his face, she said, wasn't one she'd soon forget.

22

On November 29, driving toward the Bronx with Detective Bornmann, Arthur Koehler had the feeling that he was approaching the end of his long search. It had been an often irritating but generally interesting task; although he hadn't seen his family for months, he was somewhat sorry that it seemed to be almost finished.

Of course there was a chance that he was wrong, or that, even if his reasoning proved to be correct, complications would come up and the search would go on and on. But right now he didn't think so. From the National Lumber & Millwork Company, toward which they were driving, the Dorn load of pine with the planer's unique fingerprints doubtless would lead him to the doors of a number of purchasers and repurchasers, some of whom, unable or unwilling to account for their use of the wood, could be suspected of having made the kidnap ladder. At that point the police would take over.

Koehler wondered what the man who had made the ladder would be like. A sloppy carpenter—that much he was sure of; someone with no love and respect for wood.

The National Lumber & Millwork Company, he saw when they arrived, sold not only wood but a variety of building materials: cement, plasterboard, paint, and so on. The wood was neatly stacked in a two-story shed; the office records the foreman put in front of Koehler were also kept tidily.

He soon found the entry he wanted: the yard had received the Dorn lumber on December 1, 1931, exactly three months before the kidnaping. Koehler asked to see a sample of the wood. The foreman shook his head. The entire load had been disposed of long ago.

Well, Koehler said casually, he'd run into the same situation at a lumberyard in Ozone Park, and the dealer had remembered using some of the Southern pine to make storage bins—a use for which it seemed well suited. Perhaps they'd done the same thing here?

The foreman thought for a moment. He wasn't sure, but maybe they had.

Koehler and Bornmann followed him to the bins and watched while he sawed off the end of a projecting one-by-four-inch board. Koehler took out his glass, carried the wood into the light and studied it intently.

Once again the pattern fell into place—this time a perfect fit.

Along one edge of the pine strip were the blemishes carved by the defective cutter knife; along one face were the irregular scars engraved by the insufficiently protruding blade. Without counting or measuring, Koehler recognized the other matching details—the same number of knife cuts, spaced exactly the same distance apart. In every respect the marks were identical with those on the ladder's bottom rails. There was no question about it: the wood used to make the rails had been obtained in this Bronx lumberyard.

Almost tenderly, he gave the pine strip to Bornmann for safekeeping and asked the foreman if he could look at the records of sales. There were no records, the foreman said. There wasn't any need for them. The company sold for cash and cash only. It had stopped giving credit a long time ago.

Koehler studied him with dismay. On what date, he asked finally, had the change taken place?

The foreman didn't know, but he was certain that the yard was on a cash-and-carry basis when the Dorn shipment arrived.

It seemed a little ridiculous, but Koehler couldn't resist grasping at a last straw. Did he recall anyone who had bought the pine? The foreman shrugged. Customers came and went. He could hardly be expected to remember a few casual sales nearly two years ago.

Koehler looked at the strip of wood he had placed in Bornmann's hands. In a few seconds it had become worthless.

Throughout the long search Arthur Koehler's confidence had never faltered; now it did. As they drove away, Bornmann read it in the other man's expression and roughly cut through the silence between them. All right, he said, the news was bad—but look at how much they'd learned. The man who had built the ladder either lived in or was well acquainted with the Bronx. He'd been a customer of the National Lumber & Millwork yard and maybe he still was. That gave the police something to work on. They could check out everybody the yard dealt with, especially carpenters. One of them might prove to be a carpenter who owned a dark green or blue sedan and who spoke English with a German accent; a carpenter who took small pride in his work and whose handwriting showed the peculiarities of the writing in the kidnap notes. Wasn't this progress?

Koehler smiled and agreed that it was. His customary confidence returned. The police had plenty to work on, but his and Bornmann's search wasn't ended. Since they'd failed to track down the ladder-builder by one trail, they'd try another. For the unique marks on the wood he had used weren't limited to the Southern pine. There were a few on the Douglas fir rails, too.

These had been sent east from beyond the Rockies, but with a list of shipments from the western mills they could start over again. Perhaps one of the shipments would lead them back to the Bronx—and maybe, this time, to a lumberyard that still sold on credit and could supply the names and addresses of its customers. And maybe one of the customers would be the man they wanted.

23

December 19. In midafternoon the roar of a powerful engine filled the sky over Mrs. Dwight Morrow's Englewood estate. Looking up from the windows, some of the people in the house saw a monoplane in the graceful act of describing three circles and dipping its wingtips. The travelers were home for Christmas.

They had been gone only a little more than five months, but in that time they had spanned some thirty thousand miles: two oceans, four continents, twenty-one countries. The purpose of the flight was to explore possible routes for transatlantic air service. Their respective duties had been assigned with Charles Lindbergh's unfailing efficiency: he piloted the plane and noted the facts of the survey; Anne, navigator and radio operator, recorded meteorological data.

It had been an extraordinary flight. They had spent at least one night in each of the twenty-one countries. They had been reported missing several times. They had flown the South Atlantic nonstop on their way home. They had surveyed a larger area of the earth's surface than had ever before been seen by any voyager. The newspapers agreed that the Lindberghs had made a priceless contribution to man's knowledge of his planet.

They had hurried through the final stages of the trip in order to spend Christmas with their son. The baby, Jon, was not quite eleven months old when they had last seen him; now he was going on sixteen months. Then he'd only been able to make baby noises; now, the parents had heard from Mrs. Morrow, he could speak half a dozen words.

The Lockheed monoplane leveled off to Lindbergh's habitual

perfect landing; they clambered out and drove to Englewood. At about six o'clock they climbed the stairs to the nursery. Betty Gow, the baby's nurse, was waiting for them. Because of their prolonged absence, Jon Lindbergh was more accustomed to Betty than he was to his parents; she had been in charge of him since he was two months old.

Almost three and a half years ago, in this nursery in the Englewood mansion, another child had been born, had slept in this crib and been looked after by this nursemaid. On December 19, 1933—one year, nine months and nineteen days after his death—his kidnaper-killer was still at large.

24

John was still at large, but in the first weeks of 1934 the prospect of capturing him grew brighter. Or so it seemed to the city, state and federal board of strategy composed of Lieutenant Finn, Lieutenant Keaton and Special Agent Sisk. For one thing, John was beginning to dip more frequently into the ransom money, even though his native caution and thrift held him to an average of forty dollars a week; for another, his supply of the relatively inconspicuous five-dollar United States notes apparently had run out and he was now passing ten-dollar gold certificates. Soon, perhaps, he would start to draw regularly on his hoard of twenty-dollar bills, the largest and therefore the most noticeable in the fifty-thousand-dollar package Dr. Condon had given him.

There was another hopeful sign in the public's excellent response to the New York City police offer of a five-dollar reward for every ransom bill turned in. And finally, Finn had devised a plan that might well point straight to John's hiding place.

The handwriting experts had told Finn that it would be a waste of time to try to trace the kidnaper-killer through New York's bulky files of auto-license applications, but he had clung to the idea that somehow John's undoubted use of an auto could be made to pay off. Somehow—but how? When Finn thought of the plan its simplicity delighted him. John's car ran on gas and oil. Well, then, rather than charging off in all directions, asking banks and shops and restaurants and theaters and so on and on to keep an eye open for the ransom bills, why not concentrate on gas stations? John walked into the other places to make his purchases; he *drove* into gas stations. And his car had to carry license plates.

Finn sent a request to every filling-station owner in New York state: Would he please instruct his employes to write, on the bill itself, the license number of every car driven by anyone who paid for gas or oil with a ten- or twenty-dollar gold certificate or a twenty-dollar Federal Reserve note, then check the serial numbers of all such bills against the Lindbergh ransom list (a copy of which Finn enclosed) and, if any matched, immediately inform the New York City police?

So far, the auto-license numbers supplied in answer to the appeal had turned out to belong to drivers innocent of any connection with the kidnaping; but Finn had expected that there would be many false leads, and the encouraging thing was that the volume of the response had been good. He felt confident that, perhaps any day now, the license number of John's car would be reported.

His confident mood abruptly changed. The flow of ransom bills stopped altogether. Days passed without a single report.

It was clear that John had suddenly taken alarm, but why? Finn and Sisk discussed the question and decided that the answer lay in the newspapers' handling of the case. In the past, whenever the appearance of a ransom bill had been reported in the press, the flow of money had dwindled or, for a day or two, had ceased entirely. Lately, apparently feeling—as Finn and Keaton and Sisk felt—that at last the Lindbergh case was about to break, editors had assigned more and more reporters to the job of gathering up every crumb of information. Only rarely during the last few weeks had a ransom bill's appearance gone unreported in the press, with the result that John had been furnished with a running account of his activities. Quite naturally, he must have decided to take no more chances until things quieted down.

Finn and Sisk put the problem before the responsible parties and asked for their help. If the papers would keep quiet about John, his present wariness would pass. The sooner he became bold again, the sooner he would be behind bars.

This made sense; the newspaper editors agreed. No longer would John learn in his daily paper that he had exchanged still another Lindbergh ransom bill.

On February 14, Alice Murphy, cashier of the Cross, Austin & Ireland Lumber Company at 149th Street and the East River in the Bronx glanced from the office and saw two men coming across the yard. They were carrying a large plywood panel, selected from the company's stock.

Miss Murphy met them just outside the office door. One of the men—a wiry sort, she observed, with sharp blue eyes, flat cheeks and a pointed chin—explained to her in a German accent that they wanted just a piece of the plywood, cut to a certain size; how much would it cost? Miss Murphy calculated. Forty cents, she said.

He took a ten-dollar gold certificate from his pocket and handed it to her. Miss Murphy accepted it hesitantly. She had been warned about counterfeit bills; this one seemed genuine enough, but weren't gold notes supposed to be illegal?

She called across the yard to the foreman, William Reilly, but as he started toward them the man snatched back the certificate. "Never mind," his companion said, and gave the cashier forty cents.

Miss Murphy made out a sales slip while Reilly took the plywood panel to have it cut to the specified size. It would take only a minute or two, she informed her customers. They replied that they couldn't wait, they were in a hurry—they would come back later for the wood.

Miss Murphy watched them walk quickly toward the entrance to the lumberyard. It was all very odd, she thought—the questionable bill so rudely retrieved, and now their hasty departure. On impulse, she followed and saw them get into a car. As the car drove off, she wrote down its license-plate number on the sales slip she still held in her hand.

Would they come back for their purchase? Miss Murphy thought not—but at least she wouldn't have to trust her memory to identify them as the owners if they ever did.

She returned to the office and went about her work as quietly as possible, lest she disturb the two men at a nearby desk who were bent intently over the company's books. One had been introduced to her as Mr. Koehler, the other as Mr. Bornmann, and she had been instructed to show them the company's sales of one-by-four-inch Douglas fir during the three months prior to March 1, 1932.

Barely aware of the cashier's return, Arthur Koehler continued to copy from the record of sales. He had obtained a list of shipments of the Douglas fir from the far-western mills to the Bronx, and this was just another of his visits to Bronx lumberyards in an effort to trace the kidnap ladder's fir rails. However, he had not mentioned the ladder to William Reilly and Alice Murphy—or the fact that he and Bornmann were working on the Lindbergh case.

The wave of kidnapings continued to rise.

In April, the *Atlantic Monthly* published three poems by the dead child's grandmother, Mrs. Dwight Morrow. Commenting on them, the reviewers said that they expressed the beliefs of all parents who, horrified by the Lindbergh crime, feared for the safety of their children.

On May 18, President Roosevelt signed a bill stiffening the Lindbergh kidnap law. As amended, the law defined as a federal offense the sending of a kidnap or ransom note across a state line and authorized the death penalty for kidnapers who transported their victims from one state to another and did not return them unharmed.

One afternoon late in August, Dr. John F. Condon was riding in a bus along Williamsbridge Road in the Bronx.

Although he had not acted on his threat to follow John to Australia if double-crossed, the old man had been far from idle in the two years and three months since the discovery of the baby's body. Pursuing various tips and suggestions received in his mail, he had traveled at his own expense up and down the eastern seaboard from Montreal to Miami, but had found no trace of John and his accomplices.

Southbound, the bus was nearing the Pelham Parkway intersection when, glancing out the window, Dr. Condon saw a man walking in the opposite direction, apparently heading for a strip of woods close by. Dr. Condon stared, hardly believing his eyes. But he could not mistake that wiry figure and flat-cheeked face. There he was, the man who had lied to him and betrayed his trust, the man he had sworn to track down and bring to justice if it took him to the end of his life—*John*.

Dr. Condon leaped to his feet, shouting to the driver to stop the bus. But they were just crossing the busy, double-lane parkway, and the driver, who knew his excited passenger, explained that he couldn't stop in the middle of the traffic. He pulled up as soon as he could, on the opposite side of the intersection. Dr. Condon hurried out and back across the parkway; but John had disappeared, probably into the trees, and the old man saw that it would be hopeless to try to follow him.

He telephoned the New York office of the Justice Department's Division of Investigation and told them that there could be no doubt about it: John was right here, right now, in the Bronx.

25

Or was he? Finn, Sisk and Keaton could not help wondering if Dr. Condon had mistaken someone else for John. The drought of ransom bills continued. Had John fled? Was he, even, still alive? Or had he simply determined to take no chances and continue to lie low?

Whatever the case, there was little for Finn and Sisk to do but turn again to the maps on which the colored pins patterned the past appearances of ransom money. Almost five of the original fifty thousand had been recovered since the discovery of David Marcus' twenty-dollar note in April 1932, and the maps bristled with pins; but Finn and Sisk found small consolation in that as day followed day without further reports.

Then, on September 5, the National Bank of Yorkville notified them that a ten-dollar gold note on the Lindbergh ransom list was included in a deposit made by a Third Avenue grocery store. The store's proprietor, Salvatore Levitano, when questioned, remembered very clearly how the certificate had come to him. A customer had offered him the ten-dollar gold note in payment for a *six-cent* purchase. If business weren't so bad, he would have told the fellow to beat it. Even so, he had had plenty to say before handing over nine dollars and ninety-four cents in change.

Could he describe the customer?

He could, in detail. The description tallied. The customer was John. Dr. Condon had been right.

Two more Lindbergh ten-dollar gold notes turned up in two vegetable markets a block apart on Second Avenue in Yorkville, and on September 8 the Chase National Bank on East Fordham Road in the Bronx reported a twenty-dollar gold certificate. It was traced to the nearby Exquisite Shoe Store. Albert Shirkes, the clerk who had accepted the ransom bill, said that on the day before he had sold a pair of women's black suede shoes, size 7½C, price $5.50, to a man. He described the purchaser: John.

There were additional calls on September 10. They increased the next day, and the next, and the next. Apparently confident that enough time had elapsed for him to operate safely again and reassured that he was succeeding by the absence of newspaper stories about him, John was up to his old habits on the east side of upper Manhattan, in Yorkville and the Bronx. But in one respect his pattern of behavior had changed: he was consistently paying for each small purchase with a ten- or a twenty-dollar gold note.

On their ransom maps, Finn and Sisk saw the fine web of lines between the red and green pins slowly draw tighter.

A few minutes before ten o'clock Saturday morning September 15, a dark blue Dodge sedan turned into a Warner-Quinlan service station at 127th Street and Lexington Avenue on the east fringe of upper Manhattan and stopped beside a gas pump.

Walter Lyle and John Lyons, the two attendants, came forward. Lyons lifted a water-can and took off the car's radiator cap; Lyle, the day manager, picked up the pump hose and removed the cap of the gas tank. He addressed the driver in his pleasant southern accent: "Fill her up, sir?"

"No," said the man behind the wheel. "Just five gallons of Ethyl."

Lyle stood draining in the fuel and Lyons started to polish the windshield. The driver climbed out and Lyle glanced at him. He had spoken with a foreign accent, German or something close to it, and he was dressed like a mechanic. Lyle studied his face—V-shaped, with high cheekbones, flat cheeks, a pointed chin. The manager took pride in his memory for faces and he was confident that he had never served his customer before. He withdrew the hose-spout and replaced the cap on the Dodge's gas tank. "That's ninety-eight cents," he said.

The other drew an envelope from his inside coat pocket, took out a ten-dollar gold certificate, and gave it to Lyle.

Lyle fingered it uncertainly. Warner-Quinlan had warned its attendants to be wary of all bills of large denomination, as they might be counterfeit, and to be particularly careful about accepting gold notes, as their use was illegal; on top of that, the New York City police had sent the station a copy of a circular letter asking employes to watch out for gold notes and to compare their serial numbers with the Lindbergh ransom list, a copy of which had been attached. Lyle had put the list beside the cash register in the station's tiny office, but a few weeks ago, faded and torn, it had been thrown away. He remembered, though, that both his employers and the police had made the same request: write down the auto-license number of every customer who paid with a suspicious bill.

He saw Lyons looking on curiously. The customer spoke with a slight smile. "They're all right. Any bank will take them."

"You don't see many of them any more," Lyle said.

"No," the other agreed. "I have only about a hundred left."

Lyle went to the cash register and counted out two pennies and nine one-dollar bills, then returned and gave the man his change.

The sedan drove off and Lyle stood watching it. He took the gold note and a pencil from his pocket and wrote the license-plate number, *4U–13–41,* in an end margin on the back of the bill, then added the state initials, *N.Y.*

Shortly before noon, John Lyons strolled to the Corn Exchange Bank at 125th Street and Park Avenue with the morning's receipts. He asked Miran Ozmec, the teller who took care of him, to exchange the ten-dollar gold note for two five-dollar United States notes. Ozmec agreed, and put the certificates with other bills that had been deposited. Later, as usual, they all would be turned over to the head teller.

John was seldom absent from Lieutenant Finn's thoughts; even when he tried to relax and put the too-familiar, tantalizing figure completely out of his mind, John found a way to return.

Sunday the sixteenth was no exception. Finn was at home in Neponsit, Long Island, with his wife and four daughters, listening to Walter Winchell on the radio. Winchell's syndicated column was a national favorite and his Sunday-night nine o'clock newscasts over NBC were extremely popular.

The familiar voice, now staccato, now slow and sardonic, commented tersely on the news of the week, then announced that Lindbergh ransom bills were being exchanged in Manhattan and the Bronx in ever-increasing numbers. Finn sat up. Winchell addressed New York City's bank tellers. "Boys," he said, "if you weren't such a bunch of saps and yaps, you'd have already captured the Lindbergh kidnapers."

Winchell went on to other matters, and Finn sat back. He wondered what effect, if any, the broadcast would have on the case.

The next day, Monday the seventeenth, Charles and Anne Lindbergh landed at Clover Field in Santa Monica, California, after a leisurely flight from the East. Their low-wing monoplane, the fast and powerful craft that had carried them on the trail-blazing journey of the year before, was grounded for repairs, and they had rented a small blue Monocoupe for the cross-country trip. They had come to California partly on business and partly for pleasure; there were airline affairs to be discussed with Jack Maddux, an official whose guests they were to be at his home in Inglewood; and they looked forward to seeing Anne's sister, Elisabeth, now Mrs. Aubrey Neil Morgan, following her recent marriage to a wealthy Welsh businessman who lived in nearby Pasadena.

Will Rogers' ranch, overlooking the Pacific, was just outside Santa Monica, and the Lindberghs would have liked nothing better than to visit their old friend and his wife; but the Rogers were vacationing in Europe.

Back east, in North Haven, Maine, Jon Morrow Lindbergh was with his maternal grandmother at her summer home. His second birthday had been celebrated there a month ago, with both the family and the servants in high spirits. Charles and Anne had romped with the little boy on the lawn and, racing back and forth and barking excitedly, Thor, the big watchdog, had joined in the fun.

On Tuesday the eighteenth, head teller William R. Strong of the 125th Street and Park Avenue branch of the Corn Exchange Bank began to check out some deposits. Returning from lunch at

VIOLET SHARPE
Violet was English, 28, a bit "temperamental" but never uppish. Everyone on the Morrow staff liked her. The butler's liking had grown into a warmer interest and the other servants thought he would soon pop the question.

Wide World

BETTY GOW AND OLIVER WHATELEY
A slender, attractive young woman, Betty enjoyed and was proud of her position with the Lindberghs as the baby's nurse. She and Oliver and Elsie Whateley—the butler and housekeeper-cook—had come from Scotland to domestic service in America.

Wide World

HENRY BRECKINRIDGE
Lindbergh's friend and adviser, he impressed Dr. Condon at once; obviously he was a gentleman, courteous, well-spoken, and well-dressed. (*Figure at far left.*)

Wide World

JOHN F. CONDON
AND ALFRED REICH
Dr. Condon, 71, had the body of a much younger man, thanks to his lifelong devotion to athletics. He lived in "the most beautiful borough in the world, the Bronx," as he often said. Outraged by the kidnaping, he wrote at once to his favorite newspaper, the Bronx *Home News,* offering his services and his savings to help in restoring the stolen child to its mother's arms. Al Reich, an ex-heavyweight boxer, was one of Dr. Condon's closest friends.

UPI

GASTON B. MEANS
53, with a substantial stomach and the easy tongue and affability of a successful former salesman, Means had lived a varied life, including service as a Department of Justice agent.

UPI

EVALYN WALSH McLEAN
She had had a premonition, when she was the young wife of a Washington newspaper publisher, that their son—called by the press "the hundred-million dollar baby"—would be kidnaped and held for ransom.

UPI

UPI

JOHN HUGHES CURTIS
A big man, tanned, muscular, Mr. Curtis was well known and well liked in Norfolk. He had repaired boats for rum-runners and it seemed reasonable that the gang would get in touch with him.

Wide World

GUY HAMILTON BURRAGE
It was on the admiral's cruiser, the *Memphis,* that Charles Lindbergh returned to America after his famous flight. In view of this exceptional link, would not he be bound to listen with respect to anything the admiral had to say?

HAROLD DOBSON-PEACOCK
An Englishman, he had been called abroad in 1927 to become rector of the Episcopal cathedral in Mexico City, where he had met the United States ambassador, Dwight Morrow, and his charming family. Certainly, the dean felt, he should be able to identify himself satisfactorily to Charles Lindbergh.

UPI

one o'clock, he resumed the task and soon came to a pack of bills turned over to him by teller Miran Ozmec. Among them he found two ten-dollar gold certificates.

If he had time, Strong meant to compare the serial numbers of all the bills in his possession with those listed in his copy of the Lindbergh ransom circular; however, lately he'd been asked to pay particular attention to gold notes, so he decided to check the present two while they were at hand.

Strong took out his list and looked for the serial numbers of the certificates. The first did not appear; the second, *A73976634A,* did.

He went to the assistant manager and reported his find, and his superior telephoned Special Agent Sisk at the New York office of the Justice Department's Division of Investigation. Sisk listened, thanked the official, and summoned Special Agent William F. Seery.

A veteran operative, Seery had been running down ransom-bill reports for a year and a half. Only that morning he had traced two of the Lindbergh gold notes to a couple of shopkeepers who had deposited them with the Irving Trust Company; typically, the trail had ended at their doorsteps. Nothing about the new report indicated that the result would be different, but Seery was a patient man; he took down the information Sisk gave him and promised to notify Lieutenant Finn and Lieutenant Keaton of the find. He did; Finn arranged to meet him at the bank. Keaton said he'd send Detective Corporal William Horn of the State police.

When all three had arrived, they examined the ransom bill. Except for its serial number, they saw nothing that distinguished it from the ten-dollar gold certificates previously recovered. Corporal Horn turned the note over. On an end margin there was a penciled notation. He inspected it closely and made out a few figures and letters: *4U-13-41, N.Y.*

It looked like an auto-license number. Finn was sure of it— perhaps one jotted down by a gas-station attendant in answer to his request. He asked to see the teller who had received the bill.

Miran Ozmec said he hadn't noticed the marking on the gold note and couldn't recall the depositor, but the deposit slips might give him a clue. They were put before him. At Finn's suggestion, he took from the pack only the slips which bore the names and addresses of filling stations.

They proved to be gratifyingly few—just three—but Ozmec hesitated. He couldn't be positive, he said, which one was the slip in question.

Finn solved the problem by copying all of the names and addresses; pocketing the gold note, he set out with Seery and Horn to run it down.

Four blocks away they came to a service station of the Warner-

Quinlan chain and Finn showed the bill and its notation to the manager, Walter Lyle. Did he recognize it? Sure, Lyle said; it was an auto-license number and he'd put it there himself. He called to his assistant, John Lyons; they described the customer who had tendered the certificate and related the conversation that followed.

Finn glanced at his companions; although he was careful to preserve his official calm, he couldn't keep a trace of jubilation from his face. The customer was John. And the key to John's whereabouts, the license number of his car, lay in the palm of Finn's hand.

They drove back to the bank and Finn telephoned the New York State Motor Vehicle Bureau. He read the license number slowly and distinctly: *4U–13–41*. Then he turned the key:

Who, he asked, was the owner of the car carrying that license? What was his name and his address?

There was a delay and Finn held the line; then the answer came. Finn carefully wrote it down:

Richard Hauptmann, 1279 East 222nd Street, the Bronx.

26

It seemed to Finn that dawn of the next day—Wednesday September 19—would never come.

Finn, Special Agent Sisk, Lieutenant Keaton, and nine other men —a picked force of New York and New Jersey police officers and agents of the Justice Department's Division of Investigation, all in plain clothes—were hidden in and among the tall brush and trees of a thickly wooded northeast section of the Bronx. Throughout the night, a great many more men had shared their vigil; never before had the woods of this sparsely populated area seen such furtive, busy human traffic, centering around a small frame-and-stucco house; but as the ghostly predawn grayness began to filter through the trees the others had vanished, according to plan.

The carefully chosen twelve who remained were divided into three groups, each made up of detectives, agents and troopers. From their vantage points, a strategic triangle blocking any possible escape route, they kept their field glasses trained on the magnet that had drawn them here—the house at 1279 East 222nd Street, where Richard Hauptmann lived.

The light intensified; Finn could make out the details of the house's casual architecture.

It was a two-story frame building, finished in pale tan stucco, with an attic, the second story slightly set back. Standing in a plot thick with rank weeds, goldenrod, and mountain daises, it was neither new nor really old. It faced East 222nd Street; a short flight of steps and a walk led from the front entrance to the street. The builders had given the house a generous supply of windows. Needham Avenue—far less an avenue than a heavily rutted country lane lined with aged oaks and poplars—ran along the house's east wall, cut off in back by the woods, where the underbrush was four or five feet high. An unpainted one-car garage faced Needham Avenue from the other side. In contrast to the rest, its two doors, which opened outward, had been painted; their red surface and the six small panes of glass in the top of each showed bright in the new day. They were fastened with a large padlock. Behind the garage a corrugated-tin fence enclosed a garden in which neatly spaced green tufts grew. Radishes, Finn thought.

Chiefly, of course, he was thinking about the man inside the house, wondering if Richard Hauptmann was an early riser. Dudley Shoenfeld, too, was in Finn's thoughts. The evening before, he had returned to headquarters after taking down Hauptmann's name and address from the Motor Vehicle Bureau and had traced 1279 East 222nd Street on his police map of the Bronx. It had given him a bit of a start to see that the suspect's house was inside the hypothetical hunting ground Dr. Shoenfeld and he had drawn on the map not quite two years ago. The psychiatrist's theory had been that John lived in a German community within that rough rectangle; their hopes for a swift capture had foundered on the discovery that no such community existed either inside or near it. Yet here was John's house—if, to be sure, Richard Hauptmann really did turn out to be John.

Would they have got to him earlier if they hadn't been put off by the "German community" theory? Pretty doubtful, Finn supposed; after all, the populated part of the rectangle covered about one square mile.

Finn had had an active night. First, he had given Sisk and Keaton his views as to how the arrest should be carried out. Since it was by no means certain that Richard Hauptmann was the kidnaper and murderer, it had seemed wise to gather the immediately available facts about him before moving in for the arrest. Finn, Sisk and Keaton had dug up all the information they could get, while others watched the house. They had learned from the New York State Motor Vehicle Bureau that Richard Hauptmann had been born in Germany not quite thirty-five years before, that he was a carpenter and that he had registered the same 1930 Dodge sedan each year back to 1931, when its original color had been dark green; it had been painted its present dark blue after the year of the kidnaping, 1932.

The files of neither the New York City Police, New Jersey police nor the Justice Department's Division of Investigation had proved to contain a case history of Richard Hauptmann; Finn thought this encouraging. Didn't the absence of a criminal record, together with the known facts about the suspect, bear out Shoenfeld's synthetic portrait—an amateur in crime, a German alien who lived in the Bronx, a man accustomed to working with wood, just a few years older than Charles Lindbergh—who was now 32? Even the name *Hauptmann*—in German "head man" or "chief"; in the German army, "captain"—didn't it key with Shoenfeld's observation about the kidnaper-killer's sense of omnipotence?

Finn, Sisk and Keaton had pondered the argument in favor of not making the arrest too hastily. Given enough rope, Richard Hauptmann might hang others beside himself—his accomplices. It was true that not a few of the official investigators and at least one layman, Shoenfeld, were convinced that John had played a lone hand from the beginning. And there wasn't a single scrap of positive, irrefutable evidence pointing squarely to more than one man, for all the talk about gangs. But Dr. Condon was sure that John had had one accomplice and maybe two, Italians, probably.

None of this was conclusive, but wouldn't it make sense at least to give Hauptmann a chance to lead the way to any possible accomplices? Trail him when he left his house? Assign a German-speaking detective to try to get on friendly terms with him? If he led them nowhere, revealed nothing, it would at any rate furnish a fair amount of proof that he *was* a lone hand.

The argument had its points, but the overwhelming factor against it was that it was too risky. Two and a half years had been devoted to finding this house, this man. Make him suspicious now, bungle the arrest in the smallest detail, and he might be gone forever.

Then what *was* the safest strategy? Move in from all sides and arrest him in his house? There was a flaw here, Finn had said. To hold Hauptmann for any length of time, they would need evidence to prove that he had guilty knowledge of the crime. There was no guarantee that they would find such evidence in the house; he might very well have hidden the ransom hoard somewhere else. No, they would have to allow Hauptmann to leave the house and then arrest him at a likely spot. He was continually on the alert for opportunities to exchange the ransom bills and so there was every chance that he would carry at least one of them with him, sufficient evidence to keep him under lock and key while his captors went to work on him.

Sisk and Keaton had agreed.

The sun rose higher in the clear sky. In the tension of waiting, the watchful men were sharply aware of the multitude of small sounds in the woods—leaf rustle, bird cry. Tiny white specks, like lively scraps of paper, fluttered over the garden behind the garage: butterflies. The scene must look entirely normal from the house, Finn assured himself; nothing to hint of their presence, nothing to betray the carefully hidden black Ford sedans, three of them, parked not far away. When the time came, he and Special Agent Seery and Detective Corporal Horn would ride in one car; in another, Keaton, Sisk and Detective Chester Cronin; in the third, Detective Sergeant John Wallace, Detective William Wallace and Trooper Dennis Duerr—a fair balance of the three investigative forces. The remainder of the small group would stay behind to keep watch on the house.

A man stepped out from the front door.

He closed the door behind him, came down the steps, strolled toward Needham Avenue. Finn's field glasses brought him into sharp focus. Medium height and weight, long legs, a wiry, muscular build. His unhurried gait showed a supple balance. If Finn had been asked to describe John, from all he knew of him, he would have described this man.

The man turned into Needham Avenue, walked to the garage, unlocked the padlock, drew open the double doors. A couple of minutes later a dark blue four-door Dodge sedan backed out. Finn's eyes sought the license plate: *4U–13–41*.

The long-legged man got out, closed and locked the garage doors, returned to his car, then drove over the rutted lane to 222nd Street. The Dodge swung west. The watchers, bent low, had started toward their cars as he was padlocking the garage. Finn glanced at his watch: five to nine.

The blue Dodge led a short, discreet procession, spaced so prudently behind it that its driver could find nothing in his rear-view mirror to alarm him. The Dodge was in no hurry. It moved south, in the direction of Manhattan, through Bronx Park and down Park Avenue in the Fordham section of the Bronx.

Detective William Wallace of the New York City police was driving the first Ford; Trooper Duerr was beside him and Sergeant John Wallace, also of the State police, was in the back seat. Duerr was becoming a bit apprehensive. It was nearly nine-twenty. They'd already driven a couple of miles, and right ahead, on East Tremont Avenue, there was some pretty heavy cross-traffic, in which it would be easy to lose the blue Dodge.

Then, in the block before East Tremont, the Dodge slowed. Duerr saw that a city sprinkler truck was in its way. This was the moment to spring the trap, Duerr thought, but before he could say so, Detective Wallace stepped on the gas, the car leaped forward and slammed in alongside the Dodge, so that it could not cut around the sprinkler.

The police car was still moving as Duerr, pistol in hand, bolted out of his seat and shouted to the Dodge's driver to pull over to the curb. Seconds later Sergeant Wallace, running around the Dodge, slid into its front seat and jabbed his gun at the driver's ribs. The driver stared at them, then carefully edged his car to the curb.

The two other police cars parked behind it. Finn got out of one, Sisk and Keaton came from the other. They motioned to Sergeant Wallace, and he half pulled, half led the Dodge's driver to the sidewalk and flicked a pair of handcuffs onto his strong, bony wrists.

"What is this?" the handcuffed man said, speaking for the first time. "What is this all about?"

No one answered. Finn, Sisk and Keaton were too busy looking at him, while a detective's hands scurried over his body, feeling for weapons.

His hair was a muddy blond. Fairly prominent cheekbones stood out above flat cheeks and a somewhat pointed chin, a "triangular" face. He had blue, deep-set eyes and a small mouth. His hands were large and looked as if they'd done a lot of work. He wore a gray double-breasted salt-and-pepper suit, good material but far from new, over a blue shirt and a patterned blue tie. Gray socks, low brown shoes. Physically, he fitted all the descriptions given of John by those who had encountered him; and the sketch James Berryman of the Washington *Star* had drawn from those descriptions bore a striking resemblance.

And his few words had been marked with a strong accent, a German accent, Finn had no doubt. Surely this was John—Richard Hauptmann.

The first search had yielded no weapons; Finn, Sisk and Keaton launched a more systematic search. Keaton drew out a wallet from Hauptmann's left hip pocket and found that it contained twenty-nine dollars: a five-dollar bill, four singles and a twenty-dollar gold certificate. Special Agent Seery, who had joined the group, checked the certificate's serial number against the Lindbergh ransom list, but not in Hauptmann's view. It matched.

He had said nothing more and the men around him had been silent against the background hum of traffic; but now, when the questions came, they came fast and insistently. Where had he got the certificate? How long had he had it? The accented voice replied calmly: he had made a habit of gathering gold notes for the past two years, because he was afraid of inflation—he'd seen it happen in Germany and didn't want to go through it again. He had managed to save three hundred dollars in gold certificates, getting them from banks and shopkeepers and so on, wherever he could. But then he had concluded that his fears were foolish and he'd started to spend his savings. The gold note they had taken from him was the last he had.

If that was so, why had he told the attendants at a Warner-Quinlan service station just a few days ago that he had about a hundred left? Was that true, or was what he had said now true?

Well, no, Hauptmann admitted; he had not told them the truth just now. He did have about a hundred left.

Where were they?

"Up at the house. Up at my house in a tin box."

During these questions and answers, a call had been put through to Inspector John A. Lyons, Finn's superior and the officer in complete charge of the Lindbergh case for the New York City police. Lyons had said he'd leave at once and join the group at the intersection of White Plains and Gun Hill roads as the arresting party traveled back toward Hauptmann's home.

Richard Hauptmann was led to a police car. The small procession, no longer so discreet, and now with the blue Dodge in the rear, driven by an officer, swung around and started for the frame-and-stucco house on 222nd Street.

As they drove the questioning continued.

27

In the apartment on the second floor of the house, Anna Hauptmann was giving her son a bath.

Mannfried Richard Hauptmann, whose pet name was Bubi, would be one year old on November 3, a little more than six weeks away. He was a fine, healthy boy, blond-haired, blue-eyed, and he enjoyed his bath as much as his mother enjoyed giving it to him. Presently Anna lifted him up, dried him briskly until his skin glowed shell-pink, and carried him to the bedroom window and stood there looking out. It was a beautiful day and she thought it would do them both good to be in the sunshine for a while.

As she started for the door with the baby in her arms, Anna noticed that it was almost eleven o'clock. Earlier, she had had breakfast with her husband, had seen him off to work and then had given the apartment a good cleaning. They paid fifty dollars a month for the five rooms—living room, two bedrooms, kitchen and bathroom—renting the apartment from Max Rauch, who lived with his seventy-one-year-old mother in the ground-floor front.

Anna Hauptmann was a willing and conscientious house-cleaner; she took pleasure in every domestic chore and was proud of the way her home looked. Much of the furniture was quite new and some of these recent purchases were expensive—the walnut bedroom suite she had long wanted for Richard and herself, the ivory crib for Bubi, and the radio for the living room. The radio was very impressive, even luxurious, in appearance; after all, it had cost nearly four hundred dollars. Anna thought herself lucky. She had Bubi, and Richard, a fine husband, devoted to his family. Lately, it was true, he had begun to complain a little about the twenty dollars a week he gave her to run the house and ask if she couldn't get along on less (which was certainly possible, Anna admitted; she was a thrifty housewife), but he could be as free-spending as anyone when something took his fancy—the radio, for instance. He was maybe a bit closemouthed and Anna had never felt that he shared all his thoughts with her, but wasn't that so with most German husbands?

Without bothering to change from her flowered wrapper and bedroom slippers, she went downstairs to the back yard, where she had hung out Bubi's newly washed clothes to dry and let the baby crawl around on all fours in the grass. The sun felt fine on her skin, which was inclined to freckle. She had a comfortable figure of medium height, blue eyes, and ample rust-blonde hair.

Bubi explored the yard and Anna placidly watched him. By and by she became aware that someone was watching her—a man, standing in the dirt lane that bordered the house. She had never seen him before, she was sure. Why should he be so interested in her? Anna glanced away, looked back; he was still staring. His intent gaze disturbed her so much that she was hardly conscious that some cars had stopped in front of the house.

The man walked toward her. She ran to Bubi, picked him up in her arms.

"What's your name?" the stranger asked.

Anna thought: And what business is that of yours? But she answered nevertheless:

"I am Mrs. Hauptmann."

"Where is your husband?"

"Why," she said, "he went to work."

The inquisitive stranger took something from a pocket. It glittered in the sun; it was a badge, a police badge. "Come upstairs," he said. "The police want to ask you some questions."

She was dumfounded. Clutching her child, she looked around and saw her friend Louisa Schuessler, who lived with her husband and daughter in the ground-floor rear apartment, watching from a window. Anna beckoned to her to come and take Bubi. Then she and the man with the police badge went upstairs.

The men in the apartment made it seem almost alien to her. There were a great many of them, some in police uniform. They were shoving the furniture around, opening drawers, busily prying. She stared, aghast, but the first man nudged her on. They went into the bedroom. Richard was sitting on the bed.

Anna ran to him. "Richard," she cried, "what is this?"

He said nothing, but someone else said, "Never mind, you'll find out pretty soon."

"Richard," Anna said, putting her arms around him and holding him close, "did you do anything wrong?"

"No, Anna."

"Tell me! Tell me if you did anything wrong!" she insisted.

A commanding voice said sharply, "Take that woman outside!"

Someone led her into the hallway. The door to the other bedroom, the nursery, was open, and she could see men searching through Bubi's closet and fingering the crib. His clothes and toys were scattered over the floor; the nursery furniture Richard had made for his son—a rocking chair, a high chair and a playpen painted bright yellow and green—had been toppled over and tossed aside.

Anna had been on the verge of tears; the sight of the child's ravaged nursery made her weep.

While she had been bathing Bubi and taking him out into the sunny yard, Inspector John Lyons and a few reinforcements had joined the party that had made the arrest; they had all driven to the house on 222nd Street. The search for evidence had started at once, but first Finn wanted to see the tin box their captive had spoken of. Hauptmann had brought it out, a small metal box with a combination lock, opened it, and pointed. "There is the hundred or so," he said.

Lyons, Sisk and Keaton had joined Finn, crowding in for a closer look. The "hundred or so" turned out to be $120 in six twenty-dollar gold coins. This wasn't what they had in mind, Sisk had explained; they had been talking about gold *certificates,* the same as the twenty-dollar gold note in Hauptmann's wallet. He had told the Warner-Quinlan gas station people that he had about a hundred left. Where were they? Gold was gold, Hauptmann had replied, shaking his head; he had meant these coins all along.

Someone had given him a sudden push and he had sat down abruptly on the bed. The men standing over him had resumed the drumfire of questions. Where were the rest of the gold notes? How had he got hold of them? Wasn't it a fact that he had extorted them from Charles Lindbergh? That the gold notes were part of the ransom Lindbergh had paid, thinking his baby son would be given back to him in return?

Until this moment, no one had mentioned Lindbergh's name. It left Richard Hauptmann unruffled. He knew nothing about the ransom payment, he said; he wouldn't know the money if he saw it. And he had shrugged a little and met their eyes as if to ask, patiently: What next?

Special Agent Seery had dangled a pair of new black suede women's shoes in front of him. They had been found in the bedroom closet. Hadn't he purchased the shoes a week and a half ago with a twenty-dollar gold certificate? Hauptmann had inspected the shoes; yes, he agreed, he had. And here, next, was a ten-dollar gold note with his auto license penciled in the margin. Hadn't he used it to buy five gallons of gas, just four days ago? Hauptmann had nodded. Well, then, how did he explain the fact that both of these notes, plus the gold certificate found in his wallet, were part of the Lindbergh ransom?

Hauptmann's blue eyes had stared blankly at the demanding men. He couldn't explain, he had said; he'd told them before—the money had come from banks, stores, many places. Maybe the people there could explain how they happened to have the gold notes.

Around his stolid figure, in the bedroom, and throughout the rest of the apartment, the search had continued. Thoroughly instructed, the searchers knew what they wanted but so far had rooted out nothing of real significance—letters, a few lottery tickets, snapshots of the Hauptmanns with other people at parties and picnics; a hunting rifle; an extraordinary pile of Hudson sealskins (he had been asked to explain this unusual cache and told them that for the past two years or so he had been doing a little buying and selling of raw furs); seventeen memorandum books with notations in German, useless to the searchers until translated; a German-English dictionary. And several maps, maps of the kind free for the asking at service stations. Among them were maps of New Jersey, where the Lindberghs had had their home on the night of the kidnaping, and Massachusetts; it was in Massachusetts coastal waters, John had written, that the boat *Nelly* and the stolen child would be found.

Also an expensive pair of German field glasses. They could mean much or little; at any rate they were interesting, because the searcher who found them had recalled that the police had reasoned that on at least a few occasions before the kidnaping the kidnapers must have posted themselves in the Sourland woods at night and studied, through powerful binoculars, the domestic routine inside the Lindberghs' home. Remembering this, he had shown the glasses to Hauptmann.

"What did you use these for?"

Hauptmann had paid the glasses scant attention.

"I am a lover of nature."

What the searchers really wanted were the three principal threads of evidence which, when found and knotted together, could be looped around Richard Hauptmann, and perhaps Anna too, in a web from which he could never escape, it would be so tight, so impossible to explain. One thread was the ransom money—some forty-five thousand dollars of it was still missing; the second was the ransom notes—clues to these might be in the apartment, to betray the writer; and the third thread came from the kidnap ladder—its special kinds of wood and unique markings could well point to this German carpenter, patiently sitting on the bed, as the man who had built and used the ladder.

The ransom bills naturally came first. Not only were there a great many of them—4750 bills had been handed to John—but there was excellent reason to believe that Hauptmann possessed all or at any rate some of those unspent. If the unused bills were in the apartment, they should be easy to find; if they were hidden outside, he would have to be persuaded to lead the searchers to them. They would represent a great step forward, for then Richard Hauptmann could be formally charged with extortion—and time would be on his captors' side, time in which to piece together evidence that would point to him as the kidnaper and murderer.

There were tangential strands of evidence associated with the bills, every serial number of which had been recorded: the paper and string they had been bound with—matching samples still lay waiting inside the J. P. Morgan and Company vault. And the ransom box, the careful copy of Dr. Condon's antique ballot box, with brass fittings and a veneer composed of five different kinds of wood, split on one side. As a final, unassailable method of identification, Dr. Condon had kept the key to its lock.

The searchers' narrowing quest came to the bed onto which Hauptmann had been pushed. Get up, he was told. He moved to a chair beside the window. The searchers pulled off the bed's coverlet, blankets, sheets. They hauled the mattress off and ripped it apart. No gold bills, nothing. Hauptmann glanced indifferently at the destruction.

But downstairs, the searchers had struck gold: two Lindbergh ten-dollar gold notes. Mrs. Pauline Rauch, the elderly woman who lived with her son Max in the downstairs front, had responded helpfully to questioning: yes, Richard Hauptmann had given her a gold certificate just the day before, the eighteenth, in partial payment of his September rent. She fetched it willingly. And she had another, hidden in an old eyeglass case of hers, where she had put it for safekeeping after the upstairs tenant had paid last January's rent.

The downstairs-rear tenants—Victor Schuessler, an unemployed upholsterer, and his wife, Louisa—had no gold certificates, but they had freely contributed bits and pieces of information about their friends Richard and Anna, and no doubt people in the nearby houses would round out a picture of the Hauptmanns' life at 1279 East 222nd Street.

In the bedroom, Sisk and Corporal Horn were separately concerned with the clothes closet and a chest of drawers, Horn burrowing through each drawer while Sisk was turning out pockets and linings and trouser cuffs, feeling inside shoes, and finally tapping the closet woodwork and plaster. He remembered that the toxicologist, Dr. Alexander Gettler, reporting to Finn after examining the recovered ransom bills through his microscope, had said that most of them had a musty odor, as though they had been buried for a long time. Why not inside the apartment walls? But Sisk was not too closely engaged to neglect an occasional swift glance at the man in the chair by the window. Hauptmann sat in the same pose of patient indifference, and yet when he thought no one was watching—or so it seemed to Sisk, apparently wrapped in his search, in fact alertly observant—he would raise himself slightly and peer out the window.

Sisk convinced himself he wasn't imagining this cautious maneuver, and that it was a maneuver, not idle chance. He came out of the closet and walked to the window.

"What are you looking at when you sneak those looks out the window?"

The deep-set eyes inspected him calmly. "Nothing," Hauptmann said.

Sisk took a look outside for himself. It was an unremarkable scene, little of possible interest in sight except the small frame garage, about fifty feet away. An electric wire stretched from the window-well above Needham Avenue to the roof of the garage. The wire had been noted and inquired about, and Hauptmann had explained that it was part of a burglar-alarm system he had rigged up a couple of years ago. Demonstrating, he had pressed a button beside his bed, flooding the garage with light. Plenty to scare off any thieves in the night, after his car.

Surely a reasonable explanation. But maybe there was another. Sisk pointed to the garage.

"Is that where you have the money?"

"No," Hauptmann said. "I have no money."

Sisk had ample reservations about that. He left Hauptmann and told Inspector Lyons and Lieutenant Keaton about the furtive glances out the window and the suspicion they had planted in his mind. In this, he was being faithful to the working agreement arrived at by the three investigative forces, federal, New Jersey and New York City police, that they would exchange evidence and advice; Sisk was the head federal agent in the house, Keaton the chief Jersey officer, and Lyons, Finn's superior, the top New York man.

The three went to the garage. It was small, fifteen by eleven feet; a random multitude of domestic paraphernalia had been neatly stowed inside—a wash boiler, a silk bassinet, a baby carriage, stiff-bosom shirts still in their laundry wrappers, trunks, folding chairs, a folding cot, countless tin cans, and other odds and ends. The floor was made of heavy planks, eight inches wide, two and a half inches thick, most of them scarred and charred as if by fire, and splattered with a car's oil drippings.

The two middle planks tilted loosely under their feet. They got a crowbar and pried up these wobbly planks. The soil underneath appeared to have been dug into and smoothed over not long ago. They spaded into it. Some twelve inches down they struck metal. Wiping away the dirt, they saw a metal jar. It was heavy; they tugged it out and forced off the lid. The jar contained a few inches of water.

Anna Hauptmann had reclaimed her child from the helpful Louisa Schuessler and, with the baby in her arms, stood watching and fearfully wondering on the patch of lawn in front of the house. She could not begin to understand this sudden tumult that had fallen on their peaceful home. Richard had told her he had done nothing wrong; then why were all those prodding, impudent, impatient men ransacking the house and the garage? Since she had been steered out of the bedroom she had answered question after question, told all she knew about her and Richard's recent life—it was simple enough—but when she in turn had asked questions, why were they here, what were they looking for, she had been brushed aside with little or nothing in reply.

It was half-past twelve. Hugging Bubi, she raised her arm and wiped her eyes. Then she saw Richard. Handcuffed between two men, he was brought down the front steps. She could only stare, unable to speak, and Richard hardly looked at his wife and son. The two men and their prisoner got into a car at the curb and the car drove away.

Anna sought out an officer. Where were they taking her husband?

This time she got a reply: To the Greenwich Street police station in Manhattan.

Why?

He shook his head.

At half-past two, some other men led her to another car and told her, when she asked, that they were taking her to the same place.

28

The 2nd Precinct police station at 130 Greenwich Street on the lower West Side was a venerable building, close to the El tracks with their occasional rattling thunder, and through the years little of great note had left a mark on its desk sergeants' blotters. That was why the drab, out-of-the-way station had been chosen for this preliminary reception of Richard Hauptmann—*Bruno* Richard Hauptmann, Lieutenant Finn reminded himself, was the suspect's full name; apparently his first name was seldom if ever used. And Finn, of course, approved of the choice; to a very limited extent it went along with his friend Dudley Shoenfeld's ideas as to how John should be handled. If Hauptmann had been brought to police headquarters, constantly exposed to reporters' attention, the world would have known at once about his arrest. But 130 Greenwich Street was a backwater, infrequently troubled by the press.

Shoenfeld had reasoned—and, to Finn, very convincingly—that for the best results the arrest and the handling of the suspect should be conducted quietly, with great care. Subject him to the customary brusque treatment and he would be confirmed in his belief that he lived in a hostile world and would respond by sealing himself behind a contemptuous silence. That might very well be so; but the New York City Police Department (since the arrest had been made in New York, New York police detectives were scheduled to put the actual questions to the prisoner in the coming interrogation) wasn't run by a psychiatrist, and Finn knew that he would be arguing against a stone wall if he attempted to persuade the brass that Richard Hauptmann should be handled according to Shoenfeld's prescription—taken to a quiet private apartment and casually and informally questioned as a psychiatrist might question him, to put him at his ease, in effect to disarm him.

The questioners were not casual and informal. They threw off the wraps.

A few hours ago, Hauptmann had been accused simply of extortion, but so far the evidence to back it up—the major part of the ransom money—hadn't been found. Now the questioners stepped up their attack by charging him with kidnaping and murder as well.

But here too there was little to show in the way of proof. It was true that physically he closely resembled the man Dr. Condon had dealt with and the man described by Perrone, the cab driver, and when they identified him, face to face, the case against him would gain weight. How much more it would gain, how conclusive it would be, if fingerprints matching his could be produced from the Lindbergh nursery! But the State police had found no fingerprints—and with one exception, the kidnaper's footprints had been so badly smudged as to be worthless. The exception was the single large print in the yellow-red clay outside the Lindbergh home. If someone had made a plaster cast of that print, and if the cast fitted Hauptmann's shoe, it would certainly jar his steadfast imperturbability—but a cast hadn't been made.

To Finn, Sisk and Keaton, the board of strategy, the first objective was to identify the prisoner with the crime through the classic police principle of time, place and presence. Later, as they planned it, he would be confronted with the evidence in hand; but there were three dates that more or less staked out the Lindbergh case, and if Richard Hauptmann could not supply an alibi for each occasion, a formal charge could be lodged against him, with a pretty good chance of making it stick.

The three dates were March 1, 1932, when the Lindbergh baby had been stolen; April 2, 1932, when Dr. Condon had given the fifty thousand dollars ransom to John; and November 26, 1933, when a movie theater cashier had received one of the ransom bills from a customer whose manner had nettled her so much she couldn't forget his face. All three touched the foundations of the case: kidnaping and murder, extortion, prolonged possession of the ransom money. The last of these would be reinforced, of course, by still another date: May 1, 1933, when "J. J. Faulkner" had turned over $2980 in Lindbergh gold notes to the Federal Reserve Bank—but the teller could recall nothing about "Faulkner." He might have been Hauptmann or an accomplice; without a description the incident could not serve to build the case.

They brought Richard Hauptmann into a room that resembled a thousand other rooms in a thousand other police stations, sat him in a wooden armchair, and grouped around him. The flat clear light picked out the details of his calm face. The wiry body revealed no tension. For a while captors and captive looked at one another in a silence broken only by the distant groaning rattle of the El.

Then it began.

On Tuesday, March 1, 1932, hadn't he been in or near Hopewell, New Jersey?

No, the quiet, accented voice replied. He'd never even heard of Hopewell until after the kidnaping.

But he'd frequently visited New Jersey—worked there?

Not so often. A carpentry job now and then.

As a matter of fact, he'd helped to build the Lindbergh house, hadn't he?

Hauptmann shook his head. No.

Well, then, he'd visited a friend on the job—or else he was acquainted with the Lindbergh servants, Betty Gow and Oliver and Elsie Whateley—or maybe Violet Sharpe. He'd been inside the house and had a good look at the way it was laid out.

No. No. He didn't know any of those people, the captive said positively. He'd never been in the Lindbergh house or even on the grounds.

Why lie? Tuesday night, March 1, he'd not only been in the house but in the nursery! He'd stolen the Lindbergh baby from his crib——

Hauptmann cut off the accusing voice. No, he hadn't. He had never even seen the Lindbergh baby.

Oh, yes, he had! He had seen the baby twice—alive and dead!

No, no. They'd got the wrong man.

Well, all right, another questioner said—then how did he account for March 1?

Tuesday?

A Tuesday, yes.

Well, that was a long time ago, a long time—two and a half years, so it was hard to remember, but Tuesday. . . . The captive reflected. Well, he was working then for an apartment house, he remembered—the Majestic, at 72nd Street and Central Park West in Manhattan. That morning he'd got up at the usual time, six or so, and driven his wife to Fredericksen's bakery-lunchroom, about a mile away, on Dyer Avenue in the Bronx. Anna was working there then as a waitress. Then he had driven back, put the car in the garage, and taken the subway downtown and spent the day doing odd jobs at the Majestic. He had come home at about six and driven to the bakery some time before seven. Every Tuesday and Friday his wife had to work late and so he made a habit of eating supper with her there, at Fredericksen's. At nine she was all done, free to leave, and they'd drive home together. That Tuesday was the same as the others. At nine o'clock or maybe fifteen or twenty minutes later, if they'd stayed to talk to friends, he had driven Anna home and they'd gone right to bed, because the next day they both had to get up early.

Was that the only proof he could give of what he had done on March 1, the fact that it was a Tuesday?

Well, no, but it was a long time back, and every Tuesday was such a regular thing it helped him to remember. The next morning he'd driven Anna to the bakery again, put the car back in the garage, and taken the subway to work. On the way, he'd read about the kidnaping in the paper.

Hauptmann's voice, somewhat singsong in inflection, died out on the last syllable. He looked around, almost expectantly, as if to see who would question him next, but for the moment no more questions came.

There would be time enough, Lieutenant Finn was thinking, to test this alibi for the first of the three dates. If it proved to be true, then Richard Hauptmann could not be the actual abductor. The Lindbergh baby had been stolen sometime between eight and ten o'clock of the night of March 1, probably at a few minutes past nine—when, according to Hauptmann, he had just left or was about to leave a Bronx bakery.

They proceeded to the next date. Hauptmann sat up a little straighter in his chair; he was as calm as ever.

He was familiar with St. Raymond's Cemetery, of course?

He knew where it was, sure, the captive said readily. He'd once visited a friend who lived not far from it, maybe six years ago. But he'd never gone inside it.

And he was also familiar with Dr. John F. Condon?

He'd never seen him or spoken to him but he knew who he was —most people who lived in the Bronx had heard of the old man.

Wasn't it a fact, the questioners suggested, that Richard Hauptmann knew both Dr. Condon and St. Raymond's Cemetery quite well? That on the night of Saturday, April 2, 1932, he had met the old man there and had received from him fifty thousand dollars in Lindbergh ransom bills?

No, no.

Hadn't he written fourteen notes, several of them to Dr. Condon, for the purpose of extorting the money from Charles Lindbergh? Wasn't that why he kept a German-English dictionary in his apartment, to help him spell the difficult, unfamiliar words he had had to use in the ransom notes? Wasn't it true that he was the man Dr Condon called John?

Hauptmann shook his head. No, he said flatly. None of that was true.

Then what *was* true? What was he doing on April 2, 1932?

Why, the prisoner told them, he was working at the Majestic, same as before. But he happened to remember this Saturday well because it was his last day—it was the day he quit. As usual, he got home at about six o'clock and at seven or so his friend Hans Kloeppenburg had come. Yes, Hauptmann went on, he remembered it well, because on the first Saturday of each month Kloeppenburg would bring his guitar, and the two of them, Kloeppenburg with his guitar and he with his mandolin, singing old German songs, would enjoy an evening of music together. At midnight, maybe before, Kloeppenburg would leave. That was how he had spent April 2. It was a custom, the first Saturday night of each month.

Had anyone else been present?

Yes. Anna, his wife, had been there.

Lieutenant Finn thought: That too can be checked. He watched Hauptmann even more intently, because now one of the questioners had produced a tiny, tightly folded wad, wafer-thin, and was holding it in front of the suspect. He glanced at it, looked up inquiringly.

Did he recognize this?

Hauptmann studied it, said nothing.

They unfolded the wad and spread it out. It was a five-dollar Federal Reserve note, so sharply creased that it still was divided into eight crisp squares.

Recognize it now?

Hauptmann bent his head forward a little and inspected the note more closely. No.

Wasn't he in the habit of carrying certain bills folded up like this?

He shook his head. No.

Was he fond of the movies?

Hauptmann shrugged. Once in a while he liked to go, in the neighborhood where he lived.

But sometimes he went when he was away from his neighborhood?

Hauptmann looked blankly at the questioner.

About ten months ago hadn't he gone to the Sheridan Square Theater right here in Greenwich Village and used this folded five-dollar bill to pay his way in?

No, no—he'd never been down here in Greenwich Village before now. This was the first time.

Think again! Sunday night, November 26, 1933——

The suspect's blank face suddenly became mobile with expression, and he cut in: November twenty-sixth? Why, that was his birthday! Wait a minute, wait a minute——

His face contracted, cleared again.

Sure, now he remembered! There had been a little party for him at his house, just his wife and a couple of friends—

The five-dollar note was waved in front of his face like a small green warning flag.

This was a Lindbergh ransom bill, he was told, and it could be proved that he had once owned it, just as it could be proved that he had possessed other ransom bills. Now, where was the bulk of the money? What had he done with it? They knew he hadn't worked since the spring of 1932—

(They knew it, all right, Finn thought; the neighbors had given them that information.)

—yet he'd always seemed well supplied with cash. He'd sent Anna on a trip to Germany, taken her to Florida, gone off himself on hunting trips to Maine. He'd spent $396 for a radio, $56 for a hunting rifle, $109 for a canoe, $126 for a pair of binoculars. How had he managed to do all that without working? What was his secret?

Well, he'd played the stock market, the suspect explained. He'd been successful in the market.

Finn considered the prompt, easy explanation and admitted to himself that maybe it wasn't so far-fetched as it sounded. One of the expensive items that had come to light in the search of Hauptmann's home was a receipt for $190, paid for investment advice supplied by *The Magazine of Wall Street*. So far, they'd only looked into his safe-deposit box, stopping at the Central Savings Bank at Broadway and 73rd Street en route to the police station from the Bronx; there was no cash in the box. They would know more about his tale of Wall Street bonanzas when they checked with his brokers and inspected his bank accounts.

Hauptmann sat waiting in his chair, hands relaxed on its arms. The five-dollar bill had failed to awaken a stir of recognition in him; now other objects were produced for his scrutiny.

First, the chisel that had been picked up on the Lindbergh grounds on the night of the kidnaping.

He looked at it curiously and said that he had never seen it before.

Next, a child's woolen sleeping suit.

He shook his head. He had never seen it before.

A child's thumbguard, stained with rust.

No, he had never seen it before.

The room was silent.

Suddenly, a pointing finger drilled forward out of the circle of questioners and leveled at Hauptmann's face. A voice filled the room:

"Didn't you build a ladder and put it against the Lindbergh

house, and didn't you go up that ladder and into that room and kidnap that child?"

A spark might have shot through Hauptmann. His body trembled and he gripped the arms of the chair and his blue eyes seemed to kindle and blaze—or so the watching Finn thought. And for the first time Hauptmann's voice was not disciplined. He shouted:

"No!"

The accusing voice roared:

"And didn't you abandon that ladder and chisel and murder that child and strip that sleeping suit and thumbguard from its body?"

"No, I did not!"

The room was quiet again. Hauptmann slumped back in the chair and his strong hands relaxed. He waited for more questions.

In another room, other officers led Anna Hauptmann over much the same ground. The resemblance ended there; she had none of Richard's discipline. As the questions continued, she moved restlessly in her chair and clasped and unclasped her hands, and her voice reflected the fear in her eyes. Her freckled skin was flushed and damp.

March 1, 1932—what was she doing, that night? What was her husband doing? It was too far back, Anna said, she couldn't remember whether Richard was with her that evening or not. What day of the week was it, March 1? A Tuesday, she was told. Oh, she said, Tuesday!—then Richard must have been with her, because every Tuesday she worked late at Christian Fredericksen's bakery while his wife, Katie, took the night off, and every Tuesday at about seven Richard came and ate his supper there and waited to drive her home.

Every Tuesday? Weren't there some Tuesdays when Richard didn't come to the bakery? Oh, no, Anna assured them, it was a regular thing!

What about April 2, 1932, a Saturday, the first Saturday evening of the month?

Anna was quick to answer. That was Richard's musical evening, so he was at home with his mandolin. And Mr. Kloeppenburg was there too. Because Richard's musical evenings were a regular thing, just like his coming to the bakery.

November 26, 1933—where had Richard been then?

Oh, that was easy—at home, of course! Where else would he be? November 26 was Richard's birthday, and, like always, she had given him a little party.

Well, the questioners said, let's talk about the money, Mrs. Hauptmann. She had told them that she had stopped working in December 1932 and her husband had been unemployed since spring of that year. How had they managed? Where did the money come from?

Why, Anna said, they had saved, both of them. They had put away several hundred dollars a year from their salaries. And Richard had made investments, he was making money in Wall Street.

Was that what Richard had told her?

Yes, of course.

He was making money in Wall Street?

Yes, of course!

Didn't she know that it was Lindbergh ransom money?

Anna stared at them. At the house, she had asked in vain for information. Now she had been told. It came too suddenly for her to grasp. She didn't understand, she said in a small voice.

And so they explained: Richard, her husband, had kidnaped the Lindbergh baby. He had extorted fifty thousand dollars from the baby's father, and he had been arrested with some of that money on him.

Anna's mouth opened, not to speak but in a reflex of pure amazement. Slowly she put her hand over her mouth. She examined the watching faces, and then took her hand away and cried out:

"It is not so! He could not do such a thing!"

But he had done it, they told her.

No, no, she said, stammering, it was impossible, it was a crazy idea—Richard was a good husband, a good father—why, they had a baby of their own, Mannfried, and Richard loved him, there couldn't be a better father! She tried to explain some more, but the words choked her, and she hid her face in her hands.

They watched her while she sobbed, her sturdy body shaking.

She wiped her face. Presently she was able to speak again. She remembered how shocked and upset she was when she heard about the Lindbergh baby—she was at the bakery when she heard the news. She had felt pity for the poor parents.

"It made me sick," she said. "I prayed it would be brought back to them." Richard could never do such a thing, never—her Richard, Bubi's father? There must be some explanation——

The circle of men watched her. She had seemed to them, in her behavior, her response to their questions, to be a typical German housewife who knew little of her husband's activities outside their home and who accepted as the truth anything he chose to tell her. But wouldn't that unquestioning acceptance make her the most trustworthy accomplice Richard Hauptmann could possibly find? And how could he more profitably share the ransom money than with his wife? On the other hand, even if she had had no part in the crime, and in fact was unaware that Richard was the kidnaper, did it seem likely that she could be ignorant for two and a half years of what must have been his extraordinary interest in the Lindbergh case? Wouldn't she have been bound sooner or later to learn or stumble upon the truth?

If so, then her shock, her dumfounded face, her tears were a performance. Was Anna Hauptmann, the German *hausfrau,* so superlative an actress?

That was even harder to believe.

Her protests died away. She watched them, waiting. The questions started again.

While the questions continued in the two police-station rooms, the search continued in Richard Hauptmann's home and garage. The prime quest was for the ransom money, but other evidence was highly desirable, since it would tighten the authorities' hold on their captive—such things as samples of his handwriting matching the writing in the kidnaper's notes, paper matching the kind on which the notes had been written, an instrument or device that looked as though it might have been used to make the overlapping circle imprints which had served as the unmistakable signature on every note, and the tool that had punched the curious three holes which completed the identification.

And Arthur Koehler, the government wood expert, had asked the police to look for certain items. First, of course, the kind of carpenter tools that had fashioned the kidnap ladder: a handsaw and a plane (the ladder-builder's plane, Koehler said, had had a dull, uneven blade, and perhaps still had). Second, the various kinds of wood that had gone into the ladder: four kinds, Southern pine, Douglas fir, ponderosa pine and birch. And Koehler was most anxious to locate a strip of wood with a pattern of square nailholes, or with the nails still in it. If it could be found, Koehler said, it would be extremely damaging evidence.

So far, results of the search were disappointing. The most encouraging discovery was that Richard Hauptmann subscribed to the Bronx *Home News*: the paper was delivered daily to his home. Encouraging, of course, because Dr. Condon had chosen the *Home News* for his appeal to the kidnapers and to offer his services as go-between, and in the next day's mail had received their reply.

Could anyone but a regular reader of the paper have answered so promptly?

Ten hours had passed; Richard Hauptmann was still in the chair. He had been in it with only the briefest necessary pauses. Between changes of the teams of questioners he had dozed a little, and finally he had asked for something to eat, not much; milk was his favorite. He was very tired and his eyelids blinked a lot but his manner was essentially the same; his control had lapsed only once, when he had shouted his denial at the roaring voice and pointing forefinger.

Anna had been permitted to go back to her child, left in her niece's care, but with the warning that they were not finished with her.

Other men came into the room where Richard sat, and Finn, Sisk and Keaton, the board of strategy, nodded to their superiors: Inspector Lyons, New York police; Francis Fay, head of the New York office of the Division of Investigation; and Colonel Schwarzkopf, New Jersey State police. The board of strategy had decided, and the three superior officers agreed, that the time had come to test Hauptmann's repeated denials that he had written the ransom notes or knew anything about them.

They had a well-nigh immaculate trap.

In May 1932, Albert Osborn had devised a handwriting test to betray the author of the notes; since then more than a hundred suspects had written the significant paragraph, innocent-sounding when dictated but studded with words, syllables, and letters which, if written in a certain way, would proclaim that the writer had written the ransom demands. Only superficial and therefore meaningless similarities had occurred in the specimens submitted for Osborn's expert inspection.

Among all the suspects who had thereby cleared themselves—at least to Osborn's satisfaction—not one had been given an explanation in advance of the test's vital purpose. That careful casualness was now to be discarded. The board of strategy thought there was nothing to be gained, and perhaps much to be lost, in concealing the reason for the test. In the first place, Hauptmann could hardly fail to guess that it possessed an important connection with the crime; in the second, it was so shrewdly put together that even though forewarned the author of the notes would have to be phenomenally lucky or phenomenally, deliberately adroit to skirt its lavish pitfalls.

But regardless of the test's results, if and when Richard Hauptmann went on trial it might seem tricky, unfair, prejudicial to the prisoner's rights, if in court he could swear that in taking the test he had not known what he was doing, because he had not been told—all the more so since as yet he had no lawyer to advise him.

Well, he would know, all right; Inspector Lyons made it perfectly clear. He told Hauptmann that they would like him to submit to a handwriting test which would help prove whether or not he was telling the truth when he declared that he had not written the Lindbergh ransom notes. The test would be dictated to him and he would be allowed to spell the words in his own way. Was he willing to take the test?

He answered at once:

"I would be glad to write because it will get me out of this thing."

Sergeant Thomas Ritchie of the State police took over. He gave the prisoner pen and paper and instructed him that he was to write the dictation word for word. Hauptmann took the pen and sat intently waiting. Slowly, Ritchie read aloud the first sentence of the test paragraph; slowly, Hauptmann began to write.

Again, Lieutenant Finn's thoughts returned to the past and Dudley Shoenfeld's hypothetical rectangle. In the spring of '33, Leigh Matteson, a newspaperman, had suggested, and Finn had agreed, that auto-license applications carrying German-sounding names, with addresses that fell inside the Bronx rectangle, might include the kidnaper's. Of course there would be a lot of them in the Motor Vehicle Bureau's files, but the searchers would have valuable signposts to look for: Dr. Condon's description of John's physical characteristics and the even more significant characteristics Osborn had pointed out in the writing in the ransom notes. The experts had poured cold water on the suggestion; the information given on a typical application form, they had said, was partly printed, partly abbreviated, with so little script that he might as well forget the idea.

Finn hadn't forgotten, although he had done nothing about it, not then. It seemed to him that the experts had missed the scheme's real value. It wouldn't have been necessary to prove conclusively through a comparison of handwriting that any one of the suspects was John. Just to single out the suspects would have been enough: given ten or twenty the police could have kept them under watch and eliminated the innocent until they narrowed the list down to the possibly guilty *one.*

And as things had worked out, the *one* might have been Richard Hauptmann. In these last few days, Finn had obtained Hauptmann's license applications for the past four years, back to 1931, when he had bought and registered the Dodge sedan. Taken together, they had been quite revealing, the 1931 application particularly so. Not only had they supplied the elusive, wearisomely hunted-for name and address, and the confirming statistics as to age, height, weight, color of hair and eyes, plus the *x*—in the word *Bronx*—that looked as if two *e*s had been placed back to back, and the hyphenated New-York; also, the first application contained two clues that stood out as if under a white light. In answer to the question "Were you convicted of any felony or misdemeanor since April 15, 1930?" the conscientious and truthful Hauptmann had written, in script, *"Past red lihgt. Paid fine 5$."*

Throughout the ransom notes the writer had characteristically transposed *gs* and *hs* and, invariably, had placed the dollar sign after the figures.

Wouldn't these application forms have turned up, if the search through the Motor Vehicle Bureau files had been carried out?

It was difficult not to conclude that Richard Hauptmann might have been found a year and a half ago.

29

Anna Hauptmann had gone back to the Bronx, but not to 1279 East 222nd Street. A miniature war might have been fought in the apartment. Fortunately, her niece, Maria Mueller, lived not too far away, and with the police's consent, Maria had been quick to offer a temporary home for Anna and Bubi. The police had added, though, that Anna must be on hand at 1279 first thing the next morning, when the search would continue. Did they want her to help them tear her home apart? They had not explained their reason.

Bubi was asleep when she reached Maria's. Maria was full of questions, but when she saw her aunt's drawn face and shadowed eyes she insisted that the older woman must go straight to bed. It was a bad night for Anna; again she seemed to see all the men around her and hear their questions, question after question, and finally the terrible, the overwhelming question—*Didn't she know it was Lindbergh ransom money Richard had been spending?*

Richard! Richard—the Lindbergh baby—Richard!

Soon the police would have to learn that it was crazy.

She got up, still tired, gave Bubi his breakfast, left him in Maria's good care, went to 222nd Street. She could hardly bring herself to look at the littered floor, some of it uprooted, the tangled furniture, the broken wall plaster. She was standing silently in the midst of the wreckage when the police began to arrive, two of them—detectives, they said they were—and then three more. It was barely nine o'clock.

Yesterday, Anna had asked in vain what they were looking for; today she knew—anything that would connect Richard with the crime, the awful crime he had had nothing to do with; and therefore she knew that all this hunting and pulling things apart was just so much senseless destruction. By and by it seemed that they too realized there was nothing to be found in the apartment. Beckoning to her to come with them, they went downstairs and crossed Needham Avenue to the garage Richard and a friend of his had built.

Here too, Anna saw, the police had been at work; floor planks had been ripped up and the tidy piles of household goods scattered about. She watched as the men moved slowly around the garage, inspecting floor, walls, ceiling. An hour passed, another; still they searched. Now one of them, a friendly man who had seemed a little apologetic for invading her home—Detective James Petrosino—was examining Richard's workbench, where he had made many useful things for the house. A board was nailed above the bench across two uprights in the south wall of the garage. Detective Petrosino looked at the board. He touched it, tapped it, then yanked it off.

Anna saw that there was a narrow shelf behind the board, in a kind of compartment. There were two bundles wrapped in newspapers on the shelf.

Detective Petrosino carefully lifted the bundles and took off the wrapping. Inside each one Anna could see a thick pack of bills with gold seals.

She heard the searchers excitedly talking. A few words were enough to tell her what they had found:

"Ten-dollar gold notes . . . Lindbergh ransom bills."

Detective James Petrosino's companions were Detectives Edward Murphy and Frank Dunn; the two other officers were Sergeant John Wallace, New Jersey State police, and Special Agent Leon Turrou of the Division of Investigation. Petrosino hadn't liked the idea of pulling apart the woman's home under her eyes but it was necessary; in case any evidence turned up, it could hardly be said later that it was planted. Certainly she could not say so about this rich find.

Edward Murphy noticed another board, wider than the first, nailed across some uprights beneath the workbench. He removed the board and saw a one-gallon shellac can resting in the recess of a window. Lifting it from its hiding place, he pried off the lid. Two cloths were wedged tightly at the top of the can. Under them were several bundles, wrapped like the first ones.

The other men turned to Anna Hauptmann. What did she know about this money? Where had it come from? Who put it there?

She shook her head. Dully she said she knew nothing, nothing, nothing.

The men inspected their find. All the bills were gold notes, and all were tens and twenties. The first two bundles were tens only, a hundred in one pack, eighty-three in the other; $1830 in all. The shellac can yielded ten bundles amounting to $1000 each, another bundle $990, the last bundle $940, adding up to $11,930. The grand total was $13,760.

It couldn't be said for a fact that all of them were Lindbergh bills until each serial number was checked with the ransom list, but James Petrosino didn't feel much doubt about that. He looked at the silent, sad woman. Now she must return to the police station with them, he said.

There were 390 tens and 493 twenties in the garage hoard, and every serial number checked with the list of Lindbergh ransom bills. Added to the $5100 previously recovered, $18,860 of the total had been found. As for the balance of $31,140, it seemed to the investigators that when Richard Hauptmann was confronted with the new find he would have little choice but to admit that he was the extortionist and lead them to it.

Lieutenant Finn was no handwriting expert but it did not require a specialist's knowledge to see if Hauptmann had fallen into one of the snares strewn through Albert Osborn's test; therefore he had looked eagerly at the lines written by the prisoner and, sure enough, had seen the telltale transposed *g* and *h*. Then Finn had gone off to get some sleep, more confident than ever that the man in the hard chair was the author of the ransom notes. The sheets of paper had been dispatched to Osborn for painstaking appraisal.

But for Hauptmann there had been no more than scraps of uneasy sleep, if that; no sooner had his eyes closed, at long intervals, than a fresh, alert relay of questioners had jerked him into wakefulness. By two o'clock of the afternoon of Thursday the twentieth, he had been questioned almost continuously for twenty-four hours. His face seemed gray and loose, the flesh sagging as if pulled down by invisible fingers, and fine red strands had crept into the corners of his tired eyes. But his voice remained astonishingly clear, his manner composed.

The questioners launched a new attack.

Why had he lied when he said he had no more gold certificates?

Hauptmann peered at them, rubbed his face, said nothing.

What about these, found in his garage? They showed him the money, still bundled in newspapers.

He looked at it. There was no sign that he was taken aback. Then he said calmly that he had lied, because he was afraid that if he told the truth he would be prosecuted for keeping gold, which he knew was against the law.

But this was ransom money, they pointed out. Lindbergh money.

He shook his head. He didn't know anything about that, he told them. The money wasn't his.

Wasn't his? Then whose was it? How did it get into his garage?

It belonged to a friend, Isidor Fisch. Fisch had asked him to take care of it for him while he went on a trip.

The name brought a pause, because it seemed familiar; it had turned up somewhere just a while ago. Then one of the questioners ran it down in his memory and murmured to the others that a couple of letters from Fisch, or anyway someone with the same name, had been found in the Bronx apartment.

All right, they said, resuming the attack, maybe he'd better tell them about this Isidor Fisch.

Well, Hauptmann explained, like himself, Fisch was German. He was a fur trader and they'd been partners in several fur deals. It had worked out pretty well—between them they'd made maybe ten thousand dollars. Then Fisch had got to thinking about his partner's success with stocks and had figured he ought to play the market too. But he'd had very bad luck, so bad that Hauptmann had had to give him two big loans. Well, Fisch's health wasn't good, and just before last Christmas he'd decided to visit his parents in Germany, in Leipzig. Before he left he'd brought some of his things to Hauptmann to keep until he got back. One of these things was a cardboard box, a shoe box, tied with string. Hauptmann had put it on a closet shelf and forgotten about it. Then, about two weeks ago, just by chance he'd found that it had money in it. It was a surprise to him, a big surprise, of course, because it was the first time he knew what was inside the shoe box. A heavy rain had soaked through the closet ceiling and the box had got wet and the money was damp, so he'd taken the money to the garage and wrapped it in newspapers and hidden it. Then, a few days later, he had started to take from it, because Fisch still owed him for the loans. He felt he was only taking what belonged to him. He hadn't known it was Lindbergh money, or of course he wouldn't have touched any of the bills.

It was a lot to say and it tired him. They waited while he rested a little. Then they asked where Isidor Fisch was now.

He was dead, Hauptmann answered. He had died of tuberculosis in Leipzig, almost six months ago.

The police's careful secrecy was not impregnable and in the middle of the afternoon word leaked out that a hot suspect in the Lindbergh kidnaping had been captured and a good deal of ransom money recovered. The case seemed about to break.

Also, word got out where the suspect was being held. Reporters and photographers came rushing to the old station house. Greenwich Street traffic congealed in an unholy jam; the sidewalks overflowed. Soon there was a mob, and not merely curious; talk about the kidnaping and the murder, and the consciousness of their own acute discomfort, stirred the pushing, sweating crowd into a mood of wanting to settle things here and now with the prisoner, whoever he was. Squads of police arrived to back up the overmatched cops on the scene, with instructions to keep everyone moving, clear the street and sidewalks; but the order was unenforceable. The best that could be done was to maintain a precarious control.

But now there was a diversion, and the mob's temper changed.

Since the secret was out, there was no reason not to send for the eyewitnesses who could be expected to identify the suspect and connect him with the crime; earlier, their appearance—at least one of them was very well known—could have given the game away, even if they had resisted the temptation to drop a few hints.

If the witnesses positively identified him, there were two who could put Hauptmann close to the scene of the crime on the day it occurred and thereby link him with the kidnaping and murder. They were Amandus Hochmuth, who lived near the Lindbergh estate, and Ben Lupica, the Princeton Prep student who had driven past it. Together or separately, Dr. Condon and Joseph Perrone, the Bronx cab driver who had delivered a ransom note, could connect Hauptmann with extortion. Possession of the ransom money could be established through half a dozen witnesses, ranging from Cecile Barr, the movie-theater cashier, to the gas-station men Walter Lyle and John Lyons. Of equal importance now was an East Side storekeeper who had been given one of the ten-dollar gold certificates as far back as March 1, 1933; he might prove that Hauptmann was lying when he said that the newly discovered cache of gold notes had been turned over to him by Isidor Fisch in *December* of '33. The storekeeper had told detectives that he'd remember his customer if he saw him again.

Late in the afternoon, a police car made its embattled way along Greenwich Street and got as close to the station house as it could. Two detectives stepped out. A third man followed them. His name ran through the crowd, rose to a shout:

"Jafsie!"

His tall figure was unmistakable; none who had seen the many pictures of him in the papers could forget it. Erect, dignified as ever, Dr. Condon did not acknowledge this evidence of fame. Indeed, the great, thrusting crowd, the tumultuous atmosphere, struck him as singularly out of keeping with the serious task awaiting inside the station house. Furthermore, he did not feel at his best. He had been summoned from his home in such haste by the two detectives that he had had no chance to shave or to change from the old, unpressed blue suit he was wearing.

Firmly hanging onto his black derby, he strode along the noisy lane cleared for him and entered the station.

Inside, the atmosphere was no better; in fact, Dr. Condon decided, it was worse. Newspaper people jammed the aisles and stairway and they all seemed to be shouting at him. The uproar was hellish. The old man raised his head a notch or two higher, squared his shoulders, and plunged after his escort. With enormous difficulty they got to the fourth floor and into a large room.

Here at least it was quieter. A police official sat behind a desk at the far end of the room and along one side some twenty men stood in a ragged line. Dr. Condon had been asked to inspect many line-ups in connection with the case and he had an idea most of these men were detectives, though of course none was in uniform. The official at the desk introduced himself: Inspector Lyons. Now, he said, he was sure Dr. Condon understood why he was here. They had a suspect, and he was in that line-up. If Dr. Condon felt positive one of them was John, the man he had dealt with in the ransom negotiations, he was to step forward and put his hand on the man's shoulder.

Dr. Condon nodded and turned to the line-up. Keenly, methodically, he studied the faces in the bright light, one by one. The face and figure he was looking for were stamped imperishably on his mind. Even if that picture needed freshening (and it did not), he had had a glimpse of John only a month ago, when the old man had halted a bus and unavailingly pursued him.

His searching eyes paused.

There he was.

The same, or almost the same—the sallow face maybe a little fleshier, but still pointed, still flat-cheeked; eyes and mouth expressionless as always; the figure unmistakably lithe and muscular even under the rumpled double-breasted suit he wore.

John.

The long hunt was over. All I need do now, Dr. Condon was thinking, is to follow instructions and step forward and put my hand on his shoulder—and say, "This is the man."

There is the man who lied to me and double-crossed me. There is the man who stole and murdered an innocent child, the golden-haired baby I vowed I would find and place in its mother's arms. There is the man I swore I would follow to the ends of the earth. He knows it, and he knows that I know it.

But although he knows it, Dr. Condon's thoughts continued, obviously he has refused to admit to the police that he is John. Perhaps —perhaps I can succeed where the police have failed.

It seemed to the old man that he had an excellent chance of succeeding. His years were rich in experience; he had dealt with many kinds of men, often in difficult circumstances; not only was he a teacher, he was also a student of the human mind. And surely his knowledge of John surpassed the police's knowledge; at one point John and he had been very close together, when they had spoken of intimate things, things that could not fail to move any heart, even a criminal's—even a child-murderer's. If there was one person in the world to whom John would be likely to admit, "Yes, I am John," surely it was Dr. Condon!

And it could not be denied, Dr. Condon confessed to himself, that succeeding where the police had failed would give him a certain satisfaction. He was only human, and his dignity, his self-esteem, had suffered at the police's hands. His role in the Lindbergh case had been purely disinterested from the beginning, but on several occasions the police had cast a sort of sneering doubt on it. They had implied that he knew more than he chose to tell, that he was a wily old bird moving in devious ways to thwart the execution of justice. They had even thought—some of them, anyway, in the New Jersey State and New York City police forces—that he had had a share of the gold extorted from Charles Lindbergh.

Dr. Condon therefore did not step forward and put his hand on Richard Hauptmann's shoulder. Instead, he turned back to Inspector Lyons and asked for a favor.

Lyons looked puzzled. What was it?

Dr. Condon said he would like to proceed in his own fashion.

Lyons considered. Well, all right, he said, not enthusiastically; go ahead.

Granted freedom of action, Dr. Condon walked slowly along the line-up. He did not put his hand on John's shoulder but merely touched him. Then he touched three more men—detectives, he felt confident. He asked these four if they would please step forward, and with gentle little guiding pushes formed them into a new line of his own.

Dr. Condon asked them one by one to please tell him their names. When it came to John's turn, he replied, "Bruno Richard Hauptmann."

And the old man thought, Yes, that's his voice, just as I remember it: thick, deep, with a strong German accent.

Again he went from one to the other and asked the same question.

"Have you ever seen me before?"

Three of them answered truthfully, at least so far as Dr. Condon knew: "No."

But John lied. "No," he said.

Dr. Condon returned to Inspector Lyons. He had another request. He would like to have a pencil and paper. They were given to him. The old man found a table and sat down at it, frowning thoughtfully.

During both his meetings with John, he had listened carefully to the other's every word and the tone of his voice, so carefully that later he had been able to mimic John's voice for the police on phonograph records. Dr. Condon searched his memory for those words, and they sprang into life, with such vividness that he might have been sitting once more on that bare bench, or standing in the cemetery with the imitation ballot box in his hand, hearing the telltale phrases.

Yes, *telltale* phrases; that was what he wanted! Phrases so interwoven with the kidnaping and extortion that when John repeated them their significance might thrust deep into him, shatter his stolid demeanor, force him to admit who he truly was.

On one piece of paper Dr. Condon wrote:

It is too dangerous. I stayed already too long. He would smack me up.

On a second piece of paper he wrote:

Did you got it, the money? I will send you the sleeping suit of the baby. Your work was perfect.

He got up and gave the first paper to the first of the three detectives in the little line.

"Read it aloud, please."

The old man listened with head bowed and slightly tilted.

"The next man, please."

The second detective read the words, and the third. Dr. Condon gave the other piece of paper to John alone to read aloud, and listened to the well-remembered voice, speaking the well-remembered words. Dr. Condon intently studied his face as he read. If the words affected him at all, he did not show it.

Once more Dr. Condon slowly passed along the line, asking each one if he was sure he had never seen him before, and again three men answered truthfully and again John—or Hauptmann, as Dr. Condon now thought of him; Richard Hauptmann—lied.

The old man lingered directly in front of Hauptmann.

"Are you sure?"

Hauptman said at once, "I never saw you before."

Dr. Condon went back to his table, while Inspector Lyons and the other officers in the room continued to stare. Hauptmann's shield still seemed impenetrable, but the old man fancied he knew a way past it into his heart. On a third piece of paper he wrote:

What would your mother say? She would cry.

He handed the paper to Hauptmann and told him to read it aloud, listening intently as the other obeyed.

Had his voice faltered after the words *What would your mother say?* Had it hesitated again before reading the word *cry?* Dr. Condon was standing very close to the other, and to his ears it seemed so. But Hauptmann's face remained impassive, and he did not make the admission—that yes, he was John—for which the old man was eagerly waiting.

Slowly, in deep thought, Dr. Condon walked back to Lyons' desk and requested another favor: Would they let him speak privately to Hauptmann? The inspector consented, and Dr. Condon led Hauptmann to an empty corner of the room, where any words they exchanged could not be overheard.

This was his last chance, the old man knew. Now or never he must succeed where the police had failed. Quietly, he said:

"Können Sie Deutsch sprechen?"

At least there was an answer:

"Ja."

Heartened, Dr. Condon said pleadingly:

"Wahrheit ist besser, Richard."

Anxiously he watched for the effect of his plea: "The truth is better, Richard." He could see none.

An idea occurred to Dr. Condon: perhaps some poetry would soften Hauptmann, persuade him at this last moment to speak the truth. An appropriate verse, in German, came readily to mind. He whispered it to the other:

> *"Willst du immer weiter schweifen*
> *Sieh das Gute liegt so nah*
> *Lerne nur das Glück ergreifen*
> *Denn das Glück ist immer da."*

He waited again, turning over the meaning of the verse in his mind: "Will you always seek still farther, See the good that lies so near. Learn at once to grasp your fortune, Then happiness is always there."

Hauptmann's face did not change.

It was a bitter moment for Dr. Condon, but he had done his

best. He returned to the inspector's desk and said that he was finished.

Almost at once, it seemed, the quiet room turned into a carnival. Police officials and a swarm of reporters and photographers surged around Dr. Condon, flash bulbs flared, excited voices rang in his ears—"Which one is John? . . . Look this way, Jafsie! . . . Dr. Condon, look at me! . . . Which one is John? . . . Jafsie, Jafsie, look this way!"

Dr. Condon barely kept his temper in check. A man's life hung on the words he would speak, and the appalling atmosphere in which he was asked to say them was a disgraceful parody of the processes of law and justice he revered. He determined to teach these shouting men, the police and press, a good lesson. He knew that Richard Hauptmann had been arrested with a ransom bill on him and that a great many more had been found in his garage. That was plenty of evidence for the police to charge him with extortion.

And so he said that for the time being he was withholding his identification.

A voice loud enough to be heard above the tumult bawled at him that either he could pick out John or he couldn't. *Which of the four men was John?*

Dr. Condon said firmly that at the present time he would not declare an identification.

The news had spread across the country, and in Inglewood, California, reporters raced to the Maddux estate, where Charles and Anne Lindbergh had been staying, only to learn that the young man and his wife were not available for an interview, had nothing to say. In fact, they were no longer there. Norman Schwarzkopf had telephoned the news to Lindbergh a few hours earlier; since it would be several days before Charles would be obliged to return to New York and face Hauptmann, he and Anne had decided to go into seclusion.

For their hiding place, they had chosen Will Rogers' nearby Santa Monica ranchhouse—he and his wife were still in Europe, a caretaker was in charge and their home was the Lindberghs' to use whenever they wished. It seemed fairly unlikely that reporters would look for them there.

In this refuge, looking out on the tranquil Pacific, Anne tried to prepare herself for an ordeal she dreaded: the essential public exposure of her private grief. The tragic past would be reborn in the trial of the person—or persons—accused of murdering her dead child.

Part Three

THE TRIAL

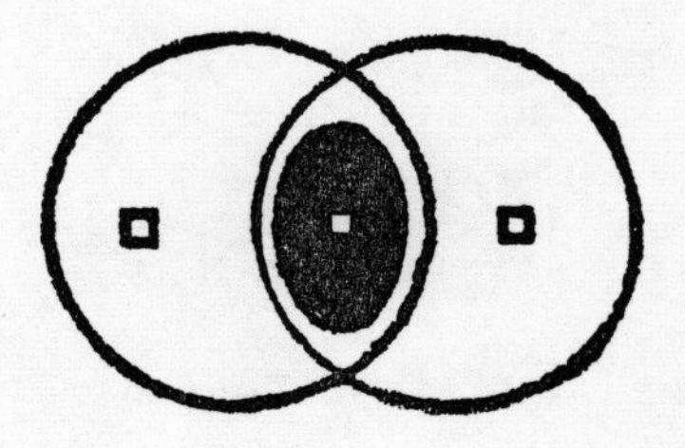

1

Flemington's town constable heard the news with mixed feelings: the legal tussle to extradite Bruno Richard Hauptmann from New York to New Jersey had been won and he would be tried in the Hunterdon County Courthouse. It was gratifying to know that Flemington would have its day in the sun, but its solitary police officer would have his work more than cut out for him. Hundreds of strangers would be in town. Hundreds? Thousands, maybe.

In normal times, the task of maintaining the peace in Flemington was not arduous. New York City was only sixty miles away, but Flemington was another world. Its citizens went to bed early, and there weren't many more than twenty-seven hundred of them. They lived in decent elderly houses with white walls and green shutters and a good deal of ornamental woodwork, kept their sidewalks clean and regarded the town constable mainly as a source of reliable weather information.

Flemington had been settled by the Dutch in the seventeenth century but took its name from Samuel Fleming, who set up as an innkeeper in the peaceable hamlet in the 1750s. Some seventy years later the courthouse, symbol of Flemington's eminence as the Hunterdon County seat, was built on Main Street.

It was a handsome building, two and a half stories high, of native stone with a white stucco façade and four Doric columns in the Greek revival style, although the Colonial cupola reminded the townspeople that this was, after all, America. The county jail, small but quite modern, was directly behind the courthouse. The town constable examined its appointments in preparation for the new tenant, reflecting that an earlier one, also involved in the Lindbergh case, had waited here to be tried: John Hughes Curtis, the Norfolk boatbuilder.

The Union Hotel, the only hotel in Flemington, faced the courthouse directly across Main Street. It was a lumbering affair of nondescript vintage and architecture, four stories tall. A commodious porch ran across its front, with double-deck balconies above. Business was sparse inside, but the ground-floor front porch enjoyed sociable afternoons and evenings and heard much chat about affairs of the day as town gossips rocked in their chairs and inspected drowsy Main Street.

Then Main Street came to life.

Friday night, October 19, three sedans containing a dozen New Jersey detectives drove into town at about half-past ten. In a fourth car, which they escorted, Richard Hauptmann sat handcuffed between Captain John Lamb and Lieutenant Arthur Keaton of the State police. A thousand restless and inquisitive people (the town constable's estimate) had gathered around the entrance to the jail; some of them, not trusting Flemington's street lights and determined to see all, had brought flares. In this garish light they watched Hauptmann's guards lead him from the car into the jail. The crowd was silent, staring. The prisoner was impassive.

Twelve State troopers stationed themselves outside.

The staff of the Union Hotel was still wondering how to cope with the huge problem the prisoner had brought to town with him. They had on hand messages from some nine hundred people—from all over the world, it seemed—requesting rooms for the duration of the trial. Many were sharply specific, stating that their rooms must be the best the hotel afforded; others, with wild incomprehension, spoke of suites; and at least one dwelt on a special diet which the hotel's kitchen must be prepared to dish up for him.

There were fifty rooms in the Union. The last few vacancies were taken by newspaper and radio reporters long before the great bulk of messages arrived; and even before that, six rooms on the top floor had been reserved for the trial jurors. Flemington housewives, quickly learning about the problem and the opportunity it offered, began to make ready their spare rooms or, when there was none, double up the family's sleeping arrangements. It soon became apparent that even these emergency measures would not suffice. Flemington was booked solid. The overflow would have to be content with quarters in the Trenton hotels, twenty miles distant.

The front porch of the Union Hotel buzzed with interesting items. No less than three hundred reporters, many of them star reporters, some of them famous novelists turned reporter for the trial—Walter Winchell, Edna Ferber, Arthur Brisbane, Fannie

Hurst, Damon Runyon, Kathleen Norris, Alexander Woollcott, Adela Rogers St. John—were coming to Flemington. Also, great figures of the stage and screen, United States senators, crooners, concert singers, social celebrities; and, of course, people who never missed any important event—a World Series, a prize fight, a murder trial—had announced that they would attend. An atmosphere of eager expectancy spread from the hotel porch through the town. Faces never before seen by the townsfolk except in their newspapers and magazines were glimpsed on Main Street, many, it was true, behind dark glasses, but recognizable nevertheless. Foreign accents were heard. Raoul de Roussy de Sales was in Flemington, sent by *Paris-Soir,* and Lionel Shortt of the London *Daily Mail,* and Dixie Tighe of the London *Daily Express.* A great criminal lawyer, Samuel Leibowitz, had been engaged by a radio network to comment on the progress of the trial, and professional colleagues, no less familiar with the law's intricacies, were to analyze the events in the courtroom for rival networks.

A phrase that hardly seemed inflated traveled from mouth to mouth and back again: this was to be the trial of the century.

And the world was not to miss a word of it. Telephone and telegraph technicians swarmed over the old, dignified courthouse, trailing wires behind them. They stitched wires over the floors and up the walls and into the garret, the center of their humming web. Here, cramped places were made for forty telegraph and cable operators, who would sit shoulder to shoulder and flash out each word practically as it was uttered in the legal cockpit below. They were prepared, the wireless companies stated, to transmit a million words a day.

The weather sharpened; Christmas was in the air.

Some of the strangers in town were saying that because of the crime's atrocious nature and the veneration in which the dead child's father was held, the Lindbergh case couldn't possibly be tried on its merits—Richard Hauptmann would never receive a fair trial. *Wrong,* Flemington replied with a united voice, absolutely wrong! No Hunterdon County jury would prejudge any defendant; Hunterdon County people were fair-minded, you could count on that.

Sounds of young voices floated through the crisp evening. The fair-minded Hunterdon County people's children were chanting carols outside Richard Hauptmann's cell.

But when was the trial to start? Flemington's constable understood that there had been something of a tussle over the date, too. The man who would prosecute, Attorney General Wilentz, had wanted it to begin on November 14, but the prisoner's counsel had said that wouldn't give him enough time and had proposed December 11; but *that* would run it through the Christmas holidays, not so good for the jurors; and, therefore, finally prosecution and defense had agreed to start the trial on the very first practical date after New Year's Day—Wednesday, January 2, 1935.

Tuesday night, January 1, was clear and cold; the rooftops were white under a lingering mantle of Christmas snow. Tomorrow promised to be a fine day.

2

Morning sunshine flowed over the white roofs. In nearby Trenton, Justice Thomas Whitaker Trenchard shaved, breakfasted and made ready for court. He thought it wise to slip a bottle of cough syrup into the pocket of his jacket, in case of any trouble with his throat. He did not expect any trouble—in fact, he had been resting in bed for the last two days, to make sure that he was fit for the sheer physical strain of the trial—but it was just as well to be prepared.

Judge Trenchard was seventy-one, a sedate, handsome, gray-haired man. His face, rather high-colored, customarily had a paternal look, and his manner in the courtroom had been described as one of sympathetic benevolence; for all that, he was a stickler for the proprieties. He had been sitting on the New Jersey Supreme Court bench for more than twenty-eight years and was starting his fifth consecutive seven-year term as a Supreme Court justice. His reputation throughout the state was second to none: Judge Trenchard's decisions were well known for the muscular thought behind them and their clarity of expression. To this refusal to countenance the slipshod in thought or word he owed his sterling record: he had never been reversed in a murder trial.

The judge waited in his chambers while the ten-o'clock bells were rung. The court crier pronounced the ancient words, *"Oyez! Oyez! Oyez!* All manner of persons having business with this Court . . . on this second day of January in the year of Our Lord One Thousand Nine Hundred and Thirty-five, let them draw nigh, give their attention, and they shall be heard."

Judge Trenchard entered the courtroom and took his place on the bench. The trial of Bruno Richard Hauptmann could begin.

Today, only a hundred or so spectators had been permitted to attend. The jury was to be selected, a delicate process that did not allow for the normal distractions of a trial audience. Those inside could hear the murmurs and occasional jeers of the crowd in the street; but by and by, under the indifferent stares of the guarding State troopers, the noise died down. Other troopers were posted throughout the building, keeping an eye on its furnishings, many of them valuable antiques.

The courtroom itself was a high-ceilinged hall with yellow walls, five large windows on either side and two more behind the judge's dais. The old benches, somewhat resembling church pews, could accommodate no more than five hundred spectators; to prepare for the weeks to come—the prosecution estimated the trial would last four weeks—folding chairs had been borrowed from the Flemington Fair and squeezed in wherever possible.

At the rear, a gallery looked down on the court, and here the press reigned, uncomfortably. Pine boards, squared off in eighteen-inch spaces, served as writing tables. One hundred fifty reporters——there was not conceivably room for a hundred-fifty-first—sat jammed at them.

Seventy talesmen, the raw material of the jury, were seated at the back of the courtroom.

Attorney General David T. Wilentz rose and moved the trial of the State of New Jersey against Bruno Richard Hauptmann; in his turn Chief Defense Counsel Edward J. Reilly announced that the defense was ready.

Anthony Hauck, Jr., and C. Lloyd Fisher came forward to get on with the tedious and all-important business of examining and cross-examining prospective jurors.

These two had faced each other before. Hauck, District Attorney of Hunterdon County, had pleaded the State's case against John Hughes Curtis in this courtroom, and Fisher, a stocky, thirty-eight-year-old native of Flemington, had defended him. Today they were in secondary roles. It was hardly Hauck's fault. He, rather than David Wilentz, would be the chief prosecutor if Hunterdon County had the money to pay for the trial, but it hadn't; the State itself was obliged to foot the bill, and the constitution plainly stated that in such circumstances the attorney general must take command.

Defense and prosecution had agreed they would alternate in examining and cross-examining the talesmen: if defense had the first turn with the first talesman, prosecution would have first with the second. It fell to Lloyd Fisher to examine Charles Walton, a slight, serious-looking man who said that he was fifty-five, a machinist, married, the father of four children.

Fisher pressed to the point:

"Mr. Walton, have you formed any opinion as to the guilt or innocence of the defendant in this case?"

"Not exactly, no," Walton said.

"Have you read the Winchell column in the *Daily Mirror*?"

"No, I haven't."

"Or heard his broadcast?"

"Well, occasionally."

"And from what you have heard in his broadcast, you have formed an opinion?"

"No, not necessarily," Walton answered, and paused and considered, and said again, "No."

These were vital questions for the defense; Walter Winchell had come out flatly in his newspaper columns and radio broadcasts with the opinion that Richard Hauptmann was guilty of the kidnaping and murder. Winchell was known to be in the confidence of a great many extremely important people. Didn't it stand to reason that he knew what he was talking about?

Fisher seemed to be satisfied with Charles Walton on this score. He moved on:

"Do you feel, Mr. Walton, if you were permitted to sit on this jury that you would be guided by the evidence and render a fair verdict in accordance with the evidence as presented to you?"

"Yes, I would, sir."

"And do you understand that rule of law that the defendant is innocent until he is proved guilty beyond a reasonable doubt?"

"Yes, sir.

"And would you be willing to give him the benefit of that reasonable doubt?"

Charles Walton said that he would.

There was another matter, an exasperating one. A person or persons unknown had mailed to every prospective Lindbergh case juror at his home a pamphlet detailing the experience (fictitious) of an aviator (fictitious) whose child had been kidnaped. The pamphlet was satiric in tone; at least prosecution and defense reckoned that that was the idea, for the anonymous author was certainly no Jonathan Swift. But who could tell what effect it might have had?

Yes, Walton admitted, he had received a copy of the pamphlet, but he affirmed positively that it had not influenced him with respect to Richard Hauptmann one way or the other.

Lloyd Fisher indicated that he was satisfied, and Anthony Hauck took over for the prosecution.

"Mr. Walton, have you any conscientious or religious scruples against capital punishment?"

"No."

"I understood you to answer Mr. Fisher, as to whether or not you had formed an opinion, that you said, 'not exactly.' "

"Well," Walton said, with a quick explanatory gesture—a habit of his, Fisher had noticed—"well, not to any extent, not more than anyone else would that read the paper."

"In other words, even though you might have been affected in some small manner, you could be guided by the evidence and by law as charged to you by the Court solely?"

Walton nodded. "Yes."

Hauck, too, was satisfied. The man seemed intelligent and alert and his record spoke for a stable character: he had worked for the same company for the past twenty-five years. Charles Walton stepped into the jury box. The first juror selected, he automatically became foreman.

3

Maybe in the future, David Wilentz thought, he would find this questioning and cross-questioning of talesmen tedious or even downright boring; right now he didn't. It was fascinating. And grim, too, considering what might depend on each question, each answer: the life of that man over there, sitting behind his counselors.

This was David Wilentz's first murder case—his first criminal case of any kind, although he was Attorney General of New Jersey, chief prosecutor for the State, head of State's counsel. The grab bag of political circumstance had determined that. He was thirty-nine, very young for the office. Governor A. Harry Moore had appointed him attorney general last year after Wilentz, a vigorous and eloquent Democrat, had persuaded a majority of voters in traditionally Republican Middlesex County to switch over to the other side. He knew his law; a New York University Law School graduate, he had been admitted to the bar in 1919 after returning a lieutenant from the war; and although in this case he was up against one of the toughest, wiliest and most successful trial lawyers in the business, Wilentz was confident he was going to come out on top and put Richard Hauptmann in the electric chair.

As a private citizen, as a voter, if given the chance to vote for or against capital punishment, Wilentz would have voted wholeheartedly against. He thought the law barbaric. But it was New Jersey State law and he was the attorney general and if he did not fight tooth and nail to win the last full measure of the punishment the law decreed, he would be derelict, and that was one thing that would never be said of Attorney General David Wilentz.

He was all light and shadow, swift as mercury, with a rapier wit and tongue and a d'Artagnan poise to go with them, and more than a little of a d'Artagnan face, thin and dark under a magnificent head of black hair. That intrepid swordsman would have approved of his taste in clothes: away from the court's majesty, David Wilentz liked to wear an off-white felt hat, brim snapped down in front and on one side, a velvet-collar Chesterfield and a flashing white silk scarf. He cut a dash. His bright eyes regarded the world with humor and tolerance and unfailing interest. He was married and the father of three children, who liked him very much.

His eyes were studying Richard Hauptmann and another man, who sat three chairs away from the accused, in the same row—Charles Lindbergh.

Hauptmann had been led into the courtroom between two State troopers, followed closely by a deputy sheriff in plain clothes. Lindbergh had come in not long afterward, striding through the hush left by the prisoner's appearance. In a light gray suit with no vest, his familiar, gangling, still-boyish figure had deepened the hush. Wilentz's bright eyes had watched carefully, had seen Hauptmann glance up as the father of the dead child took his seat and then quickly look away. Charles Lindbergh, Wilentz had noted, didn't look at Hauptmann at all. Wilentz had noted something else. As he sat, chin in hand, watching Hauck and Fisher, studying each prospective juror, Lindbergh would lean forward occasionally and his gray jacket would fall open a little, revealing beneath it a pistol in a shoulder holster.

Wilentz knew that Lindbergh had had an excellent chance to inspect the prisoner. A week after Hauptmann's arrest, he and Lindbergh had been in the same room, the large private office of Samuel J. Foley, District Attorney of the Bronx. Lindbergh, who had just flown east with Anne, had requested the meeting, a meeting only he, not Hauptmann, would be aware of. Long before, still striving to come to grips with the author of the ransom notes, the young father had disguised himself in cap and dark glasses; he had put on the same disguise before coming into Foley's office and seating himself with a group of detectives. Then Hauptmann had been brought in. District Attorney Foley had instructed the prisoner to walk around and sit down and get up and repeat, over and over, in different tones, now in a quiet voice, now shouting, the words "Hey, Doctor! Hey, Doctor, over here!"—words Lindbergh had heard when John had called out his directions to Dr. Condon from the darkness of St. Raymond's Cemetery.

For ten minutes Lindbergh had watched Hauptmann walking back and forth, obediently following instructions: "Hey, Doctor! Hey, Doctor, over here!" No, Wilentz thought, he hardly needed to look at him now.

Lindbergh was obviously very much caught up in the questioning of the talesmen. The accused man, Wilentz thought, made an absorbing sight. Asked for a word to describe his attitude, you would have to say *confident.* Even cheerful. Hauptmann glanced around a lot, often met Wilentz's eyes coolly. He chatted with his counselors as if he and they were a group of spectators who had dropped in to watch the trial rather than a man accused of kidnaping and murder sitting with the men who hoped to save him from the chair.

An absorbing sight; as an individual, an absorbing study—all that he had learned about Richard Hauptmann bore that out, Wilentz thought. The psychiatrist Dudley Shoenfeld held that the crime was compulsive and to bolster his arguments had cited examples of the defendant's behavior, taken from the composite portrait of Richard Hauptmann which had been painstakingly pieced together out of information obtained from the German province where he was born and brought up, from friends, neighbors, acquaintances, from his wife, Anna—and, of course, from Hauptmann himself.

Was the crime compulsive, the result of a puzzling tangle of psychic twists? What kind of man was Richard Hauptmann? What was his history? Studying the man so close at hand, here in the dramatic present, Wilentz's mind furled back the years to Richard Hauptmann's past. . . .

Things were bad, that Christmas of 1918, when Bruno Richard Hauptmann came home from the war—bad in the little town of Kamenz, in Saxony, his birthplace, and bad all over Germany. It was hard for his widowed mother to offer much of a welcome in their small home; she was grateful to God for His mercy in having brought back her son from the terrible war, but two of Richard's brothers had been killed in it and he himself wounded and gassed. So much in such a young life! He was just past nineteen.

For twenty months he had been a machine-gunner on the Western Front. The machine-gunners were something of an elite, the key men in every battle, the chief killers, the mass-killers. Now, no longer important, Richard could see little to look forward to. He was pretty well equipped for work—eight years of general schooling; two years in a trade school, where he had learned a good deal about carpentry and machinery—but there was no work. There was an uneasy peace, but no work and very little food, and no one could hold out much hope of improvement tomorrow or even the day after tomorrow.

On a cold spring evening in March, Richard took matters into his own hands. With Fritz Petzold, a young friend from his regiment, he went to the neighboring town of Bernbruch, climbed a ladder to a second-story window in the home of the burgomaster, Herr Schierach, forced it open and slipped inside.

The total haul was three hundred marks and a silver watch. Richard gave Fritz half the money; the burgomaster's watch he kept for himself.

The next night they took in some more money, without having to leave Kamenz; they robbed the leather-tanner Eduard Scheumann's home. A few evenings later, again in Kamenz, they made away with some two thousand marks in securities, two hundred in cash and a gold watch and chain.

Very encouraging. Richard proposed some daytime work and gave Fritz his army pistol to use if anything went wrong. On a road outside town they saw two housewives hurrying home from market, pushing fat perambulators loaded with foodstuffs. Food was as precious as gold, even more precious; it was tightly rationed and sometimes even gold couldn't buy it. Richard ordered the women to stop. Instead, they did their best to escape, screaming a little, hanging on for dear life to the baby carriages. Richard yelled: "We'll shoot! We're radicals!"—*radicals* was the scare-word in those days. Fritz aimed the pistol and the panting women gave up. Richard and Fritz took the food and their victims' food-ration cards.

But there were no more easy pickings, and before the end of March they were arrested and convicted of all four robberies. Richard was sentenced to prison in Bautzen for five years and one week. He wrote at once to the Spartacists, the radical revolutionists, and appealed for help: "I have always been a faithful Spartacist," he said. There was no reply.

Four years later, in March 1923, Richard Hauptmann was paroled.

In spite of the shame, there was a welcome home from his mother. Richard had always been her favorite; and, making much of him, she said she hoped there would be no more trouble.

There was, very soon. He was arrested early in June while trying to sell some strips of leather belting. The police said he had stolen it from a pottery, a sawmill, and a machine shop. Hauptmann said he hadn't, insisted he hadn't known the belting was stolen goods. He was put away in the local jail to await trial. Two days later, permitted to stretch his legs in the jailyard, Hauptmann casually strolled through an open gateway. He departed from Kamenz with a finishing touch; the next morning, the police found his prison clothes in a neat bundle on the jail doorstep. A note attached read: *Best wishes to the police.*

But it wasn't enough to make his escape from the tinpot Kamenz jail. Hauptmann was a fugitive from justice and he wanted to get out of Germany entirely. He had no money and no passport, but there were other ways. Late that same month, in Hamburg, he stole on board the SS *George Washington,* shortly to sail for New York, and hid in a hold.

He was used to hard times; that journey was very hard. The food and water he'd brought weren't enough and he was getting a little feverish from thirst when, a couple of days before the ship was due to dock, a crewman discovered him.

The U.S. immigration officials questioned him on Ellis Island; Hauptmann said his name was Perlmeyer and that he'd been forced to try to get into America like this because he hadn't the money to come in as he knew he should. The mildness of his treatment at their hands astonished him; they didn't even photograph or fingerprint him, said he shouldn't try anything like it again, and handed him over to the captain of the *George Washington* to be returned to Hamburg.

The trip back was far more pleasant.

The captain was at the gangplank to make sure with his own eyes that the stowaway was put off the ship. Hauptmann made him a promise. Soon, he said, he would sail again with him on the *George Washington.*

A month later, in August, he did his best to live up to his promise but was discovered before the ship left her pier. He knew it would go hard with him if they turned him over to the German police, so he jumped from the deck, swam to the pier, clung to a piling underneath until the ship sailed and it was safe to make his way to shore.

Sopping wet, bruised, scratched, he had lost none of his determination.

A third attempt was successful. Disguised and displaying a stolen landing card, Hauptmann walked down the gangplank and found himself triumphantly ashore in New York City.

It was November 1923, a few days before his twenty-fourth birthday. He had a few American pennies in his pocket—enough for a post card. Hauptmann addressed it to his mother. He was in America, he wrote.

A few months later, on January 1, 1924, another German traveler arrived in the new world, but more respectably: Anna Schoeffler had paid for her passage to New York and was in possession of a legitimate passport. And she would not be altogether a stranger, alone; an aunt, who had mastered English and the ways of the new country, lived in Queens, a borough of New York, and had offered Anna help and guidance. Not that she shouldn't be able to look after herself; she was twenty-six and this wasn't the first time she had been away from home—just recently she'd been living in Switzerland, where she had worked as a waitress. Back home in Germany, in the village of Markgroeningen, there wasn't any decent work for a young woman; Anna's father, a saddlemaker, barely scratched out a living.

Anna was soon employed in New York as a housemaid. That spring she met a young man whose background was much the same as hers. His name was Richard Hauptmann.

They got on well together—looked well together, too. Anna thought it was admirable, the way Richard had buckled down and advanced himself so quickly after such a short time in New York; he had climbed from a sixteen-dollar-a-week dishwasher's job to one as a mechanic and then as a dyer, and finally, taking advantage of the building boom and his knowledge of carpentry, had gone to work as a carpenter, averaging fifty dollars a week.

And he was thrifty, as Anna was; he had opened a bank account right away and saved everything over the twelve dollars or so a week it cost him to live. His habits were plain and sensible. He never drank schnapps; beer only, and not enough of that to do any damage. He liked cards but never gambled for high stakes. He was musical, his taste ranging from concerts and operas to the country songs of his youth and his army life.

Anna stood high in Richard's esteem; she was a real woman, not one of these short-skirted, rolled-stocking, bobbed-hair flappers. She wasn't afraid of work, could keep going as long as he could, seemingly tireless. Always neat, of course. True, her earnings—around fifty-five dollars a month—couldn't compare with his, but she was careful and knew every penny's worth and believed as religiously in saving as he did. It didn't matter to Richard that she was two years older; it was the good honest stuff she was made of that counted. Before very long he was growing sentimental and calling her Anni.

They were married on October 10, 1925.

Richard and Anna Hauptmann set up housekeeping in a small Manhattan apartment, a year later moved to another apartment, in the Bronx. Anna got a waitress' job in a neighborhood cafe. The pay was better; Richard was doing wonderfully, sometimes earning ninety dollars a week. Living as simply as they did, they could almost make out solely on Anna's pay, so that Richard could put practically all his income in the savings bank to gather interest. With pleasure, with pride in each other, they watched the money grow.

But the newspapers were telling dazzling stories about big sums made overnight in the stock market. Richard began to dip into their savings and his salary to speculate. The language of Wall Street, the frequent phone calls and visits he made to a man he called his broker, were beyond Anna's understanding, but she knew it was risky and disapproved of it and told Richard so.

It was their only difference. They lived a quiet, happy life, making friends with people in the neighborhood and in Yorkville, the German center a few miles away. Their leisure hours did not always come at the same time, but aside from that stock-market business Anna never worried about her husband and his activities when she wasn't with him, not even in the autumn, when he was away for days at a stretch, up in Maine for the hunting and fishing; he loved the outdoors. His friends had much the same tastes. A particularly good friend, Hans Kloeppenburg, came around regularly with his guitar for a musical evening with Richard and his mandolin.

By the summer of 1928, their savings enabled Anna to visit the old people in Markgroeningen. She found quite a change from prosperous America; and, moreover, her father had grown deaf and her mother was chronically ill. Anna stayed with them as long as she could—four months. It was a sad parting, and she felt a little guilty, leaving them old and sick in that dreary place, when she had so much to look forward to.

Richard had made up for Anna's absence by seeing more of his friends, the harmonious Kloeppenburg in particular. There were lots of week-end picnics on Hunter Island, just off the shore of Pelham Bay Park in Long Island Sound; swimming and boating too—Richard had a canoe, now—games and horseplay and beer-drinking and songs from the old country, sung in the mellow light of the campfire. Very few at these hearty German gatherings were more popular than Richard Hauptmann.

Anna joined the picnics and overnight jaunts—camping out in a tent—as often as she could; she worked Saturdays and every other Sunday. In June 1929 she went to work as a counter girl and waitress for Christian Fredericksen, a Danish baker who with his wife Katie ran a bakery-lunchroom on Dyer Avenue in the Bronx. The hours were longer—Anna had to be on the job at seven every morning, and Tuesdays and Fridays she had to stay late—but she made more money, up to thirty-three dollars a week including tips.

The savings account comfortably increased. It was really surprising how the dollars mounted up, with interest! No reason why they shouldn't take a long holiday. Richard bought a nice Dodge sedan in March 1931, and when the fine summer weather came along they set off with friend Kloeppenburg for California, where Richard's sister lived.

They didn't get back home until early October. Somehow the old apartment looked small and dull and they moved to a top-floor apartment at 1279 East 222nd Street, a few blocks away.

There was quite a hole in their savings account; well, they'd fill it soon enough, Anna thought; but she was wrong. The building trade fell off; work for carpenters was scarce. All through that winter, 1931–32, the slump continued—got worse, if anything—and the odd jobs Richard was able to find couldn't begin to touch his former handsome earnings.

Early in April 1932 he made a dramatic announcement: he was through with carpentering! He had figured out a foolproof system for making money in Wall Street and intended to spend all his time on it—it would be stupid not to. The news gravely worried Anna, but she tried to keep her fears to herself.

To her delight and admitted surprise, Richard's prediction turned out to be nothing less than the truth. He had discovered the trick of playing the market and never losing! Luxuries they had both wanted were now within their reach, and the second-story apartment blossomed out in new furnishings. Richard enjoyed showing off the furniture and other purchases to his friends. And their affluence would make it possible for Anna to pay another visit to Markgroeningen, for her mother's seventieth birthday. Couldn't Richard come with her? He would like to, he said, and they could afford it, but he should stay at home to keep an eye on his investments. In fact, he admitted, there was another, more serious objection—that old trouble.

The old trouble wasn't a secret to Anna; he had told her about his rash deeds as a young, bitter war veteran, his arrest, his years in prison, his escape, and his illegal entry into the United States. The truth was, he was still a fugitive from the law. His mother longed to see him, as she said again and again in her letters; what a happy time it would be for all of them, for Anna, for him, and for the two old ladies, a family reunion! But it was impossible.

Yes, Anna said, she could see that the risk would be too great. Well, she would call on Richard's mother in Kamenz and they would put their heads together, and maybe something could be done.

Anna sailed in July 1932 and returned in October. She had been as good as her word, had visited Richard's mother in Kamenz, and they had consulted a lawyer. He had advised patience. In another year the statute of limitations would automatically put an end to the threat of imprisonment and Richard Hauptmann would be able to come and go to and from Germany without fear.

Good news!—Richard was delighted with it. Anna, though, was less than pleased with the state of things that greeted her on her return.

She had barely sailed, she learned, when Richard had taken up again with the jolly Hunter Island crowd, the same people he'd seen so much of during her earlier absence. But there was a new name, a name he mentioned often—Gerta Henkel. Who was she? A very sociable young woman. She was married, but it didn't seem to bother her. She had invited Richard to drop in for a cup of coffee on his way downtown in the mornings to watch the board at his broker's office, and this cozy coffee-with-Gerta arrangement had become a habit. Gerta's husband, Karl, an easygoing fellow, apparently remained undisturbed by the implications—or possibilities—which to Anna Hauptmann were intensely disturbing. Richard introduced her to the Henkels; her attitude was cool.

She decided she had worked long enough and informed the Fredericksens, at the bakery, that she was quitting.

A few months later, Anna became pregnant.

On November 3, 1933, a son was born to Richard and Anna Hauptmann. A perfect child, blond and blue-eyed. His parents worshiped him. They named him Mannfried Richard, but quickly found a nickname, Bubi.

Gerta Henkel's name was no longer heard in the well-furnished apartment at 1279 East 222nd Street.

Richard wrote to his mother in the summer of 1934 to expect the three of them for Christmas. Her pleas had become urgent; she was getting very old—she would soon be seventy—and was hungry for the sight of her grandson. Richard looked forward to the trip. He knew Germany had changed—was still changing under its new leader, the dynamic man called Adolf Hitler. It was interesting news but it did not really touch Richard deeply. With the rise of the Nazis, many of his friends had burst out with patriotic fervor and formed sports clubs that were actually political in purpose, intensely nationalistic. They had urged him to join one and he'd done so but had promptly left after learning that sports were secondary in the organization's life. There was too much bossing around, too many small leaders trying to act big. The idea of being one among many, of being told what to do, had never appealed to Richard Hauptmann. He liked to make his own decisions and carry them out alone.

On September 19 he was arrested and accused of kidnaping and murder. . . .

David Wilentz's mind returned to the present from its excursion into the history of the prisoner and his wife. He saw that another man in the courtroom was studying Richard Hauptmann. Dr. Shoenfeld was here as a privileged spectator; he was very much involved in the case.

Recently Wilentz had seen a great deal of the psychiatrist. An extremely interesting, indeed a fascinating person, he had found him. He wished he could share the thoughts that obviously were engrossing Dudley Shoenfeld right now.

Dr. Shoenfeld was thinking that, since several of the facts which had been pieced together fitted his original theoretical portrait of the kidnaper-killer, perhaps he was not very far wrong in his further speculations, based on Richard Hauptmann's casual biography.

Surely, the dominant trait he had attributed to the unknown—his sense of omnipotence—had been amply demonstrated, had it not? What else could one call the young Richard Hauptmann's unhurried escape from jail and swaggering return to embarrass the police with a derisive note of good wishes? Or his persistent, undismayed attempts to enter the United States in the face of extreme hardship and successive setbacks? Weren't both part of his compulsive drive, his refusal to acknowledge that any adversary was more powerful than he? Didn't this explain, too, his cocksure attitude here in court—a complacent belief that he would not be found guilty of having committed the Lindbergh kidnaping but would go free?

And to go further: in his unconscious mind had Richard Hauptmann drawn a parallel between his hard, solitary stowaway's journey across the Atlantic against severe odds and Charles Lindbergh's dangerous solo flight over the same waters? For his initial venture into crime, had he chosen to rob the burgomaster of Bernbruch for the same reason that later prompted him to choose Lindbergh's home—because they were the most important, the most powerful men in their communities?

And Hauptmann's choice of names. Obviously, no fugitive from justice could be expected to give the authorities his right name, particularly not when he was trying to enter the country illegally, but why had he said his name was Perlmeyer? Of course he thought he had consciously, deliberately chosen the false name; in fact, as psychiatric studies in other cases had shown, an unconscious choice had been involved. It was at least possible that the *Perl* of Perlmeyer—a feminine name; Perl: Pearl—was an unconscious revelation of an unconscious feminine identification within Richard Hauptmann.

Next, consider his child's name. Ordinarily the name of a newborn child was a bit of give and take between the parents, but Shoenfeld was convinced that Mannfried Richard was wholly the father's wish, which had prevailed over or possibly was chosen without Anna's opposition. The use of his own name, Richard, was of course simply the typical manifestation of the masculine ego projecting itself, but Mannfried was a curious and perhaps significant choice. This was venturing rather far in the realm of theory, but in Hauptmann's unconscious did the name Mannfried literally mean *man freed*—freedom from danger, from detection, from arrest, after the many months during which he had evaded the police? The child was conceived almost exactly one year after the kidnaping and murder. Had the birth of his own son made compensation in Hauptmann's unconscious for the death of another's son?

Another aspect of the baby's given name: was there a link between Mannfried and Manfred? Baron Manfred Albrecht von Richthofen, Germany's wartime hero of the skies, the "Red Knight," ace of aces, had so captured Hauptmann's imagination that on the eve of the trial (so Shoenfeld had learned), in his cell, he was immersed in Floyd Gibbons' biography of von Richthofen.

All this was speculation, but perhaps, Shoenfeld thought, he might be pardoned for it, since the disciplined science of psychiatry had not been given an opportunity to get at the truth. The usual routine had been followed. Five psychiatrists—four representing the prosecution, one the defense—had probed Richard Hauptmann's mind for a total of six hours and had filed separate reports. The diagnosis for the defense was still a secret between its lone alienist and Hauptmann's lawyers, but David Wilentz had shown Shoenfeld the findings for the State. Hauptmann's intelligence, judgment and memory, his knowledge of the difference between right and wrong and of the relationship between cause and effect, his understanding of the nature and quality of his acts—all were normal, the four alienists had agreed: Richard Hauptmann was sane.

It was no more and no less than had occurred in criminal cases for the past ninety years, and very likely the same sort of thing would go on for a good many more; cut and dried, quick and neat, satisfying no one (least of all the alienists called upon to examine the man) and nothing except the State's demand for a legal ruling on his "sanity" or lack of it. With the report in hand, David Wilentz could dispute a plea of "insanity" if the defense cared to make one —which it did not.

The entire interpretation was absurd, of course, as Wilentz had agreed. During the weeks in which he had shaped the State's case against Hauptmann, the attorney general had revealed a keen interest in the psychological makeup of the defendant and the psychic motives for his acts. Working closely with him, Shoenfeld had found Wilentz sympathetic to a psychiatrist's point of view. To his and to any psychiatrist's mind, the rule of law followed by the courts since 1843—the M'Naghten Rule, which decreed that the accused is "sane" and therefore responsible for his criminal acts unless at the time of the acts he did not know what he was doing or did not know that it was wrong—was indefensible. Countless studies had proved that nearly all "insane" persons understood the nature of their acts and knew when their acts were wrong. But to commit a crime because of a compulsive psychic drive—an "irresistible impulse," if you wanted to call it that—wasn't this a symptom of mental illness? And wasn't this the case with Richard Hauptmann?

Shoenfeld thought so. There was no evidence in Hauptmann's

past to support it but the psychiatrist still clung to his original suspicion: the kidnaper-killer was in a state of dementia praecox. Whether or not he was right, or whether Richard Hauptmann was in any way mentally ill, was a question that only a long and careful analysis of his personality could conclusively answer.

Hauptmann might be willing to cooperate in such a study but the State of New Jersey was not.

Anthony Hauck and Lloyd Fisher, alternately questioning and cross-questioning, were making progress: four more jurors had been selected. Mrs. Rosie Pill was a fifty-five-year-old widow, a grandmother, and the kind of attentive and understanding listener grandmothers were supposed to be; or so Hauck and Fisher thought. Mrs. Verna Snyder was a country blacksmith's wife who weighed some 261 pounds, which did not detract from her commendable qualities, and while she said she wasn't sure how she felt about capital punishment, she was willing to determine the case on the evidence.

Charles Snyder, not related to Mrs. Verna, was forty, a farmer, the father of two children; he had a canny look about him and obviously appreciated the responsibility of being a Lindbergh-case juror. He was followed by Mrs. Ethel Stockton, thirty-two, a mother, quite pretty. She seemed a cut above the others in intelligence; moreover, she had spent several years as a stenographer for a former district attorney and was quite at home with the law. That was all right with Hauck and Fisher.

4

Sixty miles of good highways lay between Flemington and New York City; a couple of hours for the casual driver; but to get Richard Hauptmann across those sixty miles had required exactly one month and a great deal of thought on David Wilentz's part. One slip in his cautious maneuverings and Hauptmann might very well have remained on the other side of the Hudson River, where his lot certainly would not have been easy but infinitely more comfortable than the harsh legal welcome that had awaited him in New Jersey. In New York he would have had to try to wriggle out of a case of extortion and collateral offenses; here in Flemington it was a case of kidnaping and murder.

Wilentz had realized the true extent of the problem soon after Hauptmann's arrest on September 19.

The trouble was partly a question of law, partly a question of evidence. No matter what developed, Hauptmann could not be prosecuted under the federal kidnap law. And New Jersey's new, improved kidnap law did not apply to his case. Both laws had been enacted after the kidnaping of the Lindbergh baby and of course were not retroactive.

The solitary path to Hauptmann's trial on a capital charge—the archaic New Jersey legal code, stemming from the old English common law—was so studded with rocks and ruts and other dangers for the unwary that Wilentz quailed at the thought of traveling it. The worst obstacle was the old kidnap statute itself; it barely recognized the crime, which was quite modern, neither defining it as a felony nor providing the means to punish it adequately. And without direct evidence to show where, when and how it had been committed, murder might be hard to prove.

By comparison, New York's case against Hauptmann was simplicity itself. In the course of one week he was indicted by a Bronx County grand jury for extorting fifty thousand dollars from Charles Lindbergh and was arraigned on bail of one hundred thousand dollars, a sum conservatively calculated to be beyond his ability to raise. The final step, if it had to be taken, would be the trial. But the Bronx district attorney, Samuel J. Foley, was as anxious as Wilentz to keep the case out of the Bronx courts. For one thing, if Hauptmann should be acquitted of extortion—although that hardly seemed likely—it would make it more difficult to convict him of kidnaping and murder; more important, not only the State of New Jersey but the nation itself, and many other countries, had been revolted by the Lindbergh crime and public opinion demanded that Hauptmann be tried on the ultimate charge.

For the present—in September, just after his arrest—Hauptmann was safely under lock and key and would remain so until Wilentz could indict and extradite him in a manner any court of appeal could uphold.

Foley pressed his charge of extortion with efficient chronological dispatch. A parade of witnesses testified to the prisoner's threatening demands in letters for fifty thousand dollars, the anxious efforts to negotiate with him, the delivery of the ransom in the Bronx cemetery, his steady exchange of ransom bills for purchases, and, finally, his secret possession of more than a fourth of the money.

Quite a bit more! Five days after the initial find of $13,760, the police had come across another cache in the wall of Hauptmann's garage. Removing a cross-board from between two uprights, they had discovered that the inner edge of the board, which had rested snugly against the wall, was neatly drilled with five holes. A roll of ten-dollar gold notes was tucked inside each hole; eighty-four of them altogether, $840, all Lindbergh bills.

In another hole in the same panel, they had found a small loaded pistol.

The new strike brought the total find to $14,600. Added to the $5100 previously retrieved, $19,700 of the ransom was accounted for. The balance, $30,300, was still being hunted, but in the light of Hauptmann's expenditures there could be little doubt that a good many of the gold certificates still outstanding had found their way back to the U.S. Treasury without detection as ransom money.

Hauptmann explained the new garage lode as he had explained the others: the money had been entrusted to his care by Isidor Fisch. The holes, drilled three years ago, had been intended for small tools; at the same time he had chiseled a hollow in the board to hold the pistol because he didn't have a permit for the weapon and felt he shouldn't keep it in the apartment. When he'd removed Fisch's money to the garage, the two-by-four panel with its deep-set holes had seemed an ideal place for some of the bills, and so he had put it to that use and nailed it with the face pressed to the wall so that the money couldn't be seen.

Yes, of course, he knew that it was against the law to hoard gold certificates, but there were two good reasons why he couldn't turn them in—one, the money wasn't his, it was Fisch's, and although Fisch was dead the cash would have to be accounted for to his brother, who was coming to America to settle the deceased's affairs; and two, nearly a year had passed since the government's final warning to gold-hoarders, which meant that if he tried to turn in the gold notes he might be heavily fined or imprisoned or even deported—if they learned he was in the United States illegally.

So he had hidden the money. The pistol had had nothing to do with it.

Wilentz wasn't so sure. The pistol was a Lilliput, a three-inch-long German automatic of extremely small caliber. It was said that during the war German soldiers had used such weapons with deadly effect by concealing them in their hands, raising their hands in pretended surrender, then suddenly shooting down their captors. A very useful thing to have around you if you were the object of a nationwide search as the kidnaper and killer of the Lindbergh baby.

A pretty good argument could be made out for taking the simple way and trying Hauptmann for extortion. Under the maximum penalty he would be imprisoned for twenty years—and if the courts accepted the conviction for felony imposed by the Kamenz authorities after he had fled, this sentence could be doubled. He could get ten years for illegal possession of gold; illegal entry into the United

States, violation of the Sullivan law (possessing firearms without a permit), lesser offenses against the peace and dignity of the State of New York—all carried jail terms; in sum, they would put Richard Hauptmann behind bars for the rest of his life.

But that would be begging the question. A child had been stolen and killed, and justice would not be served until his kidnaper or kidnapers would be fairly tried and convicted and made to pay in full.

There was the headache. Hauptmann—and any possible accomplices—could not be made to pay in full under the old New Jersey kidnap statute. Its penalty was not death. And it was death the public called for.

Very well, then, David Wilentz thought—since death was the only punishment that would satisfy the clamor, why not rule out kidnaping and indict Hauptmann for first-degree murder? Maybe kidnaping could be tied in somehow. But the indictment would have to be foolproof, would have to withstand attack and deliver the prisoner into New Jersey's hands despite any action Hauptmann's attorney might take.

Wilentz put his legal experts on the task.

There was ample evidence that Hauptmann had killed the Lindbergh baby, but it was all circumstantial. No one had seen him strike the child or leave the nursery with the baby in his arms or flee with it across the Lindbergh grounds. And if you thought—as many thought and strongly believed—that he was not alone in the crime, that it was a conspiracy, and that Hauptmann had never set foot in New Jersey in connection with it but had let his accomplices carry it out, then he could not be extradited for murder unless his fellow conspirators also were indicted.

Wilentz put no stock in the conspiracy theory; he was sure it was a one-man job. But some of the people who'd investigated the crime, men whose opinion one had to respect, held that while it was certainly possible it still seemed improbable that the kidnaping was all Hauptmann's work. And what about the two Italians Dr. Condon had mentioned? And Alice Murphy's story? Recognizing Hauptmann from his newspaper pictures, she had told the police of the incident in the Bronx lumberyard and described Hauptmann's companion, apparently also German. He hadn't been found and Dr. Condon's Italians hadn't either.

But there was full agreement on one point: Anna Hauptmann was in no way involved in the crime. Her attitude, her actions, everything the police knew about her demonstrated that she had known nothing of her husband's secret life, and they let her go.

Well, Wilentz thought, you could argue for or against the lone-wolf theory, but you couldn't dispute this: in the two and a half years since the kidnaping and murder, only a single suspect had been found who could be directly connected with it.

Wasn't that evidence enough that Hauptmann alone was responsible?

And so the problem was to find a law which would embrace the peculiar nature and circumstances of the Lindbergh crime and provide the death penalty if the accused should be found guilty.

Poring over New Jersey's antiquated legal code, Wilentz's aides came upon a statute they were confident would do nicely.

Burglary, as defined by the law, was "illegal breaking and entering a dwelling house at night." In the strictest sense, the legal experts asked one another, wasn't the abduction of Charles Lindbergh, Jr., burglary? And burglary was a felony. Well, if a person was killed in the commission of a burglary, whether his death was caused intentionally or accidentally, it was murder, murder in the first degree. So the law stated. The thing to do, then, was to proceed on the theory that the child lost its life as a result of Richard Hauptmann's entry into the nursery with, in the musty words of the statute, "intent to steal and commit a battery"; therefore he was a murderer, wilfully or not, and must answer for his crime.

So far, so good. But would such a contention stand up in court; if accepted by a jury, would it then be upheld by a court of appeals?

Wilentz and his assistants looked deeper into the matter. It was prickly with questions. Where had the baby's death occurred? In Hunterdon County, where the kidnaping—the burglary—took place, or in Mercer County, where the body was found? And where and when had the act of burglary been completed? Was it over with the moment the burglar stepped out of the second-story window, the baby in his arms, or was he still executing the burglary as he raced away? Could it even be proved that he had burglarized the house?—the window through which he "broke and entered" was unlocked, and had been found in that condition after the kidnaping. And even if no one disputed the contention that the death was the result of the burglary, could Hauptmann be placed at the scene of the crime? Could it be proved that *he* was the burglar?

These weren't the only questions; all of them ranged over the entire theory, questioning jurisdiction, intent, cause and effect and, of course, proof.

But the questions didn't worry David Wilentz. Point by point, any challenge could be answered through the circumstantial evidence in hand, supported by contradictory decisions before the bar. The primary question which would have to be answered if the indictment was to succeed dealt with *presence*: if Hauptmann was solely guilty of the crime, as Wilentz contended, he would have to be placed in the nursery on the night of March 1, 1932. But even this wouldn't have to be proved conclusively. In an extradition hearing, which was what Wilentz was concerned with right now, the burden of proof was on the accused. Hauptmann would have to persuade the Bronx court that he was *not* in the Lindbergh nursery at the time of the kidnaping.

What was the evidence against him? Several eyewitnesses had identified him after his arrest and a few were ready to swear they had seen him in the vicinity of the Hopewell place on or shortly before March 1. With the trial still to come, Wilentz certainly wasn't inclined to detail the State's case; he was confident that the testimony of one such witness, Millard Whited, would furnish enough evidence of its kind for extradition.

Proof that Hauptmann had been in the nursery could be supplied through a link of circumstances. Albert Osborn was firmly of the opinion—and was prepared to demonstrate why—that Hauptmann alone was the author of the ransom notes; next, Dr. Condon had overcome his reluctance to "declare an identification" of Hauptmann as John—after a lengthy interview with the prisoner in the Flemington jail, the old man had assured Wilentz that Hauptmann was John, John was Hauptmann; and, finally, Arthur Koehler had come forward with some astonishing and dramatic evidence that Hauptmann had built the kidnap ladder.

In reverse chronology, testimony of the three would establish that on the night of March 1 Richard Hauptmann had propped a homemade ladder against the wall of the Lindbergh house, had climbed it and crept into the nursery (in talking with Dr. Condon outside Woodlawn Cemetery he had betrayed that he was familiar with the room), had stolen the child (proof of which lay in his return of the sleeping suit) and had left behind an extortion note written in his own hand.

Again Wilentz had no intention of prematurely disclosing his all-out attack; he decided that Osborn's testimony alone would satisfy pretrial audiences that Hauptmann had indeed been inside the Lindbergh nursery. Whited and Osborn would be his key witnesses; the first would link the suspect's physical, the other his probable, presence to the time and place of the kidnaping. There would be a good many other witnesses, of course—if need be, Wilentz was prepared to unleash his full attack—but he felt sure that just the bare outline of his case would convince the New York court and extradite Hauptmann to New Jersey.

Early in October, in Flemington, Wilentz asked the Hunterdon County grand jury to indict Richard Hauptmann for murder. Judge Trenchard led the twenty-three members of the panel through the confusing phraseology of the law. The attorney general, Trenchard said, would present evidence to show that the accused deliberately entered at night the dwelling of Charles and Anne Lindbergh in Hunterdon County "for the purpose of committing a battery upon and stealing in his clothing" the Lindberghs' infant son, and that in the commission of the burglary the accused caused the child's death.

If the jurors believed that Hauptmann struck the child during the act of burglary and that it died from the blow, or that the blow was not wilful but accidental; or that either way it was not inflicted in the course of the burglary but while Hauptmann was fleeing with the child; or that the blow occurred in one county (Hunterdon) and death resulted in another (Mercer)—then, in each instance, they should find Hauptmann guilty as charged.

After four and a half hours of testimony and less than an hour of deliberation, the grand jury handed down an indictment—short but covering a lot of ground, permitting great freedom in the presentation of evidence. It avoided any mention of burglary in order to prevent Hauptmann from pleading guilty to the lesser charge and thus escaping the death penalty if convicted of the capital offense.

The indictment read:

> The grand inquest for the State of New Jersey in and of the County of Hunterdon upon their respective oaths present that Bruno Richard Hauptmann on the first day of March, in the year of our Lord one thousand nine hundred and thirty-two, with force and arms, at the Township of East Amwell, in the County of Hunterdon aforesaid, and within the jurisdiction of this court, did wilfully, feloniously and of his malice aforethought, kill and murder Charles A. Lindbergh, Jr., contrary to the form of the statute in such case made and provided and against the peace of the State, the government and the dignity of the same.

Wilentz expected criticism from at least some members of the profession, and he wasn't disappointed. One veteran of the criminal courts, Clarence Darrow, saw no evidence whatever that Hauptmann was implicated in the child's death; a strong case could be made against him for extortion, but not murder.

The wheels of extradition began to turn. Governor A. Harry Moore of New Jersey formally requested Governor Herbert H. Lehman of New York to surrender the prisoner to the Hunterdon County authorities, and Lehman promptly signed a release. Hauptmann's attorney, James M. Fawcett, secured a writ of habeas corpus, postponing the execution of the warrant, and a week later, in the

Bronx County Supreme Court, Richard Hauptmann did his best to prove that he could not possibly have been inside the Lindberghs' home, near Hopewell, New Jersey, on the night of March 1, 1932—because at that time he was in Christian Fredericksen's bakery in the Bronx. Three defense witnesses agreed with him, but none of them—including Hauptmann himself—could back up the claim with anything stronger than the fact that March 1, 1932, had fallen on a Tuesday. It followed, they said, that Hauptmann had been in the bakery, because every Tuesday it was "a regular thing" for him to be there.

Justice Ernest Hammer, presiding, was not convinced by the "regular thing" theory: in his eyes this was not conclusive proof that Hauptmann had not been at the scene of the crime on the night of the kidnaping and murder; the writ of habeas corpus was dismissed. The judge granted a period of grace for Fawcett to appeal the ruling. The attorney's plea was denied.

At long last, Richard Hauptmann traveled the sixty miles to Flemington. And now he was facing trial.

Wilentz's confidence in the outcome of the trial came chiefly from his confidence in himself, but also it stemmed from the good staff work that had preceded this day in the old courtroom and from the assurance that he had able men on the State's side. The first of them was Hauck, still at work examining the prospective jurors; next there were Assistant Attorney Generals Joseph Lanigan and Robert Peacock; and finally Special Assistant Attorney General George K. Large. Large was a local man, a former judge, actively practicing law in Flemington; his special appointment to the staff had seemed wise to Wilentz's assistants because the jury would accept it as evidence that the State's case wasn't being run by a bunch of big-city foreigners. These fair-minded Hunterdon County people knew and liked and respected George Large as a friend and neighbor.

The number of jurors grew: Elmer Smith, a forty-two-year-old insurance salesman, father of a three-year-old son, took his place next to Mrs. Stockton; the panel was now half complete. Juror number seven went to the first chair in the second row of the jury box; he was Robert Cravatt, the youngest so far, twenty-eight, unmarried, the educational supervisor of a Civilian Conservation Camp. He seemed solemn, sensitive, a bit uncomfortable with the thought of having to decide whether a man should live or die. Philip Hockenbury, fifty-eight, followed, a family man who worked for the railroad in a small job; he looked steady, conscientious. Then came George Voorhees, fifty-four, a farmer, the father of three young children.

Everything was progressing smoothly. Pretty soon, Wilentz knew, the even tenor that had prevailed so far would be dramatically disturbed. He could count on his opponent, "Big Ed" Reilly, for that.

5

Edward J. Reilly sat at the defense table, directly facing the judge's bench and the small arena in which the case for and against Richard Hauptmann would be fought out. The prisoner, sitting just behind his chief defender, seemed perfectly composed and even cheerful, as Wilentz had noted, but the quality of Edward Reilly's aplomb was clearly superior. The atmosphere was congenial to him; he visibly relished the smell of the legal cockpit. He could have steered his way blindfolded from jury box to witness chair to defense counsel's headquarters. Accumulated in a hundred courtrooms, the patina of success shone on his imperial person. Ed Reilly had defended more than two thousand clients, nearly all of them in murder cases. His record of acquittals was so astonishing that to mention it sounded like a boast. He mentioned it often.

He was fifty-two. By dint of persistent feeding his tall figure had grown a mandarin stomach, and his massive face was permanently flushed. He believed in dressing to accommodate the average man's idea of titanic prosperity, and today he wore, as he always did in court, a dark morning coat, white carnation in buttonhole, striped gray trousers and spats. Even when he whispered to a jury his presence roared at them. But he whispered seldom. His voice, normally orotund, was a creature of dazzling complexions: it bullied and blustered, it palpitated with references to home and mother and the harsh cruelty of fate, it glowed with bonhomie, and, the next instant, poured out the vials of wrath.

In Brooklyn, his home, it was said that when Big Ed was trying a case the other Brooklyn courts speedily emptied of all but judge, jury and opposing counsel, who found it in their hearts to wish that they too were watching "the Bull of Brooklyn"—a newspaper phrase—at work. Leaving the courtroom, he was accustomed to find a waiting admiring throng, many of whom would then follow at his heels. He shook hands prodigally, and prodigally spent his handsome fees.

He loved beautiful women, sometimes with more ardor than prudence; four marriages had foundered in a nasty sea of alimony. Despite this, despite his thinning hair, his girth, his florid face, a hopeful romantic feeling clung to him.

Reilly had assumed command of Richard Hauptmann's defense on November 2. He owed the post to a variety of circumstances.

First, it had been suggested to Anna Hauptmann that her husband's interests would be best served by a famous criminal lawyer rather than a comparative unknown such as James M. Fawcett, however well qualified; and since the suggestion had been accompanied by a substantial offer of help, she had agreed. Richard, too, agreed, when told by her that a New York morning newspaper would pay the costs of his defense in return for exclusive stories about him and Anna's efforts to prove his innocence. Richard was not so concerned as she; he felt that he would be his own ablest defender; still, it was difficult not to be impressed by Edward Reilly's reputation, and then too, all their money had been tied up by the State of New Jersey.

James Fawcett retired from the case.

But the arrangement was not to the liking of rival New York papers. Most of them had tried to break it, and the New York *Evening Journal* had succeeded, lavishly topping all previous offers. The Hauptmanns, the new understanding ran, would talk only to Hearst reporters, and the *Journal* would control all news of defense activities.

Promptly, Reilly had selected his staff—young Fisher, with a good law background and, perhaps even more important, one of Flemington's own sons, presentable, nice-looking; Frederick A. Pope, self-assured, courtly; and Egbert Rosecrans, an authority on constitutional law—both, like Fisher, of sound New Jersey stock.

Someone pointed out to Reilly the significance in American history of these last two names, and it amused him to pretend that he, who had started out as an insurance clerk, had two Civil War generals on his staff.

Well, in this campaign they would know the sweet taste of triumph! Their commanding general firmly believed that Richard Hauptmann was innocent.

Reilly had said as much shortly after his appointment. The newsreels had recorded his image and his voice, declaring that "a man must be considered innocent until he has been proven guilty . . . a mere accusation of guilt is not proof of guilt." He had concluded by saying that although he was new to the case, he had inquired deeply enough into it to be persuaded beyond the shadow of a doubt of "the innocence of my client."

Reilly had been far from idle in the past two months, studying the case and his client, and had frequently reaffirmed his belief in Hauptmann's innocence. Nothing in his behavior had given the lawyer reason to question it. The three other defense counselors felt as he did. And yet although Hauptmann's demeanor, as a defendant accused of an atrocious crime, was reassuring, they were not altogether happy about it. His cool detachment, his placid air, might very well ruffle a jury. He seemed to live behind a shield.

Certainly it had withstood their efforts to get close to him, to make him see that they must have his faith and trust if they were to present a truly united front to the foe. Pleasantly he had turned aside their importunities after reaching that point of information about himself and his activities beyond which no trespassers, however friendly, were to be permitted. It had been irritating at times to feel in him a kind of reserved superiority, a suggestion, implied rather than stated, that they would do best to rely on him as the grand marshal in the coming fight—that their parts, while valuable, would be secondary.

After several meetings with him in the Flemington jail, one no more rewarding than another, the single argument Reilly and his staff had carried away was Richard Hauptmann's granite insistence that he was not guilty of the kidnaping and murder.

Of course a good case could be made in his favor, despite Hauptmann's refusal to cooperate beyond his interior boundary line. His criminal record in Germany could be laid to the turmoil of those years, the brutal role into which the war had plunged him while still hardly more than a boy, the poverty at home, the threat of starvation shadowing the land. And was it not a fact that in the eleven years following his arrival in America he had not once seriously fallen afoul of the law? Were not his wife and their friends ready and able to testify that he was a kind husband and loving father, a good neighbor, a sober, conscientious man of good will? *He*—guilty of kidnaping and killing a child?

Yes, the indications that he *was* guilty were diverse and damaging—but they were all circumstantial in nature. They could all be answered in kind. Albert Osborn's contention that Richard Hauptmann had written the kidnap notes could be refuted by other handwriting experts' contentions that he had not. Millard Whited's identification could be dismissed by the testimony of old acquaintances, who had seldom known him to tell the truth. As for Dr. Condon—how adroitly he had contradicted himself! First he had failed to identify Hauptmann, finally had succeeded, in the process seriously opening to doubt his veracity if not his eyesight.

Possession of the money had been and would be answered by Hauptmann himself; and if it could be proved that Isidor Fisch had placed the gold notes in his hands, the weight of evidence would seem to swing in favor of the defense—for then it could be said that Fisch, not Hauptmann, had reconnoitered the Lindbergh home and surrounding country; that Fisch, not Hauptmann, had written the ransom notes; that Fisch, not Hauptmann, had climbed into the nursery; and that Fisch, not Hauptmann, had received the Lindbergh gold certificates. To every charge the State made, the answer could be Fisch. He was dead, and could neither affirm nor deny his guilt—but if it was shown that the ransom money originally belonged to him, the prosecution would have to square that fact with its assertion that Hauptmann alone had engaged in the crime.

It was no secret that the State's case rested on the "Hauptmann alone committed the crime" theory, although officially David Wilentz hadn't said so; officially he had been discreetly silent on all aspects of the case, particularly the charges he would deliver at the trial. But it shouldn't be hard to draw him out, the defense thought. It was the defendant's right, again and again upheld, to know the charges which the prosecution would level against him. In this respect the indictment was almost as reticent as the attorney general; it accused Hauptmann of murder, and that was all. It did not begin to be enough as a foundation on which defense counsel could build. Exactly where, when and how would the State claim the murder had been committed?

The defense drew up a dozen questions which, if answered, would expose the State's case in advance of the trial, saving the most pointed and, for the prosecution, the most embarrassing question for last. It was:

By what method does the State contend Charles A. Lindbergh, Jr., met his death?

List in hand, Reilly called on his opponent with a polite request for a bill of particulars. Wilentz refused, as expected. Reilly appealed to the New Jersey Supreme Court to make him comply.

The presiding justice, Judge Trenchard, was not so helpful as defense counsel hoped he would be, ruling that eleven questions already had been answered by the indictment. But he held that the last question was valid and that the prosecution must give the defense the details of how the baby had been killed, if it knew them.

A small triumph but significant, Reilly and his staff agreed. There could be little doubt that the State did not truly know and could not truly say whether the child had been killed in his crib, or in the descent of the ladder, or during the flight from the scene—or even whether his death was wilful or accidental—and an official admission of ignorance would weaken the case against Hauptmann.

The triumph was short-lived. Wilentz's reply was a masterpiece. At once forthright and evasive, it answered the question to the Court's satisfaction but without even a hint of the confession of ignorance Reilly had hoped for. The manner of the child's death was no mystery, Wilentz pointed out; the medical examiner, Dr. Charles H. Mitchell, had said in his official diagnosis after the autopsy: *The child died of a fractured skull caused by external violence.* And so the State would contend.

Ed Reilly knew how to take a defeat gracefully, in the confident expectation of better days to come. "External violence" was a catch-all that could embrace any number of death-blow theories—Wilentz could take his pick. He wouldn't ask any more questions, Reilly announced, and wouldn't file a further appeal.

But Fisher, Pope and Rosecrans were less disposed to make a show of polite submission. On another issue they mounted a sharp attack, charging that the State, having failed to wring a confession of guilt from Richard Hauptmann after weeks of grilling, was trying to exhaust him, mentally and physically, and break his morale. They indicated the isolated seven-by-nine-foot cell in the Flemington jail, where he awaited trial. Day and night, around the clock, whether the prisoner was awake or trying to sleep, the cell and the corridor directly outside were brilliantly lighted; and day and night, in the cell and the corridor, police guards followed one another, silent, impassive men, forbidden to speak to Hauptmann except in reply to his questions, and then only in the barest terms. What was this, the defense lawyers asked, if not a form of the Chinese "sleepless torture," calculated to undermine the prisoner's resistance, ultimately to destroy his spirit?

Wilentz had referred the charge to the accused man's chief custodian, Sheriff John H. Curtiss. The sheriff was not impressed; the prison arrangements would remain as they were. "We propose to guard the prisoner against any contingency," he said.

Well, Reilly told his staff, Curtiss couldn't be blamed, if you faced the facts. He was understandably on the alert against any such incident as that which had seriously embarrassed another sheriff, Sheriff John J. Hanley, while Hauptmann had been in his care in the Bronx County jail.

Early one morning, after the usual breakfast of prunes, bread and coffee, a routine kitchen check of the returned trays had revealed that Hauptmann's pewter spoon was missing. It was an unusually large spoon, and Sheriff Hanley could think of a variety of ways in which an ingenious mind could put it to use. He had ordered Hauptmann to hand over the spoon. Hauptman said he'd never been given the spoon in the first place. Guards stripped him and searched his clothes while others searched the cell: nothing. Plumbers uprooted the wash-basin and toilet. The spoon was found after three hours, but not in one piece. The long middle part of the handle, which had been bent into a hook, was fished from the wash-basin drain. The remaining three pieces—the largest of which, the spoon cup, had been split in half to form a flat knife-edged blade—were lodged in the pipes below the toilet bowl.

Hauptmann had had the spoon about sixty minutes. In that time he had sharpened all four pieces into weapons of a sort by scraping the edges against the steel bars of the cell or the iron frame of his cot. Then, no doubt suspecting from the sheriff's urgent approach that the kitchen had reported the missing spoon, he had got rid of the pieces as best he could.

Just what had he had in mind? Escape? Had he thought the hooked piece could be used to pick the cell lock? It couldn't; the cell locks were buttressed by a master lock which could be opened only by throwing an electric switch in the warden's office. Suicide? The blade was sharp enough to slash his throat or wrists, and his necktie, his belt, and even his shoelaces—anything offering the slimmest means to self-destruction—had been taken from him when he'd been brought to the jail. But his mood was the same as it had been ever since his arrest: calm, controlled, almost indifferent. Hardly the attitude of a man intent on killing himself!

Hauptmann, of course, had refused to say anything. Sheriff Hanley had doubled the guard and instructed the kitchen to serve the prisoner's meals on paper plates, with paper cups for his coffee, and paper spoons and forks.

Despite the close watch, the bright lights, the defense had to admit that their client was bearing up remarkably well. Weekly physical examinations showed that his health hadn't suffered, might even have improved. He ate heartily and slept soundly. And once in a while, as he took a turn up and down the narrow, almost naked space to which his world had been reduced, he treated the silent guards to a bar or two of old country music, a song from far-off Kamenz and happier days.

Hauck and Fisher reached agreement on the tenth juror. She was Mrs. May Brelsford, thirty-eight, a stepmother, clubwoman and leader in local civic affairs.

As Judge Trenchard adjourned court for the day, the opinion of both sides was that so far the jury had shaped up well. A few weeks ago, *The Law Journal* had said:

"Due to an aroused and inflamed public sentiment by reason of the prominence of the victim and the atrocity of the crime, and the unprecedented publicity which every step and phase of the investigation has been given by the newspapers, it will be difficult to secure a jury for the trial of Hauptmann in New Jersey, the members of which shall possess the fair, impartial, and unbiased minds deemed essential to the proper administration of the criminal law."

Hunterdon County people had dismissed such fears. The jury, well-balanced, soberly respectable, seemed qualified to justify their faith.

The next morning, Thursday, January 3, a sixty-year-old retired carpenter, Liscom Case, was added to the panel, despite concern about his health; he had had some heart trouble, but it was evident that his keen mind had not been affected.

The twelfth juror soon joined the others—Howard Biggs, fifty-five, a pleasant, inconspicuous bookkeeper.

The jury for the trial of Bruno Richard Hauptmann was complete. They stood in the old jury box, to be sworn.

Much as if they were the cast in a play, a list of names went out over the wires from the telegraph center in the garret of the courthouse:

Judge

Thomas Whitaker Trenchard

Counsel for the State	*Counsel for the Defense*
David T. Wilentz	Edward J. Reilly
Anthony Hauck, Jr.	C. Lloyd Fisher
Joseph Lanigan	Frederick A. Pope
Robert Peacock	Egbert Rosecrans
George K. Large	

Jury

Charles Walton, machinist (foreman)
Mrs. Rosie Pill, widow
Mrs. Verna Snyder, housewife
Charles Snyder, farmer
Mrs. Ethel Stockton, housewife
Elmer Smith, insurance salesman
Robert Cravatt, camp educational supervisor
Philip Hockenbury, railroad worker
George Voorhees, farmer
Mrs. May Brelsford, housewife
Liscom Case, retired carpenter
Howard Biggs, bookkeeper

It was not necessary, of course, to list the central name, that of the man whose fate these twenty-two people would decide.

6

Duly sworn, the jurors resumed their seats, and David Wilentz got up.

Outside, the weather was clear and cold, a fine New Jersey winter day; inside the courtroom it was tropical. Steam heat had brought the temperature to a comfortable level hours ago, but by now body heat had sent it soaring far beyond. The courtroom was packed. Its ancient space had been argued and fought over as the crowd had come piling in, with the removal of the restraints imposed by selection of the jury. Judge and jury, opposing counsel, prisoner and witnesses could move, could turn, could stretch out; for the spectators, such freedom of action was an impossible luxury. If one itched and scratched, his neighbor felt it. Not only were these unfriendly neighbors jammed into the prescribed seats; they sat on the radiators and stood on the tables; they had wedged themselves into the entranceways, the aisles, the window recesses; and above their heads the windowpanes wept in a permanent mist of humidity. The coughs and sneezes that any crowd brings with it seemed to be amplified by the ferocious heat. The attorney general's opening words served as a cure.

"May it please your Honor——"

The crowd stared at the young, dark-haired prosecutor. Even in the furnace air he looked cool and smart and sure of himself. His voice had a hard, clear tone, and his vivacious hands underlined his words.

It was the law, Wilentz told the jury, that when a person was killed during the course of a burglary, the killing was first-degree murder; also it was the law that the murder occurred in the county where the blow was struck, even though death itself occurred in a different county. The final point was irrelevant to the case at hand, as they would see, for the State would show that both the deathblow and the death occurred in the same county—Hunterdon County, where, in the vicinity of Hopewell, Charles and Anne Lindbergh had made their home.

Wilentz paused, and the crowd stared at Charles and Anne.

Charles sat in the same chair from which he had so closely surveyed each prospective juror. His friends, Henry Breckinridge and Norman Schwarzkopf, sat on either side. He was not disappointing to see, as some idols were, in the flesh; he looked fine, the crowd thought, exactly the Lindy of all the photos and the newsreels—maybe a little too thin, though, a little drawn.

Anne was not far from him. She looked very young—a slight figure, almost a girl's. She wore a jacket and skirt of black silk, with a touch of delicate color in the shell-pink waist, and a black satin beret; she had pushed her blue fox fur off her shoulders. Her face was pale; but, except for a shadow left by sorrow, it looked serene.

Wilentz was speaking again, moving into the charge.

On the first evening of March 1932, this distinguished couple's only child, Charles Augustus Lindbergh, Jr., a blond, blue-eyed infant of twenty months, a happy, delightful little boy, had been murdered—and his murderer sat in the courtroom. The State would prove that Bruno Richard Hauptmann, alone and unaided, planned the crime, prepared for it and executed it.

The prosecutor's voice rose:

"He broke into and entered at night the Lindbergh home with the intent to commit a battery upon that child, and with the intent to steal the child and its clothing. And he did. Then as he went out that window and down that ladder of his, the ladder broke. He had more weight going down than he had when he was coming up. And down he went with this child. In the commission of that burglary that child was instantaneously killed when it received that first blow."

The crowd saw that the dead child's mother had bowed her head. They knew that a fresh and sorely felt loss added to the burden of the old tragedy Wilentz was bringing back to life. Only a few weeks ago, Anne's older sister, Elizabeth Morgan, had died in California after an emergency operation for appendicitis.

Wilentz spoke as if he could see before his eyes, in the sweltering courtroom, the scene outside the Lindbergh home on that bitter, wind-ridden March night—Hauptmann, attempting to flee, finding the double burden of ladder and child too difficult to carry and casting aside the ladder; and then, still on the grounds of the estate, ripping the sleeping suit from the small body—because, Wilentz cried, roughly gesturing, as if in performance of the same act, "he didn't need the child, as we will show you; he needed the sleeping garment!"

And the final scene in the brief history of the stolen child. It was the first convenient spot Hauptmann came to, Wilentz declared, a dark tangle of the Sourlands woods. Hastily clawing at the damp earth, the kidnaper scooped out a shallow grave and buried the little body face downward.

Wilentz's voice trembled and fell:

"And on he went—to complete the rest of his plans in this horrible criminal endeavor."

The crowd stared at Richard Hauptmann. Their eyes could take in the three at a glance: Hauptmann, Charles and Anne.

Hauptmann sat between two State troopers. His arms were folded on his chest. Wilentz's lashing words had not seemed to flick the surface of his calm and watchful attitude.

A new scene formed before the jurors as the prosecutor drew them inside the Lindberghs' home, let them share the moment, "the hysterical moment," he called it, when it was discovered that the baby was missing, and took them from room to room as Anne and Betty Gow and Elsie Whateley "looked through closets, looked here and there, looked through places they knew the child would not be, but just looked, in the hope that springs eternal in the human breast."

He lingered over the scene. Then his pace swiftened, running through the succeeding hours, days, weeks, months, drawing in Colonel Breckinridge and Dr. Condon, the vain, blind reaching out for the stolen child—Woodlawn, St. Raymond's Cemetery, the ransom-money box, the note telling where the baby would be found—mounting to the climax:

"And Lindy," Wilentz cried, "Lindy, who could find a speck at the end of the earth—Lindy couldn't find his child, because Hauptmann had murdered it."

Somberly, he took the jury back to the Sourlands thicket and the accidental find:

"The moisture in the ground had still preserved the face a little bit, so that it was white when it was turned up, and twenty minutes after the air struck it, it had turned black. The body was horribly decomposed——"

A communal gasp rose from the courtroom. Anne's head was still bowed; Charles steadfastly watched David Wilentz. Hauptmann, arms folded, sat apathetically.

—but, Wilentz said, a souvenir remained of the dead child's last night of life, the little flannel nightshirt; and there were distinguishing physical characteristics, still recognizable:

"There was the prominent forehead under the blond hair; there was that typical nose, and the overlapping toes of the Lindbergh child."

Wilentz told of Hauptmann's arrest and the discovery of the ransom money in his garage. Then, as if asking Hauptmann, he asked:

"Where did you get it?"

And, in a voice filled with irony, he gave the essence of Hauptmann's reply:

"Why, a partner of mine, an associate of mine, a friend of mine—now dead—gave it to me."

The crowd saw that Anne had raised her head and was watching Wilentz as steadily as Charles had been watching him from the beginning.

Wilentz came to the final phase of the argument, a point-by-point exposition of the defendant's guilt, which he said the prosecution would show in detail and prove beyond a reasonable doubt.

"The State of New Jersey," the Attorney General of New Jersey said in a voice that was measured, slow and deadly, in contrast to its earlier passion, "will not compromise with murder or murderers. We demand the penalty for murder in the first degree."

Like a swordstroke, he slashed the edge of one hand into the palm of the other. He was finished; he sat down.

And Edward Reilly rose. He allowed the jury a moment or so to look at him: tall, immaculate, supremely assured. His fine deep voice said:

"If your Honor please, I move now for a mistrial on the impassioned appeal of the attorney general, not being a proper opening, but merely a summation and a desire to inflame the minds of this jury against this defendant before the trial starts."

Judge Trenchard did not require long to reach a decision. "The motion is denied."

Free to proceed, Wilentz called the State's first witness, the first building block in his over-all plan to construct an edifice of guilt so overwhelming in sheer detail, so precisely put together—an orderly chronology, from the kidnaping night to Hauptmann's arrest and the following investigation—that the jury would ignore or at least would not be swayed by the fact that all of it was circumstantial evidence.

Walter E. Roberts, a civil engineer and surveyor, came to the stand. With maps and charts drawn by his own hand he established the location of the Lindbergh house and the relationship between the rooms and corridors. The information was pertinent but, for the jury, dull; their interest, strung so taut by Wilentz's opening, obviously lagged.

Then it revived.

"Mrs. Anne Morrow Lindbergh."

Anne was sworn, and sat down. She clasped her gloved hands in her lap, but they would not be still, betraying her serene face; the fingers broke loose, wandered apart, were brought together again and disciplined—again stirred and wandered.

Quietly, Wilentz asked his witness to tell about the events of Tuesday, March 1, 1932, in her home.

Anne's answering voice was quiet, too, but firm, and its pleasant tones carried to the farthest boundaries of that swarming territory where the crowd stood and sat—and listened, entranced, whereas a little while ago, during Walter Roberts' monotoned recital, the crowd had coughed and sneezed and gossiped and complained about its neighbors' obnoxious manners.

Because the baby was suffering from a three-day cold, Anne said, she had decided to keep him at the Hopewell house rather than return with him to her mother's estate in Englewood. She had telephoned Betty Gow, the baby's nurse, and asked her to join them, and had gone for a short walk after Betty arrived. Returning, she had paused alongside the house, where the ground was quite muddy, and tossed some pebbles at a nursery windowpane.

Wilentz made a point of this:

"You say you did walk in the mud there?"

"Yes."

"So that in the afternoon—in the vicinity of that portion of the house which would be immediately underneath the second-floor southeast window—you left your footprints?"

"I did," Anne said.

There could be no mystery, then, about those footprints, if the defense had been considering trying to link them to an unknown woman involved in the kidnaping.

Anne told how, later on, she had played with the little boy and had helped Betty Gow to put him to bed after the nurse had hastily improvised a flannel nightshirt, cut from a petticoat, to keep him snugly warm.

Wilentz permitted some seconds to pass before asking his next question. His tone emphasized its importance.

"Was he a normal child?"

The crowded room was absolutely still.

The kidnaping had left a wake of cruel rumors—*Did you know the truth about the Lindbergh baby? There was something wrong with it . . . it was an idiot, they say*—and the trial had given them a new, ugly life, and a new significance: would the defense suggest that the whispers pointed to the true, secret motive behind the kidnaping?

Anne raised her voice:

"*Perfectly* normal!"

She said it proudly. Continuing, she described her son as healthy and playful and able to talk as well as the average child of his age. His hair was a light gold, she said, and his eyes were blue.

"Was his hair curly?" Wilentz asked.

Her head had been erect, her blue eyes meeting his sympathetic gaze; now she lowered it and looked down at her restless hands and clasped them tightly. She answered in a whisper:

"It was curly."

Wilentz turned and brought forth a small wardrobe of children's things, some much used by time and weather, and handed them to her and asked if she could identify them as the garments her son had worn on the night when she last saw him in his crib. One by one Anne took them—the flannel nightshirt; the sleeveless woolen shirt; the sleeping suit; a wire thumbguard—and looked at them carefully and put them in her lap for a moment or two before surrendering them and saying yes, they were her child's.

The clothes were placed in evidence, and Wilentz asked the witness to continue with her account of the night. Anne told of leaving the nursery and going down to the living room, of her husband's arrival about an hour later and their dinner, then their short talk before the fire and the rather longer talk in the bedroom. Then Charles had bathed and dressed and gone downstairs to the library, and she had prepared for bed.

She paused. Some eager watchers in the crowd thought that Anne Lindbergh had reached the limit of her discipline and that, any moment now, they would see her cry; but she did not. She said:

"I had caught a cold from the baby. After my husband left I rang the bell for Mrs. Whateley and, when she came, asked her for a hot lemonade to take before going to bed. I then drew a bath for myself. After I'd taken my bath, Miss Betty Gow came in to me through the hall door and asked me if I had the baby and, hearing that I did not, asked me if my husband had the baby, and I sent her downstairs. I went into the baby's room through the connecting passage, looked hastily at the bed, and found it to be empty."

When she went into the nursery, had she observed any changes in its appearance?

"I saw no change in the room at all."

Did she notice the bedclothes in the crib?

"The bedclothes were apparently untouched," Anne replied, "as though the child had been taken out. The pins were still fastening the bedclothes to the mattress."

Safety pins?

"Yes."

And they were still securely fastened?

"Yes."

Wilentz thanked her for bearing with him so well; he had no more questions.

The chief of the defense staff got up. Reilly's voice was gentle:

"The defense feels that the grief of Mrs. Lindbergh needs no cross-examination."

Anne left the witness chair.

Some of the watching eyes managed to find Anna Hauptmann's place in the packed room. Her face looked flushed; but that could be from the steamy air. The heat was worse than ever.

The State called Charles Lindbergh to the stand. His tall, thin figure rose and moved in its gangling stride to the chair and sat down easily. He crossed his legs and folded his hands on a knee, his elbows resting on the chair arms.

The crowd saw Hauptmann lean forward and peer at the man in the chair and then lean back again. His eyes stayed on Lindbergh.

The young man's self-control was famous; it was plainly evident now in his composed face and clear, even voice as Wilentz led him through his activities after arriving home on the evening of the crime.

The attorney general spent some time over the peculiar sound Charles had heard while chatting with Anne on the living-room sofa. When he heard it, Charles said, he had had a vague impression that perhaps the slats of an orange crate had fallen off a chair in the kitchen. It hadn't seemed important, not then.

"Was it the sort of noise that would come with the falling of a ladder?"

"Yes, it was," Charles agreed, "if the ladder was outside."

Wilentz went without further pause to the discovery that the baby was missing. How had he learned of it?

"I was reading in the library," Charles remembered, "and Miss Gow called to me in a rather excited voice and asked me if I had the baby. I immediately went upstairs into the nursery, and from the appearance of the crib I realized that something had gone wrong. The bedclothing in the crib was in such condition that I felt it was impossible for the baby to have gotten out himself. The bedclothing was standing stiffly enough so that the opening where the baby had been was still there—the clothing had not collapsed."

Had he noticed anything else?

Yes, he had—an envelope on top of the radiator grating which formed the sill of the southeast corner nursery window.

Wilentz produced the envelope. Charles identified it and the note inside, and both were placed in evidence. Then the prosecutor read aloud the odd scrawl in which the note was written, stumbling a bit over the syntax, the misspelled words, and describing to the jury the unique signature of overlapping circles and holes.

He asked the witness to go on, please.

The police had come, Charles said, and outside the house, in the raw dark, their flashlights had found a ladder lying several feet southeast of the nursery window. They found, too, in the mud below the window, the holes left by the ladder's feet, and a man's footprint.

Then reporters and photographers had arrived, and the news had spread around the country and around the world.

The mail had brought a second note. Wilentz displayed it and Charles nodded and said yes, that was it. The note was placed in evidence, and again the prosecutor read aloud to the jury:

"Dear Sir: We have warned you note to make anyding public or notify the police. Now you have to take the consequences. . . ."

The wintry dusk had gathered over Flemington. The day's session was adjourned.

The court reconvened the next morning at its usual hour, ten. Charles Lindbergh returned to the witness chair; Anne, the crowd was quick to note, had not come with him. Those fortunate enough to have gained a place today as well as yesterday observed that David Wilentz was wearing a different suit, whereas Edward Reilly had remained faithful to his morning coat, striped trousers, and spats; but the choice blossom in his lapel was fresh.

Wilentz's questions drew Charles in memory back to the plundered nursery and further evidence of the crime: the yellowish-red clay smudges he had noticed after the little boy had vanished. They were the length and width of a man's foot, Charles said, so that while the prints were not distinct and complete, he was certain they had been made by a man's tread. As for the ladder and chisel, neither was part of his property, the witness continued; he had never seen them before.

Wilentz took him through the collaboration with Colonel Breckinridge and Dr. Condon—the long-drawn-out negotiations, the return of the baby's sleeping suit, the trip with the ransom money to St. Raymond's Cemetery and his wait in the car while Dr. Condon went alone to deal with John. Then, some two to three hundred feet away:

"I heard very clearly a voice coming from the cemetery, to the best of my belief calling Dr. Condon."

Wilentz asked, "What were the words?"

"In a foreign accent: 'Hey, Doctor.'"

"Since that time have you heard the same voice?"

"Yes, I have."

Wilentz waited a moment.

"Whose voice was it, Colonel, that you heard calling, 'Hey, Doctor'?"

"It was Hauptmann's voice," Charles said decisively. And for the first time he looked straight at the prisoner.

It seemed to some in the crowd that Hauptmann's sallow skin was invaded by a slow, reddish tide. He shifted slightly in his seat between the two guards.

Charles' gaze left him and returned to Wilentz. With meticulous care, the prosecutor led the witness through the expectant hours after the fifty thousand dollars ransom had been exchanged for a note purporting to tell where his son would be found, the search for a boat that didn't exist, the desperate efforts to renew contact with the kidnapers.

"And finally, on May 12, 1932, were you called back to Hopewell?"

"Yes," Charles answered, "I was."

"And did you visit a morgue in Trenton?"

"Yes, I did."

"Did you see the child again?"

"I saw the child's body."

"You saw the body in the morgue?"

"Yes."

"So that you did not get the money back and you did not get your child?"

"I did not."

Wilentz's lively hands made a concluding gesture. His aides saw that their chief was content: as had been expected, Charles Lindbergh had made a strong and convincing witness; and now the crime was outlined and even filled in here and there with small blocks of evidence. Then, too, the *corpus delicti* had been established, proof that the dead child was the Lindberghs' son.

Wilentz surrendered the witness to the defense.

Ed Reilly's elegant, bulky figure got to its feet. His lieutenants, aware of the formidable task facing their chief, who must now attack not only a strong witness but a famous, revered man, could detect no sign of diffidence in Reilly's manner as he leisurely approached the stand, where Charles Lindbergh calmly awaited him. The two surveyed each other.

"Are you a peace officer of the State?" Reilly asked.

Charles said no, he was not.

"Are you armed, Colonel?"

Wilentz was up at once with an objection. Judge Trenchard seemed a bit disconcerted; he asked to hear the question again. His information, here, lagged behind the crowd's: they read the newspapers, which were banned to judge and jury for the length of the trial. Reporters had seen and written about the shoulder-holster pistol beneath Lindbergh's jacket on his first day in court, and their discovery had sprouted a rumor: the bereaved father intended to kill Hauptmann. Additional gossip stated that Lindbergh was resolved to put the pistol to deadly use if insinuations were drawn in court from baseless rumors about his private life.

The question, the judge was told, was, "Are you armed, Colonel?"

Judge Trenchard said he could not see that it was material. Ed Reilly remarked, a shade ironically, "I thought it was." Then Lindbergh cut in, saying he didn't mind answering. No, he was not armed.

Reilly got on with his work. Concerning the Colonel's estate: Had he been aware of any hostility on the part of the local, long-time inhabitants around and about Hopewell while his home was being built or after he and his family had moved in, prior to the kidnaping?

No, the young man said, he hadn't.

But Reilly seemed to doubt it. Wasn't it possible that such hostility could have cropped up? After all, the Lindberghs were outsiders, and outsiders proverbially were viewed with distrust, and changes resented—and they had brought great changes: an impressive house, a large estate, sealed off to the country folk, blocking many short-cut paths and roadways they had been accustomed to use.

Charles could not agree with this inference.

The defense attorney swung off on a new tack. In staffing the new house—with Oliver and Elsie Whateley and Betty Gow—what inquiries had been made into the servants' character, what investigations of their background? In short, what action had Colonel Lindbergh taken to assure himself that he was hiring the proper sort of people?

He had talked to them, Charles said, talked to each of them for half an hour or so.

"Beyond that, did you go any further?"

"Beyond that," Charles replied firmly, "I never go any further."

The Whateleys and the baby's nurse had come well-recommended, and although he wasn't sure it seemed likely that his wife had looked into their backgrounds.

"At the time of the kidnaping," Reilly pressed, "did you not want to find out the antecedents of everybody in the house?"

"That was thoroughly done by the police."

Reilly's face, turned toward the jury, registered polite astonishment. Again looking at the witness, he asked:

"Did you not make any effort as a father to find out the backgrounds of the people that were in the house the night your child was snatched away?"

"I placed my entire confidence in the police."

"Well, Colonel, as a man of the world, you certainly must have known that some of the police are not infallible, did you not?"

"I think we have very good police," Charles told him.

The crowd laughed, and Judge Trenchard rapped for order. In the new silence, Reilly underlined his last question by implying that Charles Lindbergh's confidence in the forces of law and order was a good deal less solid than his answer indicated, since it had been more or less restricted to the New Jersey State Police; other agencies that had wished to help had been fairly ignored.

Moving ahead, Reilly invited the witness to point out to the jury, on the diagram of the house's interior, how one would walk from the nursery to the outside grounds without using the front stairs. Charles got up and traced a path down the servants' staircase past the kitchen to the garage and outside into the parking area.

"Did you examine the parking space that night for any footprints?"

"No," Charles said. "There would be no use, because it is covered with a loose gravel."

"The question is, did you look, Colonel?"

"No."

The dialogue between witness and attorney covered the Lindberghs' custom of spending the weekdays on the Morrow estate in Englewood and the week ends in their newly completed home near Hopewell, and Reilly narrowed the exchange of questions and answers to the week end directly preceding the crime and the decision not to return to Englewood on Monday, as they normally would, because of the baby's cold. That Monday, Charles had gone to his office in New York City, leaving Anne with Charles, Jr., and the Whateleys, and his work had kept him so late that, rather than make the long drive back to Hopewell, he had decided to spend the night in Englewood and get an early start on the next day's schedule.

"How did you communicate with your wife that you would not be home Monday night?"

"I believe that I called her that evening by phone."

"Did you talk to the butler?"

"He might have answered the phone," Charles said, reflecting. "I don't remember."

"But he would know that you were not coming home Monday night after you finished talking to your wife, wouldn't he?"

"He probably would."

"And Mrs. Whateley would be very likely to know—she was the cook, wasn't she?"

"It is quite probable," the witness agreed.

"But the outside world would not know that you were not coming home Monday night, would it?"

"Very few people would know that."

"Very few people would know that you were going back to New York again on Tuesday, would they, Colonel?"

"Very few people know what I do."

"Yes," Reilly said affably. "So that a person in the outside world, or a gang in the outside world, on Tuesday, March the first, would have no knowledge as to where you were?"

"Well," Charles countered, "that depends on their organization."

"It wouldn't depend on any information you gave, would it?"

"Well, not with knowledge."

Reilly wished to know about the young man's activities in New York on the day of the crime, and Charles recounted them. At about five-thirty or six he had telephoned Anne to tell her he was coming home.

"Did the butler answer?"

"Very likely he did."

Now, the attorney went on, about the evening, after Lindbergh had arrived home—wasn't there a dog in the Hopewell house that Tuesday, the night of the crime . . . ?

Yes, there was, Charles agreed—a little fox terrier, a gift from his mother.

Reilly observed warmly that it was a very affectionate breed. Hadn't Colonel Lindbergh found this to be true, that the little dog was playful, and friendly with every member of the household?

Charles had to qualify that. Playful, friendly? Reasonably so. A fox terrier, of course, was very high-strung——

Very nervous?

Very nervous, yes.

A good watchdog?

No, not particularly.

At any time between his arrival that night and his discovery that the baby was missing, had he heard the dog bark?

Not that he recalled.

Had the dog behaved in any way to suggest that someone was prowling outside the house?

No. But he wouldn't expect such a reaction from the fox terrier.

Reilly seemed annoyed. Sharply, he pressed the point:

"Anyhow, the dog was around and you have no recollection now that the dog indicated there was anything unusual about the house?"

"No, I have not," Charles' unruffled voice informed him.

The attorney pondered, gently dangling his massive black-rimmed glasses. He wished to return to the time of Lindbergh's arrival that evening, he said. Before dinner, the Colonel had gone upstairs to his bathroom to wash? Yes. And the bathroom adjoined the baby's room? Yes. But he did not enter the nursery? No. And he heard no suspicious noise from the nursery? No. With Mrs. Lindbergh, he had returned downstairs—to the dining room? Yes. Sitting at the dining table, neither he nor his wife could see the main hallway, could they? No. Nor the servants' staircase? No.

"Colonel, while you were in the dining room—if the front door of your home was opened by someone—anyone could have gone up the main stairway of your house and taken the baby out of the crib, couldn't they?"

Charles said, "I don't think so."

"It would have been physically possible, would it not?"

"I think it would be very improbable that it could be done without our knowing it."

"Why?" Reilly demanded.

"The front door did not open easily—and there was no door closed between the dining room and the front entrance."

"Then would it be possible for anyone in the house, who knew the house, to take the baby out of the crib and bring it down the main stairs—and to a window?"

"It might have been possible," Charles admitted.

Reilly suggested, "Let's take the other course, Colonel. If there was disloyalty in your home, would it be possible for a person acquainted with the home to take the baby out of the crib and descend the servants' staircase and hand it to someone in the garage yard while you were dining?"

"It would have been possible. . . ."

The timbre of Reilly's flexible voice deepened; the glasses in his hand swayed like a metronome as he tolled off his points:

The house was fairly well lighted that night and the windows were without curtains, so that from the outside the movements of the occupants could be observed; the southeast corner nursery window, through which it was claimed the child had been taken, was closed but unlocked both before and after the baby's disappearance, and of course Betty Gow, the nurse, knew that these particular window shutters were warped and could not be locked; oddly, although it was admitted that in stealing in and out the window, anyone would have to grasp the window frame or sill or shutters, no fingerprints had been found; oddly, too, one of the yellow-red clay smudges in the nursery, a footprint, the Colonel had said, was on a suitcase resting on its side directly beneath the window——

Pausing, Reilly turned away from Charles and brought his encompassing gaze to bear on the jury, and he continued to look at them as he resumed, in a tone of disbelief:

— didn't it seem strange that a man weighing 175 to 190 pounds hadn't stepped through the fabric of the traveling case, a man with a baby in his arms—enough weight, the State contended, to crash through the rung of a ladder a moment later?

David Wilentz sprang up.

"Will you please face the witness when you are asking him questions?"

Amiably deferring to his opponent's request, Reilly went on:

So far as the Colonel knew, had strangers ever visited the nursery? No.

The baby had not had much contact with strangers, had he?

No; only friends.

Reilly repeated the words, with an eloquent pause between them: Only—friends. The Lindberghs lived a rather reserved life and so the baby was not accustomed to strangers, just to his parents and Betty Gow and the Whateleys and relatives and servants at the Morrow estate and perhaps a few others?

Charles nodded. Yes.

Now, there'd been no cry from the nursery that night; even though the child was still sick, recovering from a cold, it had not called out?

So far as he knew, Charles replied, it had not.

Reilly let the implication stand. It seemed clear enough: if a stranger had stolen into the nursery and lifted the baby, perhaps sleeping fitfully, from his crib, wouldn't the child have awakened and cried out?

Thoughtfully surveying the jury, Reilly gave them a few moments to digest this; then, returning to Lindbergh, he led the witness back in memory to his desk in the library, facing the curtainless window that was directly beneath the southeast corner window of the nursery above. The young father had sat there for perhaps a half hour, with the kidnaper's alleged escape route in his line of vision, yet he had seen no one pass the bare window outside and had heard only the ordinary sounds of a windy night. And then Betty Gow came—came down the front, not the back, stairs—and announced that the baby was missing?

"Yes."

Reilly wished to know Miss Gow's condition, as it appeared to the Colonel.

"When she called to me and asked me if I had the baby, her voice was quite excited."

The attorney asked if she was hysterical.

"No."

Crying?

"I do not believe so."

Yet she was greatly attached to the child, and the child was attached to her?

"I believe so, yes."

In fact, with the exception of the child's mother, she was closer to the child than anyone else?

"She was with the child more than anyone else."

She was the child's companion, and the child was growing up practically alongside her?

"Yes."

Again, Reilly was content to let his thoughtful silence speak for him, saying, perhaps louder than words: then if Betty Gow, anything but a stranger, had lifted the child from the crib—to take him who knew where? down the back stairs and then to the garage, to hand him to someone waiting, by prearrangement, in the parking space?—of course the baby wouldn't have cried out. Not in his nurse's sheltering arms! Later, while he was being spirited away through the noisy night, any amount of crying could never have raised the alarm.

Having brooded over this second, weightier implication, the defense chief picked up another thread. The State contended that one man, Richard Hauptmann, had stolen the child; but hadn't Colonel Lindbergh voiced his belief that a gang was responsible—in particular, the Purple Gang of Detroit? Wasn't that why he had arranged for Rosner and Spitale and Bitz to use their influence with the underworld?

Charles couldn't agree. It had been suggested to him, he said, that the underworld might know what had happened to his son and, if so, that these three men could find out. He had employed them because he was determined to use every means of recovering the baby.

Touching briefly on the possibility that a personal enemy of Charles Lindbergh, or enemies in the aviation world, had kidnaped and killed the child—a supposition the witness received skeptically—Reilly moved to the immediate aftermath of the kidnaping: Dr. John F. Condon had sent a letter—an advertisement, one might say—to the Bronx *Home News* and, soon after it had been published, had telephoned Lindbergh at Hopewell, to say that he had received a note addressed to the Colonel, a note with oddly overlapping circles on it.

Hadn't it seemed strange to Lindbergh to receive a call of this nature from someone he didn't know?

"Not under the conditions, no," Charles replied. "Something like that had to happen."

Did he know anything about the symbols? Had he tried to decipher the ones on the ransom notes?

"I had thought about it considerably."

Was he aware that symbols were the basis of theosophy—and that Dr. Condon had taught theosophy?

"I didn't know what his subjects were."

Hadn't it struck him as peculiar that Dr. Condon's letter was answered immediately after it appeared in the Bronx *Home News*?

"We considered it; but we realized that after the original circumstance the sequence of events would probably be peculiar, not according to the ordinary logic of life."

But hadn't it occurred to him that the master mind of the crime might have both placed the advertisement and answered it himself?

Charles had not permitted his feelings to color his tone of voice, but now he spoke with naked contempt for the question:

"I think that is inconceivable from any practical standpoint."

Reilly was not dismayed. Wasn't it true that in every important development thereafter Dr. Condon had acted alone, unseen? That Lindbergh and his associates and the police had had no direct knowledge of what Dr. Condon was doing? Had simply relied on what he told them?

For example, take the night on which the fifty thousand dollars ransom was paid. Dr. Condon knew he could expect Lindbergh to bring the money to the old man's home in the Bronx that evening because the previous kidnap note had instructed the Colonel to be prepared for the pay-off. And soon after Lindbergh's arrival the doctor's doorbell rang and he went to the door alone and came back with a new note of instructions.

But no one saw him receive the note. Lindbergh didn't see him receive it, did he?

"No. I stayed in the back of the house."

Reilly nodded. And the note directed them to a florist's shop across from St. Raymond's Cemetery, and they set out for it, just the two of them, no police, and Dr. Condon went—again alone!—to the designated spot at the florist's shop and came back and handed to the Colonel another of the same sort of note he had turned over to him before?

"Yes."

"But," Reilly emphasized, "you did not see him pick it up?"

"I couldn't."

Then, alone again, Dr. Condon went into the cemetery and held a conversation with someone?

"That is what he told me, yes."

And came back and took the fifty thousand dollars and went away again—alone?

"Yes, he went alone."

And came back without the money but with a fresh note!

Reilly's tone and mobile face expressed the absurdity of it for the jury. Then to the witness:

Had Dr. Condon told Lindbergh that he was in contact with a gang?

"No. He told me the man that he contacted spoke of others."

And that had led the Colonel to believe that it was a group?

"It didn't lead me to believe very much, but there seemed to be no reason why it shouldn't be."

Hadn't he believed, too, that John Hughes Curtis, the Norfolk boatbuilder, was in touch with a gang, and that this gang held his infant son?

"I did—with reservations."

In fact, at the trial of Curtis, after it had been established that Lindbergh had repeatedly tried and failed to contact the gang aboard the schooner *Mary B. Moss* off Norfolk, the Colonel had given the following testimony; and Reilly read from the Curtis trial transcript:

> "The question came up at that time as to what course to pursue. I could offer no distinct reason for believing that Mr. Curtis had not been in contact with these people, and, according to the information he had given me, in my mind he certainly was either in contact directly or indirectly with the people who had been in possession of our child. I felt that it was essential to devote every effort to find out who these people were and if possible to bring about a return of the baby, and if not, bring about their apprehension."

The Colonel had said this on the witness stand when Curtis was on trial, hadn't he?

"Yes—but I found out later that Curtis was not telling me the truth."

Reilly shifted to new ground.

Had Colonel Lindbergh suspected Violet Sharpe of any connection with the crime?

Charles said no, he had not.

In spite of the fact that she had been questioned by the police, and that they had subsequently questioned her again, and that she had taken poison, had committed suicide, rather than face her questioners again?

Violet Sharpe had taken poison, Charles granted; that much was certain.

Reilly speculated about Red Johnson, a frequent visitor to the Morrow servants' quarters—had he, perhaps, been friendly with Violet Sharpe, to the extent of taking her out?

Charles said he didn't know.

But he *did* know, didn't he, Reilly asked, quickening his pace, that Johnson had been apprehended by the immigration authorities for being in the United States illegally?—that Johnson had been permitted to leave the country voluntarily and was now living abroad?—and that neither Johnson nor Betty Gow was in the United States when Hauptmann was arrested, but that Betty had been brought back to testify for the State?

And finally, after a pause:

"Do you know of any effort that has been made by the State to bring back Red Johnson?"

Charles said, "So far as I know, the question never came up."

Regally, the defense chief waved his glasses, signifying that he was finished. David Wilentz chose not to re-examine the witness, and Charles left the stand and returned to his familiar seat between Breckinridge and Schwarzkopf.

Constable Charles Williamson of the Hopewell police was called and examined by Wilentz. He corroborated the evidence of crime in the Lindbergh nursery and on the grounds of the estate and described the small body the truck driver, William Allen, had led him to. The prosecutor showed him a photograph. Was this the child he had found dead? Yes. And were these the garments clothing the body? Yes.

Again, proof that Charles Lindbergh, Jr., was the *corpus delicti*.

Reilly challenged. Had the constable ever seen the Lindbergh baby alive? No. And despite the condition of the body, he claimed that it was identical with the happy, healthy figure of the child in the photograph?

Well, Constable Williamson said, the face was the same.

He was followed in the witness chair by Elsie Whateley, the Lindberghs' housekeeper and cook. Reviewing through her memories the domestic scene inside the Hopewell house during the afternoon and evening of March 1, 1932, Wilentz spoke so feelingly of the little boy, his healthy good looks and playful charm, that Reilly complained, declaring that his opponent was not examining in a seemly manner but was striving to take advantage of and further excite the jury's natural sympathy. Wilentz shrugged; Mrs. Whateley looked with calm eyes at the indignant defense lawyer and waited for his flurry to subside. Her composure as a witness matched Charles Lindbergh's.

Wilentz wished to hear about the discovery that the baby was missing, as the housekeeper had learned of it. She was in the kitchen fixing a hot lemonade for Mrs. Lindbergh—?

Yes, and Mr. Whateley was there too, and Betty Gow ran downstairs and asked Mr. Whateley if he would go to the Colonel at once, because the baby was gone, and he went up, and the witness asked Betty what she meant, and she said, "Why, Elsie, the baby is gone."

"In what manner of voice?" Wilentz asked.

"She was terribly upset, of course."

And then?

The witness went upstairs too and asked the Colonel where Mrs. Lindbergh was, and he pointed to the nursery. And:

"I went in and she was standing beside the crib and I stood by her."

Yes?

Yes. And the witness urged Mrs. Lindbergh to dress, and helped her, and with Betty Gow they started to search for the baby, started to search the house, and from time to time the witness heard Mrs. Lindbergh whisper, "Oh, God."

Then?

Then all three sat in the living room and waited. They didn't do anything else; just sat and waited.

Without speaking? In silence?

Without speaking. In silence.

Wilentz moved on from that tableau of the nurse, the housekeeper, and the young mother, waiting. A dog, a little fox terrier, had been in the house that night: what sort was he? Barking? Quiet?

"I always thought he was sharp," Elsie Whateley said. "If he heard a noise, he would bark, as a rule, but the wind was so bad that night you couldn't hear anything."

The prosecutor did not seem too happy with this delineation of an alert pet that, as a rule, would challenge untoward sounds; Charles Lindbergh's recollection of the dog's temperament had been quite different.

Where was the terrier between seven-thirty and ten o'clock that night?

"He was in our sitting room, in his basket," Elsie replied.

And the servants' sitting room was situated in the downstairs west wing of the house while the nursery was situated in the upstairs east wing?

"Yes."

Wilentz was satisfied: a barker or a nonbarker, placid or nervously alert, the dog would have needed extraordinary senses to apprise him of an intruder upstairs in the other wing that windy night. The prosecutor thanked Mrs. Whateley, and Reilly came forward.

Wasn't it a fact that for approximately one full hour on the night of the crime, from approximately nine to ten o'clock, the witness and Betty Gow had been out of the Lindberghs' sight?

Elsie remembered that she and Betty had gone to the Whateleys' bedroom to look at a new dress——

And wasn't Oliver Whateley out of *their* sight for the same length of time?

He had stayed downstairs in the servants' sitting room, to read—Elsie remembered his saying so——

Reilly pressed for more details; the exchange went on. In the jury box, juror number three, Mrs. Verna Snyder, had grown a little drowsy from the heat and the long afternoon of testimony. The hour was late. Court was recessed for the week end.

The jurors prepared themselves for the trip back to their hotel. In normal times, crossing Main Street from the courthouse to the Union Hotel was a matter of a few seconds. The trial had made it a formidable undertaking, equivalent, the jury had discovered, to running the gantlet. They were a privileged group, theoretically isolated from the outside world; but as they made their way across the street, through a corridor cleared by the police, the outside world defied the theory. The enormous crowd struggled to touch them, pat them, yank souvenirs from their clothing, and yelled encouragement and advice: "Burn that Dutchman! Send him to the chair!"

The jurors longed for peace and quiet. In theory, they would find it in their well-guarded hotel rooms; but this too proved not to be the case.

They occupied six rooms. The eight men shared four of them, two to a room; the four women divided the other two. On the floor below, directly beneath their rooms, an emergency radio station had been installed. Even through the din of crowded Main Street, the souvenir-sellers' and newsboys' shouts, they could hear the news-broadcasters and lawyer-commentators describing the trial and speculating about its future.

7

Flemington's constable did not recognize his town. It had begun to change weeks ago; during this first week end of the trial the change assumed appalling dimensions. Saturday wasn't too bad, a relatively small chaos, but on Sunday the world seemed to explode. He wondered if the streets of New York and Philadelphia and Trenton and Camden and Newark and Jersey City, and all points round about and in between, were deserted; they must be!

The roads leading to Flemington were clogged. Sunday drivers reckoned their average speed at maybe three miles an hour. Many families that had set out hopefully to see the sights, the courthouse, the jail, catch a glimpse of all the celebrities, perhaps take a side trip through the Sourland woods, where the baby's body had been found, despaired and turned back before coming within miles of the abominable traffic jam that was Flemington; after having bawled themselves hoarse in a fruitless struggle to unlock it, scores of State troopers despaired too.

But sixty thousand sightseers, give or take a few hundred, got there.

Once in Flemington, they discovered that it was extremely difficult to get out. The old courthouse, seen from above, looked like a hive surrounded by a buzzing black swarm. The swarm did not seem to move, except on its ragged fringes, where fresh thousands heaved and panted, striving to penetrate it, and at the courthouse doors, which were the common goal. Some five thousand treasure-seekers triumphed over bitter opposition and gained the interior of the building and, eventually, the holy of holies, the courtroom itself. They hunted for portable fragments of its fame, hacked slivers from chairs and tables, tugged at wired-down antiques, endeavored to hide spittoons under their coats, and argued with the frantic guards. They sat in the jury box, cried "Hey, look at me! I'm Rosie Pill!"—this juror's name had swiftly soared to eminence through its radiant singularity—strutted like Reilly, posed as Wilentz, sat in Lindbergh's chair, and in Hauptmann's, and waited their turn to peer at the tumultuous courtroom from the dignity of Judge Trenchard's seat. They investigated closets and storerooms for souvenirs, wrangled over mops, bars of soap, rolls of toilet paper, and cut their initials into any yielding surface. They clambered to the telegraph eyrie in the attic and did their best to dismember the cables. They shattered the guards' nerves, and happily wore themselves out.

Elsewhere, the week end was quiet.

Charles and Anne Lindbergh were staying at Next Day Hill, the Morrow estate in Englewood, and there was ample room in the staff's quarters for Elsie Whateley and Betty Gow as guests of the family. Betty had gone to Scotland last summer on a leave of absence to visit her mother; the visit had stretched out and she was still in Glasgow at the time of Hauptmann's arrest. Her return, to testify at the trial, had been requested by Wilentz's office and paid for by the State of New Jersey.

Elsie and Betty had many memories to talk over, sharpened by the questioning in court. They spoke about Oliver, Elsie's dead husband, that good, quiet, faithful man, and then Elsie mentioned Henry Johnson—had Betty ever heard from him again? Yes, she had. Betty's tone was affectionate as she told Elsie that Red Johnson was living quietly—and, she had no doubt, happily—in Oslo, in his native Norway. He had married a Norwegian girl and not long ago they had opened a small greengrocer's shop. Quite a change for him from his old seafaring days!

Betty's voice became bitter. She did not like that man Reilly, she informed Elsie; she did not like him at all! The terrible things he had hinted at, about her, the baby's nurse, when he had asked Colonel Lindbergh all those questions! How could he possibly think such things? It was despicable, and she did not know how she would be able to hold her temper and not tell him what she thought of him when her turn would come in the witness chair and he would boom out his questions and his nasty implications at her in that big voice of his.

Elsie said calmly that Betty must do her best to keep her feelings under control, as she had kept hers, and remember that Mr. Reilly was simply playing his part for all it was worth, trying to build up something out of nothing. After all Betty had nothing to be afraid of, nothing to hide.

In Flemington, Anna Hauptmann was with Bubi at the rooming-house owned by an elderly woman, Mrs. William Opdyke, where she had moved just before the start of the trial, to be close to Richard. For her, too, the week end was quiet; the people from the Hearst papers, who guarded Anna as she walked to the courthouse and back, and stayed with her in court, kept other reporters and photographers away, and also would-be friends and curious strangers.

A slow and apparently inexhaustible tide of sightseers' cars rolled past the Morrow estate and the white house near Hopewell that Charles had built for himself and Anne and their baby. Another tide lapped around Richard and Anna Hauptmann's home in the Bronx. And all week end long the back road through the Sourlands woods was filled with cars searching for the patch of ground where Charles Augustus Lindbergh, Jr., had been laid in his careless grave.

8

Betty Gow was the first witness called by the State on Monday morning. She had taken pains with herself and, conscious of looking her best, did not flinch under the staring eyes as she walked to the chair. It seemed to some in the courtroom that her manner and her tone of voice, even her accent, responding to David Wilentz's questions about the course of events before the crime, were modeled on Anne Lindbergh's.

Mrs. Lindbergh enjoyed looking after the baby herself during the week ends in the new home near Hopewell, Betty said, and so as usual the nurse had stayed in Englewood until, on Tuesday, her employer had sent for her. The afternoon had passed peacefully. Just before the little boy's bedtime, Betty had given him a physic. He hadn't liked it and had spilled some down his nightclothes, so she had undressed him and, since he still had a slight cold, had hastily run up a flannel shirt to wear next to his skin.

Wilentz handed Betty an infant's flannel petticoat and then the torn and rotted flannel nightshirt which had been placed in evidence for the State and asked her if she recognized them. Yes, Betty said at once; she had cut the cloth for the shirt from the petticoat; and, with the prosecutor's encouragement, she faced the jury and held the two pieces of the same fabric so that their scalloped edges matched. Next she identified the remaining garments in which she had dressed the baby before putting him into his crib and, finally, the thumbguard which she had tied securely to one of the wrists of the sleeping suit. Its fastening tapes were still tightly knotted in the way she had bound them that Tuesday night.

So there he was, Betty continued, ready for bed at last, and she had tucked him into the crib, fixing the bedcovers firmly to the mattress with safety pins, and Mrs. Lindbergh and she had closed and locked the nursery window shutters—all except those at the southeast corner window. Evidently they had warped and couldn't be locked, although both young women had done their best. Then Mrs. Lindbergh had left the nursery. Betty had waited until the baby was asleep and left too.

Wilentz wanted to know at about what time that was?

Just eight o'clock. She had looked at her watch.

"What made you look at your watch?"

"Just to see the time," Betty said composedly.

Well, then, downstairs, in the servants' sitting room, she had sat down to dinner with Elsie Whateley, while the little fox terrier watched from his basket and Oliver Whateley occupied himself in the pantry close by. Henry Johnson had telephoned, and after chatting with him for a few minutes Betty had returned to the sitting room and made herself comfortable with the radio and a magazine until Elsie had invited her to the Whateleys' room to see a new dress. They had stayed there, talking about this and that.

And then?

She had looked at her watch, Betty said, and seen that it was almost ten o'clock, so she had left the Whateleys' room and walked along the upstairs hall and into the nursery. She hadn't put on a light but had kept the nursery door open so that the soft glow from the hall lights would come into the room.

Why hadn't she put on a light?

"It wasn't my habit to," Betty replied, almost severely. "I didn't want to startle the baby."

Wilentz nodded, and asked her to go on.

She did not. He looked at her, a little puzzled, and asked her again—please continue. At last she resumed; and it became apparent that the memory of the next few minutes in the nursery had undermined Betty Gow's self-control.

"I crossed to the French window," she began, and faltered, and began again, her voice coming in little gasps, until she managed with a visible effort to steady it, "—crossed to the French window and closed it and plugged in the electric heater and stood for a minute waiting for the room to lose its chill. I crossed to the crib and bent over with my hands on the rail and——"

Again she had to pause.

"—and discovered that I couldn't hear the baby breathe. I bent down, felt all over for him and discovered that he wasn't there."

Her voice had lost its careful accent. She found a handkerchief and pressed her face into it, and wept.

By and by she wiped her eyes and said, into the intense silence:

"I thought that Mrs. Lindbergh might have him, and I went out into the hallway and into Mrs. Lindbergh's room. I saw her coming from the bathroom and asked her if she had the baby. She looked surprised and said no, she didn't.

"I said, 'Well, where is the Colonel? He may have him.'

"She said, 'Downstairs in the library.'

"I turned quickly and ran downstairs to the library, where I saw the Colonel sitting at his desk, reading.

"I said, 'Colonel, do you have the baby?'

"He said, 'No. Isn't he in his crib?'

"I said, 'No.'

"He ran past me upstairs and into the baby's room. I followed him and from there entered Mrs. Lindbergh's room. He didn't say anything. He ran into his closet, came out again with a rifle and all three of us went into the baby's room.

"He said, 'Anne, they have stolen our baby.'

They. Not *Anne, our baby's been stolen* but *Anne,* they *have stolen our baby*.

Then who were *they*?

David Wilentz knew and therefore did not linger at this point. He knew not because Charles Lindbergh had told him but because, knowing Lindbergh's history and, far more important, knowing the young man himself, as the attorney general had come to know him in the days before the trial, he knew there could be only one answer. In that moment of discovery, of anger and of mortal anguish, Lindbergh had meant by *they*—the crowd: the great, demanding, ever-pursuing, ever-present crowd, which if it could, in its insatiable curiosity, would leave untouched not a shred of his privacy—would tear his clothes apart, pluck hairs from his head, reach into every corner of his life—would suffocate him and his in its fever to possess him, the idol, the famous one who had grown to fear his fame.

Somehow, to Charles Lindbergh, the crowd—not any part of it, not a few individuals; nothing like that; simply the anonymous faceless staring reaching, reaching crowd—had seemed to be responsible for this ultimate invasion of his precious private life, which with an increasing sense of hostility he had endeavored to keep hidden from it.

Wilentz saw that Lindbergh's face had flushed a little. The prosecutor turned and took up the thumbguard from among the State's exhibits and turned back to Betty Gow.

A bit earlier, he said, she had identified the thumbguard as one she had firmly tied to a wrist of the sleeping suit the Lindbergh child was wearing on the night he was stolen. Would she now describe the circumstances in which the thumbguard was found?

Betty said that that had happened about a month later, after lunch one day. Elsie Whateley and she were in the habit of taking walks down the driveway——

Wilentz interrupted to ask if she meant the driveway on the grounds of the Lindberghs' place, and Betty said yes. Well, they had strolled to the gate, chatted a while with the State troopers posted there, and then on the way back, both Elsie and she had noticed—at almost the same instant—a small metal object on the driveway. Betty had recognized it at once and picked it up.

The prosecutor held out the thumbguard for the jury to see. He asked Betty:

"Was it then in the same condition as it is today in this courtroom?"

"Exactly that condition."

"Still knotted?"

"Still knotted."

Wilentz glanced meaningfully at the jury's intent faces. He had told them in his opening address that Hauptmann, in his flight, while still on the Lindbergh grounds, had torn the sleeping suit from the baby's body, because "he didn't need the child, as we will show you; he needed the sleeping garment." Apparently ripped loose from the sleeping suit so abruptly that the securely tied fastenings were still knotted, surely the thumbguard furnished circumstantial proof of the kidnaper's presence and actions and plans—so Wilentz's glance implied.

All right, then, he continued: Miss Gow had seen and recognized the thumbguard. And nearly six weeks later—on the twelfth day of May, in a Trenton morgue—had she felt another shock of recognition?

Yes, Betty said, she had.

A child's body?

Betty's fingers tightened on her handkerchief. Yes.

"Whose body was it?"

The baby's nurse said, "Charles Lindbergh, Jr.'s."

Wilentz thanked her, and sat down. Betty looked past his neat, slim figure and saw a much larger figure rising from the defense staff's table and slowly approaching her, and braced herself for Edward Reilly's assault.

If she had expected a thunderbolt, she was pleasantly disappointed. Reilly smiled at her and said, with some concern, that perhaps Miss Gow would like to rest before she resumed?

No, Betty did not think she would.

Would she be kind enough, then, Reilly asked gently, to go back a few years and begin with her domestic service in Scotland?

Betty obliged. She had been employed since she was fourteen, and had come to the United States in the spring of 1929.

"Under what name did you enter?"

"Bessie Mowat Goway."

Reilly's face registered polite interest. And where had she worked after her arrival in America? He listened attentively as he was told, Detroit, and murmured *Ah, Detroit!* and seemed to brood over the name. Detroit, he murmured again, Detroit. . . .

Betty watched him warily.

Still musing, it seemed, Reilly strolled back to defense headquarters and picked up a folder and consulted it. Bringing the folder with him, he returned to Betty. Surely, he observed, Miss Gow must have become acquainted with several young men in Detroit—what were their names?

David Wilentz cut in with a sharp objection: Defense counsel was engaging in a fishing expedition. He did not go further, did not state the purpose, as he took it to be, of the expedition, an attempt by Reilly to link the witness with the Purple Gang.

Judge Trenchard placed the matter in balance; at present the question seemed irrelevant, he told Reilly, who seemed hurt and surprised by the objection; but later on, if the defense showed him to be mistaken, he would allow it.

Reilly sighed. He looked sadly at the folder and regretfully riffled the papers inside it, shaking his head. Betty wondered, and the jury wondered: What was in those papers?

Reilly restored the folder to the defense table. He started up again, more briskly. Some time after her associations in Detroit, Miss Gow was employed by the Lindberghs and became friendly with Red Johnson——?

Betty interrupted. The name was *Henry* Johnson. Only his friends were privileged to call him Red.

Her questioner stared at this admonishment. Then:

"You were very fond of Red Johnson, weren't you?"

"*Mr.* Johnson?" Betty said stingingly. "Yes, I was fond of *Mr.* Johnson."

"And this Red Johnson——"

"*Mis-ter* Johnson!"

There was a titter in the courtroom. Reilly gave ground. Would Miss Gow please tell how she and *Mr.* Henry Johnson had met?

Betty said that they had met in North Haven, Maine. She was at the Morrow summer place and Burke, the first chauffeur, had introduced her to Henry Johnson, who was working as a deck hand on Thomas Lamont's yacht. Later, in Englewood, she and Mr. Johnson had spent a good deal of time together.

Reilly brought the witness to the week end preceding the kidnaping. Miss Gow had learned on Friday that the Lindberghs and their baby son would be spending the week end at Hopewell; on Monday, Mrs. Lindbergh had telephoned her at Englewood and said that she was staying on because of the baby's cold. Of course, Mrs. Lindbergh had told her mother, Mrs. Morrow, too; but among the servants, only Betty Gow knew that the baby would remain at Hopewell——

Betty interrupted to say that very likely, she couldn't be sure, she had told some of the help.

Reilly's tufted eyebrows rose in an expression of interest. Why would she do that?

Oh, no particular reason—it would just be natural for someone in the Morrow house to ask about the little boy and for her to explain that he had a cold and was being kept where he was.

Had Miss Gow told Violet Sharpe?

The witness couldn't remember.

Had she told Henry Johnson?

As she recalled it, the witness had.

She had told Red Johnson that Mrs. Lindbergh and her baby son were staying on at Hopewell? When had she told him that? And why?

Betty neglected to reprove her questioner for his unwarranted use of Henry Johnson's nickname and did not even emphasize the Mister as she replied that on Monday night she had gone riding with Mr. Johnson and she had mentioned the change in Mrs. Lindbergh's plans.

The eyebrows went up again. Had she told other outsiders, too? And tradespeople? And strangers?

Betty said indignantly that she had not.

So that only Betty Gow and the Whateleys knew at first hand that the baby would be in the house in Hopewell that Monday night and perhaps the next night too, and Miss Gow had confided this knowledge to Red Johnson and very likely to Violet Sharpe and——

Betty's voice, much broader in accent than when she had first taken the witness chair, pointed out that there were other ways of finding out—after all, the telephone came into the house!

The telephone? Did she mean that one of the servants she *might* have told *might* have deliberately passed on the information to someone outside?

Well, no. No, Betty didn't mean that.

Surely she didn't suspect that the phones were tapped?

Of course she didn't!

Reilly paused and shrugged and gazed rather helplessly at the jury. It seemed they were back where he'd started—with the fact that only three people, outside of the Lindberghs and the Morrows, were originally acquainted with the change in plans. These three were Betty Gow and Oliver and Elsie Whateley; and so, with Miss Gow's help, he would like to have a closer look at them as they were on the night of the crime.

The courtly airs that had graced Reilly's voice were gone, leaving not so much as a shadow of concern for his witness' ease of mind and physical comfort in the chair. His voice rattled at her like a drill sergeant's:

At about half past eight on the night of the kidnaping in Hopewell, she had received a telephone call from Red Johnson?

Betty did not shrink from the battering voice but matched it with a vigorous *Yes*.

She had taken the call upstairs in her room? Yes. The Lindberghs were downstairs at dinner and the Whateleys were——? In the kitchen. The baby had been put to bed? Yes. And so far as she knew, there was no one on the second floor, just she and the child? So far as she knew, no one.

"Where was the telephone call from?"

"From Englewood."

"Did you trace it?"

"No, but I understood——"

"What number in Englewood?"

"I don't know, but——"

Reilly shouted, "*Don't you know it was from Hopewell?*"

Wilentz jumped up, one hand flung out toward Reilly; the significance of the question was still suspended between prosecutor and defense counsel as Betty shouted back:

"No, I don't know that!"

The courtroom stirred; Judge Trenchard called for order. Wilentz, his protesting hand still outstretched, said that defense counsel's question was based on a statement which was not a fact. Defense counsel angrily declared that it was his privilege to test the witness' credibility and accused his opponent of wilfully intervening at the most important place.

Betty sat bolt upright in the chair, ridged cheek muscles clamping her mouth shut on her brawny Scots temper, which had all its battle flags flying. Reilly's face, dangerously red, turned back to her.

She certainly knew, did she not, when Mrs. Lindbergh called her to Hopewell that Tuesday morning, that she could not keep her engagement with Red Johnson that night?

Yes, of course Betty knew that.

"Why didn't you phone him then?"

"I did call his house. He wasn't there. I left a message where he could find me——"

But she had just been out with him, the night before.

Betty nodded. Well?

Dwelling heavily on the words, Reilly asked, "What was the great importance of the second night?"

Wilentz was up with another objection, but Reilly's question continued: Was it necessary for her to say good-by to him again on Tuesday night—hadn't Monday night's farewell sufficed?

Again Wilentz objected; it was barely noticed as Betty, catching Reilly's sardonic, stately word, shouted:

"No, it didn't suffice!"

For the first time, Reilly unleashed the full power of his grand-opera lungs, a Götterdämmerung roar: *Or had Red Johnson really telephoned her to find out if the coast was clear?*

That mighty blast needed no emphasis; still, he emphasized it by staring triumphantly at the jury. The crowd babbled, and the old judge sharply asked for order.

Reilly had refilled his lungs. He became elaborately sarcastic, recalling that it had been touchingly pointed out how devoted Betty Gow was to the Lindbergh baby—how she had rubbed the little boy's chest with Vicks ointment, and fed him a physic, and made a nightshirt to help keep him warm—yet, though he still suffered from a cold, by her own admission she had *not once* visited the nursery to see how he was for two hours, from eight o'clock, when she left him asleep, until ten, when she found him gone. Was this typical of her conduct as a devoted nurse?—or had she stayed clear of the baby's room as part of a conspiracy?

Why was it so important for her to spend an hour with Elsie Whateley looking at a dress? Elsie Whateley's bedroom window faced in the same direction as the windows of the nursery, did they not?

"Yes," Betty said.

"At any time while you were with Mrs. Whateley in the room, was an electric light put on and off?"

"Yes."

"And anyone in the fields, knowing the house, would know that it was the Whateleys' room?"

"If they had studied it," Betty qualified, "yes."

"What time did you go upstairs to look at the dress?"

"About nine o'clock."

"At nine o'clock you left Whateley on the ground floor?"

"Yes."

"And that is the last you saw of him—until after you discovered that the child was gone?"

"Yes."

Reilly paused for a long look at the jury. He resumed:

"The child was well acquainted with Mr. Whateley, wasn't he?"

"Yes, I believe so."

"But the child was not accustomed to strangers?"

"No, not strangers."

"And you have testified that after leaving the ground floor of the house at nine o'clock, you did not see Whateley again until the whole thing was over?"

Betty made no answer, and Reilly did not press for one, seeming to feel that the conclusion was inescapable, as his thoughtful glance suggested to the jury. He followed by asking how Miss Gow would describe the fox terrier, the household pet?

Betty said that the Whateleys had trained the dog and generally looked after it. It usually tagged after Mr. Whateley, the butler, as he went about his work.

"So that anything Mr. Whateley did or Mrs. Whateley did around the house would not excite any suspicion on the part of the dog, would it?"

Betty granted that. "No, I wouldn't think so."

"You didn't hear the dog bark once that night, did you?"

"No, I did not."

"When strangers came to the door you heard the dog bark, didn't you?"

"Yes, as I remember it, he did."

Reilly permitted himself another pause, then inquired where Betty and Mrs. Whateley had last seen the terrier, when they had gone upstairs at nine o'clock?

They had last seen it, Betty told him, downstairs in the servants' sitting room.

And where had they last seen the butler?

In the servants' sitting room.

Reilly nodded significantly. Earlier in Miss Gow's testimony, he continued, she had described the casual stroll that by pure chance had led her and Elsie Whateley to find the baby's thumbguard on the driveway of the Lindbergh estate—the driveway, which had seen a lot of use since the kidnaping. Now, he asked, measuring and underscoring his words, in actual fact hadn't the witness *dropped* the thumbguard there and simply picked it up?

Betty measured and doubly underscored her answering words. *No, she—had—not.*

Was she sure?

She was positive.

The defense chief said incredulously, "And yet with all these police officers and with all the inclement weather for the month, and with everybody searching those grounds day after day, night after night, you would have this jury believe that you could pick up in broad daylight on that road this bright, shiny thumbguard in the same condition it is——"

Wilentz called out that the thumbguard was not shiny.

Reilly waved his hand toward the State's exhibits. "I will leave it to the jury whether it is bright and shiny!"

No, he needn't leave it to the jury, Wilentz fired back; it was not shiny.

"And it isn't muddy and it isn't rusty!" Reilly's big voice declared.

Betty brought him up with a start. The thumbguard had been a good deal muddier when she found it, she said; she had brushed some of the dirt off.

Reilly said hotly, "What do you mean by saying it was in a much muddier condition, when you told the attorney general this morning that it is in the same condition as it was when you picked it up?"

"It can't possibly be in the same condition when it has been handled by people," Betty instructed him.

Reilly stared. "You are a very bright young lady, Miss Gow, aren't you?"

"I am!"

The crowd broke into laughter and then applause as she sat smiling cockily at him.

Until now, despite his occasional interventions and rulings, to most of the crowd Judge Trenchard had been little more than a background presence, a symbol rather than an alert, thoughtful, actively participating individual; suddenly he was clothed in a severe majesty which dominated the room. He rapped for silence and coldly surveyed the crowd, and the applause and laughter ebbed and died in a last uncertain handclap and foolish giggle. He would not tolerate such demonstrations, he said; in the event of another, the courtroom would be cleared.

"You may proceed," the judge told Reilly.

But Reilly had had enough for the present. He suggested that they recess for lunch.

Returning, he plunged into a new exchange with the witness, the questions ranging from the Lamont yacht to City Island, off Pelham Bay Park (Betty said she had never visited the yacht or City Island), the Lindbergh nursery and Detroit, Violet Sharpe and Dr. John F. Condon (Betty had never gone out socially with Violet, she said, and had never met the doctor until after the baby was stolen).

Reilly let the jury share his disbelief: "And you say that you never visited with Violet Sharpe any yacht or boat owned by Dr. Condon?"

"No, I didn't."

The defense chief indicated that he had gone as far as he wished. David Wilentz rose for redirect examination.

He established that the relationship between Betty Gow and Henry Johnson had been honest and attractive; both were young and very fond of each other. And they had met in a natural course of events: she spent most of her time with the Morrows, he worked for Lamont—and Dwight Morrow and Thomas Lamont were friends.

Wilentz asked if Miss Gow recalled when Senator Morrow had died?

Reilly interposed, stating that the question was incompetent, irrelevant, immaterial. "Sad but incompetent," he added.

Well, the prosecutor replied, not without irony, defense counsel had been so profusely concerned with the dead—Violet Sharpe and Oliver Whateley—in its examinations that he thought he might be pardoned if he included the name of someone deceased who was really related to the case.

"By no stretch of the imagination," Reilly appealed to the judge, "should the name of the distinguished Senator be tied up with the names of the persons mentioned."

But Judge Trenchard did not agree, and Betty was allowed to respond with the approximate date of Dwight Morrow's death. The redirect questioning went on. Before long, Wilentz was finished; he thanked the witness and helped her from the stand.

9

Nothing in his appearance betrayed it, but the young prosecutor was not altogether satisfied at this point. The first phase of the State's case was well along, the foundation blocks fairly laid: the fact of the kidnaping was established and the method clearly indicated—the kidnaper, Richard Hauptmann, had climbed a ladder to the nursery's southeast corner window, thrust apart the warped shutters, raised the unlocked sash, crept to the sleeping child and then retraced his steps in flight. But Wilentz felt no assurance that Reilly, in his cross-examination, had not managed to blur this simple, vivid picture and present to the jury a more convincing one of his own.

Reilly's picture showed Betty Gow, not Hauptmann, taking the baby from the crib and handing him to Oliver Whateley (or was it to Oliver's wife, Elsie?—it wasn't quite clear, but that was only part of Reilly's purpose). Then the picture showed Oliver—or Elsie—slipping down the servants' stairway to the garage and giving the child to a confederate waiting outside the garage doors. As for the broken ladder: why, Reilly had seemed to say, it hadn't been used at all; it was just a ruse. The footprints inside the nursery and in the mud outside? Red herrings, deliberately put there. In short, there was nothing to the State's contention that Hauptmann had broken into the house and carried off the child alone and unaided. Reilly's picture portrayed the kidnaping as an inside job with outside help.

Were the jurors convinced? Did they find this interpretation plausible enough to question the charge? The prosecutor wondered. It was too early in the game to hope to read their faces with any degree of accuracy, but if Reilly had succeeded in planting a single seed of doubt the best thing would be to uproot it before it had a chance to grow and irretrievably shadow the State's case. The accusing finger must be drawn away from the Whateleys and Betty Gow—and from Henry Johnson and Violet Sharpe and Dr. Condon—and pointed again at the defendant.

The blurred picture of Richard Hauptmann coming to the house in the dark of night and climbing into the nursery must be put back into focus.

Wilentz decided that the way to restore the picture's original clarity was to introduce and emphasize the evidence of Hauptmann's entry—the ladder, the two holes it had left in the mud beneath the nursery window, the footprints, and so on. There were witnesses waiting who could accomplish this, State troopers and detectives who could describe with authority what they had found at the scene of the crime.

The prosecutor summoned to the witness chair, in turn, Joseph Wolfe, Lewis Bornmann, Frank Kelly and Nuncio De Gaetano.

Reilly countered with confident scorn. Police witnesses were an old story to him from his battles in the Brooklyn criminal courts and the memory of past victories against them showed in his brusque tone as he launched into his cross-examination.

All four officers said they had observed a "large" footprint in the soft clay beneath the southeast window of the nursery. Reilly wanted to know *what* size footprint, *what* shape, where was the proof of it?

Trooper Wolfe insisted that it was a man's footprint, right or left he didn't know. Detective De Gaetano couldn't exactly say that it was a footprint at all—it was peculiarly ridged along one side and he hadn't seen any accompanying print. None of the witnesses had measured it, although Wolfe had thought while peering at it that the print was made by a shoe slightly larger than his own and De Gaetano had guessed its length by holding the handle of his flashlight parallel to it, its width by using the palm of his hand. None of them had preserved the print; Corporal Kelly had taken pictures of it but (although all admitted this was important material evidence) not even a plaster cast had been made.

Finally, in spite of the fact that the Lindbergh servants and the baby's nurse were or should have been under suspicion, Detective Bornmann hadn't compared the size and shape of the print with Oliver Whateley's footprint, had simply taken the butler's word for it that he hadn't gone outside the house that day until after the crime was discovered. What proof was there, Reilly asked, that Oliver Whateley had *not* left the all-important clue?

The witnesses were nettled by the defense chief's jabbing voice; he did not spare them, but he saved the sharpest edge of his contempt for their treatment of the ladder. Kelly had detected no fingerprints on it and De Gaetano hadn't bothered to look for mud on the bottom rung as evidence that the ladder had been used. Worst of all, it had been bandied from hand to hand, taken apart and put together again; almost all of its nails had been pulled out with no proof that the same nails had been put back; and one side rail had been sawed in two with a new strip of wood added to hold it together.

In sum, the flimsy affair David Wilentz was so eager to place in evidence as the kidnaper's means of entry could not even be said to be the same ladder found on the Lindbergh grounds.

Judge Trenchard asked the question Reilly's attack seemed to make obvious. Did the defense object to the admission of the ladder as evidence?

The defense objected most strenuously, Reilly replied, on the ground that there was no evidence to show that the ladder had been used to enter the Lindbergh house on the night of the crime and that it was not in the same condition as when it was alleged to have been used.

Reilly was not content to let his objection rest at that. He gave the reins to Frederick Pope, who had something of a specialist's —at any rate a hobbyist's—knowledge of wood and had impressed his chief with it. Pope developed the complaint at length. The defense insisted, he told the judge in a small summation of his own, that the ladder could not be introduced until it had been traced through every person who had possessed it from the time it was found until the present.

Judge Trenchard glanced toward Wilentz and said that he thought it would be desirable if the prosecution would show in whose custody the ladder had been and what had been done with it before it was offered in evidence; meanwhile, he would allow it to be submitted for identification.

Wilentz took this with an inner grimace. Hardly an inviting prospect—a path as tedious for the jury to travel as for him to lead them over it. But it had to be done. He turned to Bornmann, the first to take charge of the ladder. Adjournment for the day could not be very far off; the prosecutor was grateful when it came.

Tuesday brought a thick fog to Flemington—weather scarcely less dull, Wilentz could not help feeling, than the recital that had been imposed on him. He had traced the custody of the ladder as quickly as he could; even so he sensed that he had lost the jury's interest. But he had thought of one move he could make without actually departing from that prescribed path that might be just the thing to win back his audience.

He called Amandus Hochmuth.

Mr. Hochmuth had been waiting with bright anticipation for his turn on stage, and it had pleased him to reflect that although the defense attorneys knew that he was there as a witness waiting to be summoned by the State, they couldn't know exactly what he would have to say. He got up and started toward the witness stand. Someone offered him a hand but he declined it. He was eighty-seven, small and frail, and his years rested heavily on his thick gray hair, but he had trimmed his beard and pointed up his mustache for his day in court and he meant to manage by himself. He climbed to the chair and sat down and smiled, not without triumph. His body shook a little and his head wavered and his hands—he was annoyed to discover—were trembling, so he folded them and put them securely in his lap. Then he straightened his shoulders with a touch of the discipline he had learned—ages ago, it seemed—in the Prussian army and awaited the Court's pleasure.

Wilentz's questions took him back to the day of the crime and the incident he had observed shortly before noon from his front porch while gazing at the juncture of the county highway and the lane to the Lindbergh place.

"I saw a car coming around the corner, pretty good speed," Mr. Hochmuth said in a firm, somewhat accented voice, "and I expected it to turn over in the ditch. And as the car was about twenty-five feet away from me, the man in there looked out of the window like this—"

He tried to imitate the driver's expression.

"—and he glared at me as if he saw a ghost."

"The man you saw," Wilentz asked, "is he in this room?"

"Yes."

"Where is he?"

"Alongside the trooper there." And old Amandus Hochmuth pointed his trembling finger at Richard Hauptmann.

The lights in the courtroom dimmed and flickered out.

The windows were little more than vague oblongs, painted gray by the fog, and the courtroom was plunged into half-darkness. The crowd whispered. Then someone laughed and said that the old man had done it with his talk of ghosts. A funereal voice that seemed to come from the group of defense lawyers—it could have been Reilly's—agreed that Amandus Hochmuth was responsible, but indirectly: a higher power had observed that he was lying and had blotted out the lights to prevent further false identification. Another voice, which quite possibly had its source in the prosecution, briskly disputed this view. Instead, the failing lights were an omen of things to come; prison lights dimmed during an electrocution.

The courtroom lights came on again. The old witness blinked. Reilly questioned the identification—at whom exactly had he pointed?

"Would you mind stepping down, please," Wilentz said to Mr. Hochmuth, "and showing us?"

The witness manipulated himself out of the chair and down from the stand, stood for a moment to get his breath, then slowly began to walk toward the man his shaky finger had indicated.

Richard and Anna Hauptmann watched him approach. Hauptmann had listened with a slight smile to the identification; now his sallow face was expressionless. Anna's skin was flushed, as it usually was in the courtroom's heat. She had been lucky today. No special seat was reserved for the prisoner's wife, but this morning she had contrived to get one quite close to Richard's regular chair; she could almost touch him.

Panting a little, Amandus Hochmuth came to the end of his journey. He craned his head forward and stared full at Hauptmann. Then he reached over and put one hand on the prisoner's knee.

He kept it there for a moment or two. Hauptmann slowly shook his head, again, again, again.

Mr. Hochmuth withdrew his hand. Hauptmann leaned over the trooper next to him and bent toward Anna and, smiling, spoke to her. *"Der Alte ist verrückt,"* he said.

Anna nodded. If Richard said the old one was crazy, he must be.

Accompanying Hochmuth back to the stand, Wilentz asked to have recorded that the witness had indicated Bruno Richard Hauptmann.

The echo of his words had barely died when, from the telegraph center in the courthouse garret, the news that the defendant had been positively identified, had been placed near the scene of the crime on the day of the crime, went out over the wires.

The prosecutor resumed and pressed gently toward the point which would connect Amandus Hochmuth's testimony to that of the preceding witnesses—possession of the kidnap ladder—in a way the defense had not bargained for.

Was there a ladder in the car?

Yes, the old man said, there was.

Reilly rose to the attack. He allowed no time for preliminaries, each question almost jostling the other:

Hadn't the witness seen Hauptmann's picture in the newspapers, and hadn't a State trooper pointed him out to the witness in court? Wasn't the witness' eyesight poor, his memory weak, his mind inclined to wander? Indeed, hadn't he once been an inmate of an asylum?

Wilentz cut in sharply; the witness was being badgered and not allowed to answer. Judge Trenchard intervened, and Amandus

Hochmuth spoke up; with a belligerence to match Reilly's, he denied everything the lawyer had said.

Reilly's manner softened. How would the witness describe the man in the car? How was he dressed?

Mr. Hochmuth wasn't sure. All that he really remembered was a red face and glaring eyes.

Reilly turned his ripe face toward the jury. A face redder than his?

The old man paused. Well, he ventured, it was very red.

Reilly watched the jurors' eyes move from his florid complexion to that of the prisoner. Richard Hauptmann's face had been described by reporters as pale, almost cadaverous; the police had called it sallow.

It definitely was not red.

Through a methodical succession of witnesses, David Wilentz had traced the custody of the ladder from Bornmann to Kelly to Captain John Lamb to Arthur Koehler; and now, with the wood technologist still on the stand, he again offered the ladder in evidence.

Again, defense counsel opposed it. Frederick Pope said they objected for the same reasons as before: the ladder had been altered since it had been found originally; moreover, the attorney general had failed to place it in the hands of every person who at one time or another had experimented with it. It had been taken here, there and everywhere and, until its course had been fully traced and the defense was given an opportunity to examine everyone who had handled the ladder, it was immaterial and irrelevant.

Pope finished scathingly: "There is absolutely no connection either by circumstance or by direct evidence between this ladder and the accused, this ladder is not evidential against the accused."

Satisfied, he sat down. Wilentz went toward the bench and spoke pleadingly. The ladder already had been connected to the scene of the crime and was evidential for that reason alone, but in addition its custody had been proved beyond reasonable doubt. And if the defense was upset because the ladder had not been related to the defendant, it was needlessly concerned. They had his promise for that. His voice rose:

"We will run it right into Hauptmann!"

Pope got up. The defense could not accept the attorney general's promise; as matters stood, the ladder was not admissible. Facing the bench squarely, he emphasized his concluding words: a man was on trial for his life and was entitled to the Court's protection.

Prosecution and defense waited for Judge Trenchard's ruling. He spoke with his customary conciseness:

"For the moment I will defer the admission of this ladder in evidence."

Arthur Koehler had remained on the stand as a silent witness of the discussion; now he stepped down, and Wilentz summoned Lieutenant John Sweeney to take his place. The prosecutor had set out to show that the ladder was the kidnaper's means of entry to the nursery and he was determined to accomplish it through the Newark police officer.

Shortly after the crime, had Lieutenant Sweeney and others placed the ladder against the east wall of the Lindbergh house? Yes, Sweeney said, they had. Placed the legs in the two indentations in the mud? Yes—they had fitted perfectly. And had they found that the top of the ladder rested within reach of the southeast corner window of the nursery? When the top section was removed, Sweeney specified, yes; the ladder rails had nestled some thirty inches below the window sill. And had they made a further discovery? Yes; in the masonry where the rails had come to rest there were two vertical scars or scrape marks in which were lodged small splinters of wood.

Wilentz paused a moment to underscore their significance; then: Had Lieutenant Sweeney climbed the ladder? No, he had not; it was broken and in no condition to use—but he had propped another ladder in a parallel position and climbed that. Wilentz repeated: A parallel position? Yes—the top rungs of both ladders on the same level. And had he then climbed through the window into the nursery? Yes. Any difficulty? None at all.

How had he got in?

"Put my left knee up on the window sill and then squirmed around and put my right foot in and stepped down on the floor."

And how much had the lieutenant weighed when he had climbed into the nursery with such ease?

"A hundred and seventy-five pounds," Sweeney said.

Wilentz let his glance rest on Hauptmann. Even now, his wiry, muscular body appeared to be close to the same weight.

The prosecutor relinquished Sweeney to the defense. Reilly advanced with an air of pleasant anticipation. He was back on familiar ground—another police witness.

When Charles Lindbergh, Jr., had been put to bed, he pointed out, the southeast corner window of the nursery had been closed and its shutters drawn together as tightly as their warped condition would allow. After the child was stolen, the window was found closed as before and the shutters only partly open. In the course of Officer Sweeney's experiments, had he drawn back the shutters?

Sweeney considered. Well, no.

Raised the window? No. Closed the window? No. Pushed the shutters together? No.

In short, he had climbed in and out of the nursery while the shutters were thrust wide apart and the window flung wide open?

Yes.

Reilly's expressive brows rose with slow astonishment.

He moved on. Officer Sweeney had said that the tips of the ladder rails rested some thirty inches below the window sill, had he not? Yes. And the top rung of the ladder was several inches below the tips? Yes. Well, standing on the top rung with his hands in the air, how had he kept his balance?

The witness explained that he had reached up and grabbed hold of the window casing.

Reilly savored this. And climbing out of the nursery—feet first? Yes. What had Sweeney done with his arms?

The lieutenant replied that with one he had held on to the casing, with the other to the sill.

"Both arms were busy?"

"Yes, sir."

"And then you would lower yourself thirty inches until you felt the grip of the ladder?"

"Yes, sir."

"And reach down to get a purchase—to balance?"

"Yes."

Reilly paused in wonderment. Officer Sweeney could do all this while at the same time *carrying a bundle in his arms?*

A bundle?

Why, yes—a bundle to simulate the stolen child.

The witness flushed and said with some confusion that he hadn't experimented with a bundle.

Oh. So he *hadn't* carried a bundle while climbing out of the nursery?

No.

Reilly nodded and sat down.

Wilentz rushed forward into the breach. *Could* the witness have carried a bundle made up to resemble the baby while climbing from the nursery?

Sweeney gratefully responded to the opening: Yes. Yes, of course he could.

And *could* he have carried both the bundle and the ladder for some seventy feet after he reached the ground?

The lieutenant settled back comfortably. Certainly! It wouldn't have been difficult at all.

Reilly was up again. But he *hadn't* carried a bundle when he climbed out of the nursery, had he? No. And he *hadn't* carried the double load for seventy feet? No. In other words, he was merely speculating as to what he *might* have accomplished *if* he had conducted his experiment properly?

Sweeney capitulated. Yes.

Wilentz made no effort to conceal his anger. He flung a final question at the witness:

"*You* didn't take the Lindbergh child out of the window, did you?"

10

The attorney general suggested to the others at the prosecution's table that it was time to thrust at the heart of the case, at Hauptmann himself. They agreed. The extortion phase of the crime offered several openings. Wilentz chose to deal the first blow through John Joseph Perrone, the Bronx cab driver.

A small, husky man, black hair carefully smoothed down, Perrone wiped his glasses and stared earnestly at the prosecutor. Wilentz led him straight to the point: eleven days after the Lindbergh kidnaping a man had stopped his cab in the Bronx and given him an envelope—a ransom note, it turned out later—to deliver to Dr. Condon.

"Who is the man who gave you that envelope?"

"Bruno Richard Hauptmann."

"Is he in the room?"

"Yes, sir."

"Come down and point him out, please."

Perrone had picked the defendant from a police line-up on the day after his arrest and now he walked over to him confidently and put his hand on Hauptmann's shoulder.

"This is the man."

Hauptmann said calmly, "You're a liar."

Only those close to him heard his quiet voice. Reilly was one. He wanted the defendant's words placed in the record as his answer to the accusation. Judge Trenchard said he hadn't heard an answer, nor had the court stenographer, and he was inclined to let the record stand for the present—later, if Reilly insisted, witnesses might be asked to clear up the point.

Resuming, Wilentz underlined the accused's suspicious behavior while arranging with Perrone to deliver the envelope and then sought to enmesh Hauptmann in a web of his own making—the spot where the transaction took place, the cab driver testified, was about two miles from Woodlawn Cemetery, six miles from St. Raymond's, one mile from Dr. Condon's home and three miles from Hauptmann's apartment.

Repeated objections by the defense had made Perrone nervous; having achieved this, Reilly went at him in cross-examination with a bullwhip. But the witness regained his professional composure and hung on stubbornly. He had stopped his cab under an arc light and had got a good look at the other, could even recall his clothes—a soft brown hat with a beveled, upturned brim and a double-breasted brown coat.

Since he recalled so much, Reilly said, did he also recall the man's hands? He hadn't noticed them, Perrone answered. Hadn't noticed when the man passed over the envelope whether his hands were bare or gloved? No.

Reilly demanded in a trumpeting voice if this was what the witness had been instructed to say. Was someone afraid that if he admitted the man was bare-handed it would have to be admitted too that there were fingerprints on the envelope?—obviously not Hauptmann's, or the prosecution would have made a great show of it! Hadn't the witness been told to forget what he'd noticed about the hands?

"No, sir," John Joseph Perrone said with cab-driver stolidity. "Nobody said anything to me."

It was the best Reilly could do; he sat down.

Wilentz began to set the stage for the entrance of a star witness, the Bronx's most famous citizen, Dr. John F. Condon. Milton Gaglio and Max Rosenhain testified to the parts they had played in the old teacher's efforts to help the Lindberghs. Wilentz was pleased with their performance in the witness chair; Reilly was not. He was still casting doubt on the validity and pertinence of their roles as the afternoon drew to a close.

Once more the jurors prepared themselves for the turbulent crossing through the waiting crowd to their hotel. Prosecution and defense retired, the former to mull over the hazards and—they hoped—the rewards of the coming day, Reilly to hold another of his affable after-court press conferences, which he had invited since the trial's beginning. He liked to favor his friends of the press and expansively answered their questions.

Richard Hauptmann paced his cell in the county jail next door. After so many hours of listening to so much talk, he wished to talk himself. The words welled up in him and he was thirsty for answering words. A dozen times he strove to get his guards to talk with him. Under the permanent glare of the prison lights, their faces—friendly? hostile? he could not tell, they were so carefully impassive—merely stared back at him. Machines, not men. But of course that wasn't true. He knew they were forbidden to speak. If only Anna were here—his Anni, his Bubi. But no, he wouldn't want Bubi to see him in a prison cell.

The guards changed shift through the night and watched the prisoner walk back and forth, back and forth. Often he would shove a cigarette into his mouth and lean forward against the door, his hands gripping the bars. The guards would light the endless cigarettes for him.

Wednesday January 9; foggy, drizzly.

Cold and damp despite coats and blankets, miserable but hopeful, a couple of hundred people had kept vigil around the courthouse throughout the night. By dawn there were a thousand waiting to get in to hear the testimony that, they told one another, might decide the whole case, might put Hauptmann in the chair. Jafsie was going to talk. Jafsie was going to tell all! "I come here clear from California!" a woman's voice sang out proudly. "Clear across the country to see Jafsie on that stand!"

The crowd grew steadily. Finally the doors opened and the guarding troopers stepped aside and the proud Californian and the others changed from friends to sudden enemies in the fight to enter. A few more than six hundred managed to jam into the sweltering courtroom.

Wilentz and his aides were awaiting Dr. Condon's appearance with a mixture of confidence and apprehension. Some of them had come to believe, through knowing him, that he was unpredictable, as downright eccentric as they had heard. Certainly he was too long-winded for his own good or anyway for theirs; loquacity was always a dangerous quality in a witness. For the past two and a half years he had talked freely and given the press so many different stories—some, perhaps, in the happy conviction that he was merely playing with the reporters' innocent susceptibilities—that counsel for the State could not really feel sure just what his testimony would be. There *should* be no difficulty when he was asked to identify the man he had known as John, but who could tell? The first time he had been brought face to face with Hauptmann, Dr. Condon had refused "to declare an identification"; the second time he had stated that Hauptmann and John were one and the same. Would he follow through on the stand or go back to his original enigmatic attitude?

The attorney general was very much aware of these uncertainties but believed that the most vulnerable part of Dr. Condon's record in the Lindbergh case was that he had asked to get into it. The public, and therefore probably the jurors, still seemed skeptical about his motives in volunteering for the presumably risky job of negotiator. *Was* it risky? It certainly wasn't, if the role had been arranged in advance! Of course that was nonsense, Wilentz thought—Dr. Condon's true and only motive lay in his staunch, God-fearing, patriotic, sentimental heart—but jurors weren't immune to nonsense. And Ed Reilly would work on that question of motives. He would work on Dr. Condon all over! It was possible to think (Wilentz preferred not to) that Dr. Condon was simply made to order for Big Ed.

One more bit of stage dressing was necessary. Wilentz attended to it by calling Alfred Reich, Dr. Condon's friend and good companion. Al briefly told the modest assistance he had rendered. His days with Dr. Condon had not bred in him an equivalent garrulity, Wilentz reflected. He thanked Al and pronounced the long-awaited name.

The old man rose and took the stand. The courtroom was silent. Every eye was on him.

The years since the kidnaping had dealt kindly with Dr. Condon; his better-than-six-foot frame was as sturdy as it had been on that long-ago night when, outraged by the news, he had offered his savings and his services through the medium of his favorite newspaper. He had dressed in seemly black for this, his first time in a witness chair. Mrs. Condon had tucked a crisp white handkerchief in the breast pocket. The old-fashioned watchchain hanging across his vest looked as solid and dependable as he.

He sat back comfortably in the chair and crossed his legs and gently wagged one of his high black shoes.

Wilentz placed a glass of water on the judge's bench, inches away from Dr. Condon's hand. Dr. Condon thanked him.

The attorney general led the witness into the prelude to his testimony. It was a difficult journey from the start. Asked where he lived, Dr. Condon responded lyrically, "In the most beautiful borough in the world, the Bronx." Lloyd Fisher of the defense sprang to his feet, citing the witness' answer as an opinion and demanding that it be stricken from the record—in his opinion, *Flemington* was the most beautiful place in the world.

Undoubtedly there was merit in both views, Judge Trenchard observed. Could they please proceed?

Wilentz desired nothing more but, as he feared, the going scarcely improved. Dr. Condon's recitation of his college degrees seemed to last forever and the prosecutor was forced to interrupt; he was fully satisfied, he said, that Dr. Condon was privileged to be called *Doctor.* He turned to the manner in which the witness had made a living and Dr. Condon set out on the story of his life.

Again Wilentz intervened. "You have been a teacher, haven't you?" he prompted.

The old man seemed hurt. "Not all the time. I was compelled——" He hesitated and inspected Wilentz's face, on which the prosecutor was endeavoring to preserve a pleased, interested expression. Dr. Condon was not deceived. He wished to let the young man know that he knew he thought the old man was talking too much, and so he raised his hand and put it over his mouth and asked in the piping tone of a kindergarten scholar:

"Did I make a mistake?"

"No, no," Wilentz said heartily.

Dr. Condon picked up the thread of his narrative. His father had had eight children and it had been a struggle to support the family. As a youth, with his sights set on a teaching career—indeed, seven of the eight young Condons had become teachers—he had realized the magnitude of the load on his father's shoulders and had determined to ease it. It was not so much that he had been *compelled* to help as that he had wished to help, or had thought it his duty to help, and therefore he had gone to work, while studying for his chosen profession, in order to contribute to the family budget.

In full possession of these facts, Wilentz moved abruptly to the evening of April 2, 1932, framing his questions in such a manner that Dr. Condon was confined to simple answers.

At about eight o'clock that evening the witness had set out in an automobile with Colonel Lindbergh?

Yes.

And where had they gone?

Wilentz regretted the question the instant he put it—he had slipped; it was too loosely phrased. Dr. Condon at once embarked on a description of the incomparable Bronx; risking his displeasure, the prosecutor asked if they could please just have the name of his and the Colonel's destination. A look of petulance came into the old man's face but cleared up as Wilentz artfully drew him on.

They had gone to Bergen's flower shop, Dr. Condon said, and there found a note directing them across the street to St. Raymond's Cemetery, and inside the cemetery he had met the man called John and had handed over a wooden box containing fifty thousand dollars in ransom money.

Wilentz emphasized the point. "Who did you give that money to?"

"John."

The prosecutor let the answer stand for a moment, then almost casually inquired, "Who is John?"

On edge, he waited for the answer. Would it be unmistakably clear or enigmatic?

Dr. Condon said in a ringing voice, separating each syllable of the name:

"John is Bru–no Rich–ard Haupt–mann!"

Frowning, he stared at the accused. Hauptmann stared back unwaveringly. Then, very slightly, he shook his head. Charles Lindbergh leaned forward, watching Dr. Condon.

Jabbering voices from the crowd broke the courtroom's hush, and Judge Trenchard rapped for order. In the attic, the telegraph wires were alive with news for the evening's headlines: JAFSIE IDENTIFIES HAUPTMANN.

Wilentz said, "Now let's go back to the beginning," and firmly and carefully led the witness over the strange path he had traveled as the third man, the intermediary between Lindbergh and the accused kidnaper-killer, John-Hauptmann, Hauptmann-John. Again and again Dr. Condon declared that the two were one, and he enriched his statements with gestures and more than a little acting, now portraying his own role and now John's, showing how they had done this and how they had done that, imitating John's accent. He paused after an exceptionally dramatic exchange between his own voice and John's and said he wished to apologize to the court for being a poor mimic.

Nearly three hours had passed. There was little else to be gained from the old man, Wilentz thought; in a moment it would be time to yield him to Reilly's hip-shooting cross-examination. He rapidly assessed the testimony, probing for weaknesses.

On the whole it had come off extremely well; Dr. Condon's mind was surprisingly alert and he had told his story clearly and convincingly if not concisely. To the most worrisome question—his peculiar interest in the case—he had given a plain, affecting answer without the point's having been raised. He had said to John "I promised Colonel Lindbergh and Mrs. Lindbergh to help get their baby. That is what I am out for—nothing else," and John had told him not to worry, before long he would be given the little boy—"You can put the baby's arms around Mrs. Lindbergh's neck."

Dr. Condon had paused in his testimony and, as if still unable to fathom the mind that had produced those words, looked long and searchingly at the prisoner. "And I believed it," he said bitterly.

But if the old man's motive was unimpeachable, if he was so

anxious to help the Lindberghs, why had he made no effort to capture John?

It had not been necessary to ask the question; Dr. Condon had answered as if he were able to read Wilentz's mind:

"I did not go to catch him. I wanted the baby."

The identification of Hauptmann was of course the one point of vital significance; it had to be absolutely solid, with no loopholes through which the defense could escape. Despite Dr. Condon's eloquent performance, it wasn't quite foolproof. Or rather, Wilentz thought, Reilly-proof! Doing his utmost to make it so, he asked the witness if he had been questioned by the police after the baby was found dead. He had, Dr. Condon replied. And had he given the police a description of John? Yes, he had.

How had he described John at that time?

Again Dr. Condon sketched the portrait he had drawn so often: the muddy blond hair and deep-set eyes, the high cheekbones, small mouth and pointed chin, the pale complexion, the heavy accent—he hadn't been sure at that time whether it was German or Scandinavian. He filled in the figure beneath the well-remembered face—in boxing circles, he said, John would be called a middleweight: wiry, muscular. He wished to leave no doubt of his ability to estimate height and weight: "I have trained about ten thousand athletes in my life and they couldn't deceive me about those inner muscles."

The jurors' eyes turned to Hauptmann. The description fitted exactly.

Wilentz moved to cap it.

The description the witness had just given was the same description he had given the police?

Yes.

And he had given the police this description long before Bruno Richard Hauptmann was arrested?

Oh, yes; more than two years before.

Wilentz thanked the witness, and meant it. Dr. Condon courteously inclined his head. He glanced at the courtroom, an audience he was supremely aware of. They were all staring at him. He could sense their excitement. Well, he was ready for the coming battle, and he looked over at the defense chief's burly figure as with elaborate leisure Reilly got to his feet.

He approached the witness stand with a friendly smile. Dr. Condon's knowledge of the sporting world must be vast and authoritative, he remarked. Dr. Condon accepted the tribute with a smile no less friendly, and like two good friends they chatted about athletes' training and the weight classifications for the boxing ring. Reilly confessed that he was not too clear about the Marquis of Queensberry rules, which he understood governed the manly art. Dr. Condon's smile broadened as he explained their niceties. Reilly thanked him for his lucid instruction and inquired, as one would ask an oracle:

"What am I—a heavyweight?"

Dr. Condon considered. "You a heavyweight? May I look?" He stepped down and felt Reilly's arm muscles. "This doesn't hurt you, does it?" he asked solicitously.

"No, not a particle."

Dr. Condon nodded and resumed the stand. "Undoubtedly a heavyweight," he announced.

Laughter in court.

Reilly easily mastered it. "And I take it you yourself are a heavyweight?"

"Yes."

Reilly's smile changed. "So," he said with a thin edge of sarcasm, "we start even."

Dr. Condon's smile changed too. "Right," he replied with an edge of sarcasm of his own. "That is, physically."

A gale of laughter. Reilly was not pleased. The Doctor's poise was admirable, he said; he must have studied acting.

No, Dr. Condon said, he hadn't—but he'd taught it.

Had he taught theosophy too?

The question was put quickly, but Dr. Condon was not taken off balance. No, he had never taught theosophy.

Reilly pressed ahead. But he was familiar with signs, he'd had experience with signs?

No, not really. He might have picked up some incidental knowledge of them while preparing lectures——

He'd read books on symbols?

No, never——

"You are not the John Condon who signed—in the Public Library of New York, two weeks before the kidnaping—for the German Koch's *Book of Signs*?"

Dr. Condon began, "I never took——" but Wilentz swiftly interceded. "Just a minute, please, Doctor." He addressed the bench: the question was improper; there was no evidence that any such thing had occurred.

Reilly objected in his turn. Wilentz listened with rising temper; he had no wish to go into it but he was as familiar as defense counsel with the reason for the question. Walter Winchell had written that shortly before the kidnaping a person who became prominently involved in the case had gone to the New York Public Library and borrowed a book by a German, Rudolf Koch, on theosophical symbols. But Reilly must know by now as well as Wilentz did that the signature on the library application slip wasn't Dr. Condon's but that of a Philadelphia art student, John Cond*ax*; his use of the incident could only be explained as a deliberate attempt to prejudice the jury against the witness.

Glancing at the old man, Wilentz saw that he was impatient to deal with the question himself. Perhaps that would be better, after all. The attorney general withdrew his objection.

Dr. Condon said emphatically that never in his life had he applied for a book at the New York Public Library—on theosophy or any other subject.

Reilly lifted his expressive brows. Dr. Condon lifted his, too.

Well, Reilly said heavily, they'd see about that at the proper time, when they produced the library slip.

He moved on. Since the summer of 1932, when the police had taken full charge of the Lindbergh case, Dr. Condon had become more or less a gentleman of leisure——

The witness bridled. He'd never had a day's leisure in his life.

But he *was* retired—and he'd traveled around the country a good deal, hadn't he? In fact, hadn't he returned only two days ago from a motor trip to Massachusetts?

Dr. Condon dissented again. It was not a motor trip but a mission. He had lectured in the town of Rockland.

Motor trip or mission, did the witness remember being in a town called Taunton?

Dr. Condon said he did.

"Did you have a conversation with the druggist?"

"Yes."

"And did you tell him that you had not yet discovered John?"

"No, sir!"

Reilly continued as if he had not heard. "And didn't you say to the druggist, 'They haven't caught John yet—I'd give ten thousand dollars to find him'?"

"Are you finished?" Dr. Condon inquired with a pitying smile.

Reilly nodded. Dr. Condon boomed out:

"No such thing!"

More laughter. Reilly spoke over it. "You're enjoying your day in the sun, aren't you, Doctor? Your first day in court, testifying—you're enjoying it?"

The crowd giggled. Dr. Condon quenched that. "No, sir," he said reprovingly, slowly shaking his head. "I feel sad."

Reilly's voice filled with scorn. Sad? Why, for weeks Dr. Condon had been looking forward to this day, boasting to news reporters of what he would say on the witness stand, what he would do to the cross-examiner——

The witness did not agree. The reporters hadn't told the truth; everywhere he had gone they had questioned him and tried to trap him and ridicule him—but, he added with scorn to match Reilly's, they hadn't succeeded.

Had the druggist in Taunton tried to trap him, ridicule him?

No.

Oh, he hadn't! And what was the druggist's name—Donegan?

Yes.

Wilentz was armed and ready for this. New York newspapers had made much of a rumor that the Taunton druggist had given defense counsel an affidavit declaring that Dr. Condon had told him John was not Hauptmann. There wasn't a word of truth in it, as Reilly knew; he had returned to his earlier device of using hearsay to reflect on the old man's credibility.

Rising and facing the bench, Wilentz waved an envelope and said he had here a letter which he would like to exhibit to the defense counsel; it might help him in his examination. Reilly answered hotly that he stood in no need of assistance from the attorney general; but Wilentz, undeterred, continued:

"If your Honor please, I present to the Court an unsolicited letter from Mr. Donegan."

"Now I object to this!" Reilly shouted. "If it keeps on, I will make a motion for the withdrawal of a juror!"

Wilentz bowed sardonically. "I will withdraw the offer."

If this was a victory, Reilly did not seem to think so; never before had he looked so genuinely angry. He forged on. Two weeks ago hadn't Dr. Condon told a waiter in a Manhattan restaurant that Hauptmann was not John?

No, he had not.

And in Miami, Florida, hadn't he told reporters that Hauptmann was not John?

No.

And he had never once told *any* newspaperman or waiter or druggist that Hauptmann *was* John—had he?

Dr. Condon replied firmly that he had never discussed the connection in public, had neither affirmed nor denied it. "I make a distinction between 'identification' and 'declaration of identification,' " he explained.

"I am to understand that you split hairs in words?" Reilly asked.

A better mimic than he had professed to be, Dr. Condon refrained from matching his opponent's mocking tone. "No hairs at all," he said gravely. "A man's life is at stake and I want to be honest."

"In the Greenwich Street police station you said it was not the man——"

"No, sir, I did not."

"You never said it *was* the man!"

"I never said it was or was not."

"Because you are not sure?"

"Because I made the distinction between declaration and identification. Identification meant what I knew mentally; the declaration meant what I said to others."

"You were brought there for the purpose of identifying Hauptmann?"

"I was, yes."

"And you didn't identify him, did you?"

Dr. Condon frowned at Reilly and spoke as if he were addressing an impudent pupil. "I take exception to your language. When you divide the identification and declaration, you make it appear as though I were dishonest, and I am not. I won't——" But this was not a schoolroom; he was not the supreme authority here; and, suddenly realizing his position, Dr. Condon paused and sought advice from the man who was. He turned to the bench and asked, "Is that too severe, Judge?"

Judge Trenchard could take appeals from opposing counsel in his stride; this was a new experience. It visibly surprised him. He cleared his throat. "No," he said.

Dr. Condon resumed the lecture. "I want you to know, Counselor, that identification is purely a mental process after the senses have distinguished; declaration is when I tell it to others."

Reilly did not propose to linger in the unwanted role of schoolboy; he set out to do some teaching himself. Whether Dr. Condon realized it or not, he said severely, he was talking to plain people! —and he gestured to the jury. To plain people, identification meant only one thing: picking out a person.

He bore in. Until today, Dr. Condon had never picked out the defendant in a court of law, had he? No, the witness admitted. Not even when the defendant was on trial for extradition? No. In fact, the Doctor had not even testified at the extradition trial, had he? No. The State hadn't asked him to, had it?

Dr. Condon was silent. Reilly became derisive. "You—with the secret locked in your heart—you were not called, were you?"

"No."

And this was after he saw Bruno Richard Hauptmann in the police station?

The old man confirmed it.

Reilly spread his hands and looked at the jury as if to ask, Is it necessary to go on? Isn't it plain that the prosecution didn't call Dr. Condon at the extradition trial because he wasn't at all sure that Hauptmann *was* John?

The defense chief changed his flexible voice to go with a new line of attack. He became quite pleasant. Dr. Condon became quite pleasant too. He had determined to help the Lindberghs get their baby back by March 7, six days after the child was stolen, the Doctor said. And then he had sent a letter to the little Bronx *News*?

The adjective disturbed Dr. Condon. Little? The Bronx *Home News*? With a circulation of a hundred and fifty thousand and more?

"I resent that!"

Whether the witness resented it or not, he knew of the Associated Press, didn't he? And the United Press? And other press agencies? And the fact that they reached every city and hamlet in the world?

Yes, Dr. Condon replied, he knew all of this.

"Then why did you pick a local Bronx paper with a circulation of a hundred and fifty thousand, with all of New York's six million people, to insert your ad?"

Dr. Condon said with remembered indignation, "Because the New York papers all led toward one miserable fellow I thought was innocent—Arthur Johnson."

Wilentz wondered if this was a slip of the tongue or faulty memory; of course the old man meant Henry Johnson.

Reilly ignored the error. "Did you know Red Johnson?"

"I did not."

"Why should you, a Doctor of Philosophy, a professor at Fordham, decide that you would protect Red Johnson, a sailor on a yacht, unless you knew him?"

Dr. Condon leaned forward, his hands clenching the chair arms. "I'll tell you why: Because I always hated to see an underdog and always gave him a chance throughout my life, and I had heard that Arthur Johnson had nothing to do with it—from many people."

"What people?"

Sailors, Dr. Condon retorted, and yacht repairers in the shipyards on City Island. He had questioned many of them, and all agreed that Johnson was not the kind of fellow to turn kidnaper.

"How would they know this inconspicuous Danish deck hand?"

"I don't know that he is Danish," Dr. Condon said, measuring the words carefully. "I didn't know that he was inconspicuous, judging from his treatment."

Laughter; applause. Judge Trenchard did not seem to mind. But Reilly did. Had the Doctor's *well-informed* City Island friends also told him that Red Johnson had telephoned Betty Gow at Hopewell at half past eight on the night of the crime?

"I knew that the night of the kidnaping."

Apparently he didn't understand the significance of his reply. Wilentz and his aides were taken aback. Reilly leaped at the opening. He had contended from the start that Dr. Condon either was involved in the kidnaping or had guilty knowledge of it; here was a chance to show it.

"How did you know that if you were not in contact with Red Johnson?"

"Why," Dr. Condon said, confused, "I knew it because it was spread around——"

"The night of the kidnaping?" Reilly boomed.

Dr. Condon lifted his finger to remonstrate, saying, "Now, your English again——" but the defense chief refused to let him finish.

"You said you knew that the night of the kidnaping!"

"That it *occurred* the night of the kidnaping."

"You said you *knew it* the night of the kidnaping!"

A look of surprise came into the old man's face. "Did I say that?"

"Yes, you did."

Dr. Condon was perplexed. But, he said, he did not know, he had never seen, Red Johnson—— He broke off, bowing his head apologetically. He meant to say, Mr. Arthur Johnson.

Reilly had had an earlier lesson in etiquette on this score; it did not seem to have helped him. "Are you in the habit of calling deck hands 'Mr. Arthur Johnson' with a bow?"

Dr. Condon said grandly, "I am. This was my father's teaching. I never heard of a man who shouldn't be called *Mister* in the United States. We have no lords or dukes or earls here."

The prosecution relaxed. Reilly had bungled his chance to discredit the witness, had not only permitted him to get out of an awkward hole but to emerge as the victor.

So the Doctor had decided that because the newspapers were accusing someone he didn't know of the kidnaping, a deck hand on the Lamont yacht—Red Johnson—he ought to go to his assistance, and he had sent a letter to the Bronx *News*——

Dr. Condon corrected him with some asperity: Bronx *Home News;* and Arthur Johnson was not his chief reason for writing the letter.

Reilly accepted the reproof with a mock bow. In any case, the Doctor hadn't bothered with the big metropolitan dailies, had he?

No, he hadn't, the witness agreed with a mock bow.

No! Because he knew when he wrote the letter that the kidnap gang was waiting for its appearance in the Bronx paper——

He knew nothing of the kind, Dr. Condon cut in.

"Within twenty-four hours after it was published in that little paper a letter came to you, did it not?"

"Yes."

A reply from the kidnapers?

Dr. Condon nodded. Yes.

Reilly left it at that, confident that only one conclusion could be drawn. Displaying the two notes the witness had received in answer to his published offer—one addressed to him, the other to Lindbergh—the lawyer drew the old man through the events that followed.

Dusk clotted the courtroom windows. Judge Trenchard ruled the session closed.

Dr. Condon looked fresh and vigorous the next morning and neat as a pin; Reilly's lapel carnation was from the same excellent stock. After a bit of sparring between the two heavyweights, the witness got into the body of his story, recounting the two meetings with John and the search for the boat *Nelly*. He was prone to use several words where a couple would do and now and then contradicted himself (but never seriously, Wilentz was glad to note); and he alertly perceived and avoided the traps Reilly placed in his path.

The defense attorney struck off on a new line. Had Dr. Condon ever discussed the kidnaping with his City Island neighbors?

Yes, many times.

On April 10, 1932, had he told them that he believed the baby had been carried off by a gang?

He couldn't remember.

Had he said that a woman was involved?

Wilentz objected to the line of questioning and was sustained. Reilly changed his tack. Just a month ago, in a Manhattan restaurant, had the Doctor talked to Marcus Griffith of the New York *Inquirer*?

Yes.

And had he told the reporter that the baby's body was brought *back* to the spot where it was found buried—that he knew this to be a fact?

Dr. Condon reflected. He didn't remember having said that, he ventured at last.

"You won't say you didn't say it?"

"I won't say I didn't."

After studying the defendant in the police line-up, hadn't the witness been so uncertain that Hauptmann was John that he had asked for photos of the accused in order to study him further?

Dr. Condon said he had made no such request.

Reilly sauntered a few steps away from the witness stand, and David Wilentz leaned forward; he was beginning to think that the defense chief was at his most dangerous—at any rate his most unexpected—when he took the trouble to seem indifferent. At this moment Reilly looked like someone's prosperous uncle with nothing more on his mind than an excellent lunch. What was he plotting? The prosecution had heard several rumors, one of them quite nasty. Was it about to materialize?

In a dreamy voice, Reilly asked the witness if he had ever been associated with Public School 35 in Manhattan.

Indeed he had, Dr. Condon replied proudly; he had been the principal.

And when he had left it, back in 1902, where had he gone?

He had been transferred to Public School 97.

Reilly strode back to the witness stand. His voice was suddenly very much alive:

"By whose request were you transferred?"

Dr. Condon seemed surprised by the question and took a few moments to reply. "By my own."

Not in the least avuncular, Reilly shoved his face close and demanded, "Weren't you transferred not at your request but at the request of teachers in the school?"

"No, sir!"

"Weren't you transferred to another school because of conduct——"

Here was the rumor, all right, in ugly fact. Wilentz jumped up, charging that the witness was being assassinated by inference, but Reilly's voice roared over his:

"——conduct unbecoming a gentleman with a woman teacher?"

"No!" Dr. Condon shouted.

They glared at each other. Wilentz was at the bench. He objected to the character of defense counsel's cross-examination, he said angrily, not only with respect to the present witness but past and future witnesses as well.

Reilly left Dr. Condon and insisted that the prosecutor's remarks be stricken from the record. Judge Trenchard declined to order it, and then, as Reilly was silent, asked if the defense was going to continue.

No, Reilly said. He sat down.

Wilentz considered that Reilly had scuttled his own rumor, but he wanted to tidy up a few loose ends. He waited for Dr. Condon to calm down. The inference had been drawn that he knew when and how the Lindbergh baby was placed in its grave—but wasn't it a fact that he had no knowledge whatever of the burial? Yes, it was, the old man answered; even now he knew nothing about it. And the matter of the phone call Henry Johnson had made to Betty Gow on the night of the crime: the Doctor had told defense counsel that he knew of the incident the same evening—was this correct? No, of course not, the witness replied firmly; he hadn't known of the call until several days after the kidnaping, when he'd read about it in the papers.

The attorney general retired to the prosecution table. Reilly got up. Had Dr. Condon ever had trouble in his lectures expressing himself in English? The reply came as expected, while Reilly's brows arched whimsically: No! Then it was amazing, was it not, that with his mastery of the language the Doctor in one breath had made a positive statement about the phone call and in another had denied it?

Dr. Condon refused to take the bait. He had been mistaken, he said sincerely; he was sorry.

The frank admission of human fallibility drew a complimentary murmur from the crowd. Looking annoyed, Reilly went to the defense table; apparently he had helped the witness rather than hurt him. He returned with a photograph and displayed it to Dr. Condon. Was he familiar with the man in the picture?

Dr. Condon studied it. No, he said at last, but he had taught forty thousand persons and he might have seen him.

Had he seen him after handing over the ransom money?

No, not that he recalled.

Would he say positively that the man in the photo had not called on him several times after the ransom had been paid?

Dr. Condon replied stiffly that until he was informed when and where the meetings took place and what was said at them, he would say nothing in any manner of voice.

Reilly gave the photo to a clerk to be marked for identification: it was a picture of Isidor Fisch.

Dr. Condon was ready and waiting for a new assault. Reilly announced that he would trouble the witness no further.

It seemed to Wilentz that the old man was disappointed.

"Is that all?"

"That is all, sir," the attorney general said gratefully, smiling.

Dr. Condon stepped down. He had sat in the witness chair for nearly five hours and felt, he had to admit, a wee bit tired; but as Wilentz called the next witness he forgot his weariness and, a spectator again, watched and listened alertly. The next witness was Colonel Henry Breckinridge, a man of impeccable reputation who had it in his power to set to rest once and for all the old doubts concerning John F. Condon's true motives in entering the Lindbergh case.

In answer to Wilentz's lead, inviting corroborating testimony, Breckinridge described his part in the case as Charles Lindbergh's friend and legal adviser. He had practically lived with Dr. Condon from the time they first met until it became tragically clear that their efforts had been useless. Dr. Condon had done nothing during those weeks without his knowledge and consent.

The prosecutor wished to pin this down in detail. Had Colonel Breckinridge ever discussed with Dr. Condon the question of whether or not the ransom money should be paid?

Yes, he had.

And had Dr. Condon ever suggested that it *should* be paid?

He had not.

In fact, wasn't he *opposed* to handing over the money?

The witness replied that Dr. Condon wanted it to be a C.O.D. delivery, the cash in exchange for the child.

And he was overruled?

He was overruled.

Wilentz went further:

"Was there ever one cent paid to Dr. Condon for the time and effort and expense that he underwent in connection with his contacts with you?"

"No, sir."

Wilentz was satisfied. Breckinridge's concise answers, in keeping with his no-nonsense look of military efficiency, could not have failed to make an excellent impression, surely dissolving any skepticism left in the jurors' minds.

Reilly cross-examined. Wasn't it true that at the beginning of their association Colonel Breckinridge knew nothing about Dr. Condon and that privately he had questioned the Doctor's motives for writing to the kidnapers in the Bronx *News*? Indeed, hadn't the question so disturbed him that he had written two letters to Dr. Condon bearing counterfeit symbols in order to test his integrity?

The witness agreed with the first two points. The last he firmly denied.

Reilly drew him to the Condon home on the night of the ransom payment: the money was ready, waiting; Lindbergh, Breckinridge and the others present expected to receive instructions from the kidnapers at any moment. Then:

"The door bell rang. Dr. Condon disappeared from the room and in a short time re-entered with a note. Correct?"

No, the witness said. The Doctor's daughter, Myra, had accompanied him: the note was delivered in her presence.

Reilly bore in. Had he *seen* it delivered?

No.

Did he *know* who delivered it?

No.

Had the note-bearer ever been found?

No.

Had neither come forward of his—or her—own free will to help solve the case nor been apprehended?

No.

Had anything prevented Dr. Condon or the others in the group from taking the messenger prisoner?

Nothing.

Reilly shook his head as if in despair. "Colonel, as a member of the Bar of the State of New York, didn't you consider it your duty to apprehend any person who had any connection with this case?"

"Yes, sir."

"Why didn't you do it that night?"

Breckinridge said evenly, "Because I was serving what I thought was a superior duty—to recover the child alive."

"But you had the person who delivered the note—and you had the note——?"

"Yes, sir. But we didn't have the child."

A few minutes later Myra Condon Hacker was called to the stand and Reilly tried once more to extract aid and comfort for the defense. The "person" who had delivered the note to her father, Myra testified, was—as she had long ago reported to the police—a young man in his twenties, very slim and dark. She had never seen him again.

Reilly looked more cheerful and repeated the words as if he liked the taste of them. Young? Slim? Dark? Foreign, perhaps? He confidently produced the picture of Isidor Fisch. Wasn't this the man?

No, Myra said, it was not.

The old schoolteacher was content. A day of triumph! Vindicated at last!—all doubts and suspicions and ugly innuendoes finally laid to rest. Could any fair-minded man say *now* that John F. Condon had had a criminal hand in the kidnaping—or had profited by it?

As he came out of the courthouse a cheer burst from the waiting crowd and the State trooper escorting him whispered that the most important parts of the testimony had been passed on by spectators inside. Dr. Condon smiled and waved and shook hands with enthusiastic strangers, whose good wishes warmed his heart as he started the trip home to his beloved Bronx, jewel of boroughs.

11

The next day—Friday January 11, eighth day of the trial—court attendants unrolled five huge photostats and flattened them against a wall rack. The black oblong sheets were stroked and looped with wavering white lines, samples of the defendant's handwriting and the writing in the kidnap notes. The script was so greatly enlarged that it could be read from the press gallery. It looked to the jurors as if an awkward giant, painfully unsure of his spelling, had written it.

The fourteen original ransom notes, enclosed in cellophane, lay in a neat stack at Wilentz's elbow. It was his intention to place every one of them in Hauptmann's hands and prove that he was their author. The attorney general had introduced this crucial phase of the prosecution the previous afternoon. Following him, his associate counsel George Large had established through several police officers —Horn, Ritchie, Lieutenant Finn, Colonel Schwarzkopf—that during the long interrogation of Hauptmann after his arrest he had willingly agreed to submit to a handwriting test and that the police search for evidence had produced additional specimens of his penmanship: a promissory note, an insurance card, applications for auto licenses. The defense, in the person of Lloyd Fisher, had struck hard at the exhibits and done its best to bar them, but Judge Trenchard had admitted them in evidence.

Wilentz had questioned Treasury agent Frank Wilson in an effort to introduce the bundle of gold notes, amounting to $14,600, that had been found in Hauptmann's garage, but here Fisher's opposing argument had succeeded; unable to place the money in evidence, Wilentz had had to be content with submitting it for identification. He had managed, however, to use the witness for another blow at Hauptmann: Frank Wilson said that so far as he knew not a single ransom bill had turned up anywhere after the day the defendant was taken into police custody.

Lloyd Fisher had parried by calling Wilson's attention to a Treasury matter in which he had taken a personal interest. Wasn't it a fact that one J. J. Faulkner had deposited $2980 in Lindbergh gold certificates in the Federal Reserve Bank of New York?—that handwriting experts had reported the writing on the deposit slip wasn't by Hauptmann's hand?—and that the man who had deposited the money had never been apprehended? The witness had agreed. Actually, wasn't this Faulkner dead, Fisher had asked, a suicide? Hadn't he jumped from the tower of the Chrysler Building in Manhattan on the very day the newspapers announced Hauptmann's arrest? But here Wilson couldn't agree. Yes, the suicide had been identified as J. J. Faulkner, but careful investigation had proved that he wasn't the man who had deposited the gold notes in question.

The witness had left the chair and the huge photostats had been carried in, setting the stage for the State's handwriting experts.

An elderly gentleman slowly approached the stand. His snow-white hair and mustache emphasized his ruddy face; he was dressed in a dark suit and his shoulders were somewhat bowed. He climbed to the chair with the caution of age, adjusted his glasses and took out a tiny black microphone, which he held in readiness to amplify the State's questions for his failing hearing. He was Albert Osborn, who had written an impressive number of books on graphology and whose appearance in many earlier trials testified to his position as an authority in the field he had made his life work.

Reilly dourly regarded the old newcomer and was moved to comment for the edification of the defense staff, who vividly recalled their chief's jousts with another elderly gentleman, the robust champion of the Bronx, and his earlier exchange with an even more senior citizen, Amandus Hochmuth. "This isn't the trial of the century," he said out of the side of his mouth, "it's the trial of the centenarians."

This wasn't quite fair of Reilly. Mr. Osborn was only seventy-four.

Joseph Lanigan of the prosecution came forward to examine the witness. Albert Osborn's opinion of the writings in evidence was well known; he had stated it unequivocally during the trial to extradite Hauptmann from New York to New Jersey; nevertheless, Lanigan led him toward the familiar conclusions as if they were new, introducing the graphologist with emphasis on his excellent reputation. The evidence was purely circumstantial—no one had actually seen the defendant write the kidnap notes—and the most Osborn could do was declare what he believed and why. The jurors would subscribe to his views, Lanigan knew, only if they were confident of his authority.

The witness responded admirably in a loud, clear voice, and Lanigan gave him free rein. He said he had devoted a good deal of time before the defendant's arrest to the question of who had written the kidnap notes—had compared them with the handwriting-test specimens the police had taken from more than a hundred suspects. The similarities he had found were superficial.

Then, last September, Richard Hauptmann had provided the answer. As was customary, the police had dictated the test paragraph to him three times, changing the paper each time. All three of his written paragraphs showed differences in style, which indicated to a graphologist that the writer had been dishonest, had partly disguised his hand.

In doing so, he had seriously erred.

The disguise he had used—perhaps the only one he was accustomed to—was the same disguise he had employed throughout his writing of the ransom notes.

But when he had written in his natural hand, elsewhere in the test paragraphs, his style was identical with the script in his personal papers—the promissory note, insurance card and auto-license applications.

And so with one hand he had correctly identified himself as Richard Hauptmann and with the other unmasked himself as the author of the ransom notes.

Of course, Albert Osborn continued, style was only one of several ways in which he had exposed himself. The same peculiar spelling, the same oddly transposed letters, the same clues to the writer's German origin—in short, the same unique combination of characteristics appeared in all of the writings in evidence.

The old man stepped down from the chair and used a pointer to indicate, on the photo-enlargements, the matching characteristics in the scrawl of the ransom notes and the defendant's acknowledged script. Naturally, he said, the same distinctive traits threaded throughout the notes proved that the same person had composed them; still further evidence of this lay in the curious symbol, including the three holes, with which some were signed and the impatient references some notes made to statements in others.

Mr. Osborn was bound up in his demonstration but the jurors were growing restless and Lanigan saw Judge Trenchard glance at the courtroom clock. Wishing to underline the cardinal point before the week-end recess, the lawyer asked if it was Osborn's opinion that Richard Hauptmann had written all the ransom notes.

Yes.

And that of course included the original note left in the Lindbergh nursery?

Of course.

Lanigan thought the inference was obvious. If Hauptmann alone had engaged in the extortion, wasn't the note in the nursery his confession that he was the kidnaper too?

A stray lady dog had wandered into Flemington along with the thousands of more intelligent sightseers and, friendly and hungry, had attached herself to a member of the press. He had named his new friend Nellie, in honor of an earlier friend, and had taken her to the extra, emergency bar that had been set up in the Union Hotel to accommodate the rush of business. The new bar was a tremendous success with newspaper and radio reporters and visiting celebrities and sightseers but lacked a name. Nellie had settled that. After having been fed beyond her wildest dreams, she had been adopted as the mascot of Nellie's Tap Room.

It was jammed as usual this Friday evening and the sound of jovial discussions mingled with the street sounds and the voices of the radio commentators in the broadcasting station on the third floor—such famous radio figures as Gabriel Heatter and Boake Carter, men with fine resonant voices—and penetrated at last in a nightmare hubbub to the jurors' rooms above.

They did not sleep well. But the next day brought a welcome change. Constable Oden Baggstrom, who was in charge of the jury's guards, had suggested to Judge Trenchard that it would do them good to get away from their locked rooms for a spell. As it happened, the constable owned a bus, and he could take them for a nice turn around the country, of course avoiding any of the places named in the trial. The judge and counsel had agreed. But the weather was poor and the judge had said that the jurors must be sure to dress warmly and wear rubbers—if anyone didn't have rubbers, he would be glad to supply them. Mrs. Verna Snyder did not have rubbers. A guard went shopping and bought a pair of lady's rubbers and charged them to Judge Trenchard and came back and put them on Mrs. Snyder himself.

While the jurors were enjoying their spin, feeling like prisoners released from a rowdy jail, the State's prisoner was enjoying a respite from the tedium of his quiet jail. Sheriff John Curtiss, who was in charge, had given Anna Hauptmann permission to visit her husband for an hour on Saturday afternoon.

Anna had come from the Bronx. She was still living at Mrs. Opdyke's rooming house here in Flemington but the elderly lady had found the lively Bubi too much for her nerves. She couldn't even stand her own grandchildren, she had told Anna, when they were brought to see Grandma. Anna would have moved except that there wasn't an empty room to be found and she couldn't think of leaving Flemington, and so she had put Bubi in her niece Maria Mueller's care, as she had done once before, just after Richard's arrest. She would visit the little boy as often as she possibly could until the end of the trial, when of course they would all be together again—Richard, Anna and Bubi, the bad dream behind them. Richard drank in every word. Again and again she had to describe Bubi's latest antics. The prisoner laughed and smiled. The hour came to an end far too soon. They parted with loving reassurances. Bubi's father slept more comfortably that night.

Sunday was not too bad—for the jurors and State troopers, and for Sheriff Curtiss, who was resolved that the courthouse would not be subjected again to the indignities of the last week end and had ordered it closed to visitors. Radio and newspapers had announced his edict, and the bad weather aided him by keeping many people at home. Nellie's Tap Room was quiet. Nellie drowsed on a full stomach. The jurors napped.

Monday morning Joseph Lanigan resumed his examination of Mr. Osborn. Then Reilly had his chance; but the old graphologist held firm, admitting no possibility of error: the evidence that Richard Hauptmann wrote the ransom notes, he said patiently, was "irresistible, unanswerable and overwhelming."

Reilly retired, the witness stepped down, and Wilentz took over. He had planned to continue with other handwriting experts, but even now the jury's attention was wandering and here and there in the crowd spectators yawned and dozed.

The attorney general called Hildegarde Alexander to the stand.

The courtroom woke up. Reilly mentally revised his statement that this was the trial of the centenarians.

He was not indifferent to the charms of the female figure and Miss Alexander's was praiseworthy. She was young and blonde and tall. In her black cloth coat with wide mink collar and mink-trimmed hat to match she looked like a fashion model—which in fact she was, in the Manhattan garment district.

Confident of his audience's attention, Wilentz drew the pretty witness on. She lived in the Bronx and was acquainted with Dr. Condon, whom she had met back in 1923, when she was a high-school girl. She had had an afternoon job as cashier in a Bronx theater where Dr. Condon was an occasional patron, and the manager, well aware that he held stern views on companies that employed youngsters who should be in school, had introduced him to Hildegarde and explained that she went to high school in the morning.

One evening in March 1932—when the ransom negotiations were in progress, as later events proved—Miss Alexander had gone to make a telephone call in the waiting room of a railroad depot in the Bronx and had seen Dr. Condon talking with the telegraph operator. She remembered the incident well because she had noticed that someone else in the room was watching the Doctor, studying him intently from a distance of about fifteen feet. The witness had thought nothing more about it until she saw Richard Hauptmann's picture in her newspaper. She recognized him instantly as the man who had been watching Dr. Condon.

It distressed Reilly to have to assail such a conspicuously likable young woman, but duty was duty. Her motive, according to him, should be obvious to the feeblest intelligence—she was movie-struck and hoped that her bravura performance would result in a Hollywood contract. He thrashed over the waiting-room story but Miss

Alexander would not be budged: it had happened just as she had said, and Bruno Richard Hauptmann was the man.

Lanigan resumed for the State, to develop the attack Wilentz temporarily had abandoned. In slow succession, seven handwriting experts testified that in their careful judgment the accused was the author of the ransom notes. The evidence was necessarily repetitious and the demonstrations with the charts fell into a monotonous pattern. It stretched over the rest of the day and continued throughout Tuesday and Wednesday—findings gave way to conclusions and conclusions gave way to opinions and all of them to general apathy.

For the first time it was possible to get a seat in the courtroom without fighting for it.

Reilly's lieutenants, whom he regarded as "country lawyers," did their level best to deepen the boredom.

Fisher, Pope and Rosecrans, taking turns, challenged witness after witness, attacking the entire body of the testimony and arguing the issue at such length and at times with such irrelevance that Judge Trenchard rebuked them. Reilly too was annoyed and told them he could see no reason for prolonging the tedium through this exhaustive cross-examination. The country lawyers disagreed, pointing out that the graphologists were the first of the State's formidable array of technical witnesses and that if the defense devoted hours and days of unrelieved dullness to handling them, the jurors might become so fed up with the whole thing that they would dread the prospect of listening to more experts and perhaps disregard *all* technical evidence.

Reilly shook his head. Wrong strategy! But he wouldn't put his foot down. Let the boys have their fling. If you could call it that.

The interminable session wound to its weary end. Clark Sellers, the final witness, in effect summed up for all the State's handwriting analysts. The evidence that Richard Hauptmann had written the kidnap notes was so complete, he said, that the defendant might as well have signed his name to every one.

12

Taking their seats the next morning, the jurors noted with relief that the giant photostats were gone.

The State was ready to reintroduce a vital phase of its case. The fact that Charles Augustus Lindbergh, Jr., was dead, that the small body found in the Sourlands was his, had been touched on in earlier testimony, but the time, place and manner of his death had not been settled. Herein lay the whole basis of the charge against the defendant.

Wilentz delegated Robert Peacock of his staff to put the *corpus delicti* before the jury so positively that it could not be successfully challenged. The young assistant prosecutor methodically tackled the task with William Allen, the Negro truck driver who had stumbled upon the grave, and Orville Wilson, who had accompanied Allen on his return to the spot that rainy afternoon. Then, through Trooper Andrew Zapolsky and Inspector Harry Walsh, Peacock established that it was the body of the Lindbergh baby, the one witness having identified it by comparing the face, still fairly well preserved, with a photograph of the child, the other having matched the remnant of a blue-silk-stitched flannel petticoat, given to him by Betty Gow, with a nightshirt on the body.

Peacock took the next step with Walter Swayze, the coroner, who testified that he had removed the corpse to his Trenton funeral parlors, where first the nurse and then the father had confirmed its identity. Drawing up a certificate of death had been a routine matter.

Lloyd Fisher had struck at the identification by inference rather than direct assault. The woods in which the body lay—well inside Mercer County, he pointed out—were quite close to St. Michael's Catholic orphanage, true? And a great many children, including very young children, lived there, didn't they? The witnesses had been taken off balance by his questions and had replied so aimlessly that Fisher was sure the jury couldn't miss his meaning. The State had established that the small body was badly decomposed. Did it seem likely that the face could be recognized or the torn, rotted garments identified? Wasn't it reasonable to think that the body might very well have been that of a child from the nearby orphanage? At any rate, Fisher told himself, if this line was relentlessly pursued the prosecution might be forced to supply absolute proof of the *corpus delicti,* an extremely difficult thing to do.

Reilly capped the cross-examination by wringing from Walter Swayze the admission that he had signed the death certificate without having personally determined the facts of death, and that he was simply an undertaker, not a physician. This seemed to detract from the State's initial triumph, when—over Reilly's vigorous opposition—Judge Trenchard had admitted the certificate in evidence.

Wilentz called Dr. Charles Mitchell, the Mercer County physician, to the stand.

He testified that he had performed an autopsy on the corpse while the coroner looked on. Although the body in general was in a bad way the facial muscles had not deteriorated, and in comparing the face with a portrait of Charles Lindbergh, Jr., he had found it to be the same child. Yes, the facial expression could be termed good.

Wilentz glanced at the child's father. His face was pale. The lips were drawn in and there was a deep line in each cheek.

The prosecutor went on to the next essential point. As the result of his autopsy, could Dr. Mitchell say what caused the child's death?

"There was no question as to the cause of death," the witness replied promptly. "The child died of a fractured skull."

Reilly spoke up, demanding that the witness confine himself to the question and his remark be stricken from the record.

Dr. Mitchell obliged. "The child died of a fractured skull."

Wilentz continued: And was the fracture the result of external violence?

"It had every indication of it."

It was an extensive fracture?

"Quite extensive." The witness illustrated this by tracing the path of the fissure on his head. "It was a very extensive fracture," he amplified.

Would he give his opinion as to the time of the child's death?

Frederick Pope intervened. It was obviously impossible for the witness to express such an opinion; it appeared that none of the child's vital organs, which might have a bearing on its death, had been available—certainly there was no evidence that Dr. Mitchell had examined them. And so who could say whether death resulted from the skull fracture or some other cause? Finally, the fracture might have occurred long after death. At best, whatever the witness said in reply to the attorney general's question would be a guess.

The witness was an experienced physician, Judge Trenchard said sharply; he had studied the fracture and had described its extent. Couldn't he tell what relation it had to the cause of death?

No, Pope answered, he couldn't—assuming, as seemed to be true, that the body was so decomposed the doctor was unable to determine whether there was another cause.

Trenchard rejected this. The witness could answer, subject of course to defense counsel's cross-examination.

Wilentz asked again if he would give his opinion as to the time of the child's death.

"I would say that death occurred either instantaneously or within a very few minutes following the fracture."

It seemed complete to the attorney general: the child had received a blow on the head and had died at once, or nearly so. The blow had been caused by a fall from the ladder in the kidnaper's hasty flight, as previous witnesses had indicated. All the elements of the charge against the defendant were in place.

But Pope had raised some doubt. Would it stick in the jurors' minds?

How to settle it? Wilentz deliberated, then addressed the witness. When he performed the autopsy, parts of the child's body were missing, were they not?

"Quite a lot of them."

Including certain organs?

"Yes."

And had their absence prevented him from determining the cause of death?

"Not by any means." The child had to be alive when the blow occurred, the witness explained, because a blood clot clung to the inner wall of the skull at the point of fracture; had the child been dead there could not have been a coagulation of blood. The time of death was indicated by the extent of the fracture. It was so severe that the child could not possibly have survived it for more than a few minutes.

Now could there be any question about the corpse in the Sourlands woods? Wilentz didn't think so; but the answer was too crucial to be left to chance. Lloyd Fisher's inference that the child was an orphan missing from St. Michael's stood untouched. It would be taken care of, the prosecutor felt confident, when the jury heard a new witness he had sent for.

Reilly countered along the line Pope had laid down. Since so very few of the child's organs were available for study, wouldn't Dr. Mitchell admit that his examination had been perfunctory?

No, Dr. Mitchell would not.

But surely he knew that the Lindbergh child—if it *was* the Lindbergh child—was sick with a cold and suffering from congestion of the lungs. Couldn't it have choked to death?

The witness said that he had thoroughly explored that possibility and ruled it out.

Reilly persisted. The night of March 1, 1932, was cold and windy and the child was scantily dressed; might it not have died from exposure?

In the circumstances counsel described, the child very likely would have died within twenty hours. But the autopsy had shown that these were *not* the circumstances. Death had occurred, the witness summed up, in the manner he had stated.

His voice was calm, as it had been throughout. This seemed to irritate Reilly. Where was the proof of the precious blood clot the doctor had found? Had he photographed it? No, Mitchell replied, he hadn't but he recalled it exactly as it had looked. Reilly rode over the words. And he still pretended that his examination was acceptable?

The word *pretended* stung. Mitchell flushed. He would like counsel to know that he had been a physician for forty years. He had performed approximately a thousand autopsies, at least a hundred of them on children. In his opinion, his examination had been a mighty fine job.

Reilly subsided. The autopsy report was admitted in evidence.

Early in the afternoon Wilentz returned to the ransom money, this time offering not the entire bundle but a single bill. He traced the possession of a ten-dollar gold note from an unidentified motorist to two Warner-Quinlan service-station attendants, Walter Lyle and John Lyons; from them to a Corn Exchange Bank teller, Miran Ozmec, who hadn't noticed an auto-license number penciled on the back of the bill; and to his superior, William Strong, who hadn't noticed it either, but who *had* observed that the bill's serial number appeared on the Lindbergh ransom list; then to Lieutenant Finn, Corporal Horn and Special Agent Seery; and finally, through their investigation, to the motorist who had started the whole sequence, Richard Hauptmann—after his arrest he had admitted giving the note to Lyle, and both Lyle and Lyons had identified him.

Wilentz submitted the bill as evidence. The defense had insisted throughout the march of witnesses that it was in no way connected with the charge of murder against the defendant. Judge Trenchard thought this argument absurd and overruled it without pause.

Now the entire issue of the ransom money could be explored; with Seery on the stand Wilentz pressed his advantage, placing in evidence other gold notes the defendant had used for purchases and the one found on him at his arrest. The prosecutor was well into the money hidden in Hauptmann's garage—$14,600, all in Lindbergh gold certificates—when the witness he had sent for arrived.

Another federal investigator, Thomas Sisk, was waiting to follow Seery, ready to add to the evidence of extortion, but Wilentz motioned him back and brought Mrs. Elmira Dormer to the witness chair.

On March 1, 1932, was Mrs. Dormer employed as custodian of St. Michael's Orphanage near the village of Hopewell?

"Yes, sir."

And how many children lived there?

"Three hundred and six."

Of all ages?

"Their ages were from two weeks to sixteen years."

Were any of the children missing on March 1?

"None were missing. They were all accounted for."

Wilentz moved to the day Charles Lindbergh, Jr., was found dead. And May 12, 1932? Was any child unaccounted for then?

"No, sir. We know all the children and we account for them every day."

So that there was no question whatever that on both occasions not a single child was missing from the orphanage?

"No, sir."

Wilentz picked up a ledger and turned toward the defense. It was St. Michael's record of attendance for the year 1932, he said, and if they proposed to dispute the testimony he would offer the ledger in evidence; if not, he would disregard it.

"There is no dispute," Reilly told him almost indifferently.

Wilentz was anything but indifferent. Then the defense conceded that the *corpus delicti* was *not* that of a child from the orphanage?

Lloyd Fisher rose to counter the question, but with an impatient gesture Reilly cut him off: "I will say now there has never been any claim but that it was Colonel Lindbergh's child."

Wilentz nodded, more than satisfied. It was an admission of complete defeat on the issue, going far beyond the demand of his question.

Fisher looked stunned, as if he could not believe his ears; his amazement gave way to anger; he said vehemently to his chief, "You are conceding Hauptmann to the electric chair!" Then, with an exclamation of disgust, he strode from the courtroom.

Hauptmann, in his chair directly behind the defense table, moved uneasily. He had heard Reilly praised to the skies, his reputation described as second to none, but the defendant had come to repose more confidence in Fisher.

Certainly Fisher seemed to think of Richard Hauptmann not as a name, a stranger, a pawn, but as a human being, a husband, a father, a man with feelings; and he visited him often in his cell and was quick to reassure him and always asked after Anna and Bubi—a sturdy, sympathetic fellow with a good-looking, friendly face—yes, someone who could have been a friend in the old days of hunting trips to the Maine woods and songs around the campfire.

And now he had walked out, angrily. Was he gone for good?

Hauptmann made as if to get up, then sat back, remembering the guard on each side.

Reilly's cross-examination of Mrs. Elmira Dormer of St. Michael's was desultory; after a few minutes, with the waiting witness, Thomas Sisk, on the stand, Wilentz returned to the subject of the ransom. Sisk spoke calmly about the capture of the defendant and his unsatisfactory explanation of the ransom bills traced to him and proceeded to the Hauptmanns' apartment and the search for the great quantity of Lindbergh money still outstanding. In the bedroom, Sisk related, the defendant's furtive glances out the window had led him to believe that the money was hidden in the garage, but a hasty search had produced only a metal jar containing a few inches of water, and the prisoner had disclaimed any knowledge of it. But during the next day's questioning he had admitted that three weeks earlier the jar had contained ransom money.

Hauptmann had been straining forward, shaking his head with increasing agitation. Sisk's culminating words galvanized him. He jumped up, catching the guards unaware. Hunched over, hands thrust out, his sallow face flushed, he started toward the witness stand.

"Mister, Mister, you stop lying!" he shouted.

The guards grappled with him. He was strong enough to pull them ahead a short way; then their superior weight won and they heaved him back to his chair. His thick voice rose again:

"You are telling a story!"

Lindbergh turned and looked at him. It was only the second time, so far as the spectators in the silent courtroom could remember, that the father of the dead child had looked at the accused, and it was hardly more than a glance.

Thomas Sisk was not perturbed. Judge Trenchard said into the silence that he would suggest that the defendant behave with decorum and make his observations quietly through counsel.

Wilentz led Sisk back to his story.

The prisoner's knotted muscles relaxed under his guards' grip; he sat slumped in the chair. A few moments later he straightened. Lloyd Fisher had returned to the courtroom and was walking swiftly toward the defense table; he had learned of the outburst from an attendant. Before sitting down he put his hand on Richard Hauptmann's shoulder.

13

Once more, on the following day, Wilentz drew his audience into the hunt for the ransom money. A series of police witnesses testified that, according to Hauptmann, the twenty-dollar gold note in his wallet at the time of his arrest and the $120 in coins in his strongbox was all the gold he owned. Later he acknowledged he had lied; the searchers had discovered three rich lodes of gold certificates, $14,600 in all, in his garage. And they had found a chest of carpentry tools, including a handplane.

The money and the tool chest were received in evidence—as was another State exhibit, a small board wrapped in cellophane. Wilentz asked Inspector Henry Bruckman to explain its significance.

Bruckman was chief of New York's division of detectives in the

Bronx. He was on familiar ground in describing the board's history; he had told it at Hauptmann's extradition trial. The story began on a day in September 1934.

Monday September 24 was the fifth day following the arrest of the defendant. A good deal of evidence had been turned up to tie him to the kidnaping; the garage search had been particularly rewarding. It seemed strange, Bruckman thought, that the hunt through the apartment itself had produced almost nothing worth while. Surely it should contain a clue to at least one of the prisoner's suspected roles of kidnaper, murderer and extortionist! Of course they'd given the garage a thorough going-over; well, then, they ought to tackle the apartment in the same way.

The inspector spoke to his superiors and got permission to strip the flat down to the lathwork.

Bright and early the next morning a team of carpenters and investigators began to rip into the apartment. Wiping plaster dust from his face, Bruckman went into the nursery and studied a closet, empty except for a shelf and a clothes pole. He asked one of the carpenters to remove them so that he could get inside. It was a narrow closet, difficult to turn around in, and Bruckman chose to back into it. He stood for a moment with his back pressed to the wall; the light was too dim to reveal anything and he borrowed a flashlight. Its beam paused on the inside trim above the doorway. There seemed to be a smudge there—no, a notation of some kind. The inspector put on his glasses.

Pencil jottings. He looked closer.

2974 Decatur. And beneath: *S*—the second letter was blurred—*DG 3-7154.*

The pencil scrawl fell neatly into place in Bruckman's mind. It was Dr. Condon's address and phone number; the blurred letter after the *S* of course was an *E. SEDG*—Sedgwick. And, most important, it was Dr. Condon's *old* number, which he had changed ten days after the kidnaping to a private listing, Sedgwick 3-1177.

Wasn't this proof that Hauptmann was dealing with Dr. Condon during the ransom negotiations and hadn't been given the money by his friend Isidor Fisch, as he insisted he had?

Bruckman probed farther in the telltale closet. And here, on the inside of the door, were more pencil markings: *$500,* followed by what seemed to be the serial numbers of two bills.

The inspector ordered the trim-board and door removed. The board came away without disturbing the nails, revealing a shallow recess in the wall. It looked as if it might have been made to hide ransom bills, but the space was empty.

Bruckman took his find to the office of the Bronx prosecutor.

District Attorney Samuel Foley, and Hauptmann was brought from his cell to explain the notations, if he could.

At this point in the witness' account of that September day, David Wilentz thanked him for his testimony and called on Foley's confidential secretary, Benjamin Arac, to complete the story. Arac quickly picked up the thread from his stenographic notes and described the scene in the Bronx district attorney's office.

The trim-board was shown to Hauptmann. He readily acknowledged that the wood was from his apartment but was a bit hesitant about the writing on it. Yes, he said, the figures were in his hand but he didn't know about the words—they were hard to make out.

Samuel Foley agreed; the writing *was* smudged. Why? Had the prisoner tried to rub it out?

Hauptmann shook his head.

But he recognized it as a notation of Dr. Condon's address and phone number, didn't he?

No, he didn't.

Foley went on. Why had he written this information about Dr. Condon on the inside of a dark closet?

Well, Hauptmann said, he couldn't be sure but most likely he had gone into the closet to put fresh newspaper on the shelves and had come across the Doctor's address and phone number in a news story he chanced to read. He was a bit interested in the Lindbergh case, just like everyone else, and so he must have copied down the information on the board in front of him. That was a habit of his, he explained, writing down little things of interest—but usually he wrote them on one of the kitchen walls.

Was that the best explanation he could give for writing the memo?

"It is the only explanation I can give."

What about the numbers penciled on the back of the closet door?

Hauptmann replied that they were a record of two big bills—five-hundred- or thousand-dollar bills, he didn't recall which—that his friend Isidor Fisch had turned over to him to buy stocks. He was a little nervous over having so much cash at home, so he had noted down the serial numbers and for a time had hidden the bills in the secret hollow behind the trim-board.

Neither of the numbers appeared in Foley's copy of the Lindbergh ransom list and if in fact they had been five-hundred- and thousand-dollar bills they couldn't be kidnap money anyway; the biggest bills Dr. Condon had handed to John were twenty-dollar notes.

Foley returned to the crucial point. Did Hauptmann remember the date when he wrote down the Doctor's address and phone?

"No."

But he did remember writing it?

"I must write it, the figures; that's my writing."

Then didn't it seem that he had written the words too?

The prisoner held fast to his original doubt—the words were barely legible; he could hardly read them.

Foley pressed hard for a full admission. No use. "I don't know," Hauptmann said.

Benjamin Arac closed his steno notebook and Wilentz yielded the witness to the defense.

Reilly's cross-examination carried little challenge. Hauptmann had answered Foley's questions of his own free will, Arac admitted, but the prisoner's attorney was not present to advise and protect him and, so far as the witness knew, no one had bothered to tell him that he would be within his constitutional rights if he refused to make a statement.

That was enough for Reilly, and for the time being at least the incident of the closet was closed.

John Hughes Curtis, the Norfolk boatbuilder, had been a faithful reader of his newspaper during these days, and as the columns of trial testimony mounted he came to the conclusion that in one place the record must be set straight. Early in the trial Charles Lindbergh had asserted there was no truth to the story that Curtis was dealing with the kidnapers; but the State of New Jersey hadn't proceeded on that theory—it had put Curtis on trial, accused him of being "actually in contact with the kidnapers," and convicted him of obstructing justice by not disclosing the gang's whereabouts to the police. True, his jail sentence had been suspended, but that hadn't removed the stigma of guilt.

And also he was out one thousand dollars, the fine he had paid.

Certainly the record should be set straight! He was entitled to a complete exoneration.

Plus the fine.

In return, he would go to Flemington and identify Bruno Richard Hauptmann as one of the kidnap gang. Wasn't that a fair exchange?

Curtis telephoned Colonel Schwarzkopf, told him what he had in mind, and proposed that they let bygones be bygones. But on one condition. "In fairness to me," he explained, "Colonel Lindbergh must agree to pose for photos showing us shaking hands. My reputation has been damaged through my efforts to aid him. I know Hauptmann is one of the men I dealt with. But I am entitled to vindication and I make this request in fairness to my wife and my children."

Schwarzkopf promised to put the offer up to Lindbergh and call back. He did. The answer was no.

The subject of the offer was busy in his cell this week end. On Friday, a few hours before court was recessed, the prosecution had introduced a new aspect of its case, and to Richard Hauptmann it seemed all-important.

Four witnesses had explored his brokerage accounts, bank deposits and so on over the past several years, but he knew their testimony was only small-arms fire compared to the big gun the State would introduce on Monday in the person of an expert from the Treasury Department. Hauptmann felt confident, though, that when the time came for him to testify in his defense he would be able to answer every question about the money.

He asked for pencil and paper, sat down on the cell cot, and began to make notes.

The big gun appeared as scheduled—a small man, William Frank, whose cool, unfussy manner testified to a lifelong diet of facts and figures. He placed his brief case beside the witness chair, identified himself as an agent of the Intelligence Unit of the United States Treasury Department, and then, at Wilentz's bidding, set out to clear a path through the thick green maze of the defendant's financial affairs.

Hauptmann listened intently. During the weeks of imprisonment before the trial, the Treasury man had questioned him at length about his earnings, holdings and expenditures, had taken him page by page through the notebooks the police had found in his apartment—his meticulously kept records of his and Anna's income over the years of their marriage and the various results of his stock transactions. Now he would learn the outcome.

Wilentz knew that it would be a complicated piece of testimony; he would have to keep careful check on the witness, boil his findings down. He drew the accountant on.

In analyzing Richard and Anna Hauptmann's finances, William Frank said, he had found that on April 2, 1932, the date of the ransom payment, the couple's total wealth amounted to $4941.40. Most of this was in a mortgage; the remainder consisted of $203.90 in cash in the Central Savings Bank in Manhattan and fifty shares of Warner Brothers movie stock with a total market value of $100.

But starting with April 2 the Hauptmanns obviously had struck it rich: up to September 19, 1934, the day of the defendant's arrest, they had used a spectacular sum of cash, a good many thousands of dollars—and of course Hauptmann had several thousands more at home when he was taken into custody.

Frank consulted a paper from his brief case and ticked off his findings during the two-and-a-half-year period: $16,942.75 deposited in the Hauptmanns' brokerage accounts; $9073.25 deposited in their bank accounts; $3750 paid for a new mortgage; $14,600 in gold certificates (ransom money) and $120 in gold coins on hand in their apartment and garage. Altogether, their assets during the thirty months after April 2, 1932, came to $44,486.

But even this figure didn't tell the whole story, the Treasury expert's dry voice continued. On the final day of the accounting—September 19, 1934—the Hauptmanns' total wealth (mortgages, stocks, savings, an assortment of raw furs, the hidden gold certificates and coins) was $40,529.02. Add to that their expenditures during the period after the ransom payment—$15,530.63 spent as much on luxuries (hunting and vacation trips, a radio, a canoe, binoculars and the like) as on necessities—and you had a grand total of $56,059.65. Subtract their assets on April 2—$4941.40—and their earnings over the period—$1167.81—and there remained $49,950.44. The source of this money was unaccounted for, and since it was just a few dollars shy of the $50,000 kidnap payment it could be presumed to be ransom money.

Wilentz led the accountant to a new set of figures, which seemed to picture Richard Hauptmann as a man who was anxious to get hold of a large sum of cash because he had been bitten by a well-known bug. The defendant had taken his first fling in Wall Street in November 1929, Frank said, and had played the market more or less steadily every year since. From 1929's modest stock transactions—$1196—he had stepped up his activity to $6913.13 in 1930; $2836 in 1931; $4905.25 in 1932 (the year of the ransom payment); $256,442.15 in 1933 (three brokerage accounts); and $10,982.50 in 1934 up to September 19, when he was arrested.

The figures were impressive, particularly the great surge in 1933, and the witness' manner—almost that of a human tabulating machine—was no less so; but to Reilly, rising to cross-examine, they presented a prime target. He aimed at the bull's-eye, the accounting of the defendant's stock investments and bank deposits, which he politely asked William Frank to give in detail. The witness obliged. He described every transfer of money by the Hauptmanns in all of their savings accounts before and after April 2, 1932, and named every stock they had bought and sold and the dates and sums of money involved.

Reilly listened with keen interest. He coughed, cleared his throat, then inquired if all this didn't go to show that the defendant dealt in a great many stocks—?

"Yes, sir," Frank said.

That he was constantly in the market, trading—buying one day and selling the next—?

"Yes, sir."

That he frequently made small profits in the course of a few days—?

"Yes, sir."

Reilly coughed again. In fact, in one month hadn't the defendant earned a thousand dollars in this way—?

"Yes, sir."

Then didn't it appear that the witness had attributed to the Hauptmanns a quantity of cash they never had? Although at intervals their brokerage accounts seemed to show a great amount of money, weren't these really paper figures?—traveling transactions?—the results of the defendant's constant trading in the market? In actual cash, weren't only a few thousand dollars involved?

Frank shook his head. His analysis of the accounts was correct.

Reilly produced a small storm of coughs. He retreated to the defense table for a glass of water, drank deeply and returned to the fray. "It is nothing unusual for a man to go into Wall Street with a five- or ten-thousand-dollar bankroll, is there, and buy and sell on margin if he can get credit?" he demanded hoarsely.

"No, sir," the witness granted. "It is not unusual."

"I think that is all," Reilly said, turning away; but before he could reach his seat the cough seized him once more and attained alarming proportions.

"Mr. Reilly," Judge Trenchard called.

Reilly looked around inquiringly. His face was purplish. The judge beckoned to him and he came to the bench.

Judge Trenchard's health had been bearing up splendidly but he was as much concerned for others' well-being as for his own and Reilly's spasms had distressed his paternal eye. He had debated between a couple of the remedies with which he was equipped and decided on the handier as calculated to afford Reilly less embarassment. "Try these for your cough," he suggested gently, and pushed a box of lozenges across the bench.

Reilly gratefully accepted. He popped a pellet into his mouth, went back to the defense table and sat down, sucking hard.

David Wilentz, re-examining the witness, observed with mild surprise that there had been a good deal of talk about Hauptmann's profits in the stock market—but his losses hadn't been mentioned. There *were* losses, weren't there?

"Yes, sir," Frank told him. "There were losses in excess of profits."

Seemingly perplexed, Wilentz repeated the phrase. Did that mean that in spite of all his winnings the defendant had ended up with a loss?

"A net loss. Yes, sir."

Wilentz bore in sharply. And what was the total sum of his loss from stock speculations?

The witness consulted his figures: $9132.29.

Hauptmann had explained after his arrest that he was able to live nicely without working because of his successes in the market. Well, Wilentz reflected, that was one less alibi he could count on.

The attorney general struck at Reilly's "paper figures" in the brokerage accounts. Up to April 2, 1932, Frank declared, the defendant had never dealt in Wall Street to the extent of $50,000 a month, but after that date he had—month after month.

Pausing, Wilentz asked himself if he had forgotten anything. Yes, he had; and again he addressed the methodical William Frank, whose salvos had been quiet but devastating. In the eight years between 1924 and 1932, how much money in silver coins had the Hauptmanns deposited in their bank accounts?

$1.47.

And how much in silver had they deposited in the two and a half years between April 2, 1932, and September 19, 1934?

$453.25.

The comparison should register a direct hit with the jury, Wilentz thought. Could there be any explanation for this extraordinary accumulation of coins other than that Hauptmann had been busy converting ransom bills throughout the latter period and was partly paid off in small change?

It seemed to the prosecutor that too much attention could not be given to the significance of April 2; also, he decided to introduce the two other revealing dates in Hauptmann's history. He had told the police that on the day of the ransom payment he was working as a carpenter at the Majestic, an apartment house at 72nd Street and Central Park West in Manhattan—and on March 1, the day of the kidnaping, too. The State's next witness, Edward Morton, the employees' timekeeper at the Majestic, took a different view; his records showed that Hauptmann had not been hired until March 21, 1932—three weeks after the crime—and that on the following April 2, the Saturday of the payoff, he hadn't reported for work. He had put in a full day on Monday, the fourth, but that was the last they'd seen of him at the Majestic; he'd quit without giving any notice or explanation.

The third significant date was November 26, 1933. Hauptmann had said that of course he remembered it because it was his birthday; he'd been at home that evening, celebrating with friends.

But Mrs. Cecile Barr declared from the witness chair that he was in Greenwich Village that night. No, she couldn't be mistaken—he'd walked up to her cashier's booth at Loew's Sheridan Square Theater and—and here was why she remembered him—tossed toward her a five-dollar bill that was folded in a very peculiar way. It had struck her, too, that although the night was bitter this customer wore no overcoat.

Reilly had finished his cough drop and taken out additional insurance with a few more swigs of water, and his voice was unencumbered and caustic. With such a remarkable memory, the cashier no doubt could recall *every* customer who gave her a five-dollar bill, *every* customer who came to the theater without an overcoat——?

No, of course not, Mrs. Barr replied patiently, but this one she couldn't forget. And she glanced over at Richard Hauptmann as if to emphasize it.

14

Tuesday January 22, fifteenth day of the trial.

David Wilentz girded himself for another test of strength over the ladder. Twice before he had tried, and twice failed, to establish it as the kidnaper's means of entry; but he promised himself that this time he would place it in evidence no matter what obstacles defense counsel threw in his path. Too much of the State's case depended on the ladder to permit it to remain in limbo.

He recalled Detective Lewis Bornmann to the chair.

In his original appearance the witness had described the discovery of the ladder, with one of its dowel pins still in place, and the three-quarter-inch chisel, and Judge Trenchard had permitted all three exhibits to be marked for identification. Again Wilentz showed Bornmann the chisel and again he identified it, and the prosecutor offered it in evidence. Despite defense objections, it was admitted.

One down and two to go, Wilentz thought. Now for the real test. He brought out the ladder.

Bornmann identified its three sections and traced its custody from hand to hand, explaining what had been done to it and why and concluding with the flat statement that in spite of its alterations it was substantially in the same condition as when it was found—the ladder the kidnaper had abandoned on the Lindbergh grounds.

The attorney general faced the bench. He said quietly, almost indifferently, "We offer the ladder in evidence."

Judge Trenchard glanced at the defense table and Frederick Pope got up. He seemed bored. "And, of course, we object to the introduction of the ladder in evidence," he said, "for the reasons which have already been indicated to the Court."

The judge knew those reasons very well; so did Wilentz; but Pope recited them again. He might have been talking about an elderly relative he did not particularly care for, the state of whose health he was obliged to report. The ladder had traveled from person to person, from place to place, and it had been handled and tinkered with so much that in effect it wasn't the original ladder. And the prosecution still hadn't produced every person who'd had charge of it at one time or another.

Pope summoned up a show of force for his final point against the tiresome ladder. "There is a still further and even stronger objection," he declared. "There is no connection between this ladder and the defendant here on trial. No one has even suggested that this ladder was ever in the possession of this defendant. No one has even suggested that he had anything to do with building it. It is therefore immaterial, irrelevant, and we submit that it should not be introduced in evidence."

Wilentz addressed the bench. "Does your Honor want a reply?"

Judge Trenchard asked Pope if he had overlooked the testimony of the old gentleman, Mr. Hochmuth, to the effect that on March 1, 1932, he saw the defendant in possession of the ladder?

With a polite smile, Pope ventured to correct him. Amandus Hochmuth had testified that he saw a ladder in the defendant's car; he hadn't said that he recognized the ladder—that it was *this* ladder.

The judge nodded and looked inquiringly at Wilentz. He was ready with every ounce of persuasion he could bring to bear. Possession of the ladder *had* been proved, he said, and its alterations were the result of efforts to bring it into the courtroom where it now stood, so that a jury could decide whether or not the accused was its owner and thus guilty or innocent of the crime.

Now it was up to Judge Trenchard. His thoughtful eyes considered Wilentz and Pope, no less tense at this moment of decision, and then the ladder itself.

"I feel constrained to admit this ladder in evidence," he said, "and it will be admitted."

Wilentz permitted his locked-up breath to escape. He brought the dowel pin to Bornmann, on the stand; the detective identified it and it too was received in evidence, despite Pope's objections.

The attorney general gave the witness to the defense and sat down to plan his next moves. The test of strength had cleared the path to the wood testimony; he could have it whenever he wished, but first there was some unfinished business to attend to.

Few events of any consequence had served to lighten Millard Whited's life as a logger or to prepare him for the extreme prominence that had come his way with the Lindbergh case. His testimony at the extradition trial had had great weight in bringing the prisoner to the Flemington courtroom. And here he was, too, in the same courtroom, spang in the public eye. He sat awkwardly in the witness chair, his countryman's face watchful and guarded as he reviewed the steps that had put him there.

Remembering the story he had told of having seen a stranger in the vicinity of the Lindbergh estate shortly before the kidnaping, Captain John Lamb of the State police had been anxious for Whited to meet the suspect, after Hauptmann's arrest, and if possible identify him as that stranger. Whited hadn't liked the idea at all. He had left his Sourlands farmhouse long ago and, when the State troopers finally found him, was busy on a logging job in a Pennsylvania lumber-mill village. The thought of going to the Bronx County jail and exposing himself to reporters and photographers—and losing a day's pay, maybe more—was too dismal to consider. He had changed his mind only after Trooper Joseph Wolfe solemnly swore he'd be paid back every cent lost on his job and that there'd be no publicity.

But there had been publicity, plenty of it. After he had identified Richard Hauptmann as the stranger, Millard Whited had seen his face staring at him from the front pages, with lots of print presumably explaining his new importance. He'd had to admit to himself that he enjoyed it. He imagined there'd be more pictures following his present session on the witness stand. Such was fame. He only hoped these lawyers wouldn't ask him any embarrassing questions.

David Wilentz's opening questions, inviting his testimony, put him at ease and Whited settled more comfortably in the chair. Again he recalled how on two occasions during the last two weeks of February 1932 he had observed Hauptmann at the border of the Lindbergh estate, and how in the early morning of March 2, a few hours after the kidnaping, Lieutenant Arthur Keaton and other State police officers had come to his farmhouse and he had told them about his encounters with the stranger.

Wilentz didn't want to leave any loose ends hanging. He asked why Whited hadn't got in touch with the police after Hauptmann's arrest—hadn't he read about the suspect in the papers?

No, the witness said, he had not.

Why not?

Millard Whited knew where this would lead. He supposed the newspapers would make much of it and that people who read the papers would say of him, "Just a hillbilly." He hesitated, embarrassed.

Wilentz delicately amended the question. It was not his wish to offend the witness, but—couldn't he read?

Well, there it was. Millard Whited shook his head. No. At least, he explained, not enough to exactly *understand* the papers.

Wilentz retired and Lloyd Fisher got up for his first cross-examination since he had left the courtroom and then returned to comfort Hauptmann. It seemed to him that the witness added to his inability to understand the printed word the inability to distinguish fact from fiction, and he pounded hard at Whited's story.

He had told the court that the second time he saw the stranger he was about a mile and a half from the gate to the Lindbergh place, whereas at the extradition trial he had estimated the distance at three quarters of a mile. Either he had a poor memory or he was a bad judge of distance. Or maybe the explanation was that he hadn't seen the stranger at all?

He certainly had seen him, Whited insisted.

Fisher shrugged. When the police came to his farmhouse early that March morning, they hadn't told him about the kidnaping, had they? Hadn't he assumed that they'd come to question him about a robbery in Blawemburg, a village a few miles away, just two evenings before? In fact, hadn't he been pretty sure that they suspected him of being the robber?

Not waiting for a reply, the young lawyer read from the transcript of the extradition trial:

"Naturally, what was in my mind was that they came there thinking I was a thief."

Whited's words, weren't they?

The witness agreed.

That was the first thought that went through his head when the police knocked on his door—?

Yes.

——and to protect himself, to divert suspicion, he had invented his story of the prowling stranger?

No. The story was true.

Fisher contemptuously dismissed the denial. What *was* true was this: although Whited had talked to two of the police officers for more than fifteen minutes, he couldn't identify either of them—whereas he had identified Hauptmann as his mythical prowler after having seen him for only a few seconds from a moving truck and, in addition, after having been shown two photographs of him just before picking him out from a police line-up in the Bronx. All of this *was* true, wasn't it?

Whited said yes, it was.

A new witness, Charles Rossiter, a traveling salesman, took the stand. He had been driving to Philadelphia on the Saturday evening preceding the Tuesday of the crime and at about eight o'clock, just north of the Princeton airport, had come upon a man kneeling behind a car, fixing a flat. Rossiter was a good Samaritan; he stopped and offered to help, but the man told him he could handle the job alone. The good Samaritan lingered for a few minutes to make sure, watching in the beam of his headlights.

When he saw the newspaper pictures of Hauptmann after his arrest, Rossiter recognized him as the man who hadn't wanted help. He told the police, was taken to see the prisoner, and identified him.

Cross-examining, Reilly laced into the witness's memory. Charles Rossiter cheerfully admitted it wasn't the best in the world; he forgot lots of things and occasionally mistook strangers for friends. But he was not wrong about Richard Hauptmann. Richard Hauptmann was the flat-fixer on the Princeton road.

The attorney general saw that there was still enough time to begin his final argument before court was recessed for the day. He was rather looking forward to it, since he proposed to rub a little salt into the wounds left on defense counsel by the admission of the ladder. Pope had said that there was no connection between it and the defendant, no evidence that he had built it or that it was ever in his possession; and Wilentz remembered very well his promise to run the ladder right into Hauptmann. Well, either he or Pope was wrong. The jury would decide for itself very soon now, after it had heard the testimony about the secrets that could be pried by an expert from that seemingly prosaic and uncommunicative substance—wood.

He called Max Rauch to the witness stand, observing as he did so that the most placid person in the courtroom—with the possible exception of the judge—was the man who was waiting to describe and illustrate those secrets.

Arthur Koehler was a very patient man.

Since his earlier appearance on the stand, aborted by the defense attorneys, he had calmly bided his time, watching David Wilentz at work with a craftsman's appreciation of the dexterity displayed by the young prosecutor in attempting to build a capital case out of bits and pieces of circumstantial evidence. The foundation of the case, which of course was the charge itself, murder in the first degree, could not be convincingly established without Koehler's help. If it could be proved that Richard Hauptmann built the ladder as well as wrote the ransom notes, Wilentz had pointed out, it would be constructive evidence that he planned to steal and did steal the baby and thus, in the eyes of New Jersey law, was responsible for the child's death. Place the ladder in Hauptmann's hands and the case would be solid.

Once again Koehler glanced at the prisoner's hands. How often he had pictured them to himself during his long search!—the hands of a careless carpenter with scant feeling for the wood he used—the hands that had crudely fashioned the kidnap ladder. Koehler hadn't the slightest doubt of that, and he was confident the jury would agree.

Wilentz had warned him that the defense would fight his testimony every step of the way, indeed would oppose his very right to testify. For although Koehler had served as a witness in civil cases and once, years ago, in a criminal court, a wood technologist was a rare, even an exotic figure and enjoyed little or no professional standing in criminal jurisprudence. Ed Reilly, who had made himself a widely read man, had been forced to consult a dictionary to find out what Koehler really was and had reported, to his associates' and his own amusement, that this placid-looking chap was a xylotomist.

But even that bone-rattling word didn't completely define Koehler; it said nothing of his work as a wood detective. When it became clear to the defense that he was speaking not only as a wood technologist—or xylotomist!—but also in effect as a wood *criminologist,* and that among other things he intended to trace a few feet of lumber in the ladder from the forest in which it had grown right down to Richard Hauptmann's hands, they would do their best to dismiss his entire testimony as absurd.

Arthur Koehler was not worried.

After his original hunt for the ladder-builder had ended in disappointment, he and Detective Lewis Bornmann had set out on a different trail. With a new list in hand—shipments of Douglas fir from far western mills to the Bronx during the period prior to the kidnaping—they had toured Bronx lumberyards in an attempt to trace the uniquely scarred fir rails in the ladder to the man who had built it. This too had stopped short of the goal, and Koehler had gone back to his normal duties in the Forest Service Laboratory. Often during the following months he had turned the ladder over in his thoughts, wondering where the careless carpenter was and how he could be found.

One morning his newspaper informed him that a prime suspect was in police custody in New York. The man was a carpenter named Bruno Richard Hauptmann and he lived in the Bronx. The words—*carpenter, Bronx*—could hardly have been more significant to Koehler. He needed all his patience in the next several days. Then word came that Norman Schwarzkopf of the Jersey State police had requested the wood technologist's superiors to give him a leave of absence and lend his services for the second time to the Lindbergh case, and he left his Madison home for New Jersey. Arriving at State police headquarters, he was driven to the Wilburtha barracks, where he found that Schwarzkopf had fitted out a laboratory and also arranged for him to live there as a jealously guarded guest, every word of whose potentially vital investigations the police chief meant to keep from the papers.

Koehler saw why Schwarzkopf had delayed in sending for him. The day before his arrival, police carpenters had razed the garage Hauptmann had built next to his Bronx home, and every strip of wood in it lay neatly stacked in the laboratory-workshop awaiting Koehler's meticulous inspection. The nails, too; not only those extracted from the wood but others, unused, found in the garage, for him to compare with the ladder nails. And the prisoner's tool chest was there; it had been removed from the garage along with an eighteen-inch-long wood block plane with a two and one-half-inch blade discovered on a shelf above the workbench. Koehler saw at a glance that the blade seemed dull and uneven, which meant that it would scar wood with a pattern as distinctive as a man's signature, just as a handplane had scarred every rail and cleat of the kidnap ladder.

There was the usual assortment of carpenter's tools in the chest. Koehler lingered over a set of chisels. They were of various sizes; it struck him that a three-quarter-inch chisel, such as the one that had been left on the Lindbergh grounds, wasn't among them. That chisel had a white beechwood handle stippled with brownish dots; there was one here like it in that respect and its brass ferrule showed the same pattern of milling. It too bore a Stanley trademark.

Koehler experimented with the tools. His own chief tool was his microscope; its powerful eye brought the scientist's eye to bear on the wood. His first interest was to find samples of the four kinds of wood that had gone into the ladder—Southern pine, Douglas fir, ponderosa pine, birch—which bore the same slovenly markings as the ladder: the identifying tracks left by a carelessly used handsaw and chisel and the nicked bit of a handplane. But even while he pursued this quest Koehler was keenly alert to another matter. When he had examined the three-piece ladder on his first visit to Wilburtha his attention had been arrested by the characteristics of the left-hand Southern pine side rail in the top section—Rail 16, he had numbered it. This particular board had been used before it was fitted into the ladder, used somewhere indoors, because there were four nailholes free of rust in one end of the rail. The holes were square rather than round, having been made by old-fashioned square-cut nails, and they were spaced irregularly, the distance between them varying. They varied in other respects, too—in depth, width and the angle at which they penetrated the wood. All in all it had seemed to Koehler that the four holes in Rail 16 formed a unique pattern that couldn't be duplicated even if four identical cut nails were driven into the same strip of Southern pine ten thousand times.

It followed that if a second piece of wood was found with precisely the same pattern of nailholes—or with four cut nails protruding from it in matching position—it *had* to be the wood to which Rail 16 originally was attached; Koehler had calculated that the chance that, at some time prior to the kidnaping, the two boards had *not* been nailed together was mathematically almost nonexistent.

If a piece of wood with the matching pattern of holes could be found among the lumber from Hauptmann's garage, or in his apartment, it would prove without a doubt that he had built the kidnap ladder.

It had not occurred to him then, Koehler reflected, that all his work on the ladder might turn out to have been in vain: the prosecution had had to fight stubbornly for its admission as evidence. The defense had been well advised to seek so manfully to block it. Well, it was coming very close to home now.

Max Rauch had left the witness stand. Koehler had not paid too much attention to his testimony; he knew its central point. The young associate prosecutor, Robert Peacock, had employed three witnesses to turn back to November 1931 and trace a carload of lumber from the Dorn mill in McCormick, South Carolina, to the firm of Halligan & McClelland in New York City and then to the National Lumber & Millwork Company in the Bronx. The significance of the shipment, as Peacock had brought out, was that part of it consisted of one-by-four-inch Southern pine boards faintly scarred by a defective knife in a lumber-mill planer (the testimony showed that it was the Dorn mill planer) and the same blemishes in the same places appeared on both of the ladder's bottom side rails, which also were one-by-four Southern pine. Thus, it could be assumed that the ladder-builder had obtained the wood for the bottom rails from the Bronx lumberyard.

The third witness, David Hirsch, part owner of National Lumber, was still on the stand. Peacock sought to trace the single strip of Southern pine from which the two rails had been cut to its ultimate destination.

Had Richard Hauptmann ever been employed by National?

Occasionally, yes.

Had he ever bought lumber from the company?

Sometimes.

When was the last time?

The witness opened a sales ledger, ran his finger to an entry, and replied that Hauptmann had made his last purchase on December 29, 1931.

And how much had he paid for the wood?

Nine dollars and thirty-two cents.

Koehler felt certain that the purchase had included a single strip of Southern pine almost imperceptibly blemished by a defective cutter knife, although of course the National sales ledger gave no clue. The Dorn shipment had arrived at the Bronx yard on December 1, 1931; Hauptmann's purchase four weeks later allowed him plenty of time to build the ladder and use the yellow pine for its legs.

Little profit in speculating on *ifs*, but Koehler couldn't help remembering, with a certain wryness, his visit to the lumberyard more than a year ago. He had been given a sample of the Dorn pine with cutter markings that exactly matched those on the ladder's bottom rails and was confident that the wood for them had been obtained at National. But when he'd asked to see the sales records the foreman was sure that they hadn't kept any at the time the Dorn lumber was sold. He was wrong, as David Hirsch's testimony showed. If the sales ledger had been found that day, Richard Hauptmann might have been captured some nine months earlier.

The next day, Wednesday January 23, a cold wind flung gusts of snow against the courtroom windows.

Lewis Bornmann took the stand again; Koehler nodded to his old companion. Robert Peacock led the detective back to September 26, a week after Hauptmann's arrest. The prisoner's flat was pretty well torn up; to extend the search, Bornmann raised a hatch in the ceiling of a small linen closet off the hall and lifted himself into the attic. Two police carpenters followed him into that dark, dusty, slant-roofed space and, poking around with flashlights, they hunted for more of the Lindbergh money.

The attic was unfinished, floored along its center by one-by-six-inch tongued-and-grooved boards of Southern pine but with the joists, and the laths and plaster below them, exposed on both sides of the flooring where the roof slanted low. Bornmann's eye paused on a board at one edge of the floor. It was only half as long as the others. He knelt for a closer look. His flashlight picked up a sprinkle of sawdust on the laths and plaster beneath one end of the board and a saw cut a quarter of an inch deep extending at an angle into the adjoining board. Then that was why the floorboard was too short: someone had sawed it in half and taken away the missing piece.

Robert Peacock briefly delayed the witness' account to let a previous bit of testimony sink in. Yesterday the owner of the house in the Bronx, Max Rauch, had told the Court that on October 15, 1931, when the Hauptmanns moved into their apartment, the attic floor was intact. Satisfied that the point had not escaped the jurors, Peacock turned back to the witness and he picked up the thread of his story.

Still examining the cut board, Bornmann saw something else of interest: there were several square nailholes in the joists, the exposed beams that had supported the missing strip of flooring.

Closer, closer, Koehler thought. How very close the ladder was now!

Peacock carried the witness on. Some time after Bornmann's discovery, the carpenters had removed the half-length floorboard and ten cut nails in it and Bornmann had taken them from the attic for safekeeping.

Challenging for the defense, Frederick Pope bitingly pointed out that since the police had virtually annexed Hauptmann's flat after his arrest, and that even after their search was ended Bornmann had rented the apartment from the building's owner, locked it up, and placed a guard over it, thus sealing off the entrance to the attic, the court had only the detective's word for it that the board in question, in evidence for the State, actually had been part of the attic floor.

The implication was sharp and Peacock moved to blunt it. Hadn't the defense counselor overlooked the fact that there was also a photo in evidence which showed the floor as Bornmann had found it?

Pope rewarded this with a sniff. Photos could be misleading. And the floor could have been treated so that the picture would show only what the police wanted it to show.

The implication had become almost an assertion. Peacock summoned the two police carpenters who had helped Bornmann remove the board. They confirmed the detective's findings.

It was far from conclusive but Peacock felt it would do for the present. He returned to the prosecution table and David Wilentz glanced across at Koehler.

Koehler nodded. He was ready.

The Court wasn't. Judge Trenchard interrupted the proceedings for lunch.

15

The jurors sat down to lunch, as usual, in the dining room of the Union Hotel. Their passage across the street from the courthouse was relatively tranquil; the wind's snow-edged bite kept all but the hardiest indoors and the jury was spared the usual shouted advice to "put that Dutchman in the hot seat." But, as usual, they heard much comment while they ate. In theory, they were secluded by the screens that separated them from the rest of the dining room, crowded with the trial's spectators; in fact, they were exposed to the violent opinions of dozens of noisy amateur judges. They lunched in bedlam.

In their absence, a new set of stage properties was arrayed in the courtroom theater.

Returning, the jurors stared at the wall rack that had held the handwriting photostats. Now it exhibited huge photo-enlargements and drawings of various portions of wood, illustrating the texture and the marks and scars left by plane and saw and chisel and other man-made, man-operated tools. The handwriting photostats had become boringly familiar, lapped around by a sea of testimony; the jury wondered if this new display, so vivid and interesting at first sight, would also slowly sink into dullness.

Judge Trenchard took his seat. It was pleasant to see a truly professional judge after the wiseacre judges of the dining room.

The courtroom was quiet. David Wilentz said, "The State calls Arthur Koehler."

Koehler got up and walked to the stand, and a reporter with a taste for statistics whispered to a friend in the press gallery that this was the State's seventy-ninth witness.

The seventy-ninth witness for the State of New Jersey *vs.* Bruno Richard Hauptmann was a middle-aged man, rather stooped, fairly bald, neatly dressed. The forest groves he had loved and wandered among in his boyhood and young manhood had not left on him the weathered cheek and rugged cut of the woodsman of fact and fancy; his complexion and demeanor belonged to the laboratories of his later years.

His manner impressed the jury. They had a notion they were not going to be bored.

In answer to Wilentz's request for his credentials, Koehler said that he was the chief wood-identification expert for the United States government. He had been professionally engaged in testing and investigating wood for the past twenty-one years and, as an authority in his field, on various occasions had testified in court. He had a working knowledge of carpentry and the tools of the trade. He had been asked to enter the Lindbergh case by the State of New Jersey and his superiors in the Forest Service and as a result had thoroughly examined the ladder in evidence.

Koehler's voice was pleasantly matter-of-fact, and the jury had no difficulty in hearing every word. Wilentz led him on, drawing attention to the left-hand Southern pine side rail in the top section of the ladder, Rail 16. Had Mr. Koehler detached it from the ladder in order to conduct an experiment in the attic above Richard Hauptmann's apartment?

Yes, he had.

And what relationship, if any, had he found between the ladder rail and the half-length floorboard in evidence that later had been removed from the attic?

Frederick Pope swiftly intervened, saying that the witness could establish a relationship between the two boards only by expressing his opinion, and it was the defense's view that he was not qualified to express such an opinion.

Judge Trenchard seemed puzzled. "Do you say that he is not qualified as an expert on wood?"

"We say that there is no such animal known among men as an expert on wood," Pope retorted. Wood technology, he continued, whatever its merits, was not a science that had been recognized by the courts and therefore the witness was not in a class with fingerprint experts, ballistics experts, handwriting experts. The witness might testify as a carpenter or as someone with experience in examining trees, tell what he saw and what he did, but he could not qualify and speak as a wood expert. Pope gestured toward the jury. "We say that the opinion of the jurors is just as good as his opinion and that they are just as qualified to judge whether there is any relationship between those two pieces of board."

Wilentz replied with some heat that if defense counsel meant to question Mr. Koehler's qualifications, he might have done so while the witness was being introduced rather than wait until the start of the wood testimony.

The judge considered him for a few moments. "I don't want to stand on form, Mr. Attorney General," he said good-naturedly, "and I don't think you do."

In his turn, Wilentz considered him. Judge Trenchard was the last man in the world to speak idly. Those few words might be a warning not to take refuge in a technicality. If he did, the defense could construe it as an attempt to forestall further challenge of Koehler's right to testify, which they could take advantage of should the final verdict go against them. Warning or not, it was better to be safe. "No, sir," he said respectfully.

Very well; if the defense wanted qualifications, they would get them! Wilentz took Koehler back to his college years, developing a picture of a man devoted heart and soul to his subject, rounding it off with a reference to the brief case he had put beside the witness chair. What was in it? Fifty-two bulletins and pamphlets on wood.

Perhaps Mr. Koehler would be kind enough to read the titles aloud? The witness did. And the author's name? Arthur Koehler.

"Let me interrupt a moment," Judge Trenchard said, and turned to the defense table. "Mr. Pope, do you still want to question this witness as to his expert qualities?"

Reilly laid a restraining hand on Pope's arm and rose in his stead. "May we preserve our rights to this extent and have the Court pass upon the witness's qualifications?"

The judge nodded. "I would say to counsel now that I deem this witness to be qualified as an expert."

Wilentz permitted that to sink in and then returned to Rail 16 and the question that had been left hanging: What relationship, if any, had Koehler found between the ladder rail and the attic floorboard?

He had found that at one time the two pieces were one piece. The original strip of wood had been cut in half.

And what had led him to believe that?

Well, several things. First, the nailholes——

Wilentz beckoned him to the display in the wall rack and gave him a pointer with which to indicate the characteristics of the two boards, vastly magnified by the photo-enlargements. Simple and clear as they were, Koehler's easy voice made them simpler and clearer as he took the jurors with him step by step through the dusty attic above the Hauptmann flat.

He had learned about the attic—and, more particularly, about the missing portion of flooring and the square nail holes in the joists—from his old friend Lewis Bornmann, and had thought at once of Rail 16, which had served some other purpose before it was used in the kidnap ladder. It too showed square nailholes. Removing the rail from the ladder and carefully wrapping it, Koehler had set out for the Bronx. The spark of excitement that had died at the dismaying end of his original search in a Bronx lumberyard was burning again, and he felt that this time it would stay alive.

Following Bornmann, he squeezed through the open hatch in the ceiling of the Hauptmanns' linen closet and saw that the attic floor was exactly as the detective had described it. The two men knelt beside the open slit at one edge of the flooring, unwrapped the ladder rail and placed it over the exposed beams. The four nailholes in one tip of the rail appeared to rest on a matching pattern of nailholes in one of the joists. But was the same pattern pursued beneath the surface of the beam, in the varying angles of penetration? One of the holes in the ladder rail slanted sharply.

They would soon find out. Bornmann took four square-cut nails from the ten that had been pried out of the half-length floorboard still in place and gave them to Koehler, who inserted them one by one into the holes in the rail and lightly tapped them with his thumb. One by one the nails sank smoothly into the wood until the nailheads were flush with the face of the board.

Could anyone doubt that this ladder rail had once been nailed to this attic beam? Koehler saw that Bornmann certainly didn't; he was grinning.

There was additional proof. As it rested on the joists, the entire length of the ladder rail ran precisely parallel to the adjoining floorboard. Koehler was convinced that this juxtaposition could not possibly have occurred if the nails had found the two patterns of holes to be less than a perfect match.

The wood expert paused. Seldom before had the courtroom been so quiet. And it was not the peaceful hush of ennui. Those in less favored seats strained to see and hear. The jury, occasionally somnolent after lunch, was brightly alert and attentive. They might have been twelve model pupils in a model schoolroom listening to a model teacher.

Wilentz was gratified. He drew the witness to the basic point: he had said that originally the ladder rail and the attic's half-length floorboard were one piece of wood. Why so?

In reply, Koehler moved his pointer to another part of the display.

Peering down at their experiment in the attic, the two men saw that while Rail 16 lay as a direct extension of the abbreviated floorboard, a one-and-one-fourth-inch gap separated the ends. It seemed to Koehler that the space explained itself. On the laths and plaster beneath the end of the floorboard lay a scattering of sawdust, and opposite the board-end a saw-cut angled slightly into the adjoining board. The original board, then, not only had been sawed in two but the portion that was removed and fashioned into a rail for the ladder also had been sawed off at one end, doubtless because the ladder-builder had judged it to be too long for his purpose.

There was still another bit of evidence that the floorboard had been cut apart, and it did nothing to alter Koehler's conviction that the ladder-builder was a sloppy workman: the half-length strip in the flooring projected well beyond the joist at the point where it had been sawed, so that the end hung free of support. Would the carpenter who had laid the attic floor when the house was built have left it in that condition? Koehler thought not.

He looked once more at the gap separating the two board-ends. Despite the space between them, the continuity of the wood was plain to see: the grain of the ladder rail corresponded precisely with the grain of the floorboard.

But Frederick Pope was up again.

"I object to this unless the gentleman *saw* the missing piece of wood about an inch and a quarter wide. I object to his testifying that there is any matching of the grain between these two boards. It seems quite obvious that you could take almost any piece of Southern pine showing that general grain and draw them far enough apart and together and manipulate them so that you might get a comparative continuity of grain. I object to any expression of opinion as to whether or not these two boards were at one time one board—unless the gentleman will tell us what he knows about the missing piece an inch and a quarter wide."

Glancing at Wilentz, Koehler felt sure the attorney general was aware that he had told all he knew about the missing piece of wood, which of course he had never seen. And the other promptly moved into the breach. The witness had testified that the two boards were connected. Could he not tell how he knew this on the basis of his experience as a wood technologist and his examination of the wood in question?

"I will overrule the objection," Judge Trenchard said.

Koehler's pointer turned to the photos and drawings illustrating the two strips of Southern pine. Every year, a tree girdled itself beneath the bark with a new layer of wood; these layers were known as the annual rings, which told the tree's age and rate of growth.

There were the same number of annual rings in Rail 16 as in the severed floorboard.

But the rings varied as the tree grew, running narrow and wide in no particular sequence and turning light in the spring and dark in the summer.

The same pattern of rings was present in both pieces of wood, with one difference: the rings were wider and more distorted in the end of the floorboard than in the end of the ladder rail.

Koehler explained that this apparent discrepancy was due to a knot which distorted the grain. The closer any grain came to a knot, the more distorted it was. The grain at the end of the floorboard was greatly distorted.

But the rings in the end of the ladder rail were distorted too, not so much as those in the companion board because they were farther away from the knot. This showed that the influence of the knot in the floorboard had spread through the missing one-and-one-fourth-inch-wide piece and into Rail 16.

Trees were like people, Koehler observed; the pattern of growth was never precisely the same in one as in another—but the pattern of the two Southern pine boards matched. In number, curvature and variation their rings corresponded. It followed that they were of the same tissue. At one time they had been one piece of wood.

Wilentz said, "I notice that the ladder rail is not as wide as the attic board. Will you explain that?"

Koehler had noted the difference the moment he saw the garret flooring; it was composed of one-by-six tongued-and-grooved strips and Rail 16 fell short of this width and description. But there was a ready explanation and he gave it now. Both edges of the ladder rail had been shaved with a handplane whose blade was dull and uneven and had left minute ridges on the wood.

The attorney general went to the tool chest in evidence, took out the wood block plane found on a shelf above Hauptmann's workbench, brandished it for the jury to see and placed it in Koehler's hands.

Was this the plane used on the ladder rail?

It was.

How did he know?

"Because when I plane a piece of wood with this plane it makes ridges the same size and the same distance apart as those on the ladder rail."

"Would any other plane make those ridges?"

"No. That would be out of the question."

Wilentz turned to the judge. He wished the witness to demonstrate by planing a piece of wood and comparing the imprint with the ridged pattern on the edges of Rail 16.

Objection by Pope: there was no evidence that the bit of the plane was in the same condition as when the plane was found in the defendant's garage and so the demonstration should not be allowed.

Judge Trenchard disagreed; Pope took a new position. He would like to ask the witness what kind of wood he proposed to plane.

Koehler displayed the wood he had selected for the test. Ponderosa pine, he informed Pope.

And that was different from Southern pine, and much softer, wasn't it?

It was different, yes.

If they were going to have a demonstration, Pope ventured to think that the wood planed ought to be the same kind as the wood of the ladder rail, Southern pine, not a piece of soft pine or soft poplar or something like that.

He didn't have a piece of Southern pine that he could use, Koehler said, but if he could offer a suggestion——

"We don't want any suggestions from the witness," Pope snapped.

"Let the attorney general examine him," the judge said sharply.

Wilentz picked up the thread: What had Koehler tried to say?

He wanted to explain, Koehler replied, that the same imprint of the handplane appeared on the ladder cleats—the steps—as well as on the ladder rail and that the cleats were ponderosa pine.

It was said in a gentle voice, which did not in the least blunt the point of this thrust at Pope. Perhaps defense counsel would think twice, Wilentz reflected, before again employing an insulting tone in referring to the quiet man on the stand. To underline the riposte, he asked:

"Is the piece of wood upon which you will demonstrate the same type, the same quality of wood that makes up those rungs in the ladder?"

"Yes."

With the Court's permission, Wilentz said, the witness would proceed with his demonstration. Judge Trenchard granted it and also allowed Koehler to select one end of the bench as the most appropriate place to clamp the wood in a vise.

Koehler's audience was completely bound up in his preparations; Juror Number 11, Liscom Case, watched with professional interest. He was a retired carpenter. Another retired carpenter, Richard Hauptmann, seemed almost indifferent.

As a youngster, Koehler began, he had amused himself by putting a piece of paper on a penny—or on a nickel, if he happened to be that wealthy—and rubbing a pencil over the paper to bring out the penny's Indian head or the buffalo on the nickel. It produced a clear, complete impression, and he intended to use the same technique to show the imprint of the handplane on wood.

First, so that there would be a basis for comparison, he would make an impression of the test surface before it was planed. He placed a sheet of onionskin paper over the edge of the ponderosa pine strip clamped to the bench and rubbed a pencil briskly back and forth over the paper until the impression was distinct. It was marked for identification. Koehler picked up the plane, set himself alongside the wood and thrust at the edge until a long shaving peeled off. He covered the shaved surface with another onionskin sheet and again rubbed energetically, then repeated the performance with a third sheet placed over a ponderosa-pine cleat in the ladder. These too were marked for identification.

Wilentz exhibited the three sheets to the jury, while Koehler pointed to the impressions they bore. The first sheet showed the curved grain of the wood; the second showed more—a pattern of little ridges. The third impression precisely matched the second.

It could not escape a carpenter's eye—or a judge's, or a housewife's —that the demonstration proved Arthur Koehler's point: the handplane he had used on the sample wood had been used at some previous time on the ladder steps and Rail 16. The track of the blade was the same.

The attorney general drove the point home: it was Richard Hauptmann's plane. Lest there be any question about it, he placed in evidence a wood bracket that had been removed from the defendant's garage; this too, Koehler testified, bore the pattern left by the plane's blade.

Wilentz gave the witness the chisel found on the Lindbergh grounds and asked if it also was one of the tools employed in building the ladder. Koehler said he couldn't be sure—but it was evident that a chisel of the same three-quarter-inch size had been used.

The defense, through the stubborn Pope, objected. For the witness to say that an ordinary three-quarter-inch chisel was used to make the ladder didn't connect it with this chisel in any way. That was obvious!

Well, Judge Trenchard began mildly, perhaps it was a circumstance for the jury to consider——

Pope cut him off. It might be a circumstance if the chisel was found in Hauptmann's garage, but it was found some forty miles from there—

The judge cut in himself; his mildness was gone. "Yes. And it was found, was it not, under the southeast window of the nursery?"

"Somewhere on the Lindbergh estate," Pope said, shrugging. "I don't remember where."

"Where the ransom note was left—which has been traced to this defendant."

Pope stared. "We don't agree to that!"

"I know you don't, but I am telling you what the evidence tends to show. Therefore, I think that these pieces of circumstances must be given over to the jury to consider. That is my ruling on the matter."

The defense attorney had flushed. He seemed about to speak; thought better of it; sat down.

Wilentz drew the witness on. He was satisfied that a three-quarter-inch chisel was used to cut the recesses for the ladder cleats, Koehler said, and though as a rule this size chisel was part of a carpenter's equipment, there wasn't a three-quarter-inch chisel in the defendant's tool chest. He carried the ladder itself close to the rail of the jury box and pointed to the places where a chisel had gouged into the wood. Then, using the chisel Wilentz had given him, he gouged into a sample strip. Again he made paper impressions. Again the impressions matched. Either this chisel or one just like it had been used by the ladder-builder.

Wilentz had saved for the last the testimony which, he had thought—all else failing, as Koehler had not failed—would be bound to capture and impress the jury, since it embraced a truly prodigious feat of detection. He led the witness into that long saga. Koehler described how he had entered the case, long before Hauptmann's arrest, and how by means of some almost imperceptible marks a lumber-mill planer had carved in a strip of Southern pine he had traced the ladder's bottom rails from a South Carolina lumber mill to the Bronx lumberyard where, as it was later shown, Hauptmann provided himself with wood.

The wood expert returned to the photo-enlargements to explain the technical puzzles he had solved; the usual adjournment hour was well past by the time he finished.

Court was recessed. Richard Hauptmann got up slowly. He had looked like a casual spectator, untouched by tales of a boy's experiments with pennies and nickels and paper and pencil; but as the story told by the man who had been that boy mounted steadily to its climax, his indifference had fled, he had moved frequently in his chair, had crossed and uncrossed his wiry legs. He seemed older. He did not glance around for a last look at Anna before his guards led him from the courtroom back to the cell with its permanent glare.

Others repaired to more comfortable accommodations, where the lights were shaded. One was Edna Ferber, the novelist, who was attending the trial as a special correspondent for *The New York Times* and the North American Newspaper Alliance. The distaste stirred in Miss Ferber by certain aspects had become strong enough to be called revulsion; she sat down to tell her readers why. It was considered chic to be seen at the trial, she wrote; for women, certain things added to the chicness—a mink coat, for example, and lavish use of the word *divine* and other hallmarks of the Café Society set—*Darling! Isn't this too, too divine? Isn't this wonderful?*

Yes, wonderful, the writer went on—horrible and sickening and wonderful. She felt like resigning from the human race and cabling Hitler "Well, Butch, you win." All the spectators, she thought, should be turned away—the hungrily staring crowd, like vultures, anxious to watch a living thing writhe just a little longer, like the mob of French *sans-culottes* at the guillotine with their knitting needles. Yes, clear them all out!—all except the people definitely connected with the trial. Miss Ferber listed them: The judge, the jury, the lawyers, witnesses, reporters and special correspondents. "For the jammed aisles, the crowded corridors, the noise, the buzz, the idiot laughter, the revolting faces of those of us who are watching are an affront to civilization."

A brand-new souvenir made its appearance tonight in Flemington's streets and caught on like wildfire. Women snapped them up and pinned them to their coats or hung them from their necks like a multi-armed crucifix, also made of wood—cute little miniature kidnap ladders, only ten cents each.

The jurors dined in the usual noise and retired to their rooms. The broadcasters, commenting on the day's testimony, were going strong in the radio station below. "Who's that one?" a juror asked a colleague, after listening for some time to a resonant, tireless, beautifully polished voice.

"Boake Carter, I think. Why?"

"Damn him."

Arthur Koehler returned to the stand the next morning. Wilentz showed him a photograph of the defendant's dark blue Dodge sedan.

Had the witness disassembled the three-piece ladder and tried to fit it into the car?

Yes, he had. When the three sections nested together they lay on top of the front and back seats with several inches to spare.

More information about the ladder: Koehler pointed out that although it was roughly fashioned, only someone with a knowledge of carpentry could have built it—because it had been necessary to fit the dowel pins snugly in their holes and to cut recesses in the uprights so that the cleats would be flush with the rails.

Wilentz caught up the word. The cleats? They were the steps, weren't they?

Yes.

There was quite a distance between them—?

The attorney general didn't wait for a reply but glanced at Hauptmann and continued:

"A little fellow like me would have a hard time climbing a ladder with steps so widely separated, wouldn't he?"

"Yes," Koehler agreed.

"A man about five feet nine or ten inches would have an easier time, wouldn't he?"

"Somewhat easier, yes."

The attorney general was satisfied. He yielded the witness to Frederick Pope.

He attacked the whole body of the testimony. Koehler was imperturbable in defending it. The morning was still young when the defense counselor broke off this discouraging engagement.

David Wilentz rose—not a tall man, a rather small one but with a commanding and confident air. "The State rests," he said.

It was twenty minutes past noon, Thursday January 24, the seventeenth day of the trial.

16

Crossing to the Union Hotel for lunch, the jurors noticed that today's street crowd seemed larger than usual; the State troopers forcing a passageway knew why: Word had got out that the prosecution was finished and that the first witness for the defense might be Richard Hauptmann himself.

Returning from his lunch, Judge Trenchard surveyed the courtroom without pleasure. More than once its atmosphere had reminded him of a carnival; or, rather, that of the main tent of a circus. All Flemington was a carnival; its atmosphere seeped into the courtroom, the scene of the chief attraction. He had done his utmost to keep it in check; and now again he spoke sternly to the jammed rows of gigglers and chatterers. The room was quiet.

Egbert Rosecrans, tall, thin, very proper, rose for the defense and respectfully addressed the bench:

"If the Court please, I desire to make a motion for a verdict of acquittal."

He listed his reasons. The State had failed to prove that the crime alleged was accomplished in Hunterdon County and therefore the Court was without jurisdiction, the venue having been improperly laid in that county instead of in Mercer County, where the *corpus delicti* was found and where it could be presumed that the blow had been struck and death had occurred.

There was no evidence to show that a wilful, deliberate and premeditated murder had been committed.

Next, while the State contended that the child's death was murder, having resulted from a statutory burglary—the purpose of which was to steal the child's sleeping garment—there was no statute in New Jersey law in which the crime of burglary was defined as such. And there was no evidence that the defendant had committed the common-law definition of burglary, as the baby's garment had not been shown to be of value. Since it had not been proved that a burglary had occurred, the defendant could not be convicted of murder.

Furthermore, the other acts of which the defendant was accused—building the ladder, writing the ransom notes and collecting and spending the ransom money—had occurred in the State of New York and therefore were outside the Court's jurisdiction.

Finally, the evidence that the defendant had written the ransom note found in the Lindbergh nursery did not prove that he was in the nursery on the night of the crime, and the testimony of witnesses who placed him near the scene of the crime was inconclusive. The State alleged that one man, Richard Hauptmann, had accomplished the kidnaping and thus was guilty of murder. In the defense view, the evidence to support the charge was insufficient.

Judge Trenchard glanced at Wilentz. "Does the attorney general care to be heard?"

Wilentz attacked the argument, so forcefully and in such detail that his reply began to have the sound of a summation; and so he swiftly closed: The State respectfully submitted that there was not only sufficient but overwhelming evidence of the defendant's guilt, and it demanded that he answer the charge.

The judge allowed only the barest pause. "The motion for direction of acquittal will be denied," he said.

Glancing at Reilly, the jurors waited for him to rise to deliver the defense's opening statement; but it was Lloyd Fisher who got up. A sound move, a reporter noted. He, and no doubt the jury, well remembered Fisher's angry words to Reilly, and had observed other signs of strain between the "big-city lawyer" and the "country lawyers." The choice of Fisher for the opening would demonstrate that they were, after all, united in a single cause. And he made a good impression—young, nice-looking, obviously believing heart and soul in the defendant's innocence.

"If it please your Honor"—he walked toward the jury box—"and ladies and gentlemen of the jury——"

He took another couple of quick steps; and then, with an occasional gesture and in a candid, eager voice, so filled with the marrow of his belief that it made Rosecrans' seem bone-dry, launched into his address.

He was keenly aware of the importance of the trial and the gravity of the charge, he said, but confident that when the jurors were given the true circumstances they would acquit Bruno Richard Hauptmann.

The defense would prove that Hauptmann was not in the Lindbergh nursery or even in the State of New Jersey on the night of the crime, March 1, 1932; that he was not in St. Raymond's Cemetery on the night of the ransom payment, April 2, 1932; that he was not in Greenwich Village passing a ransom bill on the evening of November 26, 1933. The defense would show that on all three of these crucial dates Hauptmann was somewhere else.

Other testimony on which the State rested its case could be dismissed, too, as the jury would see, and the defendant's finances, which the prosecution had blown up until they far exceeded his actual cash, would be explained simply and clearly, so that there could be no question but that he had obtained the money honestly.

It seemed obvious, Fisher said, that the police had bungled the case. Their bungling showed particularly in their handling of the *so-called*—he underlined the words contemptuously—kidnap ladder, which in no way now resembled the ladder found on the Lindbergh grounds. The defense intended to demonstrate the difference, proving that the ladder in evidence could not possibly be identified as the kidnap ladder. Therefore, all the testimony concerning it was of no consequence.

The defense would prove its case with competent witnesses, but he must caution the jury—and Fisher's tone was disarming in its frank friendliness, that of a man who has nothing to hide—not to expect anything like the array of witnesses supplied by the State. The defense couldn't afford it. Every penny Hauptmann owned had been tied up by the State. His counsel was in no such favorable position as the prosecution, which could and did use the official resources of New Jersey, New York and the United States to press the case. To put it bluntly, the defense was fighting with its back to the wall—but when the facts were established, the jury would see that Bruno Richard Hauptmann was innocent.

Fisher looked at Hauptmann, sitting between the two guards, and smiled, a visible expression of the sturdy confidence with which his speech had closed.

Reilly got up. He too looked at the defendant, the stolid face, the wiry figure dressed as it had been every day of the trial in double-breasted gray suit, much creased, blue-and-white polka-dot tie and blue shirt, and smiled and said, with a return to his avuncular manner:

"Bruno Richard Hauptmann, take the stand."

The defendant seemed anxious to be there; his long legs covered the distance in a few strides. One of his guards followed him and stood behind the witness chair. Hauptmann was sworn in. He sat down, crossed his legs, leaned forward a little and intently watched Reilly.

David Wilentz addressed the bench for the jury's benefit, lest they should think that the guard behind the chair was to thwart any wild notion of escape; or, worse, signified the defendant's presumed guilt rather than his presumed innocence. The guard's position had been approved by both counsel, the prosecutor explained, simply a routine precaution to forestall any disturbance.

He yielded the floor to Reilly. Reilly was splendidly at ease, as much at home as if he were within the walls of his own house, talking to a dearly loved nephew who had been away too long, whose travels were a matter of interest, but certainly not concern, to the older man. He led the witness through the formative years in his native Saxony. For all their seeming casualness, the questions were carefully phrased, inviting little more than *Yes* or *No;* but bit by bit Richard Hauptmann's early life took shape—his schooldays, finished when at fourteen he was apprenticed to a carpenter; his enlistment in the army when he was seventeen; the next twenty months under fire on the Western Front; his return home after the war was lost, older than his years—nineteen—and faced with the grim prospect of making his way in bitter, hungry Germany.

Hauptmann's answering voice was low-pitched, without nervousness. He had laced his stubby fingers together. The accent that had clung to him marked some words strongly.

And it was during this period immediately after the war that he was convicted of—Reilly hesitated, gently chose an inconspicuous word—of an offense?

Yes.

The uncle-attorney drew him through other offenses that had followed it. Hauptmann's answers were almost inaudible; Reilly sauntered over to the jury box, thus without pressure forcing him to raise his voice.

Finally, in 1923, he left Germany——?

Yes.

—and entered the United States after hiding on board a ship?

The memory seemed to please Hauptmann; he smiled, and Reilly smiled too. Yes.

Well, it wasn't an exploit to be ashamed of, they seemed to agree, overcoming all obstacles to reach the New World. Reilly showed the way; more cheerfully, the witness followed. Jobs had been easy to get and each had led to a better one. He was not a man to squander his earnings. "I opened right in the beginning a bank account," he said proudly. Two years after arriving he married a young German woman named Anna Schoeffler and they set up housekeeping, much in the manner of an average American couple.

Reilly signaled a halt; turning to the bench, he asked for permission to suspend Richard Hauptmann's testimony until after two other witnesses had appeared—purely a matter of convenience; they were from New York and the man's business was an exacting one of careful timing. Judge Trenchard put it up to Wilentz. The attorney general said that so long as Hauptmann resumed the stand, the State would not protest.

The defendant returned to his regular chair; the guard followed.

Reilly called Christian Fredericksen to the stand. A small man, not at all at ease, he identified himself as the proprietor of a bakery and lunchroom at 3815 Dyer Avenue in the Bronx, where Anna Hauptmann once worked as counter girl and waitress. He spent most of his time at his ovens; minutes were important with bread and pastries; and Anna had been hired to help his wife, Katie, in the front of the store. Tuesday and Friday evenings Katie went to the movies or visited or took it easy at home and Anna stayed late and looked after the customers by herself.

Reilly strolled toward the jury box. And was this the way it was in March 1932?

Why, yes.

"On Tuesdays and Fridays during March 1932, what time would Anna be through with her work?"

"Oh, I would say around nine o'clock."

"And who would come and take her home?"

"Her husband usually come," the baker said. "As a rule, he always come."

"He would drive her to work at seven in the morning and come back with the car at night and take her home?"

"Yes."

"Do you know that March 1, 1932, was a Tuesday?"

"Yes."

"And Anna worked late on Tuesdays—?"

"Yes."

Reilly was facing the jury. His voice took on more volume, not because he feared it might fail to reach the witness but because of the importance of the question.

"Do you say, Mr. Fredericksen, that—to the best of your recollection—Bruno Richard Hauptmann called for his wife that night, Tuesday, March 1, 1932?"

Christian Fredericksen gave the question careful thought. After some moments, he addressed Reilly's broad back:

"My best recollection is that Bruno usually called for her. He must have been there that night, too, but I can't swear to it."

Reilly walked over to the witness. And did he also recall when Mrs. Fredericksen returned from her evening off on that night?

Well, it seemed likely that she returned when she usually did on her nights off—at ten or eleven o'clock.

Reilly surrendered the witness to the prosecution. Wilentz began matter-of-factly: Of course, Mr. Fredericksen knew that March 1, 1932, was a Tuesday simply because when he was questioned after the defendant's arrest a detective had told him it was——true?

True.

And so he couldn't be sure whether his wife was in or out of the store that Tuesday night?

The little baker said firmly that she was out every Tuesday. Tuesdays Katie was always off.

"And so you think that Mrs. Hauptmann must have been there because your wife was off?"

"Absolutely."

"But Hauptmann wasn't there that night, was he? You didn't see him there that night, did you?"

"I can't swear to it."

"You can't remember. You don't know whether you saw him there or not?"

"No."

"So you don't know whether he was there at all?"

A sigh was heard: Christian Fredericksen's. Not weariness, not exasperation; distress.

"I can't swear to it."

That was enough for Wilentz. Reilly came forward to replace the testimony in what seemed to him to be its proper frame.

"You are giving us your best recollection—is that right?"

"That is it," the baker said gratefully. "Yes, sir."

Katie Fredericksen followed Christian to the chair and Reilly drew her over the same ground. If there had been a feeling of uncertainty in some of her husband's replies, there was none in Katie's. She recalled March 1, 1932, very well, because it was a Tuesday and as usual she had taken the evening off and Anna had stayed in her place; she couln't be mistaken because when she and Christian read and talked about the kidnaping the next day it made her think particularly of the night before, when the terrible thing had been done.

Wilentz challenged again. Since Mrs. Fredericksen was sure she wasn't in the store that Tuesday evening, how could she be sure that Anna Hauptmann was on duty?

Katie replied with the conviction of a woman who knows her husband better, perhaps, than he knows himself. Anna was dependable; but if she *hadn't* been on duty and stayed on duty, Mr. Fredericksen would have complained about it in the morning. And he hadn't said a word.

But Mrs. Fredericksen hadn't *actually seen* Anna in the store that night?

No, Katie said, she hadn't.

The Fredericksens' testimony was finished; Richard Hauptmann resumed the chair, again with the guard behind him. Reilly took him through his life with Anna. The years were good to them, he said; carpenters were in demand and he was seldom out of work, in fact sometimes worked overtime. And Anna was steadily employed, too, and they were able to run the house on her earnings and put his away, some in the bank, some in a safe place at home.

Reilly underlined the point. He kept some of their savings in the house?

"Yes, always. That is a habit I have."

A good deal of money?

Well, at the end of 1929 he had maybe thirty-five hundred dollars in cash hidden away at home, and in the summer of 1931 a little over four thousand.

His story moved to Hunter Island. Starting in 1928—he thought that was about right—he had enjoyed many week ends there with his German friends. These were good memories; he spoke fondly of picnics and games and singing on the island's southern shore.

At last Reilly came to the year of the crime.

On Saturday, February 27, 1932, had he gone to the Reliance Employment Agency in Manhattan—?

Yes.

—and through this agency secured a job?

At the Majestic, yes. On Monday the twenty-ninth he had sharpened his tools and taken them to that apartment house, at 72nd Street and Central Park West, and put them in the carpenters' shop so he would be all ready to work the next day.

The next day would be Tuesday, March 1, 1932?

Yes.

And did he work at the Majestic apartment house that day?

Four months before, at his police questioning, Hauptmann had recalled that he did work on that March 1, his thoughts going back two and a half years; but now he shook his head. When he reported to the Majestic the construction superintendent had told him that he couldn't start until March 15. He had returned on that date and worked at the job until Saturday, April 2, when he quit—because, although he had been promised a hundred dollars a month, he found that he'd get only eighty.

But he *was* at the Majestic that Saturday, April 2?

Oh, yes; it was his last day there. The following Monday he had gone back simply to get his paycheck and had been told that he would have to wait a couple of weeks.

Reilly returned to the significant date, well remembering that the Majestic's timekeeper had declared for the State that Richard Hauptmann had not turned up that day.

"Do you say positively that you did work on April 2?"

Hauptmann's deep voice said, "Positively."

But to Reilly the matter was too important to dismiss with even so firm a response; he asked for an accounting.

Hauptmann said that he had left his apartment at seven that Saturday morning, and except for an hour off for lunch he had worked through the day until five. He had arrived home at six or so. Anna was there. Around seven, his friend Hans Kloeppenburg had come with his guitar. On the first Saturday evening of every month they got together and fooled around with some music, he on his mandolin, Hans on his guitar—sang old songs, laughed, had a good time. It always lasted till nearly midnight. It was a regular thing, a habit they'd formed.

Reilly summed it up.

"On the night of April 2, 1932, after you came home from work in the neighborhood of six o'clock, did you leave your home?"

A young man in the courtroom, the most deeply involved of all the trial's spectators, leaned forward in his seat. On the night of April 2, 1932, he, Charles Lindbergh, was sitting in Al Reich's Ford coupé at St. Raymond's Cemetery when he heard a man's voice call to Dr. Condon, "Hey, Doctor." Not long afterward, the ransom payment was exchanged.

The defendant answered firmly, "No, sir."

"You were in your apartment all the time?" Reilly asked.

"All the time."

It was half-past four in the afternoon; Court was adjourned. Head up, confident, Richard Hauptmann walked between his two guards toward his cell.

17

He looked well-rested, alert, anxious to get on with his testimony, when he resumed the witness chair the next morning. David Wilentz thought he'd never looked healthier.

Listening to Reilly's opening questions, designed to establish Hauptmann's friendship with Isidor Fisch, the attorney general reflected that the two men must have seemed unlikely friends: the lithe, muscular Hauptmann with his darkish blond hair and the obviously ailing Fisch, black-haired, underweight and pale. There could be no question, though, that they had been friends.

Wilentz knew a good deal about Isidor Fisch. During those sleepless hours in the Greenwich Street police station after his arrest, Hauptmann had told his questioners that Fisch was dead—had died in Leipzig, Germany, several months before. The gold notes found in his garage, he had explained, belonged to Isidor.

Lieutenant Finn's detectives had set out to gather some facts on this mysterious figure.

Through extensive investigations in New York and Leipzig, they learned that in 1925 Isidor Fisch and his good friend Henry Uhlig, both nineteen, had left Germany for America. They had lived together in a New York apartment, shared friends and interests, and become citizens. Isidor's health wasn't too good; colds bothered him a lot; he thought that a trip home might serve as a tonic and, on May 12, 1932—marked by the sensational news of the discovery of the Lindberghs' baby's body—he had applied for a passport, with the idea of sailing for Germany on the *Leviathan* in July.

But then Uhlig lost his job and couldn't find another; he stubbornly insisted on moving alone to a cheap furnished room rather than burden his friend. Isidor was so upset that he put off his trip. In August, he moved to a furnished room near Uhlig's, on the upper East Side of Manhattan. His health didn't improve; by the next summer he had developed a chronic cough that shook him painfully. He thought he'd better get back to the old country while he could to see the parents and brother and sister for whom his heart longed. Uhlig agreed to go with him.

They sailed on December 6, 1933. And on March 29, 1934, in St. George Hospital, Leipzig, Isidor Fisch died of tuberculosis of the lungs. His sister Henna, his brother Pincus, and Henry Uhlig were at the bedside.

Reilly's questions continued. He had been told by the witness that he and Fisch had met at Hunter Island early in March or April 1932. No one introduced them; things were free and easy on the island; they just fell into talk and took to each other. Fisch informed his new friend that he was a fur trader and Hauptmann responded that he was by way of being a trader too—trading stocks. Played the stock market, in other words. Fisch was interested, so much so that early in May he proposed a partnership: each would keep on with his specialty, Fisch buying and selling furs, Hauptmann stocks, but they'd invest equally in each enterprise, in which each of them would have a half interest—Fisch putting up money to buy stocks, Hauptmann giving Fisch money for furs. Profits and losses, of course, would be split fifty-fifty.

So, the witness went on, in the middle of May he gave Fisch six hundred dollars to invest in furs, and in August Isidor gave him money for stocks. The partnership had worked out well. Hauptmann wasn't certain just how much he'd made from the fur business, but several times Fisch had handed over different sums, clear profit.

Their friendship waxed in this balmy atmosphere and Isidor frequently visited the Hauptmanns' flat. The night before he left for Germany he had called at the apartment to say good-by.

Reilly asked, "Did Fisch have anything with him—bundles or anything—the night before he sailed?"

"No, sir."

"Before he sailed, did he leave anything with you for you to take care of while he was away?"

"He left two suitcases," Hauptmann replied.

"What else?"

"Four hundred fur skins—Hudson seal."

"What else?"

Hauptmann said, "A little box."

Reilly was interested in this box. He invited the witness to describe the circumstances in which, on a previous visit, Isidor Fisch had given it to him.

It was on a Saturday evening, Hauptmann remembered, a few days before Fisch sailed.

And——?

"Well, Fisch was throwing a party when he left for Germany. It was at his request in our house. We invited a couple of friends and about nine o'clock or a short while before, Fisch came and got a little bundle under his arm. I answered the doorbell—my wife was in the baby's room. We went in the kitchen and Fisch said, 'I leave it, I leave something, if you don't mind, keep care of it and put it in a tight place.' I didn't ask what is in it; he only said that is paper in it. I thought maybe they are——"

Wilentz, rising, stopped him. "Just a minute."

Hauptmann's steady voice continued, "——they are bills and receipts."

The attorney general told the bench that he objected to the witness' opinion. With an air of sweet tolerance, Reilly translated for Hauptmann's benefit. "Tell us what you did," he said, "not what you thought."

The witness complied. There was a broom closet in the kitchen—that is, a closet where his wife kept her brooms, mops, soap, polish, things of that sort—and he had put Fisch's little bundle on the top shelf.

Months passed. Word came that Fisch had died in Leipzig, but the bundle on the closet shelf slipped Hauptmann's mind. Then, on a rainy Sunday in the middle of August 1934, he went to the closet for a broom:

"The broom is on the left side in the closet. And when I took the broom I must hit the box with the broom handle, and I looked up, and I saw that it is money. I damaged the box."

Reilly asked, "And you saw money?"

"Yes."

"In the box?"

"Yes. Soaking wet."

He explained. There was a leak in the roof; a ventilation pipe extended from the roof through the broom closet in his kitchen and he guessed the shingles didn't hug the pipe tightly enough, so that whenever there was a heavy rain, the water flowed down the outside of the pipe into the closet and spread over the shelves. He had complained to the landlord several times but the leak hadn't been fixed.

Reilly brought him back to the box. It had gotten wet——?

Sopping wet. That explained why he saw the money—the broom handle had knocked through the wet cardboard.

"Did you take the box down?"

Yes, he did. There was so much water, the water was so thick it ran down his arms as he lifted the box from the shelf. He put it in a pail and carried it to the garage, tore off the sodden paper wrapping and saw that it was a shoe box. Inside the box were four bundles wrapped in thin brown paper, with wads of newspaper wedged between them; these too were drenched. He removed the money—all gold certificates—and squeezed out the water as best he could. Even so, the gold notes stuck together. He left them that way without attempting to count them and put them in a basket to dry. Covering the basket, he placed it on a top shelf of the garage, directly beneath the roof, put another basket on top of it and nailed two vertical strips of wood to the shelf so that the money basket couldn't be seen. Two weeks later he took down the basket; the gold certificates were fairly dry and he counted them, withdrew a few and spent them.

Reilly returned to the witness' financial transactions with Isidor Fisch. When his partner sailed for Europe, Hauptmann had twelve thousand dollars "in stock on margin," he said. Fisch owned two thousand five hundred of that and "said he got twenty-one thousand dollars of furs." Fisch needed cash when he left and suggested selling the furs, but Hauptmann felt it was a bad time to sell. Instead, a few weeks before the other sailed, he drew a check against his stock account and gave Fisch two thousand in cash as a loan.

Reilly went to the kidnaping.

"On the night of March 1, 1932, did you enter the nursery of Colonel Lindbergh——"

Hauptmann's emphatic words cut through:

"I did not."

"——and take from that nursery Charles Lindbergh, Jr.?"

"I did not."

Yesterday, Reilly reminded him, he had spoken of that March 1 in a general way; would he now please tell the jury where he was and what he did that day from the time he got out of bed in the morning until he went to bed at night?

Well, Hauptmann began in his steady, confident voice, he woke up about six that morning, March 1, 1932. Between six-thirty and a quarter to seven he drove his wife to work in his car—Fredericksen's bakery, a good mile away, where Anna had to be on duty at seven. He didn't go into the shop; just dropped Anna, then drove back to the house, put the car in the garage and went to the White Plains Avenue subway station, a six- to nine-minute walk. The subway took him down to 72nd Street and Broadway where he got off and walked to the Majestic Apartments. In the carpenters' shop the foreman told him to see the superintendent; when he did, the super told him he couldn't start work that day. Well, so he left his tools in the shop and went down to the Reliance agency to get back the ten-dollar fee he'd paid. The Reliance people put him off, told him to return the next day; maybe they'd have a good job waiting for him. He made the rounds of some other agencies but there wasn't anything doing at them and so he applied at Radio City, which was going up then, a big building job. Nothing there either. So he went home, got there about five. Since it was Tuesday, one of Anna's late nights at the bakery, with Katie Fredericksen taking the evening off, he drove there at around seven, ate supper at the bakery and then took the Fredericksens' police dog for a walk—this was a regular thing—while waiting for Anna to finish. He walked as far as the Boston Post Road; on the way back, a man waiting at a gas station asked about the dog.

Reilly stopped the account. He asked deliberately:

"At about what time of the night?"

"Between eight and half-past eight."

"Between eight and half-past eight," Reilly repeated, glancing at the jury. Across the Hudson River, in New Jersey, near the village of Hopewell, during this same stretch of time the kidnaper must have been approaching the new white house, perhaps had paused, surveying it in the damp, windy night—a last pause before the act itself.

After telling the inquisitive man that the dog belonged to Christian Fredericksen, Hauptmann continued, he returned to the bakery and at nine o'clock or thereabouts drove Anna home. He put the car away and they went to bed.

"I ask you again," Reilly said earnestly: "Were you in Hopewell, New Jersey, on March 1, 1932!"

Hauptmann said, as earnestly, "I was not."

He got up at his usual time the following morning—six—drove Anna to the bakery, drove home, garaged the car and started for Manhattan by subway. He bought a paper just before getting on the train. It was then he learned that the Lindbergh baby had been kidnaped.

Reilly motioned to a court attendant and the three sections of the kidnap ladder were placed in direct view of the defendant and the jury. Hauptmann watched with interest.

The lawyer turned from the ladder to the witness.

"Did you build this ladder?"

"I," Hauptmann said, half-proudly, half-scornfully, "am a carpenter."

His tone said: That is answer enough. It was not enough for Reilly. He said again, his raised voice quelling the laughter in the courtroom:

"Did you build this ladder?"

"Certainly not."

"Come down and look at it, please."

The witness left the stand and examined the ladder. His forehead wrinkled.

"Looks like a music instrument," he observed, with what appeared to be genuine wonder that such a contraption could be put together.

More laughter. The judge's gavel cut it off. Hauptmann resumed the chair. It didn't look like a ladder at all, he commented; he didn't see how a man could use it.

Reilly proceeded to other evidence employed by the State against him.

Had he taken any wood from the attic over his apartment and used it as a ladder rail?

No.

Left a chisel on the Lindbergh grounds?

No.

Written any of the ransom notes?

No.

"On April 2, 1932, were you in St. Raymond's Cemetery and did you receive fifty thousand dollars from Dr. Condon?"

"I did not."

Hauptmann had said previously that he had not left his flat that night, his regular music evening, but now he recalled that at about half-past eleven he drove Hans Kloeppenburg to his streetcar.

Reilly moved on. Of course, the witness had excellent reason to remember November 26?

Yes, it was his birthday.

On the night of November 26, 1933, had he gone to the Sheridan Square Theater in Greenwich Village?

No, he had not. He had spent the evening at home celebrating his birthday with a few friends.

He hadn't tossed a Lindbergh ransom bill, folded in eight parts, at the theater cashier?

He had not. He had never set foot in Greenwich Village in his life, up to the time the police took him there.

Reilly wished to account for a third occasion, brought up by the State through a singularly attractive witness. A young lady, he said, a Miss Alexander, had declared that in March 1932 she saw Hauptmann secretly watching Dr. Condon in a Bronx railroad station. *Had* he watched the old man in the circumstances described?

He was familiar with the station, the witness replied, but he had never been inside it.

After lunch, Reilly walked to the witness stand holding two duplicate sheafs of photostats, copies of the defendant's bank and brokerage transactions that defense counsel had told the jury would be explained. He gave Hauptmann one set, kept the other. The witness, calmly accepting his set, took from a pocket the notes he had made in his cell the week end before, to help his memory. He pulled out a yellow pencil and poised it above the papers and waited, alert, interested, confident.

Methodically, with the air of accountants studying important business figures, they moved through the years following Richard Hauptmann's arrival in America. The witness said that at the end of 1929 his total wealth—which embraced a $3750 mortgage, the money he and Anna had put in the bank, and the considerable cash of his own that he kept at home—amounted to approximately $9000.

And was it about this time that he became interested in Wall Street?

Yes. He had made his first investment in the stock market with $2800 he withdrew from the bank on November 1, 1929.

Reilly's questions guided the witness back to his partnership with Isidor Fisch and the brokerage sheets of Steiner Rouse & Company, through which, Hauptmann said, Fisch had played the market.

Clarifying this, Reilly asked if the arrangement was that, even with funds Fisch supplied, Hauptmann alone dealt in stocks and the account was in his name?

Yes.

They went on, tracing the transactions on the brokerage sheets through the year in which the witness said he had first met his friend, the year of the crime, 1932. On September 15, Hauptmann had deposited $170 in cash with Steiner Rouse. He took it from $4300 he had hidden at home, he told Reilly.

Reilly held up a forefinger, pinning the jury's attention to his next question.

Was one dollar of that cash—or *any* cash the witness had deposited in this account at *any* time—Lindbergh ransom money?

No.

Reilly nodded at the jury. There you are, he seemed to say.

Back to figures. In August 1932, Hauptmann remembered, as always carefully studying his own notes and the photostat records, for the first time Fisch had given him money to purchase stocks. It was in cash. Later, too—whenever Fisch gave him money—it was in cash. As the records showed, on September 19 the witness had deposited this first sum from Fisch, $582.50, in his account at Steiner Rouse. On October 7 he had put in $860 supplied by Fisch. February 1933 had been a particularly busy month; but the $700 deposited in cash on February 27 was his own money—he had withdrawn five hundred of it from his and Anna's joint account in the Central Savings Bank and the remaining two hundred was his share of the profit from one of Fisch's fur deals.

Witness and attorney seemed to be in a snug account-book world of their own. Questions and answers fell into a pattern, a precise, almost predictable duet.

March 1, 1933. Hauptmann had deposited eight hundred and fifty in cash in his Steiner Rouse account. Where had the money come from?

Fisch.

April 28. Hauptmann had deposited two thousand five hundred in cash. The money was from—?

Fisch.

May 3. Hauptmann had deposited two thousand five hundred seventy-five dollars in cash——?

Fisch.

Throughout May and into June there had been a good deal of trading, buying and selling——?

Yes.

And then June 7. Hauptmann had deposited two thousand two hundred twenty-five dollars in cash. Money from—?

Fisch.

All through June and July there had been a heavy purchase of stocks?

Yes.

And on July 24 Hauptmann had put four thousand five hundred in cash into his account?

Yes. The witness added that that was the last bit of money Fisch gave him to invest in the market.

"Fisch put in that four thousand five hundred in cash to cover the overlapping margin; is that correct?" Reilly asked.

"Yes, because I bought very lightly that month for myself."

"And in that month you did about forty-nine thousand three hundred dollars worth of business on the books of Steiner Rouse?"

"Yes."

"Where the month before you did fifty thousand?"

"Yes."

"The month before the debit balance that you owed Steiner Rouse was seven thousand nine hundred seventy-three dollars and seventy-two cents?"

"Correct."

"And at the end of July it was reduced by profits and deposits to four thousand thirty-eight dollars?"

"That is right."

Reilly went on to the winter of 1933 and the witness called his attention to November 14, when he had withdrawn $2057 from his brokerage account. He had cashed a check in that amount at a Yorkville bank, he explained, and given two thousand to Fisch for his trip to Germany, keeping the other fifty-seven dollars for himself.

There was one other thing he wished to clear up: prior to Fisch's departure, Hauptmann had used his share of the fur profits to pay for his and the family's expenses; but after Fisch sailed, in December, and the fur business languished, he regularly drew from his brokerage account to pay his living costs.

Reilly moved ahead. After Fisch left, Hauptmann had continued to deal in stocks, using only his own money, hadn't he?

That was right.

"And in January 1934 we find the account very active, don't we?"

"Yes."

"Buying the second, third, fourth, fifth, ninth, eleventh, twelfth, fifteenth, sixteenth, nineteenth and twenty-fourth?"

Hauptmann checked off the dates. "Yes."

"Selling the third, fourth, fifth, tenth, seventeenth and eighteenth?"

"Yes."

Reilly paused for a significant glance at the jury; it must be plain, certainly, that he was drawing in on the contention he had made during his bout with the State's financial expert, William Frank. Yes, these brokerage accounts seemed to show a great deal of money but it was far more show than reality. In fact, Reilly had claimed, it was mostly paper money—traveling transactions—the results of the defendant's steady trading in the market.

"In January," he resumed to Hauptmann, "when you were dealing for yourself, no cash was placed in the account, was there?"

"Only a little—eighty dollars in dividends."

And in February 1934, he sold more stocks than he bought—?

Yes.

"So that your debit balance dropped from nine thousand six hundred forty-one dollars and sixty cents in January to one thousand three hundred thirteen dollars and three cents at the end of February; is that right?"

Yes, that was right.

But on February 26, 1934, he had deposited $1350 in cash in his brokerage account; where had this money come from?

The witness explained that on February 16 he had taken $1500 from Steiner Rouse to lend to a friend, but they'd disagreed on terms and so he'd put almost all the cash—$1350—back in his account.

And except for eighty dollars in dividends, this $1350 was the first money he deposited with Steiner Rouse since July 24, 1933, when he put in Fisch's $4500?

Yes.

"So that the account was carrying itself in August, September, October, November and December 1933 and in January and February of 1934, *without the inclusion of a dollar of your money except the dividends I have referred to?*"

Reilly bore down heavily on the last words. Hauptmann answered:

"That is correct."

Diligent, exact, wasting no words or gestures, the attorney reached farther into the witness' financial history. On March 1, 1934, Hauptmann said, he collected a couple of dividends and bought and sold at will throughout the month, with the result that the balance he owed Steiner Rouse rose from $1313.03 to $12,746.08 on March 31.

But he put no cash in his account.

In April, he bought and sold again—some $27,000 worth of trading—and at the end of the month his debit balance was $11,144.94.

But he put no cash in his account.

In May, he reduced his debit to $9000; in June to $6511.57; in July to $3800; and on August 31, 1934, he had wiped out the debt, was out of the red and in the black with $1242.41 to his credit.

And in all these months he put no cash in his account.

Reilly condensed the pages of figures, the questions and answers, the ground they had covered so far, in one sentence:

"From the day in July 1933, when Fisch put in four thousand five hundred dollars until September 14, 1934, when this account at Steiner Rouse was closed, isn't it a fact that the only cash you put into it were small dividends and one thousand three hundred and fifty dollars of the fifteen-hundred-dollar check that you drew?"

Hauptmann's reply, too, was in effect a summation of all his answers:

"That is correct."

Reilly turned to another financial matter. On March 15, 1933, had the witness deposited $1250 in his bank account?

Yes; that was when President Roosevelt had directed everyone who owned gold to turn it in for other forms of currency. Hauptmann said he had deposited $750 in gold certificates and $500 in gold coins.

And were any of the gold certificates Lindbergh money?

No. All of it, notes and coins, had been part of the $4300 he had hidden in his apartment. He had held on to it—not even putting it in his bank or brokerage account—because he was afraid of inflation. Then the President had made it illegal to keep gold and he'd taken the whole sum to his bank.

"And when you put in the seven hundred fifty in gold notes, you made out a deposit slip?"

"I did."

"And you handed it in the window?"

"I did."

"In a bank you had been trading with for years and years?"

"Trading with for eight years."

A few of the more acute listeners in the press gallery thought that Hauptmann's explanation didn't seem to fit; then they remembered that President Roosevelt had called in all gold on April 5, 1933, three weeks after the March 15 deposit. But that hardly changed one significant aspect of the deposit: would the Lindbergh kidnaper have risked apprehension by turning in a pack of gold certificates to a bank—any bank—where their serial numbers might be checked against the Lindbergh ransom list?

Assuming of course that Hauptmann was telling the truth—that they were gold certificates. The deposit slip wouldn't show.

The money chapter was closed. Attorney and client seemed confident that it had gone off well. Hauptmann was smiling, not cockily; an easy, good-feeling smile. He might have smiled just such a smile looking at stock prices on the board when the financial tide chanced to be running in his favor.

Reilly opened a new chapter. As before, when dealing with its basic material—the police—his tone and manner reflected many past victories. He asked the witness:

"When you were taken to the New York City police station, were you beaten by the police?"

Wilentz was up with an objection but Hauptmann spoke over it: "I was."

There was no confession of guilt by the accused which his counsel could claim had been obtained by force, Wilentz said to Judge Trenchard, and therefore the question was not material to the case.

The judge thought perhaps the point was not quite so simple. The State had introduced handwriting specimens taken by the police and police witnesses had testified that the tests were executed voluntarily. If the question was limited to these tests, and whether or not the accused had submitted to them willingly, it would be allowed.

Reilly boiled it down:

"Were you beaten—yes or no?"

"Yes, sir."

Where and when?

The second evening after his arrest, in the Greenwich Street station. That was the first time the police had required him to write.

"In writing," Reilly said with even more than his usual care, "did you spell the words of your own free will or did they tell you how to spell them?"

"Some of the words they spell it to me."

"How do you spell *not*?"

"N–O–T."

"Did they ask you to spell it N–O–T–E?"

Hauptmann said firmly, "I remember very well they put an *e* on it."

"How do you spell *signature*?"

"S–I–G–N–A–T–U–R–E."

"Did they tell you to spell it S—I—*n*—G——"

"They did."

"—N–A–T–U–R–E?"

"So when they were dictating the spelling, that was not your own free will in spelling, was it?"

"It was not."

Here, certainly, was grist for Wilentz's mill, some reporters thought. *Signature* was a key word. It had appeared—spelled si*n*gnature—in the original note left in the Lindbergh nursery; and John, in his conversations with Dr. Condon, had used it—and pronounced it si*n*gnature.

But in preparing the handwriting test, Albert Osborn had purposely left it out. It would hardly be a valid test, he had felt, because the newspapers had given so much publicity to the ransom-note writer's misspelling.

Reilly forged on. If the police had told the witness what to write, why had he submitted to the tests?

"They forced me. They said, 'You won't get any sleep. You got to write.'"

The police had kept after him for hours, Hauptmann continued. He was exhausted but they wouldn't let him sleep. Every time he dozed off they jabbed him in the ribs and said, "You write."

And after the writing tests——?

"I got the treatment. It wasn't home at all."

But later, when he was removed to the Bronx jail, he had given a statement to the Bronx district attorney in which he said he was being treated fairly?

Hauptmann explained again: the statement applied only to the Bronx jail. The result of his treatment in Manhattan was that he had lost over thirty pounds.

Reilly thanked him. The direct examination was over. Glancing at the man who would conduct the cross-examination, Hauptmann shifted in his seat, touched his polka-dot tie; but it was not a nervous gesture. Reilly and he had got along so well that he seemed perfectly comfortable in the chair, content to be where he was.

Without visible apprehension, he watched Wilentz approach. The courtroom waited for the prosecutor's first assault; but it was Hauptmann who, against all custom, spoke first.

He said he would like to explain that in testifying to his financial transactions with Isidor Fisch he had spoken from memory because they hadn't kept records of their dealings with each other.

"I see," Wilentz said helpfully. "What you mean is that everything you have said about your financial transactions is your best recollection and there may be a difference here or there——?"

Exactly what he meant.

Well, the attorney general observed, they'd come to that later. He continued, quite pleasantly:

"You have had an opportunity in this Court, and you still have an opportunity, to tell the whole truth—"

Hauptmann cut in quickly. He had told the truth.

"So that you now stand on the story you have given?" Wilentz asked.

Yes, he did stand on it.

"And the story that you swore to before a court in the Bronx?"

The witness hesitated. To a certain extent, yes.

Reilly had touched gently on Richard Hauptmann's criminal past in Germany. Wilentz was not gentle. He did not use the word *offense*. He spoke of robberies, arrests, broken parole, and underlined with mock surprise the first crime: Hauptmann had *climbed a ladder* to a *second-story window* and broken into the house of the *most eminent citizen* of the neighboring town. And subsequently he had held up two women who were *wheeling baby carriages.*

The witness chair had become uncomfortable. For the first time Hauptmann took out a handkerchief and wiped his face. He began, half angrily, "Everybody wheels baby carriages—" but Wilentz's harsh voice overrode him, moving on to later events: he had entered the United States illegally, uninvited, had enjoyed the opportunity to make a living here, and then—in the period following the Lindbergh crime—had begun to arrange for his return to Germany when the statute of limitations would protect him from being jailed as a fugitive from justice.

All that was true, wasn't it?

Yes, the witness said reluctantly; it was true.

Wilentz took out a small red account book and showed it to Hauptmann. It was easily recognizable as still another of his belongings that had been confiscated by the police. They'd come up with many others, after his arrest.

The attorney general gave him time to study the pages. Then:

"Is that your handwriting?"

"Yes."

Wilentz was standing beside the chair; he turned to another page, pointed.

"And is that your handwriting—that one word?"

Hauptmann did not answer. The attorney general waited. No answer. The witness stared at the word. He looked around, looked back at it. Still no answer.

"Or," said Wilentz with bitter humor, "did some *policeman* write it?"

At last Hauptmann spoke, unevenly:

"I—I can't remember every word I put there."

Wilentz pointed to some numbers on the same page. "Are they your figures?"

"They must be my figures."

"That is your word, then, isn't it?"

"I can't remember if I ever put it in."

The crowd had been waiting for a blunt, tough assault; they heard it now. Wilentz seemed to enjoy delivering it.

"Either it is your handwriting or it isn't! Is it your handwriting?"

"It looks like my handwriting."

"Now, tell me, how do you spell *boat*?"

Hauptmann said carefully, "B–O–A–T."

Wilentz shouted:

"Why did you spell it B-O-A-D?"

His voice, his pointing forefinger, leveled at the open book, seemed to force Hauptmann back against the chair's hard spine. He looked away, then asked if he could examine the book. Wilentz gave it to him, and the witness turned the pages. Yes, he said finally, it was just as he thought, the account book was probably eight years old. Over the years, one's writing improved.

Wilentz asked if that meant that at one time he had spelled *boat* B–O–A–D?

No, he didn't think so.

The forefinger jerked in front of Hauptmann's face. "You spelled it in there, didn't you? Tell the truth now! Didn't you spell it in there?"

Lloyd Fisher rose to object and Frederick Pope followed. "It isn't *twice* objectionable, is it?" Wilentz inquired.

Fisher said it certainly was. Judge Trenchard, settling the issue, said that it wasn't necessary to demand that the witness tell the truth.

The witness put away his handkerchief as Wilentz attacked again. Was the word B–O–A–D in his handwriting or wasn't it?

Hauptmann answered, falteringly, that he wouldn't say yes and he wouldn't say no. He couldn't remember putting it in the book.

"The reason you won't say yes or no is because you know you wrote *boad* when you got the fifty thousand from Dr. Condon—isn't that right?"

"No, sir."

Wilentz took one of the kidnap notes from the State's exhibits, the note Dr. Condon had testified John had given him in exchange for the ransom money. The prosecutor put it in Hauptmann's hand, saying, "*Boad Nelly*. Look at it."

The witness looked. "No."

"Look at it again! Look there!"

Hauptmann's eyes followed the pointing finger. The words it pointed to read:

> the boy is on Boad Nelly it is a small Boad 28 feet long. . . .

He looked up. Wilentz asked:

"You come from Saxony, don't you?"

"Yes."

"In Saxony they use *d* instead of *t*, don't they? All the words are *boad* instead of *boat*, and things like that——?"

"Some of them, yes."

"And you spelled the word *boat* as B–O–A–D because that's the way they would spell it in Saxony; isn't that it?"

Hauptmann shook his head. In Saxony they might pronounce it with a *d* but they spelled it with a *t*.

The prosecutor swung over to a new line of attack. Hauptmann had said that he was a carpenter?

"I am."

But he hadn't worked regularly as a carpenter since April 1932?

"That is correct."

Instead, he spent all his time trading in the stock market?

"Yes."

And every dollar that had gone into his brokerage account—whether his own money or money given to him, so he claimed, by Fisch—he had delivered to the broker himself?

"Yes, sir."

He alone had turned over the money to the broker; Fisch hadn't given the broker a penny?

"No."

And of the two persons who had known about the partnership and the stock investments Hauptmann said he had made for his partner and friend, one—Isidor Fisch—was dead?

The witness nodded. Then he murmured, "Unfortunate."

Wilentz nodded too, but not compassionately. His expression seemed to say: Unfortunate indeed!—notably for Isidor Fisch but also for the State, whose task otherwise would be far simpler.

The prosecutor moved to an exhibit in which he saw more significance than was immediately apparent, thanks to his conversations with the psychiatrist Dudley Shoenfeld. The exhibit was a board from Hauptmann's garage. He had drilled a series of holes in it.

The witness noticed, didn't he, Wilentz asked, that the holes in the board were round, just like the circles in the signature on the ransom notes?

Hauptmann said, for once as if to a not very bright person, "When you drill a hole, it has got to be round."

"Yes, I know that. But you don't need a round hole to put money in, do you?"

"It wasn't prepared for money."

Oh, no? Hadn't he told the Bronx district attorney that he had drilled five holes in the board to hold money, the same money the police found in the holes, Lindbergh money, eight hundred and forty dollars in gold notes?

No, no, the witness protested; the holes were intended to hold small tools.

But he *had* used the holes to put the money in?

Later, yes.

Wilentz pointed to the sixth hole, an oblong shape. Why had he made this?

Hauptmann crossed his legs, uncrossed them; his fingers wandered apart, locked together again. He said, almost inaudibly:

"To put something in."

"*What* did you put in?"

"It wasn't money," Hauptmann whispered.

"Answer the question!"

"I put something in there."

"Answer the question!"

Reilly got up. Objecting to the prosecutor's line of questioning, his manner was that of a reasonable man whose patience has been tried too far. "I say that unless ransom money was in that particular hole of which he speaks," he concluded, "the admission of what he made it for or what he did is incompetent, immaterial and—dangerous."

Judge Trenchard didn't agree; the witness must answer.

"*What did you put in?*" Wilentz cried.

Hauptmann's diminished voice said:

"I put a small pistol in it."

A loaded pistol?

Yes.

And stuffed the other five holes with bills?

Yes.

At a quarter to five, past the usual time, the judge called the session to an end. Hauptmann left the chair that had grown so hard. Again he walked between the guards toward his cell. There was no trace of a smile on his lips and the lightness was gone from his step.

18

The slim lady dog that had wandered into Flemington in search of a meal would never have recognized herself in the prosperous mascot of Nellie's Tap Room. Besides a stomach, she had developed a taste for beer and an ear for music. One of her reporter friends had introduced to the tap room the schnitzel-bank song that enlivened German-American beer halls in Manhattan, a descendant of old German rhymed lessons in which the teacher pointed to drawings on a chart and demanded corroboration of his belief that this was a house or a tree or a mountain or an elephant or whatever.

The crowd in Nellie's sang their own version this Friday night:

Ist das nicht ein ransom box?
Ja, das ist ein ransom box!
Ist das Fisch ein clever fox?
Ja, Fisch ist ein clever fox!

Ransom box?
Clever fox!

Ist das nicht ein sing*nature?*
Ja, das ist ein sing*nature!*
Ist das nicht peculiar?
Ja, ist damn peculiar!

Sing*nature?*
Peculiar!

Ist das nicht ein ransom note?
Ja, das ist ein ransom note!
Ist das nicht ein Nelly boad?
Ja, das ist ein Nelly boad!

Ransom note?
Nelly boad!
Sing*nature?*
Peculiar!
Ransom box?
Clever fox!

They sang these and other verses again and again and again and yet again. Hearing her name, or what in pardonable error she took to be her name, Nellie the mascot enthusiastically responded and joined in the fun. The music and her happy barking rose to the jurors in their rooms above.

In his cell, the prisoner's depression had gradually lifted as he immersed himself in the familiar and reassuring world of his brokerage and bank accounts and the notes he had made. He checked and rechecked the figures. After some hours of study, calm and confident again, he lay down on the cot, apparently feeling—as one guard later remarked to another, when the new shift of guards relieved them—that the jury's verdict would be decided in his favor by the accounting he had given of where the money for his stock-market ventures had come from.

If that was Hauptmann's belief, one special correspondent did not agree with him. Putting down for *The New York Times* his impressions of the day's testimony, Alexander Woollcott wrote that if any one of the "saucer-eyed mob of sightseers" in the courtroom professed to have gathered "either from what Hauptmann said or from the way he said it so much as a single ray of new light on the question of his guilt or innocence," then he or she was possessed of "faculties of divination which ordinary mortals must worry along without."

Mr. Woollcott thought that in the minds of the crowd a verdict already had been reached, and without benefit of testimony—all a matter of emotion. Leave out, he wrote, "the lonely and itching women" who saw in Richard Hauptmann a figure "so physically attractive as to be above all suspicion of doing anything unkind and who, if he didn't have a wife, would be flooding his mail with offers of marriage," and there was still a herd of muddleheads to whom any man on trial was automatically a martyr and a charming fellow to boot.

The special correspondent, a bachelor himself, rather plump, who had yet to receive love-addled proposals from spinsters itching or otherwise, did not believe that these lonely women and underdog-champions could think at all.

David Wilentz was treated to a great deal of praise over the week end. Columnists, special correspondents, news broadcasters and the rank and file of the press were almost unanimous in the opinion, abundantly offered to the attorney general, that his attack was getting home—Hauptmann's defenses were crumbling. A few more sledgehammer blows would break that much-touted man of steel. What a victory, to have a collapse, a complete confession, on the witness stand!

Snow covered the serene countryside. Sleighs appeared round and about Flemington and young people sang songs that were young in their great-grandparents' day while the little bells danced and jingled and the horses breathed white plumes into the cold still air.

Visiting Richard on Sunday afternoon, Anna found him relaxed and cheerful and looking forward to the good times that would follow the jury's verdict.

19

Hauptmann walked to the witness stand on Monday morning with a confident air; the guard took his regular post behind him.

If the amateur strategists who had advised Wilentz over the week end counted on seeing him begin with a sledgehammer attack, they were disappointed; the attorney general moved into his examination almost casually.

The defendant had always been very careful about figures, hadn't he? Very careful about money, too?

Yes, Hauptmann agreed in a quiet voice, he had been careful about both.

And from the day he arrived in America and started to earn a living he had kept an account——?

Well, not from the day he arrived; perhaps a couple of years later—1925.

Little books in which he painstakingly jotted down the various moneys he and his wife earned and spent and loaned to others and deposited in the bank and invested in stocks and so on?

Yes.

And of course every entry, every item, in the account books was honest and truthful; the figures were correct?

Yes, but—

So that whatever he wrote in his own account books in his own hand was true?

Hauptmann began, "But there is one thing I did not put—"

"No *buts,*" Wilentz cut in.

"—I saved money besides that my wife should not know. I put nothing in the books."

Wilentz almost seemed pleased to hear it. "Oh. In other words, you were hiding it from your wife?"

The witness nodded.

"You were hiding a lot of things from your wife, weren't you?"

"No, sir. It is only the money I kept."

"When was the first time you met Mrs. Henkel—Gerta Henkel?"

"Summertime, thirty-two," Hauptmann said calmly.

"Where?"

"Hunter Island."

"Was Mr. Henkel there when you met her?"

"I can't remember."

"Who introduced you to Mrs. Henkel—nobody?"

"It doesn't need much introducing out there," Hauptmann explained, smiling a little.

Wilentz smiled too, not pleasantly. "That was when your wife was away, wasn't it? She was in Europe then?"

"Yes."

The prosecutor nodded, glancing at the jury. He returned to the account books. It was established, then, that everything in them was accurate but some things had been left out because the defendant wished to conceal them from his wife?

Yes.

"When you found fourteen thousand dollars or more in gold, how did you feel? Did you cry? Did you laugh? Were you happy or were you sad?"

"I was excited."

"Did you say anything? Did you holler out, 'Anna, look what I found!'?"

"No."

"Did you tell your wife?"

WOODLAWN CEMETERY GATES

Against the background of trees and tombstones, a dim figure masked by a handkerchief faced Dr. Condon. A deep voice asked if he had brought the money.

Acme

All Law Enforcement Officials, Wardens of Penal Institutions, Etc.

Reproduced below will be found specimens of the handwriting represented by two notes smitted by the alleged kidnapers in the Lindbergh case:

cross the street and
lk to the next corner
d follow whittemore ave
he soud

take the money with
u . come alone
and walk
I will meet you

The boy is on Boad Nelly
it is a small Boad 28 feet
long. two person are on the
Boat. the are innosent.
you will find the Boad between
Horseneck Beach and gay Head
near Elizabeth Island.

Wide World

THE WRITING IN THE RANSOM NOTES

Posters were widely distributed of the clumsy misspelled note sent to the Lindberghs and Dr. Condon demanding $50,000 for the return of the child.

UPI

BRUNO RICHARD HAUPTMANN

The suspect's hair was a muddy blond. Fairly prominent cheekbones stood out above flat cheeks and a somewhat pointed chin, a "triangular" face. He had blue deepset eyes and a small mouth.

THE SUSPECT'S GARAGE
The police ransacked it, scattered the tidy piles of household goods, ripped up the floor planks, dug into the earth beneath.

INS

THE FLEMINGTON COURTHOUSE
Telephone and telegraph technicians swarmed over the handsome old building. They stitched their wires up the walls and into the garret, the center of their humming web. The telegraph companies said they were prepared to transmit a million words a day.

Acme

THOMAS WHITAKER TRENCHARD

Judge Trenchard was 71. His decisions were well-known for the muscular thought behind them and their clarity of expression; he had never been reversed in a murder trial. Before leaving for Flemington, he thought it wise to slip a bottle of cough syrup into the pocket of his jacket.

UPI

Wide World

THE JURY

Left to right, front row: Elmer Smith; Mrs. Ethel Stockton; Charles Snyder; Mrs. Verna Snyder; Mrs. Rosie Pill; Charles Walton, foreman. Second row: Robert Cravatt; Philip Hockenbury; George Voorhees; Mrs. May Brelsford; Liscom Case; Howard Biggs.

"I did not."

Wilentz seemed shocked, as if he had never dreamt that such things could be: a husband who did not tell all to his wife!

"You *didn't* tell your wife?"

Hauptmann was nettled by the other's exaggerated reaction. "No."

Wilentz's opening casualness was gone. Was that the defendant's way of being honest with her, a woman who had slaved till all hours in a bakery, who had turned over her earnings and savings to him, given him every dollar she had in the world?

He had turned over his money too, Hauptmann replied sharply. They had shared everything they saved and spent——

"You were partners?"

"Yes."

"But when you found fourteen thousand dollars in gold, no more partnership——"

"Why should I make my wife excited about it?" Hauptmann demanded.

Wilentz appeared to think that this was a strange kind of concern. He pressed on. And what reason did the defendant have for not telling her about the other money, the money he saved and neglected to note down in his little books?

It was to be a surprise, Hauptmann said; he planned to use the savings to build a house for his wife.

Wilentz shifted his ground. After he was brought to Flemington, had the defendant asked for a German-English dictionary?

Yes.

This one? Wilentz held out a book.

Hauptmann briefly inspected it. Yes.

"Is that where you learned to spell the word *signature* correctly?"

"No, sir."

Wilentz turned to the exhibit table and picked up the original ransom note, which had been found in the Lindbergh nursery. He held it out for the witness to see, indicating with a forefinger the spelling of the word as it appeared in the note's final sentence:

> Indication for all letters are *singnature* and three holes

Of course the defendant recalled that the handwriting experts had pointed out several examples of this peculiar transposition—*n* before *g*—in the photo-enlarged specimens of script?

Yes.

"It's a habit of yours, isn't it—putting *n*s where they don't belong?"

"No."

"You do it often, don't you?"

"I don't remember doing it at all."

Wilentz handed him a slip of paper.

"Is that your check?"

Hauptmann studied it. "Yes."

"What is the amount of that check?"

"Seventy-four dollars."

Wilentz asked slowly, "How do you spell *seventy?*"

The check was in Hauptmann's hand; his eyes were on it, and he could not have misunderstood the question. But he did not reply.

"Well?" Wilentz asked, with the air of a man who is enjoying himself. "How do you spell *seventy?*"

"Seventy?" Hauptmann repeated, as if in doubt. The muscles moved in his flat cheeks. "I guess——"

Wilentz reached out a forefinger and tapped the paper. "Read it from here. You wrote it. *Seventy*. Read it. Nice and loud."

Hauptmann's voice was very low. "That is——"

"Loud, now!"

"S," the low voice pronounced, "E——"

Staring at the check, he stopped.

"Loud, now!" Wilentz taunted him. "S–E—what?"

"S–E–N——"

"S–E–N?" Wilentz cried.

Hauptmann whispered, "Yes."

"Senvety?"

"Senvety, yes."

"You have an *n* in there, haven't you?"

"Yes."

"The same *n* as you have in *singnature*——?"

Frederick Pope rose from the defense table. "That is not true. How he spells *signature* and how he spells *seventy* are two entirely different things."

Wilentz shrugged it off and rephrased the question. "Didn't you place the *n* in *senvety* just as you placed the *n* in *singnature*—and for the same reason?"

Again Pope intervened: The witness had testified that he did not place the *n* in *singnature,* did not write the word *singnature,* did not write the ransom note; therefore the question was manifestly improper.

Judge Trenchard overruled him. Wilentz resumed:

"Answer the question, sir."

The witness' answer was a flat no; he had not.

The reporters who had noted a naked flaw in Hauptmann's defense left by this same misspelled word—he had testified that the police had told him how to spell it when he had taken the handwriting test—waited confidently for Wilentz to exploit it, but he went on to something else. The handwriting experts, he continued, had pointed out another peculiar error in the specimens of script, the habitual transposing of *gs* and *hs* in words such as *right* and *light*——

Hauptmann said politely that there were so many of the experts talking he couldn't remember.

Wilentz turned to a page in one of the account books. "You bought Curtiss-Wright Aviation stock?"

"Yes."

"Spell *Wright* as you have it here so the jury will know how you wrote it."

Hauptmann glanced at the words, then spoke reluctantly, "W–r–i–h–g–t."

"W–r–i–h–g–t?"

"Yes."

"Just like in the ransom notes—*h–g–t* in *light,"* Wilentz pointed out. "Isn't that right?"

Pope was up again; Wilentz left the question unanswered, observing that the same mistake appeared in other writings the witness had acknowledged were his. Little words containing *ghs,* such as *light* and *night* and *right*—they gave him a lot of trouble, didn't they?

Hauptmann was apologetic: he wasn't very good at writing English, so he made mistakes—

Yes, with one-syllable words he made mistakes, Wilentz cut in, but he hadn't made any mistakes with a three-syllable word like *signature,* had he? Oh, no, of course not! "You could spell *signature* without the *n,* couldn't you?"

Unruffled by the sarcastic, badgering tone, Hauptmann said yes, he could.

Wilentz produced still another account book, the little red book he had shown Hauptmann on Friday. He gave it to him again. Wasn't this a record of expenses he had written down during a trip to California he had made with his wife and his friend Hans Kloeppenburg?

Hauptmann studied the pages a second time. Yes, it was.

Wilentz singled out a page. And didn't this entry—$2.25—refer to a boat ride the three had taken?

Yes, it did.

And in writing it down he had spelled the word *boat* b–o–a–d, hadn't he?

Yes.

Once more it was clear that Wilentz was enjoying himself. When had they left for California, he asked——in July 1931?

Yes.

So that during the summer of 1931—six months or so before the *Boad Nelly* note was given to Dr. Condon—Richard Hauptmann had spelled *boat* with a *d* instead of a *t*—?

Yes.

—and therefore it was not true, was it, as he had testified earlier, that he had written the word *boad* (if he had written it) in the book some eight years ago and that prior to 1932 he had learned to spell it correctly?

The witness was silent, then shook his head. When he had first looked at the book he hadn't realized it was an accounting of the California trip, he said calmly; he had simply been puzzled by the word *boad*. He had been wrong about that.

Wilentz pronounced a date, April 2, 1932, said it again, slowly. A momentous date, wasn't it? In exchange for the *Boad Nelly* note, Dr. Condon had given Hauptmann fifty thousand dollars on that date, hadn't he?

"Me? *Fifty thousand dollars?*" the defendant said, as if bewildered.

Wilentz said ironically, "Yes. You recall that was his testimony." He moved on. Prior to that exchange, earlier in the day of April 2, 1932, Hauptmann and his wife owned fifty shares of Warner Brothers movie stock—and that was *all* the stock they owned?—a balance of $203.90 in their bank account?—a mortgage?

Hauptmann agreed.

Altogether, a total wealth of $4941.40?

No, the witness said; there also was $4300 in cash he kept hidden at home.

Wilentz favored him with a knowing smile. "That was the cash you were hiding from your wife?"

"Yes."

And where at home had he hidden the money?

In a trunk inside the living-room closet. The trunk was full of clothes and household things which were stored and removed as the season called for.

Curious to know more, Wilentz went along with the witness. The trunk was dry inside, where he kept the money?

Of course.

The closet where he kept the trunk—it was locked?

No.

But the trunk was?

Yes.

"Who had the key?"

"I got a key."

"Did your wife have a key?"

"No, sir."

"The trunk was the safest place in your house—is that right?"

"I guess it was the safest place."

"That is why you put the money there?"

"Yes."

"So safe that you were sure you could keep the money out of the sight of your wife?"

"Well," Hauptmann said reasonably, "I know my wife goes only two or three times a year in this trunk."

"That is what I say," Wilentz told him. "So safe that you thought you could keep it away even from your wife—isn't that right?"

"Yes."

"And that is the only place you kept this money that you kept in hiding?"

"Yes."

Wilentz drew him back to previous testimony. During direct examination he had said that in 1929 he had about $3500 in cash hidden at home?—and in 1931 a little over $4000?

The defendant nodded. Yes.

And he also agreed that everything he had written down in his account books was honest and accurate——?

Yes, except that he hadn't put in—

Impatiently, Wilentz concluded for him—hadn't put in the money he'd hidden from his wife. But the figures in the accounts were correct?

Yes.

Wilentz picked up the little books, one at a time, and showed them to the witness.

1926. At the end of the year Richard and Anna Hauptmann were worth $3758. He had written it down, hadn't he?

Yes.

1927. At the end of the year they had $5780—$112 of it in cash at home. He had put it down, hadn't he?

Yes.

1928—$6666?

Yes.

1929——

Wilentz paused, looked up from the accounting. "You were doing pretty well in 1929—saved quite a lot of money, you and your wife?"

"Yes, we did."

"You worked as a carpenter then, didn't you?"

"Always worked as a carpenter."

"Yes, and your wife worked hard too, didn't she?"

"Yes."

"And you saved money?"

"Yes."

"And you wrote in the book to show what you had?"

"Yes."

Wilentz read the figures: at the end of 1929 the Hauptmanns had a $3750 mortgage, $2850 worth of stocks, $900 in the bank, $150 owed them by friends they'd lent money to, and—

Again the prosecutor paused. He pointed to the page.

"Tell us what the next words are."

Hauptmann read, " 'Was at home.' "

They had $16.59 in cash at home?

Yes.

Not $3500 in cash at home?

No.

That was in his own handwriting, wasn't it?

Yes.

And his total assets for the year were $7666.59?

Hauptmann shook his head. He hadn't put into the book the extra money he'd earned from special carpentry jobs, money he'd put into the trunk—

Wilentz interrupted. Then how much did he say he was worth at the end of 1929?

The witness considered the question. Well, nine or ten thousand.

But in the book he said he was worth $7666.59.

"Yes, except the money my wife——"

"Oh, yes. Except the money you were hiding from your wife?"

"Yes."

"Did you ever have that much money when you were in Europe?" Wilentz said with a small unfriendly smile.

Hauptmann smiled broadly. "I got billions."

"Billions in Europe?"

"Sure," Hauptmann said, enjoying the joke. "Inflation it was."

Laughter in court. Wilentz's voice rose:

"This is a sort of hallucination with you, isn't it—this billions business?"

The laughter mounted; Judge Trenchard silenced it.

Wilentz went back to the books. 1930—the same meticulous accounting, page after page, week after week, right to the penny, the amount of money he earned, the amount Anna earned and so on, down to July of that year—when the accounts were discontinued?

Yes.

Wilentz adjusted the points of his breast-pocket handkerchief; not that they needed adjusting. His tone of voice was almost indifferent, as if he expected little or nothing from his question:

And Anna—was she hiding some of her money from her husband?

The husband was not indifferent; he seemed startled. He said, frowning, "Well, I am not—I don't know——"

His reaction was a surprise to Wilentz. "You don't think she did, do you?"

"Everybody got his secret, I guess," Hauptmann said, still frowning.

"Do you think your wife *was* hiding money from you?"

"I really don't know."

"You wouldn't say she wasn't, would you? You wouldn't give her the benefit of the doubt?"

"I don't think so."

Wilentz turned toward the jury, spreading his hands in a gesture that seemed to say: He wants the benefit of the doubt in your judgment of him—a benefit great indeed!—but won't extend even a small grace to his wife!

He turned back; the exchange continued.

In his counsel's examination, Hauptmann had testified that in the summer of 1931 he had a little over four thousand dollars in cash at home?

Yes.

How much would he say he had hidden away in the spring? To be exact, in May 1931?

Between $3900 and $4000.

In cash?

Yes, in cash.

And in May he had received a letter from his broker asking for $74.89, hadn't he?

Yes.

Wilentz observed banteringly that he wasn't doing very well in the stock market in 1931, was he?—in fact, he was a better carpenter than he was a speculator! While he was earning a few dollars as a carpenter and Anna a few as a waitress, Wall Street was taking away hundreds! He lost three thousand dollars or so up to April 2, 1932, didn't he?

The defendant explained that when he was on a carpentry job he wasn't able to watch the brokerage board and so his investments had gone badly. He couldn't attend to both interests at the same time.

Wilentz, no longer bantering, took him up: Yes, his investments had gone badly, and so his broker had told him that $74.89 was needed to protect his account; and after receiving this request he had written in reply to the broker—a letter dated May 21, 1931—

He gave Hauptmann the letter and told him to read it aloud.

" 'Dear Sir,' " the defendant read: " 'Please, will you carry on my debit, $74.89, until May 25th. By this time I will settle my debit balance from $74.89. Very truly yours, Richard Hauptmann.' "

Wilentz took back the note and resumed after it was placed in evidence. In May 1931 the witness' broker had asked him for $74.89 and in reply he had asked the broker to wait four days for the money?

Yes.

Why? He had between $3900 and $4000 in cash tucked away in his trunk!

Yes, Hauptmann broke in, shifting in the chair—but he had made a rule never to touch the money in the trunk.

Never to touch it? But his broker was going to sell out his stocks if he didn't hurry and put up the few dollars needed! Only $74.89! Wilentz repeated that modest figure; then:

"Where *did* you get it?"

"It was probably a paycheck coming."

"You didn't take it from the trunk, though, did you?"

Hauptmann shook his head.

"And the reason," Wilentz told him bluntly, "the reason you didn't take it from the trunk is that you didn't have anything in the trunk! Isn't that it?"

"No. As a rule, I never touched the money in the trunk."

Wilentz's tone proclaimed that it was absurd, a tale for children, not for a jury. Thousands of dollars lying handy in the trunk and he didn't touch them! Money in the bank, too, and stocks and mortgages!

Hauptmann intervened: Why should he sell a mortgage to cover $74.89?

The prosecutor seized the new opening. Ah, but of course it wasn't necessary to sell a mortgage, was it?

No.

But if he *had* wanted to, he was well aware that his wife wouldn't let him—?

Well, yes.

"And that is why you didn't use the mortgage—because Anna wouldn't let you. Isn't that right?"

Hauptmann didn't reply; he turned his face away.

Wilentz kept after him. What eventually happened? Did he pay the $74.89 or let his broker sell the stocks?

The witness couldn't remember. "Let me refresh your recollection," Wilentz said, and consulted a piece of paper. Hauptmann, he said, had taken fifty dollars from his bank savings and given it to the broker on account; months later, in December 1931, the broker had sent him a telegram demanding the balance, $24.89. Many phone calls and letters had preceded it.

Wilentz emphasized the date: December 2, 1931—exactly three months before Charles Lindbergh, Jr., was kidnaped and a note demanding fifty thousand dollars ransom was left in the nursery.

"At the end of 1931 you were running very low in money, weren't you?"

Hauptmann couldn't agree.

"You had lost a lot of money?"

Yes, that much was true.

"And that is why you took some time to pay this $74.89—because you were getting down to where there was no money left. Isn't that right?"

Again the witness disagreed. He hadn't been willing to borrow from the trunk and so had had to wait a bit before the cash was handy.

Wilentz said contemptuously, "You weren't such a good stock-market operator, were you?"

The question seemed to sting Hauptmann. He stared at his questioner's sardonic face. Then he said:

"The first time you get in the stock market, you have to pay for it."

"And the first time you build a ladder you don't build a good one, do you?"

Hauptmann said angrily, "I never build a ladder."

Wilentz thrust ahead in his chronology of dates and drew Hauptmann to the small farewell party he had described in his flat on December 5, 1933. Isidor Fisch had arrived carrying a bundle under his arm, Hauptmann said, and had asked him to take care of it; he had put it on the top shelf of the broom closet in the kitchen, where Fisch turned it over to him—?

Listening carefully, the witness could find no fault with the introduction; he nodded.

And when Fisch gave him the bundle—the shoe box—he told him to keep it in a dry place?

Yes.

And a safe place?

Yes.

"How much money was in that box?"

The tone was abrupt, demanding; Hauptmann studied his questioner.

"You counted it many times. How much was in the box?"

The witness spoke carefully: "I find out later it was close to fifteen thousand dollars."

"How close?"

"Say fourteen thousand eight hundred."

"You don't know the exact amount?"

"Not exactly."

Wilentz flicked him with a smile.

"When you found that money and took it to the garage to dry and put it into a basket, you didn't count it, did you?"

"No."

"You let it lie in a basket all night and you didn't count it?"

"That is right."

"You let it lie another night and you didn't count it?"

"That is right."

Again the prosecutor's tone was hard and sharp.

"The reason you didn't count it was because you knew, didn't you?"

"I didn't know anything—"

"Thousands of dollars of strange money—you find it and you don't even count it. Is that right?"

"It was hard to count."

"Hard—?"

"Because it was wet."

Wilentz ignored the explanation.

"For two weeks you left that money in the basket without counting it, didn't you?"

"I counted——"

"After it dried, two weeks later, you counted the money, didn't you?"

"—always when I took the dry ones out; I counted the dry ones."

"It took two weeks for you to count the money?"

"Yes."

"For two weeks you left gold lying in the basket and didn't know how much was there?"

"That is right."

"The trunk was a safe place, wasn't it?"

"It was."

"The trunk was a dry place, wasn't it?"

"Yes."

"When you had money and you wanted a safe place for it, you put it into the trunk, didn't you?"

"Yes."

"Everything dear to you in this world, the thing you loved the most—money!—you kept in that trunk because it was safe and dry——?"

Hauptmann seemed to have recovered from Wilentz's reflection on his skill as a stock-market operator; in answering, he was almost facetious. "That," he said, "is not the way I lose most money." And he smiled.

Wilentz didn't smile. "You kept all the money you had in that trunk because you thought that was the best place to keep it?"

"Yes."

"Yes." Wilentz paused. "Fisch was your best friend, wasn't he?"

"Not my best friend."

"You knew he was sick?"

"Yes."

"Here was your sick friend, going home, and he asked you to keep this box in a dry place?"

"Yes."

"You knew from the day you moved into that house that that closet was a wet place; you had complained about it. But even though you knew it was a wet closet, even though Fisch told you to keep the box in a dry place, you put it in the closet—?"

"Because I couldn't go into the front room and I couldn't go into the middle room either when Fisch gave me this package," Hauptmann explained.

"That night?"

"That night."

"Who was going to stop you?" Wilentz inquired. "Weren't you the boss of the house?"

"Yes, but I got somebody in the front room and my wife was in the baby's room, and so I put it in this closet, and I forgot all about it."

Now Wilentz smiled.

"So you forgot all about it!"

"Yes."

"But finally you found it?"

"Yes."

"Because a broom hit it? A broom hit the box and you saw money?"

"Yes."

Wilentz slanted off from the central line, to approach it from a new direction. The witness had first met Gerta Henkel in the summer of 1932, he had testified; and later, her husband Karl——?

Later, yes.

And through the Henkels he met Fisch?

Hauptmann shook his head firmly. No, no; he had met Fisch on Hunter Island.

Hadn't the Henkels introduced him to Fisch?

Yes, but Fisch and he were already acquainted.

Wilentz crossed to the prosecution table and brought back a few sheets of paper. Hadn't the witness told the police in his explanation of how he met Fisch that Fisch lived in the same house as the Henkels and that when he went there to visit the Henkels they introduced the two? Hadn't the witness said, "I was sitting with a family named Henkel and Mr. Fisch came downstairs for company—"?

Well, Hauptmann granted, probably he had.

Wilentz said harshly, "Isn't that where you met him?"

"Yes——"

"Isn't that where you were introduced to him?"

"—but it doesn't mean first," Hauptmann finished.

"When *did* you meet Fisch?"

"First part of March or first part of April."

"Isn't it a fact that you are saying that you met Fisch before June because you are attempting to account for the moneys that you deposited *before* June?"

"Positively not."

Well, Wilentz said with his unfriendly smile, then why hadn't he told the police that he and Fisch already were acquainted when the Henkels introduced them?

He hadn't told the police because the questions had come so quickly he wasn't given the chance, Hauptmann explained.

Wilentz shook his head, in simple disbelief or as a comment on the police's regrettably impatient methods. He took a short stroll away from the witness stand, as if to illustrate that he had all the time and patience in the world, stopped at the exhibit table and picked out the small board he had placed in evidence through Inspector Bruckman.

He showed the board to the witness. Of course he knew what this was?

Hauptmann amiably agreed: A piece of wood-trimming.

From a closet in his flat?

He really couldn't say; it was an ordinary piece of trim that might have come from any place.

"That is your handwriting on it, isn't it?"

"No," Hauptmann said calmly.

Wilentz didn't seem to believe his ears. "What?"

"No, sir."

The prosecutor tore off the cellophane wrapping and shoved the board close to the witness, pointing to the penciled scrawl: *2974 Decatur,* and beneath it *S* followed by the blurred *E* and then *DG 3–7154*.

Wasn't that his writing? Hadn't he written those figures?

Hauptmann glanced at the writing, pleasantly shook his head. No, he couldn't remember putting them down.

He had remembered better when he was questioned by District Attorney Foley in the Bronx, hadn't he?

Well, the witness said reasonably, he was a little excited then.

Was he also excited when he testified before Justice Hammer in the Bronx County Supreme Court?

Yes, he was.

He hadn't told the truth on those occasions—is that what the witness was trying to say?

Hauptmann seemed to search for the right words. Well, he meant he wasn't thinking then.

But since then he'd learned to be careful? He realized now that the trim-board found in his apartment with Dr. Condon's address and phone written on it in the witness' hand was a serious thing——?

No reply. Wilentz pressed on. The witness had told District Attorney Foley that he recognized the board, that it was from a closet in his flat and that the figures at least were in his writing; he had explained that he must have been reading about the Lindbergh case while he was putting fresh newspaper on the closet shelves and must have copied down Dr. Condon's address and phone because he had a habit of jotting down things of interest—

Hauptmann broke in. He couldn't have known where the wood came from because one piece of trim was like another, and he hadn't said that the figures on it were in his writing—only that they *looked* like his writing. And finally, while he liked to jot things down, it would have been foolish for him to write on the inside of a dark closet where he couldn't read it.

Wilentz demanded, "Did you tell District Attorney Foley the truth about this board?"

He hadn't given any thought to what he said.

"Did you tell him the truth?"

Hauptmann sought to put his answer another way. Wilentz wouldn't have it.

"Did you tell him the truth?"

"I told him the truth, yes."

"Did you tell the truth about this board in the Bronx County Supreme Court?"

Again Hauptmann hesitated. Wilentz drummed the question at him, twice, three times. Finally:

"I say no."

"You *didn't* tell the truth there?"

"No," Hauptmann said.

He asked for permission to explain; Judge Trenchard granted it. When Foley had talked to him about the board and asked if the writing was his, he hadn't said yes and he hadn't said no, because he couldn't remember putting it down; and later, in the Bronx court, when he was asked again, he had said yes without thinking—he could have just as easily have said no.

Wilentz had taken a few restless steps during the explanation;

impatiently he resumed, calling the witness' attention to the serial numbers penciled on the back of the closet door the police had removed from his apartment. He had told Foley they were a record of two big bills Fisch had given him to buy stocks. Did he still say this notation was in his writing?

Yes.

And how big were the bills—$500 or $1000?

He didn't recall.

Wilentz ridiculed it. Didn't *recall*? Didn't know whether they were $500 or $1000 bills?

Well, he knew they were one or the other.

Didn't know whether he had hundreds or thousands?

No, he——

So hard up for cash that he couldn't get his hands on a few dollars to give his broker, and he didn't know whether he had hundreds or thousands lying around the house?

The picture suggested by these scornfully incredulous words seemed to amuse Hauptmann; he smiled at the prosecutor. It was a mischievous or perhaps a rather superior sort of smile, and it got under Wilentz's skin. He glared at the man in the chair.

"This is funny to you, isn't it?"

The smile vanished. "No."

"You're having fun—smiling at me——"

"No."

"You think you're a big shot——"

Hauptmann's body seemed to bunch together and he said, angrily, contemptuously:

"Should I cry?"

"—bigger than everybody, don't you?" Wilentz finished, shouting.

"No—but I know I am innocent!"

Wilentz pounded away; a few more sledgehammer blows, his advisers had said, would break Hauptmann; and here was the attack, hard and vicious. Most of those admiring advisers were in the press section. They leaned forward eagerly.

"You're the man with *will power*——"

Hauptmann's cheek muscles stood out. He gripped the chair arms, twisted his body from side to side.

"You wouldn't tell if they murdered you, would you?" Wilentz cried.

"*No.*"

The word was like a pistol shot, flat and deadly.

"Will power is everything with you, isn't it?"

"No, I am innocent!" Hauptmann shouted. "That keeps me the power to stand up!"

"Lying, when you swear to God that you will tell the truth!"

Hauptmann shoved out his right arm, palm forward. He was trembling; the guard behind the chair moved as if to restrain him. His voice seemed on the edge of hysteria:

"Stop that!"

"Didn't you lie under oath, time and time again?"

"No, I did not!"

"Lies, lies, lies!" Wilentz shouted. "But you're not smiling any more, are you? It has gotten a little more serious, hasn't it?"

The guard hadn't touched Hauptmann. His body gave a shudder; then he had himself under control. "I guess," he said, and it was like an apology, "—I guess it isn't any place to smile, here."

Four words spoken proudly by the prisoner occurred to Wilentz. " 'I am a carpenter,' " he quoted, mocking him.

Hauptmann said no less proudly, "I am!"

"That was funny, wasn't it?" Wilentz said; certainly the courtroom had laughed, when Hauptmann had said the words as if in dismissal of the shabby ladder.

"No, sir, there was nothing funny about it."

"You had a good laugh, didn't you——?"

But Frederick Pope was on his feet, angrily objecting. "I think this has gone just about far enough!"

Wilentz turned away from the witness and spoke to the bench. Perhaps they might have a recess?

Pope agreed; more than agreed. "I think we ought to come back to this courtroom and see if we can't get down—"

"What do you mean by that, Mr. Pope?" Judge Trenchard asked.

"I mean this patent abuse of the witness! It is about time we protested against it."

"Whenever you have any occasion to protest, make your protest to the Court and the Court will deal with it. It always has and will continue to do so."

Pope looked sulky. He sat down.

Well, the press gallery observed, Hauptmann hadn't broken. Seemed near it, though. Perhaps after the recess——

But Wilentz resumed quietly; no sledge hammer. He went back to the subject of Isidor Fisch. During their so-called partnership, Hauptmann had given his friend $5500 in cash——

No, Hauptmann said, he hadn't.

Wilentz studied him. Hadn't given Fisch $5500 from his private bank account?

No.

Wilentz brought a letter from the prosecution table. After Fisch's death, the witness had written to his friend's family in Germany, describing his partnership with Fisch and asking about the estate?

Yes.

Wilentz handed him the letter. In it, he had told them that he had given Fisch $5500 in cash from his private bank account?

Hauptmann replied without looking at the letter. Yes.

Was it the truth?

No, it wasn't.

"My God," Wilentz said, "don't you tell *anybody* the truth?"

Lloyd Fisher objected; the judge sustained him.

The truth was that Fisch owed him the money, Hauptmann explained. It was a business debt, but to avoid going into his transactions with Fisch in detail, he'd simply said that he'd given his friend the cash from his private bank account. Actually, he didn't have such an account.

Then he had lied to them, hadn't he?

Yes, he had lied.

Wilentz pressed on, bitterly accusing the witness of having lied to Fisch's family in other respects—for example, when he suggested to them that they appoint him administrator of the estate and neglected to tell them that he had found more than fourteen thousand dollars of his friend's money.

Once more Hauptmann explained: He hadn't found the money until a few weeks before he was arrested.

But he was taking from the money, wasn't he? —he'd spent part of it——?

He was entitled to it. Fisch owed it to him.

A couple of months earlier he had written that all he had of Fisch's was a couple of trunks worth nothing, hadn't he?

Yes.

He hadn't said anything about the shoe box?

No, because he had forgotten about it.

Even after he found the box, and found the gold notes inside it, he hadn't written——?

Because he knew Isidor's brother was coming to America to settle Fisch's affairs.

"Oh," Wilentz said, lavishly scornful, "I see. You were saving the secret for Fisch's brother!"

"Yes. I wouldn't keep the money."

"Oh, of course not. You weren't going to keep the money——"

"But," Hauptmann said, "I was going to keep what was coming to me."

Slowly shaking his head, Wilentz stared at him.

The day's session ended.

20

Tuesday January 29, twentieth day of the trial.

The axis on which the State's case slowly swung was the date of the ransom payment, April 2, 1932; in the prosecution's view, that day—or night—divided Richard Hauptmann's life into a dramatically contrasting before and after. Wilentz had pinpointed the date time and again during the weeks of testimony; this morning, he took it up once more.

He reminded the defendant that he had accounted for the day of April 2, a Saturday, by saying that he had worked at the Majestic Apartments and that he had quit at the end of the day because he had been promised a hundred dollars a month and found he was being paid only eighty. On the other hand, the Majestic's timekeeper, a man presumably in possession of the facts, had testified that Hauptmann hadn't worked that Saturday, hadn't quit until the following Monday, April 4. The timekeeper had produced records to prove it.

But he had worked at the Majestic on April 2, 1932, Hauptmann answered firmly, no matter what anyone said.

And he'd quit because he was to get eighty dollars a month, not a hundred as he'd thought?

Yes.

Wilentz turned to his associates at the prosecution table and was given a sheaf of photostats, copies of the Majestic's payroll during the period; he turned again to the witness and pointed out his name and his pay—$3.33 a day.

Didn't $3.33 a day mean that he was getting $100 a month?

Hauptmann was silent.

Didn't it mean, too, that he hadn't quit over a few dollars' difference in salary, as he had said, *but because he had come into a fortune?*—fifty thousand dollars in extortion money?

No; that was *not* the reason.

Wilentz developed the theme. Just look at the luxuries he and his wife had enjoyed after the ransom was paid! —a splendid new radio, purchased in May for $396; an expensive, high-powered pair of German field glasses, bought in July for $126; Anna's trip to Europe the same month, at a cost of $706; two hunting trips, one to Maine, the other to New Jersey, for which he had paid $150, plus $56 for a hunting rifle, a gift to Karl Henkel, who accompanied him; $100 for a motor trip to Florida; all those carefree week ends on Hunter Island—now and then footing the bill for his convivial friends, perhaps? —and a canoe for their greater pleasure, a matter of $109.

The prosecutor paused, then capped the recital: And all that time he had been unemployed!

Hauptmann denied it: He had been busy in the stock market and had made money; had made money from the furs, too.

Wilentz ignored the explanation. How much would he say he had earned as a *carpenter* after April 2, 1932?

A couple of hundred dollars.

Wilentz nodded, satisfied, then moved to a new vantage point, displaying deposit slips the defendant had filled out at one of his banks during the period in question, all showing large deposits of silver coins.

Previously, when the prosecutor had implied that the defendant had spent most of his time after the fifty thousand dollar payment converting the bills into small change, Hauptmann had listened stolidly from his seat between the two guards; now, in the witness chair, he purposefully addressed himself to setting the evidence into the correct perspective. He never paid attention to the entry lines on deposit slips, he told Wilentz, and so a sum of money he had jotted down after the word *Silver* might properly have belonged after the word *Bills,* and the other way around. Even now, looking at the slips, he recalled some of the deposits and saw they were listed in the wrong place.

Wilentz greeted this with a smile; he seemed confident that the answer exposed its own flaws to anyone who had ever filled out a deposit slip and submitted it for a bank teller's inspection.

But the witness would admit, wouldn't he, that he had circulated Lindbergh money?

Hauptmann stared at him. No.

Hadn't he said that he spent some of the gold notes he found in the shoe box?

Yes, but—

Ransom bills?

—but he hadn't known it was Lindbergh money; he'd learned that after he was arrested.

Driving over the reply, Wilentz asked it he hadn't been circulating gold notes for a couple of weeks before then—that was true, wasn't it?

Yes.

Because he needed money?

Oh, no.

Why, then?

Simply because the bills were handy—he'd used a few to pay expenses, instead of taking money from his brokerage or bank accounts.

This was in September 1934?

Yes.

And he wasn't trying to convert the ransom bills into small bills and coins——?

Absolutely not.

If this was so, and he needed cash for expenses, why had he deposited in one of his bank accounts a couple of hundred dollars in silver and bills at the same time he was spending the gold notes? Why hadn't he used the money he deposited to pay for his living costs?

Hauptmann frowned. He had already explained, he said: the gold notes were handy.

And he didn't think it strange that he was using ten- and twenty-dollar gold certificates to pay for ordinary expenses while at the same time he was putting small bills and coins in the bank?

Hauptmann's frown deepened as he considered the question. Wilentz didn't help him. He hoped, the prosecutor said solicitously, he wasn't *confused?*—surely not that!

No, Hauptmann snapped, why should he be? He hadn't used the bank money because it was in an account in Mount Vernon his wife didn't know about and he was saving the money bit by bit to pay for their long-hoped-for trip to Germany.

Oh? Wilentz's tone was arch. Still another secret he kept from his wife?

The accused evidently did not consider this worthy of remark; his expression, a reporter noted, was contemptuous. It did not dismay Wilentz, who returned to the cache in the garage. How many gold notes had Hauptmann spent?

Twelve, maybe fifteen.

"How many did you intend to spend?"

"All I did spend. I wouldn't have spent any more."

"You were going to stop—even if you hadn't been arrested?"

"Yes."

"What were you going to do with the balance?"

"The other certificates?"

Yes, Wilentz assured him, that was what he meant: the other certificates.

"Give them to Fisch's brother."

"Why did you take twelve or fifteen if you weren't going to touch the others?"

Hauptmann said truculently, "I tell you there is no special reason for it."

"And the rest you were going to give to Fisch's brother?"

"My intention was to give him twelve thousand dollars."

As he listened to the earlier explanations, Wilentz's face had been skeptical if not downright incredulous; but now he seemed to go along with the defendant, if with a touch of playfulness.

He was going to give Fisch's brother only $12,000 when his friend and partner had entrusted him with about $14,800?

Again Hauptmann explained. Fisch owed him money and he meant to settle the debt. There was some $2800 involved—the $2000 he gave Fisch when his friend left for Germany and the rest due him from stock investments—and when the gold notes were dry he wrapped $2000 separately and put it aside and tucked $800 more into the holes drilled in the board. In this way he would be in no danger of losing the money that belonged to him, as he might be if he turned the full amount over to Fisch's brother: there was nothing in writing to establish the debt; the brother might refuse to acknowledge it.

Yes, yes, Wilentz murmured, he quite understood the need for such common-sense precautions—but how would the brother know about the gold notes hidden in the garage?

The defendant said he would show him the money.

He hadn't said anything about it in his letters to Fisch's family?

He intended to.

Why hide the money in the garage? He had bank accounts, a safe-deposit box——?

Yes.

And, above all, he had that trunk!

Yes.

When he hid money of his own—the money he kept from his wife—he put it into the trunk?

Yes.

Not the garage?

No.

Quite so; not the garage, the trunk. Wilentz paused. Well, now, for that matter, why hadn't he turned in the gold notes to the Federal Reserve Bank? He knew that it was against the law to hoard gold, didn't he?

Yes, he knew. But nearly a year had gone by since the government's final warning about keeping gold; he might be closely questioned and punished, especially if it was found out that he was in the United States illegally. Anyway, the gold wasn't his.

Hadn't he said to the police, after his arrest, "I was afraid they would hook me up if I turned it in"?

Hauptmann considered. He couldn't remember, he said; but if he had, it was in reference to the explanation he had just given.

The prosecutor went back to the object that had engaged so much of his attention, the trunk: despite all its virtues as a hiding place, hadn't Hauptmann been just a little bit uneasy when he made the California trip with Anna and friend Kloeppenburg—with over $4000 in cash lying at home?

He hadn't left the money at home, the witness promptly replied;

he had packed it in a satchel and left the satchel with his uncle in Brooklyn, not telling him what it contained.

This seemed to astonish Wilentz. Wouldn't it have been safer to put it in a bank?

Yes—but then his wife would have found out about the money.

She didn't know about his account in Mount Vernon, did she?

Hauptmann hesitated. He wasn't altogether sure.

Well, then, Wilentz pointed out, he could have opened a new account in some bank in the city——

The witness shifted in the chair. No, she would find out about it.

How? If he didn't tell her, how would she know?

Well, she—— Hauptmann paused. She would find the bankbook.

Wilentz smiled, an understanding smile, a sort of between-friends, man-to-man smile. He could have hidden the bankbook where he hid the money—in the trunk! Why not? They both knew how safe the trunk was!

Hauptmann shifted again; his hands clasped and unclasped. No, impossible—that is, it wouldn't have been the thing to do—he always kept his bankbooks in the writing table.

Honestly, now, wouldn't it have been safer—and just as much a secret from his wife—if he had put the $4000 in a bank and hidden the bankbook in the trunk?

No. No.

Wilentz threw off the tone of sweet reasonableness. The fact was, it didn't matter, did it?—because there was no money in the trunk?

There was.

When he was arrested, had the police found any money in the trunk?

No.

Wilentz echoed, emphasizing it: No.

Because, Hauptmann said, because he had removed the savings a long while before.

Wilentz briskly fetched Hauptmann's account books from the exhibit table and reminded him that he had acknowledged that the notations in them were in his handwriting and were correct. He had testified, too, that Fisch had given him some $15,000 to invest in stocks and that he had given Fisch $2000 just before his friend sailed.

Yes.

But the truth was, Wilentz said in a hard voice, that all the money he ever got from Fisch was $2000, and the $2000 he gave Fisch—if he ever had given it—was to square matters between them.

Hauptmann replied sharply that that was not true.

The prosecutor shoved the books into the witness' hands and pointed to an entry. There it was: $2000 received from Fisch—that and no more.

But there *was* more—much more!

Where was it written down?

He had explained before that the accounts were incomplete——

Wilentz flipped the pages, pointed again. The witness had testified that he made several profits from the furs; what did the books say?

Hauptmann read aloud: $1737.51.

And that was the total profit, wasn't it?

No; he had said in the beginning that Fisch kept the fur records—

Wilentz moved ahead, pressing his examination to a close, using the letter of sympathy Hauptmann had written to Fisch's family after his friend's death to point out that although he said he and Fisch became partners in the spring of 1932, the first transaction between them mentioned in his letter was in the spring of 1933, a full year after the ransom was paid.

The afternoon was wearing out. Reilly followed Wilentz, endeavoring to smooth over the furrows the attorney general had left; before long, court was adjourned.

Wednesday morning, Reilly took the witness back over the day of the crime and the day of the ransom payment, reaffirming his innocence and pointing out that when he circulated the twelve or fifteen gold notes during the two weeks before his arrest he showed that he was unaware of the deadly nature of the money by spending it openly—without disguising himself or changing his car's license plates. And while the attorney general had devoted much time to the letters Hauptmann had written to Fisch's family, where were the letters the family had written to Hauptmann? They had been in his apartment when it was searched by the police!

Reilly finished, surrendered the witness once more to Wilentz; again the exchange grew sharp. At last the prosecutor turned away. "That is all," he said.

Hauptmann got up, stretched a little; he had a rather relaxed look, not tired, not worried. Followed by the guard, he began to walk toward his regular seat in the courtroom. He had answered questions for a total of seventeen hours; Wilentz's duel with him had lasted for eleven of them.

After a few steps he paused. He turned and looked at the jury and slowly smiled.

21

Anne Lindbergh had preceded her husband on the witness stand; Anna Hauptmann followed hers.

For the first time it occurred to some spectators that there were several points of similarity between the two women. Their Christian names were almost identical. Each was the mother of a baby son, Anne Lindbergh's second child, Anna Hauptmann's first. Their husbands were world-famous.

The similarities ended there. Anne's family background was one of great wealth, Anna's of decent poverty. Anne was fragile and dark-haired; Anna had a buxom figure and rust-blonde hair. Anne had dressed for her appearance on the stand in a jacket and skirt of black silk and a blue fox fur. Anna wore a navy-blue dress, with a cowl neck from which pleats ran through the heavy crêpe blouse, and a small black felt hat that somewhat resembled a trench cap and left a fringe of curls exposed. A white medallion hung from her neck on a black ribbon. She wore two rings, the gold wedding ring and a white-gold engagement ring set with small stones.

Reilly helped the witness into the chair and began in a quiet voice to lead her through her arrival in America and friendship with Richard, but he had to raise his voice and ask Anna to raise hers. He looked around, annoyed. The courtroom was jammed with a crowd equal if not even superior in numbers to that which had struggled into the building to see Anne Lindbergh. Again, people were standing on tables, sitting on radiators, were wedged fast in the aisles and into the window recesses. Again, they whispered, coughed, sneezed, complained of the insufferable conditions. Judge Trenchard relieved them. Everyone who was standing, he announced, must leave. The guards enforced the order. The complainers regretted their complaints.

Reilly resumed his sympathetic questions; Anna's accented voice could be heard quite clearly in the new hush. She seemed composed, but her eyelids blinked rapidly half a dozen times over the blue eyes as she began each answer. She watched Reilly devotedly, as if her life depended on him.

Yes, Richard and she met and were married and they worked hard and saved their money. She started to work at the Fredericksen bakery in June 1929. Mrs. Fredericksen took two nights off a week, Tuesday and Fridays, and as a regular custom Anna worked until eight o'clock on those nights.

"Did the Fredericksens own a police dog?" Reilly asked.

Anna blinked her eyes. "Yes."

March 1, 1932, was a Tuesday, Reilly went on; and on that night had her husband called for Anna at the bakery?

"Yes, he did."

"At what time?"

"Maybe it was seven o'clock, maybe quarter after, maybe quarter before. I don't know exactly the minutes."

"How long did he remain there before you and he left to go home?

"He was there until we went home together, about half-past nine, quarter to ten."

"You went right home?"

"We did."

"And after you arrived home did you remain there?"

Anna replied firmly, "Yes."

At a few minutes past nine on Tuesday night, March 1, 1932, Anne and Charles Lindbergh were chatting in front of their fireplace when Charles turned his head and, in answer to Anne's question, said he had heard a sound, a sound like breaking wood. They did not investigate.

Did Anna remember, in March 1932, about what time in the morning Richard went to work for the Majestic? She remembered that he would drive her to the bakery, where she started in the mornings at seven, and then go right to work. Now, Reilly continued, another date that had been spoken of a good deal, April 2, 1932, a Saturday—could she remember who was in her house that night? Hans Kloeppenburg was with her and Richard then, Anna told him, for a musical evening and a little card-playing.

She would remember her husband's birthday, wouldn't she? She would indeed. November 26. How about November 26, 1933? That was a Sunday, Anna said, and some friends were at their place for a birthday party, her niece and Paul Vetterle and Isidor Fisch and of course Richard and she.

Reilly asked about Gerta Henkel, and Anna replied that she had met Mrs. Henkel through Richard.

"In connection with Mrs. Henkel and your husband, have you ever entertained the slightest suspicion concerning his infidelity toward you?"

Anna flushed. "Mrs. Henkel was not only a friend of my husband, she was my friend too."

"Did you ever entertain any thoughts or opinions that your husband was untrue to you?"

"Never."

As for Isidor Fisch—some information about him, please. Well, Anna had met him late in 1932 at the Henkels' house, where he lived. He and Richard were in business togeaher. The Hauptmanns had given a farewell party for him on a Saturday night, about four days before he sailed for Germany. Anna was in the baby's room when he arrived at the apartment that night and so she couldn't see if he brought any packages or bundles with him; but about a week before he sailed, or maybe a few weeks, he brought a suitcase with things he didn't want to take to Germany, and some boxes, like cardboard boxes, with furs, and a valise—"filled with books in," Isidor Fisch said.

Reilly nodded. "How tall are you, Mrs. Hauptmann?"

Anna said she believed she was five feet four inches tall.

Then could she reach the top shelf in the broom closet next to the sink in the apartment?

Well, she would have to stretch herself.

"Did you know anything about any box, shoe box, cardboard box, on the top shelf?"

"No, I never used that shelf."

Reilly wished to know more about the closet, anything in connection with any water Anna may have found there and where the water came from. Anna began with the shelves. There were three, on the right side. On the first she kept a box with shoe polish and brushes, and soap and powder. On the second, an electric iron, and bottles of polish, and cleaning rags. And on the third, the top shelf——

"I believe I put up some few bundles of shelf trimming there, what I didn't use. There is a pipe, I don't know what for, and this goes through the ceiling, and the water came down on the pipe and on the top of the ceiling, and I noticed a few times that even my mop was hanging on the left side in the closet sometimes was very damp. The water came through the closet, through the ceiling, and many times the shelves were wet, and even down on the floor I had to put a pot."

Reilly's expression was that of a man ordinarily little interested in closets, mops, brooms, shoe polish, shelf trimming. He moved on to Anna's earnings; had she kept a record?

"Yes, we put it down in a book."

How much had she earned altogether since she came to America?

"Well, I would say around seven thousand dollars, a little over seven thousand dollars."

She saved most of it?

"Oh, yes!"

She and her husband had a joint bank account where they put all the family funds?

"Not all."

But all her savings were put there?

"Yes."

"You trusted your husband and he trusted you?"

"Sure."

Wilentz objected. "I move the part about the husband trusting her be stricken."

Agreeably, Reilly cut his question in half. "You trusted your husband, didn't you?"

Anna's blue eyes gave him a long look. "Who shouldn't trust a husband?"

"I don't know," Reilly said. Then this much-married man paused and added, in a tone the courtroom had not heard him use before, a little sad, altogether human, "That speaks well for some of us."

He glanced at Wilentz. "The witness is yours."

There was a ground swell of sympathy from the crowd for the woman on the stand as the attorney general approached her. He was swift, adroit, intelligent, and, as he had proved, capable of a battering-ram attack; she was a rather plain, rather dumpy housewife, capable of—what? Hard work, and, as she had proved, immense loyalty. Now the two were opponents. He would tear into her account of the three significant dates, the night of the kidnaping, the night of the ransom-money exchange, the night when a movie-theater patron had tossed an oddly folded bill to the cashier. Surely Anna Hauptman was no match for David Wilentz.

Anna watched him with apprehension and dislike. His violent exchanges with Richard had hardly prepared her to regard him with favor. Far more than that, he was a man professionally committed to obtaining Richard's death. For him, the death of her child's father would mean victory. She mustered what resources she had to stand up to his onslaught.

But Wilentz had a surprise up his well-tailored sleeve for her, for the crowd, and for the defense. It soon became evident that he was ignoring the three dates. Instead he was asking—and in a quiet, respectful voice—about the furs and other things Isidor Fisch had left with the Hauptmanns: books, clothing, an electric lamp, some pictures. Anna and Richard looked them over together, she said, after they heard that Fisch was dead in Germany. Then Richard stored them in the garage, except for the furs, which they put in the closet in the baby's room.

Wilentz seemed to muse. Then:

"You worked very hard, Mrs. Hauptmann, didn't you?"

"I did."

"And until 1932 your husband worked very hard too, didn't he—and saved money?"

"He did."

"And you and your husband were quite happy?"

Anna smiled. The crowd had not expected to see her smile during the cross-examination.

"We were, very."

Wilentz smiled, too. "And the money you saved as the result of your hard work," he said respectfully, "you put it in the bank, didn't you?"

"Yes, I did."

"And then finally your husband started to gamble in the stock market?" he asked, as if a little distressed. "Is that right?"

"Yes."

"And then he lost some money?"

"I guess so," Anna said reluctantly. But she had warmed under his sympathetic interest.

Almost as if he were a neighbor chatting over the back fence in the sun, Wilentz inquired about Anna's domestic arrangements—familiar, congenial territory for her; she prided herself on her exemplary housekeeping. The neighborly Wilentz seemed to be chiefly concerned with the interior economy of a closet, the same broom closet in the kitchen which Anna had described to Reilly. It was a closet to which she went every day? Yes. She went to the closet every day but she never saw a shoe box on the top shelf?

Anna said she didn't know what was on the top shelf.

"You never saw a shoe box there?"

"I didn't."

"From November or December 1933, the month and the day that Mr. Fisch was last at your home, until September 1934, you never saw a strange shoe box on the top shelf of that closet?"

"I never had anything to do with the top shelf. I didn't use it for my—" she hesitated "—for myself."

Wilentz was less neighborly. He appeared to be reverting to the man she disliked: the prosecutor. He brought out a photograph of the broom closet and asked Anna if it correctly showed the position of the shelves. Yes, it did. And the apron hanging on the hook there, he continued—she used to take her apron and hang it up there? Yes. She had no trouble hanging it up there?

"Oh, I could hang it up," Anna said.

"Now see if that hook isn't above the top shelf."

She said guardedly, "I see that."

"And you know if you stood a few feet away from it you could see everything on that top shelf?"

"Why should I stay away a few feet and look up there?"

The friendly neighbor had vanished. Wilentz was altogether the prosecutor. He demanded, "Will you please tell me if it is not a fact that if you stepped away from the closet a few feet, if the door was open, you could see everything on the top shelf?"

"I don't think so."

He shook his head. "You did your own cleaning, Mrs. Hauptmann?"

"I did."

"And of course you cleaned the closet once in a while?"

Anna said indignantly, "I *do* clean closets!"

"How often did you clean this closet?"

"Almost every week."

"Did you ever clean the shelves?"

"I did."

"Did you ever clean the top shelf?"

"I never use the shelf."

"Did you ever clean the top shelf? That is all I want to know! If you didn't, say so."

The good, faithful housekeeper stared at him. Her freckled skin was flushed. At last she pronounced three words that might have been acid in her mouth:

"No, I didn't."

He was relentless. "Never cleaned the top shelf? You cleaned the first shelf, didn't you?"

"I had to clean the first and the second because I had my stuff there."

"So you cleaned the first shelf, and you cleaned the second shelf, but you never cleaned the top shelf?"

"No, I didn't use it!"

Wilentz said quietly, "You don't really mean that, do you, Mrs. Hauptmann?"

"No, I didn't use that!" the good housekeeper said again.

But she used to keep something up there, he pursued—what was it she had told Mr. Reilly? Shelf trimming? Yes, Anna said, shelf trimming; her niece had given it to her and she couldn't use it in the house and so she put it on the top shelf.

"Of course it wasn't dirty up there, was it? You didn't let dirt and dust accumulate, did you?"

"What should I do up there?" Anna cried. "I put that stuff up there and I left it there!"

He became interested in another closet, right next to the broom closet; from November and December 1933 right up until September 1934 she kept groceries in this second closet? Yes. She had never had to move the groceries out because it was wet in there? No, there was no water in that closet.

Back to the broom closet. Besides the trimming material, hadn't she kept a tin box on the top shelf? Yes, Anna remembered, she had. She kept soap coupons in the tin box? Yes. How often would she put the coupons in the box? Once every three months, four months. Then from November and December 1933 until September 1934 she must have taken down the tin box at least two or three times? Maybe she did, Anna admitted.

"To take that tin box down, you had to reach into that closet?"

"Yes."

"And into that top shelf?"

"Yes."

"You didn't see any shoe box there?"

"No, I didn't."

"You did not?"

"I didn't look!"

Pausing, Wilentz glanced at the jury and then at the good housekeeper's husband, who had testified that he had put Isidor Fisch's shoe box—which later had proved, Hauptmann said, to contain almost $15,000—on the top shelf. Anna had just said she didn't see it. She had quickly added that she didn't look.

Hadn't she also kept cleaning rags in the closet? Yes. Had she kept them on the first shelf, second shelf or top shelf? Anna said she had kept them on the top shelf.

The prosecutor observed sardonically, "It was a pretty busy closet, a pretty busy shelf, wasn't it? Shelf trimming—old rags—coupons, a tin box. Do you remember anything else that was up there?"

"I don't know."

Wilentz's glance lingered on the jury again, on the housewives who were among its members. His questioning gaze seemed to ask: This conscientious, thrifty housekeeper would never have looked on the top shelf of her cleaning-materials closet? No? But if she *had* looked and *had* seen the strange box her husband has testified was there during all those months, wouldn't she have wondered what it was and what was in it—and opened it?

It now appeared that Wilentz had not intended to ignore altogether the three dates, at least not the first date, the date of the kidnaping. "You remember, of course, Mrs. Hauptmann, that you were a witness in the Bronx in the proceedings in which your husband opposed his return to New Jersey?"

No one caught up the words *his return;* certainly not Anna. "Yes, I do," she said.

"I want to read to you a question that was directed to you in the Bronx and your answer," he continued, and quoted, " 'When your husband was arrested recently, Inspector Bruckmann spoke to you about this case, did he not?' Answer: 'Somebody spoke to me.' Question: 'And did you not tell Inspector Bruckmann and others who were there present that you had no recollection at all of what happened March first, 1932, and that it was too far back, that you don't know whether your husband was with you or not?' And didn't you answer, 'I did tell him that'?"

Anna said nothing.

"Did you tell that to Inspector Bruckmann?"

Anna asked him to read it again, please. The prosecutor did so, slowly.

"Did you tell Inspector Bruckmann that?"

"I was asked," she began, and paused, her eyelids blinking. "Someone asked me if I remember that night of the kidnaping and I said I do."

"Yes, ma'am," Wilentz said politely.

"And then someone asked me about the first of March and I said I didn't know if this was the first of March. I couldn't remember that, and I said it was too far back. I couldn't remember the first of March."

"You didn't know at the time that March the first was the night of the kidnaping, is that what you mean?"

"I didn't know it was the first of March."

Wilentz moved in to end it. "And so when they asked you about March first, you said, 'That's too far back; I can't remember whether my husband was with me or not'?"

Her voice was slow and heavy. "When they asked me about the first of March I believe I said that."

The prosecutor turned away, turned back. "Whatever your husband did in the garage with reference to taking those pieces of board and putting money in them and hiding them, that was done without your knowledge, wasn't it?"

"I didn't know anything about that," Anna's slow voice replied.

"And when that money was found, it was a surprise to you, wasn't it?"

"It was."

Wilentz bowed his head a little, as if to thank her. Their chat was finished.

Reilly hurried forward. Yes, Anna told him in answer to his question, she could see no more than the edge of the broom closet's top shelf, from the floor. And she hadn't any doubt at all that Richard had been with her on the night of March 1, 1932.

Anna left the stand. A pleasant-looking young man with blue eyes and a schoolboy complexion followed her; he was Elvert Carlstrom, a former resident of the Bronx, where he had found that the Fredericksen bakery was a good place to eat. He remembered March 1, 1932, very well, he continued to Reilly, couldn't help but remember it—March 1 was his birthday. That particular March 1 he'd had a job in Dunellen, New Jersey, looking after a new, unfurnished house owned by a Mr. Christensen. New York wasn't too far away and the Bronx bakery was a friendly spot, nice people. On the night of March 1, 1932, Carlstrom got there around half-past eight. The waitress had a smile for him.

"Did you see anybody else?" Reilly asked.

"I saw that fellow sitting right down there," the witness told him.

Reilly gestured to Hauptmann to rise. "The defendant?"

"That's right. He was sitting at the front table."

"Did you see a picture of him in the newspapers after his arrest and associate it with the man you had seen in Fredericksen's?"

"Yes."

Wilentz took over. There were other people in the bakery that night? Yes, four or five. Would he describe them, please? Well, no, he couldn't. And yet he remembered the defendant! Yes, sure, Carlstrom explained, because the man had been laughing—laughing at him.

Just where in the Bronx had Mr. Carlstrom lived before he moved away? About five minutes' walk from the bakery. Lived by himself? No, with a family named Larsen. And in Dunellen, when he'd been caretaker of the new house? He'd lived right there in it, alone, the witness said. But wasn't it unfurnished? Yes; he'd slept on a mattress on the floor.

The winter dusk had gathered; court was adjourned.

Rosy as the new day, Elvert Carlstrom faced Wilentz again.

"You lived in Dunellen in this house alone, you testified yesterday. Is that correct?"

"Yes," the witness answered promptly. "I did."

"Now the Mr. Larsen you talked about yesterday, will you take a look over there? Stand up, please, Mr. Larsen."

A man got to his feet not far from the prosecution's table. Wilentz continued:

"Is this the Mr. Larsen you talked about?"

"Yes."

"He worked with you at Dunellen, didn't he?"

"Yes."

"When he worked there, he stayed there?"

"Yes."

"He didn't go home to the Bronx each night, did he?"

"No."

"He stayed and slept in the house in Dunellen with you, didn't he?"

"Yes."

"You never said a word about Larsen staying in the house, did you?"

The witness said defensively, "Because you never asked!"

"You never said a word! 'Alone,' you said, didn't you?" Wilentz pressed.

Elvert Carlstrom's pink cheeks were a little pinker; he did not answer. The attorney general left him to his unhappy silence.

Reilly strolled over. The witness remembered the man in the

bakery the night of March 1, 1932, because he'd laughed at him, something anyone would remember. But why had he laughed?

"I said something to the waitress in English, and my English wasn't so good," Carlstrom explained. "So he laughed. That is why I get mad."

Reilly smiled tolerantly at the jury, thanked the boyish Carlstrom and called his next witness, Louis Kiss. Mr. Kiss was a very quiet man; a little louder please, Reilly requested. His business? He was a silk painter artist.

"What is that?" Judge Trenchard inquired.

Painting on silk, wall decoration, Kiss told him. Reilly resumed: How had he become interested in the Hauptmann case? Well, he'd read in the papers about the dog, the police dog, and remembered the night of March 1, 1932, when he'd been in Fredericksen's bakery in the Bronx.

"Tell us how you came to be there," Reilly said.

"I was supposed to take two pints whiskey to a friend of mine in the Bronx." But he'd lost his way and stopped in at the bakery for directions and coffee. A dog ran in, big police dog, and a man followed and told the waitress in German something about the dog. The whole business—losing his way, the bakery, the dog, the man—was firmly tied in Kiss' mind to March 1, 1932, because later he had recognized the man in the newspaper pictures of Bruno Richard Hauptmann.

Wilentz, cross-examining, wanted to know what had happened to the whiskey. Kiss said he had delivered it to his friend. Whose name was ——? Leo Singer. What kind of whiskey?

"My whiskey," Kiss said quietly.

"What kind?"

"Rum," Kiss whispered.

"What?"

"Rum."

"Where did you buy it?"

"I made it."

"You manufactured rum at the time?"

"I bought alcohol and I put in those flavor."

"How long did it take you to make this rum?"

"Ten minutes."

"How much did you sell it for?"

"Dollar and a quarter a pint."

"Did you add your carfare to the cost?"

"No, no, sir," Kiss said strongly, "I never did that."

The crowd laughed, recognizing in him a figure only recently departed, with the repeal of the prohibition amendment, a figure that often had described itself as a decorator, an interior one—the

ANNA HAUPTMANN
AND EDWARD J. REILLY

"Who wouldn't trust a husband?" Anna asked Reilly; and he, a much-married man, observed, "That speaks well for some of us." The chief defense counsel was 52, with an astonishing record of acquittals. He believed in dressing to accommodate the average man's idea of titanic prosperity.

Wide World

Wide World

LLOYD FISHER

One of Flemington's own sons, his presence was counted on by Reilly to persuade the jury that the defense was not an alien force arrayed against the New Jersey-born Wilentz.

Acme

DAVID WILENTZ

Young for his office—he was 39—the attorney general knew that he was matched against one of the toughest and most successful trial lawyers in America.

LINDBERGH AT THE TRIAL
He carefully studied the prospective jurors. As he leaned forward, his jacket fell open, revealing a pistol in a shoulder holster.

UPI

NORMAN SCHWARZKOPF, ANNE MORROW LINDBERGH AND MRS. DWIGHT MORROW
Chief officer of the New Jersey State police, Schwarzkopf had known nothing but praise until the kidnaping. Charles and Anne Lindbergh's confidence in him remained firm. Anne Lindbergh was present twice during the trial; the first time, to testify; the second, to accompany her mother and return home with her after testimony in defense of Violet Sharpe.

Wide World

Acme

ALBERT S. OSBORN
The State's chief handwriting expert was 74. Reilly, remembering other elderly witnesses, notably Dr. Condon, was moved to comment for the benefit of his staff: "This isn't the trial of the century; it's the trial of the centenarians."

UPI

THE KIDNAP LADDER AND THE ATTIC FLOORBOARD
Was one of the rails of the ladder used in the kidnapping cut from the same piece of wood as the floorboard from the defendant's attic? The state said it was.

ARTHUR KOEHLER
His reputation as a wood-identification expert had grown over the years; some people said he was infallible in his chosen field. The kidnap ladder challenged his talents, and he set out to trace it to the man who built it.

Acme

Acme

ELLIS PARKER AND ELLIS, JR.
In his son's eyes, and many others', Ellis Parker was America's greatest detective, if not the world's, but his critics said that the Chief of Detectives of Burlington County, New Jersey, often skated close to the edge of the law he was sworn to uphold. He had conducted twenty thousand criminal investigations and failed to win convictions in only ten cases.

Wide World

HAROLD HOFFMAN
The Governor of New Jersey was 39 in 1935. A Republican, he had won office in the face of the New Deal landslide; his neighbors in South Amboy had always said he would go far. Above all things he loved to preside over the revels of the Circus Saints and Sinners.

UPI

PAUL WENDEL
He and Ellis Parker had been friends for twenty years. Wendel, a former attorney, had complete faith in the famous detective, with whom he worked on the Lindbergh case. (*Figure at right.*)

purveyor of forbidden spirits, the bootlegger. The judge's gavel admonished them.

Wilentz was content, for the time being. The name of Kiss' customer, Leo Singer, had been noted down: perhaps he too would have his day in court.

August Van Henke took the stand. Yes, he told Reilly, he certainly remembered March 1, 1932; the next day everybody had been talking about it as the night of the kidnaping. That night he had been at a gas station in the Bronx near Dickerts Park and had seen a man with a police dog. Van Henke had lost his own police dog the month before and he'd thought maybe this one was his; but the man had told him no, said his name was Hauptmann and the dog belonged to a baker, Fredericksen.

Reilly sat down; Wilentz rose.

"What is your name, sir?"

"August Van Henke."

"Who is August Wunstorf?"

"That is me."

"I thought you said your name was Van Henke?"

Well, the witness said, yes; he used the name Wunstorf once in a while—family trouble, he explained.

"Who is August Marhenke?"

"Me."

"So you are August Van Henke *and* August Wunstorf *and* August Marhenke?"

"All me, yes."

Had he, all three of him, ever run a speakeasy? No. Well, then, a restaurant? Yes. Hadn't it been raided several times by the police? Yes.

Anna, Carlstrom, Kiss and Van Henke had placed Hauptmann in the Bronx as the child was stolen. Reilly moved on. Lou Harding, who identified himself as a laborer, said he had been repairing Washington Road in Princeton, New Jersey, on the afternoon of the same March 1 when two men stopped in a car and asked him how to get to the Lindbergh house. He directed them to the best of his knowledge. No, neither of the men was the defendant. Yes, he'd looked over the car; it was dark blue. And there was a ladder in it. Early next morning he'd told his story to the police and they'd taken him to the Lindbergh estate and there he had seen the same ladder.

"Look at the ladder that was offered in evidence," Reilly said, "and tell me if it is the ladder you saw in the car."

Lou Harding inspected the ladder. "Yes, something about like that."

The attorney general inspected the witness' past. He had been convicted of crimes? Notably assault and battery on a woman? Or, to put it more simply, an attack on a woman?

Lou Harding did not like the definition. It was carnal abuse, he said.

John Trendley, a handwriting expert, was the defense's first witness the next morning, February 1. He had devoted careful study to photographic copies of the handwriting exhibits in question and, for a period of two hours and fifteen minutes, in Trenton, had looked at the originals of the ransom notes.

Reilly said slowly:

"And as a result of your study and examination of the ransom notes and the admitted Hauptmann writings, are you in a position to render an opinion as to whether or not the defendant wrote the ransom notes?"

"In my opinion he did not."

Answering Reilly's careful questions, John Trendley explained in detail why he was confident his opinion was correct, pointing out that the word *were,* a misspelling of *where,* in Hauptmann's admitted writings, had not appeared in Mr. Osborn's giant photostats, and that many words in the ransom note found in the nursery also had been omitted. Trendley thought these omissions significant.

Reilly handed him the nursery note. "From your examination of this, would you say it was written by a person's free hand or a disguise?"

"I think it was written by disguise."

"Part of it is written and part printed; is that correct?"

The witness nodded. "And I think he made the attempt with his left hand."

"So we find that Mr. Osborn, with this nursery note as a comparative test upon which he makes his observations and opinion to the jury, picks out the word I-S, 'is,' and compares it with the I-S's of Hauptmann's admitted writing—is that correct?"

"It is."

"Picks out the word *singnature* and compares it with nothing on the chart from Hauptmann's writing?"

"That is correct."

"In your opinion would that be sufficient to send a man to the electric chair?"

Joseph Lanigan of the prosecution objected; the judge sustained him. Reilly turned to the *x*s in the ransom notes and the admitted writings. There was a difference between them, Trendley said.

Reilly sat down; Lanigan attacked. The witness had based his opinion on only a little more than two hours' study of the original ransom notes—wasn't *that* correct? Yes, Trendley replied, but he had offered his services to the defense after far more prolonged examination of reproductions of the notes in the newspapers. He stuck firmly to his opinion and summed up by declaring that the line quality in ransom notes and admitted writing was not the same; in the latter the shading was graduated and uniform, with clean pen movements and no roughness, which was not true of the former.

His manner of speech was deliberate; it seemed to the jury that all handwriting experts were men who took their time. The day was well along when John Trendley, unbowed by the State's assaults, left the stand.

Peter Sommer followed in the witness chair. He was a fingerprint expert, he told Reilly, trained in precise observation. Around midnight, March 1, 1932, he was a passenger on the Weehawken ferry, running between New Jersey and Manhattan. Among the others on the ferry were two men whom he remembered very well. Reilly gave him a photograph of Isidor Fisch. Was that one of the men? Yes, the picture strongly resembled him. When they got off at the Manhattan ferry slip, the two men helped a lady with a baby onto the Forty-second Street crosstown streetcar.

Reilly produced a photograph of Violet Sharpe. Was that the woman with the baby?

"I would say that she resembles her very strongly."

How did she behave?

"She appeared very nervous."

And the baby?

"The baby was wrapped in a blanket. The blanket slipped and I noticed the baby was dressed in a one-piece nighty. The baby was blond, I would say about two years old."

"Thank you, Mr. Sommer," Reilly said with much meaning. David Wilentz came forward, but time was running out and court was recessed for the week end. The attorney general wasn't displeased; he wished to have his investigators look into the past life of Peter Sommer, fingerprint expert.

22

The State possessed an inestimable advantage in the investigators whose energies lay at its disposal. There were hundreds if not thousands of them, members of the New York City police, the Justice Department's Division of Investigation, and the New Jersey State and city police forces. The defense's announced witnesses had been investigated more or less at leisure; no sooner would an unannounced or surprise witness take the chair than a detective or trooper would leave the courtroom, step to a telephone and pass on the new name, and city, state and federal men would open their files; if they were barren, inquisitive men would appear in the witness' home neighborhood.

By the next morning, Saturday, February 2, Wilentz knew a good deal about Peter Sommer. He may or may not have been a fingerprint expert but indisputably was a professional witness who testified in courts for a price. He had been known to threaten to change his testimony if not paid promptly. His precise observation seemed to be at its most precise when directed to the size of the figures on U.S. currency. Wilentz looked forward to a few words with him in court on Monday morning; so far, the defense's witnesses had turned out to be a pretty shabby bunch, except for Trendley. The attorney general had not been awed by Reilly's statement that a spectacular list of witnesses would prove his contentions right down to the ground. Reilly had broadcast radio appeals for witnesses. Hardly a sign of quiet strength.

Lloyd Fisher was with Hauptmann this Saturday morning. He visited him often; Reilly was almost never there, Rosecrans and Pope seldom. The prisoner said:

"Where are they getting these witnesses from? They're hurting me!"

Fisher was silent. He could not have agreed more thoroughly, and Rosecrans and Pope were in accord with him. But Reilly was the boss. They believed in laying down one line of defense and holding fast; Reilly, in opening up defense theories wherever circumstance led. Not that he didn't have a basic theory. Alibi, alibi, get the alibi! Put Hauptmann in the Bronx the night of the kidnaping and the hell with the State's dozens of witnesses! Was Hauptmann a magician? Was he superhuman? Could he be in the Bronx and climbing through that nursery window at the same time?

"Tell Mr. Reilly he's got to find out if they are honest, good people before they are witnesses for me!"

Fisher promised. Much good it would do, he thought. He patted the prisoner's shoulder and left.

The jury went for another jaunt in Oden Baggstrom's bus.

On Sunday, Anna Hauptmann dressed Bubi in new clothes for the great occasion, his first visit to his father since the beginning of the trial. He wore a white knit jacket, blue blouse, knee-length blue pants and white socks and shoes. His silky blond hair had been brushed and brushed and was brushed again and again during the trip from Maria Mueller's in the Bronx to Flemington. It was brushed a final time just before they entered the jail.

Richard knew that permission had been granted for the visit and was waiting in high excitement. The guards kept Anna behind the visitors' screen but let the prisoner take his son in his arms. He kissed the boy's lips and cheeks and hands and hair and marveled at his beauty. How big and strong already, and only fourteen months old! Anna was smiling and crying at the same time. Richard seemed to be having trouble with his eyes when, finally, the visitors had to leave.

Monday February 4; Charles Lindbergh was thirty-three. The birthday did not keep him from his usual seat at the trial; as always since her appearance as the State's first witness, Anne stayed in Englewood with her mother.

Wilentz had his few words with Peter Sommer, who became confused and restless. He was clearly anxious to leave the courtroom; the attorney general detained him long enough to look at some other pictures of Violet Sharpe. Was this the woman he had seen with the baby on the Forty-second Street crosstown trolley? The witness would not say yes or no.

The defense called Ben Lupica to the stand. Ben had been driving home from Princeton Prep in the late afternoon of March 1, 1932, when he stopped at his family's letter box near the entrance to the Lindbergh estate. As he was reading his mail, a car, a dark blue or black '29 Dodge, came around a bend and drew up on the wrong side of the road. Ben looked at the driver and also saw two sections of a ladder in the car.

Lloyd Fisher asked:

"Have you at any time said to anybody that you can definitely recognize the defendant, Hauptmann, as that man you saw in the car?"

"No."

"Can you identify Bruno Richard Hauptmann as the man you saw in the car, Mr. Lupica?"

The witness said firmly, "I cannot."

Wilentz, cross-examining, was less inquisitorial than fatherly. His tone seemed to say: Go thou, Ben, and sin no more. Hadn't Ben told him, in the presence of Anthony Hauck and several other people, that Hauptmann resembled the man he had seen in the Dodge on March 1, 1932?

"That Mr. Hauptmann had a resemblance to him," the witness agreed.

"And you say so today, don't you, Ben?"

"Yes."

"The man in the automobile with a ladder in it looked like Hauptmann?"

"He has a resemblance, yes."

The paternal Wilentz was satisfied. Fisher was not. But the witness had made no *positive* identification of the defendant as the driver of that car?

No, he hadn't.

It seemed to be a draw. Prosecution and defense left it there.

Hans Kloeppenburg came next, the song-loving Kloeppenburg. Yes, as a regular arrangement he had spent musical evenings at their apartment with the Hauptmanns, the first Saturday of each month. Yes, he had been there the night of April 2, 1932, with Richard and Anna, and between eleven and twelve Richard had driven him to the White Plains Avenue subway. Oh, yes, he'd often seen Isidor Fisch at the Hauptmanns', the last time at a farewell party for him in December 1933. Besides the host and his wife, Mrs. Mueller was there, and Mr. and Mrs. Wollenburg, and a young couple—he thought their name was Heyne—and a Mr. Schuessler. Fisch arrived around six and talked right away with Richard.

"Did you notice whether Fisch had a package or bundle with him?" Reilly asked.

"Yes, he carried a package in his arm. I would say it was about five to six inches high and seven, eight wide, and the length about fourteen inches."

"When did you last see him with that package in Hauptmann's house?"

"When Richard and Fisch both went together through the hall in the kitchen."

Wilentz wanted to know the date of the witness' first meeting with Isidor Fisch. In July or August 1932; Hans didn't know if Richard met Fisch for the first time then or before.

"Hauptmann didn't *say* anything about meeting Fisch before, did he?"

Hans shrugged. "Well, I just don't remember."

The night of that farewell party, had he seen Fisch leave? No. So he didn't know if Fisch took the package with him? No, he didn't.

Hadn't Mr. Kloeppenburg told Bronx District Attorney Foley, a little while after Hauptmann's arrest, that it was "too long ago" to remember just when he had seen Hauptmann in March or April 1932?

Hans admitted it.

Reilly advanced to seal the breach. But Hans had three good

reasons for remembering April 2, 1932, hadn't he? Yes, Hans said, smiling, he had indeed. It was the first Saturday of the month, their regular night. And the American joke about April Fool's Day, the day before. And Anna Hauptmann had said she was going to stop over to see her niece, Maria Mueller, the next day.

The attorney general said harshly:

"Isn't that the reason Hauptmann picked out the first Saturday night to get the money from Dr. Condon, so he would have you to establish the alibi?"

Hans looked shocked. "That's a very funny question," he said, not humorously. Wilentz was content to let it stand without an answer.

Mrs. Anna Bonesteel informed Reilly that she owned a restaurant in Yonkers, not far from the ferry to Alpine, New Jersey. She knew Violet Sharpe—well, hadn't known her as a *friend* but had met her through a friend a couple of months before the Lindbergh baby was stolen. Yes, Mrs. Bonesteel said, identifying a photo, that was Miss Sharpe, the same young woman who had come into her restaurant on the night of March 1, 1932, around half-past seven, very nervous, with a gray blanket on her arm—kept asking the time and opening the door and looking out. Nervous as a hen on a hot griddle. Left about half-past eight, quarter to nine, when a car stopped two hundred feet or so away; she ran out and got into it.

Wilentz had some information for Mrs. Bonesteel: Violet Sharpe had not left the Morrow home in Englewood, many miles away, until eight or half-past on the night of the kidnaping. Would the witness care to acknowledge that she had made a mistake? No, the witness would not. He showed her a photo. Was this the friend who had introduced her to Violet? It certainly wasn't, Mrs. Bonesteel declared. Have a good look, he urged. She was sure? She was sure. Who was it? She couldn't say. Well, then, he would tell her: it was Violet. Well, Mrs. Bonesteel snapped, maybe it *was*.

Paul Vetterle testified that he had gone to school in Germany with the girl who was to become Mrs. Richard Hauptmann. On November 26, 1933, he had attended Richard's birthday party; Mr. Fisch was there too, he remembered, and Mrs. Mueller. Richard arrived about four-thirty in the afternoon, wearing working clothes. They all had a nice time, coffee and cake; the radio was playing. Richard drove him to the subway station about ten.

The attorney general asked if, as a matter of fact, the witness hadn't left at *six* in the evening? No, Paul Vetterle said stoutly, it was ten.

Tuesday's session began with Philip Moses, a cab driver, distinctly not a morose type, whose face seemed pliable as putty. Around 8

P.M., April 2, 1932, which was to become famous as the night of the ransom payment in St. Raymond's Cemetery, he was cruising in that neighborhood when he noticed three men fussing around a stalled green car, 1932 model. It was in one of the lanes running past the cemetery. They hailed Moses and he drove them to Scribner Avenue, where they got into a gray car.

He hadn't always been a cabby, the witness told Wilentz under cross-examination—once was a Wall Street runner. Had done a little plumbing. Pretty good amateur actor and dancer. Did impersonations. Look! His face became seized with a fierce grin. Will Rogers!

The crowd laughed; Judge Trenchard rapped; Will Rogers vanished. "If you do that again, the consequences will be unpleasant," the judge said severely.

"I'm sorry, your Honor. I guess I got carried away."

Was the witness well acquainted with St. Raymond's? Not exactly. Could he describe any of its features? Well, gravestones. Was there a hedge around part of it? He couldn't say. The men with the stalled car—had they struck him as gangsters? That was what the witness had been saying around Flemington the past couple of days, hadn't he? The witness guessed he'd been talking with a little artistic exaggeration. No, he wouldn't want to swear they were gangsters. He left the stand in a diminished state.

The next two witnesses, Anna's niece Marie Mueller and Louise Wollenburg, confirmed earlier testimony regarding Richard's birthday party on November 26, 1933, and the farewell party for Isidor Fisch; Otto Wollenburg backed up his wife.

Mrs. Bertha Hoff told Reilly that during the summer of 1931 she stayed with friends named Budreau on their farm at Mountainville, not far from Flemington. In October 1933—no, November, "because we talked about Thanksgiving"— Mr. Budreau and another man stopped by her home in Bayside, New York City, early one afternoon. Reilly showed the witness a photo of Isidor Fisch. Was this the other man? Yes. She was positive? She was positive. Was Mr. Fisch carrying a package?

Wilentz objected to the question. Reilly's ripe face turned a deeper hue. With a flourish, he addressed the judge:

"Now, if the Court please, we might just as well face the issue. During the day, I am prepared to prove, if my witnesses get here from New York, that the man who jumped over the cemetery wall was Isidor Fisch, that the money was handed to Isidor Fisch, that Isidor Fisch—from that date on—not only approached one but many persons in New York, trying to dispose of this money. I am going to trace every connection of Isidor Fisch with this money until he left on the steamer. I hope to be able to prove by witnesses, when he arrived in Hamburg, his actions before the immigration authorities in Germany. I am going to trace everything I can to show that Isidor Fisch *and not this defendant* received the money from Dr. Condon, tried to dispose of it, tried to leave it not only with this woman, Mrs. Hoff, but other people, finally left it with Hauptmann, whose innocence will be developed by these witnesses."

His booming voice ceased.

"I can find no fault, if your Honor please, with counsel's statement that he is going to *try* to do it," Wilentz said, "and I have no objection either to his declaration here for the benefit of the jury—because he is going to be called upon to prove his statements."

He paused, then continued in a sharper tone:

"I feel very confident that there will be no such credible proof. The question right now is with reference to whether or not a person whom this witness had never seen before in her life came to her house that day and whether or not she saw him with a package."

Judge Trenchard sustained the objection. Angrily, Reilly withdrew the witness, subject to recall.

Victor Schuessler and Hilda and Otto Heyne briefly took turns in the witness chair to testify that they had been present at Isidor Fisch's farewell party on December 2, 1933, but hadn't seen him at the actual moment of his arrival.

Benjamin Heier, a young man dressed in the height of Broadway fashion, took the stand. Saturday night, April 2, 1932, he'd had a date with a very close friend, a young lady whose name he wished to withhold because of her later marriage to another party who was still alive; the young lady was dead. They'd gone driving in the Bronx. Seeking for a lonely spot, Benjamin Heier found one in Webster Avenue, not far from the wall of St. Raymond's Cemetery, and parked the car. He and his friend chatted and then again were silent. At intervals, Heier switched the headlights on and off—no particular reason. Then:

"The headlights were shining on the cemetery wall, and suddenly a man landed on the sidewalk as if he had jumped from over the wall."

"What time of night was that?" Reilly asked.

"About nine-thirty or ten, maybe."

"Did you get a good look at his face?"

"Yes, sir."

"When did you next see that man?"

"In the newspapers, when the trial started."

"And the newspaper picture was identified by what name?"

Heier said, "Isidor Fisch."

Wilentz took over. The witness had a criminal record, hadn't he? He'd once been convicted of a crime. When did he get to the cemetery that night? About nine. And remained there until——? About eleven. He saw this man jump over the wall when? The witness now thought it must have been between quarter to eleven and eleven.

"You couldn't be mistaken by an hour, could you?" Wilentz inquired.

"By an hour?"

"When you say quarter to eleven you don't mean quarter to ten?"

"No."

He was sure?

He was sure.

George Steinweg, a travel agent, testified that on November 14, 1933, he had sold a passage to Germany on board the SS *Manhattan*, sailing on December 6, to Isidor Fisch; and besides paying for his ticket, Mr. Fisch had bought some $650 in German marks. He had seemed to Mr. Steinweg to have quite a bit of money left in his wallet, and the agent remembered, too, that he'd been bothered by a heavy cold.

Wilentz asked:

"And don't you know that on November 14, 1933, Hauptmann gave him two thousand dollars for that very purpose?"

"No," Steinweg replied, "I don't know."

"So you don't know where the money came from?"

The travel agent didn't. It was hardly part of his job to inquire into the source of clients' cash.

Although Reilly had confidently reserved a dozen chairs in court for other witnesses he expected from New York, the chairs remained empty; it now appeared that he had run out of witnesses, at least for the day. They had turned shy, had chosen to cling to decent seclusion, safe from the slings and arrows of the redoubtable Wilentz and his corps of delvers into a man's past.

Judge Trenchard warned defense counsel that it was up to him to have his witnesses present. "Otherwise," he added, "something unpleasant is likely to occur."

23

Wednesday February 6, twenty-sixth day of the trial.

Mrs. Verna Snyder, Juror No. 3, had developed a cold, and it concerned Judge Trenchard. He paused at the jury box to ask how she was feeling. Better, thank you, she said with a smile.

Sam Streppone, a radio repairman, had managed to get to Flemington from New York—from that borough which was enjoying a day in the sun equal at least to Flemington's, the Bronx. Reilly showed him the familiar picture of Fisch. Yes, that man had been a customer of his; on May 10, 1933, had come into his store with a faulty radio. And he'd come back on May 14.

"Did he have anything with him?"

"Yes, sir," Streppone said. "A package."

"He left it there for how many hours?"

"From two to eight-thirty, I think."

The size of the package? Well, say the size of a shoe box.

Wilentz rose.

"You were adjudged insane some years ago, weren't you?"

"In 1928," the repairman admitted. But he'd been discharged with no psychosis—nothing wrong with him, he added defensively.

"How many times were you in an institution for mental disorders?"

"A few times."

"Eight times, six times, seven times?"

"About five times."

"Was one of the times due to the fact that you threatened bodily harm to one of the women of a charity organization?"

"Yes, sir."

"One of the times for writing filthy letters to her?"

Streppone did not like the description. "Abusive language, sir."

Reilly came to his support. "But you're now doing business in New York?"

Yes, he was.

"Under no restraint?"

"No, sir!"

The defendant was looking at Lloyd Fisher and shaking his head, as if to remind the lawyer of his protest and plea: *Where are they getting these witnesses from? They're hurting me! Tell Mr. Reilly he's got to find out if they are honest, good people!* Fisher had passed on the anguished message and Rosecrans and Pope had supported him. Reilly had brushed it off. The dissension between the two sides of the defense, "country lawyers" and big-city lawyer, had come close to an open break. Reilly stood on his record of acquittals. It was unanswerable. After the Hauptmann trial, Fisher thought bitterly, perhaps there would be an answer.

Another cab driver, Oscar Bruchmann, sat down in the witness chair and testified that he had worked for Isidor Fisch in 1930, before turning to hacking for a living. He met Fisch by chance one night in May 1933, at Broadway and Sixtieth Street in New York. Had he any particular reason to remember the incident? He certainly had: "Fisch pulled a roll of bills out of his pocket and gave me a five."

Wilentz objected and Reilly returned to his earlier theme. "We are offering this witness and other witnesses," he said, "to endeavor to show that after April 1932, down to the time Fisch sailed for Europe, he exhibited large sums of money to many people."

"I object to that statement in the record," the prosecutor said.

"I think counsel has a right to have it stated in the record," Judge Trenchard said. Reilly's recent wounds were soothed. He was through with the witness, he observed. Wilentz did not cross-examine.

The next witness, a trucker, Theron Main, continued Reilly's theme. In August 1933, cashing a check in a New York bank, he noticed a man whose face he remembered when he saw a newspaper picture of Isidor Fisch, because he'd seen him again in a bar near the bank and Fisch had given the bartender a twenty-dollar bill. It was a gold certificate, Main said. Fisch and he talked a little and the other showed him some more gold bills.

Cross-examining, Wilentz asked, "What is a gold bill, Mr. Main?"

"Well, it is yellow on one side and green on the other," the witness explained.

"The front green, the back yellow?"

Exactly.

"So there is no question in your mind that when you saw this twenty-dollar bill you saw a goldback?"

Correct.

"Don't you know," Wilentz inquired sweetly, "that the only reference to gold on gold bills was a little certificate saying it was a gold bill and that they weren't yellow or gold at all but green on both sides?"

Theron Main admitted he hadn't known.

Reilly called Gerta Henkel. The jury inspected her with interest; this was the Mrs. Henkel in whose company the defendant had enjoyed the cheerful morning cups of coffee and of whom Anna Hauptmann had spoken as a friend, her relationship with Richard above suspicion. They saw an attractive youngish woman, on excellent terms with cosmetics, no stranger to the art of eyebrow-plucking, who popped a piece of gum between her bright lips as she moved to the stand. She adjusted herself prettily to the witness chair and crossed her nice legs. A flamboyant quill was thrust through her small green hat and her green dress was trimmed with white cuffs and wide ruffled collar.

Sure, she knew Isidor Fisch; they'd gone to school together in Germany. She met the defendant in July 1932.

"Mrs. Henkel," Reilly asked, "was there anything at any time in Mr. Hauptmann's conduct toward you ungentlemanly or dishonorable?"

"Certainly not!"

"Thank you, Mrs. Henkel."

Wilentz centered his fire on the important question of the month of Hauptmann's first meeting Isidor Fisch. The defendant had testified that it was the early part of March or the early part of April 1932. According to Reilly's theory, Fisch received the ransom payment on the night of April 2, 1932; in possession of a handsome sum of money, Fisch therefore was able to underwrite the suddenly vigorous stock-market transactions of his friend and business partner Richard Hauptmann.

"Hauptmann met you in the summer of 1932, Mrs. Henkel?" Wilentz asked.

The witness replied, offhandedly, "Yop." She re-crossed her legs.

"And then he came to your house and met your husband?"

The witness answered again, "Yop." The attorney general winced.

"And while he was at your house he was introduced to Isidor Fisch, isn't that right?"

The witness abandoned her *Yops*. "Yes. But Mr. Fisch told me he had met him before."

"When you were asked by the police about it, didn't you tell them that you introduced Hauptmann to Fisch?"

"But they knew each other before that."

"You knew that when you were answering the police?"

"No, I didn't know it. I mean, I remembered it only later."

Wilentz said sharply, "It is a fact, is it not, that in July or August 1932, you introduced Hauptmann to Fisch? Answer yes or no."

"Yes, before they——" The witness paused, chewed. "I mean, before Fisch told me about it."

Wilentz nodded, sat down; Reilly replaced him. "Fisch told you afterwards he had met Hauptmann long before?"

"Yes."

"Had Fisch borrowed some money from your mother-in-law?"

"Yes, sure."

"How much?"

"Oh," Mrs. Henkel said, "over four thousand dollars."

"And he sailed without paying it back, didn't he?"

"Sure."

Wilentz came forward for re-cross-examination. "The police asked you, 'When was it you introduced Fisch to Hauptmann?' and you said, 'July or August'?"

"Yes."

"Today you have a different story, haven't you?"

"Yes, because I remembered."

"Not because you are a very good friend of Mr. Hauptmann?"

"No."

"Not because you had coffee with him two or three mornings a week?"

"Oh, my God, no!" Gerta exclaimed.

"You knew, did you not, and you have known right along, Mrs. Henkel, that it has been an important matter as to when Fisch was introduced to Hauptmann?"

"I didn't know it was important," the witness assured him. Wilentz's expression was not that of one who implicitly believes in a lady's word.

Gerta was allowed to leave the stand. On her way out, she winked at the Hauptmanns.

Dr. Erastus Mead Hudson took the chair; in answer to Frederick Pope's questions, he described his examination and silver-nitrate treatment of the kidnap ladder. Yes, he remembered the rail now called Rail 16 and recalled that at the time of his inspection it showed only one nailhole made by a square nail. Yes, if there had been four such nailholes in Rail 16 at that time, of course he would have seen and remembered them.

Court was adjourned as darkness gathered over Flemington; Wilentz would have to wait for his turn with the witness until the next day. A vital question hung in the jurors' minds: Dr. Hudson, a respected physician, admittedly an amateur fingerprint expert but scientifically trained in his hobby, had examined the ladder and demonstrated his silver-nitrate process—which had not yielded significant results—on March 13, 1932, with the permission of the State police, and observed *one* square nailhole in Rail 16. But when the ladder reached Arthur Koehler, later on, he had observed *four* square nailholes in that rail. Much later, after Hauptmann's arrest, he had matched their precise pattern to four nailholes in the joist in the defendant's attic, proving to his satisfaction that the ladder rail at one time had been part of the attic flooring. But hadn't Frederick Pope fought bitterly against admission of the ladder as evidence, claiming that it had been passed from hand to hand—*after* Hudson had seen it but *before* it got to Koehler—and tinkered with so much that it could not resemble the original ladder? Wasn't Hudson's testimony proof of Pope's claims? Who had put those three additional holes, in the exact matching pattern, in Rail 16?

Wilentz lost no time in tackling the question the following day, Thursday. A photograph taken of the ladder before Dr. Hudson examined it showed four nailholes in the part that was to become Rail 16. He gave the photograph to the witness.

"Will you admit, then, Doctor, that you were mistaken in your testimony and your recollection?"

Dr. Hudson pondered the black-and-white proof before him. "Well," he replied at last, "I would say yes."

"Thank you, sir."

Next the courtroom heard the testimony from three one-time friends, or at least neighbors, of Millard Whited, the logger who had seen the suspicious stranger near the Lindbergh place before the kidnaping. William Whithead, George Lenz and William Diehl, asked by Fisher about Millard's reputation for telling the truth, replied in turn, "No good," "Not good," "Ain't any good."

Wilentz quickly established that although Millard had never been in jail, William Whithead could not make the same boast; that George Lenz had had an argument with Millard over money which he refused to pay for lumber bought from George because Millard thought that it was stolen; and William Diehl said he wasn't able to read a statement he had signed concerning Millard's reputation.

Karl Henkel, Gerta's husband, told Reilly that he had never seen anything improper between his wife and Hauptmann and never felt there was anything improper. Wilentz returned to the Fisch-Hauptmann meeting. Karl said it was he, not Gerta, who introduced Hauptmann to Fisch.

"And that was in July or August of 1932, is that right?"

"Yes, sir," Karl said.

Walter Manley had traveled from the Bronx to testify for the defense; the journey seemed to have tired him. He was not a well man, he explained, had left his bed to come here. Judge Trenchard expressed his concern; he felt sure counsel would not unduly tax the witness, and Reilly begged him to make himself comfortable. He was in the Fredericksen bakery on the night of March 1, 1932? Yes, about quarter past seven. He saw Mrs. Hauptmann there? Yes. Anyone else?"

Manley pointed toward the defendant. "I see Mr. Hauptmann."

Wilentz asked if the witness had known Hauptmann before March 1, 1932. No. How long was Mr. Manley in the bakery that night? Maybe five minutes.

A murmur from the crowd followed the next witness to the stand and rose as he arranged his effects. He looked like a walking arboretum. He was Charles De Bisschop, of Waterbury, Connecticut; his husky build, tanned cheeks and woodsy trimmings were in sharp contrast to the scholarly Arthur Koehler, who now took a seat at the prosecution table. De Bisschop carried a small tree, maybe four feet high, which he placed beside the witness chair. Then, with Judge Trenchard's permission, he put a satchel on the judge's bench. Three seedlings went in front of the satchel and a few spruce cones, appearing from De Bisschop's pockets, were disposed around the seedlings.

He smiled at the wondering crowd.

He was a lumberman, housewrecker, general contractor, nurseryman, the witness told Pope, and often matched wood grains for cabinetmakers. Here was an example; and he investigated the satchel with his stubby fingers and produced two board slabs. The grains matched perfectly, he stated, but the boards came from two buildings, one building forty-seven years old, the other only five. Two more slabs from the satchel. Southern pine. Obtained from different lumber companies. "But the end grain compares identically the same," the witness said. Two more slabs. Bird's-eye maple, from different trees. "But they match exactly." A hunk of oak from the prodigious satchel. "See how erratic the grain is, and how it will change its course." Similar erratic changes would be found, he estimated, in twenty-five per cent of all wood.

Wilentz and Koehler had been whispering together; Wilentz got up. Could the witness tell whether two pieces of lumber were ever connected at one time?

"I can."

"What authorities have you read on the subject?"

"Well, I read them through the magazine *Farm and Forestry.*"

"What books?"

"I never read any books."

"Do you know how many knives there were in a lumber-mill planer that dressed the surface of a board, by looking at the board?"

"I do not."

Pope resumed his questions for the defense. "Have you made a study of the ladder rail, Rail 16, and the piece of wood taken from the defendant's attic?" He gave the witness the exhibits.

"I have."

And what had the witness found?

Well, he had examined them three times, and he would say that they were an entirely different board. The rings in one weren't the same kind of knot ring as in the other. "It can't match," De Bisschop continued, "not so far as the face surface of either side——" He hesitated. "This is the way it's supposed to be matched, isn't it? Which is the top? Which is the top here?"

"Just a minute!" Wilentz intervened. "Are you asking *Mr. Koehler* which is the top?"

"Why, yes."

Judge Trenchard said, "The witness ought not to ask questions. He ought to answer questions."

Before the day's adjournment, De Bisschop admitted that the

boards from the forty-seven-year-old and five-year-old buildings had come originally from two trees that were the same age.

Pope and De Bisschop began the new day with further consideration of the board from Hauptmann's attic. If the board had been nailed to floor joists with cut nails, had been nailed there for a couple of years, could it be removed from the joists without showing the marks of a chisel or a bar or a hammer or some nail-extracting tool?

"It could not," De Bisschop replied firmly.

Today, he did not even glance toward Arthur Koehler. It had been pointed out to him that appealing to the State's expert to settle a wood problem was not calculated to convince the jurors of the superiority of his own qualifications in that field.

Pope asked, "Do you see any marks of a bar or a hammer or a nail-extracting tool on the board removed from the defendant's attic?"

"No, sir, there are no marks."

Wilentz struck at the answer. "Do you mean to convey that this board in your opinion had not been nailed down to joists?"

"No, sir," De Bisschop said.

"So that you won't say that it was *not* nailed down to joists?"

"I will not."

The attorney general offered a nail in evidence; it was admitted, and he gave it to De Bisschop.

"Would you say that this nail was not used in the ladder or in the floor board?"

"This nail never was."

"Why do you say it wasn't?"

"Because there are no marks. It is an impossibility to take a nail out of lumber in as straight a condition as that."

"Would you be surprised to learn that it *is* a nail taken from the attic board?"

De Bisschop reached for words; finally he said, "I would be awful surprised."

Whatever its effect on the jury, his performance the day before had not impressed Reilly. The defense chief had made a vigorous effort to put on the stand a wood expert whose qualifications could be mentioned in the same breath with Koehler's. He had telephoned Arch Loney, a wood technician with the Public Works Administration in Washington; Reilly had been given to understand that he had some reservations about Koehler's findings. But Loney had said no, he couldn't offer to testify; the State had had about two years to study the wood in the case and he would need time that simply wasn't available—for one thing, to investigate

Hauptmann's attic for himself, to say nothing of subjecting floorboard and ladder to an examination that would not look ridiculous alongside Koehler's.

William Bolmer, the next witness for the defense, a Princeton University graduate with a civil engineering degree, owned a service station four miles from Princeton, within easy range of the Lindbergh estate; at around a quarter past one on the morning of March 1, 1932, he continued to Pope, a dark green Ford coupé had pulled into his place for gas. The car had stuck in his mind because a ladder was fastened to the running board, a very makeshift-looking ladder. A man and a woman were in the car.

"Stand up, Mr. Hauptmann," Pope said; and then, to Bolmer, "Is that the man?"

"Positively not."

Cross-examining, Wilentz asked, "Did you ever report this to the New Jersey authorities?"

"I did not."

Pope asked, "Why not?"

"I didn't recognize the description of the kidnap ladder, and in the picture I saw of it, it was extended. The ladder I saw on the car was nested, one part within another. I didn't think it was the same ladder and I didn't want to make a fool of myself talking about something I didn't know about."

Now that he had seen for himself the ladder found on the Lindbergh grounds, what was his opinion?

William Bolmer said that it was the same ladder he had seen on the Ford. Wilentz could not shake him; it was a Ford, not a Dodge.

Ewald Mielke came to the stand, and Pope established that he owned a millworking plant in Lindenhurst, Long Island. Yes, he had had a lot of experience in matching wood grains and frequently used a handplane. Nicks weren't at all rare in a plain's blade, after much use. He was extensively familiar with Southern pine; millions of feet of it had gone through his place. Yes, he had inspected Rail 16 of the ladder and the attic board.

"Mr. Mielke," Pope said slowly, "from your experience as a carpenter and practical mill man, and from your handling, dressing, working and using lumber, and from your personal inspection of the board known in this case as the attic floorboard, and from your personal inspection of Rail 16, will you tell the jury whether those two pieces of board were at one time a part of or one and the same board?"

"They are not," Mielke replied.

Wilentz's cross-examination was very much to the point. How long had the witness spent in examining Rail 16 and the attic floorboard?

"Possibly five minutes."

The attorney general nodded. Arthur Koehler's exactly opposite conclusion regarding the two pieces of board was the result of a good deal more than five minutes' study. A good deal more! Wilentz did not believe that the fact would elude the jurors when they retired to consider the State's case against Bruno Richard Hauptmann.

Mielke left the witness chair; Judge Trenchard glanced at Reilly. "Counsel may proceed."

Reilly got up. "The defense rests," he said.

The announcement created a stir in the crowd. Was that all? Had the defense played its whole hand? Did nothing else remain except the opposing sides' summations and the judge's charge to the jury?

Those in the crowd who were familiar with trial procedure knew that an important chapter of the long conflict was still to be written: the State's rebuttal.

Wilentz was ready for it, with the help of his unseen, swift corps of investigators. Their celerity was matched by his in examining the rebuttal witnesses.

Benjamin Heier had testified for the defense that on the night of April 2, 1932, between a quarter to eleven and eleven, he had seen a man jump over the St. Raymond's Cemetery wall, and that newspaper pictures of Isidor Fisch were of the same man.

Joseph Farber, an insurance broker, now testified in rebuttal that on the night of April 2, 1932, a little after ten, on Sixth Avenue, Manhattan, between Fifty-fourth and Fifty-fifth Streets, his car had been in an accident with a car driven by Benjamin Heier. As an insurance man, Mr. Farber was professionally capable of ascertaining the identity of the other driver. Fifty-fourth, Fifty-fifth Streets, Manhattan, he said, were about eight and a half miles south of St. Raymond's Cemetery.

Reilly asked if he'd had a tape measure with him. No, he hadn't, but any New York City street map would prove him to be right.

Elvert Carlstrom had testified that on the night of March 1, 1932, around half-past eight, he had seen Richard Hauptmann in Fredericksen's bakery in the Bronx.

Arthur Larsen testified in rebuttal that on the night of March 1, 1932, he had been in the new, unfurnished house at Dunellen, New Jersey, where he and Carlstrom worked; that Carlstrom had been with him all evening and that they went to bed between nine and ten.

Oscar Christensen testified that he owned the Dunellen house and that Larsen and Carlstrom had worked for him on March 1, 1932.

Mrs. Bertha Hoff had testified that in November 1933 Mr. Budreau, a friend, came to her Bayside house with Isidor Fisch, and that Fisch was carrying a package.

Wilentz produced Alfred Budreau, Mrs. Hoff's friend, who stated that he had not come to her house in October or November 1933 with Isidor Fisch. He did not know a man named Isidor Fisch.

Yes, he told Reilly, Mrs. Hoff would know him all right if he came to her house. Yes, she had spent part of a summer on his farm.

Joseph Levenson, a real estate broker, testified that he had been at the Bronx home of a Mr. and Mrs. Henry Jung between half past seven and midnight of the night of March 1, 1932. Isidor Fisch had been there, on business matters concerned with Jung and Levenson.

Reilly protested, "No one has said Isidor Fisch was in Hopewell March first." Robert Peacock of the prosecution answered: Maybe the defense hadn't said so but there'd been plenty of insinuations that it was Isidor Fisch and not Richard Hauptmann who was on the Lindbergh grounds the night of the kidnaping.

Mrs. Henry Jung confirmed Levenson's testimony, and Mr. Jung confirmed hers.

Miss Henna Fisch, Isidor's sister, brought by the State from Germany to testify, said through an interpreter that Isidor had come back to Germany in December 1933 and lived with her until he died, in March 1934, in the hospital. The only money he had amounted to around fifteen hundred marks, about five hundred dollars. She had unpacked his bags. They contained a couple of suits, a few shirts, shoes, some ties. Nothing else.

Reilly tried to question the witness in German but failed to make his meaning clear and resorted to the interpeter. Weren't there such things as safe-deposit boxes in German banks? Yes; but Miss Fisch did not believe Isidor would have hidden any money in one. During a period of six years he had managed to send home only a thousand dollars in all; and in 1932, she had sent him money.

Selma Kohl testified that Isidor Fisch had rented a room in her house from April 1932 until he left for Germany. It was the cheapest room she had: $3.50 a week.

Lou Harding had testified for the defense that on the afternoon of March 1, 1932, two men had stopped in a car and asked him how to get to the Lindbergh place, that there was a ladder in the car and that it resembled the kidnap ladder. On March 2, police had taken him to the Lindbergh grounds, where he'd seen the ladder.

William Konietzko, a Princeton police officer, now testified that it was he who had driven Harding to the Lindbergh estate. Harding had talked about the men who had questioned him but had said nothing about having seen a ladder in their car.

The parade of rebuttal witnesses halted for the day. Prosecution and defense agreed, with Judge Trenchard's consent, to resume the following morning, Saturday February 9, carrying the trial into a week end for the first time.

Saturday morning's courtroom crowd made an exciting discovery: Anne Lindbergh was with Charles. Why, they wondered, had she chosen this day to return to the trial? Was she to testify again? Her slight figure and calm, rather pale face easily dominated the crowd's attention, almost to the point of ignoring the new rebuttal witnesses.

Louis Kiss, the quiet rum-maker, had testified that on the evening of March 1, 1932, he had seen the defendant in Fredericksen's bakery and later had delivered two pints of rum to Leo Singer, a thirsty friend in the Bronx.

Leo Singer took the stand. Mr. Kiss had not delivered two pints of rum or anything else to him on the night of March 1, 1932; he hadn't even seen him that night.

Reilly was unable to budge Singer; he was no more successful in attacking the testimony of Ottilia Hoerber, who said that Isidor Fisch had come to her house on the night of April 2, 1932, and talked business with her from around seven to half-past nine.

Peter Sommer, the fingerprint expert who in the past had testified for money, had told Reilly that he had seen a woman with a baby on the Manhattan Forty-second Street trolley around midnight, March 1, 1932, and that a photo of Violet Sharpe resembled the woman; and Mrs. Anna Bonesteel later had added the information that on the same night, between half-past seven and half-past eight or a quarter to nine, Violet Sharpe, very nervous, a gray blanket on her arm, was in Mrs. Bonesteel's Yonkers restaurant.

But now Ernest Miller testified that Violet—whom he had met more or less by accident late in February 1932—had been with him and two friends, Katherine Minners and Elmer Johnson, on the night of March 1, 1932, from eight o'clock, when they had picked her up at the Morrow estate in Englewood, until around eleven, when they'd brought her back from the place where they'd spent the evening, the Orangeburg Peanut Grill.

Katherine Minners and Elmer Johnson corroborated Miller's testimony. All three held firm under Reilly's attempts to shake them.

Wilentz said, "Mrs. Dwight Morrow."

He helped an elderly woman dressed in black to the witness chair. Courtesy and respect rather than the witness' physical need lay behind his gesture; the years and heavy sorrow had not unduly marked her thin upright form. The crowd understood why Anne was here; she had accompanied her mother to court.

"Will you tell us, please, Mrs. Morrow," Wilentz asked, "about what time you saw Violet Sharpe the evening of March 1, 1932?"

"She served dinner about seven o'clock," Elizabeth Morrow told him in a quiet, precise voice which further marked her as Anne's mother, "and I did not see her after about a quarter to eight until much later in the evening—after eleven."

"Thank you, Mrs. Morrow."

Reilly got up. His respect, too, was evident. Mrs. Morrow employed a butler whose name was Septimus Banks? Yes. Did he help in serving dinner that night? No.

"Did he serve the next night?"

"The night of the second of March I was not there," the witness said gently. "You see, I was in Hopewell."

"Was the butler's night off March first?"

"He was in our house that night, but not serving."

Reilly bowed. "I think that is all, Mrs. Morrow." He was not to be outdone by David Wilentz in this, their last passage at arms over a witness: he helped her from the stand. She and Anne and Charles left the courtroom.

Wilentz said, "The State rests."

"We rest," Reilly said.

Court was adjourned.

24

The prisoner enjoyed a good night's sleep.

Anna had been given permission to bring Bubi on Sunday afternoon for a second visit. No hint of tears for anyone today; they were all smiles—not too much longer to wait for the jury's verdict and freedom. The summations, the final speeches to the jury, would come first, then the judge's charge, Richard told Anna. He had wanted Lloyd Fisher to make the summation for the defense but Mr. Reilly had said no. Reilly said he had been summing up cases for juries before Fisher was born. He said maybe this was a jury of country people but country juries and city juries were brothers and sisters under the skin because it was all a question of appealing to the human heart and the human heart didn't change.

Parting with a smile, Anna said that maybe Mr. Reilly was right.

Seventy-five to a hundred thousand people visited Flemington during the day, the State troopers estimated.

Monday February 11.

Anthony Hauck, who had been limited so far to his examination of prospective jurors, rose in the jammed courtroom. "It is customary in criminal cases, especially in Hunterdon County," he said, "for the defense to demand from the State what is known as an opening, and it is my assignment, as prosecutor of the pleas in Hunterdon County, to give this opening."

His opening was a brief statement of the facts as the State saw them. It served as a curtain-raiser; the coughers, sneezers, shufflers and murmurers had pretty well subsided by the time he was finished.

Reilly's slow approach to the jury box put the last sneeze to rest. He looked the same, a figure to command silence, but somehow was different. Simply his awareness of the life-and-death task on his hands? Yes, of course, but something more, a sharp-eyed special correspondent thought; and then spotted it. For the first time, Ed Reilly had forgotten his white carnation!

Forgotten? Well, maybe not. Maybe it was deliberate, a concession to the jury, to demonstrate that Edward J. Reilly was just plain folks, after all.

The spats remained.

A round oak table on which many of the trial exhibits were displayed had been placed in front of the jury box; other exhibits were in the wall rack, a pointer beside it. Reilly, hands clasped behind him, glanced at the table; then, with a smile for the jury, he began.

He came from Brooklyn, he said, and they were New Jersey people, yet they spoke the same language, the language of horse-sense —for it was only a little river that divided their state from his, a meandering little stream called the Hudson—wasn't that so?

The jurors settled back comfortably, smiling too.

But Reilly's face was grave, now. He took out a small black book and reverently held it high. It was a Bible. He said quietly:

"Ladies and gentlemen of the jury, I wish to give you a text from St. Matthew, 'Judge not, lest ye be judged,' and ask of you in the consideration of this case that you bring into your hearts and into your consciences the feeling that you are weighing that which you cannot give back if you take it away—life."

After a moment he put the Bible back in his pocket. At the same instant Hauptmann drew out a handkerchief and rubbed it between his palms.

The State, Reilly said, was relying on its contention that the defendant alone planned the crime. If the jury found that it was the work of a gang, or if three or four people had a hand in it, the pattern was all wrong, the State's case exploded.

The State would have the jury believe in one breath that Hauptmann was a master mind and in the next that he was dumb—that he wouldn't leave any fingerprints on a ladder but would sit talking for an hour and a half, his face exposed, with Dr. Condon!

Hauptmann—in one breath the master criminal, in the next the perfect fool! Did that make sense? Reilly shook his head. It did not! He continued:

"The first thing you have got to decide when you go into your jury room is this: How in God's name did Hauptmann, in the Bronx, know anything about the Lindbergh home? Was that possible? No. Colonel Lindbergh was stabbed in the back by the disloyalty of those who worked for him, and despite the fact that he courageously believes there was no disloyalty in the servants' quarters, I say now that no one could get into that house unless the information was supplied by those who worked for the Colonel.

"What is the evidence? That the first time he spent a Tuesday night in that house was the Tuesday night of the kidnaping. Every other week end the family only stayed over Sunday night or early Monday morning. Who knew the baby had a cold and had to stay in Hopewell on Monday? Not Hauptmann. Nobody but the Colonel, his lovely wife, his butler, his butler's wife, Betty Gow, the servants in the Morrow home and Red Johnson knew it. Betty Gow? The Colonel can have all the confidence he pleases in her. I have none. The butler?"

Reilly paused. "There was one thing in that house that would only respond to its master," he resumed, "and that was the little fox terrier—the snappiest, scrappiest dog alive, when it comes to a watchdog! And who controlled that dog's movements that night? The butler. I say the circumstances point absolutely along a straight line of guilt toward that butler and the disloyal servants. Can a man come up to a strange house with a ladder and stack it up against the wall and run up the ladder, push open a shutter and walk into a room that he has never been in before? *That* is what the State would have you believe!"

He said the words scornfully. Continuing, he addressed himself to the women on the jury.

"The moment anyone put their hand on that child, that child's cry ringing out would have brought the mother from her bedroom close by. I will leave it to you mothers if I am not right! The person who picked that child out of that crib *knew* that child—and the child knew that person! Of course," Reilly added almost parenthetically, "if instead of a physic, if the child had been doped, or given paregoric or something—then the child wouldn't cry." His clasped hands parted, swung around and spread out, both forefingers raised. "But who gave the medicine?" he asked. "Not Hauptmann. Who gave the physic? Not Hauptmann. And this little child is picked up and they would have you believe that Hauptmann, who never saw the child, never knew the child—and with a dog downstairs!—a strange man in the house, and all the doors open! —they would have you believe that this stranger to the house goes back with a twenty- or twenty-five pound child in his arms, swings himself out of the window in the darkness and is able to find the top rung of that ladder, three feet below the window shelf, that rickety old ladder, and then, as he finds himself on the window seat and his feet touching the top of the ladder, is able to turn, with the child in his arms, and feel his way down the side wall and still hold onto the child and find the ladder, so that he can come down the ladder to the part where the dowel pin joins it together, and then they say the dowel pin broke—but what they say is not evidence."

Reilly's clenched fist struck the exhibit table. "Remember the evidence of the officer who found the ladder fifty to seventy-five feet away from the house! Remember the mud between the house and the ladder! You can't walk in mud without leaving footprints, can you? But there was not a footprint between the house and the ladder! Why?"

Solemnly he spaced out the words:

"I say that ladder was a plant. I say that ladder was never up against the side of the house that night. *Now* am I right in saying that you have a right to assume from this evidence that somebody disloyal to the Colonel entered the nursery, somebody who knew that baby?"

His voice rose. "Oh, it was so well planned by disloyal people!" he cried. "So well planned!"

The jury's attention was entirely his, and not only the jury's. Hauptmann was staring earnestly at him; Anna's eyes were wide, enthralled. Lindbergh, in his customary seat between Henry Breckinridge and Norman Schwarzkopf, was studying the dramatic, commanding figure no less fixedly. There was not a cough, not a murmur or rustle of moving bodies in the courtroom.

Reilly picked up the pointer beside the wall rack and rested his massive hands on it, leaning toward the jury. Oliver Whateley, the butler, was downstairs somewhere, he continued; Mrs. Whateley and Betty Gow were talking about a dress. And somebody came in who knew the child—whether from the Lindbergh house or the Morrow house, Reilly admitted he didn't know—but those were the only houses that had servants who had contact with the child.

"And the Colonel and his wife are eating dinner, secure in the belief that they are safe. They are out of sight of the front door and out of sight of the rear door. And all of a sudden comes the signal—'*The coast is clear; they are at dinner.*' The signal? The telephone call from Red Johnson, whom Betty Gow had left only two hours before."

He straightened, raised the pointer, waved it. "Who is hiding things here?" he demanded. "Who is hiding the truth?"

The State of New Jersey had spent thousands of dollars to bring the Fisch family to America, he told the jury—their money, taxpayers' money!—only to put one of them on the stand, but the State hadn't raised a finger to bring back from Norway the man who talked to Betty Gow while the Lindberghs were at dinner—Red. Why not? *Who was hiding the truth?*

Again Reilly leaned on the pointer as he moved on to the note found in the nursery. There was a lot of wind that night, he reminded the jury, and yet with the window open, and nothing on top of the note to hold it down, it just stayed there—wasn't whisked across the room by the wind. Strange! Then the State troopers came and Kelly the fingerprint man came. There must have been fingerprints all over the nursery, Mrs. Lindbergh's, Betty Gow's, even the baby's—but did Kelly find any? None. Had somebody been instructed to wipe them off? Not a single fingerprint, only smudges. Not even a fingerprint on the glass Betty Gow used for the baby's physic! Who rubbed them out?

Reilly gave the jurors a moment to dwell on the question. Now, he said, he would like to talk to them a little while about the notes the State claimed Hauptmann wrote. He did not wish to take up the testimony of every one of the State's handwriting experts. The judge would tell the jury that expert evidence was nothing more or less than opinion evidence. And what did opinion evidence mean?

"Opinion evidence means that this man says, 'I think it is this.' Another man says, 'I think it is that.' And the wise courts and judges have decided for many years that a jury has a perfect right to disregard expert evidence altogether and use their own common sense. It is very important for the prosecution to try and pin this nursery note on Hauptmann—that is part of what I call their scenario." Reilly straightened again, waved the pointer. "But I ask you this, please: before finding that this is Hauptmann's handwriting—if you ever do, because he has denied it—please keep in mind that there is no evidence except this produced by the prosecution which puts Hauptmann in the nursery March the first, and this note places him there through the opinion, or guesswork, we will call it, of Mr. Osborn and those who followed him."

They all said that the handwriting in the note was disguised, Reilly pointed out. Was disguised handwriting—*whose* handwriting, no one could say for a fact—enough to send a man to his death? Even enough to condemn him to life imprisonment?

Could anybody honestly believe that *one man* could have planned the kidnaping, stolen the child, run around New York and New Jersey, written all the notes, followed up the notes? Did not all this planning, all this activity, have to be the work of a gang?

He wished to make himself clear. By *a gang* he meant a collection of people bent on an evil undertaking.

Reilly walked slowly to the wall rack, every eye with him, and put the pointer back where he had found it. He returned to his position in front of the jury box. Now, he said, he came to Dr. Condon.

He folded his arms across his immaculate chest. "Dr. Condon," he said, "stands behind something in this case that is unholy."

Dr. Condon rushed to the defense of a man—Red Johnson—about whom he said he knew nothing. Why so anxious to protect this poor innocent? Why——unless there was a secret connection between the two?

Dr. Condon said he went to the Bronx *News* and inserted a letter. Who saw the letter? For his part, Reilly didn't believe there was a letter, but he did believe there was a signal—the same kind of signal that passed between Betty Gow and Red Johnson the night of March 1.

Who knew anything about Dr. Condon?—except this:

Everything Dr. Condon did he did alone; and Reilly tolled out the word, emphasizing it with strokes of his clenched hand:

"*Alone, alone, alone!*"

Who went into the cemetery with Condon? No one. He was alone. Who saw him hand over the fifty thousand dollars? No one. He was alone.

"*Alone, alone, alone!*"

Reilly permitted his deep voice a few moments' grace before pronouncing the next name in his catalogue. It was Violet Sharpe's. He knew the jurors would use their horse-sense in considering this question:

Would anyone sophisticated and worldly enough to go out on the road and flirt with a fellow—as Violet Sharpe did—commit suicide because she was afraid of losing her job? No, no! Life was too sweet.

"But the net was closing in. Violet had let something drop, had given a clue. And suddenly the detectives came back and said, 'Bring Violet down here again.' Inspector Walsh and his detectives have checked up and found something—and Violet knows it. And she drains the poison. Why? Not because she was afraid about her job. She did it because the woman from Yonkers, Mrs. Bonesteel, told the truth. Sommer too. Violet was at the ferry to Alpine with a blanket and later at Forty-second Street with a child in a blanket, and that child was the Colonel's child, and while I have the greatest respect for the distinguished Mrs. Morrow, I believe she is honestly mistaken. I don't think Mrs. Morrow remembers correctly that she saw Violet at eleven or twelve that night, because it just doesn't fit in with Violet's suicide."

Reilly's voice had been quiet, in talking about Violet; now its volume and pace increased. Thirty-five thousand dollars of the ransom money was missing, he said. Where was it? If in circulation, it would be spotted immediately. He would tell the jury where he thought it was: in a safe-deposit box, under an assumed name, put there by Isidor Fisch. Some day it would come to light. God grant that when that day came the jury would have nothing to regret!

"Not a dollar of that money, of that ransom money, ever went through Wall Street or went through a bank!" Reilly declared. "One bank might slip up. But there was a bank in Mount Vernon. There was the Central Savings Bank. There was the bank the brokers did business with. There were three or more banks, and there were those brokerage accounts, and not a brokerage account and not a bank account found a dollar of this money!"

As for the writing Hauptmann did in the police station, he was anxious to write; he wished to clear himself of suspicion. What had he testified? "I wrote as I was told to write. They spelled words for me and I spelled those words as they told me to." And had a single solitary soul come back on the witness stand to contradict Richard Hauptmann on that score?

Reilly knew—who was in a better position to know?—and he would tell the jury that the New York City police were past masters in fixing evidence. "Of all the crooked evidence in this case," he said, "of all the plants that were ever put into a case, this board on the inside of a closet—where they would have you believe a man would crawl in, crawl into that dark closet, and over in a corner on a board write Dr. Condon's number as it was three or four years ago—this board is the worst example of police crookedness that I have ever seen."

Solemnly he contemplated the jury. He only hoped there were some carpenters on it, he observed. He hoped they would examine the ladder very carefully, because it was never made by any carpenter.

His eye did not linger on Liscom Case, the acknowledged carpenter on the jury; but Case's gaze never left him.

"Do you suppose the board used in the ladder was ever taken out of any attic floor?" Reilly asked. "Examine it carefully! It doesn't bear a mark from any hammer. But Mr. Koehler comes in—and here we are again with expert evidence as opposed to horse-sense—and he'd have you believe that this carpenter, Hauptmann, who could buy any kind of wood in a lumberyard, went out and got two or three different kinds of wood, and then said to himself, 'My goodness, I am short a piece of lumber! What am I going to do?' "

Reilly's tone was magnificently sardonic. "Whatever was he going to do?" he continued. "There is a lumberyard around the corner. And so he crawls up into his attic and tears up a board and takes it downstairs and saws it lengthwise and crosswise and every other wise to make the side of a ladder!"

He snorted. "You men on the jury have handled boards. Down in the Carolinas billions and billions of board feet are produced every year, and yet Koehler has the nerve to tell us that there never were two boards alike in all those billions of feet!

"Ladies and gentlemen of the jury, the case is too perfect from the prosecution's point of view and what they produced here. There isn't a man in the world with brains enough to plan this kidnaping alone and not with a gang and then sit down and make the foolish mistake of ripping a board out of his attic and leaving the other half of it there!"

The State was rich, Reilly concluded, and the defense poor; but in spite of the State's attacks, the jury could believe the testimony it had heard from the defense's witnesses, none of whom had been paid or cajoled or threatened.

He was silent. Then, slowly and with utter conviction, he said:

"I believe Richard Hauptmann is absolutely innocent of murder. And I feel sure that even Colonel Lindbergh wouldn't expect you and doesn't expect you to do anything but your duty under the law and under the evidence."

He turned and looked at the father of the dead child.

"May I say to him, in closing, that he has my profound respect. I feel sorry for him in his deep grief, and I am quite sure"—he turned back to the jury—"that all of you agree with me that his lovely son is now within the gates of Heaven."

Reilly made his audience a little bow and walked to the defense table.

Court was adjourned for the day.

25

Tuesday February 12.

A trooper said he thought this was the biggest crowd Flemington had seen since the start of the trial, and wondered why. Because everyone knew David Wilentz was going to sum up for the State today?

Maybe not, another trooper said; maybe the fact that it was a holiday had something to do with it. Lincoln's Birthday.

The most seasoned spectators, those who had managed to squeeze into the courtroom on every one of the trial's preceding thirty days, had expected thunder and lightning from Reilly, a performance to cap with a flourish his role in this, the greatest drama of his long legal life. They had been disappointed; few fireworks had marked his summation, which instead was remembered for the note of deep personal belief on which it had closed—belief in Richard Hauptmann's innocence.

And now Wilentz. Would he too hold himself in check?

The packed room waited eagerly.

David Wilentz rose and came forward to the same position his opponent had taken, beside the exhibit table in front of the jury box.

"May it please your Honor and men and women of the jury——"

Reilly had jettisoned the carnation for his final appeal; Wilentz was at his sprucest. His dark blue double-breasted suit looked new, or at least newly pressed; the striped blue tie was in harmony with it; the starched, fairly high shirt collar seemed almost as formal as Reilly's wing-tip; and two triangles of a handkerchief, their points precisely level, protruded from his breast pocket. His face was rather pale; his black hair had a glassy polish.

Even during the first words an electric restlessness was plain in the quick movement of his hand, which brandished a book.

Reilly had read from the New Testament; Wilentz read from the Old.

" 'Judge not lest ye be judged,' my adversary says. But he forgets the other Biblical admonition:

" '*And he that killeth any man shall surely be killed, shall surely be put to death.*' "

He placed the Bible on the exhibit table, as if it too were in evidence.

"For all these months since October 1934," he told the jury, "not during one moment has there been anything that has come to light that has indicated anything but the guilt of Bruno Richard Hauptmann. Every avenue of evidence leads to the same door: Bruno Richard Hauptmann.

"What type of man would murder the child of Charles and Anne Lindbergh? He wouldn't be an American. No American gangster ever sank to the level of killing babies. Ah, no! An American gangster that did want to participate in a kidnaping wouldn't pick out Colonel Lindbergh. There are many people much wealthier than the Colonel. No; it had to be a fellow who had icewater, not blood, in his veins. It had to be a fellow who had a peculiar mental makeup, who thought he was bigger than Lindy—a fellow who, when the news of the crime came out, could look at the headlines screaming across the page, just as the headlines screamed when Lindy made his famous flight. It had to be an egomaniac, who thought he was omnipotent."

The attorney general abandoned his position beside the exhibit table and walked back and forth; occasionally he slammed the palms of his hands together like a small clash of cymbals, underlining the swift rise and fall of his voice, and nothing more vividly illustrated the difference in delivery between Reilly's summation and his. He described Hauptmann as the type of man who trusted nobody, not even his wife; a man who wouldn't talk even if you killed him, a man who at gunpoint would hold up women wheeling their baby carriages.

Clash of hands. "And let me tell you, men and women of the jury, the State of New Jersey and the State of New York and the federal authorities have found an animal lower than the lowest form in the animal kingdom, Public Enemy Number One of this world—Bruno Richard Hauptmann!"

Was the case against him a frame-up? Who were the framers? Men like Colonel Schwarzkopf? Like Dr. Condon? Like William Frank? Like Arthur Koehler? Were such men crooks? They—and Betty Gow and Inspector Bruckman and dozens of other honest, decent people —had had to listen to his delightful adversary's attempts at character assassination; even the character of a dead woman, Violet Sharpe, no longer able to defend herself, had not been spared. Even Mrs. Morrow and Colonel Lindbergh himself were not altogether spared.

Wilentz halted his restless pacing, crooked a leg against the exhibit table, leaned toward the jury and spoke confidentially. He told them that Red Johnson would never have been permitted to leave the country if he had not been exhaustively checked by the police and the federal authorities; that Betty Gow had returned from Scotland by the State's invitation, her way paid by the State—of course! could a twelve-dollar-a-week maid be expected to pay her way here and back?—so as to be ready to answer any untrue charges by the defense. If she had had one scintilla of guilty knowledge, would she have returned?

"Contrast that with Hauptmann, over in the Bronx. Boy!" Wilentz exclaimed. "When he heard the State of New Jersey wanted him, did he say, 'I'll come right over?'"

Oh no, the prosecutor said scornfully; not Hauptmann; there had to be a big legal fight to get him to New Jersey. Why so reluctant, this fellow who claimed he was innocent? The evidence had demonstrated the reasons for his shyness. The evidence had tied his handwriting to the writing in the ransom notes. The evidence—which Wilentz swiftly synopsized—had placed him in St. Raymond's Cemetery on the night of the ransom payment; had brought the kidnap ladder home to his Bronx attic; had revealed the source of his suddenly expanded stock-market operations; had proved why Hauptmann had lied in saying he met Isidor Fisch in March or April 1932—lied because he had made deposits in April, May and June which he attributed to Fisch, whereas the fact was that he hadn't met Fisch until the end of July or August. Ransom notes, ladder, the baby's sleeping suit, stock-market deals, hidden hoard of kidnap money, Dr. Condon's identification, Colonel Lindbergh's identification—a complete chain leading from the violated nursery to the man here in the courtroom.

Wilentz left the exhibit table, resumed his pacing. His delightful adversary had said that if anyone who was a stranger had walked into the nursery, the baby would have sensed it, would have cried out.

"I don't think that's a fair statement of fact, men and women of the jury. I think a stranger could walk into a child's room, if the child were asleep, without the child awakening."

Clash of hands. "But let me tell you this! This fellow took no chance on the child awakening. He crushed that child right in that room, into insensibility. He smothered and choked that child right in that room. That child never cried, never gave any outcry, certainly not! The little voice was stilled right in that room. *He* wasn't interested in the child. Life meant nothing to him. That's the type of man we're dealing with."

The prosecutor's voice reached a peak. "Public Enemy Number One of the world! That's what we're dealing with! You're not dealing with a fellow who doesn't know what he's doing. Take a look at him as he sits there! Look at him when he walks out of this room today—pantherlike, gloating, feeling good!"

The jury's eyes shifted to Hauptmann. His ordinarily sallow face looked damp and reddish. He dabbed at it with a handkerchief, twisted in his chair, crossed and uncrossed his legs. Anna's eyes were closed; her lips moved without sound.

"Certainly he stilled this little child's breath," Wilentz said harshly. "Right in that room! That child didn't cry out when it was disturbed. Yanked from the crib—how? Not just taken up; the pins were still left in the bedsheets. Yanked, and its head hit up against the headboard—must have been hit. *He* couldn't do it any other way. Certainly it must have hit up against that board. Still no outcry. Why? Because there was no cry left in the child. Did he use the chisel to crush the skull at the time or to knock it into insensibility? Is that a fair inference? What else was the chisel there for? To knock that child into insensibility right there in that room."

At the defense table, Egbert Rosecrans was quickly adding to the notes he had been making. Wilentz had said in his opening address to the jury that the child died when the ladder broke and the kidnaper fell; now the prosecutor had completely reversed himself. Nothing during the State's presentation of its case had foreshadowed this new, contradictory charge. It was not Rosecrans' or the defense's business to wonder why Wilentz had left his charted course; their business was to plan for the future.

Taking breath, Wilentz leaned against the jury box. When he spoke again, he might have been talking to a group of old friends, homefolks, his kind of people, New Jersey people, shutting out the alien world. Circumstantial evidence, he said, there'd been a lot of talk about circumstantial evidence—well, sometimes it was the strongest kind. But the State did not rest on circumstantial evidence alone. Dr. Condon's identification was positive, so was the taxi driver Perrone's—nothing circumstantial there. The board in Hauptmann's closet with the handwriting on it, that wasn't circumstantial. Hochmuth's evidence wasn't circumstantial. Whited's wasn't. Lupica's wasn't. And Colonel Lindbergh's identification was not circumstantial. The brokerage accounts, the sleeping garment, the fifteen thousand dollars in the garage—not circumstantial!

"And the note in the nursery. This fellow had planned this crime. He wasn't going to let any faker come in and take that money. He had something on that note so that Colonel Lindbergh could tell, if another one came, that it was from the right party. So he put his signature on it. You couldn't reproduce it. The blue circles, the red center and the holes—*b* in blue, for Bruno; *r* in red, for Richard; holes, *h* for Hauptmann!"

That was Hauptmann's signature, Wilentz continued; and then he repeated the word, deliberately mispronouncing it. *Sing*nature. Now, let him tell the jury about that, let him show them what a perjurer Hauptmann was, a liar, lying right in this courtroom. His counsel asked him how he spelled *signature,* and he replied, S–I–G–N-A-T-U-R-E. Then his counsel asked:

" 'Did the police tell you to spell it S–I–N–G-N-A-T-U-R-E?' And Hauptmann answered, 'They did.'

"Why? Because it was spelled that way in the ransom note and Hauptmann wanted to show that he didn't write it. So he swears the police told him to spell it *sing*nature."

Wilentz slapped his hands together. "Now, men and women of the jury, take those writings Hauptmann made in the police station. Go through every one of them and you won't find the word *signature* anywhere. He was never asked to write it, right or wrong! And still he swears on the witness stand that he was told by the police to misspell it!"

It had taken the attorney general some time to put to use that glaring blunder of Hauptmann's, the press-gallery observers noted; it had not escaped the prosecution after all.

Wilentz backed it up by reminding the jury of another significant misspelling, B–O–A–D for boat, then swiftly came to his final appeal: "Mr. Reilly says the case is too perfect. No case can be too perfect, but it *is* perfect—perfect because of Hauptmann's conduct. Every piece of evidence we have he presented to us.

"There are some cases in which a recommendation of mercy might do—but not this one, not this one! Either this man is the filthiest and vilest snake that ever crept through the grass or he is entitled to an acquittal. And if you believe as we do, you have got to convict him. If you bring in a recommendation of mercy, a wishy-washy decision, that is your province, and once I sit down I will not say another word, so far as this jury and its verdict is concerned. But it seems to me you will have the courage to find Richard Hauptmann guilty of murder in the first degree."

He was finished.

A voice cried, "If your Honor please——"

Startled, Wilentz turned. A man in clerical black had risen to his feet among the spectators. Guards rushed to him; one threw a hand over the speaker's mouth, muffling his next words, so that none except the guards and others close to him heard him continue: "—I have a confession that was made to me by the man who committed this crime——"

Then he was completely silenced and half-carried, half-pushed from the courtroom.

Wilentz's angry face spoke clearly for him: Could this outbreak, this bolt from the blue, mean a mistrial? Would the whole weary fight have to be fought over again?

Judge Trenchard called him and Reilly to the bench and they spoke in low voices, while jury and spectators stared. Reilly said he knew who the man was—Vincent Burns, pastor of an interdenominational church in Palisades, New Jersey. Some time before the trial the Reverend Burns had come to him and said that Hauptmann was not guilty, that the real kidnaper and murderer had confessed to Burns in his church on Palm Sunday 1932, the year of the crime, and that Burns was convinced the man had told the truth. For his part, Reilly went on, he hadn't been impressed; Burns had struck him then as an eccentric and it seemed to him now that the minister belonged in an insane asylum.

To that, Wilentz heartily agreed.

Judge Trenchard said he'd heard no more than "your Honor" and he felt sure the jury had heard no more. Still, he would take precautions. He addressed the jury:

"It is very unfortunate that this scene had to occur but I don't imagine you heard anything except the man's first words. But if you did hear anything more, my instruction to you is that you utterly and entirely disregard it and forget the scene."

But as the courtroom crowd filed out into the jam-packed street, the last picture they carried with them was of the black-clad man's earnest face and waving arms. It was not easy to forget.

26

Thomas Whitaker Trenchard got out of bed, bathed and shaved and put on a dark brown business suit of conservative cut; his robes, of course, were in his chambers at the courthouse. It was a cold sunny morning, he observed; the air seemed bright as dew. A substantial breakfast had been prepared for him; Mrs. Trenchard knew that a long day lay ahead. He ate with excellent appetite. His throat was clear; apparently he need anticipate no trouble with his voice in delivering the charge to the jury. Mrs. Trenchard kissed him good-by.

There was a considerable crowd outside the courthouse, not so great as yesterday's, but yesterday had been a holiday, Lincoln's Birthday. The State troopers on guard looked very smart in their peaked caps and shiny boots and blue, yellow-striped uniforms, so crisp they might have been newly pressed for this notable occasion, the day of the judge's charge, the jury's deliberations, the verdict—provided the jury would not encounter undue difficulty in arriving at one.

It was Judge Trenchard's duty to make their road clear. New Jersey law granted him a good deal of freedom in framing his charge. Many states held a tight rein on the judge; in their courts he served solely as a guide to the law's technicalities and, unless he wished to risk reversal, dared not step from his narrow path to offer—directly or by implication—an opinion on the credibility of the testimony or the soundness of the contending lawyers' arguments. But New Jersey law followed its honored ancestor, English law. The judge was considered to possess a mind of his own and the discretion properly to employ it. He was permitted to emphasize testimony which to his trained eye appeared crucial. If he thought the witnesses made up a herd of sheep and goats, he was allowed to separate them.

Judge Trenchard entered his chambers, took off his hat and overcoat, gave his gray hair a brush or two, which did not really make its order more conspicuous, and donned the stately black silk. He picked up a pencil, took a sheaf of papers from his brief case, and walked into the courtroom through the door directly behind the bench. It was two minutes past ten.

The first thing that struck him was that all the lights were on, even though sunshine was streaming through the windows. Then, as always, he noticed the big American flag hanging over the jury box. The court calendar announced the date in huge black figures: 13. It was right in the defendant's line of vision.

The defendant seemed composed. Apparently he had been talking with his wife; he was leaning a little across one of his guards toward her where she sat two chairs away; now he straightened, his deep-set eyes staring at the judge. Mrs. Hauptmann's gaze followed her husband's. She did not look quite so calm. Her blue eyes blinked a few times.

Charles Lindbergh was in his usual seat. His friends, Henry Breckinridge and Norman Schwarzkopf, were with him.

Prosecution and defense counsel had been the first to rise at the judge's entrance. Wilentz was as smartly dressed as ever and Reilly, as ever, looked like a big-city financier, with blooming face and flower in buttonhole. They and their colleagues had been chatting; now they were silent.

The judge glanced at the jury. He had been rather concerned about Juror No. 3, Mrs. Verna Snyder, whose cold had not improved during the past week. She had a handkerchief pressed to her face; hastily she put it away.

The room was too crowded. The condition was not new to Judge Trenchard and he dealt with it as he had before; everyone who did not have a seat must leave, he said; then the doors were to be locked. No one was to be admitted or allowed to leave the room while he was charging the jury.

Prisoner, jury, counsel, spectators resumed their seats. There was a shuffle, a murmur.

Silence.

"Ladies and gentlemen of the jury," Judge Trenchard said, "the prisoner at the bar, Bruno Richard Hauptmann, stands charged in this indictment with the murder of Charles A. Lindbergh, Jr., in this county on the first day of March, 1932. It now becomes your duty to render a verdict upon the question of his guilt or his innocence and upon the degree of his guilt, if guilty. In doing this you must be guided by the principles of law bearing upon the case that I will now proceed to lay before you.

"In the determination of all questions of fact, the sole responsibility is with the jury. You are the sole judges of the evidence, of the weight of the evidence, and of the credibility of the witnesses. Any comments that I may make upon the evidence will be made not for the purpose of controlling you in your view of the facts but only to aid you in applying the principles of law to the facts as you may find them. You must not consider what I shall say concerning the evidence as being accurate, but you must depend upon your own recollection. You must not only consider the evidence to which I shall refer, but you must consider all of the evidence in the case."

His voice, a fitting instrument for the solemn words, was robed in dignity, yet retained its familiar paternal aspect. The jury was gravely attentive. Mrs. Snyder appeared to have forgotten her cold and her handkerchief.

"In this, as in every criminal case," he continued, "the defendant is presumed to be innocent, which presumption continues until he is proved to be guilty. To support the indictment and to justify a conviction, the State must prove the facts sufficient for that purpose by evidence beyond a reasonable doubt; and that burden never shifts from the State. If there be reasonable doubt whether the defendant be guilty, he is to be declared not guilty."

He paused, as if aware of a question in their minds: What was reasonable doubt?

"Reasonable doubt," he said with deliberate emphasis, "is a term often used but not easily defined. It is not a mere possible doubt. It is that state of the case which, after the entire comparison and consideration of all of the evidence, leaves the minds of the jurors in that condition that they cannot say that they feel an abiding conviction to a moral certainty of the truth of the charge. The evidence must establish the truth of the fact to a moral certainty, a certainty that convinces and directs the understanding and satisfies the reason and judgment of those who are bound to act conscientiously upon it.

"But if, after canvassing carefully the evidence, giving the accused the benefit of reasonable doubt, you are led to the conclusion that the defendant is guilty, you should so declare by your verdict."

Foreman Charles Walton was sitting bolt upright. Juror No. 2, Mrs. Rosie Pill, whose attention had been known to wander, had regained firm command of it.

"To make out a case of guilt," the judge resumed, "the State must establish by evidence beyond a reasonable doubt, first, the death of Charles A. Lindbergh, Jr., as a result of a felonious stroke inflicted on the first day of March, 1932, in this county. To support that charge, the State has produced evidence to the following effect. The fact of death seems to be proved, and admitted. On the evening of March first, the child was prepared for bed by its mother and its nurse, Betty Gow, at the Lindbergh home in this county. The evidence is to the effect that the child was then in good health, a normal child except for a slight cold; that the mother and the nurse securely fixed the covering about the child, and about eight o'clock closed the window and left the room; that between that hour and ten o'clock the child was removed from the bed by some person and carried away, with the clothing in which it had been put to bed.

"There is evidence from which you may conclude, if you see fit, that the person who carried away the child entered the nursery through the southeast window by means of a ladder placed against the side of the house, under or near the window, and that this occurred shortly after nine o'clock.

"You will recall the evidence of Colonel Lindbergh to the effect that, as he was sitting in his living room downstairs, he heard a strange noise about that time, the sound of wood on wood, like the striking of two pieces of wood together, like the boards of a crate falling together off of a stand or chair. He testified that he could not tell where the sound came from, and at the moment he did not think much about it. Later, at about ten o'clock, when the disappearance of the child became known, a strange and broken ladder was found, about sixty or seventy feet from the southeast window, with indications that it had been used in entering and leaving the window; and also there were the imprints of a man's shoe in the soft ground under or near the window."

The courtroom was remarkably free of its previously endemic coughs and sneezes. Robert Cravatt, twenty-eight, the youngest member of the jury, whose face occasionally had revealed a nature swiftly stirred to sympathetic response, seemed as impassive as its senior member, the sixty-year-old Liscom Case.

Judge Trenchard said, "Miss Gow and Mrs. Whateley testified that later, about April first, 1932, they found the thumbguard, which Miss Gow had securely tied to the wrist of the child's sleeping suit when she put him to bed, that they found this thumbguard in the road leading from the Lindbergh home and on the Lindbergh property, with the knot still untied, from which you may possibly conclude that the sleeping suit was stripped off of the child at that place.

"There is also evidence to the effect that there was a dirty smudge on the floor of the nursery, leading from the window to the child's crib, and a ransom letter left on the window sill. Later, the child's dead and decomposed body was found in a shallow grave, not far from the road, a few miles away, in Mercer County.

"Dr. Mitchell, who performed the autopsy, testified that the child died of a fractured skull, the result of external violence. It was a very extensive fracture. He further testified that, in his opinion, death occurred either instantaneously or within a very few minutes following the actual fractural occurrence. It is the contention of the State that the fracture described by Dr. Mitchell was inflicted upon the child when it was seized and carried out of the nursery window down the ladder and when the ladder broke.

"Now, the ladder has been placed in evidence. Its broken condition when found in the yard has been described to you.

"The fact that the child's body was found in Mercer County raises a presumption that the death occurred there; but that, of course, is a rebuttable presumption, and may be overcome by circumstantial evidence. In the present case the State contends that the uncontradicted evidence of Colonel Lindbergh and Dr. Mitchell, and other evidence, justifies the reasonable inference that the felonious stroke occurred in Hunterdon County, when the child was seized and carried out of the nursery window and down the ladder by the defendant, and that death was instantaneous; and from the evidence you may conclude, if you see fit, that the child was feloniously stricken on the first day of March, 1932, in this county, and died as a result of that stroke."

The charge, having described the State's first task, came to a natural pause at this point, and Judge Trenchard took advantage of it for a moment's rest. He resumed:

"Secondly, the State, in order to justify a verdict of guilty, must establish by the evidence, beyond a reasonable doubt, that the death was caused by the act of the defendant. The uncontradicted evidence is that the child was left by the mother and the nurse in the nursery, and the window was then closed. The evidence justifies the inference, if you see fit to draw it, that the window was maliciously opened and the child seized shortly after nine o'clock that night. You will, of course, recall the evidence to the effect that almost immediately after it was discovered that the child had been taken from its crib, there was found the ransom letter, demanding fifty thousand dollars, on the window sill, on which was placed a peculiar symbol and peculiar punch holes, and stating that directions would later be given for the delivery of the money. There is also evidence to the effect that a few days later Colonel Lindbergh received a second letter with like symbols, referring to the original ransom letter, and reiterating that directions for the delivery of the ransom money would be given. Meanwhile, Colonel Breckinridge, the friend and counselor of Colonel Lindbergh, had identified himself with the case in an endeavor to help his friend.

"There is evidence to the effect that a few days before March ninth, 1932, Dr. Condon had inserted an advertisement in the Bronx newspaper in effect offering to act as a go-between; that a few days later Dr. Condon received a letter accepting his offer and enclosing a letter to Colonel Lindbergh, telling Dr. Condon that after he got the money to put words in the New York *American* that the money is ready, and the letter to Colonel Lindbergh said Condon may act as go-between, to give him the money, with directions as to the package; and how thereafter the baby was to be found.

"This letter to Colonel Lindbergh, as I recall the testimony, contained the peculiar symbols of the original ransom letter. The evidence is to the effect that immediately Dr. Condon drove to Hopewell and conferred with Colonel Lindbergh and with Colonel Breckinridge and, with their acquiescence, he inserted the advertisement, 'I accept; money is ready.'

"Dr. Condon testified that shortly thereafter he received a letter addressed to him, and delivered to him by a taxicab driver, giving him instructions how to proceed. The taxicab driver testified that he was given that letter by the defendant Hauptmann. Dr. Condon testified that, as a result of the directions contained in that letter and another letter, he first had, on March twelfth, 1932, an interview in Woodlawn Cemetery with a man whom he identifies as the defendant, after talking with him for more than an hour. In that interview Dr. Condon said that the defendant, after having run away from the gate, said, among other things, 'It is too dangerous. Might be twenty years or burn. Would I burn if the baby is dead?' "

For the first time, several members of the jury looked away from the man on the bench at another man. Mrs. Ethel Stockton, thirty-two, the youngest woman juror, looked at Richard Hauptmann; and Howard Biggs and Mrs. May Brelsford and Mrs. Snyder, still without her handkerchief, and Elmer Smith also turned their eyes toward him; some of them, it seemed, almost unwillingly, as if pulled by the short, ugly word, *burn*. He did not appear to be aware of the word or of their gaze.

They looked back at the judge, who was speaking again.

"Dr. Condon also testified in effect that the defendant said that the baby was being held on a boat by others, that 'We are the right parties,' that the baby was held in the crib by safety pins, and he said that he would send the sleeping suit. Dr. Condon further testified that later he received the sleeping suit, and other letters containing further directions, and finally a letter directing that the money be ready by Saturday night and to put an advertisement in the newspaper, 'Everything O.K.' and that these directions were complied with by him, Condon, with the acquiescence of Colonel Lindbergh and Colonel Breckinridge, the latter of whom had been in close touch with Dr. Condon during practically the whole of the ransom negotiations.

"There is testimony to the effect that on this Saturday night, April second, 1932, there was delivered to Dr. Condon's residence a letter containing further instructions, and that as a result thereof on that evening Colonel Lindbergh, who was there waiting, drove

Dr. Condon to the entrance to St. Raymond's Cemetery with the ransom money; that Dr. Condon alighted and contacted with a man, and after some talk and some delay handed him the package containing fifty thousand dollars of ransom money, thirty-five thousand dollars of which was in gold certificates, the numbers of which bills had been taken.

"It is argued that Dr. Condon's testimony is inherently improbable and should be in part rejected by you, but you will observe that his testimony is corroborated in large part by several witnesses whose credibility has not been impeached in any manner whatsoever. Of course, if there is in the minds of the jury a reasonable doubt as to the truth of any testimony, such testimony should be rejected; but, upon the whole, is there any doubt in your mind as to the reliability of Dr. Condon's testimony?

"There is evidence to the effect that after Dr. Condon alighted with the money he was hailed by a man on the other side of the hedge, to whom he finally delivered the ransom money. Colonel Lindbergh testified that the voice that hailed Condon was that of the defendant. Dr. Condon testified that the man to whom he delivered the money was the defendant. This is denied by the defendant, and there is other testimony bearing upon the matter, and so that question becomes one for your determination.

"It is argued that Colonel Lindbergh could not have identified that voice, and that it is unlikely that the defendant would have talked with Condon. Well, those questions are for the determination of this jury, after having patiently listened to the evidence bearing upon those topics. If you find that the defendant was the man to whom the ransom money was delivered, as a result of the directions in the ransom notes, bearing symbols like those on the original ransom note, the question is pertinent: Was not the defendant the man who left the ransom note on the window sill of the nursery, and who took the child from its crib, after opening the closed window?

"It is argued by defendant's counsel that the kidnaping and murder was done by a gang, and not by the defendant, and that the defendant was in nowise concerned therein. The argument was to the effect that it was done by a gang, with the help or connivance of some one or more servants of the Lindbergh or Morrow households.

"Now do you believe that? Is there any evidence in this case whatsoever to support any such conclusion?"

Judge Trenchard's manner, earnest and dignified throughout, reminded the jury even more strongly at this point of the paternal mentor whose authority they had seen exercised at moments of crisis during the trial, and the tone in which he had addressed the two questions to them was in harmony with his manner. It seemed to bring him close, to bridge the gap between jury box and judge's bench. At the same time they were conscious of a stir among the defense attorneys.

"A very important question in the case," the judge continued, "is, Did the defendant Hauptmann write the original ransom note found on the window sill, and the other ransom notes which followed? Numerous experts in handwriting have testified, after exhaustive examination of the ransom letters, and comparison with genuine writings of the defendant, that the defendant Hauptmann wrote every one of the ransom notes, and Mr. Osborn said that that conclusion was irresistible, unanswerable and overwhelming. On the other hand, the defendant denies that he wrote them, and a handwriting expert, called by him, so testified. And so the fact becomes one for your determination. The weight of the evidence to prove genuineness of handwriting is wholly for the jury.

"As bearing upon the question whether or not the defendant was the man to whom was paid the ransom money in the cemetery, you will, of course, consider the evidence to the effect that the defendant had written the address and telephone number of Dr. Condon on the door jamb of his closet; and if you believe that he did, although he now denies it, you may conclude that it throws light upon the question whether or not he was dealing with Dr. Condon. As I have said, the defendant denies that he was the man who was paid the ransom money, and there is other testimony which, if credible and believed by you, supports his statement.

"You will consider, as bearing upon that question, the fact that a record of the serial numbers of the ransom money was retained. Now, does it not appear that many of the ransom bills were traced to the possession of the defendant? Does it not appear that many thousands of dollars of ransom bills were found in his garage, hidden in the walls or under the floor, that others were found on his person when he was arrested, and others passed by him from time to time?

"You may also consider in this connection the evidence to the effect that shortly after the delivery of the ransom money the defendant began to purchase stocks in a much larger way and to spend money more freely than he had before.

"The defendant says that these ransom bills, monies, were left with him by one Fisch, a man now dead."

Judge Trenchard paused. "Do you believe that?" he asked. "He says that he found them in a shoe box which had been reposing on the top shelf of his closet several months after the box had been left with him, and that he then, without telling anybody, secretly hid them, or most of them, in the garage, where they were found by the police. Do you believe his testimony that the money was left with him in a shoe box, and that it rested on the top shelf in his closet for several months? His wife, as I recall it, said that she never saw the box; and I do not recall that any witness excepting the defendant testified that they ever saw the shoe box there."

Again, the eyes of a good many of the jurors—notably the housewives, and the foreman, and Philip Hockenbury and George Voorhees and Charles Snyder—left the judge, to examine the housewife he had referred to. Anna's blue eyes remained on the black-gowned figure on the bench. He continued:

"As bearing upon the question whether or not the defendant was the man who took the child and left the ransom letter on the window sill, you should, of course, consider the evidence with respect to the ladder, if you find, as seems likely, that it was used in reaching the nursery. That the ladder was there seems to be unquestioned. If it was not there for the purpose of reaching that nursery window, for what purpose was it there? There is evidence from which you may conclude, if you see fit, that the defendant built the ladder, although he denies it. Does not the evidence satisfy you that at least a part of the wood from which the ladder was built came out of the flooring of the attic of the defendant?

"In this connection you should consider the marks upon the wood, and give the evidence in respect thereto such weight as you think it entitled to, after a consideration of the credibility of the witnesses who testified in respect thereto.

"The defendant has offered himself as a witness in his own behalf, and the law makes him a competent witness, notwithstanding his very deep interest in the event of the trial. His evidence is not to be rejected merely for the reason that he is interested, but his interest in the result may be taken into consideration by you as an important circumstance upon the question of his credibility, the question whether he is telling the truth. You should also consider his testimony in view of its inherent probability or improbability, in the light of all the facts and circumstances as disclosed by the evidence. It appeared on the examination of the defendant here in court that he has been heretofore convicted of crime. That testimony may be given consideration by you as affecting his credit as a witness, and for that purpose only. The defendant denies that he was ever on the Lindbergh premises, denies that he was present at the time that the child was seized and carried away. He testifies that he was in New York at that time. He denies that he received the ransom money in the cemetery and says that he was at his home at that time on the evening of April second, 1932."

The man of whom the judge was speaking sat in his usual attitude, the long, wiry legs crossed, arms folded. His face was calm. Certainly there were many in the crowd of listeners who seemed more affected by the judge's words than he. It was difficult for some listeners to believe that at one point during the State's presentation of its case he had leaped from his seat and shouted at a witness to stop lying and struggled with his guards; that at another point, when engaged in the duel with Wilentz, he had appeared to totter on the edge of an emotional breakdown. Yet he had. His discipline was not impregnable.

Proceeding, Judge Trenchard dealt with Hauptmann's denials of having been on the Lindbergh grounds and having received the ransom payment.

"This mode of meeting a charge of crime is commonly called setting up an alibi. It is not looked upon with any disfavor in the law, for, whatever evidence tends to prove that the defendant was elsewhere at the time the crime was committed, at the same time tends to contradict the fact that the crime was committed by the defendant, whereas here, the presence of the defendant is essential to guilt, and if a reasonable doubt of guilt is raised, even by inconclusive evidence of an alibi, the defendant is entitled to the benefit of that doubt.

"As bearing upon the question of whether or not the defendant was present at the Lindbergh home on March first, 1932, you, of course, should consider the testimony of Mr. Hochmuth, along with that of other witnesses. Mr. Hochmuth lives at or about the entrance of the lane that goes up to the Lindbergh house.

"He testified that on the forenoon of that day, March first, 1932, he saw the defendant at that point, driving rapidly from the direction of Hopewell; that he got in the ditch or dangerously near the ditch; and that he had a ladder in the car, which car was a dirty green. This testimony, if true, is highly significant. Do you think that there is any reason, upon the whole, to doubt the truth of the old man's testimony? May he not have well and easily remembered the circumstance, in view of the fact that that very night the child was carried away? The defendant, as I have said, denies that he was there or ever in the neighborhood; but, as bearing upon that question, you should consider the testimony of other witnesses, that the defendant was seen in the neighborhood, not long before March first, 1932, and give it such weight as you think it is entitled to, after considering the credibility of the witnesses, as disclosed by the evidence.

"The defendant has produced some testimony besides his own, that he was in New York on the day and evening of March first, 1932, and some testimony besides his own, that on the evening of April second, 1932, when the ransom money was delivered, he was at his home.

"This testimony produced by the defendant I shall not attempt to recite in greater detail. It should be given consideration by you and given such weight as you think it is entitled to, after considering it in connection with all of the other evidence in the case, bearing upon these questions and all other questions in the case, determination of which would tend to throw light upon the case.

"You should consider the fact, where it is the fact, that several of the witnesses have been convicted of crime, and to determine whether or not their credibility has been affected thereby; and where it appears that witnesses have made contradictory statements, you should consider that fact and determine their credibility as affected thereby."

Judge Trenchard paused to sip from a glass of water near at hand. It was not really needed. He had been right not to anticipate trouble with his voice in pronouncing the lengthy, precisely phrased charge. It had never faltered or grown weak.

"The evidence produced by the State is largely circumstantial in character," he told the jury. "In order to justify the conviction of the defendant upon circumstantial evidence, it is necessary not only that all of the circumstances concur to show that he committed the crime charged, but that they are inconsistent with any other rational conclusion.

"It is not sufficient that the circumstances proved coincide with, account for and therefore render probable the hypothesis that is sought to be established by the prosecution. They must exclude to a moral certainty every other hypothesis but the single one of guilt, and if they do not do this, the jury should find the defendant not guilty.

"And when the case against the defendant is made up wholly of a chain of circumstances, and there is reasonable doubt as to any fact the existence of which is essential to establish guilt, the defendant should be acquitted."

He raised a forefinger. It was the first gesture he had made.

"But the crime of murder is not one which is always committed in the presence of witnesses, and if not so committed, it must be established by circumstantial evidence or not at all. And where the essential facts and circumstances are proved, which cannot be explained upon any other theory than that the defendant is guilty of the crime charged against him, such evidence should be considered as satisfactory and convincing as that of the most direct and positive character.

"If the State has not satisfied you by evidence beyond a reasonable doubt that the death of the child was caused by the act of the defendant, he must be acquitted. But if, on the other hand, the State has satisfied you beyond a reasonable doubt that the child's death was caused by the unlawful and criminal act of the defendant while seizing, stealing and carrrying away the child and its clothing, of which unlawful act against the peace of the State, the probable consequences might be bloodshed, it is murder; and if murder, the degree thereof must then be determined.

"Now, our statute declares, among other things:

"Murder, which shall be committed in perpetrating, or attempting to perpetrate any burglary, shall be murder in the first degree.

"The State contends that the murder in this case was committed in perpetrating a burglary, and is murder in the first degree.

"I charge you that if murder was committed in perpetrating a burglary, it is murder in the first degree, without reference to the question whether such killing was wilful or unintentional; and I further charge you, as requested by the defendant, that in order to convict this defendant you must be satisfied, beyond a reasonable doubt, that the death of the child ensued from committing, or attempting to commit, burglary, at or about the time and place in question.

"Our statute relating to burglary says:

"Any person who shall, by night, willfully or maliciously break and enter any dwelling house with intent to steal, commit a battery, shall be guilty of a high misdemeanor.

"If, therefore, the defendant by night willfully and maliciously broke and entered the Lindbergh dwelling house with intent to steal the child and its clothing and to commit a battery on the child, he committed a burglary; and if the murder was committed in perpetrating a burglary, it is murder in the first degree.

"In the circumstances of this case you must be satisfied that the window was shut and that it was raised and opened by the defendant, and that he entered the house.

"There is evidence from which you may conclude, if you see fit, that the defendant feloniously, wilfully and maliciously broke and entered the dwelling house of Colonel Lindbergh in the night time with intent to steal the child and its clothing and commit a battery upon the child; that the defendant brought the ladder to the Lindbergh house in East Amwell Township in this county, and placed it up against the house near the nursery window; that shortly after nine o'clock at night he ascended the ladder, maliciously and willfully opened the closed window and entered the nursery room; that he seized the child and its clothing and carried it out of the nursery room window, and that the fracture of the skull which caused the child's death was inflicted when the child was seized by the defendant and carried out and down the ladder, and when the ladder broke."

He paused again, a final pause before his conclusion. None of his listeners watched him more intently than Charles Lindbergh. There were those in the crowd who, enslaved by the presence of this living legend, had spared scarcely more than an occasional glance for the judge, for the prisoner, for the prisoner's wife, devoting their ardent and unwearying gaze to the father of the dead child. To them, only one additional presence could have made his more satisfying: Anne's.

Judge Trenchard said:

"If you find that the murder was committed by the defendant in perpetrating a burglary, it is murder in the first degree, even though the killing was unintentional.

"If there is a reasonable doubt that the murder was committed by the defendant in perpetrating a burglary, he must be acquitted.

"I am requested to charge, and do charge, that each juror must reach his own judgment after discussion of the facts with his fellow jurors.

"If you find the defendant guilty of murder in the first degree, you may, if you see fit, by your verdict, and as a part thereof, recommend imprisonment at hard labor for life.

"If you should return a verdict of murder in the first degree and nothing else, the punishment which would be inflicted on that verdict would be death.

"If you desire to return a verdict of murder in the first degree, coupled with imprisonment for life, then you must so put it in your verdict, because the law reads that every person convicted of murder in the first degree, his aiders, abettors, counselors and procurers, shall suffer death unless the jury shall, by their verdict and as a part thereof, upon and after consideration of all the evidence, recommend imprisonment at hard labor for life, in which case this and no greater punishment shall be imposed."

The charge was finished. The time was thirteen minutes past eleven. The elderly man in black had spoken for an hour and ten minutes.

He directed the court clerk to swear in three men and three women constables to guard the jury room while behind its closed door the jurors considered the testimony and the charge they had heard and, should they wish to examine any or all of them, the exhibits that had been placed in evidence. There were more than three hundred.

Sheriff John Curtiss made his way to the judge's side. State troopers had completed their search of the jury room, he said; no dictographs, no microphones, no hidden eavesdropping instruments of any kind had been found. Judge Trenchard pronounced the four words that brought to an end the first phase of the long trial's last chapter:

"The jury may retire."

27

A spectator who was more interested than most in every aspect of the trial, because he was better informed, watched the jury pass out in single file and observed that none of them glanced at Richard and Anna Hauptmann, only a few feet away from the decorous procession. The Hauptmanns sat staring straight ahead.

Next the spectator watched Lindbergh, Schwarzkopf and Breckinridge leave. Then he devoted his attention to the activity among the defense attorneys, who one by one approached the judge.

Dudley Shoenfeld knew the reason for their activity; they were entering exceptions to the charge to the jury as the basis of a future appeal, should one become necessary. He had a good idea, moreover, of the nature of the exceptions. Some leaped to the eye, even an eye unschooled in the law's niceties. It was true that Judge Trenchard was governed by New Jersey law and that, as many of his layman listeners could not have known, Jersey law gave its judges a reasonably free hand; still, there were in his charge such leading inferences as, ". . . upon the whole, is there any doubt in your mind as to the reliability of Dr. Condon's testimony?" . . . "The [defense] argument was to the effect that [the kidnaping and murder] was done by a gang, with the help or connivance of some one or more servants of the Lindbergh or Morrow households. Now do you believe that? Is there any evidence in this case whatsoever to support any such conclusion?" . . . "The defendant says that these ransom bills were left with him by one Fisch, a man now dead. Do you believe that?" . . . "Do you believe his testimony that the money was left with him in a shoe box, and that it rested on the top shelf in his closet for several months?" . . . "If [the ladder] was not there for the purpose of reaching the nursery window, for what purpose was it there?"

His intelligence, his manner, his appearance—his alert and benevolent sympathy for their, and indeed everyone's, ills and complaints! —had earned for Judge Trenchard, the psychiatrist felt sure, a position of formidable authority in the jurors' minds. Coming from such a dominant figure, would not such clear-cut guideposts to his opinion as had appeared in the judge's charge have an almost overwhelming effect on them?

Well, Dudley Shoenfeld reflected, that remained to be seen. He wondered how long it would take the jury to reach a verdict.

Hauptmann was led from the room back to his cell, a guard holding each arm. He had a parting nod and smile for Anna. One of his counselors had a parting pat on the back for him: it was Lloyd Fisher. Reilly was chatting affably with reporters, who had swarmed down from the press gallery. The courtroom was losing its recent dignity in a tumult of talk, and Wilentz proposed that it be cleared except for those who had an official or professional right to be present during the wait for the jury's decision. Judge Trenchard agreed. The crowd did not. The judge prevailed.

Complaining, the crowd straggled out, some energetically helped by the guards, to join the larger and constantly growing crowd in the street.

Fifteen minutes past twelve.

Judge Trenchard left the bench for the privacy of his chambers; he soon reappeared and asked Sheriff Curtiss to order a generous supply of sandwiches and coffee from the Union Hotel. It was within a New Jersey judge's power to bar food from a locked-in jury if he thought they needed the spur of hunger to hasten their deliberations; Judge Trenchard was no more capable of doing this than of refusing the resources of his portable medicine cabinet to a cough-wracked attorney. Besides, he was hungry himself. Presently, he and the jury ate.

In his absence, the courtroom began to look like an unusually sociable newspaper city room, without the typewriters, which were banned, but with the cigarette smoke. Reporters and special correspondents gossiped, compared notes, sauntered, sat and lounged in previously sacred territory; an industrious few wrote.

A *New York Times* special correspondent remained in the deserted press gallery; he wished to be alone with his thoughts. He was an Englishman, Ford Madox Ford, a novelist much less widely read than Special Correspondent Edna Ferber, with whose work his had little in common. Today, his memories of the war, in which he had soldiered and seen much death, weighed heavily on Mr. Ford. He stared down at the littered, noisy, hazy courtroom and seemed to see the smoke of fire and shell drifting over the fields of France and hear the insane staccato of the machine guns. By and by he began to write.

If he were a member of the jury, he wrote, he would vote for acquittal. He would vote for acquittal and hold fast to his vote until the skies fell, and he fancied he would be backed by a throng of somber shadows.

He could not forget that the man waiting to learn the jury's vote once was a boy of seventeen in the muddy, death-stinking trenches. Was not the boy's brain warped by the actions of the men who had made the war? If the verdict should brand him guilty, would not the guilt be theirs? Would not the hundreds of thousands of boys who had perished in the war cry down such a verdict, if their dead throats could speak? Among the living, would not some reasonable doubt remain?

Ford concluded:

"And the affair cannot but have, however unjustly, the aspect of the most famous and fortunate man in the world versus a miserable shred of human jetsam. And there is too much class hatred in the world already and the passion for bloodshed is too keen."

The prisoner's cell was directly beneath the jury room. It could have been a thousand miles away, for all the sound of discussion that reached Hauptmann. He had sat down on the cot under the everlasting glare of the lights when the guards brought him to the cell and closed and locked the door. They thought he looked about the same. He smoked and walked a little. The rule of silence still obtained. He did not try to break it.

He lay down for a while. His eyes were open.

He got up and walked some more.

Time passed.

Time passed slowly in the courtroom. A bored reporter asked a guard, also bored, "How do they usually handle things here when a jury's reached a verdict? I mean, is there any special sign of it?"

"Yes, there is. They've got a special custom in Flemington, I don't know how old, I guess it goes back for years. They ring the court-house bell when the jury's ready to come in."

In his chambers, Judge Trenchard was endeavoring to speed the time by considering various legal matters. He went to the court-house's law library to look up a statute and discovered that he had been preceded in those chaste and secluded quarters by a group of men huddled over some object of veneration. Reporters, he guessed. There was a scramble among them as they became aware of the newcomer. The judge caught a glimpse of cards, a pile of money. He found his book and with a nod and smile left them.

Three P.M.

Someone knocked on the inner side of the jury-room doors. Chief Constable Oden Baggstrom unlocked them. Foreman Charles Walton said, "We need a magnifying glass."

The glass was brought; the doors were locked again. Word of the request reached the languid, smoke-filled courtroom and a guessing game got under way. Why did the jurors want a magnifying glass? To compare the writing in the ransom notes with the specimens of

Hauptmann's admitted handwriting? Examine the marks left by mill plane and handplane and chisel and saw on the kidnap ladder? The pencil jottings on the strip of door trim taken from the Bronx apartment? A devout wish was heard: that they didn't want to inspect *all* the exhibits through that solitary glass.

The short winter day, longer to some in the courthouse than summer's longest, began to die. At six o'clock Judge Trenchard speculated that the jury could do with a bit of dinner; at any rate, his inner man was beginning to call. The meal, again supplied by the Union Hotel, exactly resembled lunch: sandwiches and coffee.

Hauptmann was provided with more substantial fare; he ate little of it. He walked and smoked. Around seven o'clock he asked to see Lloyd Fisher. The answer was no; New Jersey law forbade visiting between counsel and client while the jury was out.

Jersey law also forbade jurors to leave the jury room until they had agreed on a verdict or become hopelessly deadlocked. Judge Trenchard reminded Oden Baggstrom of the stipulation, in case there was any doubt among the jurors. He would see to it that they were fed—sandwiches everlasting, coffee everlasting—and of course any request for medical attention would receive an immediate response—Mrs. Snyder's cold still bothered him—but they were going to stay in that room until they agreed or agreed to disagree, if it took all night and all the next day and all the following night.

The tenth hour of their deliberations passed. Well, the judge informed Sheriff Curtiss, he'd wait another hour or so; if they hadn't come in by that time, ten or eleven, he intended to go home for the rest of the night. If they reached a verdict after he left, it was to be given to him in a sealed envelope at ten the next morning, when court would reconvene.

An Associated Press reporter in the courtroom was observed to be jealously watchful of his brief case. It was a pretty bulky brief case. He sat with his hands tenderly folded over it and when he felt the need to stretch his legs it went with him. His care was not ill advised; the brief case contained neither paper nor pencils nor sandwiches nor even a bottle but a short-wave radio set. Two code signals were engraved on the reporter's mind. He was resolved to beat the courthouse bell to the news. When tokens of an imminent verdict appeared, an inevitable tightening of the atmosphere, chief constable hurrying from jury room to judge's chambers, guards doubly vigilant to see that no word got out by hand signal from the windows to reporters watching on nearby roofs, he would flash the first code signal to a receiving set manned by an AP telegraph operator in the courthouse attic: jury coming in. The second signal would follow: the verdict.

That was the plan.

He muttered his code signals like an incantation, noticing that it was nearly ten o'clock. The jury had retired at 11:21 in the morning. It seemed a long, long time ago; it *was* a long time ago! Obviously they were split; some of them, or maybe only one of them, must be holding out. For what?

The watching guards saw a twitch in Hauptmann's cheek. During the last hour or so he had barely paused in his pacing. They wondered that he did not clap his hands over his ears. A man could pray for deafness, here, as men in a quiet world pray for health and happiness. Outside the cell's walls the night had become a jungle, alive with screaming, hooting voices. Occasionally the voices would embrace and become one voice, one mob-howl:

"Kill Hauptmann! Kill Hauptmann! Kill Hauptmann!"

The mob's ten thousand faces looked blank, clown-white, in the huge glare of the spotlights set up for newsreel crews. A little girl danced and lifted her skirts to catch a camera's eye; fathers and mothers hoisted their children and told them to wave and smile. A man with rock in hand came running and hurled it at the courthouse and proudly yelled to see it smash the lovely ancient fan-shaped window over the portico. His triumph doubled; the lights in the courtroom went out. Some rock!

But it was not that marvelous rock that turned the trick, though perhaps the marksman would always think so. After six minutes of searching in the confused darkness, a guard's flashlight found the trouble in the courtroom fuse box; one had blown. Jury-room lights, prisoner's-cell lights stayed steady.

A messenger told Sheriff Curtiss he was wanted by Chief Constable Baggstrom. The sheriff hurried to attend, then ran to the judge's chambers. David Wilentz followed him. The attorney general came out at twenty past ten and nodded to Colonel Schwarzkopf. The troopers he had hand-picked for duty in the courthouse quickly pulled down to their full length the heavy dark green window shades, spreading despair among the rooftop watchers, and mounted guard there and at the doors. The courtroom shook off its apathy; surely these portents were unmistakable. The AP man opened his brief case and flashed the agreed-on signal: jury coming in.

He waited anxiously. Then a deep sad voice spoke in the night and set his fears to rest: the courthouse bell was tolling.

Richard Hauptmann asked, "What's that?"

One of his guards said to another, "Don't they ring the bell when the jury's coming in?"

"Yes."

The street mob roared. Even that furious sound was not enough to deafen the prisoner's quick ears; he heard footsteps and looked around and saw two men approaching, a State trooper, a man in plain clothes. Each held a pair of handcuffs. He said, "Why handcuffs? They never put on the handcuffs before!"

The trooper said, "Doesn't mean anything special, just regulations."

The prisoner was locked between the two, right wrist to trooper's left, left wrist to deputy sheriff's right.

The bell still tolled.

Up in the garret, the coded radio signal had flashed home beautifully to the receiving set; but the long wait had produced in the telegraph operator's mind a small but important confusion. It seemed to him that his man with the brief case down in the courtroom had decided for some reason or other against sending the first warning signal that the jury was coming in and instead had flashed that they and the verdict were already in and that they had found Hauptmann guilty of murder in the first degree but had recommended mercy, which made a sentence of life imprisonment mandatory. His telegraph key clacked and in their heavy metal beds the presses began to turn and thunder; Press Radio News picked up the bulletin and passed it on to the broadcasting networks. HAUPTMANN FOUND GUILTY, GETS LIFE IMPRISONMENT. A clear news beat, except that it was wrong.

Sheriff Curtiss and five troopers led the way into the courtroom. The prisoner looked awkward and slow, as if unaccountably his fine trim body had aged or turned arthritic. Then the courtroom watchers saw the reason. He was not used to manacles. Obviously they bothered him; he seemed to wish to hide his captive wrists. It was a clumsy, embarrassing business, getting into his seat. He kept his head down. He heard his name and looked up. Anna had come in. She smiled; he couldn't smile.

A friend's arm curved around his shoulder. Lloyd Fisher said cheerfully, "This is only the beginning, Richard. Don't show a sign." Hauptmann nodded, glanced down apologetically at the handcuffs, and Fisher shrugged and smiled.

Eleven hours and fourteen minutes after they had left the courtroom, the jury returned.

The watchers searched their faces for a clue to the verdict. They had an ashy pallor; they were very tired. Mrs. Snyder's eyes were puffy and red-rimmed. Had she been weeping? Why? But perhaps it was only from her cold. Mrs. Rosie Pill's lips moved; was she biting them? The young, responsive Robert Cravatt looked serene; was that significant?

They entered the box and sat down. Sheriff Curtiss went through the door behind the box to the judge's chambers.

Charles Lindbergh's usual seat was empty. A trooper told a newspaper friend he understood the Colonel had returned to the Morrow place in Englewood to be with Anne when the verdict was announced; they'd hear it soon enough. Henry Breckinridge sat beside the empty chair.

The mob's roar had dwindled, died to nothing; aside from an occasional tinkly pop as boys shattered old flash bulbs, the street was as quiet as the courtroom.

Richard and Anna Hauptmann watched the judge's door. He did not appear.

Sheriff Curtiss came out and Wilentz, Reilly and Fisher got up and walked over to talk with him. He nodded and turned back through the door.

Why so long? Hadn't everyone waited long enough?

"He hasn't gone home, has he?" the newspaperman whispered to his friend the trooper.

"He's here, all right."

"It's ten forty-three. Almost ten minutes since the jury came back."

"Here he is."

Judge Trenchard walked to the bench, rapped twice with his gavel and sat down. The jury was polled; answering "Here," their voices' tone told nothing else. The judge nodded to the court clerk.

"The jury will rise!"

Then the judge spoke.

"Let the defendant stand."

Hauptmann got up so quickly the men locked to him were caught off guard. The bands yanked at their wrists. Their prisoner stared earnestly at the judge.

The court clerk said:

"Members of the jury, have you agreed upon your verdict?"

"We have."

"Who shall speak for you?"

"The foreman."

"Mr. Foreman, what say you: Do you find the defendant guilty or not guilty?"

The defendant's eyes did not move from the judge.

Foreman Charles Walton said:

"Guilty."

It was a whisper. The court clerk hastened to prompt him: he must announce the verdict formally. Charles Walton's hand fumbled at a pocket; the fingers shook. He drew out a folded paper and looked at it as if surprised to find it there. He had difficulty unfolding the paper.

"Read in a louder voice," the clerk said confidentially.

The foreman's voice sounded oddly cracked, now deep, now high, as if he were a boy, very nervous, whose voice was changing.

"We, the jury, find the defendant, Bruno Richard Hauptmann, guilty of murder in the first degree."

No recommendation for life imprisonment. *If you should return a verdict of murder in the first degree and nothing else,* the judge had charged, *the punishment which would be inflicted on that verdict would be death.*

Anna's eyes blinked. Hauptmann stared at the judge.

"Members of the jury," the clerk said briskly, "you have heard the verdict, that you find the defendant, Bruno Richard Hauptmann, guilty of murder in the first degree, and so say you all?"

"We do."

The AP man with the brief case flashed a second signal and the AP man in the garret realized that someone had blundered; how many verdicts could any one jury declare? He informed his organization's members over the wires that the first bulletin was in error. The correct news was HAUPTMANN GUILTY GETS DEATH.

Ed Reilly asked, "May we have a poll?" Judge Trenchard nodded; the clerk repeated his question and each juror in turn repeated the words Walton had read. Lloyd Fisher said to no one, "This is a cry for blood."

Hauptmann's guards sat down. The steel links tugged at his wrists and he sat down too. Anna's face was carefully stiff; they didn't look at each other. David Wilentz, the victor, did not seem to know what to do with his victory. The judge reminded him of the necessary next step.

"Do you wish to make a motion for sentence, Mr. Attorney General?"

Wilentz gave a little start. "The State moves for immediate sentence," he said.

An eager messenger had got out of the courtroom and raced to a second-floor window. He threw it open and shouted, "Guilty—death!" The mob screamed. Hearing it, Fisher murmured again, "A cry for blood."

Judge Trenchard said, "The defendant may stand."

Hauptmann stood up. The guards were alert this time and rose with him.

"Bruno Richard Hauptmann, you have been convicted of murder in the first degree. The sentence of the Court is that you suffer death at the time and place and in the manner provided by law."

The mob was still screaming. Judge Trenchard set the execution for the week beginning Monday, March 18, 1935. Then he said:

"You are now remanded to the custody of the sheriff."

Hauptmann's guards started him toward the door. Fisher hurried over and whispered, "Remember, it's only the beginning!" The prisoner half nodded. His wife watched him go. The instant he was through the door her heavy face creased and sagged, and she wept.

Time: ten minutes to eleven.

They marched the prisoner to his cell and unlocked the handcuffs. Breaking the steel bands seemed to break a steel rod in his body; he doubled over and fell. His face hit the floor. They lifted him to the cot. He put his hands over his bruised face, and the guards heard Richard Hauptmann sobbing. They had not thought that he would ever cry. It embarrassed them.

An argument began in Nellie's Tap Room: why had the jury taken so long?

The jurors had agreed among themselves never to talk; still, there were rumors; and new rumors came in with each new arrival at Nellie's. One rumor received the most support. There had been five ballots, this impressive rumor claimed. The ballots weren't signed. The first ballot was seven for the chair and five for life imprisonment. The five who voted for life were Mrs. Snyder, Mrs. Pill, Elmer Smith, Philip Hockenbury and Robert Cravatt. On the second ballot the two women joined the majority. Hockenbury gave in on the third ballot and voted for death. The fourth brought Smith's vote for death. Robert Cravatt surrendered on the fifth. The rumor declared he had not yielded for all those hours because no confession from another's lips in later years could give life back to Richard Hauptmann, once the chair had held him in its burning arms.

Flemington's constable watched the great host begin to straggle off into the night. The carnival was over; but he did not think his town would ever be the same again.

Tiny wooden ladders lay discarded in the filthy streets.

At times throughout the night the prisoner wept; at times he whispered: "Little men, little pieces of wood, little scraps of paper."

Part Four

THE APPEAL

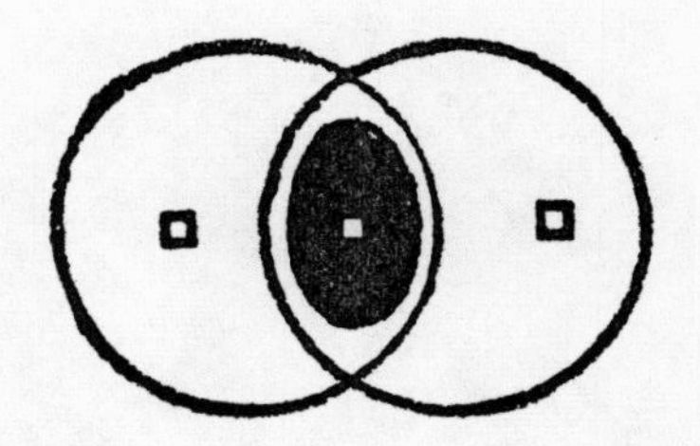

1

The trial of Bruno Richard Hauptmann had lasted for six weeks. It had been argued in a million and a half words, and the official transcript filled thirty typewritten volumes.

A great many more words greeted the verdict. Since the evidence was mainly circumstantial, some people thought the death sentence too severe. "The entire trial left me with a question in my mind," Eleanor Roosevelt told reporters who had asked for her opinion. "While I have no sympathy for Hauptmann, I can't help wondering what would happen if it were an innocent person on trial." She did not believe in capital punishment, the President's wife added, but whenever the law demanded it, the law should be carried out.

The New York Times had this to say:

> The long trial at Flemington, the charge of the judge and the verdict of the jury established a crime but did not clear away a mystery. We do not yet know exactly what happened on that tragic night at Hopewell. This is a leftover disappointment of the case. One motive which millions of people had in reading every scrap of the testimony was the hope that either the evidence of the police or the admissions of Hauptmann would show precisely who the kidnaper was and what were his preparations and methods of operation. As it is, they remain an unsolved mystery. This was admitted by the presiding judge, who told the jury that the State had been unable to present positive evidence identifying the prisoner at the time and place of the original crime, and that circumstantial evidence alone had to be depended upon. That was certainly strong enough to prove beyond a doubt that Hauptmann had guilty knowledge of the outrage and was at least an accessory. The jury became convinced that it was but a step, and a justified step, from that to finding him guilty as

> a principal. This is as far as the trial took us. Nothing but a confession or the turning up of new evidence can now be expected to throw further light upon a mystery which has all along been one of the most puzzling in criminal annals.

But the New York *Daily News* thought that the jury's verdict:

> . . . will put a crimp in the snatch racket from which it won't recover for a long time. The poor little baby didn't die in vain. Everybody in this country who has children can feel a little safer today than yesterday.

For Betty Gow, the trial had capped the long ordeal of the crime itself and the following investigation. Reilly's attack on her in the witness chair still hurt. "To insinuate that I knew more about the tragedy than I made known to the court was most unjust," she said to friends. "I'm sure he wouldn't have been allowed to do that in Britain. He shouldn't be allowed to do it in America." And so she had decided to try to put the whole painful experience behind her. Rather than re-enter Charles and Anne Lindbergh's service, as she could if she wished, she was going back to Scotland. After a farewell party in Englewood, friends drove her to the Cunard-White Star Line pier and the SS *Berengaria*. A woman in the mob of reporters, photographers and onlookers tugged at Betty and swung her around, saying "Let's have a look at you!" Betty cried "Let me alone!" and clenched her fist and struck the peering face. She hurried to her cabin and locked the door; she had had enough of crowds.

The same night, Friday February 15, in the Englewood house, Mrs. Morrow was making final preparations for a journey of her own. She was to leave for Mexico the next day to reopen the mansion outside Mexico City where the Morrows had lived during Dwight Morrow's term as U.S. Ambassador. Mrs. Morrow had always been fond of Mexico and she was looking forward to her return. Harold Nicolson, who had made a name as a writer while still in the British diplomatic service, was to be a special guest there. He was writing a biography of her husband and needed her assistance. Such congenial work should help to dull the recent, tragic past.

On Saturday morning, three sedans set out on the twenty-three-mile journey from Flemington to Trenton and the New Jersey State prison. Hauptmann was in one of the cars; fourteen State troopers made up his armed escort, in turn escorted by a score of cars crammed with press. They got to the main gate of the prison at half-past ten. Hauptmann seemed to ignore the crowd that had gathered to watch his arrival; his face expressionless, arms linked by handcuffs to a guard on each side, he was steered toward the massive entranceway. It was a curious architectural mixture, copied in part from New York City's famous prison, the Tombs. Serpents, eagles, rams, and mythological creatures, with a scattering of kneeling human figures, decorated the stone walls; someone had topped off this Oriental profusion with a white, New England-style cupola.

Hauptmann was given a physical examination; he was photographed and fingerprinted and his hair was cut off. He put on the regulation blue shirt, blue trousers and heavy shoes, and became Prisoner Number 17,400. By this time most of the prison's population had gathered in the mess hall for the midday meal. Hauptmann was led past the hall on the way to his cell. The men knew who he was. As he walked on, their jeers and hisses followed him.

He had been assigned Cell Number 9, on the lower tier of the death house. Half a dozen other convicts under sentence of death were on the upper tier, but Hauptmann was alone in his row of cells. His immediate neighbor, its entrance only a few steps away, was the electric chair chamber.

The cell door was shut; the guards began to leave. Hauptmann called after them. Could he have a Bible?

2

The day before, he had signed a petition declaring himself a pauper and asking the State of New Jersey to help pay for an appeal. He and Anna Hauptmann were penniless, and even routine moves to reverse the trial verdict would cost a great deal. Petitioning the state was regarded by his four lawyers as an elementary but essential step because of its bearing on the far more pertinent move to follow: obtaining a writ of error, which would automatically postpone the execution pending a review of the trial by the Court of Errors and Appeals. But the writ would require them to file a transcript of the trial testimony, a print job that would cost from eight to eleven thousand dollars. Perhaps Hauptmann's pauper's oath would persuade Judge Trenchard to pass the expense on to the state; a New Jersey statute provided that where a defendant was convicted of murder in the first degree and swore that poverty prevented him from appealing, the judge who sentenced him could order the state to supply him a copy of the trial record.

Frederick Pope had assured reporters that in their determination to see justice triumph the defense were ". . . four musketeers, all for one and one for all"; but on Monday the eighteenth the antagonism between Reilly and Fisher sharply revealed itself. The point of difference hung on Reilly's interpretation of what he called "the gentlemanly practice of law." David Wilentz was away on a vacation in Miami Beach. With the writ of error still to be obtained, Reilly held that it would not be proper to take any of the steps leading to the appeal until their opponent returned. After all, such a short delay wouldn't hurt their client's chances.

Fisher held otherwise. It was Hauptmann's life that was at stake, he reminded the courtly Reilly, and for a man sitting alone in the death house each day gone was a day irretrievably lost. Not a day, not a minute should be sacrificed, Fisher said, demanding that they move at once to win an appeal; and, not waiting for further niceties, he saw Hauptmann, explained the situation, and received from him signed authority to act without delay, however the vacationing Wilentz might feel about it.

That Thursday, February 21, Fisher got the writ of error. It required that a copy of the trial transcript be filed on March 12.

And so now the money problem had to be solved in a hurry. There was a simple and dramatic way to tackle it: appeal to the public, tell them that Richard Hauptmann was innocent, the case against him a police frame-up, carefully rigged to answer the clamor caused by the kidnaping and the long failure to find the murderer; and, with the public's sympathy enlisted, ask for a defense fund to carry the fight to the higher courts.

The four musketeers saw eye to eye on this, and so did Hauptmann, who appointed Fisher trustee of the fund.

Six days later, the fund made its first move with its strongest card. In Yorkville, the center of New York's German-American colony, Anna Hauptmann stood on the stage of a large hall, nodding and smiling in answer to the ovation from an audience of twenty-five hundred who had burst into cheers at sight of her figure, familiar to all of them through the newspapers. Three thousand more were still trying to get in.

Reilly performed the unnecessary introduction, after telling the crowd that the presence of Charles Lindbergh, "America's greatest hero," at every session of the trial had influenced the jury against Richard Hauptmann, and that somewhere in the United States, "laughing at the authorities," was the real kidnaper. Lindbergh's name brought hisses and boos, Hauptmann's cheers.

Anna spoke. It was clear that she didn't have to rely on English here, and so she used the easier German. For months, she said, she and Richard had suffered one torment after another—Richard, her husband, who was innocent. She appealed to their noble hearts to help her fight for his life and liberty.

Forty ushers passed baskets along the crowded rows. Each usher wore a green armband bearing the legend *Hauptmann Defense Fund.* Their movements were coordinated with military precision; their parent organizations, all pro-Nazi—the German Legion, Friends of the New Germany, the American Legion of National Socialists, and others—had become handy in staging political and money-raising rallies.

When the contents of the baskets were counted up, it was found that some $700 had been contributed to the fund, to be added to the $625 collected from the twenty-five-cent admission charge.

Anna made her second appeal on Sunday March 3. To a German-American audience in Passaic, New Jersey, she pleaded, again in her native language: "Help me get a new trial for my husband. Whatever you give will help me and our baby." Her listeners responded with a total of $1200. Next she appeared in the Bronx. Fifteen hundred people turned out, each paying a fifty-cent head charge. The ushers with the green armbands did a prosperous preliminary business selling pamphlets stamped with the crooked Nazi cross and a four-page leaflet called *The Gentile Front;* but reporters were assured by the chairman of the rally, repeating assurances given after the earlier rallies, that the meeting had no political, pro-Nazi, anti-Semitic overtones—there was no connection between the sale of the pamphlets and the Hauptmann Defense Fund. One of the speakers had mentioned Wilentz's name; it came out *Wilensky* and brought jeers. The chairman declared that it had been a slip of the tongue.

Anna described a visit she had paid to Richard the day before. "He asked if Bubi had any new teeth," she told the hushed gathering, "and he asked for a picture of him and the little dog he plays with." The baby was now sixteen months old.

Hauptmann had found that he could help the defense fund simply by signing his name. Checks had begun to arrive at the prison for him, and the flow increased. It was true that the great majority were made out for a dollar, and it seemed evident that the senders were concerned less with his welfare than with their interest in his signature as a collector's item; but their motives did not matter to a man in the shadow of the electric chair, and he endorsed the checks with no qualms.

Anna's public appearances continued throughout March; the fund grew promisingly, and there were still many German-American communities in the East to visit, to say nothing of the great midwestern cities. But on April 3, she brought Richard shocking news. Mr. Reilly had submitted his bill—for twenty-five thousand dollars.

The Hauptmanns agreed that Reilly should be dismissed. Anna wrote him a registered letter telling him so. "Mr. Reilly should know, if anybody should," she said to reporters, "that the defense fund has not any such sum as he demanded for his fee. We are struggling very hard to get our defense fund to meet the appeal's expense." From now on, Mr. Fisher would be in charge.

Reilly did not receive his dismissal in silence; he said that the figure of twenty-five thousand dollars had been agreed to by both the Hauptmanns. At that, he'd been generous—"if I'd tried this case in New York my fee would have been one hundred thousand dollars." As for their plea of poverty, he knew for a fact that there was more than enough money to pay him in the defense fund, which was deposited in a Flemington bank in Fisher's care. If necessary, Reilly concluded, he would sue and tie up the fund.

His bill remained unpaid at the end of April. Reilly obtained a court order in Brooklyn Supreme Court requiring Anna Hauptmann to show cause why she should not be enjoined from disposing of any of the funds collected through the public appeals, why a receiver should not be appointed to contain these funds and why the court should not decide on the fee that Edward J. Reilly should be paid for services rendered.

3

The month of June was a gratifying one for the Lindberghs; both received high public recognition. Anne's turn came first. At the Smith College commencement, while Charles watched, she received from President William Allan Neilson the honorary degree of Master of Arts.

In conferring the degree, President Neilson said:

"Anne Morrow Lindbergh, B.A., Smith, 1928, Hubbard gold medalist of the National Geographic Society, poet, pilot, navigator, radio operator, co-explorer with her husband of the unflown air routes of five continents and two oceans, who has proved to an admiring world the compatibility of imagination and practical dexterity; of sensitiveness and fortitude; of modesty and daring; the pride of her college, the glory of her country."

A few days later, the Rockefeller Institute for Medical Research announced that, thanks to the successful completion of a mechanical heart, for the first time the vital organs of humans and animals could be kept alive and functioning indefinitely outside their bodies. Charles Lindbergh was the inventor of this "chamber of artificial life," complete with its mechanical lungs, artificial blood supply and synthetic air. The method, as reported in *Science,* the official publication of the American Association for the Advancement of Science, consisted of the transplantation of an organ, or of any part of the body, into a sterile chamber, and of its artificial feeding with a nutrient fluid through the arteries.

The New York Times observed that the announcement of the invention, "regarded as one of the most sensational in the annals of medicine and of science in general, which opens up vast untrodden fields for peering into the mysteries of life's most vital processes and of life itself, is made even more dramatic by the fact that one of the two men who have at last succeeded in making this dream of science come true is the same man who eight years ago was the first to span the Atlantic from New York to Paris in an airplane.

"Colonel Lindbergh's associate in this epoch-making task, regarded by scientists as of vastly greater importance to the future of mankind than Colonel Lindbergh's epic flight, is the Nobel Prize winner, Dr. Alexis Carrel of the Rockefeller Institute."

Two months before, Lindbergh had told Transcontinental and Western Airways that he wished to be free for a time of his duties as technical adviser, to avoid the inevitable publicity attached to his activities for the airline and to devote himself more to personal matters, which meant putting the final touches to the mechanical heart. Its success encouraged him to continue his explorations in this fascinating field.

4

On Thursday, June 20, counsel for the defense, now reduced to three—Fisher, Rosecrans, and Pope—appealed to the Court of Errors and Appeals, New Jersey's highest tribunal, to reverse the verdict convicting Bruno Richard Hauptmann of the kidnaping and murder of Charles Augustus Lindbergh, Jr., and the death sentence.

The court sat in pleasant surroundings, the comparatively new annex to the State House in Trenton. The windows looked out on the Delaware River; heavy purple carpet muffled the lawyers' and judges' footsteps; and the general public was kept out—circumstances far different from those in which Hauptmann's life had first swung in the balance, nearly half a year ago, in the hot, crowded courtroom in Flemington.

The hearing began at 10 A.M. Usually made up of sixteen judges, on this occasion the court was reduced to fourteen; Justice Trenchard was disqualified because he had presided at the trial, and there was one vacancy.

Egbert Rosecrans, the defense's expert on constitutional law, argued for Hauptmann, who was prevented by law from being present to hear the attack his counsel had devised. Rosecrans contended, as the briefs had, that the verdict could not be upheld because the defendant's rights, guaranteed by the Fourteenth Amendment, had been contravened: he had been deprived of his liberty, and was in immediate hazard of being deprived of his life, without due process of law. Also, his rights under the Sixth Amendment had been flouted: he had not been tried by a jury of the district in which the crime had been committed. Since the trial had been held in Hunterdon County, and the crime had taken place in adjoining Mercer County, the court in Flemington in fact had had no jurisdiction, had had no business trying the case—a point Rosecrans had argued, unsuccessfully before Judge Trenchard.

Indeed, Rosecrans continued, the very basis of the State's charge against Hauptmann—"that he was guilty of murder during the commission of a felony in the crime of burglary"—had no legal precedent. "The State indulged in legal gymnastics to spell out its theory that the death of the child ensued from the commission of a statutory burglary. The circumstantial evidence as to burglary was highly technical, the charge being that the house was entered by night with intent to steal a sleeping garment of no proven value, and with intent to commit a battery upon a two-year-old infant. There was no proof of any jimmying of the window or other evidence that the window had actually been the means of entry."

So the brief had argued, and so Rosecrans argued now. And in fact, he went on, wasn't there clear proof that there had been *no intent* to steal the sleeping suit, since it had been returned? In any event, burglary was not a statutory crime in New Jersey, and by legal definition—even of simple larceny—a garment that had not been proved to be of value could not be offered as proof of theft with any hope of winning a conviction. Even assuming that a burglary had been committed, which he most certainly was not admitting, the theft was petty larceny, not grand larceny, therefore a misdemeanor, not a felony, and consequently the child's death was not first-degree murder—an argument based on New Jersey law at the time of the crime, under which burglary was one of the five crimes on which a first-degree murder conviction could be obtained as a result of a killing executed during, or as a result of, the commission of such a crime.

Nothing so clearly demonstrated the weakness of the State's case, Rosecrans maintained, as the two theories—one contradicting the other—which Attorney General Wilentz had given the court as to the manner in which the baby had been killed. In his opening address, Wilentz had promised to prove that the child was instantly killed when the kidnaper fell from the broken ladder; but in his summation, the prosecutor had charged that Hauptmann had crushed the little boy's skull while he still slept in his crib.

"This new theory," Rosecrans told the fourteen judges, "injected into the case for the first time in the attorney general's summation, involved a wilful, deliberate and premeditated killing in all its essentials. The defendant had no further right to cross-examine and introduce new evidence to combat this new theory." In effect, Hauptmann had been accused and then barred from answering the accusation.

But then, Rosecrans said, Wilentz had repeatedly overstepped the bounds of propriety and fairness one had a right to expect of an officer of the State. He had expressed his personal opinion as to the defendant's guilt, commented freely on facts not in evidence, and appealed to prejudice through inflammatory remarks. He had bullied and tried to break Hauptmann with "the virulence and venom of the nearly barbaric advocate who tilted in the lists for the case of his principal."

Next, Rosecrans directed the court's attention to Judge Trenchard's charge to the trial jury. The defense lawyer said that he was of course familiar with the ruling in this, his native state, to the effect that judges may fairly comment upon the evidence; but surely Trenchard had gone far beyond! His charge had been argumentative to a degree which made his comments on the State's evidence an act not of the arbiter but of the advocate.

Rosecrans picked up his copy of the defense brief and read from it:

> The function of the Court is to conduct the trial in such a manner that the jury may pass fairly and intelligently upon the guilt of the accused and base its determination upon the evidence offered by both sides and upon nothing else, and without the slightest attempt to impute anything but a single-minded purpose to fulfill his multifarious duties as a firm and capable moderator and presiding justice in a case tinged with world-wide interest, the defendant nevertheless respectfully insists that the comments made upon the evidence by the trial judge had the intrinsic tendency of controlling the jury in their view of the fact, and the comments

> of the Court as to particular facts only emphasized, to the disadvantage of the defendant, any other facts of a cognate character which might be found in the evidence of the defendant, Hauptmann.
>
> The defendant further respectfully insists that notwithstanding what the Court said in regard to the jury's recollection of the evidence as being active and pertinent, every factual comment made by the Court became, by the very mention of the trial justice, elevated to the authority of an established and demonstrated actuality by reason either of the emphasis which the Court placed upon the particular incident, by the modulation or tone of the Court, or its grammatical or rhetorical emphasis of interrogation.

Putting the brief aside, Rosecrans looked up at the judges. What was the trial jury to think, he asked—what *could* it think—when, in referring in his charge to the defense counsel's contention that the kidnap-murder had been committed not by the defendant but by a criminal gang with the help of the Lindbergh or Morrow servants, Judge Trenchard had asked—asked the jury!—"Now do you believe that?"

Rosecrans let the words linger in the quiet air. "Whether the kidnaping was done by a gang with the help or connivance of the servants was a circumstance for the jury to consider," he continued, "it is impossible to escape the conviction that under the conditions prevailing the probability of help or connivance of someone on the inside is a far more reasonable hypothesis than any theory advanced by the State."

Was Judge Trenchard's question to the jury justified? Rosecrans thought not.

Trenchard had been unfair in other respects in his charge, the lawyer held. He had thrown doubt on the testimony of key defense witnesses and given undue emphasis to the testimony of witnesses for the State, Amandus Hochmuth, for example, and Albert S. Osborn, the star handwriting expert. Osborn had concluded, Judge Trenchard had pointed out, that the evidence that Hauptmann had written the ransom notes was "irresistible, unanswerable, and overwhelming." What was this, if not elevating "to the authority of an established and demonstrated actuality"?

Rosecrans turned to the testimony of some of the other key witnesses for the State, notably that of Colonel Lindbergh himself. Was it really possible for the Colonel to identify the voice of a man he had heard speak *two to three hundred feet away?* And could anyone seriously accept Mrs. Cecile Barr's statement that the man who had tossed a ransom bill into her cashier's cage—on a dark night, remember!—was Hauptmann? And Arthur Koehler's testimony. Were sensible people expected to believe that a rail of the kidnap ladder had been part of a board in the attic of the house where Hauptmann lived? Wasn't that stretching things to the point of fantasy? And he wished to remind the Court that Koehler's testimony, almost the whole of it, had been contradicted by a practical lumberman, speaking for the defense.

Concluding this phase of his argument, Rosecrans declared that none of them—the witnesses he had mentioned and the rest: Dr. Condon, Colonel Schwarzkopf, Frank Wilson, Whited—had proved anything of consequence. In judging Hauptmann guilty, the jury had gone against the weight of evidence.

It was twelve minutes past one, and the judges recessed for lunch; they returned a few minutes after two. Rosecrans launched his final attack. The atmosphere and conduct of the trial had made a mockery of justice, a veritable Roman circus. Even before the trial had started, biased, exaggerated newspaper stories—which the people who were to become members of the jury could not help reading—had inflamed the jurors' minds against the defendant, causing them to forget the essential rule of law that a man is innocent until proved guilty beyond all reasonable doubt. This prejudice, and the resulting inability to think and reason calmly, had been increased by the mob spirit which had swirled around the trial itself; the jurors had been exposed to the comments of spectators, the cries of newsboys hawking headlines, the radio broadcasts delivered just a few feet away from their quarters in the Union Hotel—all of which had been critical or downright condemnatory—the repeated outbursts in the courtroom, and, perhaps above all, by the daily presence of Charles Lindbergh, constantly presenting to the jurors the living picture of a bereaved father, for whose sorrow the world demanded a sacrifice.

The true prosecutor of Bruno Richard Hauptmann was Charles Lindbergh, and the sacrifice demanded was Hauptmann's life.

In the light of all these facts, Rosecrans said finally, one could only conclude that the defendant's interests had been unfairly prejudiced, his conviction unjust. He asked the Court to reverse the verdict.

Aside from rare moments of dramatic emphasis, his manner had been that of the bookish student of constitutional law. David Wilentz, rising to reply, offered a striking contrast. In denying each accusation defense counsel had made, he was vigorous, harsh, sarcastic. Following him to the floor, his associate Joseph Lanigan challenged Rosecrans' interpretation of the law. Richard Hauptmann, they maintained, was guilty as charged and deserved the death sentence.

The Court adjourned at four o'clock. It would be autumn, Lloyd Fisher knew, before the fourteen judges came to a decision. But he and Rosecrans and Pope felt confident that that decision would be in Hauptmann's favor. A simple majority vote would reverse the conviction; a tie would sustain it.

In any case, the order for execution would be put off until the Court had decided for life or death.

Throughout the summer, defense counsel followed any leads suggested by their constant preoccupation with the case. Reilly's efforts to tie up the defense fund until he got his twenty-five thousand dollars had been defeated, but the fund itself, which had finally grown to some thirty thousand dollars, had been largely used up. Anna Hauptmann's appeals to the public had run dry, and no more was to be expected from that source; her midwest tour had had to be canceled after an unsympathetic reception in Chicago.

The summer months passed. On Wednesday, October 9, the Court of Errors and Appeals handed down its judgment. Justice Charles W. Parker had been chosen to write the opinion. In twelve thousand words he answered the long list of Rosecrans' contentions.

First, there was evidence to show that Charles Augustus Lindbergh, Jr., *had* been subjected to a fatal blow in Hunterdon County, and therefore the trial had properly been held in that county, even though death itself may have occurred in another county. The theft of the child and his sleeping suit from his home, followed by the surrender of the sleeping suit—merely as proof that the abductor had the child and was qualified to negotiate for ransom —indicated that the abductor intended to commit larceny, which established the crime. The variant theories presented by the State in the opening and closing of its case as to the manner of the child's death had not been harmful to the defendant, for, in submitting the case to the jury, the court had taken cognizance solely of the first theory, death from a fall.

It was not only the right but the duty of a trial judge to comment on the evidence and give the jury his impressions of its weight and value, and such comments could not be held in error so long as the ultimate decision on the disputed facts was left to the jury. The trial verdict was not against the weight of evidence—indeed, the conviction was the one verdict to which the evidence inescapably led—and no legal error could be attributed to Charles Lindbergh's presence in the courtroom, or to demonstrations from spectators, or to press and radio reports on the case, adequate arrangements having been made to prevent the jurors from being unduly influenced and prejudiced against the defendant.

The decision of the Court of Errors and Appeals was unanimous, Justice Parker concluded. The evidence, though circumstantial, pointed to guilt from so many directions that there was no room for reasonable doubt. No verdict other than the one found by the trial jury was justified.

The appeal for the verdict's reversal was denied.

Lloyd Fisher gave himself the duty of bringing the news to the man in the death house. The decision had gone against them, he told Hauptmann, and there was no use pretending that it was not a grave setback to their hopes. But hope remained, and for his part, Fisher regarded the fight as only begun.

Hauptmann was silent, turning away from the lawyer and staring at a picture of Anna and Bubi on his cell wall. Presently his sad face turned back to Fisher and he said in a low voice that it was the eve of his tenth wedding anniversary. "Won't this be a terrible anniversary present for my Anni?" he asked, but it was hardly a question.

Six days later, on October 15, defense counsel won a second stay of execution, to permit an appeal to the United States Supreme Court.

On November 12, Egbert Rosecrans petitioned the Supreme Court to review the action of the New Jersey Court of Errors and Appeals. That court, he declared, had erred in sustaining the conviction, because the defendant's constitutional rights had been jeopardized and he had not been given a fair and impartial trial.

As before, Rosecrans cited his careful, detailed reasons.

5

The new governor of New Jersey, Harold G. Hoffman, who had succeeded A. Harry Moore, felt that his state's Court of Errors and Appeals was mistaken in regarding the Lindbergh case as solved and finished, which was certainly the meaning of its refusal to reverse the verdict. How could the case really be closed when so many loose ends were still dangling? He wasn't alone in this opinion; *The New York Times* had said pretty much the same thing, and so had many people, here at home and throughout the nation—throughout the world, for that matter. And although some newspapers were offering a huge price to Richard Hauptmann for his own story of how he had kidnaped and killed the Lindbergh baby, on the other hand they were urging his defense counsel to dig up new evidence and prove his innocence.

Even if you brushed aside these things, Governor Hoffman thought, it was impossible to deny that Hauptmann had not been tried in an unprejudiced atmosphere. Hate and bias had played a part in the jury's decision to inflict the ultimate punishment.

Harold Giles Hoffman was not a man to let such reflections roost lazily in his mind.

He was a native of the state that in paying him its highest honor had done so with the additional flourish of electing him, a Republican, in the face of a Democratic landslide. His home town was South Amboy, where his father had been a railroad detective. A stocky, energetic boy, young Harold was bound for big things, friends and relatives said—a real go-getter! He wasn't long in proving them right. He set out for the World War as an infantry private and came home a captain, with a record of military achievement to show that he deserved the rank. In 1925, at twenty-nine he was a candidate for the office of mayor of South Amboy, and won—the youngest mayor in the state. Two years later he ran for Congress, and won. He ran for Congress a second time, and won. It was true that his legislative record listed only one bill to his credit, but the nature of that bill did him no harm: it made it possible for Gold Star Mothers to travel to Europe at public expense to see the graves of their soldier sons.

Congressman Hoffman didn't serve out his second term; he was recalled to New Jersey to become Commissioner of Motor Vehicles. Then came his greatest triumph. On November 6, 1934, he was elected governor, youngest in the nation. He had staged a whirlwind campaign. "Harold would blow into town like a reincarnation of old Doc Beasley's medicine show," a friend said. "You couldn't tell whether he was selling civic reform or Indian bitters."

The new governor had remained faithful to sleepy South Amboy, on the banks of the Raritan. His wife, Lillie, and three daughters, Ada, fourteen, Lillie, nine, and Hope, four—looked on him as a wonderful husband and father. Ada was the governor's favorite. During his campaign, the smiling, enthusiastic little girl was often at his side on the platform, reciting a poem she had composed:

Lucky, plucky, happy fella,
Once he's started, he won't stop.
And he'll win this darned election!
I should know—'cause he's my Pop!

Governor Hoffman had a round, cheerful face, and it was plain where Ada's friendly smile had come from. Some Republican political leaders thought he would make a fine Vice-president, or even President. He had the winning habit, which was rare among Republicans these days. And he couldn't be beat for sheer popularity. Was there anyone who didn't like him, even Democrats? He was a great joiner. He belonged to the Methodist Church and to the Masons, the Rotarians, the Shriners, the Odd Fellows, the Eagles and the Elks. But his favorite group was the eagerly eccentric Order of Circus Saints and Sinners, which performed good works with money raised at dinners and lunches and entertainments attended by public figures who seemed to enjoy being hit on the head—in a manner of speaking—with bladders by clowns. Phony telephones squirted water in their august ears and disgusting messes appeared on their dinner plates. Governor Hoffman loved these revels. He put on a fake mustache and painted his nose, pounded the backs of cabinet members and performed ingenious practical jokes of his own concoction. He drank Scotch, which he liked, and made speeches; his reputation as an after-dinner speaker was second to none.

He was thirty-nine this year, 1935.

Hoffman was reinforced in his doubts concerning Hauptmann and the "closed" Lindbergh case by the fact that an old, respected friend, Ellis Parker, was doubtful too. Rather more than doubtful, Parker was just about convinced that Richard Hauptmann was innocent, or at least that he had been no more than a minor figure in the hands of the real criminals.

Parker had said this to the governor many times. And if Ellis said the case was *not* solved, then, Hoffman thought, you could be sure it wasn't.

Ellis Parker was a redoubtable figure. Some people called him America's outstanding detective, if not the world's. Like the governor, he had begun his chosen career fairly early in life. Back in those days, in 1892, when he was twenty-one, Ellis often fiddled at country barn dances. He was fiddling at one when his horse and buggy were stolen. Ellis pondered the problem. He knew everybody in the neighborhood and fancied he knew them well enough to be able to declare which ones would steal a horse and buggy and which wouldn't. After completing his list of those who would, he reduced it to a finer list: those who so hankered for a horse and buggy they would ignore the consequences of stealing a horse and buggy belonging to a man so cool, thoughtful and determined as Ellis Parker. He made calls on these people. Two days later, Ellis was driving around in his buggy again.

This feat decided his career.

He became chief of the Burlington County, New Jersey, detective force at twenty-two, something of a prodigy, and still held that post in 1935. The years had spread his fame far beyond the state. He had conducted twenty thousand criminal investigations, including 236 murder inquiries. His extraordinary record showed that he had failed to win convictions in only ten of these cases.

Ellis Parker was not a Scotland Yard type. He cared little for police protocol, dressed sloppily—his necktie wandered unheeded far below the notch of his collar—and he was fat and bald. His blue eyes could hardly be called piercing. His favorite smoke was a corncob pipe. Though a Quaker, he was anything but guarded in his speech, which was of a quality sometimes described as bluff—in fact, Mr. Parker cursed and swore. He lived in a fifteen-room house in Mount Holly, New Jersey, and was the father of fifteen children, of whom seven had died.

Despite his success, or perhaps because of it, the Chief of Detectives of Burlington County had his critics, who said that in serving the law Ellis Parker pretty often skated damn close to the edge of it. He preferred to go after a murderer by locking up everybody with even the vaguest connection with the crime and keeping them in jail until they had explained to his satisfaction why they didn't belong there. This strategy was patterned on the method that had cracked the horse-and-buggy case; it might be rough and ready, Parker said, but by Jesus it worked.

With Ellis Parker's opinion to back him, Governor Hoffman had taken an unusual step. One night in October, a week after the Court of Errors and Appeals had upheld Hauptmann's conviction, the governor had paid a secret visit to the man in the death house—secret, that is, to everybody except the prison warden, Colonel Mark O. Kimberling, who was not only a good friend but who owed his appointment to Hoffman. Kimberling had made clear to the governor that trouble might be expected if the newspapers got wind of a visit to Hauptmann's cell; prison regulations provided that only a condemned man's relatives, counsel and religious advisers could see him without court order; but Hoffman was set on interviewing the prisoner and the warden found an excuse to remove the guards from the death house so that the governor could come and go unobserved.

His talk with Richard Hauptmann hadn't changed the governor's mind one way or the other; he was convinced neither of Hauptmann's guilt nor of his innocence, only of the need to inquire further into the case. Hauptmann, gratified by the unexpected visit, promised not to mention it even to his lawyers.

Harold Hoffman continued to think about the case in the following weeks. Finally, he decided to act.

He announced on December 5 that notwithstanding the judicial decisions that had been and might in the future be handed down, he would ask New Jersey's Court of Pardons to grant Richard Hauptmann a personal interview should he decide to throw himself on the mercy of the court and plead for a commutation of the death sentence to life imprisonment. The governor held that the Court of Pardons, of which he was an ex-officio member, had been created for the sole purpose of reviewing the trial of a defendant from a standpoint above the law, after all legal measures for the defendant's relief had been explored. In Hauptmann's case, of course, some of these measures were still open: even if the Supreme Court refused to intervene, a basis for a new trial might be found, or he might win a writ of habeas corpus from the federal court, or his counsel might turn up new evidence; but Hoffman was announcing his intention anyway.

The announcement brought questions; reporters asked why he was taking so much interest in the case, which hadn't seemed to stir any special reactions in him before. Had he by any chance seen Hauptmann?—visited him, maybe?—learned anything other people didn't know? Hoffman answered that he had been disturbed for months by several aspects of the case. He wasn't concerned about Hauptmann as a person, but *was* concerned about truth and justice. And yes, he admitted, having said so much he might as well tell them more—he *had* seen Richard Hauptmann in his death-house cell.

The next day, the governor's words were in headlines. Much criticism followed. It appeared that his visit to Hauptmann was not only unprecedented and illegal; it impugned the integrity of the New Jersey courts and, by extension, of the whole American judicial system. By casting doubt on the trial and conviction, Hoffman was making a brazen attempt to exploit the celebrated case for personal publicity that would improve his chances of nomination for high office at the Republican National Convention in June of next year.

The governor wasn't ruffled. The fate of Richard Hauptmann, he said, was "one with which the dimensions of American justice will be measured by all Americans and the world." It was the right of every convicted man to present his case to a Court of Pardons, a court of mercy, and nothing about Hauptmann's case justified suspending that right. Hoffman promised that if and when Richard Hauptmann appeared before the Court of Pardons, he would be heard without prejudice.

Reporters dug up the fact that Hoffman had had a number of discussions with Ellis Parker about the case. Both denied it, but it looked very much as if the governor had retained Parker to make his own investigation. Hoffman had hardly made a secret of his opinion that the State police had acted with something less than intelligence and efficiency. Was he now aiming to discredit Colonel Schwarzkopf and replace him as head of the organization when his term expired in June '36?

That notion opened up other, highly interesting speculations. If Hoffman got rid of Schwarzkopf, then he'd be certain to slide his man Kimberling into the berth. Ellis Parker would be given a new State detective bureau, and ultimately—if his mentor should become the next President of the United States—would replace J. Edgar Hoover as chief of the newly expanded Federal Bureau of Investigation, which, since its recent elevation from division to bureau, had quickly become known as the FBI.

All this might or might not be so. But some students of the New Jersey political scene felt that a good deal more than a wholesome desire to see justice done lay behind Harold Hoffman's action and statements. Cynically, they attributed his handsome words to a sharp political rivalry which the coming national elections had sharpened even more.

These people said that the rivals were Governor Hoffman and Attorney General David Wilentz; one a Republican, the other a Democrat; both still young, or at any rate youthful, and both with promising political futures. They had matched each other in their rise to the two most important posts in New Jersey; and they could look back to days in the same Jersey school, when the rivalry had started.

But lately David Wilentz seemed to be getting the better of it —at any rate, so far the Hauptmann case had done more for him than it had for Harold Hoffman. Wilentz had won the case and in the winning made his face and name familiar to every voter. Was it Hoffman's idea to try to throw the case wide open, to discredit Wilentz's handling of it, and to emerge himself as the champion of the underdog?

He might be able to get rid of Schwarzkopf, the cynics remarked, but he couldn't kick Wilentz out of his way. Wilentz was Attorney General of the State of New Jersey by grace of A. Harry Moore, the Democratic ex-governor, now U.S. Senator, who had appointed him in 1934 for a term of five years. He could be removed only by impeachment, which was most unlikely, considering that the state legislature was heavily Democratic.

On Monday December 9, in a single typewritten line, the Supreme Court of the United States rejected Bruno Richard Hauptmann's pleas for a review of the judgments against him; and on Friday the thirteenth, which happened to be Justice Trenchard's birthday, the judge again sentenced the prisoner to die, the execution to take place during the week of January 13, 1936.

Warden Kimberling waited for the defense counsel to arrive at the prison and break the news to Hauptmann. None of them showed up. He could hardly permit the bitter word to reach the death cell through the prison grapevine, the warden reflected, and commissioned an officer to tell the condemned man.

Presently the officer reported back to his chief. The news that he had only another month to live hadn't seemed to shake Hauptmann; he'd actually thanked the messenger for letting him know the Supreme Court had refused to act, and in quite a cheerful voice.

"He seems to have some kind of feeling he's going to get out of it," the officer said.

6

On Sunday the fifteenth a family group met at the Morrow home, Next Day Hill. Mrs. Morrow had come up from Mexico to attend the meeting; Constance and Dwight, Jr., were there; also Aubrey Neil Morgan, who had moved to the house after his wife Elizabeth Morrow Morgan's death.

Charles and Anne were the central members of the meeting, which had been called to discuss a question that had grown steadily in their minds since Jon's birth: could they risk living any longer in America?

Recent events had given the question an urgency that at times seemed almost fearful to the young parents. Their minds had been conditioned, as much as parents' minds ever could be, to a phenomenon that defied reason, because its authors were not reasonable human beings—the savage letters threatening Jon. Charles' experience covered wider latitudes than Anne's in this alien country, though she too had come to be familiar with its population of the hate-filled, the maladjusted, the insane, or the merely resentful. He had met these people, through their letters, immediately after returning from his famous flight. It was only to be expected, his advisers had told him—one of those often-quoted penalties of fame which to the unknown seem blandly and exasperatingly fictitious. Then he had married Anne, and she had been accorded her share of the vindictive tribute. In an attempt to get away from its atmosphere, Charles had chosen the lonely acres near Hopewell and said to his friend Colonel Breckinridge,

"Please buy me that"; here, he had thought, he and Anne and their baby might have a chance to escape into the obscurity he had not known how to value when it was his.

After the kidnaping, the letter-writers multiplied from the hundreds to the thousands to the tens of thousands. It was possible to think of the Hopewell house as a frontier stockade, still beleagured, even though the cherished possession it had been built to protect was gone.

The Lindberghs had moved from the empty house to Next Day Hill, and for a while the letters had dropped off: but Jon's birth had ended the lull. The threats doubled, tripled, when Richard Hauptmann was condemned to die. The majority of the letters were held up by the various post offices and then forwarded to Lindbergh's New York office, where they were carefully read through and referred to the appropriate authorities for investigation, if it seemed to be warranted. The usual but not unvarying veil of clumsy anonymity was pierced and, in cases of patent insanity, the writers were turned over to institutions. A score of other correspondents, comparatively sane—they merely demanded money under threat of a second kidnaping—were arrested and jailed.

The Yahoo tribe was greedy for malice; they itched to hate. There were people who were paid to pander to them and did so with bold enterprise. Jon attended a nearby nursery school, where one of the teachers drove him every day and brought him home. These peaceful travels were twice interrupted. The first time, as the car carrying the little boy drew up to the school grounds a makeshift curtain dropped from the back of a nearby parked truck; two glinting eyes peering from slim tubes focused on Jon. After a few terrifying moments, the truck sped away. An alarm went out for it. The State police ran it down some hours later. The truck contained news cameramen.

The second time, not too long before today's family meeting, a car shouldered Jon's to the curb and several figures scrambled out. The teacher dropped the steering wheel and drew the little boy close. Their frightened faces stared at the cameras jammed in at them. These were dramatic shots, captured by the same newspicture syndicate that had sent the truck on its tour of duty.

It began to seem that tension and uncertainty were part of Jon's daily life, tagging along with him to school and back. Charles and Anne took him out of the school; he had been kept at home ever since.

Then, just over a week ago, a kind of climax had arrived. Governor Harold G. Hoffman, the Lindberghs read, was not satisfied with the Hauptmann verdict, openly doubting the convicted kidnaper's guilt and indicating that he meant to investigate the case.

Charles was appalled. He and Anne were convinced that Richard Hauptmann was the kidnaper and killer; apparently the tragedy was not to be allowed to die but stirred up again, used and prolonged by a politician whose announced intention could only seem to them to be that of an opportunist. Also, it was said that Hoffman meant to get rid of Norman Schwarzkopf as head of the New Jersey State Police. Charles felt this as a blow at a friend in whom he had complete faith. Colonel Schwarzkopf, he believed, had done his utmost during the long search. It looked to him like a partisan mixing of politics into the sound guidance of a police organization that had answered his needs to the limit of its ability.

As the Lindberghs could have predicted, the governor's announcement left a new wake of threats, threats demanding money, threats to kidnap and murder. The Supreme Court's refusal to review, and Justice Trenchard's setting of a new date of execution, spurred the letter-writers into even more frenzied activity.

And so Charles and Anne had asked themselves if they could risk staying in America. If not, where could they go to find the normal lives Charles had spoken about in his statement to the newspapers just after Jon's birth?

They had pretty well settled on the answer. They wanted unworried days and nights, Charles for the new scientific problem his friend Alexis Carrel had posed for him, Anne for her writing. They thought they could find privacy in England.

Charles had been in England twice, immediately following the Atlantic flight and again in 1933 when he and Anne had flown there from America after stops at Greenland and Iceland, on their trip exploring possible routes for transatlantic passenger air service. They had come away with grateful memories of a minimum of flash bulbs and reporters' questions.

They put up the question and the likely answer for the family's opinion, and the family agreed.

Wherever they finally settled in England, Aubrey Morgan said, he could make the first part of their stay a bit easier. As they knew, his father still lived on the Morgan family estate in Wales, at Llandaff, near Cardiff, and he'd be delighted to have them there until they found a place of their own.

That was the decision, then. Maybe, in time, the atmosphere at home would change, or maybe, for their and Jon's sakes, they would have to stay abroad; but of course, the Lindberghs said, they would never give up American citizenship.

Charles went to Washington the next day and told a few government officials who were trusted friends. He wanted to get out of the country as quietly as possible. The way to guarantee it, he learned, was with diplomatic passports, which would be obtained for him.

Then he consulted Basil Harris, vice-president of the United States Lines, who said that to make sure the Lindberghs' leaving would be kept secret he'd handle the arrangements himself. A big liner, as public as a hotel, was out of the question; the best thing would be a freighter with limited passenger accommodations. Here was one, sailing in a few days: the *American Importer,* 7590 tons, due to dock in Liverpool on December 30. Harris would see to it that the ship's officers wouldn't know in advance the identity of their three passengers.

Lindbergh paid the regular one-way fare for a family of three, two adults, one child—$293, including tax—and, thanking Harris, also arranged for Aubrey Morgan's passage to England on a faster ship, the *Westernland,* sailing the same day, which would give Morgan the chance to prepare for their arrival at the family home in Wales.

Late Saturday evening, the twenty-first, Charles and Anne made their farewells at Next Day Hill; if all went well, Anne's mother and sister would join them in England after the turn of the year. They had hired a cab for the trip to the pier, rather than take one of the family cars with their well-known license plates. The cab brought them to the West 20th Street dock in Manhattan just before midnight. All was quiet.

Then, in their cabin, they waited.

Sailing time came and went.

Could anything have gone wrong? Charles left the cabin to ask. The delay had nothing to do with his and Anne's presence, he learned; the radiomen had threatened to strike, and it was impossible to tell how long the ship might be held in port.

Three hours later the strike threat was lifted and the *American Importer* headed out toward the Atlantic, carrying her voluntary exiles from their native land. Her course would be just a little south of the path the *Spirit of St. Louis* had flown over, eight years before.

7

But their exile could hardly remain a secret; and when the story broke, Lindbergh wanted to be sure that it came from a sympathetic source. Some days before, he had told a newspaperman friend, Lauren D. Lyman of *The New York Times,* about their decision and the reasons for it, and it was arranged that Lyman's account would appear in his paper on Monday the twenty-third, when the *American Importer* would be well out at sea.

The Times' front-page exclusive story rapidly spread by radio across the country and around the world. President Roosevelt declined requests to comment on the news; Congress had adjourned for the Christmas holidays and this usually dependable well was dry; but newspaper editorials made up for it.

The New York *Herald Tribune's* chief editorial writer spoke for most of his colleagues:

> The departure of Colonel and Mrs. Lindbergh for England, to find a tolerable home there in a safer and more civilized land than ours has shown itself to be, is its own commentary upon the American social scene. Nations have exiled their heroes before; they have broken them with meanness. But when has a nation made life unbearable to one of its most distinguished men through a sheer inability to protect him from its criminals and lunatics and the vast vulgarity of its sensationalists, publicity-seekers, petty politicians and yellow newspapers? It seems as incredible as it is shocking. Yet everyone knows that this is exactly what has happened.
>
> Colonel and Mrs. Lindbergh have endured with great courage burdens which no one had a right to put upon them. If they have finally decided that too much has been asked of their patriotism, nobody can blame them.
>
> The excesses of American habit and temperament are an old story. They have yielded prime virtues such as hospitality and generosity. But they have produced not less barbarism and cheapness and it is high time that the nation reviewed these facts candidly, and accepted the truth about its faults. The slow, hard task of curbing the violence of its public moods cannot be too speedily begun.
>
> The Lindberghs can live with some freedom in England, not only because there has been, it is said, no recorded case there in recent times of a kidnaping for ransom, but even more, because of the adult public sense of good taste, restraint and respect for individual rights and privacies which underlies the British freedom from crime. Now that Americans have driven one of their leading men to flee in secrecy from a life which they made intolerable for him, they would do well to meditate upon the value of those virtues.

The New York *Daily News* dissented:

> On the other hand, Colonel Lindbergh has always invited publicity by shunning it, after the manner of Greta Garbo. We do think he would have been pestered less if he had acted

more as a popular hero is supposed to act, and been less embarrassed in the public gaze.

Mayor Edward J. Kelly of Chicago said the family's flight was un-American.

Others thought the blame for their exile should be brought closer to home; in fact, to one individual. The Trenton *State Gazette* said:

> It is easy to believe that Governor Hoffman's strange interest in the welfare of Hauptmann was the determining factor that influenced their decision. What reason would they have for confidence in security when the Chief Executive of the State manifests such extraordinary concern in the welfare of a felon convicted of the most heinous of crimes?

Dr. John F. Condon took up his pen, dipped it in his home-made ink, and addressed the editor of *The New York Times*. In his stately hand he wrote:

> During all wars there is a fair exchange of prisoners, and sometimes one country will reap the reward of gain, while the other loses by the negotiations.
>
> During times of peace there are exchanges of men whether directly, or indirectly, even to the disadvantage of our own country, which really means a profit for some foreign country.
>
> The latest exchange between the United States and a foreign power seems to be the loss of our great "National Hero," Col. Charles A. Lindbergh, in exchange for whom we retain and detain Bruno Richard Hauptmann, with whom I exchanged $50,000 and received in return a promissory note to return our beloved "Eaglet," Charles A. Lindbergh, Jr.
>
> I beheld the anguish of Mrs. Anne Morrow Lindbergh, in the throes of blessed motherhood, and promised to return her beloved baby to her arms, or give my life in the attempt.
>
> The Colonel and Mrs. Lindbergh gave me a note of authorization to act as intermediator in this greatest and most disastrous case of all time, excepting the Crucifixion of the divine Son of Man.
>
> I accepted the Colonel and Mrs. Lindbergh's invitation and for three years and ten months, night and day, near and far, I worked assiduously to restore the baby, or run down the cowardly knave who climbed a ladder, nailed together in three sections, to carry out his nefarious scheme.
>
> I saw with deep satisfaction $49,680 of the $50,000 which

I gave in the hand and on the arm of the carpenter returned to the G-men under that great chief J. Edgar Hoover, and the New York Police Department, under the friend of my boyhood, Col. John J. O'Ryan, as Commissioner in New York City, from the Bronx, the most beautiful "Borough" in the world.

Yes, but the ashes of the darling baby, victim of a fiend urged by greed of gain, and seeking pleasure, are mute witness of the Crime, while within every American's breast there is a beating of the heart, tolling the death-knell of every gangster, while the Stars and Stripes fly from every staff and masthead. . . .

In conclusion will the Courts stand as a tribunal, only to be swept out of power by an individual for sake of political aggrandizement, or will the representatives of the people stand firm and defy gangsterdom, or individual marauders while we trade National Heroes like Col. Charles A. Lindbergh and his family for the discarded miscreants of other countries who lie, cheat, kidnap and murder, depending upon the loot and spoils to serve as a cache to free them from the toils and meshes of the law?

Col. Lindbergh told me that he would remain a citizen of the United States.

He will return in triumph to us and the U.S.

May God speed that return. JAFSIE

The *American Importer* had taken a Christmas tree on board, and on Christmas Eve it was put up in the ship's small lounge. Charles and Anne hadn't forgotten to pack a supply of bright ornaments and three big Christmas stockings, and they decorated the green branches and hung up the stockings, ready for Jon's eyes.

At midday, Tuesday the thirty-first, the freighter nosed toward her Liverpool pier. A great crowd was there, more reporters and photographers, police said, than Liverpool had ever seen. But Sir Philip Game, commissioner of Scotland Yard, had received a cable from New York's police commissioner, Lewis Valentine, soon after the *American Importer* had sailed, asking him to make special preparations for the Lindberghs' arrival, and Sir Philip had stationed a heavy guard on the wharf.

Anne came down the gangplank first, smiling, a newspaperman thought, "weakly, unhappily." Charles followed, hatless as usual and without an overcoat, despite the cold, damp weather. He carried Jon in his arms. A waiting car drove them to the Adelphi Hotel in Liverpool.

They stayed in their three-room suite that afternoon and night, which was New Year's Eve, and for the next three days, while a private detective stood guard at the door. No reporter or photographer was allowed to come in.

Aubrey Morgan took the family to Llandaff on the fourth day of the new year, 1936. They arrived after dark. It was very quiet; after New York and the Liverpool crowds it seemed to be the other end of the world. But Morgan hadn't left anything to chance. Ten constables on bikes patrolled the approaches to the estate and others on foot were posted around it.

They entered the big house. And there, gaily sparkling in the hall, was another Christmas tree.

Jon, in his father's arms, clapped his hands.

8

Governor Hoffmann was annoyed with Dr. Condon. After the Supreme Court had refused to review the case, Richard Hauptmann had petitioned the New Jersey Court of Pardons for clemency, following the governor's lead; and now, on the very eve of the day that had been set aside for the court to hear Hauptmann's plea, Dr. Condon was leaving the country for a holiday—a long holiday, the governor understood.

At the very least it was inconvenient, and perhaps much more. True, the old man's presence wasn't required at the hearing, but there was no telling what the hearing might lead to; and if a new investigation was called for, Dr. Condon would certainly be one of the first to be questioned. This sudden departure, with David Wilentz's approval, seemed suspicious to Hoffman. In fact, he thought, quite a few things about Condon were suspicious. A national magazine which was never noted for reticence had just published an article by him, the first of a series; Hoffman had obtained a manuscript copy of all the articles, and the account the old teacher gave of his activities in the Lindbergh case included several statements so at odds with his sworn testimony at the trial that in effect he shot his story full of holes.

The outstanding instance was his blunt, no-two-ways-about-it assertion that more than one person was involved in the crime; that he, John F. Condon, had seen or heard at least *two* of Hauptmann's accomplices.

He had been so eager to tell his story that he had written about the trial while it was still in progress, and had been rapped on the knuckles by the American Bar Association, which had deplored this somewhat premature bit of self-advertising as "decidedly out of place." And just a month ago he had told a reporter in Lynn, Massachusetts, that he had been offered a quarter of a million dollars if he would change his testimony and put the blame for the crime on Isidor Fisch.

Surely, Governor Hoffman thought, it wasn't too much to ask just who were these accomplices! And where had the $250,000 offer come from?

Where was the dividing line between fact and fancy in the old man's courtroom testimony and his tales out of court?

And then too, in the governor's opinion, Dr. Condon's behavior after the trial discredited him as a reliable witness as much as his written and spoken revelations. First, he had lectured on the case to church and civic groups; next he had decided to set out on a vaudeville tour. Announcing the tour in *Variety,* the show-business weekly, he had referred to himself as "the most enigmatic, colorful and widely publicized personality in America." In defense of this switch from the role of retired educator and first citizen of the Bronx to the somewhat gaudier one of show-biz entertainer, he contended that he had spent thousands of dollars of his savings on the Lindbergh case and hadn't been paid back a penny.

As it turned out, the vaudeville tour had barely got off the ground; after two local appearances, his scheduled visit to Plainfield, New Jersey, had been so strongly protested by the local clergy that the whole project was canceled.

Governor Hoffman wondered what action he should take, if any, to prevent Dr. Condon from leaving on his holiday. He could ask the attorney general to hold him, but on what grounds? Perjury? Even so, was there any reason to believe that Wilentz would agree? Once the old man was on the high seas, it would be the devil of a job to bring him back. The governor had asked his legal advisers about this and they had explained that since Dr. Condon would depart without having been named in an arrest warrant, he couldn't be considered a fugitive from justice. He was sailing for Cristobal, Panama; a process server would have to be sent there and a request for extradition relayed through the Attorney General of the United States to the Secretary of War and then to the U.S. Army officers in Panama who administered the Canal Zone. Out of the question.

About all he could do, Hoffman decided, was to announce that he wanted Dr. Condon held for questioning regarding discrepancies in his story and see what would happen.

He called in his press secretary.

That night, Friday January 10, the Grace liner *Santa Rita* sailed from her Brooklyn pier. Dr. John F. Condon and daughter Myra were among the passengers.

Richard Hauptmann's request to plead his case in person had been refused by the Court of Appeals, despite the favorable recommendation of its presiding officer, Governor Hoffman. On Saturday the eleventh, defense counsel asked the court to commute the death sentence to life imprisonment. Counsel argued all the more urgently because of the knowledge that State Prison Warden Kimberling had fixed an exact time for the execution: 8 P.M., Friday January 17. Six days away.

The defense's hopes had been raised for a while by an unexpected development. Two weeks ago, Hoffman had received a letter asking the Court of Pardons to grant clemency because Hauptmann was innocent. The letter was signed *J. J. Faulkner*. This was a familiar name—the name that had been signed to an exchange slip when $2980 in gold notes, all ransom money, had been turned in at the Federal Reserve Bank of New York on May 1, 1933. And there was no conclusive proof that "Faulkner" had ever been caught.

The governor had given both the letter and the exchange slip to a handwriting expert, who said that in his opinion they had been written by the same person. Later, after studying photo-enlargements of the samples, he changed his mind. Just before the Court of Pardons hearing, Hoffman had shown the defense lawyers the expert's final report. There was no similarity whatever; the "Faulkner" letter was either a hoax or an attempt to interfere with justice.

But the defense felt that their chances with the Court of Pardons were reasonably promising. It was an eight-man court. Politically, its members were split down the middle, four Republicans, four Democrats. Say they split down the middle, too, in their vote on Hauptmann. In that case, surely the presiding officer, the governor, would give the defense every benefit of the doubt! The fight might still be won.

The arguments were concluded and the court retired to deliberate. Six hours passed. The court's judgment was ready: with Governor Hoffman dissenting, the conviction of Richard Hauptmann was upheld, his pleas for clemency denied.

Lloyd Fisher brought the grim news to the death house. There was very little left now that they could hope for, he told Hauptmann—one or two legal maneuvers, and even these seemed foredoomed. He thought he'd better speak as frankly as he could, and he wanted Hauptmann to weigh his answer well.

"Richard, if you have any confession to make, it is the time to make it."

"I am innocent," the condemned man said. "I have never changed my story and I never will."

On Monday January 13, Fisher petitioned the United States Circuit Court of Appeals in Trenton for a writ of habeas corpus on the well-tried ground that the defendant's constitutional rights had been violated.

On Tuesday, Judge Warren Davis declined to issue a writ, saying that to do so in effect would be to overrule the Supreme Court of the United States. He also refused to grant a stay that would give Fisher time for further appeal.

Three days were left before the appointment in the execution chamber.

Racing against time, Lloyd Fisher asked the U.S. Supreme Court for permission to file for a writ of habeas corpus. He had little faith in this; he placed more in Anna Hauptmann. Earlier, she had appealed to the public to help her Richard; now, Fisher told her, she could appeal to one man, Harold Hoffman—ask him for a stay, a reprieve, a delay of execution, to stave off that fast-approaching hour, eight o'clock next Friday evening—just a little more time, time in which to fight!

Bubi was now a little more than two years old. To shield the boy and herself from the merciless publicity, Anna had resumed her maiden name—Schoeffler—and moved to an apartment at 2505 Lorillard Place in the Bronx. Not for anything, of course, would she miss her regular visits to the Jersey prison, and she had been just as faithful in calling on the defense lawyers, in case their drive to save Richard faltered—which, she was glad to admit, it never had.

Then, as the days and hours began to narrow down to the one day, the one hour, Anna had taken a room in a Trenton hotel, the Stacy Trent, to be as close to Richard as she could. She did not have far to go to the governor's office in the State House on this Thursday morning, January 16.

In thirty-three hours Richard was scheduled to die.

Anna was brought into the governor's office and he looked up from his desk and said "Yes, Mrs. Hauptmann?" His round face was serious; hardly the grinning clown's face of the Circus Saints and Sinners. Indeed, he looked like a governor.

Richard was innocent, Anna said. She begged Hoffman to grant a stay of execution, so that the lawyers would have another chance to save the life of an innocent man.

"Are you going to see your husband soon, Mrs. Hauptmann?"

Yes, she said; as soon as she left. Unless the governor stopped the execution, it would be her last visit.

"Tell your husband that his only chance is to tell the truth," Hoffman said.

His only chance is to tell the truth; but he *had* told the truth, he had always told the truth! Still, as Anna hurried from the handsome office to the death cell, she felt that the governor had meant to encourage her. She said as much to Richard, after repeating the message word for word. But he shook his head impatiently. What was the good of their talking about it? He had told her, told the lawyers, told the judge, told the jury, told everyone everything that had happened, all that he knew, the truth, never anything but the truth. Go back to the governor, he instructed Anna; ask him to come to the prison.

"Tell him I must talk to him!"

She rushed back to the State House. The governor was waiting. Anna translated Richard's German into English.

All the governor said was "Thank you."

She waited. He indicated the interview was over.

Anna returned to her hotel. There seemed to her little left but despair.

She had barely gone when a secretary came in with a message for Hoffman: Chief Justice Charles Evans Hughes had just announced that Fisher's request for permission to apply for a writ of habeas corpus was denied.

Governor Hoffman realized that he was face to face with his moment of decision. If the Lindbergh case was not to be closed in a very few hours by Hauptmann's execution, it was up to him to keep it open, by granting a stay.

Perhaps it wasn't so simple as that. Even if he decided that he should, *could* he grant the stay? The question had been argued by lawyers and newspapers ever since they had learned that the governor had involved himself in the case. Attorney General Wilentz had told Hoffman that even as governor of New Jersey he had no legal authority to grant a reprieve later than ninety days after a criminal's conviction, and to support it had cited the ruling Justice Bennet Van Syckel of the New Jersey Supreme Court had handed down in the 1890s, which had been upheld repeatedly in subsequent court decision. And since nearly a year had passed since Hauptmann's conviction, it was clear that the governor was powerless to act.

Strictly speaking, maybe so, Hoffman thought; but on several occasions his predecessors in office had ignored the Van Syckel finding. And he knew that if he granted a reprieve, Warden Mark Kimberling would honor it.

But he had better make haste slowly. He told a secretary that he would like to see Wilentz and Anthony Hauck, the Hunterdon County prosecutor.

Hoffman informed the two men that he felt he had no alternative but to order a stay. There were too many doubts about the case in the public's mind to let Hauptmann die without the State's making a final effort to determine if justice had been done. And executive precedence was on his side, he pointed out to Wilentz. Here were the figures: Since 1906, six Jersey governors had granted fourteen reprieves, although in every case the ninety-day limit had expired. But there was a far more important consideration. "My heart," the governor said, "my conscience and my sense of duty impel me to grant this reprieve."

David Wilentz said it was well known that he was opposed to capital punishment, and if any evidence could be brought forward that materially altered the case against Hauptmann he would be the first to go to court and seek clemency. He very much doubted that anything could be gained by reopening the case, and in cold fact it would be bound to be interpreted as an attack upon everyone connected with the investigation of the crime and the prosecution of the criminal—still, he wouldn't stand in the way.

Hoffman turned to the other. All right, Hauck said, he'd go along with the attorney general.

The governor thanked them. He would grant a thirty-day reprieve.

Wilentz volunteered to add thirty to sixty days to that, simply by not asking Judge Trenchard to sentence Hauptmann again until the reprieve had run out. Under the law, the new date of execution could not be set less than four weeks or more than eight weeks from the day the judge wrote the order.

Richard Hauptmann could look forward to at least two or three more months of life.

Lloyd Fisher and Frederick Pope hurried to the death cell with the wonderful news. Hauptmann seemed calm. He had expected to be spared, he said. But Anna was ecstatic and burst out with a jumble of German and English. "God be thanked! I hope the truth comes out now."

Others were less than grateful. The Trenton *Times* declared in a front-page editorial that Harold Hoffman had openly violated the state constitution, flaunted the highest court decisions, betrayed the interests of justice, dishonored himself and disgraced New Jersey by converting it into an international laughingstock. He had sacrificed all moral and legal right to serve as the state's chief executive. The state legislature should impeach him and throw him out of office.

Few members of the legislature appeared willing to accept the newspaper's angry challenge, and old political hands explained that there was little likelihood of even a motion for impeachment—the Democrats were happy with all the criticism, feeling that it had served them well, and the Republicans were hardly eager to attack their party's most prominent state figure.

Governor Hoffman believed in meeting criticism head-on. On Friday, the seventeenth, he issued a statement in which he said that if impeachment was the price he must pay for daring to follow the dictates of his conscience, he was ready to pay it; in granting a reprieve he had only exercised a right that the framers of the state's constitution gave its governors. He went on:

> I have never expressed an opinion upon the guilt or innocence of Hauptmann. I do, however, share with hundreds of thousands of our people the doubt as to the value of the evidence that placed him in the Lindbergh nursery on the night of the crime; I do wonder what part passion and prejudice played in the conviction of a man who was previously tried and convicted in the columns of many of our newspapers. I do, on the basis of evidence that is in my hands, question the truthfulness and mental competency of some of the chief witnesses for the State; I do doubt that this crime could have been committed by any one man, and I am worried about the eagerness of some of our law-enforcement agencies to bring about the death of this one man so that the books can be closed in the thought that another great crime mystery has been successfully solved.
>
> I make no apology for granting a reprieve in this case. During this period we may calmly consider some of the baffling phases of the crime and the subsequent trial of Hauptmann. I intend to give to the public, in due course, my reasons for entertaining doubts that I have expressed and I intend to direct the State police to continue their search for any other person or persons involved in the crime. Colonel Lindbergh, Colonel Schwarzkopf, and many others have repeatedly expressed the opinion that the crime was perpetrated by more than one person, and there is no justification now for abandoning that belief.

The governor pointed out that Hauptmann had steadiastly refused to change his story in spite of the great rewards that awaited him if he did. Sid Boehm of the New York *Evening Journal* had told him and others present that his paper had offered Hauptmann seventy-five thousand dollars to be left to his widow and baby son in exchange for an exclusive confession of guilt—and Hauptmann had rejected the offer. And when he had been told that his only chance to save his life was to go before the Court of Pardons, say "I was guilty," and throw himself upon the mercy of the court, again he had said no.

Hoffman's statement concluded:

> I am moved by no maudlin sentiment in this matter. I am the father of three children, I look upon kidnaping as the most dastardly of crimes, and I shared the horrors that struck the hearts of people throughout the world after the murder of the Lindbergh baby.
>
> I am interested in the preservation of that thing we have rather proudly called "Jersey Justice," and I hope that real and full justice will finally be done in this case. A stay of a comparatively few days cannot defeat that end.

The reprieve was big news in England. Charles and Anne Lindbergh had nothing to say.

9

Harold Hoffman's statement failed to calm his critics, but it was given a sympathetic reception by those who agreed with the governor in finding it hard to believe that one man, of ordinary intelligence, had perpetrated "the crime of the century" —and baffled some of the country's topnotch detective brains for the next two and a half years.

This was a moderate view, in contrast to the interpretations of extremists, who said that the prosecution hadn't come near the real criminals, that Richard Hauptmann was only a small cog in a large conspiracy, and that Lindbergh, Schwarzkopf and others close to the case were well aware of the fact.

Major Frank Pease was one of the extremists. The major, who did not otherwise identify himself, claimed in a forty-four-page pamphlet that the kidnap-murder was an act of vengeance executed by the OGPU, the Soviet secret police, against Dwight W. Morrow, and that Hauptmann had been only one of the agents who had carried it out. The fact that Morrow had died the summer before the crime had not deterred the Reds from revenging themselves on his family, Pease explained.

The reason was obvious—Morrow's activities in Mexico. At the time of his appointment as United States ambassador, relations between the two countries were strained. The Mexican government appeared to be leaning more and more to the left; American lives and investments were threatened. Major Pease said that the Soviet ambassador, a woman, and "her numerous staff of propagandists, provocateurs, saboteurs, agitators, and spies" were striving might and main to establish a Communist government in the United States' southern neighbor. Using all his great political and financial strength, Dwight Morrow had thwarted the attempt, and the foiled Russian plotters had vowed to make him pay.

The major offered no evidence but asked many knowing questions. Hadn't Betty Gow and Violet Sharpe formerly been employed by Communist-controlled English cooperative organizations? Wasn't Henry Johnson, Betty's boy friend, called Red *not* because of the color of his hair but because he belonged to the seamen's branch of a Red trade union? Hadn't Hauptmann been an admitted Spartacist, one of the violent radicals who, directly after the war, had tried to swing the German revolution into out-and-out Bolshevism?

Colonel Schwarzkopf and other authorities in the case restrained themselves from replying to Major Pease's challenges, but the chief of detectives of Burlington County, Governor Hoffman's friend Ellis Parker, wrote to the major that the crime was unsolved, unquestionably, and that he was doing what he could to clear it up. And from Baltimore, Maryland, came an opinion from a prominent author, editor and critic:

> My dear Major Pease:
>
> Your theory is at least plausible and deserves to be heard. My own belief, like yours, is that Hauptmann is undoubtedly guilty, but that it is impossible to imagine him committing the crime alone. And I share your confidence in Parker, the New Jersey detective.
>
> Sincerely yours,
> H. L. Mencken

Pease was not the only one to write a pamphlet on the subject. In a series of leaflets addressed *To The American People,* a group of twenty-five men and women who called themselves the Committee of Witnesses charged that the crime was an act of reprisal against Lindbergh by German and Japanese business interests, and that their guilt had been concealed by powerful figures in Wall Street, who had seen to it that the truth was suppressed by the capitalist press.

The Committee wrote that in the summer of 1931, when Herbert Hoover was president, the Republican-ruled State Department had encouraged Charles and Anne Lindbergh to fly to the Orient. China was looking to the sky; already a small fleet of American planes was making occasional flights from Shanghai. But Japanese troops were moving rapidly to occupy Manchuria, and it was expected that Shanghai would fall; worse, the Deutsch Luft Hansa Company, subsidized by the German government and international bankers friendly to Japan, was pressing the Chinese government for a contract that would give its planes a monopoly. As a semiofficial spokesman for the United States, the Committee continued, Lindbergh might be counted on to freeze out Luft Hansa and win the contract for American aviation interests. And so he had!—obtained a long-term agreement from the Chinese, making it possible for American planes with American pilots to link up Shanghai, Peiping, Nanking, Canton, Hankow, Chungking, Chengtu and other key points with a continuous passenger-and-mail air service.

Lindbergh's intervention, the Committee said, dealt Luft Hansa a lethal blow. Huge investments were wiped out and the men who had lost them were incensed. They had decided to steal the Lindberghs' baby son, delude the American people into believing it was the work of a criminal gang by demanding a ransom, and then secretly compel Lindbergh and his associates in the U.S. air industry to grant certain concessions in China in exchange for the child.

But the baby had been killed, and the out-of-pocket planners had had to abandon their scheme.

The Committee of Witnesses explained that they were privy to the plot because telltale evidence had fallen into their hands: instructions sent from the Orient to German agents in America. Richard Hauptmann and Isidor Fisch were two of these agents. Included with the directions was a complete description of the house and grounds at Hopewell, with particular attention paid to the nursery and the servants, who would help carry out the plot. Also included was the identifying symbol, an ingenious combination of two interlocking circles outlined in blue, the insignia of Luft Hansa planes in China; a solid red oval in the center, where the circles overlapped, to suggest the red ball of the Rising Sun on Japanese military aircraft; and three holes, part of a common code signature used by German secret agents in communicating with one another.

The Witnesses said that a few days after the kidnaping they had notified Charles Lindbergh, Colonel Schwarzkopf and others in a position to act of the identity of those responsible, and had supplied documentary proof. Nothing had been done about it. Throughout the long search for the child and for his abductors and murderers, and throughout the trial, the Witnesses had demanded suitable action, but they had to report that every request had been ignored and their evidence suppressed.

The Committee could only conclude that the rich and powerful Old Guard of the Republican Party regarded the crime as merely the unfortunate outcome of a family quarrel between domestic and foreign financial giants and that the truth should never be told. All decent Americans should punish the Republican party by voting against its candidates in the coming national elections.

10

Harold Hoffman had promised that he would give his reasons for questioning that the Lindbergh case had been satisfactorily settled. Going over the evidence, some of it merely puzzling, some highly suspicious, all of it demanding explanation, he thought that perhaps the time had come to do so.

First, there was the matter of Dr. Condon. Of course a few contradictions were to be expected, particularly from a man of his age, but the governor felt that in several instances Condon's discrepancies undermined the State's case. And an affidavit had come to hand that threw new light on his role in the trial; it declared that after originally failing to identify Hauptmann as John in the Greenwich Street police station, the old man had been intimidated by the police, who had reminded him that he was the sole person who had dealt with John and followed with the threat that if he didn't positively say Hauptmann was John he would be indicted as an accessory after the crime. Condon had given in. It seemed to Hoffman that any doubt in Jafsie's mind had been stifled by fear.

It had to be admitted that Condon had radioed Wilentz from Panama offering to return at once and answer any questions Governor Hoffman wished to ask, but the inspiration for that might have come from Wilentz, who had replied that there was no need for him to change his plans.

And what about Colonel Henry Breckinridge, Lindbergh's friend and adviser? During the trial, Breckinridge had told about various events in Dr. Condon's home on the night Condon and Lindbergh had set out to pay the ransom but had neglected to say that—according to other evidence Hoffman had received—he had followed them in another car and had been in the immediate vicinity of St. Raymond's Cemetery when the old man exchanged fifty thousand dollars for a worthless note of instructions. Why hadn't Breckinridge seen fit to mention this? Had he kept silent because he couldn't corroborate everything Condon had testified to about the transaction?

The State's case seemed awry in other respects. The official inventory of Hauptmann's apartment listed two letters he had received from Isidor Fisch's family after his friend's death. The letters contained statements which could not have failed to help Hauptmann. Was that why they hadn't been presented at the trial?

As for the handwriting experts who had testified for the State: everyone knew that photography played tricks on the eye—how could they be so positive, in identifying Hauptmann's writing with that of the ransom notes, that they were citing what they actually saw rather than what the exaggerations of photo-enlarging led them to see?

And Arthur Koehler. A man to be respected, nobody would deny that, honest and intelligent and dedicated to his work—but surely he had tried to prove the impossible! Was it reasonable to think that any criminal, however naïve—worse than naïve, idiotic!—would abandon at the scene of the crime a ladder built partly of wood taken from *his own attic?* Didn't it sound almost as if the evidence in the Hauptmanns' attic had been planted?

All this was damaging, but Hoffman thought it only brushed the surface. There were more serious reasons for doubt, and he was getting still others. Lieutenant Robert W. Hicks, a Washington criminologist Hauptmann's counsel had referred to him, had come up with some interesting clues. And of course Ellis Parker, working independently, was making his own investigation.

Lloyd Fisher and his colleagues were anxious to help but there wasn't much more they could do. The defense fund was gone and efforts to replenish it had failed. Hauptmann had even written his autobiography, thirty-six thousand words in painstaking German script, hoping to sell it, but so far no one had made a bid. If the editor of an astrology magazine hadn't become interested in the case and offered to pay for a private investigation, they wouldn't have the benefit of Lieutenant Hicks' services.

The governor told himself that it wasn't enough. If the discrepancies were to be resolved, the whole truth pried out, the State of New Jersey would have to make a new official inquiry. Strictly speaking he need give the reasons for it only to the State police, but he had promised to justify his stand to the public, and it would be just as well to accomplish both at once.

On Thursday January 30, at State police headquarters, Colonel Schwarzkopf received a letter and a brief from the governor. The letter directed him to renew his investigation of the kidnap-murder of Charles Augustus Lindbergh, Jr., and make "a thorough and impartial search for the detection and apprehension of every person" connected with it. He was not satisfied, Governor Hoffman wrote, that the execution of Bruno Richard Hauptmann would be full punishment for the crime; there was too much evidence that others had participated in it, and allowing them to go scot-free would be as grave an offense against justice as would the execution of an innocent man. The governor knew that Schwarzkopf thought it a remote possibility, but "a complete and searching inquiry may prevent a tragic error." In any case it would resolve the doubts of a great many people. He would expect a weekly progress report.

Schwarzkopf turned to the brief. It posed nineteen questions to which Governor Hoffman wanted answers:

> Who was the person to whom John had said, during a telephone conversation with Dr. Condon, that the latter wrote articles for the newspapers? Who was the Italian who had spoken curtly to John, apparently directing him? Was he the same person or someone else?

Schwarzkopf ran down the incident in his mind, remembering that Dr. Condon had said it had taken place during an early phase of the ransom negotiations, when he had distinctly heard over the phone the Italian words *statti citto.*

> Who was the woman, also apparently Italian, who had spoken so mysteriously to Dr. Condon, telling him (he said) to meet her at the Tuckahoe station?

Schwarzkopf remembered the old man had said that she had promised to deliver a message to him, and since he hadn't heard from John for some time he had been inclined to believe that he would get a note of instructions from her; but although he had kept the rendezvous, she hadn't.

> Why hadn't the State police questioned Dr. Condon about the $250,000 bribe he said he had been offered? Since Hauptmann was in prison and couldn't have made the offer, who was his alleged accomplice?

This, Schwarzkopf knew, referred to the statement Condon had made to a newspaper reporter some weeks ago. He had claimed that it was an attempt to make him change his story and pave the way for clemency for Hauptmann by putting the blame on Isidor Fisch.

Not without irony, the governor summed up his questions in another question:

> Is not Dr. Condon, whose word was so greatly relied upon by the prosecution, believed when he says, "I am still convinced that more than one person is involved in this crime"?

The brief then pointed out that in his earlier statements Charles Lindbergh had been of the opinion the crime was the work of a gang and that Condon had been in touch with the gang, the actual kidnapers. Then why had he entered into negotiations with John Hughes Curtis? What did Curtis say, or show to him, that persuaded him that Curtis was dealing with the kidnapers? Was the deciding factor Curtis' description of a member of the gang, called John, who exactly tallied with Jafsie's description of *his* John? Wasn't it true that, shortly before the Hauptmann trial, the State had brought Curtis to Philadelphia and put him up at a hotel, paying all expenses; that he refused to say that John—*his* John—wasn't a member of a gang; and that consequently the affidavit he gave to Assistant Attorney General Robert Peacock wasn't used as part of the State's case?

And how did all this fit in with the State's accusations against Hauptmann and against Curtis, who had been charged with having known the whereabouts of the abductors and wilfully withholding this information from the authorities? "Was the State right," Governor Hoffman asked, "in obtaining a conviction of Curtis based on obstructing justice after having had contact with a 'gang' of kidnapers—or was the State right in prosecuting Hauptmann as a 'lone wolf'? Since it is evident that the prosecution was wrong in either one case or the other, is it not obvious that the State and the courts are not infallible and that every possible inquiry is warranted before final action is taken in this important case?"

Schwarzkopf hadn't expected to escape untouched; but when they came, the blows were relatively mild. Hoffman quoted a statement he had given to the press a month or so after the kidnaping in which he had expressed the opinion that two gangsters, Harry Fleisher and Abie Wagner, were connected with it. More damaging, perhaps, was his stated conviction—in which Inspector Harry Walsh joined—that Violet Sharpe was implicated in the crime.

There was more. Did it seem possible that one of the baby's thumbguards could lie in the driveway to the Lindbergh house for a whole month without being found? Wasn't it easier to believe that it had been deliberately put there, just before its alleged discovery, by accomplices inside or outside the household? Since the thumbguard had been found by Betty Gow and Elsie Whateley, the implication, Schwarzkopf thought, was clear; but what would be their motive?

Finally, J. J. Faulkner. Since everyone agreed that the $2980 exchange slip signed with this name was not in Hauptmann's writing, the governor wanted to know why the search for Faulkner had been abandoned.

Colonel Schwarzkopf telephoned Wilentz. Yes, he had received a copy of the brief, and so had the newspapers. The two men agreed to meet the next day to discuss what to do.

After they had talked it over, Wilentz issued a reply to the questions. It was very much to the point. Hauptmann and Hauptmann alone was guilty of the crime.

Schwarzkopf's position hardly permitted him to behave so cavalierly. In an answering letter, he promised the governor his full cooperation and asked to have any new evidence that had come into his superior's possession.

A few days later he wrote two more letters, one to J. Edgar Hoover of the Federal Bureau of Investigation, the other to Commissioner Valentine of the New York City police, asking them to reassign to the Lindbergh case the same agents and detectives who had made the original investigation. The police commissioner's reply, obviously carefully composed, applauded Schwarzkopf's zeal and said nothing about lending a hand. United States Attorney General Homer Cummings, answering in a letter for Hoover, was less diplomatic. In view of the fact that nothing of any consequence had happened in the Lindbergh case since Hauptmann's arrest, the Department of Justice was not interested in devoting more time and attention to it.

11

But a private citizen in the nation's capital was interested in devoting more time and attention to the case, even though the memory of her lost $104,000 and the abuse of her confidence by the cynical Gaston B. Means still rankled. Mrs. Evalyn Walsh McLean was dissatisfied with the declared solution of the crime and felt that its loose ends should be gathered up. She had read with sympathetic attention about Governor Hoffman's activities, which seemed to her courageous and commendable. Surely Bruno Richard Hauptmann was not solely guilty!—and surely the other, unnamed criminals should be run to earth and punished!

How could she help?

She had been taken for a ride, as the man in the street would say (a thrilling one, admittedly; whatever else might be said of him, Gaston Means was not lacking in flair), and Mrs. McLean didn't care for another. She would deal only with fully accredited people, not with a falsely penitent rogue (now behind bars, with some fourteen years of his sentence still to run). She was acquainted with Robert Hicks, the Washington criminologist who was working with Governor Hoffman on the case, and she would ask him if her good offices could be used.

Lieutenant Hicks referred Mrs. McLean's question to Hoffman, and the governor answered at once that of course she could help. Help was badly needed—financial help. The defense fund was broke and the New Jersey legislature felt diffident, at best, about spending taxpayers' money to aid their chief executive's investigation.

Hoffman was sure he had an excellent idea how to use additional money. Richard Hauptmann alone knew all the facts; only if he would tell them could the case be brought to a quick, and genuine, close. But he kept on insisting that he was innocent, had nothing to confess, and Lloyd Fisher backed him up. Who could make Hauptmann talk? There was a man in New York who might turn the trick, Sam Leibowitz, the famous criminal lawyer. Governor Hoffmann told Hicks to sound out Mrs. McLean on the idea; if she thought well of it, the governor would try to get Leibowitz to enter the case.

Mrs. McLean replied through Hicks that she would gladly pay for the lawyer's services.

On Thursday evening, February 6, Hoffman had a talk with Leibowitz in New York. Leibowitz was by no means a stranger to the case; the governor had listened to his comments over the radio on the trial while it was in progress. The lawyer didn't shilly-shally about the trial's conclusion that one man was responsible for the kidnap-murder; he said it was "nonsense."

The governor suggested that Leibowitz visit Mrs. McLean and see if they could come to mutually satisfactory terms. Leibowitz was amenable. That Sunday, he went down to Friendship, Mrs. McLean's Washington place.

At forty-three, Samuel Simon Leibowitz was as energetic and colorful in his public life as he was sedate in his private one, which he spent chiefly at home in Brooklyn with his wife Belle, his twin sons Robert and Lawrence and his daughter Marjorie. He had a solid, healthy body, an infinitely expressive face and voice, a booming laugh, and hair that was thinning out. His quick eyes reflected the dauntless curiosity of his mind. He had worked his way up in the world from humble beginnings as the son of a Rumanian immigrant on New York's Lower East Side, a forcing ground for talent. After graduating from Cornell, he began to practice civil law as a member of a large law firm, and after two years was making thirty-five dollars a week. But if those years were lean, the discovery they led to held promise: he found that he had a virtuoso's gift for criminal law. His first exercises in the field, performed gratis, restored poverty-stricken thieves to their friends and their relations; by and by, in 1919, he opened his own office. Within a few years he had defended so many underworld figures so successfully that Al Capone retained him in the matter of a triple-murder charge. Capone's instinct was sure: his young lawyer brought him off scot-free.

By 1932, when he was thirty-nine, Sam Leibowitz was the best-known criminal lawyer in New York, and deserved to be: he had defended seventy-eight men charged with murder in the first degree and had won no less than seventy-seven acquittals; even the seventy-eighth case was not a conviction but a disagreement, hardly a blot on his shield. These triumphs were not due to sheer legal sleight-of-hand or theatrics, although they had their part; Leibowitz believed in preparing his ground as thoroughly as a Duke of Wellington, and after drying a freshet of tears or calming a voice raised high in denunciation of the prosecution's wiles he could argue on equal terms with medical or ballistics experts.

For the past three years, in addition to his regular practice Leibowitz had served without fee as chief defense counsel for the Scottsboro Boys, the nine young Negroes who had been indicted in 1931 in Scottsboro, Alabama, on charges of having raped two white girls while all were hitching a ride on a freight train. By 1936 the case had been fought twice to the Supreme Court, stirring violent partisanship: either the girls were models of virtue or, in another view, their morality was somewhat less than unconquerable, having been trifled with if not stamped on by lily-white (epithelially speaking) admirers. The battle wasn't over. It brought Leibowitz international attention; even his bitterest critics did not say that that possibility had been his reason for entering the case.

In the same living room where, a few weeks less than four years ago, Gaston Means had pitched his tale, Sam Leibowitz told Mrs. McLean how he felt about the Lindbergh case. The key, of course, was Hauptmann. If he refused to change his story, only new and conclusive evidence would reopen the case. He was willing to talk to Hauptmann, Leibowitz said, but until then he couldn't promise to engage in his defense. If he did, Mrs. McLean replied, she would pay him a retainer of $10,000 and another $15,000 if he succeeded in solving the crime.

Lieutenant Hicks was delegated to prepare the way for Leibowitz' appearance on the small, somber stage of the death house. Hicks did so by speaking to Anna Hauptmann, telling her that a world-famous lawyer was interested in coming to Richard's aid, with Governor Hoffman's approval; but, he added, if Mr. Leibowitz did join the defense staff, it would mean that he rather than Lloyd Fisher would have to be recognized as its chief counselor. Would she and Richard agree to this? Anna said she would ask Richard.

She brought the news and the question to Richard the next Tuesday, February 11. Anna thought it would be fine to have Mr. Leibowitz on their side, and she recited some of his achievements, as described to her by Hicks. Mr. Fisher was a true friend but it seemed there wasn't much more he could do. They wouldn't be getting rid of him; they could never do that; they would simply be bringing in a powerful new ally—if Richard said yes.

Hauptmann thought it over. Good, he said.

Thursday February 13 marked the first anniversary of the conviction, with no recommendation for mercy, of Bruno Richard Hauptmann—surely an appropriate day to usher in a man in whose stated opinion the verdict was nonsense. Sam Leibowitz was introduced to Hauptmann by Anna. The two men inspected each other. Leibowitz had seen many pictures and read many heavily flavored descriptions of Richard Hauptmann, but the lawyer was a stranger to the convict.

Leibowitz did not spend time on generalities but started with facts. The thirty-day reprieve the governor had granted would expire the day after tomorrow and some time during the next week Judge Trenchard would appoint a new date for the execution. Unless new evidence was discovered, there wasn't a chance that Hauptmann would not keep that date with the chair. Even if two of the State's main witnesses—Dr. Condon, who had identified him as the man to whom he had given the ransom money, and Amandus Hochmuth, who had placed him near the scene of the crime on the day of the crime—should waver, even if they should contradict themselves under aggressive examination, justifying a new trial—even then, Leibowitz said flatly, Hauptmann would be convicted again. That was his estimate of the state of things, and he knew what he was talking about.

There was one hope, and if Hauptmann thought there was any other reason for hope he was cruelly deluding himself. If he didn't wish to sit in that chair next door, he would have to tell the truth and name the people who had carried out the crime with him.

The lawyer was silent. Hauptmann stared at him.

Leibowitz had read about Richard Hauptmann's cold blue eyes and his icy reserve and his steely will and all the rest of it.

Hauptmann's shoulders trembled. He bent his head; he wept.

Anna took him in her arms.

For a while Leibowitz listened to the unlikely sound of Richard Hauptmann sobbing and to Anna's pitying voice. Well, he said, he would leave now. Maybe they would think over everything he had said. He would come back for another talk on Sunday.

When Leibowitz returned to the cell, he brought with him two bound volumes of the trial transcript. He wasn't alone. The second man to enter the cell had been there before, to offer solace; he was the Reverend John Matthiesen, a Lutheran minister of Trenton.

Hauptmann seemed calm. The lawyer opened the big books. Now he said, he was going to show the prisoner's trial testimony to him from the point of view of the law. Here were the weak spots; and his swift finger burrowed through the pages and ran down the questions and answers and drew hard invisible lines under the crucial words, the faltering words that seemed to shout: this *isn't* the truth! Once in a while he would look up from the pages and seem to talk at random, but it was anything but that; he was prying into and attacking the "icy reserve," the "steely will." Then he would go back to the testimony and riddle its thin fabric.

At last Leibowitz closed the books. He had spent three and a half hours in the cell. He thought he had made progress; he didn't, after all, exactly count on seeing Richard Hauptmann cry every time.

He would pay him another visit in a few days, Leibowitz said, and left.

That evening he reported to the governor in his South Amboy home. Hoffman agreed that there had been progress.

Leibowitz' third visit started at two o'clock in the afternoon of Wednesday the nineteenth. Lloyd Fisher accompanied him. In a sense they were rivals, and despite Liebowitz' announced preeminence it had been impossible to avoid a certain small battle between them for position, since their really significant rivalry consisted in Fisher's belief that his client was wholly innocent and Leibowitz' that he was anyway partly guilty; but Fisher bore the other no ill will, he wished only to help him; as colleagues, they broke the news to Hauptmann that three hours ago Judge Trenchard had signed a new death warrant.

The prisoner was to die during the week of March 30.

Leibowitz had convinced many juries; this was a one-man jury. He was determined to walk out of the cell with the jury's decision in his favor; that is to say, with a full confession. That there *was* a full confession to be wrung from Richard Hauptmann, the lawyer had not the slightest doubt. And he was going to get it. Why not? He had caused this man to weep, hadn't he? Had that ever been done before? He began his argument, while Fisher sat quietly, not interrupting.

Hauptmann's counselors, Leibowitz said—Lloyd Fisher here and Pope and Rosecrans—had made every possible legal move to save him. They had taken his case to the highest court in the country. There was nothing more they could do. So it was up to him, Richard Hauptmann. He must confess. He must admit his part in the crime and name his accomplices. Then a new appeal could be made to the New Jersey Court of Pardons. The almost certain result would be that the death sentence would be commuted to life imprisonment.

He *must* tell the truth. How could he pretend that the whole truth was set forth in his trial testimony? Look at the flaws in it —here and here and here and here! Was he going to go to his death still protesting that those lies were the truth when the truth could save him? Was he? Well?

In a voice that made Leibowitz wonder if this was the man who had wept the other day, Hauptmann said that they were not lies, they *were* the truth. He had told the truth. He had nothing more to tell.

Leibowitz retraced his argument. After four and a half hours he got the same answer.

He was beaten. He said good-by to Hauptmann and left the cell.

Reporters were waiting outside the prison gate and Leibowitz told them he'd failed, he didn't have a confession, and therefore he was withdrawing. Lloyd Fisher said that of course he and his two associates were going right on in their attempts to prove Hauptmann's innocence.

He thought a moment and added a few words:

"It must be admitted that the outlook is dark."

Governor Hoffman admitted his disappointment, but he still thought the true answer to the case would be found. He would instruct the State police to double their efforts.

Mrs. McLean was distressed by the news. She felt sure, though, that Mr. Leibowitz had done his best. He had.

12

Colonel Schwarzkopf wound up his fourth weekly report to the governor on the State police's new investigation with the names of five of his officers who, he said, had been approached by the govenor's agents and asked to describe how evidence against Hauptmann had been framed. They had been promised that in return for the information they would be guaranteed their jobs next June; the agents had told them that Schwarzkopf would be replaced as police superintendent at that time. If they didn't cooperate, they'd be fired.

If Schwarzkopf had felt angry about these alleged tactics, he had refrained from saying so in his report; but Governor Hoffman could imagine what he was thinking. It seemed to Hoffman beyond argument that some of the State's case *had* been framed; he had the proof, in statements taken from the State police files.

Whether or not anyone had gone a little too far in trying to get all the facts was of small consequence, in his opinion, compared to the deliberate concealment of a large, ugly truth.

Just a week ago he had tried to pin down and expose it. Millard Whited, the Sourlands hillbilly who had linked Hauptmann to the time and place of the kidnaping and helped the State extradite him from New York to New Jersey, had given several statements to the police. In at least one of them he had clearly lied.

Lieutenant Arthur Keaton and other officers of the State police had visited Whited at his farmhouse several hours after the kidnaping. He told them he'd twice seen a stranger in the vicinity of the Lindbergh estate during the two weeks preceding the crime. But on the following April 26, he had denied the whole thing to State detectives—he hadn't seen anyone. Then, in a statement taken by Trooper Joseph Wolfe on October 6, 1934, he had described how, after Hauptmann's arrest, Wolfe had called on him, urged him to go to the Bronx and see the suspect, and promised that if he did Whited's expenses and loss of time from his logging job would more than be made up to him.

Whited had agreed and Captain John Lamb had taken him to the Bronx County jail, where he had positively identified Hauptmann as the stranger he had said originally he saw lurking near the Lindbergh place. He had confirmed this identification at the trial—but in almost the same breath had admitted that before he was asked to pick out his suspicious stranger from the police line-up he was shown two photographs of Hauptmann.

And he had admitted that when the police turned up at his farmhouse on that March morning in 1932 his first thought was that they suspected him of being the thief who had pulled off a job in the nearby village of Blawemburg two evenings ago; they hadn't said they were looking for the Lindbergh kidnaper—at that point, Whited hadn't known the baby was missing.

This switching back and forth had struck Hoffman as highly questionable, and for nearly three hours he and Anthony Hauck and Lloyd Fisher had examined Whited. The hillbilly had freely declared that he had decided to oblige the State police and go to the Bronx partly because Trooper Wolfe had told him that if he did he'd probably get one third of the twenty-five thousand dollar reward offered by New Jersey for the apprehension of the kidnaper-killer.

Later, Hoffman had said that he thought it all boiled down to this:

(1) Whited had lied in his first story, for fear of being arrested as the Blawemburg thief; (2) in his second story, long after learning

that he had nothing to fear, he had told the truth, that he had made up the story of the stranger; (3) then, tempted by promises of payment and the chance of sharing in the reward, and having seen the photos of Hauptmann, he had switched to his original yarn and identified him as the stranger.

Whited had insisted that his first story and trial testimony were true; that he had made his contradictory second statement to the State detectives because he suspected they weren't what they claimed to be.

There the matter had rested, with Hauck ready to summon the Flemington grand jury if either the governor or Fisher would sign a complaint charging Whited with perjury; but both Hoffman and Fisher had felt that the evidence simply wasn't that conclusive.

Another identifying witness had been cast in a dubious light by the information he had given the State police—the Bronx cabby, John Joseph Perrone. After the baby's body was found, Perrone had been taken to see one suspect after another, and had partly identified several as the man who had handed him the note for Dr. Condon. And in March 1934, after looking at a suspect named Otto Steiner, who had just been taken into custody in the Bronx for burglary, Perrone had told the State police that while he wasn't completely sure, he was *reasonably* certain this was the man. Two months later he had said so again, more emphatically. But in September he had claimed that Richard Hauptmann was the man he had had in mind all along!

Governor Hoffman had asked himself just how in the world Perrone could have been reasonably sure of Steiner and absolutely sure of Hauptmann when the one no more resembled the other than Dr. Condon resembled one of Singer's midgets!

David Wilentz had displayed no eagerness to clear up these inconsistencies. Returning from his Florida vacation, he had told reporters that he would resist every attempt to recall any State witnesses for "persecution or to satisfy the whim of an individual." It was perfectly clear to the governor who the individual was.

And now here was Schwarzkopf accusing him of intimidating the police!

Hoffman called in a secretary and dictated a stiff note. He wasn't interested in receiving further perfunctory reports each week telling him in effect that another conference had been held. If Schwarzkopf felt that the Lindbergh case had been completely solved, that Hauptmann was the only one who had had a hand in it, then it was his duty to answer the questions the governor had put to him a month ago. In the meantime, he should keep in mind that the case was widely referred to as the most bungled in police history. It was in his interest as well as the public's to clear it up.

"Had ordinary sound police methods been used following the commission of the crime," Hoffman concluded, "many doubts entertained today might have been eliminated and two and a half years might not have elapsed before the arrest of a person who, through the efforts of a gasoline attendant and a bank teller, could be charged with the crime."

13

Charles and Anne Lindbergh had found the privacy they wanted. It was an almost incredible experience for them. A whole week had gone by after their arrival in Llandaff without a single appearance of their names in the British press, and very little had been printed about them in the following weeks.

But they wanted a place of their own. Mrs. Dwight Morrow's friend Harold Nicolson and his wife, the novelist V. Sackville-West, had a suggestion. The Nicolsons lived in Sissinghurst Castle, near the village of Weald, in Kent. They owned a house in the village and they thought the Lindberghs would like living there. It was called Long Barn, a big, comfortable old house. The decent, orderly people of Weald could be relied on not to interfere with newcomers, no matter how famous, and would give only a cool welcome to intrusive reporters if any appeared, which was doubtful.

Protected by the Weald and English tradition of leaving one's neighbor to his own devices, Long Barn was doubly protected by its high surrounding brick wall and location at the end of the village. Charles and Anne liked it instantly. Weald was soaked in time and tranquility. If they felt in the mood for friendly talk, the Nicolsons were nearby; and London was only some thirty miles away, if they wanted a complete change.

They began to feel like everyday people. They could look out the windows without seeing a single policeman. Not even a reporter.

Charles turned to the pursuits that engrossed him, and Anne to hers.

He fixed up a laboratory in a wing of the house. His job, or problem, which Alexis Carrel had proposed, was to cap the triumph of the mechanical heart with a mechanical kidney, no less essential to a perfusion pump—to dispose of the waste matter of the living organs placed in it—than to a human body. With test tubes and Bunsen burner he struggled for creation.

In another room Anne sent her mind traveling through the high blue reaches of her aerial voyages with Charles and tried to capture their lonely poetry in a book.

Jon had his more agile pleasures and the taste of an astonishing freedom. The reason for slackening the reins on his movements wasn't explained to him, but it was simple: England's crime records had yet to show a kidnaping. He played in the garden and greatly favored the swing that some kind swing-lover had hung from a huge tree. His mother or father often gave him a push, although that wasn't really necessary for a person of his growing independence. In return he lent his mother a hand in the garden, digging holes and putting odds and ends in them and disposing of weeds. A set of miniature tools was presented to him for these labors. After a pleasant, sunny interval Anne would thank him for his assistance and go back to her writing table and Jon would return to the swing and listen to the mysterious sounds coming from his father's end of the house and wonder about them. This was a good life.

In America, Charles and Anne saw in the British papers, kidnaping was still rather commonplace.

14

Dr. Dudley Shoenfeld was extremely anxious for the convicted Lindbergh kidnaper to escape the electric chair. The doctor's concern came not so much from the fact that many people doubted Hauptmann's guilt, a doubt Shoenfeld didn't share, as from his knowledge of the benefits that would accrue to the practice of criminal psychiatry if Hauptmann would confess and reveal his psychic drives. Such a potential bonanza would disappear with the savage whine of the electric current in the death chamber.

How long would it require to get a confession from him? More time than was left. Shoenfeld had followed in the newspapers Samuel Leibowitz' efforts to crack Hauptmann's silence. He could have foretold their failure; from all he knew of the convicted man's personality, no other outcome was to be expected.

Of course some progress had been made toward establishing psychiatry in the eyes of the law as a respectable handmaiden in the solution of a crime and the apprehension of a criminal, and Shoenfeld was grateful for the degree to which the police had permitted him to work with them; but what a great distance there was still to go! And how powerfully a searching psychoanalysis of Richard Hauptmann would illustrate to the authorities in particular and the public in general the point psychiatrists were striving to make: that a crime was merely a symptom of the criminal's mental illness.

Shoenfeld was fairly confident that Hauptmann was no exception to this rule. His early analysis of the then still-unknown kidnaper's motive and personality had suggested that the man was in a state of dementia praecox, and the facts that had come out after Hauptmann's arrest, plus Shoenfeld's careful day-by-day observations of him during the trial, had strengthened the diagnosis. But this was of small significance; the question as to whether or not Hauptmann was mentally ill hadn't been conclusively answered.

According to long-standing legal definition—the ability to know the nature and quality of the act, the difference between right and wrong—Hauptmann was "sane." But there the law and psychiatry were in conflict; to psychiatrists, the law hadn't advanced beyond the bad old days of the English bedlams, when the definition had been handed down by a learned judge. Certainly the law had every right to decree punishment for an individual of asocial behavior, but punishment wouldn't cure him of his motivating illness. The day to be fought for was the day when the law, in pronouncing sentence, would make provision for the criminal's psychiatric treatment and care, after having taken his illness into account in determining that sentence.

It was true that, once in the Bronx and once in Flemington, Hauptmann had been examined by qualified psychiatrists. But these examinations had been so confined by legal barriers that from a medical point of view they were, to say the least, unorthodox and would be disregarded in private practice. To be of genuine value, an analysis of the individual's personality must not be cramped for time and must be made with his cooperation. Dudley Shoenfeld knew that if he knew anything.

Given time, he was confident he could win Hauptmann's cooperation. But Hauptmann had barely a month to live.

What could be done?

Perhaps, Shoenfeld thought, a meeting could be arranged for him with Governor Hoffman, whose interest in the case was well known.

Who could arrange it?

Well, there was a famous columnist who seemed to have the governor's ear—

The psychiatrist and the governor met in Walter Winchell's

home. Shoenfeld explained his views. Hoffman replied that his own actions spoke for him. He believed that some of the evidence had either been framed or tampered with, and that while Hauptmann undoubtedly was involved in the crime he wasn't completely guilty. He was a father, the governor said, and he wouldn't lift a finger to save a justly convicted kidnaper and killer from the chair; no, sir!—he'd pull the switch. David Wilentz was against capital punishment; not he.

He agreed that psychiatry should have a place in the process of criminal law, Hoffman continued; indeed, he hoped to add two psychiatrists to the panel of members of the New Jersey Court of Pardons; but he was concerned with Hauptmann's fate only because he thought his execution would cut off any chance of ever finding and punishing his accomplices.

Shoenfeld listened respectfully. Then he spoke up. He had arranged for enough money to be provided to permit an exhaustive psychiatric study of Hauptmann and the kidnaping and killing, with no time limit; but it could only be done if the sentence was reduced to life imprisonment. What steps could they take to bring that about?

The technicalities of the Jersey law were such, the governor answered, that only one course was open: he, Wilentz and Shoenfeld would have to petition Justice Trenchard to permit them to examine Hauptmann. If as a result Hauptmann confessed, then the governor would convene the Court of Pardons and, with Wilentz's approval and cooperation and Shoenfeld's support, would formally appeal for a commutation of the death sentence.

The psychiatrist was doubtful of this scheme and told Hoffman why. Richard Hauptmann was convinced the governor was on his side and had assured himself that so long as that was true he wouldn't die. They would get nowhere if they examined him while the idea was fixed in his head. Even the newspapers were saying that Governor Hoffman meant to grant another reprieve.

The papers knew everything, the governor said bitterly, but he would tell Shoenfeld right now that he hadn't the slightest intention of reprieving Hauptmann without excellent cause.

Shoenfeld urged: Get that across to him! Make him and Anna Hauptmann believe that unless he confessed he was going to die as ordered during the week of March 30! *Then* they'd examine him.

Harold Hoffman promised that he would—"and in no uncertain terms." Also, he'd see if he could get Wilentz to go along with them about the examinations. But he had to add that his relations with the attorney general of the state weren't too cordial at present.

15

Dr. Condon returned home from his holiday of more than two months brimming over with health and energy, but exasperated. Didn't he have good and sufficient reason? Had a patriotic citizen ever been more put upon? It was fortunate he had always been able to control his temper, or he'd boil over.

During his stay in Panama he had followed all reported developments in the Lindbergh case, but not with pleasure. This man Hoffman seemed to have set out maliciously to impugn his character, his motives and behavior. He had implied that John F. Condon was a liar and an opportunist. He had even suggested that his vacation trip, surely more than deserved, possessed some evil significance.

Enough was enough. Dr. Condon intended to have it out with Hoffman, but on *his* terms.

No, he told reporters, he wasn't going to make the journey to Trenton, where Hoffman hatched his innuendoes and aspersions, to submit to an inquiry, but he was willing to receive the man as a guest in his home in the beautiful Bronx. He would give him a good dinner from Mrs. Condon's own hands and talk with him over cigars as long as he desired. But of course David Wilentz, as prosecutor in the case, would have to be present.

That evening, March 17, the inflammatory information was brought to Dr. Condon that Governor Hoffman could not accept the invitation so long as it included Wilentz, since in effect the latter would be acting as Dr. Condon's counsel and therefore a free and full response to the governor's questions could not be expected. Dr. Condon would have to leave Wilentz out.

He would *not,* the old man said.

There the matter uneasily rested.

But a few evenings later a telegram came from the governor and in it he sang quite a different tune. He said he was sure that Dr. Condon stood ready to cooperate in every way to clear up the doubts about the case and bring to the bar of justice anyone who had had anything to do with the crime, and in the same spirit of cooperation the governor would be glad to talk with him in his home *with* Wilentz and any other guest Dr. Condon wished to invite.

The victory was sweet. Dr. Condon could not resist making it a little sweeter. He took up his pen to compose a telegram in reply.

Yes indeed, he wrote, he was interested in justice, and he looked forward to receiving the governor whenever it would be convenient for him to come to the Bronx. Also, he would ask Mr. Wilentz. The governor understood, of course, that all questions would have to be submitted in writing beforehand. He would answer them in the same way.

The telegram got warmer.

It was interesting to note, Dr. Condon observed, that although Hoffman had been governor of New Jersey throughout the trial, he had waited until the very eve of Dr. Condon's leaving on a holiday to announce that he was wanted for questioning, and had taken advantage of his absence to hurl malicious untruths at his head. "I have concluded," the telegram went on, "because of your reported activities and of utterances attributed to you in the public press that you are disqualified from conducting an impartial examination on a fair basis. I do not believe that you have any legal authority or justification for your present activities, and I further seriously doubt your sincerity and good faith.

"Although you have apparently usurped the functions of the courts and the duly constituted investigating officials, and despite your unfairness, I have nevertheless decided to permit you to confer with me at my home as indicated above."

It was quite a long telegram. Thoughtfully, Dr. Condon wrote "collect" at the top.

Governor Hoffman shook his head over it. He had given in against his better judgment about Wilentz's presence, and now the old man wanted the questions and answers to be in writing, which in effect could mean that the answers would be dictated by Wilentz and merely signed by Dr. Condon. There'd be no point in such an inquiry; somehow he'd have to persuade him of that.

But here was an astonishing development from another quarter, some papers that U.S. Attorney General Cummings had sent the governor.

In the federal penitentiary at Leavenworth, Kansas, Gaston B. Means had confessed that *he* was responsible for the kidnaping and murder of the Lindbergh baby. Others had helped him, but not Richard Hauptmann. Hauptmann was completely innocent.

Means' confession gave the details of the crime. The whole thing had started when a mentally unbalanced relative of Anne Lindbergh, wanting the little boy out of the way, had hired him to steal and kill the child. Max Hassel and Max Greenberg had taken part in the plot. A woman, unnamed, had waited beside the ladder while Means climbed down from the nursery. He had fallen and dropped the baby. The woman and he had fled into the woods, where they had finished off the injured child.

In Homer Cummings' opinion there wasn't a word of truth in the revolting story. It bore considerable resemblance to the tale Means had told almost three years ago, in that two of the principals, Hassel and Greenberg, were dead; the third, the unidentified woman, was no doubt fictitious. The Justice Department had thoroughly investigated the previous confession and had found it to be a lie from beginning to end. Cummings said he was convinced that this new lie was a transparent attempt to gain temporary liberty.

Governor Hoffman had to agree.

Bruno Richard Hauptmann, Warden Kimberling announced from the New Jersey State prison, would be placed in the electric chair at eight o'clock in the evening of Tuesday March 31.

16

Arthur Koehler was faced with a situation that to his orderly mind seemed incomprehensible. Of course he had known that Governor Hoffman had said it was beyond belief that anyone planning such a sensational crime would be so simple-minded as to use wood from his own attic flooring in part of the kidnap ladder, when wood that could not be so positively identified could easily be obtained from an anonymous source; but hadn't Hauptmann's behavior at the trial shown that he had a blinding sense of omnipotence, as Dudley Shoenfeld had observed?

Quite apart from that, Koehler's findings had been so clear and conclusive that he couldn't imagine how any intelligent person could fail to be persuaded by them.

And yet now Governor Hoffman intended to prove that the evidence in the attic had been framed!

David Wilentz had telephoned Koehler at the Forest Service Laboratory and given him the news. Apparently it worried the attorney general, even though he had said that he knew it was a wild-goose chase. Could Koehler manage to be there when Hoffman put his theories to the test? Koehler's testimony had not only traced the ladder to Hauptmann but had placed him at the scene of the crime on the night of the crime, and it was only too obvious what the consequences might be if somehow or other the governor's demonstration cast doubt on the validity of the wood evidence.

The demonstration was to take place in Hauptmann's attic. Koehler had assured Wilentz that he would be present.

In Trenton, the attorney general supplied him with the details. Arch Loney, a wood technician in the Public Works Administration, had bolstered the governor in his belief that Rail 16, the left-hand Southern pine rail in the top section of the ladder, had not come from a floorboard in the attic, as the State had contended. Loney had questioned Koehler's findings when he read about them in his Washington paper while the trial was in progress, but he had rejected Edward Reilly's invitation to testify for the defense because there wasn't time for him to examine the ladder and the attic thoroughly. Recently, though, with the aid of Robert Hicks and other investigators acting for the defense, Loney had been conducting experiments in the attic and apparently had persuaded Governor Hoffman that there was no truth in Koehler's tie-up of the ladder rail and the attic floorboard.

Was it possible, Arthur Koehler wondered, that his calculations had been wrong? He reviewed them in his mind. His companion in the long search, Detective Lewis Bornmann, had told him that in the attic of Hauptmann's house a portion of one floorboard was missing, and that in the joists—the beams that had supported the missing portion—there were nailholes, with a sprinkle of sawdust on the lath-and-plaster flooring. Bornmann had led him to the spot and Koehler had seen that, sure enough, one of the floorboards had been sawed in half and one of the halves removed. Moreover, the board was Southern pine, as was Rail 16, and the nailholes in the exposed beams were square, as were the four holes in the ladder rail, all having been made by old-fashioned square-cut nails.

Koehler had placed Rail 16 over the joists and it fitted snugly into the open slit. Then he had taken four cut nails and, despite the irregular pattern of the holes in the ladder rail and their individual and uniquely contrasting angles, had lightly thumb-tapped the nails through the rail holes into an identical pattern of holes in one of the joists, a penetration so complete and unresisted that the nail heads were flush with the wood.

From that fact alone, Koehler thought, it should be plain beyond the shadow of a doubt that the ladder rail had once been part of the attic floor. But there was further proof. The pattern of the wood itself, the grain of Rail 16, perfectly matched the pattern of the Southern pine floorboard from which the missing strip had been cut.

What could Loney have found to contradict this evidence?

Koehler soon learned. On Thursday morning March 26, led by Governor Hoffman's stocky figure, he, David Wilentz, Anthony

Hauck, Arch Loney and Lewis Bornmann—now a detective sergeant—entered the small frame-and-stucco house in the Bronx and, while other States police officers waited in the apartment itself, entered the small linen closet off the hall and one by one squeezed themselves through the open hatch in the ceiling to the dark, musty, low-roofed attic.

They had brought with them both Rail 16 and the half-length of attic floorboard Bornmann had ordered removed for safekeeping after Koehler had satisfied himself that originally the two had been one piece. Koehler watched closely as they were fitted into the vacant space in the attic flooring. As before, there was an inch-and-a-quarter gap between the ends of the two boards. The gap was familiar enough to Koehler; when he first saw it, he surmised that that ladder-builder had found the board for Ladder Rail 16 too long and had cut part of it off.

It was pointed out to Koehler now that in every other board in the attic floor seven perpendicular nails were driven, but that in the board from which the State contended the ladder rail had been cut, *twenty-five* perpendicular nails had been driven. Didn't this indicate that the disputed board had never been part of the flooring?

No, it didn't, Koehler replied; it simply indicated that the board in question, which was at one edge of the attic floor, had very likely been the first to be laid, and for that reason had been nailed into place more tightly than the others.

Well then, he was asked, what about the fact that the disputed board was a sixteenth of an inch thicker than the yellow pine boards that were laid? And that, counting from the center of the attic, there were already thirteen floorboards on either side? With Koehler's board added, it would mean that the attic was off balance, with more floorboards on one side than on the other.

Taking these objections in order, Koehler pointed out that uneven flooring was common to unfinished attics, and that since only the middle area of the attic was floored—the joists and plaster being exposed on both sides, where the roof slanted low—whether there was an even or an odd number of boards was simply a matter of the carpenter's choice.

Another question. The half-length of board Koehler had said he had seen in the attic had been sawed straight, while the saw-cut Hauptmann was supposed to have made in removing the portion for the ladder rail was at an angle. Could Koehler reconcile the two?

He could. They had only to look, he said, to see that there was an inch-and-a-quarter gap between the ends of the two boards, representing a one-and-a-quarter-inch piece, a chunk of wood that obviously had been sawed off when the whole board had been cut apart—plenty of width to allow the saw, afterward, to attack the wood at the angle it showed.

For the time being there were no more questions. Governor Hoffman bent over beside the two loosely placed boards and started to tap the cut nails into the holes. Koehler saw the governor's intent expression change. Then he saw why.

Not one of the nails had gone cleanly full into the wood. Every one protruded a quarter of an inch or so above the faces of the two boards.

Koehler glanced at Wilentz, Hauck and the others. They looked puzzled and worried. The reason was glaringly plain. Koehler and Bornmann had sworn under oath that when they had made this same test the nails had gone in smoothly to their full length, the nail heads coming flush with the board faces.

Had they lied? It seemed so. It seemed now that neither of the two boards had been part of the attic floor, which could only mean that Rail 16 of the kidnap ladder was in no way connected with Richard Hauptmann.

Anthony Hauck was the first to break the silence in the musty attic. The nailholes had been tampered with, he told Hoffman. He had gone over the ladder evidence thoroughly before the trial and there had been nothing like this; it had been exactly as Koehler and Bornmann were to swear to. They must keep in mind that the defense's aides had visited the attic a number of times in the recent past.

Governor Hoffman retorted that to him it was a clear case of perjury. The wood Bornmann had claimed he had removed from the attic hadn't been there in the first place; the evidence had been planted.

The governor let them think over that flat statement for a minute or so and then beckoned to Bornmann and Wilentz to follow him. The three men climbed down to the rooms below.

After a while, since they hadn't returned, the others left the attic. From behind the closed door of one of the rooms came the sound of angry voices. Nobody thought it wise to intervene.

The shouting continued for some time. At last the door opened. Arthur Koehler thought his old companion-in-arms Bornmann looked pale and strained, and Hoffman and Wilentz too showed that this had been rather more than a diplomatic exchange of differing points of view between two old rivals.

Wilentz gave the others the result of the noisy conference. They had decided to test the nail holes in the joists to which the disputed boards had been nailed. The impartial test would be performed in a Columbia University physics laboratory.

Six sections, in which there were twelve nailholes, were cut out of the joists by a carpenter; early that afternoon, in the Columbia lab, a physics professor of the university studied the samples under a microscope.

There were tiny bits of wood fiber clogging the holes, the professor reported after examining a few. He wasn't sure but perhaps there was something beneath them.

Koehler took the sample pieces and, with Loney, carefully sawed the holes open. A tiny wood plug was imbedded at the base of each one.

They removed the plugs and fitted the holes together again, then placed the ladder rail and its companion board with the corresponding holes in position. Koehler nodded to Hoffman and the governor repeated his earlier experiment, inserting the nails. Now they sank in smoothly to their whole length; the nailheads were absolutely flush with the board faces.

There was another silence. Again, Anthony Hauck broke it. "Are you satisfied?" he asked Hoffman.

He was satisfied, the governor replied shortly, that Koehler and Bornmann had told the truth when they testified that the nails had fitted in the holes flush against the wood—that was all.

He spoke at more length that evening, in a statement for the press. He would offer no opinions of his own but would cite those of Hauptmann's counselors and their wood expert, Mr. Loney, who still insisted that the ladder rail hadn't come from the board which, according to the prosecution, had been removed from Hauptmann's attic.

David Wilentz said the governor's statement was nonsense. It rather amused Arthur Koehler—the neat twist that the defense had managed to impart to the events in the attic and the Columbia lab. Quite a trick! Faced with the fact that the evidence in the attic had indeed been tampered with, the defense blithely turned the finger of guilt around from its side and pointed it at the prosecution.

But Anthony Hauck wasn't amused. He was sick and tired of Governor Hoffman's acrobatics, he declared. In the name of common decency, wasn't it about time the state legislature did something to stop him?

This in turn failed to amuse Harold Hoffman, who replied vehemently. The case literally reeked with prejudice and foul play! He would gladly reprieve Hauptmann again if Wilentz or Hauck would just tell him that he had the legal right to do so; but how could sensible people expect anything from Mr. Hauck?—the man was so incompetent he had become the attorney general's errand boy! So maybe he'd reprieve Hauptmann again *without* their approval!

Thoughtful reporters brought the governor's answering blast to Hauck, and he needed little time to prepare and fire off one of his own. He and Wilentz would do everything in their power, he said, to prevent another reprieve. He was Wilentz's errand boy, was he? Well, it was all a matter of taste, but somehow he preferred to be the attorney general's errand boy rather than the errand boy of a child-murderer.

17

If Governor Hoffman and Anthony Hauck insisted on shooting angry remarks back and forth, Dr. Shoenfeld wished they would do it in private. Not in the newspapers! According to the newspaper story, Hoffman seemed to be denying the assurances he had given the psychiatrist that Richard Hauptmann wouldn't be reprieved again unless new developments warranted it and that the governor personally would see to it that everyone connected with the defense understood this. But now he had declared in effect that he'd issue another reprieve any time he felt like it. All right, maybe he hadn't really meant it, but would anyone take the trouble to explain that to Hauptmann? Could anyone convince *him* that the governor wasn't 100 per cent sincere? Now, thanks to the newspaper reports, he could hardly be blamed if he persisted in his protestation of complete innocence up to the time they buckled him into the chair, only a few days away.

If there was any hope left of persuading Hauptmann to confess, Shoenfeld thought, he'd need all the help he could get. Whom could he turn to? Well, why not the prosecutor himself?

During the long trial, he had come to know and respect and like David Wilentz; frequently they'd discussed the trial's psychological aspects. The prosecutor had said frankly that he thought capital punishment an evil thing, seldom if ever achieving its ostensible purpose of preventing crime by killing convicted criminals.

Shoenfeld telephoned Wilentz and asked if they could meet. Right away, the other said. He greeted the psychiatrist warmly, and Shoenfeld, encouraged, explained that he wished to see Richard Hauptmann's sentence commuted to life imprisonment so that a thorough psychiatric study of the crime and the criminal could be made. The governor had shot off his mouth and perhaps irremediably damaged that hope, but he would still act in concert with them, Shoenfeld was sure, if Wilentz would take the initiative and tell Hoffman that he stood ready to join the effort to get Hauptmann to confess.

Would he?

Wilentz pulled a long face. He was pretty unhappy about Harold Hoffman's behavior, he admitted; lately, *damned* unhappy. The man had been hitting him, *his* attorney general, below the belt—the wild-eyed statements he had given to the press clearly implied that Wilentz was railroading Hauptmann to his death. He wasn't interested in clapping people into the electric chair, he was interested in justice; and as he had often said, if it could be proved that a State's witness had perjured himself or that an exhibit of State's evidence had been planted or tampered with, he would be the first to take action.

He had offered Hoffman full cooperation in evaluating the evidence, and how had he replied? To take one instance, Wilentz continued, look how he had carried on during the recent inspection of Hauptmann's attic. The governor had decided that a hard-working, conscientious, honest State police officer, Lewis Bornmann, was a liar and a cheat and a conniver and so on and on—and then, taking Bornmann and Wilentz into a room below the attic and locking the door, had stormed at Bornmann, accused him of planting the evidence after Hauptmann's arrest and lying about it during the trial. He had wound up by demanding that the officer make a full confession then and there of his trickery and perjury.

God alone knew, Wilentz went on, how Bornmann had managed to keep from hitting the governor, whose language had been—well, mighty hard to take. Finally, unable to stand any longer the exhibition of wilfully unrestrained temper on one side and admirable self-control on the other, Wilentz had interrupted and simply asked Bornmann to tell the truth. And Bornmann had said he *had* told the truth. Every word of his trial testimony was true. And of course the Columbia laboratory tests had sustained him. No apology from Hoffman, though. The idea was fixed in his head that the State had framed Hauptmann. And so, naturally, here he was again talking about reprieves.

He could talk all he wanted to, but legally he couldn't grant a new reprieve, and of course he couldn't pardon the kidnaper; that was within the power only of the Court of Pardons, which had already refused a simple clemency appeal. Lloyd Fisher of the defense had just appealed to the court for a rehearing, citing newly discovered evidence, but even Fisher must know that was a forlorn hope.

The attorney general fell silent, obviously thinking things over. Dudley Shoenfeld didn't interfere.

Given the choice between a scientific study of Richard Hauptmann, with all the possible benefits, and a quick snuffing-out of his life, finally extinguishing whatever secrets he had to tell—certainly he couldn't hesitate, Wilentz resumed. It was a choice between the sane act of a reasonable society and the law of the jungle. But in asking him to join Harold Hoffman, Shoenfeld was asking a great deal! He hoped he wasn't being petty—hoped Shoenfeld wouldn't think it was political ambition that made him hesitate; politically, he considered that he had reached his zenith in the attorney general's office. But if he said yes, he would be attacked by many of the papers and a large section of the public, his motives would be cynically questioned, and undoubtedly he would get his share of the hate mail so familiar to people involved in the Lindbergh case. For himself, he could tolerate all that; public figures necessarily had to develop a thick skin; but some of the attacks would slough off on his wife and children, and who knew what the consequences might be? They must come first in his decision.

Wilentz fell silent again, and again Shoenfeld quietly waited.

Of course, the attorney general said slowly, there was also the question of honor. Perhaps it should come first. If he believed—and he did believe—that Richard Hauptmann should be given a final chance to confess, could he honorably lessen the likelihood of it by standing in the way?

All right; his answer was yes: he would join Hoffman and Shoenfeld in their effort.

"Thank you," Shoenfeld said.

But, Wilentz added, in agreeing to join them in petitioning Judge Trenchard for the right to examine Hauptmann and—if this resulted in a confession—in a plea to the Court of Pardons to reduce the sentence to life imprisonment, he must insist on Shoenfeld's making it unmistakably clear to Governor Hoffman that the attorney general's purpose was solely to bring the case to a close; it was not to be seized on by the governor as the excuse for another reprieve or for further prolonging the already wearisomely prolonged legal procedure.

Shoenfeld said he would stress that to Hoffman. The two men shook hands.

Shoenfeld hurried to the nearest phone. He got Hoffman at once. He had important news; when could they meet? The governor said he had to be in New York that night; he'd have his personal secretary reserve a hotel suite where they could talk in private.

Hoffman wasn't free until just after midnight. Shoenfeld described the day's events—Wilentz had said yes, but with a condition. Then, as he had promised, he stressed the terms of the condition. Nothing for Wilentz to worry about, the governor immediately replied; at the time he had granted the reprieve he had assured the attorney general that there wouldn't be another unless he agreed that new developments warranted it, and he meant to keep his word. Anthony Hauck had got under his collar and he was afraid he'd been guilty of some loose talk.

Unfortunately, the psychiatrist said, it was just the sort of talk that could defeat their purpose. There was no point in struggling to persuade Hauptmann to confess if he was constantly encouraged to maintain his show of innocence. The governor must not give him any more false hope. That was vital! They were close to the ultimate margin of time. Hoffman must absolutely convince Hauptmann that at eight o'clock of the evening of March 31 he was going to be put into that chair and electrocuted unless there was a full and honest confession—convince him that even the governor of New Jersey had no power to intervene.

Hoffman nodded. But Shoenfeld wasn't finished. They had to get the truth and the urgency of his only alternative through to Hauptmann in such a way that he couldn't fail to believe. How? There were two people the kidnaper trusted above all and whose belief in him had never wavered—Anna Hauptmann and Lloyd Fisher. First, *they* must be convinced. Then they must convince Hauptmann. They must tell him there was only one hope of escaping the chair. Confess! Confess!

But Anna and Fisher mustn't for a moment let Hauptmann think they were pleading with him to plead for his life; their attitude must be that *they* were begging him to live. The man's personality simply wouldn't permit him to confess if he thought anyone would interpret it as a weakness. How clearly he had demonstrated that! One of Shoenfeld's most vivid memories of the trial, he told Hoffman, was an exchange between the accused and his accuser. David Wilentz had said bitterly, sarcastically, "You wouldn't tell if they murdered you, would you?" There had been no waiting for Hauptmann's answer. He had snapped off the word, and it had had a flat and deadly sound:

"*No.*"

That *No* must be changed.

All right, Governor Hoffman said; he understood, he agreed, and he'd go to work.

Obviously he meant it.

Maybe, just maybe, Dudley Shoenfeld thought, there was still enough time. Maybe they could still win. Maybe eight o'clock of the evening of March 31 would pass and the dynamos that fed the chair would be silent because Bruno Richard Hauptmann had talked.

18

Friday March 27.

Walter Hatfield of Plainfield, New Jersey, a member of the State Court of Pardons, found a fat envelope in his mail. Twenty-five pages had been stuffed into the envelope. Hatfield began to read; casually at first. His interest rapidly picked up and he glanced ahead through the typewritten account to see if it was what it seemed to be. Then he started all over again, slowly.

The document was the confession of a man named Paul H. Wendel, who had signed it, in which he admitted to Ellis H. Parker, chief of detectives of Burlington County, New Jersey, that he and he alone had kidnaped Charles Augustus Lindbergh, Jr.

In his rambling account of the crime, Wendel said that he had stolen the little boy and taken him to a tenement in a Trenton slum. He had built a crib and made other preparations to look after him, but in spite of all his care the child had become ill. Wendel had wanted to go to a doctor but the hue and cry of the search for the baby had frightened him. Several uneasy weeks had passed. Returning to the tenement flat after a short absence, Wendel had made the horrifying discovery that the little boy had fallen out of the crib and fractured his skull. He was dead. Wendel had buried the body in the woods across the valley from the Lindberghs' home, the hasty grave that was to be found on a rainy day in May.

Walter Hatfield made some telephone calls and learned that all the other members of the Court of Pardons had received copies of the confession in their mail the same morning. They were agreed that it was an extraordinary tale, almost incredible—but on the other hand, Ellis Parker was no amateur; it was hardly likely that he would be taken in by a cock-and-bull yarn of the kind Gaston Means was in the habit of spinning and had come up with again just a week or two ago. Parker, in fact, had often declared that he was never wrong about criminals. And so Paul Wendel's confession had to be taken seriously, all the more so since on the coming Tuesday, just four days off, Richard Hauptmann was scheduled to die for the crime Wendel said he alone had committed.

But who had sent the confession to the eight men who, excluding Governor Hoffman, made up the Court of Pardons? Surely it was odd that he hadn't identified himself, and there was no sender's name and address on the envelope or the confession. Was it Parker? For a long time he'd maintained that Hauptmann was innocent, and had been working to prove it. But Ellis Parker was scarcely one to hide his light under a bushel. Lloyd Fisher, then? A few days ago the defense chief had asked the court to hear another plea for clemency, claiming that he had new evidence which seriously challenged the verdict. Was this the evidence?

Or had the governor's office mailed the eight copies? He was Parker's friend, sympathized with his views, and had encouraged his investigation of the crime; moreover, Hoffman was the presiding officer of the court. It was reasonable to assume that Parker had told him the real kidnaper had been found, had given him the confession and that Hoffman had dispatched the copies to the men in whose hands lay Richard Hauptmann's last chance. But why the anonymity? Why was everyone—someone—so shy?

Having puzzled over the mystery the Court of Pardons proceeded to try to solve it, but it was only compounded by their discreet inquiries. Lloyd Fisher said he hadn't seen the confession, knew nothing about it, but was naturally anxious to know. Ellis Parker, who could hardly profess ignorance of its existence, refused to discuss it. As for the governor: "I have never seen such a document," he said, "don't know anything about it, and certainly did not either send it or cause it to be sent." He too was anxious to read it.

A few hours later a copy was given to Hoffman, with some hastily assembled facts about the confessed kidnaper. Paul H. Wendel was fifty, a minister's son. In 1920, when he was thirty-four, a moderately successful attorney in Trenton, he had been charged with perjury, convicted and sentenced to nine months in jail. He had been disbarred from practice, and it was none other than Ellis Parker, a friend, who had tried to help by signing a petition appealing to the bar association to restore his standing. It had failed.

By 1931, Wendel had been indicted for passing worthless checks and embezzling money from an estate entrusted to his care. Warrants had been issued for his arrest but never served; Wendel had dropped out of sight. His family, still living in Trenton, said they never saw him or had anything to do with him.

The brief report noted, finally, that Paul Wendel had once spent four days under observation in the New Jersey state hospital for the insane.

The fact that this man had confessed seemed to Governor Hoffman to put quite a new light on the promise he had given Dudley Shoenfeld. Maybe the confession was true, maybe false; but it had been made to a respected law officer, whose reputation alone surely demanded that the clear and unqualified admission of guilt should be cleared up before the convicted killer in the death house paid for a crime he had always denied. Rather than a second plea for clemency for Hauptmann, which Shoenfeld was pressing for, there should be a plea for a stay of execution. Then Wendel's remarkable account could be investigated.

Even Shoenfeld would agree, the governor reflected, that the chances of persuading Hauptmann to confess weren't bright. How much less promising they would be when the man in the death house learned his innocence had been proclaimed in this recital of the kidnaping at another's hands!

On Monday, when he would preside at a meeting of the Court of Pardons to hear Lloyd Fisher's new plea for clemency, there would be an opportunity to argue instead for a stay of execution—so Hoffman concluded his analysis of the situation. At worst it would be merely a postponement; at best it would reveal the true criminal. The time wouldn't be wasted in any event. Even if Wendel's confession turned out to be false, the extra time might be just the margin in which to get Richard Hauptmann to talk.

19

David Wilentz, too, had read the confession. He would not have agreed with the governor that it demanded respect, if only because of Ellis Parker's name. How could anyone respect an account of the kidnaping that only occasionally coincided with the well-established facts and often strayed so wide of them as to become absurd?

Much more interesting than the long, wordy document itself was the peculiar way in which it had come to light. Why had the sender —and someone had mailed it; it hadn't mailed itself—chosen to remain anonymous? And above all, just where *was* Paul Wendel? Why hadn't he been turned over to the proper authorities, the attorney general's office or the State police? Who knew the answers? One man, of course: Parker. But Parker hadn't cared to discuss his accomplishment of pinning down the real kidnaper. Why not?

These questions would wait; the thing to do now was to take possession of Wendel. If his statement had been made in Burlington County, Parker's domain, which seemed likely, then it also seemed likely that Wendel was still there.

The next day, Saturday the twenty-eighth, Wilentz told Parker in a telegram that, since a confession without the criminal was worthless and the latter's absence was obstructing justice, he should deliver Paul Wendel to the authorities in Trenton or to an accredited officer of Mercer County.

Detective James Kirkham of Mercer County knew nothing of these events; they caught up with him a little before ten-thirty that evening, when an old and famous friend, Ellis Parker, sent word that a man named Paul Wendel would be turned over to Kirkham the same night at the county line near White Horse. The detective notified Erwin E. Marshall, the county prosecutor, who immediately remembered the name. Paul Wendel, he told Kirkham, had been indicted for embezzlement five years ago; the sheriff still had the warrants for his arrest. Now, finally, they could be served. Get the warrants from the sheriff, Marshall continued to Kirkham, and commit Wendel to jail on the old charge.

The detective got the warrants and drove to the county line. Paul Wendel was duly placed in his care. But this seemed to be far more than a routine matter of embezzlement. There were some papers that came with Wendel. Kirkham glanced at them, looked at them again, read them more slowly. They were a confession—Wendel's confession. *He* had kidnaped the Lindbergh baby.

What a surprise! But he might have known, Kirkham reflected, that foxy old Ellis Parker would be capable of pulling a trump card like this from his sleeve.

How quiet the old man had kept about what he was up to! Obviously the prosecutor, Marshall, hadn't known, or he wouldn't have bothered with the embezzlement warrants—what was embezzlement compared with kidnaping and murder? And so when Kirkham drove his prisoner to a justice of the peace, Charles Mulford, he arraigned Wendel on a charge of murder, and Mulford made out the papers committing him to jail on the charge, which he phrased in a sentence:

> Paul H. Wendel did wilfully, and of his malice aforethought, murder one Charles Augustus Lindbergh, Jr., and give him mortal wounds, of which said mortal wounds he languished a short time and then died.

Kirkham put these papers in his pocket along with the confession and proceeded on to the county jail, where he delivered Wendel to Sheriff Walter Bradley. His mind was so occupied with the drama of this astonishing Saturday night that he quite forgot to give Bradley the confession and the murder complaint. They stayed in his pocket.

In the lounge of the Stacy Trent in Trenton, the talk among a group of friends—David Wilentz, Anthony Hauck and Norman Schwarzkopf, Captain John Lamb and Lieutenant Arthur Keaton—lagged, started up, lagged again, and pretty well died out. It was late, well after midnight. Wilentz wondered if the expected phone call would come after all, and felt tempted to head for home. He glanced toward the hotel desk. The night clerk was on the phone. He looked up, met Wilentz's eyes and nodded.

It was the long-awaited call. Sheriff Bradley was on the wire with the news that Paul Wendel had been put in his custody and was being held on the old charge of embezzlement. Good, Wilentz said; he'd come at once. He told his friends and invited them to join him.

They arrived at the county jail a few minutes before one and saw that word about Paul Wendel and his confession had leaked out. There was a crowd around the jail entrance and the police's efforts to disperse it only succeeded in making it grow. And here came the reporters and photographers; the flashbulbs began to pop.

Wilentz and the others made their way into the jail. The noise and flaring bulbs faded as they entered a small bare room. A man was sitting there, a middle-aged, quite ordinary-looking man, with something curiously calm, even resigned, about his attitude. His indifferent eyes inspected the newcomers. Then he smiled and got up and held out his hand to Wilentz. "Gee, but I'm glad to see you," he said.

This was Paul Wendel.

Wilentz accepted the proferred handshake; Schwarzkopf, whom the confessed kidnaper also recognized, did too. Wilentz started with the all-important question. Wendel, he asked, is your statement true or false?

False, of course, Paul Wendel said, still smiling. He knew nothing about the kidnaping of the Lindbergh baby except what he'd heard or read. He had been forced to confess that he was the kidnaper.

Wilentz repeated the word. Forced?

Look here, Wendel said, and pulled up one of his trouser legs. The group stared at the livid bruises on his shin.

Wilentz said he'd like to hear the whole story from the beginning. That was fine with him, Wendel agreed; he'd waited a long, long time to tell it! So much had happened that some of it was still a jumble in his mind, but he'd be as brief and clear as he could.

He let the trouser leg fall and sat down again. Slowy rubbing the bruised shin, he began his narrative.

Early in the year, Paul Wendel was living at the Hotel Stanford, 43 West 32nd Street, in Manhattan, where you could get a room for a few dollars a week. On February 14, he was just about to enter the hotel when someone said, "Hello, Paul." It was a man he had never seen before. "You're Paul Wendel," the stranger said confidently, and Wendel admitted it. "De Louie wants to see you," the other told him.

The name was familiar to Wendel as that of a New Jersey detective attached to State police headquarters in Trenton. Did this mean that the old charges, bad checks and embezzlement, were finally going to catch up with him? The stranger seemed to think that maybe he was considering making a bolt for it, which he wasn't; he felt the iron pressure of a gun in his back and realized that the first man must have signaled to another to step up behind him. The first man took his arm and led him to an old black car parked not far away. Two more strangers were in the front seat. Wendel was nudged into the back seat. Now he saw the man with the gun, who flanked him on one side, the first stranger on the other.

The Jersey law would hardly bother with such elaborate precautions, Wendel thought; this looked like a kidnaping. But God alone knew who'd want to kidnap him! At least they hadn't blindfolded his eyes and he resolved to use them as best he could, so that he would remember the course taken by the black car and also recognize his captors when and if he saw them again.

The first man was dark, heavy-set, with a deep scar on his left hand. The others called him Harry or Spidella, and apparently he'd put in plenty of time in prison; he spoke casually of having been one of Capone's pals in the Atlanta pen, and in the Tombs here in New York the Shapiro gang had been friends of his. The driver, short and slender, with light hair and long sideburns, was called Jack. The third man, Tony, looked to be about the same height, average weight; the scars at his temples suggested that his face had been lifted. The fourth, a very neatly dressed fellow who kept pulling at his mocha gloves, was maybe five feet five, 135 pounds or so. His accent sounded French. He had a high, sloping forehead, and his companions called him Freud.

The car crossed over to Brooklyn. Brooklyn was pretty much foreign territory to Wendel but he had a vague idea they were heading toward the Sheepshead Bay section. He studied the street signs. The car turned into Emmons Avenue, made a few twists and turns, and stopped in front of a house that looked much like almost every other house on the block. Wendel couldn't see the number.

They took him to the cellar and bound him hand and foot with chains. Now Harry Spidella became informative. The information stunned Wendel. He had been brought here, he was told, to confess of his own free will to the kidnaping of the Lindbergh baby.

Spidella allowed the news to sink in. Then he added, smiling—he smiled a lot—that if Wendel *wouldn't* confess of his own free will, well, he'd be made to. And if he didn't think they meant it, he could get the idea out of his head right now. They didn't fool around. He'd heard about Judge Crater, hadn't he? Wendel certainly had; the prominent, impressive-looking judge had disappeared off the face of the earth six years ago; it had been, and was, a headline mystery. They could tell him where Crater was, Spidella observed—dead. They'd bumped him off. Plenty of others, too. Maybe Wendel would like to know how. They shoved these uncooperative people into barrels of wet cement and let it harden and dumped the barrels into the river. That *could* happen to him. Think it over, Spidella advised.

It did not seem that Spidella and his friends were bluffing. At first, when Wendel refused to confess to a crime he hadn't committed, they didn't do much, outside of threats; but as the days passed, day after day, so many that he almost lost count, and he persisted in his refusal, they strung him up by the wrists, thrust his back to a board leaning against the cellar wall, and punched and kicked him, now and again beating him with a blackjack and jabbing lighted cigarettes so close to his eyes that the little nub of fire looked as big as the sun. They showed him a bottle of acid; if he continued to hold out, Spidella said, pretty soon he'd get it in the face.

The small cellar windows had been boarded over but there was a crack between two of the boards and through this a tiny ray of light slanted to the floor and wearisomely advanced toward Wendel's bound feet and crept past them and disappeared into darkness again; it served as a clock, and by watching it he dimly knew how many days had gone by. He preferred the times when he was left alone with his personal sunbeam, but they were few. Spidella and his friends never quite gave him enough to eat and drink; he was mostly hungry and thirsty; he was filthy, too, and his skin itched under the growing stubble of his beard. Sleeping was almost worse than being awake, because it meant waking into a nightmare.

The nightmare was now a week long, according to the light ray. Wendel did not think that, physically, he could last much longer. He surrendered. Anything they wanted him to write and sign, he said, he would.

Spidella congratulated him on his intelligence. Now for the confession. Wendel wrote in longhand as Spidella dictated; but it was slow and clumsy work, because Wendel's hands were numb from the weight of the chains. Spidella described how he—I, Paul Wendel—kidnaped the Lindbergh baby. He put in a good many details, and Wendel found himself writing things about his life which he would have thought only relatives or close friends could know.

Spidella read over the completed confession and appeared pleased; then Wendel signed it. He was given something to eat and drink and was left alone to watch the sunbeam again. But he did a little more than that. He scratched his initials, *PHW,* in the cellar floor.

The next day, according to the sunbeam, Spidella returned and told Wendel the confession wasn't quite right, changes would have to be made. There was more dictating and Wendel wrote a second. Spidella liked this one, too. He seemed so affable that Wendel asked if as a great favor he could have his crumpled, stained suit cleaned and pressed. Spidella thought that would be okay, and Wendel took off the suit and it was sent out into the world beyond the boarded cellar windows.

The sunbeam leisurely described another day's travels. Spidella came in looking happier than Wendel had ever seen him. The second confession was fine!—who judged it to be fine, he didn't say. Tomorrow, Wendel could leave.

And he would have his clean, pressed suit to leave in. When the contented Spidella brought it to him, Wendel said he was grateful; and he was. Nobody had noticed his initials on the floor, and now, exactly as he had hoped, he had the cleaner's little green tag, attached to the suit to identify it, reading 907–3XV. Maybe he wouldn't be able to tell the police the street and house number, but the tag would lead them to the cleaner's shop and through its location they and Wendel certainly should be able to find the house —the one house with *PHW* laboriously scratched in the cellar floor.

On the eleventh day—or so Wendel reckoned, which would make the date February 24—he was taken out to the same black car. Jack drove and Spidella sat close beside Wendel; apparently Tony and Freud were busy elsewhere. Jack and Spidella chatted at random with the air of men who have worked soundly and to good purpose. Wendel enjoyed the drive; the world was radiant and astonishing, full of sunbeams. He began to feel more and more at home in it. The surroundings added to this feeling. They were taking him into familiar country, New Jersey. It was like going home—or almost, because when the car stopped it was in Mount Holly, a place Wendel had been often, and in front of a house he knew very well, his old friend Ellis Parker's house.

He did not have time to marvel at this. Spidella took out a pistol and pointed it at the house stoop. "You go right up to that house," he told Wendel, "and don't turn away or I'll blow your brains out."

Wendel hurried to the door and rang the bell. Ellis Parker, Jr., answered it. Out of the corner of his eye Wendel saw the old black car speed off.

The older Parker was at home, too. Wendel quickly told them his extraordinary recent history. He urged them to call the police and have the black car stopped and Jack and Spidella arrested. But the elderly detective said no, it was too late for that, and anyway there was something more important to think about—his friend's safety. It was clear that Paul had fallen into the hands of an underworld gang, and his life was probably still in danger. He would have to be hidden somewhere, some place so unlikely the gang would never hit on it no matter how hard they tried. The old man ruminated for a while and then said yes, he had thought of just the spot. He told Wendel where and what it was. Wendel had to agree, it certainly was unlikely enough!—but, he asked hesitantly, was it really necessary to hide him there? Was he really still in danger?

Parker assured him he was. And if anyone knew the devious and unpredictable ways of criminals, Ellis Parker was the man. Wendel accepted his judgment.

The Parkers turned over the comforts of the roomy old house to him and he had a bath and ate well and that night slept soundly in the guest room. He got up feeling a new man. Parker was waiting to drive him to the ingenious hideout. It was ten miles away, the New Lisbon Colony, a state institution for mental defectives. The superintendent, Dr. Carroll Jones, cordially received them and told Parker he was glad to do anything he could to help a state official.

Wendel was given an apartment in one of the bungalows at the colony. A Burlington County detective went with him, to protect him, Parker explained. First, of course, he had to sign a form voluntarily committing himself to the sanitarium.

A few quiet days passed. The gang made no move. Ellis Parker dropped in for a visit, the first since he had left Wendel there. He had been thinking the whole business over very carefully, he said, and had come to the conclusion that actually it would be a damn smart idea if Paul *did* confess to kidnaping the Lindbergh child.

Wendel stared at his old friend. You're joking, he said.

No, no, not at all! Look at it this way, Parker said seriously: There was a lot of money to be made from the confession. All Paul had to do was write a full and frank statement in which he would plead guilty to the crime, saying that he had stolen the baby while out of his mind—and now, having regained his proper senses and realizing what a terrible thing he had done, he was making a clean breast of it. The medical profession would be on his side with sympathy and understanding, the plea of temporary insanity would see to that; and then—why, there'd be so many offers for the true story of what had happened that he'd make a million dollars and be on easy street for the rest of his life!—his family too.

There was absolutely nothing to be afraid of, Ellis Parker continued. Governor Hoffman was a very close friend of his; they saw eye to eye about the Lindbergh crime, and if Paul confessed, he'd be protected right down the line. The governor was pretty unhappy about Trenchard, Wilentz and Hauck—the judge, attorney general and county prosecutor who had lorded it all over the Hauptmann trial—and Parker had been given his word that in the event of a new trial he'd replace them. More than that, Parker was sure the governor would cooperate even further by creating a special grand jury to indict Wendel. And who would prosecute? Who else but the Burlington County prosecutor, Howard Eastwood! And if Ellis Parker couldn't speak for all the Burlington County officials, he was missing his guess!

So how about it?

Wendel shook his head. He still couldn't believe his friend was in earnest. Did he realize what he was proposing? Asking an innocent man to say he was guilty of this terrible crime, a crime it would never have entered his head to commit?

Parker advised him to think it over, and left. Spidella, too, had advised him to think it over, Wendel reflected; but to have the advice and this appalling proposition come from his old, respected friend—it was incredible. Incredible! Why, the man had lied to him! It was a long time since Wendel had practiced law but he hadn't forgotten everything he'd known, and he asked the sanitarium authorities to let him borrow some Jersey law books. There it was, in black and white: Governor Hoffman couldn't replace Wilentz and Hauck; only the legislature could oust an attorney general, by impeaching him, and only the order of a Supreme Court justice could discharge a county prosecutor.

Wendel wrote a letter to Parker, citing the law and pointing out the other's mistake; but he didn't feel much better, if at all. The nightmare seemed to have come with him from the cellar of the Brooklyn house.

The two Parkers came to see him regularly during the days that followed, sometimes singly, sometimes together; but whether together or separately, they acted as a team with but a single thought—Wendel should confess. They hammered it into him, over and over and over. He almost preferred Spidella. At least he could figure out Spidella; he was a plain, simple thug; but these two men—what had got into them? What had gone wrong with their minds? Why was Ellis acting out this monstrous farce? Or was he only acting a part? Was he instead the inventor of the whole thing, nothing less than a plot to sacrifice his friend Paul?

But why? Wendel thought he knew the other pretty well; he ought to know him, after twenty years of friendship. They had even worked together on the Lindbergh case: now and again Parker would come up with a clue and would ask Wendel to help him track it down. And Wendel began to remember Parker's attitude toward the case. He had had nothing but scorn and contempt for the efforts of the State police and the federal agents to capture the kidnapers. Those blundering fools, messing around in waters too deep for them, whereas he, *Ellis Parker,* a man with a reputation second to none, had been left out in the cold, as if he were the dumbest amateur! At times the thought of this injustice had made Parker boil over, shouting and swearing.

Wendel wondered if that could be the explanation. Had Ellis become so obsessed with a driving need to prove himself the supreme manhunter, showing up all the others, that he had lost all perspective and taken off on this crazy venture?

To the Parkers' repeated and ever more urgent demands, Wendel replied with an ever more desperate request: please let me talk to Wilentz, or Hauck, or Norman Schwarzkopf! It merely irritated Ellis Parker. He was running out of patience, he warned; he would have Wendel declared insane and committed to an asylum—a real hard-boiled one, nothing like the New Lisbon Colony!—if he didn't confess pretty damn soon.

Looking at Parker, Wendel had a terrifying vision. He seemed to see the old man in the weeks and months and even years ahead basking in the glow of the fame he so greedily coveted, a fame reflected by newspaper interviews and magazine articles and books, *How I Solved the Lindbergh Case,* by Ellis Parker; *Ellis Parker, the Master Detective Who Saved an Innocent Man from the Chair; Ellis Parker, the Country Detective Who Out-thought the FBI; My Greatest Case,* by Ellis Parker; *Ellis Parker, a Real-life Sherlock Holmes.*

But more terrifying than the vision was Wendel's certainty that he was not the only one who saw it. It hung constantly, temptingly, in front of the old man's bemused eyes.

Wendel thought: I've got to get out of here!

But two men now "protected" him during the days; three at night.

He had been in his bungalow apartment—his prison—for nearly three weeks when he concluded that his only chance, as before, was to pretend to give in. All right, he told Parker, he'd confess.

The atmosphere changed. Ellis Parker became the amiable, helpful friend of the old days. They worked over the confession together. As finally approved by Parker, it ran to twenty-five typewritten pages.

Another week passed. Wendel wondered who was reading the confession, and if they would realize, as surely they must, that it was too farfetched to be true.

Late Saturday night March 28, his guards drove him to the Mercer County line and turned him over to a man who was waiting there, a detective, James Kirkham. Soon afterward, Paul Wendel found himself charged with murder.

As he finished his story, Wendel inspected the faces of the men listening to him in the small room of the county jail. Their expressions told him nothing.

In fact, David Wilentz was thinking that the narrative he had heard was even more fantastic than the typewritten confession. He could not help wondering if both had come from a disordered mind, and he sensed that the same question had occurred to Hauck and Schwarzkopf. Well, he said to Wendel, they'd better have it in writing; would he mind putting down the main points? Of course not, Wendel answered, smiling; he was used to writing statements—but this one would be true!

He wrote it in the same room. It was reasonably short but complete, and it concluded with a blanket denial that he was connected in any way with the Lindbergh kidnaping, and the accusation that Ellis Parker and his accomplices had made him the victim of a colossal hoax. Then the signature, *Paul H. Wendel.*

The crowd outside had grown, although it was now almost three o'clock in the morning. Wilentz gave the reporters a brief account of the night's events, adding that it had come to his attention that Wendel had been arraigned for murder—but of course there was no basis for that charge, none whatever, and he felt confident that Erwin Marshall, the Mercer County prosecutor, would soon set the matter to rights.

At eight o'clock the same morning, Mr. Marshall sat down to a leisurely Sunday breakfast. There was a new prisoner in the county jail, yes, but the charge was an old one, embezzlement, and Marshall had seen no pressing need to question him at the awkward early hour of his delivery to the jail—the prosecutor had said as much to Kirkham over the phone. And so his Sunday paper struck him like a thunderbolt. "Great Lord!" he cried, startling Mrs. Marshall. "Look at this!"

The headline said that Paul Wendel had been charged with the murder of the Lindbergh baby. But how could that be?—the embezzler, Wendel, accused of the murder for which Richard Hauptmann was to be executed in two days?

Marshall ran to the telephone and got James Kirkham and

asked for an explanation. The detective told him that on being given a copy of Wendel's confession, along with Wendel himself, he had assumed that it superseded the embezzlement charge and had acted accordingly. Marshall then made two more calls, to Wilentz and Schwarzkopf, and they arranged to meet at the jail at one.

They asked Wendell to tell his story again. This time it was in greater detail; a stenographer took it down. After some three hours of listening to the recital of chains and torture and an ego-blinded old man, Marshall was pretty much of the same opinion as Wilentz and Schwarzkopf: Paul Wendel was innocent *or* he was the victim not of a hoax but of a diseased imagination. The fact remained that he was technically charged with murder. Since the Court of Pardons was sitting the next day to hear Hauptmann's new plea for clemency, it was bound to be a thorny issue!

In the long run, Marshall concluded, the murder charge would have to be put before the county grand jury; but since the charge had turned out to be simply a fluke, there was no need to act hastily.

Governor Hoffman was having a busy Sunday afternoon with the press. The reporters' questions had an exasperating theme: the governor had accused the State of framing the case against Hauptmann; well, was the shoe now on the other foot—had Hoffman hatched this plot with Ellis Parker to frame an innocent man? The governor indignantly denied it.

Parker, too, denied the charge. All Wendel's wild accusations were poppycock, he said; obviously the man was out of his mind. But Dr. Carroll Jones of the New Lisbon Colony said that so far as he'd been able to see, Wendel was quite normal.

New York Police Commissioner Lewis Valentine and Brooklyn District Attorney William F. X. Geoghan announced that they would investigate Wendel's charges of having been kidnaped, imprisoned and tortured. They had his little green dry-cleaning tag to help them. And the Department of Justice said it was taking steps to see if the alleged kidnapers had violated the Lindbergh law by transporting the alleged victim across the New York–New Jersey state line.

20

Monday March 30.

At eleven o'clock in the morning, the Court of Pardons was ready to hear Richard Hauptmann's new plea. Lloyd Fisher spoke first for the defense: he felt that his client deserved the court's mercy and commutation of the death sentence to life imprisonment if only on the basis of the so-called evidence in his attic, which lately had been proved to be questionable and suspicious; an additional reason for clemency lay in Paul Wendel's confession, in which he declared that he and he alone had kidnaped Charles Lindbergh, Jr. He was quite aware, Fisher continued, that Wendel had recanted his confession, but the fact remained that he was still in the Mercer County jail charged with the murder of the child, and the State could not hold two men responsible for a crime which it had persistently contended was the work of one.

Frederick Pope concluded the argument. Then David Wilentz and Anthony Hauck spoke for the prosecution. Governor Hoffman, presiding, said no more than was strictly necessary. His own activities were rather in a shadow because of Wendel's charges; he was blameless, as he had repeatedly told the reporters; still, his position was delicate and he felt that perhaps it wasn't quite the most suitable time for him to plead for a stay of execution so that the case might be brought to a satisfactory close.

A little after five in the afternoon, the court delivered its verdict: Bruno Richard Hauptmann's plea for clemency was denied.

Fisher bowed his head dejectedly. This was the sixth time he had appealed to the courts and the sixth time he had failed. Another blow wasn't long in coming. Governor Hoffman announced that he would not grant a second reprieve.

Again, someone had to give the news to the man in the death house. Fisher set out for the state prison. He was accompanied by Warden Mark Kimberling, who had been waiting to hear the court's decision. An active time lay ahead for him. Richard Hauptmann was scheduled to die at eight o'clock the next evening. Various arrangements had to be made; the electrocution chamber must be prepared, the chair tested.

21

Tuesday March 31.

Richard Hauptmann's breakfast was brought to him and he found that he could not eat it.

The evening before, his good friend Lloyd Fisher had come to Cell Number 9. Hauptman had been waiting for the sound of his friend's footsteps. Cell 9 seemed to amplify sounds. The briefest sound, which in the outside world would pass unnoticed, seemed to double and redouble in Cell 9 and spill enormous echoes from its first thin self; or perhaps the explanation was that since there was little more to see in Cell 9 than if it were a blind man's world the ears of the man who lived there had become trained to a degree of hearing so acute that he could hear sounds which to the visitor would have been silence. With his wonderful hearing he could have lived, happily, a blind man's life, if he were free to live it in the world outside.

His friend's voice, introduced by the lagging sound of his footsteps, had told him that the news was very bad, the pleas for commutation of the death sentence had been denied. Hauptmann's eyes, sharp too, had quickly found his friend's watch and seen that before long it would be eight o'clock. At eight o'clock tomorrow night, the night of Tuesday March 31, he would not be in Cell 9; he would be in the chair, braced for the great final sound of the mighty dynamos, a sound which a deaf man, almost, could hear. He knew their sound well; he had heard it often, during his thirteen months and two weeks and three days in Cell 9.

Then Anna had come to the cell and Fisher had left. The prison rules would not permit a man's wife to see him on the day he was to die. His and Anna's life together was ending now, in minutes, seconds. They held hands. His life with his son had ended long ago, although he had not known it then; he would not permit his son to carry through his life the memory of his father as a man in drab clothes in Cell 9. But he wondered if he had been wrong. Maybe he should have seen Bubi again.

Anna said that he would see him again. She still had faith, she said. He must have faith.

But Hauptmann's faith and hope were gone. He had never believed that he was to die in that chair. They could not kill an innocent man, he had told Anna, with false witnesses and circumstantial evidence. All human beings were not so corrupt; there were honest men somewhere. Fisher and Harold Hoffman were honest men. The governor had reprieved him. The reprieve had run out; then Paul Wendel had confessed. Now, surely, there would be a new trial. But human hypocrisy was too strong. Another man had confessed, but *he* was to die!

No faith, no hope.

A sound like mad wind racing past the bare boughs of winter trees filled the cell. Anna's hand tightened on his.

"What was that, Richard?"

"Nothing, nothing."

The sound of the testing dynamos surged up and died again as she left the cell.

Then they had brought his evening meal to him, and he had not been able to eat it. Lying on the iron cot, he had buried his face in his arm. But there were other farewells that must be made, and he had called to the night guards, Fred Mayor and Charley Douglas, who were his friends, and they had given him paper and pencils. He had written half a dozen letters, the last to his mother in Kamenz. Ten days ago, when hope had been still strong in him, he had sent her a good, cheerful letter. "Human hypocrisy may go far," he had said, "but I still have so much confidence in humanity that I believe it will shy from murdering an innocent man." This last letter was hard to write and his pencil traced the German script with painful slowness, but he finished it finally and wrote good-by.

Then he had wept.

His breakfast was cold. He walked back and forth, then lay down for a while, then got up and walked again.

Footsteps. He knew prison footsteps and outside-world footsteps and these were prison footsteps. He knew the particular, careful ceremonies of the last day; other men had spent their last days as his neighbors in the death house. The ceremonies were beginning. The prison barber came in and shaved his head. Then he was given new clothes. The blue shirt and dark-striped khaki trousers were clean and crisply starched. One leg had been slit.

In his new clothes he waited, and walked, and lay down, and walked.

They brought his lunch. He couldn't eat.

The ceremonies of the day continued. They took him from Cell 9 and locked him into Cell 8. It too was next to the room with the chair but on the opposite side of the death house. Of course he knew why he had been moved, even though for a stay of only a few hours; it was to make sure that he would be alive for the chair. He might have managed to hide something in Cell 9, something to kill himself with in the last minute before the final ceremony of leading him to the chair.

He had not thought much about the chair before yesterday and today, confident that it was for other men, not for Richard Hauptmann, but now he could hardly get it out of his mind. He cried again. He was still weeping when he heard footsteps. A guard had come to say that the warden wished to visit him. He asked if he might have a few minutes to—he stumbled over the expression—to get himself together. The guard said yes. Hauptmann rubbed his eyes against his sleeve. He did not want the warden to see that he had been crying.

He heard the warden's footsteps. Kimberling said quietly he had heard the prisoner hadn't had anything to eat for twenty-four hours. That wasn't good; he must eat. Hauptmann replied in a careful, polite voice; he didn't want to eat. Then the thought of the terrible chair overwhelmed him and his voice and his courage broke. He was innocent, he cried—innocent, innocent, innocent! The whole case against him was a lie! There were no facts—all lies! The warden was a big, important man, and he could arrange with a radio station, a radio network, to let his prisoner appeal here from his cell to all America, broadcast his appeal to anyone anywhere in America who knew anything about the Lindbergh crime to come forward now before it was too late and tell the truth!

Kimberling waited until the anguished voice died. He said he was sorry but such a thing couldn't possibly be done. Then he said again that he was worried because Hauptmann hadn't eaten for so long. He could ask for anything he wanted. Any kind of food he wanted, it didn't matter what it was, they'd get it for him.

Hauptmann turned away. He would not eat, he said.

The warden left him. He lay down; his outburst had tired him.

More footsteps; outside-world footsteps. The three lawyers, Fisher, Rosecrans and Pope, entered the cell. He received them calmly, expecting no news. He noticed that they kept their eyes away from the visible tokens of the last day, his bald head, his new clothes with the slit trouser leg. He thanked them for everything they had done and by and by they shook his hand and went away.

He waited.

Footsteps. These, too, were friends'. Reverend Matthiesen and Reverend Werner were good men, they had visited him often in Cell 9 and tried to comfort him. Presently Werner left. Matthiesen asked if he would like to pray. He said yes, he would like to very much, but he was afraid his mind was too full to think of prayers. Matthiesen thought about the problem and found an answer. Even a saint, he said, a great and famous saint, St. Francis of Assisi, sometimes could not find the words to give voice to the prayers in his heart, and then he would repeat again and again the single, simple, wonderful word *God.* Perhaps the prisoner could discover solace in this way. He would leave him now, Matthiesen said, but early in the evening Werner and he would return.

As the cell door closed behind him, Matthiesen heard the prisoner speak softly:

"Gott. Gott. Gott."

David Wilentz put down his phone with a sigh. Patience was an excellent virtue and he believed he was as patient as most men but the Lindbergh case had burdened his supply to the breaking point and this latest piece of idiocy was just about the last straw.

An hour ago, in Judge Trenchard's chambers, the case had seemed to be closed at last, the execution this evening its only remaining formality. Lloyd Fisher had made a last-minute appeal to the judge for a stay of execution on the grounds that the Wendel confession had not been thoroughly investigated and that, before it was, Hauptmann should not be put to death. The thought of the events that had led to that confession had goaded Wilentz to a bitter response. The New Jersey police, he had said, hadn't found a scrap of evidence to connect Wendel with the Lindbergh crime, but on the other hand the New York City police had discovered enough to substantiate his contention that Wendel had been framed on Ellis Parker's orders. "We've had enough time to determine that this is the vilest fraud ever perpetrated in New Jersey," Wilentz had declared.

Judge Trenchard had studied the Wendel confession for fifteen minutes or so, then looked up over his glasses at Fisher and said, "It seems plain to me that this confession is incredible on its face and out of harmony with the known facts of the case. On this basis, I do not think I have the authority to interfere with the orderly course of justice."

Thus writing finis to the case; or so Wilentz had felt sure. But he had been wrong. A few minutes ago it had blown open again.

Here, back at his desk, he had received a call from Erwin Marshall. The Mercer County prosecutor had been very upset. At one-thirty that afternoon, he had told Wilentz, the Mercer County grand jury had assembled for a routine session, only to learn from its foreman, Allyne Freeman, that Wendel's admitted guilt had put a new complexion on the Lindbergh case and the jury would have to decide whether or not to indict him for the baby's murder. This had seemed pretty strange, Marshall thought, since he himself, the county prosecutor, had never been given the complaint officially charging Wendel with the murder and he was reasonably sure it hadn't been presented to the grand jury either; stranger still, only witnesses who would testify to the authenticity of the confession had been summoned to appear—Ellis Parker, his son and his secretary. Then, to cap it all, no sooner had Marshall announced that the jury would consider the Wendel case than the foreman had told him that since he had declared that he put no stock in the confession, it would be improper for him to be present—and had compelled the prosecutor to leave the room!

"What's it all about?" Marshall had asked Wilentz. "What should I do?" And Wilentz had told him not to worry; he'd see to it that something was done in a hurry.

All right; it was his problem. He considered the situation. The whole procedure wasn't only strange, it was illegal: the grand jury had no jurisdiction in Wendel's case. Even if his confession were true he couldn't be indicted for murder, for although he had said in the confession that the Lindbergh baby had been killed in Trenton, the seat of Mercer County, he also had said that the child had died as the result of an accidental fall, which certainly wasn't murder. And since the kidnaping itself had taken place in Hunterdon County (which was true enough, but not at his hands) the Mercer County jury couldn't indict him for that either.

Admittedly the grand jury was privileged to dispense with the services of the county prosecutor any time it wanted to but it was an extreme and unusual step and, in this instance, thoroughly unwarranted. And it had invited the Parkers to testify but not Wendel! Damned high-handed! Wilentz wondered what had prompted foreman Allyne Freeman to take charge so arbitrarily. Freeman was a Republican, Wilentz recalled—Erwin Marshall was a Democrat—and had persistently and unsuccessfully sought public office; at present he was being touted as a candidate for the state senate. More important, Harold Hoffman was a close friend of his. Could it be that the governor's fine hand was pulling the strings?

It was certainly possible. Paul Wendel's family would have said so. Wilentz knew they felt that Hoffman had been mixed up in Paul's kidnaping, at least from the time he had been put in the New Lisbon Colony and maybe before. Questioned by State troopers, Wendel's son and daughter had said that Ellis Parker had come and told them that their father had confessed to the Lindbergh crime, had shown them a letter the governor had written to Parker on February 27 in which their father was mentioned (Wendel had been taken to the New Lisbon Colony on February 25), had boasted of his friendship with Hoffman and asked the daughter to write a statement admitting that she and her mother had been given charge of the kidnaped baby and that the child had died while in their care. Of course they had refused. Parker had been annoyed, but not too much.

As was to be expected, the governor had denied writing any such letter to Parker, insisting that he'd known nothing about Wendel until his confession was given to the Court of Pardons.

For the present, it seemed to Wilentz, the question—was Hoffman involved or not—would have to remain a matter of curiosity; there was no evidence to support either side, only talk. The important thing right now was to get Wendel's son and daughter over to the grand jury hearing and insist that they be allowed to testify in their father's behalf until he could speak for himself.

Wilentz sent for a member of his staff who was familiar with the

Lindbergh case, briefly described the situation and told him to go to Erwin Marshall's aid.

Fifteen minutes to eight.

Warden Mark Kimberling's preparations had been completed long ago. Forty-five people had won the right to see Bruno Richard Hauptmann die. These invited witnesses had been admitted one by one to the warden's office, having successfully passed a careful screening and search of their persons both before and immediately after entering the prison. They had been waiting since seven-thirty to go down to the execution chamber.

They were getting a little restless.

With them yet apart from them, Kimberling sensed their impatience. Still he delayed. The truth was, he was uncertain of his ground. News that the Mercer County grand jury was investigating the Wendel affair had confused the issue to the point where he didn't know if he was authorized to carry out the death sentence. If the jury voted to indict Paul Wendel for the murder of the Lindbergh baby, then he could hardly execute another man for the crime!—whereas if it had voted *not* to indict, he could go ahead.

But the jury had done neither. It simply hadn't made up its collective mind. Should he proceed, or not? What a miserable dilemma! In an effort to forestall it, he had sent a message to Erwin Marshall, reminding him that Hauptmann was scheduled to die at eight o'clock and that the execution would be carried out as ordered unless official notification was received by the warden to postpone it. And there had been no reply.

Kimberling could look down on some of the ninety troopers stationed fifty feet apart along the prison walls to hold back the crowd outside—eight thousand or so strong by now and still growing. If things should get out of hand, two fire companies stood ready to turn on their hoses. In a case as hot as this, he didn't know what to expect. One of the death-house guards had been warned that he'd be killed, and the children of another had been told that they and their father would die if Richard Hauptmann died in the chair.

Five to eight. The warden telephoned Marshall. He couldn't help him, the county prosecutor said, much as he'd like to; the grand jury inquiry was still in progress. Kimberling hung up, stared out the window, conscious of the murmurings and shufflings of the people in the room with him. In a couple of minutes it would be eight and he had to make up his mind one way or the other.

When the phone rang it sounded loud as an alarm bell. Very much aware of all the watching eyes, Kimberling picked up the receiver. The caller identified himself: Allyne Freeman, foreman of the grand jury. He had been instructed by the jury, he said importantly, to ask that the execution be postponed for forty-eight hours; the Wendel investigation was still incomplete and there were some interesting new angles the jury wanted to look into.

The warden considered. In a legal sense, the situation hadn't changed, and this was a request, not an order. But it seemed reasonable, in the light of developments, and he would be well within his authority if he granted it: the death warrant called for Hauptmann's execution during the week of March 30; the day of the week was left to the warden's discretion. All right, he told Freeman, the jury could have the extra time.

He hung up and gave the news to the waiting witnesses. Two days more.

Three men were praying as one in Cell 8, Matthiesen, a Lutheran, Werner, a Seventh-Day Adventist, and Richard Hauptmann, who belonged to neither's church but who was closer to the pastors now than any member of their flocks. They prayed aloud but even in prayer the prisoner could pick up and identify the approaching sound: footsteps. Quick footsteps! Not death-march footsteps; footsteps from the outside!

Lloyd Fisher came hurrying to the cell. He was smiling.

"They've put it off for two days!"

Hauptmann and the ministers got up from their knees. They smiled at one another.

"I think this means better things for me," the prisoner said.

Now he could eat. And sleep.

Anna Hauptmann lay on her bed in the Hotel Stacy Trent. That morning she had bought a black dress and black hat and veil. She was wearing the dress now, although ordinarily she would not have thought of lying down fully clothed, particularly not in a brand-new dress. She was drowsy; the doctor who was sitting beside the bed had given her a sedative. They were waiting for the telephone. The doctor had a stronger opiate ready, just in case.

Lieutenant Robert Hicks was in the room with them. He got to the phone first when it rang. He answered quietly but after a second or two of listening he raised his voice. It was Lloyd Fisher, he told Anna—the execution had been postponed!

Her drowsiness vanished. She sat up, swung her feet off the bed. "I knew it!" she cried. "I told you so!" And she ran to the closet. She took off the black dress, carefully smoothed out the wrinkles and hung it up neatly under the black hat and veil.

When the photographers came, she was ready. The black dress

was out of sight behind the closed closet door; she was wearing a dark blue print with little red and white flowers and a green biblike collar.

The great crowd waited outside the prison walls. Again and again the troopers had shouted the news but the crowd only laughed and jeered and stood firm, not to be deceived by any ruse to get rid of them. At ten o'clock the first newsboys came yelling the extras' blazing headline: HAUPTMANN REPRIEVED. Grumbling, still not quite believing, the crowd drifted off into the darkness.

22

Wednesday and Thursday, April 1 and 2.

Harold Hoffman found himself the target of a bitter new attack. His critics charged that the last-minute reprieve proved his determination to annul the orderly process of the law. The whole sorry mess was a transparent conspiracy plotted by the governor and his cronies to set Hauptmann free. His friend Ellis Parker had forced a confession from an innocent man; his friend Allyne Freeman had used the confession to bring the Wendel case before the grand jury and pre-empt the role of prosecutor; the man he had made warden of the state prison, his very grateful friend Mark Kimberling, had blocked the execution without consulting the attorney general or any other judicial officer of the state and thus forwarded the conspiracy. If all this wasn't collusion, what was it?

In a front-page editorial the Trenton *Times* called again for the governor's impeachment.

Thirty-four Princeton University professors, led by their president, Dr. Harold W. Dodds, petitioned the state legislature to determine whether any state officials involved in the Lindbergh case should be removed from office.

Mark Kimberling announced that Bruno Richard Hauptmann would be escorted to the electric chair at eight o'clock of the evening of Friday April 3—unless the grand jury was still undecided about Paul Wendel and requested another stay.

At nine o'clock on Thursday morning the grand jury reconvened. The day of the postponed execution it had sat almost continuously until almost an hour past midnight. It had listened to three witnesses, Ellis Parker and Paul Wendel's son and daughter. Finally it had invited Erwin Marshall to return to the hearing, an invitation the prosecutor had been quick to accept.

It had adjourned with no conclusion whatever.

On Wednesday, it had received a letter from Paul Wendel in which he had asked for the opportunity to speak in his own defense, promising to waive immunity; and today, Thursday, he was the single witness scheduled to appear. Governor Hoffman and Attorney General Wilentz also would testify, but they could hardly be called witnesses. And Wendel's handwriting would be compared with the writing in the Lindbergh ransom notes.

The long day dragged on.

At midnight the grand jury voted to discontinue its investigation of the Wendel case and adjourned. Reporters were puzzled; it looked as if nothing had changed. The paradox remained: two men charged with the same crime, for which one was to be electrocuted! Just what did "discontinue" mean?

Erwin Marshall said it meant just that—the jurors had decided to drop the case; technically, Wendel was still charged with the murder because they hadn't voted a no-bill. The foreman explained that they'd taken the only course open to them: since the murder complaint hadn't been presented, they could neither throw the case out nor declare a no-bill; and without a formal charge against Wendel no action could be taken to indict him.

Where *was* the complaint, anyway? One man should know—Detective James Kirkham. He was asked. He pondered, and grew embarrassed. It seemed that after arraigning Paul Wendel he had put the warrant in his coat pocket.

It was still there. James Kirkham had forgotten it.

André Maurois, an author almost as well known in America as he was in his native France, was reminded of a story written by a compatriot. The story told of a suspected heretic seized by the Spanish Inquisition. The unfortunate victim endures indescribable torture, then is left alone in his cell. He stares at the gloomy walls, makes out a strip of light at the door. Is it opening, have they come to drag him to the final agony? But no one is there. His jailers have forgotten to lock the door! Heart beating, he steals out, reaches the end of the corridor, sees freedom ahead. A hand falls on his shoulder. "And where are you going?" a soft voice asks. The door had been left ajar deliberately in a last delicate, pitiless torment.

Maurois retold the story in the Paris newspaper *Le Figaro.* He went on:

> I am positive nobody consciously intended to inflict such punishment on the man in a death cell at Trenton. But the

fact is that it has been inflicted on him. Hauptmann was convicted on February 13, 1935, of a crime which deserves no pity. Whether he is guilty or innocent I do not know. But the fact is that a month before the date fixed for his execution the first delay was granted.

Thirty days later came another delay, and on Tuesday, a few minutes before the time for the execution, a third stay of forty-eight hours was announced to the prisoner.

This man, then, has three times awaited death on a date known to him. He has counted days, hours, and minutes. Three times during these fearful days his mind has turned, supposedly for the final time, to the horrible details of the electric chair, to the dreadful scene in that room, to the signal, the final shock and convulsions to follow. The last time his imagination was further stirred by the gruesome preparations in the death chamber, and by the shaving of his head for contact with the electrode.

This is not all. This man has a mother and a wife. For them as well these three frightful rehearsals have taken place. Three times the wife has said her last farewell, and on Monday, while leaving the prison, she saw the workmen hastily installing telegraph equipment for newspaper reporters. Nobody can picture such things without feeling pity.

Whether Hauptmann is guilty or not is no longer the question. The death of a guilty man may be necessary for the good of society. But all civilized people ought to admit that a man who, through play of unexpected circumstances, of doubts and scruples, has had the order of his execution countermanded at the last moment, should not then be forced to die.

Encouraged by "countless" letters and calls congratulating him for protesting the "unfair and extreme sentence based on an assortment of doubtful evidence and testimony" the Hauptmann jury had handed down, Clarence Darrow telegraphed Governor Hoffman and the Court of Pardons that in the interest of fair play and in "the face of such widespread public disapproval" Richard Hauptmann was entitled to a new trial.

23

Friday April 3.

Early in the morning, Lloyd Fisher moved again to try to delay the execution, wiring a plea to Governor Hoffman for a second executive reprieve, to be based, as the first had been, on the governor's interpretation of his power under the law, as distinct from the reprieve the defense had failed to win through the Court of Pardons. Fisher then sent a telegram to Anthony Hauck, the Hunterdon County prosecutor, demanding that the Hunterdon County grand jury take up the case of Paul Wendel and consider indicting him for kidnaping, which was specifically admitted in his confession.

Governor Hoffman did not immediately reply, but Hauck wired back that he had seen no complaint charging Wendel with kidnaping; if and when one was submitted to him, he would be happy to present it to the grand jury.

Fisher lost no time, dispatching his car and secretary, Laura Apgar, to pick up Anna Hauptmann at the Stacy Trent. The car headed at high speed for Flemington.

Anna was in good spirits, although not many hours remained before the time set for the execution. Yesterday she had visited Richard—another "last visit." But neither of them had believed, and she still didn't believe, that it could be the last. The omens were too promising; he had been moved back to his old cell, and he was cheerful, rested, calm; he'd been eating and sleeping well. Their parting had been almost like an everyday good-by—quite temporary. Soon they'd be together again.

In Flemington, Miss Apgar handed Justice of the Peace George Webster a typewritten complaint, prepared by Fisher, formally charging Paul H. Wendel with the kidnaping of Charles Augustus Lindbergh, Jr. The justice read it hurriedly, told Anna to sign it, signed it himself, and returned it to Miss Apgar to serve on Paul Wendel in the Mercer County jail, where he was being held for embezzlement.

Fisher wired Hauck that afternoon, advising him that the complaint had been signed and served on Wendel and asking the prosecutor to join Fisher in seeking a stay of execution until the charge of kidnaping had been thoroughly explored.

Hauck had been wonderfully prompt in replying the last time. Surely he would be no less prompt now.

Mark Kimberling, too, was busy. Wishing above all to avoid his earlier predicament, he had sought a judicial ruling in the Wendel case and asked whether there was sufficient reason why Richard Hauptmann should not be put to death at eight that evening.

First, the warden had sent a letter by messenger to Erwin Marshall, asking for his interpretation of the Mercer grand jury's vote to discontinue its inquiry; Allyne Freeman had said this to him in a telephone call, Kimberling wrote, and had added that the jury had no further requests to make of him.

All that was correct, Marshall had answered. Up to this moment, he had yet to see a complaint charging Paul Wendel with murder.

It was hardly the information Kimberling had hoped for. Just after the jury had adjourned in the first hour of Friday morning Marshall had told reporters that in his judgment Wendel was still charged with the murder because the jury hadn't voted a no-bill.

Kimberling wondered if he was to be spitted again on the same wretched dilemma. Not if he could help it! He had composed a letter asking for a clear-cut directive to guide him and had dispatched it by messenger to David Wilentz.

The attorney general's answer came a little before three. Kimberling read and re-read the significant paragraphs:

> The execution of Bruno Richard Hauptmann must be carried out in accordance with the warrant now in your possession issued to you by the presiding judge of the Oyer and Terminer of the County of Hunterdon, and within the time set forth in said warrant, unless:
>
> (a) There is a reprieve by the Governor. I have heretofore advised the Governor that he was without authority at that time to grant a reprieve. However, if an order of reprieve is served upon you by the Chief Executive, it is not your duty to question its validity, but to obey it.
>
> (b) A stay of execution by the Court of Oyer and Terminer of the County of Hunterdon.
>
> (c) Commutation of sentence by the Court of Pardons. . . .
>
> I can readily understand the reasons for your confusion [Wilentz continued]. Since the early part of December, 1935, through daily statements to the press, all from important sources, reflections have been cast upon not only the validity of the conviction but upon the officials who, only because of their sworn duty, participated in the prosecution. The seeds of distrust and the germ of suspicion have been planted until the entire nation has been thrown into unjustified confusion.

Well, Kimberling thought, that settled that; his course was plain. It was also plain that the attorney general dismissed the Wendel case as irrelevent; he hadn't even mentioned it in his list of three exceptions—and it was unlikely indeed that any one of them would keep Richard Hauptmann from the chair, since all three had been weighed and rejected within the last few days.

At five, Governor Hoffman telephoned Wilentz and asked the attorney general to please come to his office at once. He was considering a new request for a reprieve, the governor explained.

Dusk sharpened the edge of the raw wind. Low clouds rolled like a gray sea over the somber prison. One hundred Trenton policemen and fifty State troopers had formed a thin necklace around the walls. "I just hope they don't have to turn on the hoses," one of the troopers said to a shivering companion, gesturing toward the fire truck that faced the main gate.

But it didn't seem likely, not so far; and glancing at his watch the trooper saw that it was almost six. Only two more hours to go. He had been on duty since noon. The warden had foreseen trouble. Last Tuesday the mob had grown to ten thousand, give or take a few. It had been a jittery, impatiently expectant audience, eager for action. The execution scheduled for tonight hadn't pulled nearly so well. There could be scarcely five hundred in the crowd, the trooper estimated. The weather, damn cold, must be to blame; last time it had been a beautiful day—picnic weather almost. The mob had hated to leave. They had jeered and hooted and laughed at the announcement of the stay; only the newsboys' brandished headlines had convinced them.

These people weren't nearly so vivacious. They hardly seemed to believe that Richard Hauptmann was going to die tonight. The troopers themselves only half believed. Some of them knew that Governor Hoffmann was talking reprieve with the attorney general at this very minute, and there was a rumor that the Justice Department had asked for another stay so that its agents could investigate the Wendel confession. It was rumored, too, that a new witness had come forward. True or false? Anything could happen in the Lindbergh case.

Nearby church bells tolled for vespers and the rambling wind lifted the sound over the prison walls and past the sentry boxes and the buildings in the open square and brought it at last to the red-brick death house, its roof whitewashed by floodlights.

The first of the select inner audience began to arrive. Mark Kimberling had warned them that they must be in his office forty-five minutes before the time of the execution. Passing the outermost guarding line, they walked in single file along a corridor formed by two rows of State troopers in bright blue and yellow uniforms. Here there was an imitation day. The newsreel cameramen had inched their trucks up into the last scrap of tolerated space and the bald flares on the roofs dazzled the witnesses' eyes. The newspaper photographers' flashbulbs crackled like miniature lightnings. It was a kind of carnival, one official thought. He moved on toward the steps of the old brownstone administration building and glanced up at the profusion of carved figures that decorated the walls. "Just look at all that stuff," he said to a friend. "Gods and beasts and the

Lord knows what. It's like the old temple or labyrinth or whatever it was, with the Minotaur waiting inside for its victims."

"It's waiting, all right," his friend said.

The official witnesses were an exclusively male group. At the top of the steps a prison guard, spic-and-span in blue-and-white cap and blue uniform, examined their invitations and ran his hands over their bodies, relieving the State police officers of their pistols and taking cameras from a few hopefuls. They went on. Directly inside the heavy gate, in a small room off the entrance, other neat guards waited. They were more curious. They inspected the invitations as if suspicious of frauds. Their inquisitive fingers dug into hatbands and trouser cuffs and suit and coat linings. They turned every pocket inside out and lingered over a harvest of pens and pencils and matchbooks and pocketbooks and notebooks and keyholders and random papers. They tapped the soles and heels of shoes in search of hollow spaces and peered at watches like pawnbrokers.

They were satisfied.

The witnesses moved on.

One at a time, they were escorted to the warden's office. His deputy, Colonel George Selby, was stationed there. "You will be required to sign an affidavit," he told them, "swearing that you have not brought into the prison any deadly weapons, cameras, drugs or other contrabrand." A few quiet figures, women office workers, passed out the papers, and each witness signed.

They were all present and accounted for. There were fifty official witnesses altogether, some thirty reporters, six physicians, a scattering of State police officers, members of the state legislature and representatives of the governor.

Selby looked at the clock on the wall and then at his watch. Seven fifteen. "I think we can go ahead," he remarked. He led the way to the prison center, a circular space from which wide corridors radiated into the cell blocks like spokes of a wheel, and left them under the guards' vigilant eyes. He would be back before the appointed time, he said.

"Is it all right to smoke?" a witness asked the nearest guard.

It was all right to smoke.

The witnesses didn't talk much and soon even that small talk died. They found themselves watching a wall clock. The minute hand dropped down to the half hour and began the long climb toward the top. When it reached the top the prison's official time would be eight.

Four men were waiting in Cell 9, the condemned man, the two ministers and Lloyd Fisher. Fisher had been talking earnestly to Hauptmann. There was still hope, he had said. He had appealed to the governor for a new reprieve and the governor was considering the appeal right now. And a complaint had been made out formally charging Paul Wendel with kidnaping, and Anthony Hauck had agreed to present the charge to the Hunterdon County grand jury. They need not despair.

Hauptmann had listened quietly, but Fisher wondered if the words had meant anything to him. His closely shaved head bent forward a little, he was staring down past his open-necked light blue shirt at the slit in one leg of the dark-striped khaki trousers. He seemed stoically indifferent. He might have been in the witness chair in the Flemington courtroom, Fisher thought; his attitude had been the same. No, the lawyer corrected himself, this wasn't the same. Richard Hauptmann's apparent unconcern in the courtroom chair had been a kind of conceit, a reflection of his confident sense of superiority. Now he wasn't the superior man; he was stunned, broken, consumed by a devastating awareness of defeat. If he thought at all, perhaps he was thinking of the words he had said in his cell in the first shattering hours after the trial verdict—"little men, little pieces of wood, little scraps of paper."

Fisher saw that there was a piece of paper in his own hand. He glanced up and realized that Matthiesen had given it to him. It would be Richard Hauptmann's last statement, the minister said. Fisher read:

> I am glad that my life in a world which has not understood me has ended. Soon I will be at home with my Lord, so I am dying an innocent man. Should, however, my death serve for the purpose of abolishing capital punishment—such a punishment being arrived at only by circumstantial evidence—I feel that my death has not been in vain. I am at peace with God. I repeat, I protest my innocence of the crime for which I was convicted. However, I die with no malice or hatred in my heart. The love of Christ has filled my soul and I am happy in Him.

Matthiesen was looking at him as if waiting for his approval. Fisher handed the paper back and nodded. He could not really find it in him to repeat that a last hope remained. Certainly Richard Hauptmann didn't believe it. Did the ministers? Did he, even? He got up from the hard cell chair, and his client got up too. The two men faced each other. Looking at the thin, high-cheekboned face, the blue eyes, the shaved skull, Fisher's thoughts returned again to the tumultuous past, to the witness stand, to the first time he had seen his client and heard his voice. Together, they had lived through shocks and hopes and crises enough for a dozen lives.

Then he reprimanded himself for permitting his mind to betray him into resignation. There is still hope, he thought; there *is*! He shook his client's hand. Hauptmann thanked him for all he had done and all he had tried to do. Fisher held on to his hand, wondering if there would be more. There was. He had told the truth, Hauptmann said; he was innocent. Fisher tightened his hand. Yes, he said, he was convinced of it.

He left the cell.

He walked past the execution chamber, next to the cell, and hurried to the warden's office. Kimberling was at his desk, talking to George Selby. The warden turned as Fisher came up and said gravely that he had bad news for him. Governor Hoffman had called at half-past seven and said that there would be no further reprieve; as he interpreted the state constitution, he was now without power to grant a new stay. Anthony Hauck, too, had called, with this message: he would submit the complaint against Wendel to the Hunterdon County grand jury at the next regular session.

The prosecutor had chosen this last minute to reveal a taste for irony, Fisher thought; he wished him pleasure of it. For himself, he had all he could do to remember his self-reprimand: while there was life, there was hope. He met the warden's tired, watching eyes. He was tired too, but he made himself speak forcefully. The death warrant, he told Kimberling, permitted the warden to carry out the death sentence as late as Sunday midnight, April 5, fifty-two hours from now. Would he give Richard Hauptmann and his lawyer the benefit of those fifty-two hours by again postponing the execution?

Kimberling shook his head.

Now, Fisher knew, truly there was nothing left; only the chair.

George Selby said he'd better go and get the official witnesses into an orderly column. He started to leave the room, then hesitated, waiting for his chief; but Kimberling didn't move and the deputy warden went on. In a few minutes it would be eight o'clock. Kimberling preferred to wait. In the past he had seen these final minutes turn out to be not final after all. Of all the many, many people who were watching the clock, here and throughout the country and pretty well throughout the world, perhaps there was *one* who would be impelled to call before the minute hand finished its climb. And so he waited.

The minute hand reached the top of the dial, passed it.

Selby had formed the witnesses into a tidy double row in the prison's central area. They were beginning to murmur about the passing time—eight-ten, eight-twelve, fifteen minutes past eight—when Kimberling entered. There was silence. The warden spoke.

In a moment, he said, they would go to the execution chamber. But there had been persistent rumors that efforts would be made to take photographs of the man in the chair and that a demonstration would be attempted to protest the execution. He hardly needed to tell them that neither would be tolerated. Anyone who deliberately cried out or rose from his seat during the execution of the death sentence would be removed from the chamber. He wished particularly to emphasize this: If Richard Hauptmann spoke, if he indicated that he wanted to confess, then he, the warden of the prison, would do everything that needed to be done; everyone else—police officers, prison guards, reporters, physicians, members of the state legislature, all of them—must remain silent and simply watch and listen.

Finally, to put to rest once and for all the rumor that there would be an effort to photograph the scene, just before entering the chamber everyone would be searched once more, beginning with himself. Any witness who declined to be searched would be barred.

Kimberling paused. There were no questions. All right, he said, and walked to the head of the line.

It was twenty past eight.

Two abreast, in a file a hundred feet long, they began the march. Steel doors swung open at their approach and let them into the middle cell block, then through the dimly lighted mess hall and kitchen corridors and out into the prison yard. They saw that the tumbling clouds had cleared. The moon was pale but the stars seemed very bright.

Those who were in the lead could see, ahead, the chunky brick building that was the death house, and, on the roof, so sharply silhouetted in the blaze of floodlights that they might have been toy two-dimensional figures, the slowly patroling prison guards, holding bayoneted rifles.

Folding doors opened and two by two the witnesses entered the death-house courtyard. The final search Kimberling had promised was begun. The air wasn't silent, here; it was alive with a murmur like that of sea water rising in the wind. The crowd outside the walls had grown until it was perhaps two thousand strong. That was the sound of their voices.

Orderly and hushed, the witnesses stepped into the heart of the death house, the innermost core of the whole prison complex. Many of them had never seen an electrocution chamber and they peered to right and left and high and low with an almost furtive curiosity. It wasn't a big room; the bright lights made it seem smaller. Smudged, whitewashed brick walls rose to a skylighted ceiling. To their left as the witnesses came in there was a steel-grilled door leading to the death-house cells, to their right another door, giving onto the autopsy room. Directly in front of them there were ten rows of straight-back wooden chairs; and one witness, who had been here before, whispered that two rows were usually enough. He pointed to another proof that this was a night beyond the common run of execution nights; a three-foot-high strip of white canvas was suspended from a chain completely across the room, separating the ordinary, transient chairs from the permanent chair.

But they could see it quite plainly from where they sat.

It faced them. Across its arms lay a wooden board studded with large bulbs. Robert Elliott, the executioner, had been testing the current which fed the electric chair. He was a gray-haired man whose face looked patient and wise because it was so deeply lined.

The tests had satisfied him. He put the board away and moved to a cabinet set in the wall behind the chair. The cabinet's open doors revealed an instrument panel and a large wheel.

Another man came from somewhere or other and stood squarely in front of the chair. It was the warden, the witnesses realized. He looked different here. In the bright naked lights, everything looked strangely unreal, except the chair. The guards, also facing the witnesses, stood behind Kimberling. The warden's voice sounded strained. He instructed the witnesses to button their coats and keep their hands out of their pockets. Reporters who wanted to make notes could do so as long as the pencils and pads could be clearly seen. Any secret movement would be regarded as suspicious.

Kimberling motioned to a guard and the guard held up a large clock. It would establish the official time of the execution, Kimberling said. The guard turned the clock from side to side. The turning dial gathered shadows from the bright lights above and behind but the witnesses could make out the time. It was thirty-six minutes past eight.

Kimberling spoke to another guard:

"Before we call Hauptmann, I think it would be wise to telephone the central office and ask if there is any message for us. Would you do that?"

The guard nodded and left.

He came back in two minutes. There were no messages.

Kimberling looked over toward Elliott. The executioner lowered his gray head to signify that preparations were complete. Kimberling waited a little while longer, then turned away from his position in front of the chair and told the guards to bring Hauptmann from his cell.

As the door to the death house closed behind the guards, the room was absolutely quiet.

Then the door opened again, and the witnesses heard voices speaking in a foreign tongue.

One of the guards came first. Behind him there were two men dressed in black, side by side, reading aloud from German Bibles. They were the ministers, Werner and Matthiesen, who had attended the prisoner for so long. Though they tried to read as one, their voices weren't quite in unison and it was possible to distinguish between them. Matthiesen's was precise, almost crisp, against Werner's slower, deeper, sorrowful tone. Matthiesen wore glasses and the black ribbon attached to the rim swayed gently with his measured step.

Hauptmann came next. The rest of the guards followed him. The death-house door closed with a brief steel note.

The prisoner's face was pale and expressionless, the lips forming a straight tight line. The shaved head was tilted slightly to one side; he might have been about to ask a question, although his face was incurious. He barely glanced at the witnesses. His eyes were all for the chair. He walked rapidly to it and sat down in it eagerly, as if inviting the lightning, and held on to the arms with a strong grip. His head wasn't tilted any longer; it was perfectly, firmly level, the classic pose for an old-fashioned formal photograph, a serious business.

He didn't speak.

The ministers stationed themselves behind the chair and steadfastly read on.

A witness thought he saw the man in the chair try to smile, but perhaps that was a trick of the passing shadows as the guards swiftly moved and slipped a black mask over Hauptmann's face and strapped his chest and arms and legs to the chair.

Robert Elliott came forward. He had been standing by with the leather cap and its electrode, already dipped in brine, and he fitted it neatly over the shaved head and fastened it under the chin. Then the executioner stooped down and clamped a second electrode to the leg through the trouser-slit.

Elliott straightened up and walked to the control panel and put his hand tentatively on the wheel. He looked at the warden.

Standing next to the chair, Kimberling saw Hauptmann tilt his head from side to side, as if trying to adjust the cap and mask more comfortably.

The time was forty-four minutes past eight. Kimberling nodded, and Elliott spun the wheel.

Light bulbs blazed on the control panel and two thousand volts fled into Hauptmann's body and violently snapped it rigid. His compressed lips were jarred apart by the gigantic invisible fire and his clenched hands pulled and strained at the chair arms. The whine Anna had heard, like crazy wind, rose and fell, rose and fell, rose and fell a third time, Robert Elliott leaning toward the chair with each spin of the wheel, to see better, to be sure that all was working well.

At the first shock, as the body leaped, Werner's voice faltered and ceased and his head hung down, but Matthiesen continued without pause:

"I believe in One God the Father Almighty, maker of heaven and earth, and of all things visible and invisible, and in One Lord Jesus Christ——"

The three lightning bolts spun from the wheel had struck within the space of sixty seconds. The executioner switched off the current and the lights on the control panel died. Kimberling motioned to the three physicians who were to examine the body. In turn, they cupped their stethoscopes to Richard Hauptmann's chest. Howard Wiesler, the prison doctor, spoke for them:

"This man is dead."

Still intoning the Nicene Creed, Matthiesen closed his Bible and bowed his head.

Forty-seven and a half minutes past eight, the night of Friday, April 3, 1936.

In her room in the Stacy Trent, Anna Hauptmann wept and covered her face with her hands. *"Ach, Gott! Mein Richard!"*

Lloyd Fisher, waiting in the warden's office, was asked by reporters if he had anything to say. He had. "This is the greatest tragedy in the history of New Jersey. Time will never wash it out."

The crowd outside the prison, at first skeptical, finally convinced, wandered away.

Charles and Anne Lindbergh had spent a quiet evening at home in their refuge in England. Thousands upon thousands of words were streaming by cable toward the London newspapers, but the Lindberghs had not been asked to talk about the occasion; weeks before, the British press had come to an unwritten agreement not to disturb them. Jon slept soundly.

Four years, one month and two days ago, Anne Lindbergh had paused at the southeast corner of the new house near Hopewell and looked up at the second-story nursery windows, then picked up a few pebbles from the moist, clayey ground and tossed them against the corner windowpane. Presently Betty Gow, the nurse, appeared. Smiling, she turned away and came back with the little boy in her arms. She pointed down to his mother and he smiled in recognition. Anne Lindbergh waved. Betty raised the baby's hand and waved it back.

POSTSCRIPT

Kidnap is a history of the Lindbergh case from the afternoon of March 1, 1932, to the night of Bruno Richard Hauptmann's execution, but it may not seem out of place to take one step beyond the latter boundary.

Late in April 1936, five men were indicted for kidnaping Paul H. Wendel. The district attorney of Kings County, William F. X. Geoghan, had confirmed the victim's story with the help of the clues Wendel had given him. The five were Harry Bleefeld, owner of the house at 3041 Voorhies Avenue in the Sheepshead Bay section of Brooklyn, where Wendel had been held; his son, Murray Bleefeld, of Trenton, New Jersey; Harry Weiss and Martin Schlossman of Brooklyn; and Ellis Parker, Jr., of Mount Holly, New Jersey.

Schlossman had already confessed his part. Harry Bleefeld was easily found in a hospital, where he lay ill, under arrest for a later crime. Weiss was picked up in Youngstown, Ohio. He blamed Ellis Parker, Jr., who he said had told him that Paul Wendel, not Richard Hauptmann, had kidnaped the Lindbergh baby and who had deputized him as an officer of the law; to the best of his belief, therefore, he had been acting in an excellent cause and strictly within the law—the reputation enjoyed by young Parker's father was proof against any doubts. Murray Bleefeld was arrested in Albany, New York, and admitted that the entire undertaking was a plot designed by Ellis Parker to frame Wendel.

District Attorney Geoghan added a sixth indictment against Parker and he was arrested, but Governor Hoffman refused to extradite the Parkers to Brooklyn for trial, implying that he did not trust the motive behind Geoghan's actions; presumably Hoffman considered it to be wholly political. And so the Parkers remained at liberty. But Wendel took matters into his own hands. He wrote to the United States Attorney General and asked if the charges against them were not properly the concern of New Jersey's federal grand jury. The attorney general agreed. In October, after hearing Wendel's story, the grand jury handed down an indictment charging the Parkers with conspiracy under the Lindbergh law.

Harry Bleefeld had died during the summer; Schlossman, Weiss and Murray Bleefeld went on trial in Brooklyn in February of the next year, 1937. A month later they were convicted of violating New York State's kidnap law and sentenced to twenty years' imprisonment in Sing Sing.

Ellis Parker and his son came to trial before a federal court in Newark in May. Parker had often said that every criminal leaves some trace of his crime, however small, and his sagacity could not be doubted by the court after hearing one of the most important pieces of evidence pointing to his and young Parker's prime roles in the plot against Wendel: the telephone company had a record of numerous calls between the father in Mount Holly and the son in Bleefeld's home in Brooklyn.

The case was argued for seven weeks. The defense contended: one, that the Parkers had had nothing to do with Wendel's abduction; two, that if they had been involved, they were justified by their official position and their belief that Paul Wendel was the kidnaper. These arguments failed; the Parkers were convicted under the Lindbergh law. Judge William Clark said to the elder: "I have the impression that your life as a law-enforcement officer and your position in the community have given you the feeling that you are above the law, and that is the cause of your making a mockery of the processes of justice in New Jersey."

The jury asked for leniency. Ellis Parker was given six years, his son three, in a federal penitentiary.

In June 1939, after they had appealed the verdict and been denied, the Parkers went to prison in Lewisburg, Pennsylvania. On February 4, 1940, Ellis Parker died of a brain tumor in the prison hospital. His son was released late in October the next year.

ACKNOWLEDGMENTS

In the research for this book, I am indebted to a great many sources of information, but particularly to the following:

NEWSPAPERS:

In New York, N. Y., *The Times* (a very special debt, gratefully acknowledged), *Daily News, Herald Tribune, Daily Mirror, American, Evening Journal,* and *World-Telegram,* all of which day by day devoted as much space to the Lindbergh case during the four years, one month, and two days it took to run its course as they would to a small but crucial war; Bronx *Home News* (extremely helpful); Brooklyn *Eagle* and *Times-Union.*

In Trenton, N. J., the *Times* and *State Gazette.*

In Jersey City, N. J., the *Jersey Journal.*

In Newark, N. J., the *News* and *Star-Eagle.*

In Washington, D. C., the *Post, Star,* and *Times.*

In Norfolk, Va., the *Virginian-Pilot* and *Ledger-Dispatch.*

In Roanoke, Va., the *Times* and *World-News.*

In Madison, Wis., the *Capital Times* and *Wisconsin State Journal.*

In Philadelphia, Pa., the *Inquirer* and *Evening Bulletin.*

In London, England, the *Times, Daily Mail, Daily Express, Daily Telegraph,* and *News Chronicle.*

In Liverpool, England, the *Daily Post.*

In Manchester, England, the *Guardian.*

In Glasgow, Scotland, the *Daily Record & Mail* and *Evening Citizen.*

In Paris, France, *Le Figaro, Le Matin, Paris-Soir,* and New York *Herald* (European edition of the *Herald Tribune*).

In Leipzig, Germany, *Neueste Nachrichten* and *Neue Zeitung.*

RECORDS AND PAMPHLETS:

Transcripts of the trial proceedings and testimony, State of New Jersey *vs.* Bruno Richard Hauptmann; State of New Jersey *vs.* John Hughes Curtis; United States *vs.* Gaston B. Means and Norman T. Whitaker.

Transcripts of radio news broadcasts dealing with the Lindbergh crime and trial.

The "Hole" in the Hauptmann Case? by Major Frank Pease, a forty-four-page pamphlet published by the author in New York, N. Y., 1936.

A series of circulars addressed *To the American People* from 1932 to 1938 by the Committee of Witnesses and published by them in New York, N. Y.

BOOKS:

The Lindbergh Crime, Blue Ribbon Books, 1935, and *The Trial of Bruno Richard Hauptmann,* Doubleday, Doran, 1937, both by Sidney B. Whipple.

The Crime and the Criminal—a Psychiatric Study of the Lindbergh Case by Dr. Dudley D. Shoenfeld. Covici, Friede, 1936.

Jafsie Tells All by Dr. John F. Condon. Jonathan Lee, 1936.

The Lindbergh-Hauptmann Aftermath by Paul H. Wendel. Loft, 1940.

The books listed above helped me to establish a frame for the story, and to Dr. Condon and Dr. Shoenfeld in particular I owe my special gratitude for material not available elsewhere. I also consulted:

True Story of the Lindbergh Kidnapping by John Brant and Edith Renaud. Kroy Wen, 1932.

The Great Lindbergh Hullabaloo by Laura Vitray. William Faro, 1932.

The Hand of Hauptmann by J. Vreeland Haring. Hamer, 1937.

12 Against Crime by Edward D. Radin, specifically Chapter 10, "Sawdust Trail," based on the account Arthur Koehler wrote of his activities in the Lindbergh case for the United States Forest Service. G. P. Putnam's Sons, 1950.

Only Yesterday and *Since Yesterday,* both by Frederick Lewis Allen. Harper & Brothers, 1931 and 1939.

MAGAZINES:

Magazine articles dealing with the Lindbergh case were, for the most part, fanciful and speculative—efforts to outdo the news stories in the daily press. One article, however—"Who Made That Ladder?" by Arthur Koehler as told to Boyden Sparkes in the *Saturday Evening Post* of April 20, 1935—supplied a guide to Koehler's mental approach to his task in the Lindbergh case, supplementing his lengthy testimony at the trial. Many years later, shortly before he retired from the Forest Service, Koehler enlarged on this account of his activities in the case, in a report he wrote for the Government's files (as mentioned earlier, the chapter on Koehler in Edward D. Radin's book was based on this report).

In closing, I want to thank Marianna Gillespie for helping me over a particularly high hurdle at a time when it seemed out of my reach; her enthusiasm for the story, and practical solutions to vexing problems, were buoying.

GEORGE WALLER